Russian Literature of
THE
TWENTIES
An Anthology

Introduction by Robert A. Maguire

Edited by

Carl R. Proffer, Ellendea Proffer, Ronald Meyer, Mary Ann Szporluk

Ardis, Ann Arbor

Ardis Publishers
2901 Heatherway
Ann Arbor, Michigan 48104

Library of Congress Cataloging in Publication Data

The Twenties: an anthology.

Collection of prose and poetry translated from Russian.
Includes bibliographies.
1. Russian fiction—20th century—Translations into
English.   2. Russian poetry—20th century—Translations
into English.   3. English fiction—Translations from
Russian.   4. English poetry—Translations from Russian.
I. Proffer, Carl R.
PG3276.T84 1987   891.7'08'0042   87-1787
ISBN 0-88233-820-X
ISBN 0-88233-821-8 (pbk.)

Cover photograph: Alexander Rodchenko

CONTENTS

INTRODUCTION

Robert A. Maguire

From a distance of more than half a century, the Soviet 1920s stand out for exceptional achievement and promise in all fields, whether science and technology, music, painting and architecture, theater and cinema, philosophy, education and linguistics, or, of course, literature. Each seemed to impinge on the other: educational reforms on literature, music and art on theater, linguistics on social theory, technology on architecture, to create an impression sometimes of confusion, but more often of energy, innovation, and excitement. But it was literature which stood at the very center. It had long been regarded as the highest and most effective expression of the national ideals and the national identity. This conviction passed intact into the 1920s and was perhaps the decade's most important legacy to the future.[1]

Accounts of this period customarily begin with 1921 and end with 1928. The parameters are political, defining as they do the dates of the New Economic Policy (NEP), which encouraged a partial return to private enterprise in the interest of restoring an economy shattered by three years of civil war. This yielded to the First Five-Year Plan (1928-32), when all forces, including the arts, were mobilized to serve the new, overriding priorities of rapid industrialization and collectivization. Such markers are convenient, serviceable, and even valid up to a point. But there are other criteria for identifying a literary period. One is, of course, the appearance of writers with significantly new things to say. By this standard alone, the Soviet 1920s were exceptionally fecund. Nearly all the writers who have become classics began their careers or achieved celebrity then. A new literary canon took form in those seven short years, and promptly won recognition, no doubt because writers addressed the great issues of the day, and made some sense out of the welter of new experience while honoring its depth, richness and complexity. At the same time, the twenties are not coextensive with any one "great" writer, but are the result of a collective effort on the part of dozens of major and hundreds of lesser talents.

The achievement of the twenties is all the more impressive when we consider how unpromisingly it all began. To one observer from abroad, Russia in 1920 presented the following picture: "There is no paper, no ink, no machines, no transportation or telegraph, no productive labor, *there is no living Russia*. Whole generations are dying out. Not only are whole categories of people dying off, but things, institutions, science and culture as well. All movement natural to life is coming to a standstill in literature and ideas. Alas, one must make a survey not so much of life in Russia as of death, the processes of quick and slow death...."[2] Even allowing for the hostility of the writer and exaggeration for effect, this appreciation was not entirely inaccurate. Certainly 1920 stood in glaring and painful contrast with the color, vigor and variety of Russian culture in 1914, or even 1918. A mere seven or eight years, however, made all the difference. Has any comparably short stretch of time yielded such abundance? Certainly not in Russian history. There is no definitive accounting for it. But several forces were unmistakably in play.

One was a carry-over from the so-called Silver Age, which reached roughly from 1895 to 1914. Even though many of its leading writers had died, emigrated or fallen silent by 1921, so spectacular were its achievements in all the arts that not even the vast upheavals of 1917 and later could stop its momentum. All the leaders of the Revolution had come to maturity during that period, had had to take account of its values and expectations, and tended to regard it with respect, if not always with affection. Then too, some writers and literary groups straddled the great divide of 1917 with ease. Chief among them were the Futurists, who had burst on the literary world in 1912 with a manifesto entitled "A Slap in the Face of Public Taste." By their own lights they had always been "revolutionary," and they now wished, for the most part, to be numbered as active and avid supporters of the Revolution. Their most important poet, Vladimir Mayakovsky, had begun his career before World War I and went on to become the most famous poet of the 1920s. Then there were the Symbolists, or rather, one of the foremost Symbolist poets, for they had long since ceased to exist as a group: Alexander Blok. Ever since 1905 he had been publishing provocative essays urging the Russian intelligentsia to "listen to the music of revolution"; and when the Revolution of 1917 came, he publicly cast his lot with it. His poem *The Twelve,* composed in two feverish days of January 1918, is really the first piece of Soviet literature. Its importance historically is that it employs themes and images that were characteristic of Blok's earlier work, and of much of Symbolism too, in ways that were to become respectable and therefore influential by the new political and social standards. Blok died in 1921, that is, at the very beginning of what we have been calling the twenties; but the mark he left on Soviet literature shows that we must look back—as this anthology does— for a better understanding of the decade.

Another factor that shaped the personality of the twenties was the attitude of the Bolshevik regime. For the first few months after the Revolution, literary and intellectual life continued to flourish. Certainly all the external signs were good. Schools, salons and circles seemed, if anything, more numerous and lively than ever. There were groups like the Emotionalists, the Luminists, the Biocosmists, the Neo-Classicists; more substantially, the Imagists, the Futurists, the Eurasians; more ephemerally, the Communist Union of Artists of the Word, which was organized one morning and liquidated that same evening for lack of members, yet had time, in typical Russian fashion, to issue a manifesto. Literary cafes like

Domino, the Music box, and Pegasus' Stall devoted entire evenings to the recitation and discussion of poetry. Adult education centers sprang up, where famous poets offered courses in reading and writing to workers. It was an age of the spoken word. Any gathering might well turn into what one observer called an "oral journal," which was a kind of intellectual free-for-all. The printed media were lively and profuse. To be sure, blatantly anti-revolutionary journals and newspapers were suppressed at the outset of the Revolution. But the new government's first "Decree on the Press" (1918) stated that "restriction of the press, even at critical times, is allowable only within absolutely essential limits."[3] Many of the pre-Revolutionary newspapers and journals continued to publish. Many new ones of a decidedly "bourgeois" cast were established. Most of the old publishing houses were allowed to continue operating; and in 1921 more than two hundred of them still existed (although fewer than half were actually functioning). We must not, however, paint too rosy a picture. Many artists and intellectuals were hard pressed to find a place in this tumultuous new society. Mere subsistence could be a challenge. To its enduring credit, the government saw the problem, and took measures to alleviate it. One of the reasons for setting up the State Publishing House (Gosizdat) in 1919 was to create jobs for translators, editors and copyreaders. Encouragement was also given to various self-help societies, such as the House of Literati and the House of Arts in Petrograd, and the Palace of Arts in Moscow, which offered, besides readings and lectures, dormitory space, dining rooms, and libraries. In these first years after the Revolution, we can already discern the broad outlines of the government's policy towards the arts throughout much of the 1920s: a relative permissiveness, and the preservation or restoration of institutions through which literature in Russia had traditionally functioned. The main ones, in the 1920s, were literary journals and literary groups.

During this period, the Party consistently refused to articulate an official policy toward literature, in other words, to demand or sanction an official way of writing, and it also refused to allow any of the numerous literary groups to speak in its name. Diversity and competition were encouraged. To put the matter somewhat differently, the Party made an important though largely implicit distinction between two kinds of literature, political or official Party literature, and all other kinds, including fiction and poetry. Over the first, the Party maintained watchful control. For the second it showed little concern: writers were expected to be more or less sympathetic to the new order of things, but beyond making openly counter-revolutionary statements, they could write pretty much what and how they wished.

This policy, which Soviet writers have looked back upon ever since with nostalgia, was born of necessity. For one thing, the business of consolidating and extending political and economic power undoubtedly took first priority. For another, there were virtually no precedents for a

Marxist, let alone a Bolshevik, policy toward the arts. Marx and Engels had had things to say about literature, but mostly as afterthoughts. Of their disciples, Georgy Plekhanov fleshed out a theory of literature, without suggesting how or whether it should be translated into practice; in any event, he was in bad odor politically with the Bolsheviks at this time. Lenin's essays on Tolstoy, while of course Marxist, did not allow of much extrapolation for a policy toward literature as a whole. His article entitled "Party Organization and Party Literature" (1905) came to stand as the cornerstone of the official esthetic, Socialist Realism, from the 1930s on, but its original purpose was thereby broadened if not perverted, inasmuch as Lenin was referring only to what we have called "official" literature. Still another factor was a deep-rooted habit of mind that could not be changed in a mere four or five years, even by a revolution. Since at least the eighteenth century, Russians had looked to their literature as a measure of the health and vitality of their society. The paucity of literature in the early 1920s was at best an embarrassment, at worst an ominous symptom.

These were some of the elements that shaped the Party's decision to promote the revival of literature. The profoundly disaffected were to be expelled from the country, or allowed to leave. Conditions were to be created that would encourage the appearance of new writers. A first step was the establishment, in 1921, of a literary journal, *Red Virgin Soil,* which in format was a continuation of the old "thick" journals that had played such a crucial role in Russian literary life for nearly a hundred years. Under the editorship of Alexander Voronsky, a cultivated Bolshevik with an eye to quality, this journal was designed to attract new writers without imposing any strict political tests. It succeeded brilliantly, becoming the locus of much of the best writing of the twenties, especially by the so-called Fellow Travelers, who, while not proletarian in background or members of the Party, supported the new way of life and were willing to take an active part in it. Among them were Babel, Ivanov and Olesha, who are represented in this anthology as well. *Red Virgin Soil* also became an important source of Marxist literary theory and criticism, especially through the writings of Voronsky. And it quickly became entangled in the lively and increasingly acrimonious literary polemics of the decade.

For the most part these polemics centered around groups and journals. One extreme was represented by the Serapion Brothers, a loose association of writers formed in 1921, who insisted on the freedom to write as they pleased, and who steered clear of the heated disputes that were to come, even though they saw fit to state their position by issuing a manifesto. Among them were three of the writers included in this anthology, Zamyatin, Zoshchenko and Kaverin. Another extreme was struck by the Futurists, who were now organized mainly around the journal *LEF (Left Front of the Arts,* 1923-25) and later *New LEF* (1927-28). They called for the "building" of a new art, and thereby a new society, through a new language and new forms, in contrast to the art of the past,

which they considered representational and therefore dead and irrelevant
to the present. Their main target was *Red Virgin Soil,* the Fellow Travelers
and Voronsky, whom they accused of trying to resuscitate and perpetuate
that old culture. Much larger and more vocal were the proletarians. Their
first important organization had been the Proletcult (1917-21), which was
succeeded in the 1920s by several others, whose most contentious members
published mainly in the journals *On Guard (Na postu,* 1923-25), and *On
Literary Guard (Na literaturnom postu,* 1926-32). They proclaimed the
reality of a uniquely proletarian literature, and demanded that the Party
give it special nurturing and preferential treatment. Naturally, they
declared war on all non-proletarian groups and theories, such as Futurism,
but they took aim primarily at Voronsky and his journal. Voronsky found
such polemics distasteful, but staunchly insisted on the priority of
excellence, a continuity with the Russian classics, the irrelevance of most
Futurist exercises, and the unlikelihood of an identifiably "proletarian"
literature.

All the participants in these verbal wars seemed to agree on at least one
thing: the need for a new Soviet literature. The areas of disagreement were
numerous and profound. Could there be a proletarian literature at all, and
if so, was it entitled to preeminence in a "workers' and peasants'" state? Did
non-proletarian writers, especially the Fellow Travelers, have anything
positive and constructive to offer a new Soviet literature? What
connection, if any, should this new literature have to the large and
impressive literary past? Were writers best left alone to create, or should
they be brought into organizations? Did the Party have the right, even the
duty, to attempt to influence or control the direction of literature? What
indeed were the nature and purpose of literature: to reflect reality, to
disseminate useful knowledge, to serve the needs of a particular group, to
create new realities? Was literature merely a mirror of class values, or was it
the property of all mankind, regardless of class?

Such questions lay at the very heart of the long and noisy debates that
characterized the twenties. Literature was ostensibly the topic, but more
was involved. It is not difficult, for instance, to see the debate in terms of a
confrontation between elite and mass cultures, or written and oral cultures.
Broadly speaking, Voronsky and the Fellow Travelers represented a
continuation of a "high" literary culture, centered in journals and books,
whereas their opponents gravitated toward a culture of the spoken word,
whether expressed in public recitations of poetry or in the kind of verbal
play that appeals more to the ear than to the eye, as with the Futurists, or
whether, as in the case of the proletarians, oriented on the speech patterns
of the "common" man, designed for an audience still semi-literate and
expressed in genres with markedly oral origins, such as theater, folk songs,
and anecdotes. Not surprisingly, the Futurists and the proletarians were
keenly interested, as the Fellow Travelers decidedly were not, in what we
have come to call multi-media events; these tended to blur traditional

boundaries among the arts, and to assign literature a lower position in the system of priorities than it traditionally enjoyed in Russia. A further blurring was the inevitable result of the heavy proletarian emphasis on ideology, which in effect gave equal priority to all kinds of art as long as it was politically correct.

One vital consequence of these disputes was the development of a theory and practice of literature which was sufficiently Marxist in spirit to enable the Party, when ultimately it did intervene, to choose from among a number of well-explored possibilities. Another was a gradual but relentless elimination of the distinction between two literatures, official and non-official, so that Party pronouncements on the one could easily be made binding on the other. In any event, the Party by 1927 had moved to a position that favored the proletarian groups. Voronsky was dismissed from his post and soon arrested. By 1928 literature was being pressed into service. And in 1932 a Party resolution abolished all literary groups and mandated the formation of a single organization, the Union of Soviet Writers. Insofar as the twenties are synonymous with plurality, we could plausibly stretch the decade to end it here.

As Nikolai Bukharin remarked, the energies spent in writing charges and counter-charges could better have been expended in creating fiction and poetry. Even so, hundreds of writers were finding their way into print. All the major genres were being cultivated. And much of this literature still comes across as fresh and invigorating. One reason is that it deals with issues we have come to think of as quintessentially "modern," issues like the quality of life in industrialized societies, the bankruptcy of old values, or savagery masquerading as civilization. Such issues are the very stuff of twentieth-century literature, of course; but in the context of the Soviet 1920s, they became intensified and sufficiently defamiliarized to make an even greater impact on the foreign reader. For instance, the novel *We* compellingly demonstrates that the theme of "1984" was not invented by Orwell, but had been cast in its now chillingly familiar terms by Zamyatin in 1920 (though not invented by him either).

One of the major themes of this new literature was violence. It was most explicitly, graphically and tirelessly explored in literature about the Revolution and Civil War, such as Ivanov's *Armored Train 14-69,* Babel's *Red Cavalry,* Serafimovich's *The Iron Flood,* and Fadeev's *The Rout* (also translated as *The Nineteen*). But the dividing-line between soldiers and civilians was often thin, especially when the subject was civil strife. Furthermore, Russia had a long tradition of military fiction which commented, explicitly or implicitly, on the values of society at large (*War and Peace* being a prime example), and readers of the twenties had certainly not lost the habit of making the connection. That is one reason why, when military literature began to wear itself out toward the middle of the decade, its themes, character-types, and even details of language could readily be transferred to the civilian realm, especially, though by no means exclusively, in works dealing with industrialization and collectivization. For instance, Gleb Chumalov, the hero of Fyodor Gladkov's "proletarian" novel *Cement* (1925), finds, as he works to rebuild a war-shattered cement plant, that he is engaged in a battle nearly as fierce and decisive as any he has experienced during his military service. There are enemies to be overcome, spies to be unmasked, and victory to be won through supreme exertions of the will, the emotions, and the body. "Suffering and blood," we are told, "are inevitable. Blood is turned into suffering, suffering is transformed into great exploits and through the masses into world-wide struggle."[4]

Violence had other faces in this new literature. Mayakovsky, for one, considered it essential to the artistic process: the material for art is provided by the world, but it is dead until the poet does it violence in an act of creative deformation. In this sense, the artist is automatically a revolutionary, and the revolutionary an artist. Presumably this helped Mayakovsky, at least for much of the twenties, to see the Revolution—with a capital R—as a great creative force. Blok's version of violence is more complex, as is suggested by the variety of images he uses to convey it: music, spirit, speech, blood, noise, wind, snow, culture, revolution, to specify just a few. All represent a vital energy that sweeps away everything inert. One striking instance comes in the first section of *The Twelve* (which Blok says arose out of "the noise of time"), where the "merry wind ... tears, batters and pulls at/ A large banner' reading "All Power to the Constituent Assembly." The latter was a representative body elected to establish a democratic system in Russia; it met just once, in January 1918, and was dissolved by the Bolsheviks. In the image-system of this poem, it obviously is a vestige of a dead world, and as such, is appropriately depicted in printed letters, which, to paraphrase the Bible, kill, while the "spirit" (here, wind) gives life, and wafts the spoken (and therefore living) words of the common people, who are shown in constant movement throughout the poem. The contrast reaches far back into Russian literature. It became embedded in the literature of the twenties as well. One of its most skilful exploiters was Isaac Babel. His *Red Cavalry* shows us, in the narrator Lyutov, a sensitive man who, as a participant in the Russo-Polish War of 1920, is constantly forced to face violence, some of it seemingly pointless, but much of it redeeming, creative, even beautiful. One story in the collection, "Italian Sunshine," presents the gloomy figure of Sidorov, who has fought with the Anarchists and is sent back to Moscow wounded. There he encounters a smoothly running bureaucracy, and "comes to loathe" this whole world that operates "according to plan." When he is transferred to the Red Cavalry, his wound prevents him from riding, and he concludes that there is no place for him in the new Russia: "The wisdom of statesmen is driving me crazy. I am drunk with boredom." In search of the kind of violence that alone has given his life meaning, he yearns for assignment to Italy, where he will kill the King, "a nice old fellow," or to the Cheka. Babel strongly suggests that such violence is gratuitous and sterile.[5] But it focuses a problem that was beginning to take on some urgency in the 1920s, as many people began to wonder how the call for restoring order and reasonable prosperity could be reconciled with the revolutionary spirit. As early as 1920, Zamyatin had set the problem in stark (and unacceptable) relief in his novel *We,* where, in the Twenty-Eighth Entry, I-330 says: "There are two forces in the world—entropy and energy. One leads to blissful tranquillity, to happy equilibrium; the other leads to the destruction of that equilibrium, to an agonizingly-endless movement." It is clear that energy is to be not only preferred but accepted and welcomed, even though this means acknowledging that there is "no final revolution; revolutions are infinite." The entire book, in one sense, is a gloss on this distinction, and that is undoubtedly why it has never been published in Soviet Russia.[6] Interestingly enough, Mayakovsky seems to have been unable to find anything creative in the reconstruction programs of the twenties, even in the spectacular feats of the First Five-Year Plan. His suicide in 1930 was widely though not of course officially interpreted as a commentary on the Revolution.

Insofar as violence involves movement, another version of the theme is action. Many writers of the twenties pose the choice of action/non-action very clearly: to act is to engage in the process of change; change is shaped by the movement of history; to act is to ally oneself with history. It is better to be on the right side, but presumably better to be on the wrong side than not engaged at all, for one is at least involved in the movement of history. Alexander Fadeev's "proletarian" novel *The Rout* (1927) is highly instructive in this respect. It is the story of a small detachment of Red guerrillas operating in the Far East against the Japanese and the Whites. Most of them are miners, peasants and intellectuals by origin, and they are in constant conflict with each other because of old class identities and private memories. Their leader is Levinson, who is keenly aware of their vulnerability and bends all his efforts to keeping them out of action. At last the enemy is met, however, and many of the Red soldiers are in fact killed. But the nineteen survivors, including Levinson, discover that it is only the acceptance and engagement of circumstances that have forged out of them a true collective, with a single will and purpose. The one character in the novel who fails to act, by the simple expedient of running away, is Mechik. He is described as a "maximalist," that is, a terrorist, one who tries to bend the course of history to his own will. But the point, Fadeev reminds us, is not to make history as we would like to see it, but to take sides in the struggles created by history. Mechik does not die; he simply disappears; history has passed him by. The literature of the time is full of bypassed characters. In Babel's *Red Cavalry* it is Ageev ("The Two Ivans"), who has "twice deserted from the front," and is sent back to the rear as a prisoner and subjected to many dehumanizing indignities. In Leonid Leonov's *The End of a Petty Man* (1924) it is Likharev, a famous paleontologist, who at first ignores the horrors of the Civil War, then despairs and ends by burning his life's work. In Olesha's *Envy* (1927) it is primarily Kavalerov and Ivan Babichev who have slipped anchor in the old world, and cannot find one in the new.

Intellectuals, bourgeois and aristocrats tend to be the least prone to act in this fiction; workers and peasants the most. But for the best writers, the lines are by no means so clear-cut: social mobility is rampant. The military is the great melting pot: Ivanov's *Armored Train 14-69,* like Fadeev's *The Rout,* is a sociology of people of very different backgrounds who are made as one by shared experiences. This becomes the paradigm for the treatment of the civilian world too, whether urban or rural. The weaker the old class loyalties, the more successful the adjustment. Here the figure of the Jew plays a significant role. Until the Revolution, he was a secondary character in Russian literature, usually an emblem of treachery, absurdity, or ineffectualness. But in Soviet literature of the 1920s he assumed heroic stature. Major works like *Red Cavalry, The Rout,* and *Time, Forward!* (by Valentin Kataev, 1932) all have a Jew as protagonist. Weakness has become strength: a man who had been perceived as peripheral to Russian society, a man apart, easily becomes a man with the new virtue of mobility. Certainly Lyutov is represented as an outsider in every conceivable way: a Jew serving in a Cossack regiment, an intellectual among virtual illiterates, an urbanite among peasants, a Russian (culturally) among Poles, a Bolshevik among the ideologically indifferent or hostile, an agnostic among believing Jews, and so on. Levinson, of *The Rout,* acquires much of his authority over his motley unit, almost paradoxically, because he is perceived as remote, aloof, and free from allegiance to any of the social groups from which his subordinates, all non-Jews, spring. Margulies, the leader of a construction brigade in Kataev's novel, never grapples with any of the details of the work, but instead follows a larger vision that requires him to stand aside and cheer the men on. Since the Jew belongs nowhere, he can be anywhere, and in this sense he is surely one of the prototypes of the Communist activists, Jewish or not, who people the fiction of the twenties and beyond.

These were ambitious themes. And they were played out on an ambitious scale. The literature of the twenties offers not only a sociology of all the groups, classes and professions, but also a grand tour of the territories belonging to the old Russian Empire, all the way from Poland (Babel) to Siberia and the Far East (Ivanov, Fadeev), from the Arctic (Pilnyak) to the Caspian and Central Asia (Neverov). In this sense, the twenties can be seen as the culmination of the process of opening up literature to new themes, characters and locales that had begun before the Revolution, especially in the works of writers like Gorky and Kuprin. The process has been aptly called "the destruction of taboos."[7]

Given that the purpose of this literature was nothing less than to record and describe all of contemporary Russia, we are perhaps startled to find that much of it, especially in the earlier years of the decade, is drawn on small canvases and is of a decidedly gloomy cast. Much of it consists of sketches, vignettes and short stories; it tends to focus on the surfaces of the physical world, notably in its small and discrete details; it represents that world as being so sordid and fragmented as to resist any attempts to organize or interpret it; in fact, it eschews evaluations and generalization, and if essayed, shows them to be fatuous; it represents human beings as flawed and fragmented beings who move purposelessly through an incomprehensible universe in which no laws seem to operate. In these respects, it calls to mind the work of pre-Revolutionary writers like Andreev and Chekhov. Much of it is written in a manner that critics have dubbed "ornamentalism," which is a melange, within the boundaries of a single text, of various levels and kinds of speech, such as oral and literary, high and low, and of various traditional genres, such as novels, poems, letters, documents and anecdotes. Babel, Ivanov, and especially Pilnyak made ornamentalism popular, and it dominated the twenties. Whether it was, as many argue, a continuation of stylistic trends in pre-revolutionary literature, or whether it was an invention of the twenties, it nonetheless seemed eminently suited to the moods and themes of the first half of the decade.

At first, this kind of writing was widely regarded as "realistic": if it was fragmented, if its mood was dark, then it was merely reflecting the realities of a society that had been shattered by Revolution and Civil War. But as the twenties wore on, an increasing number of critics, most of them Marxists, began to express profound discontent and serious concern. As Voronsky wrote: "There have been a great many themes, but there has been no *one theme*. There have been a great many heroes, but there has been no *one hero*. People have written about a great many astonishing, amusing and sad events, but there has been nothing about *one event*. Just as in a cinema, thousands of types of human faces have flashed before us, but there has been no *one type*. Our writers have presented thousands of small details, they have crawled around in all the most remote and tiny corners, they have told us about astonishing and unheard-of things, and they have constantly left out, constantly forgotten something important."[8] That "something" was an overarching view of society. For Marxists, after all, the world, even an apparently shattered world, has coherence and purpose, and is guided by laws. It is the main business of art to show the coherence and purpose behind the welter of details. That is why many critics, Voronsky among them, were greatly distressed by the absence of novels as new writers began to appear. Apart from their awe before the great achievement of the nineteenth century, they did not regard short forms as capacious enough for the times. The magnitude of the Revolution, and the immensity of the tasks facing the new society, deserved, in fact, demanded worthy literary representation. What better than the novel to depict large-scale events in the process of change and development? For many Russians,

Marxist or not, the health of the novel was an index of society's health. That is why they greeted with enthusiasm and relief the appearance in 1924 of *Cities and Years,* by Konstantin Fedin, a Fellow Traveler. With Gladkov's *Cement* the following year, and Fadeev's *The Rout* two years after that, the proletariat seemed to have found its novelistic voice too. Given Marxist presuppositions about literature, it is not surprising that the novel became the predominant genre of Socialist Realism. But it is not the characteristic form of the literature of the twenties. In its best and most interesting manifestations, that was still very much a highly experimental literature of short forms.

What is remarkable about these writers and critics, for all their differences, is their deep conviction that literature matters, that it can and must play an active part in the life of the individual and of society. In this respect, the literature of the twenties reaffirmed a truism of Russian culture, and through the sheer force of its achievement, passed it on to succeeding generations. Even the perversions of the literary process under Stalin were motivated by a belief in the importance of literature. In recent years, strenuous efforts have been made to rectify these perversions. As this is done, the literature of the twenties is invoked again and again, as a model of idealism, lofty purpose, and high achievement.

Notes

1. Properly speaking, the term "Soviet" applies to all the national literatures created on Soviet territory. However, American popular usage makes it virtually synonymous with "Russian," as the largest and most influential of them. The anthology offered here follows this practice, and so shall I in these introductory remarks.

2. M. Vishnyak, "Na rodine," *Sovremennye zapiski,* No. 1, 1920, p. 206.

3. "Dekret o pechati," as in *O partiinoi i sovetskoi pechati,* Moscow, 1954, p. 173.

4. As translated by A. S. Arthur and C. Ashleigh, New York, International Publishers, n.d., p. 218.

5. The quotes are from the version in Isaac Babel, *The Collected Stories,* edited and translated by Walter Morison, New York, 1974, pp. 66, 67.

6. The quotes are drawn from the translation by Samuel Cioran in this anthology. See also Zamyatin's 1923 essay, "On Literature, Revolution, Entropy, and Other Matters," as in *A Soviet Heretic. Essays by Yevgeny Zamyatin,* edited and translated by Mirra Ginsburg. Chicago and London, 1980, pp. 107-12. Oddly enough, this essay made its way through the Soviet censorship and was published in Moscow.

7. D. S. Mirsky, *A History of Russian Literature,* edited and abridged by Francis J. Whitfield, London, 1949, p. 375.

8. "Na perevale," *Krasnaya nov',* No. 6, 1923, p. 315.

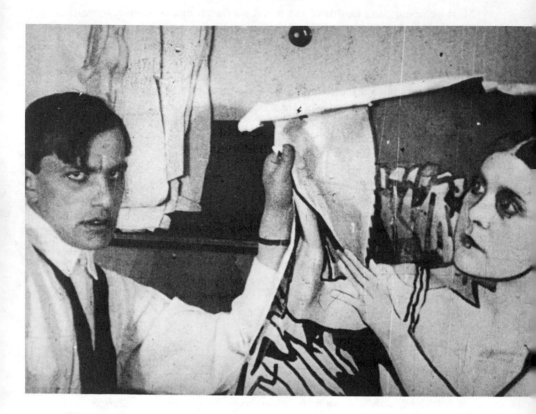

Mayakovsky and a photo of Lily Brik, in a scene from the movie *Fettered by Film.*

Russian Literature
of the

1920s

Evgeny Zamyatin.

EVGENY ZAMYATIN

Evgeny Ivanovich Zamyatin (1884-1937) was the first Soviet writer to have a novel banned by *Glavlit*, the censorship board, the first Soviet writer to go through trial by press, and the first writer to be allowed to leave Russia by permission of Stalin—through the intercession of Gorky. As these events indicate, his was an unusual personality and an unusual fate.

From the provincial world of Lebedyan, where he was born, to Petersburg, where he pursued his degree in naval engineering, to France where he ended his life, Zamyatin was always in a willfully uncomfortable position. This admirer of heresy could never belong to any group for very long: an early Bolshevik, he became disenchanted before they were in power; powerful in the Writers' Union, he refused to compromise with the politics of his time and quickly became a non-person, his works taken off the stage and the page; in emigration he refused to take part in any anti-Soviet publications, gave no political statements—and kept his Soviet passport.

Despite his status of non-person, Zamyatin had a great influence on the nascent Soviet literature. He was one of the tutelary intelligences of the Serapion Brothers group, and gave influential lectures and readings. His opinions, as expressed in reviews and conversation, were valued.

We, written in 1919-1920 is his major work. It was published in English first, in 1924, and did not come out in Russian until 1927, although Zamyatin read it to various private groups. The Russian publication by a Russian emigre journal published in Czechoslovakia was the pretext for the public persecution of Zamyatin in the late 1920s.

Preceding the works of Huxley and Orwell, and in many ways artistically superior to theirs, his novel can be read as a polemic with the works of the hugely influential H. G. Wells, a polemic fueled by Dostoevsky's story of the Grand Inquisitor. Where Wells focussed on the joys of a rational organization of humanity, Zamyatin saw the difficulties. Wells saw a finite universe, a place where there was indeed a "final number"; Zamyatin perceived a constant shifting to be the key, a shift from seeming stability to seeming chaos—both, perhaps, necessary, but certainly his affinity seems to be for the chaos, for primitive as opposed to civilized. This last idea does not really withstand close analysis, however, either when one considers who Zamyatin was (a serious engineer who built ice-breakers), or when one reads the novel carefully. In *We* the State is based on very primitive mathematics, for example. The Mefis, however, use and discuss higher mathematics—irrational numbers, non-Euclidean geometries, etc. I-330 reeducates the hero on some of these topics. And D-502 often makes basic errors in his discussions of probability, and in his narration constantly falls into false logic, false premises, etc. What does all of this mean? Perhaps that mathematics and reason are not the reason for the oppressiveness of the United State—but it is rather the lack of freedom to pursue such things on a high level. This mathematical layer of the text gives much support to the idea that this State has debased science as well as art, two areas in which the human imagination must have no constraints. Basically the State is incompetent in many ways, which explains why the Mefis can be as effective as they are. The problem of personal hours, for example, could be solved, and certainly a civilization so far in the future should be further along with rocketry, since the first ones had already been tested at the time of World War I—a development Zamyatin kept up with.

At first glance, I-330 seems to be a heroine, but further examination makes her more ambiguous. She lies and deceives, and in many ways is a temptress in this Paradise—but the snake, not Eve. In Zamyatin's work as a whole we see a constant pull towards the idea of "the main thing," which turns out to be love. In love man finds the thing worth submitting to, the thing his instincts can lead him toward. Ultimately Zamyatin sees the final good in the birth of children. In this sense O-90, at first so unremarkable, is the person who actually accomplishes something—she will have her child, and she will have it in freedom.

Philosphically, Zamyatin is drawn to Hegelian dialectic, most clear in his well-known discussion of entropy versus energy. Reason and instinct are both needed, and must be synthesized in the integrated personality. This synthetic approach is naturally reflected in his style as well. Zamyatin used a Russian rich in unusual words, but without the ornamental tendencies found in other writers of this period. He insisted that the language be as laconic as good vernacular Russian. There is a great precision in the novel's structure, and a seeming chaos in its style and meaning. Zamyatin tends toward a governing metaphor—each of his works has one key image, and everything else is subordinated to it, although this may not at first be clear due to the elliptical telegraphic style employed. Zamyatin employed punctuation, especially the dash, in unusual ways in his desire to convey the fragmentation of thought structures.

It is revealing that to this day critics cannot decide about the ending of *We*: are the forces of revolution crushed, or is that merely another false assertion on the part of the narrator? In this, perhaps, we may see the basic trait of the man of science who was attracted to the Scythians.

WE

Record 1
Synopsis: **An Announcement**
The Wisest of Lines
A Poem

I am simply transcribing—word for word—what was printed in the
State Gazette today:
"In 120 days the construction of INTEGRAL will be completed. The
mighty, historical hour is near when the first INTEGRAL will soar into
universal space. One thousand years ago, your heroic ancestors subjugated
the entire earthly sphere to the power of the United State. Awaiting you is
an even more glorious feat: the integration of the infinite equation of the
universe by means of the glass, electrical, fire-breathing INTEGRAL.
Awaiting you is the subjugation of those unknown creatures inhabiting
other planets to the beneficent yoke of reason   and perhaps still living in a
wild state of freedom. If they will not comprehend that we bring them a
mathematically infallible happiness, our duty is to force them to be happy.
But before arms—we will attempt words.
In the name of the Benefactor it is hereby announced to all the
numbers of the United State:
Everyone who feels capable is obliged to compose treatises, poems,
manifestoes, odes or other works, on the beauty and grandeur of the
United State.
This will be the first cargo which the INTEGRAL will carry.
All hail to the United State, all hail to the numbers, all hail to the
Benefactor!"
I am writing this—and I feel: my cheeks are burning. Yes: the
integration of the grandiose universal equation. Yes: to unbend the wild
curve, to straighten it out along a tangent—an asymptote—to a straight
line. Because the line of the United State—is a straight line. A great, divine,
precise, wise, straight line—the wisest of lines...
I, D-503, the builder of the INTEGRAL,—I am only one of the
mathematicians of the United State. My pen, accustomed to figures, is not
capable of creating the music of assonances and rhythms. I am merely
attempting to record what I see, what I think—more accurately, what we
think (that is it precisely: we, and let this *WE* be the title of my records). Yet

this will be a derivative of our life, of the mathematically perfect life of the United State, and if that is so, will it actually not be in itself, independently of my will, a poem? It will—that I believe and know.

I am writing this and I feel: my cheeks are burning. Probably, this is similar to what a woman experiences when for the first time she senses within herself the pulse of a new—still tiny, blind human being. It is I and simultaneously—not I. And for long months it will be necessary to nourish it with one's life fluid, with one's blood, and then—painfully tear it away from oneself and lay it at the feet of the United State.

But I am ready, just as everyone is,—or almost everyone of us. I am ready.

Record 2
Synopsis: Ballet
            Square Harmony
            X

Spring. From beyond the Green Wall, from the wild invisible plains, the wind carries the yellow pollen of some kind of flowers. Your lips grow dry from this sweet pollen—every minute you pass your tongue over them—and it must be that all the women you meet have sweet lips (and the men as well, of course). This somewhat hinders logical thinking.

But then, what a sky! Blue, unspoiled by a single cloud (what wild tastes the ancients had if their poets could be inspired by those ugly, disorderly, clumsily jostling clumps of vapor). I love—I am certain that I will not be mistaken if I say: we love—this same sterile, immaculate sky alone. On such days—the whole world is cast of that very same immutable eternal glass as the Green Wall, as all of our buildings. On such days you see into the bluest depths of things, you see certain of their amazing equations, hitherto unknown—in something most common, prosaic.

Why, just take this example. This morning I was at the launching site where the INTEGRAL is being built—and suddenly I caught sight of the machine benches: with eyes closed, in self-oblivion, the spheres of the regulators were spinning; flashing, the levers were bending to the right and to the left; the pendulum rod was proudly dipping its shoulders; to the rhythm of an inaudible music the blade of a tooling lathe bobbed up and down in a dance. I suddenly perceived all the beauty of this grandiose mechanical ballet suffused with the buoyant azure sun.

And further—in the same vein: why—beautiful? Why is the dance—beautiful? Answer: because it was a *nonfree* motion, because the whole profound meaning of the dance is precisely in its absolute, aesthetic subordination, in its ideal nonfreedom. And if it is true that our ancestors would surrender themselves utterly to dance during the most inspired moments of their life (religious mysteries, military parades), then this signified but one thing: from time immemorial, the instinct for non-freedom has been organically inherent in man, and in our present-day life— we are only consciously. . .

I shall have to finish later: the intercom has clicked. I looked up: 0-90, of course. In half a minute she herself would be here: to take me for the walk.

Dear O-!—it always seemed to me—that she resembled her name: approximately 10 centimeters shorter than the Maternal Norm—and thus seemingly turned so roundly as though on a lathe,—and the pink O—her mouth—opened wide to greet every word of mine. And moreover: the round, plump little fold of skin on the wrist of her hand—the kind that children often have.

When she entered, the logical flywheel was still humming at full force in me and because of its momentum I began to talk about the formula I had just constructed which included all of us, as well as the machines and the dance.

"Marvellous. Isn't it?" I asked.

"Yes, marvellous. Spring," 0-90 gave me a pink smile.

Well, there, how do you like that: spring. . . She talks about spring. Women. . . I fell silent.

Downstairs. The avenue was full: the post-lunch private hour, in weather like this—we usually spend on a supplementary walk. As always, the music factory was playing the March of the United State with all its pipes. In even ranks, four abreast, solemnly keeping time to the rhythm, the numbers walked—hundreds, thousands of numbers, in pale-blue unifs,* with golden badges on their chests—a state number for every male and female. I too—we, the four of us,—were one of the countless waves in this mighty torrent. To the left of me was 0-90 (if one of my hairy ancestors had been writing this about a thousand years ago—he probably would have called her by that amusing word *my*); to the right—two other strangers, a female-number and a male-number.

A sky of blissful blue, minute, toylike suns in each of the badges, faces unclouded by the insanity of thoughts. . . Rays of light—you understand: everything made of some indivisible, radiant, smiling matter. And the rhythmic measures of the brass: "Tra-ta-ta-tam. Tra-ta-ta-tam," those were the brass steps gleaming in the sun and with each step—you climbed higher and higher, into the dizzy azure.

And then, just as had been the case that morning, at the launching site, once again I perceived, as if only then for the first time in my life—I perceived everything: the absolutely straight streets, the glass pavements

*Probably from the ancient *Uniforme*.

shimmering with rays of light, the divine parallelepipeds of transparent dwellings, the square harmony of the grayish-blue ranks. To illustrate: it was as though not entire generations, but I—yes I alone—had conquered the old God and the old life, yes, I alone had created all of this, and I, like a tower, I was afraid to move my elbow lest the walls, cupolas, machines collapse in showering fragments...

And an instant later—a leap through the centuries, from + to —. I recalled (apparently,—an association by contrast)—I suddenly recalled a painting in a museum: one of their avenues from twentieth-century times, a deafening, motley, jumbled mob of people, wheels, animals, billboards, trees, colors, birds... And they do say that it was in fact like that—it could have been so. It seemed to me that it was so unlikely, so absurd, that I lost control and suddenly burst into laughter.

And immediately there was an echo—laughter—from the right. I turned: before my eyes—white—extraordinarily white and sharp teeth, an unfamiliar woman's face.

"Forgive me," she said, "but you were gazing about with such inspiration—like some mythological god on the seventh day of creation. It seems to me you are certain that you and nobody else created me as well. I am very flattered..."

All of this—without a smile, I might even say—with a certain deference (perhaps she knew that I was the builder of the INTEGRAL). Yet I could not say—in the eyes or the eyebrows—there was some manner of strange, irritating X and I could not understand it in the least, I could not give it any mathematical expression.

For some reason I grew embarrassed and with some confusion I began to justify my laughter logically. It was perfectly clear that this contrast, this impassable abyss between now and then...

"But why—impassable? (What white teeth!) One can throw a small bridge—over the abyss. Just imagine to yourself: a drum, batallions, ranks—that did exist as well—and, consequently..."

"Yes, of course: it's clear," I cried (it was an amazing intersection of thoughts: she—almost with my very same words—what I had recorded before the walk).—You understand: even the thoughts. This was because nobody is *one*, rather *one of*. We are so one and the same..."

She:

"Are you certain?"

I perceived the brows upturned at a sharp angle towards the temples—like the sharp horns of an X, again I felt bewildered for some reason; I glanced to the right, to the left—and...

To my right—she, slender, sharp, tensely resilient, like a whip, I-330 (now I saw her number); to the left—0-90, entirely different, all circles, with the childlike fold of skin around her wrist; and on the extremity of our foursome—an unfamiliar male number—double-curved, in the shape of the letter S. We were all different...

The one on the right, I-330, apparently caught my distraught look—and with a sigh:

"Yes... Alas!"

In essence, this *alas* was perfectly appropriate. But again there was a certain something in her face or in her voice...

With an extraordinary sharpness for me—I said: "There's no *alas* about it. Science is advancing and clearly—if not now, then in fifty, in a hundred years..."

"Even all the people's noses..."

"Yes, the noses," I was practically shouting now. "As long as there is—whatever basis for envy... If I have a nose like a button, while someone else..."

"Well, but your nose, forgive me, is even *classical*, as they said in olden times. And your hands there... No, do show me, show me your hands!"

I could not bear it when people looked at my hands: they were all hairy, shaggy—some kind of absurd atavism. I stretched out my hand and—in a voice as indifferent as possible—I said:

"Apelike."

She glanced at the hands, then at my face: "But there is a most curious affinity," she seemed to be weighing me with her eyes, the little horns at the corners of her eyebrows appeared fleetingly.

"He is registered to me," 0-90 opened her mouth in pink joyfulness.

It would have been better for her to remain silent—it was completely irrelevant. In general, this dear O- how could I say... the speed of her tongue is incorrectly designed, the speed per second of the tongue should always be slightly less than the speed per second of thought, and by no means the contrary.

At the end of the avenue, on the Accumulator Tower, the bell was striking a booming 17. The personal hour was ended. I-330 was leaving together with that S-shaped male number. He had the kind of face that—inspired respect, and then I saw what seemed to be a familiar face. I had met him somewhere—but then I could not recall.

Upon leaving, I-330—still X-like—gave me a wry smile.

"Come by auditorium 112 the day after tomorrow."

I shrugged my shoulders:

"If I am assigned—precisely to that auditorium you have named..."

She, with a kind of incomprehensible confidence: "You will be."

This woman had the same unpleasant effect on me as an insoluble, irrational component which has made a haphazard intrusion in an equation. And I was happy to be left alone with dear O- if only for a short while.

Arm-in-arm we passed four rows of avenues. At the corner she had to turn left, I—to the right.

"I would like so much to come to you today, to lower the blinds. Especially today, right now..." O- timidly raised her crystal-blue eyes to me.

She is amusing. Well, what could I say to her? She had been at my place only yesterday and she knew as well as I that our next sexual day was the day after tomorrow. This was simply the same case of her "premature thoughts"—as happens (at times harmfully) with a premature ignition in a motor.

Upon parting I kissed her twice... no, I shall be precise: three times I kissed those marvellous blue eyes, unspoiled by a single cloudlet.

Record 3
Synopsis: **A Jacket**
A Wall
The Book of Hourly Tables

I have looked over everything that I wrote yesterday—and I see: I did not write with sufficient clarity. That is, all of this is perfectly clear for any one of us. But how is one to know: perhaps, you, the strangers, to whom the INTEGRAL will carry my notes, perhaps, you will have read the great book of civilization only as far as the page that our ancestors did about 900 years ago. Perhaps you do not even know such ABC's as the Book of Hourly Tables, the Personal Hours, the Maternal Norm, the Green Wall, the Benefactor. It seems ridiculous to me—and at the same time very difficult to speak about all this. It would all be the same as though some writer or other, let us say, of the 20th century, were forced to explain in his novel what was meant by *jacket*, *apartment*, *wife*. But nevertheless, if his novel is translated for savages—is it really conceivable to avoid annotations concerning a *jacket?*

I am certain that a savage would look at *jacket* and think: "Well, what is that for? Merely a burden." It seems to me that you would look precisely the same way when I told you that since the time of the Two Hundred Years' War none of us has been on the other side of the Green Wall.

But, dear friends, you must do at least some thinking, it does help a great deal. After all, it is clear: all of human history, as much as we know of it, is the history of the transition from nomadic forms to increasingly sedentary ones. Does it not then follow from this that the most sedentary form of life (ours)—is at the same time the most perfect (ours). If people dashed about the earth from one end to the other, then it was only during prehistoric times when there were nations, wars, commerce, the discoveries of the various Americas. But whatever for, who needs that now?

I grant you: growing accustomed to this sedentary form did not come immediately or without difficulty. When during the time of the Two Hundred Years' War all the roads were destroyed and became overgrown with grass—for the first while it must have seemed very inconvenient to live in cities, cut off from one another by green jungles. But what of it? After man first lost his tail, he probably did not learn at once how to chase away flies without the aid of that tail. But now—can you imagine yourself—with a tail? Or: perhaps you can imagine yourself on the street—naked, without a *jacket* (it's possible that you still go strolling about in *jackets*). Here it is precisely the same thing: I cannot imagine to myself a city that is not enveloped by a Green Wall. I cannot imagine a life that is not arrayed in the figured chasubles of The Book of Hourly Tables.

The Tables... Right at this very moment the purple figures on a golden background are gazing sternly and tenderly into my eyes from my wall. I am involuntarily reminded of what among the ancients was called an *icon* and I feel the urge to compose verses or prayers (which is one and the same thing). Oh, why am I not a poet that I might sing in worthy praise of you, O Tables, O heart and pulse of the United State.

All of us (and, perhaps, you too), while yet children in school, read this mightiest of monuments to come down to us from ancient literature— *The Railroad Timetables*. But place even it beside The Tables—and you will see, side by side, graphite and diamond: both have one and the same thing—C, carbon,—but how eternal, how translucent, how the diamond gleams. Whose spirit would not thrill when you rush headlong with a roar through the pages of *The Railroad Timetables*. But the The Tables— actually transform each of us into the steel, six-wheeled hero of a mighty poem. Every morning, with six-wheeled precision, at precisely the same hour and at precisely the same minute,—we, millions of us, arise as one. At precisely the same hour, millions like one, we begin our work—millions like one we finish. And coalescing into a single, million-handed body, at precisely the very same second, designated by The Tables,—we raise our spoons to our mouth,—and at precisely the very same second we emerge for our walk and we proceed to the auditorium, to the hall for the Taylor exercises, and we withdraw to sleep...

I will be entirely frank: even we do not yet have the absolutely precise solution to the question of happiness: twice a day—from 16 to 17 and from 21 to 22 the single mighty organism dissolves into separate cells: these are what The Tables have designated as—the Personal Hours. During these hours you may see: in the rooms of some—the blinds are modestly lowered, others, to the slow steps of the March—walk in measured time along the avenue, while yet others—as I myself am doing right now—are at their desks. But I resolutely believe—let them call me an idealist and a dreamer—I believe: sooner or later—but someday we shall find a place in the general formula for these hours as well, someday all 86,400 seconds will be included in The Book of Hourly Tables.

I have had the occasion to read and hear a great deal that was improbable about those times when people were still living in a free, i.e., unorganized, wild state. But the most improbable thing always seemed to me to be precisely the following: how in those times—even a rudimentary governmental authority could permit people to live without anything resembling our Tables, without any obligatory walks, without any precise regulation of mealtimes; they would get up and go to bed whenever they took it into their heads; several historians even say that apparently in those times lights burned in the streets all night, people walked and rode along the streets all night.

I cannot comprehend any of this in the least. However restricted their intelligence might have been, all the same they should have understood that a life like that was the most genuine form of mass murder—albeit a slow one, from day to day. The state (humaneness) prohibited the outright murder of a single person and did not prohibit the partial murder of millions. To murder a single person, i.e., to decrease the sum of human lives by 50 years—that was criminal, but to decrease the sum of human lives by 50 million years—that was not criminal. Really, is that not ridiculous? Any of our ten-year-old numbers can resolve this mathematical-moral problem in half a minute; but they were incapable—with all their Kants together (because not one of those Kants could hit on the idea of constructing a system of scientific ethics, i.e., based on subtraction, addition, division, multiplication).

Moreover—is it really not absurd that a state (it dared to call itself a state!) could leave sexual life without any control. Whoever, whenever and as much as one wished. . . Completely unscientific, like animals. And like animals, blindly, they bore children. Is it not ridiculous: to know horticulture, poultry-breeding, fish-breeding (we have exact data that they knew all of this) and not know how to proceed to the ultimate step in this logical ladder: child-breeding. Not to hit upon the idea of our Maternal and Paternal Norms.

It is so ridiculous, so improbable, that now that I have written it I am afraid: what if suddenly, you the unknown readers, should take me for a malicious jokester. What if suddenly you should think that I simply wish to have my joke at your expense and I am relating the most utter rubbish with a serious face.

But first of all: I am not capable of jokes—falsehood is a secret function that enters into every joke; and secondly: the United State Science can not be mistaken. And where would any state logic be forthcoming in those times when people lived in a condition of freedom, i.e., like that of animals, apes, the herd? What could one demand of them if even in our time—from somewhere at the bottom, out of the shaggy depths,—a wild, apelike echo can still be infrequently heard?

Fortunately—only infrequently. Fortunately—this is only a minor breakdown in details: they can be repaired logically, without halting the eternal, mighty progress of the whole Machine. And for the disposal of the twisted bolt—we have the skilful, heavy hand of the Benefactor, we have the experienced eyes of the Guardians. . .

Yes, by the way, now I remember: that male number from yesterday, the double-curved one, like S,—it seems to me that I have had occasion to see him coming out of the Bureau of Guardians. Now I understand why I had that instinctive feeling of deference towards him and a kind of awkwardness when in his presence that strange number I-330...I must confess that this I...

The bell is ringing for sleep: 22 1/2. Until tomorrow.

Record 4
Synopsis: The Savage with the Barometer
Epilepsy
If Only

Up until now everything in life had been clear to me (it is hardly by chance that I have, apparently, a certain predilection for this very word "clear"). But today... I do not understand.

First of all: I was actually assigned to be precisely in auditorium 112, just as she had told me. Although the probability was—

$$\frac{1,500}{10,000,000} = \frac{3}{20,000}$$

(1,500—that is the number of auditoria, 10,000,000—represents the numbers). Secondly... But better to take it in order.

The auditorium. An enormous hemisphere of glass massifs all suffused with sunlight. Circular rows of noble, globe-shaped, closely cropped heads. My heart gently skipped a beat as I looked all around. I think, I was searching: whether somewhere above the pale-blue waves of unifs a rosy crescent would be glistening—the dear lips of O-. Then suddenly someone's extraordinarily white and sharp teeth, similar to... no, wrong. This evening, at 21, O- would come to me—the wish to see her here was perfectly natural.

Then—a bell. We rose, sang the Hymn of the United State—and on the stage appeared the phonolecturer gleaming with wit and a golden loudspeaker.

"Respected numbers! Archeologists recently unearthed a book from the 20th century. In it the ironical author tells of a savage and a barometer. The savage noted: every time when the barometer came to rest on *rain*—it actually rained. And since the savage felt like rain, he then began to remove the right amount of mercury so that the level stopped at rain (on the screen—a savage in feathers, shaking out the mercury: laughter). You laugh: but does it not seem to you that the European of that era is more deserving of your laughter. Like the savage, the European also wanted *rain*,—but rain with a capital letter, an algebraic rain. Yet he stood before the barometer like a wet hen. The savage, at least, had more daring and energy and—even though a savage—more logic: he was able to ascertain that there was a connection between effect and cause. Shaking out the mercury he was able to take the first step on that mighty road by which. . ."

At this point (I repeat: I am writing without concealing anything)—at this point I became seemingly impervious to the vivifying streams pouring forth out of the loudspeakers. It suddenly seemed to me that I had come here in vain (why *in vain* and how could I have not come once I had been assigned here?); it all seemed to me—hollow, only a shell. And with difficulty I switched my attention back on only when the phonolecturer had gone on to the main theme: to our music, to mathematical composition (the mathematician is the cause, the music is the result), to a description of the recently invented musicometer.

"By simply turning this handle, anyone of you can produce up to three sonatas in an hour. Yet how difficult that was for your ancestors to achieve. They could create only by driving themselves into fits of *inspiration*—an unknown form of epilepsy. And here is a most amusing illustration for you of what they produced,—the music of Scriabin—the 20th century. This black box (curtains parted on the stage and there—their most ancient instrument)—they called this box a piano or a *royal grand*, which shows but one more time to what extent their music. . ."

And so forth—again I do not remember, quite possibly because. . . Well, yes, I shall say it straight: because she had walked up to the *royal grand* box—I-330. No doubt I was simply struck by this unexpected appearance of her on the stage.

She was in a fantastic costume of the ancient era: a tightly fitting black dress, the white of her bare shoulders and bosom sharply defined, and undulating with her breathing that warm shadow between. . . and the blinding, almost wicked lips. . .

Her smile—a bite, directed here—below. She sat down, began to play. Wild, convulsive, motley, like their entire life in those times,—not a shadow of rational mechanicalness. And, of course, they, around me, were right: everyone was laughing. Only a few. . . but why me as well—me?

Yes, epilepsy—a spiritual illness—a pain. . . A slow, sweet pain—a bite—if only it would go deeper yet, more painfully yet. And then, slowly— the sun. But not ours, not the azure crystalline and uniform one through the glass bricks—no: a wild, soaring, scorching sun—off with everything— rip everything into tiny shreds.

The number sitting beside me on the left glanced sideways—at me— and snickered. For some reason I have a very clear memory of that: I saw— a microscopic bubble of saliva form on his lips and burst. That bubble sobered me. I was—myself again.

Like everyone else—I heard only the absurd, fussy squeaking of strings. I was laughing. I felt light and simple. The talented phonolecturer had been depicting that wild era too vividly for us—that was all there was to it.

With what pleasure I listened to our contemporary music afterwards. (It was demonstrated in conclusion—for contrast.) The crystalline chromatic progressions of merging and diverging series—and the summarizing chords of Taylor McLauren; the full-bodied/full-toned, squarely massive passages of the Pythagorean theorem; the mournful melodies of a fading oscillatory movement; the brilliant measures alternating with Frauenhofer's lines in the pauses—the spectral analysis of the planets... What grandeur! What unwavering equilibrium: And how pitiful—totally unrestricted by anything other than wild fantasies—that willful music of the ancients...

As usual, in even ranks, four abreast, everyone exited through the wide doors of the auditorium. The familiar double-curved figure flitted past me; I nodded respectfully.

Dear O- was supposed to come in an hour. I felt pleasantly and usefully excited. Home—quickly to the desk, I handed the duty clerk my pink ticket and received a permit for the right to use the blinds. We have this right—only for Sexual Days. Otherwise amid our transparent walls seemingly woven of sparkling air—we always live in full view, eternally washed by the light. We have nothing to hide from one another. Moreover it facilitates the burdensome and exalted labour of the Guardians. Otherwise who can say what might happen. It is possible that it was precisely those strange, opaque dwellings of the ancients that gave birth to that pitiful cellular psychology of theirs. "My [sic!] home is my castle"—it really must have cost them an effort to think that one up!

At 22 I lowered the blinds—and at that very minute O- entered slightly out of breath. She held out her tiny pink mouth to me—and her pink ticket. I tore off the coupon—and then I could not tear myself away from that pink mouth until the very last moment—22:15.

Then I showed her my *records* and I talked—very well, I thought—about the beauty of the square, the cube, the straight line. She listened so enchantingly and pinkly—and suddenly from her blue eyes a tear, a second, a third,—straight onto the opened page (p. 7). The ink ran. Well, now I shall have to recopy it.

"Dear D-, if only you would—if only..."

Well, what *if only*? What about *if only*? Again her old refrain: a child. Or, perhaps, something new—concerning... concerning that other one? Even if it were... No, that would be too absurd.

Record 5
Synopsis: The Square
**   Rulers of the World**
**   A Pleasantly Useful Function**

Again I am wide of the mark. Again, my unknown reader, I am speaking with you as though you. . . Well, let us say, as though you were my old comrade, R-13, the poet, with negroid lips,—of course everyone knows him. But meanwhile you are on the Moon, or Venus, or Mars, or Mercury—who knows you, where you are and who you are.

Try this: imagine to yourself—a square, a living, beautiful square. And it must tell about itself, about its life. You understand—the square would be the last one to whom it would occur to talk about the fact that all of its four angles are equal: it simply does not see this any more—inasmuch as this is so customary, so prosaic for it. And all the time here I am as well in the situation of the square. Just take for example the pink coupons and everything connected with them: for me this is the same as equality of the four angles, but for you, perhaps this is less accessible than Newton's binomial theory.

But look here. A certain ancient wiseman, by chance, naturally, said a clever thing: "Love and hunger rule the world." Ergo: in order to gain mastery of the world—man must gain mastery over rulers of the world. Our ancestors finally subdued Hunger at a heavy price: I am speaking of the Great Two Hundred Years' War—about the war between city and village. Probably for reasons of religious prejudice, the wild Christians clung stubbornly to their *bread*.* But in the 35th year before the founding of the United State—our present-day petroleum-based food was invented. True, only 0.2 per cent of the population of the earthly sphere survived. Yet in return—cleansed of the filth of a thousand years—how radiant did the face of the earth become. And, in return, those two tenths—tasted bliss in the halls of the United State.

But is it not clear: bliss and envy—these are the numerator and the denominator of the fraction called happiness. And where would the sense be in all the innumerable sacrifices of the Two Hundred Years' War if all the same there had remained some reason for envy in our life. And it did remain because "button-noses" and "classical noses" remained (our earlier conversation during the walk)—because there were many who strove for the love of some whereas no one strove for the love of others.

Naturally, once having subordinated Hunger to itself (this is algebraically equal to the sum of eternal blessings), the United State launched an attack against the other ruler of the world—against Love. Finally, this

*This word has survived to our day only in the form of a poetic metaphor: the chemical composition of this substance is unknown to us.

element was conquered as well, i.e., organized, mathematized and about 300 years ago our historical *Lex Sexualis* was proclaimed: "every number has the right—to any other number—as a sexual product."

Well, the rest—that was merely technical detail. You are thoroughly examined in the laboratories of the Sexual Bureau, the content of sexual hormones in your blood is determined—and a corresponding Table of Sexual Days is worked out for you. Thereupon you make application that on your days you wish to make use of such and such a number (or numbers) and you receive the appropriate coupon booklet (pink). And that is all there is to it.

Clearly: the reasons for envy—they no longer exist, the denominator of the fraction of happiness has been reduced to zero—the fraction has been converted into magnificent infinity. And the very thing that had been the source of innumerable, stupid tragedies for the ancients—we have reduced it to a harmonious, pleasantly useful function of the organism, the same as sleep, physical labor, the taking of food, defecation and so forth. From this you see how the mighty force of logic purifies whatever it touches. Oh, if only you too, unknown readers, would come to know this divine force, if only you too would learn to follow it to the end.

...Strange: today while I was writing about the loftiest heights in human history, all the time I was inhaling the freshest mountain air of thought,—inside it seemed somehow cloudy, full of cobwebs, a kind of four-pawed X like a cross. Or was it because of my paws and it all stemmed from the fact that they were before my eyes for so long—my shaggy paws. I do not like to talk about them—and I do not like them: they are a vestige of a savage era. Can it be that there really is in me——

I wanted to cross all this out—because it oversteps the boundaries of my synopsis. But then I decided: I will not. Let my records—like the most precise seismograph—give the curve of even the most insignificant cerebral vibrations: indeed at times it is precisely such vibrations that serve as a forewarning——

Now this is becoming absurd, this should really be crossed out: we have harnessed all the elements—there can be no catastrophes whatsoever.

And now it is perfectly clear to me: the strange feeling within—it all stems from that same square-like situation of mine that I was discussing at the beginning. And there is no X in me (that cannot be)—simply I am afraid that some X will have remained in you, my unknown readers. But I believe—you will not judge me too harshly. I believe—you will understand that it is more difficult for me to write than it ever has been for a single author in the course of entire human history: some wrote for their contemporaries, others—for their descendants, but no one has ever written for their ancestors or creatures resembling their savage, distant ancestors.

Record 6
Synopsis: An Incident
The Accursed "It Is Clear"
24 Hours

I repeat: I have charged myself with the responsibility for writing without concealing anything. Therefore, however sad, I must remark here that apparently even for us the process of the solidification, of the crystallization of life has not yet been concluded; to the ideal—several steps still remain. The ideal (it is clear) is when nothing any longer happens, whereas here... But you might prefer an example: today in the *State Gazette* I read that a celebration of justice will take place in the Plaza of the Cube in two days' time. It must be that again some number has disrupted the progress of the mighty State Machine, once again something unforeseen, unprecalculated has happened.

And what is more—something has happened to me. True, it was in the course of the Personal Hour, i.e., in the course of the time specially set aside for unforeseen circumstances, but all the same...

Around 16 (more precisely, at ten minutes before 16) I was at home. Suddenly—the telephone:

"D-503?"—a woman's voice.

"Yes."

"Are you free?"

"Yes."

"It is me, I-330. I shall fly over for you right away and we will go to the Ancient House. Agreed?"

I-330... That I irritated me, repelled me—almost frightened me. But precisely for that reason I did say: yes.

Five minutes later we were already in an aero. The blue majolica of the sky—and the airy sun—in its own golden aero was humming behind us, neither catching us up nor falling behind. But there before us, gleaming whitely like a cataract was a cloud, absurd, puffy—like the cheeks of an antique *cupid*—and somehow it bothered me. A raised forward window, wind, lips drying up—licking them involuntarily all the while and thinking about your lips all the while.

And now the hazy green spots were already visible in the distance— there, beyond the Wall. Then the gentle, involuntary skipping of my heart—down, down, down—as though from a steep mountain—and we were at the Ancient House.

This whole strange, decrepit, blind structure was enclosed all around in a glass shell: otherwise, of course, it would have crumbled long ago. By the glass door was an old woman, all wrinkled—and particularly her mouth: nothing but folds, gathers, her lips had already withdrawn inward, her mouth seemed to have become overgrown—and it was entirely improbable that she should be able to speak. But all the same—she did begin to speak:

"Well, then, my dears, you've come to take a look at my little house?" and the wrinkles began to gleam (i.e., probably because they took on the shape of radiating rays of light, it gave the impression of "gleaming").

"Yes, grandmother, I felt like it again," I-330 said to her.

The wrinkles were gleaming:

"Some sun, eh? Well, what is it now, what? Ah, you mischiefmaker, you! I know, I know! Well, alright: go on by yourselves, I better stay here, in the sun. . . "

Hm. . . No doubt my companion was a frequent guest here. I felt like shaking something loose from myself—but something prevented me: doubtless it was still that same persistent optical image: the cloud on the smooth blue majolica.

While we were climbing up the broad, dark staircase, I-330 said:

"I love her—that old woman."

"What for?"

"I don't really know. Perhaps—for her mouth. Or perhaps—for no reason. Just because."

I shrugged my shoulders. She continued—with a slight smile, or, perhaps, without any smile at all:

"I feel very guilty. It is clear that it should be not a *just-because-love*, but a *because-of-love*. All elemental forces should be. . ."

"It is clear "—I began—but I caught myself immediately on this word and stole a furtive glance at I-330: had she noticed or not?

She was looking somewhere down below; her eyes were lowered—like blinds.

A recollection: evening time, around 22, walking along the avenue, and amid the brilliantly illuminated, transparent cubicles—dark ones with lowered blinds, and there, behind the blinds— What was going on there, behind her blinds? Why had she telephoned today, and why all of this?

I opened a heavy, creaking, opaque door—and we were in a gloomy, disorderly enclosed area (in those times they had called it an *apartment*). That most strange, *royal grand* musical instrument—and a wild, disorganized, insane—like their music—motley of colors and forms. A white flat surface overhead; dark blue walls; red, green, orange bindings of ancient books; yellow bronze—candelabras, a statue of Buddha; distorted with epilepsy, defying placement in any equations whatsoever—the lines of the furniture.

I could endure this chaos only with effort. But apparently my companion had a stronger constitution.

"This is my favorite. . ." —and suddenly she seemed to catch herself—the biting smile, white sharp teeth. "More precisely: the most absurd of all their *apartments*."

"Or, even more precisely: of all their states," I corrected. "Thousands of microscropic states, eternally at war, pitiless like..."

"Of course it is clear..." I-330 said with apparent seriousness.

We walked through the room where small children's beds stood (in that era children were private property as well). And again—rooms, the glimmer of mirrors, sullen dressers, unbearably variegated divans, an enormous *fireplace*, a large bed of mahogany. Our present-day glass—beautiful, transparent, eternal—was visible only in the form of miserable, fragile, small window-squares.

"And to think: here *they loved just because*, burned and tormented themselves... " (Again the lowered blinds of her eyes.) "What an absurd, extravagant expenditure of human energy—is it not true?"

She seemed to be speaking from out of me, speaking my thoughts. But all the while in her smile there was that irritating X. There, behind the blinds, something was going on of the sort—I did not know what—that made me lose patience; I had the urge to argue with her, to shout at her (yes, exactly), but I was forced to agree—it was impossible not to agree.

Then—we stopped before a mirror. In that moment—I saw only her eyes. An idea came to me: the human being is really constructed just as wildly as these absurd *apartments*—human heads are opaque, and there are only minute windows within: the eyes. She seemed to guess—she turned around. "Well—here are my eyes. Well?" (All this, of course, in silence.)

Before me were two eerily dark windows, and within, such an unknown, alien life. I saw only a fire—she had some kind of *fireplace* of her own blazing there—and some kind of figures resembling...

This, of course, was natural: I had caught my own reflection there. But it had been unnatural and unlike me (apparently, this was the oppressive effect of the surroundings)—I definitely felt fear, I felt myself trapped, imprisoned in this savage cage, I felt myself caught in the savage whirlwind of ancient life.

"You know what," I-330 said, "go into the next room for a minute." Her voice was audible from there, from within, out of those dark windows of eyes where the fireplace was blazing.

I went out, sat down. From a small shelf on the wall the snub-nosed, asymetrical physiognomy of one of the ancient poets (Pushkin, I believe) was smiling almost imperceptibly directly at me. Why was I sitting there—and enduring submissively that smile and why all of this: why was I here—why this absurd state? That irritating, repellent woman, the strange play...

In there—the door of the wardrobe banged, there was the rustle of silk, I was restraining myself with difficulty so as not to enter there and——
I do not remember exactly why: probably, I had the urge to say very harsh things to her. But she had already appeared. She was in a short, old, brilliantly yellow dress, a black hat, black stockings. The dress was of a

very thin silk—I could see quite clearly: the stockings were very long, much above the knees,—and the neck was bare, the shadow between. . .

"Listen here, it is clear, you wish to be original, but do you really. . . "

"It is clear," I-330 interrupted, "that to be original—this means to stand out in some way from others. Consequently, to be original—this means to destroy equality. . . And what in the idiotic language of the ancients was called *being banal*—for us it means: simply to fulfill one's duty. Because. . ."

"Yes, yes, yes! Precisely." I did not restrain myself. "And you, as far as you are concerned. . ."

She went up to the statue of the snub-nosed poet and lifting the blinds to reveal the wild fire of her eyes—there within, behind her windows—she said, apparently with complete seriousness this time (perhaps in order to placate me)—she said a very intelligent thing:

"Do you not find it amazing that at one time they could have put up with such people as this? And not only put up with them—they worshipped them. What a slavish spirit! Is it not true?"

"It is clear. . . That is I wanted (that accursed *it is clear!*)."

"Yes, I understand. But you know, in essence, these were rulers more powerful than their own coronated ones. Why did they not isolate them, destroy them. Here we. . . "

"Yes, here we. . . " I began. And suddenly she—burst into laughter. At that moment I simply saw the laughter: the ringing, abrupt, curved line of that laughter, tensely resilient, like a whip.

I remember—I was trembling all over. Then I wanted to grab her—and I no longer remember what else. . . There had to be something—it did not matter what—something else to do. Mechanically I opened my golden badge, glanced at my watch. It was ten minutes to 17.

"Do you not think that it is time now?" I said as politely as I could.

"And if I asked you—to stay here with me?"

"Now listen here: you. . . are you aware of what you are saying? In ten minutes I am obliged to be in the auditorium. . ."

". . . And all the numbers are obliged to take the prescribed course in art and science. . ." I-330 said in my voice. Then she quickly drew back the blinds—she raised her eyes: through the dark windows—blazed the fireplace. "I have a doctor in the Medical Bureau—he is registered to me. And if I ask—he will give you a certificate for being sick. Well?"

I understood. Finally, I understood where all this game was leading to.

"So that's it! But you know that like every honorable number I must virtually go to the Bureau of Guardians immediately and. . . "

"But not virtually," (the sharp biting smile). "I am terribly curious: will you go to the Bureau or not?"

"Are you staying?" I reached for the handle of the door. The handle was brass—and I heard: my voice sounded just as brass-like.

"One moment... May I?"

She went to the telephone. She rang some number or other—I was so upset that I could not remember it—and she exclaimed:

"I shall be waiting for you in the Ancient House. Yes, yes, alone... "

I turned the cold brass handle:

"Will you permit me to take the aero?"

"Oh, yes, of course! Please do..."

There, in the sun, by the way out—like a plant, the old woman was dozing. Again it was amazing that her densely overgrown mouth opened up and that she could speak.

"And what about that one of yours—is she staying there alone?"

"Yes, she is."

The old woman's mouth again became overgrown. She shook her head. Apparently even her deteriorating brain understood all the absurdity and foolhardiness of that woman's behavior.

Precisely at 17 I was at the lecture. And there I suddenly realized for some reason that I had not told the old woman the truth: I-330 was not alone there now. Perhaps it was precisely this—that I had involuntarily deceived the old woman—that tormented me and hindered me from listening. Yes, she was not alone—that was what the matter was.

After 21 1/2—I had a free hour. It would have been possible to go this very day to the Bureau of Guardians and make a deposition. But I was so tired after this stupid business. And then—the legal period for making a deposition was two days. I would have time tomorrow: there was still a whole 24 hours.

Record 7
Synopsis: An Eye-Lash
         Taylor
         Henbane and Lily-of-the-Valley

Night. Green, orange, blue; a red royal grand instrument; a dress yellow like an orange. Then—a brass Buddha; suddenly he raised his brass eyelids—and sap began to pour: out of the Buddha. And from the yellow dress—sap, and over the mirror drops of sap, and the large bed was oozing sap, and the small children's beds, and then I myself—and a kind of deathly sweet terror...

I awoke: a subdued, bluish light; the glass of the walls gleamed, the glass chairs, the table. It was calming, my heart ceased pounding. The sap,

Buddha... what kind of an absurdity is that? It is clear: I am ill. I have never had dreams before. They say that among the ancients—this was a most ordinary and normal thing—having dreams. But of course: their entire life had been—this kind of horrible carousel: green—orange—Buddha—sap. But then we know that dreams—these are a serious psychic illness. And I know: up until now my brain was a chronometrically accurate, glittering, mechanism without a speck of dust, whereas now... Yes, now it is precisely as though: I can feel there, in the brain—some kind of alien body—like the finest eyelash in an eye: otherwise you feel normal, but that eye with the tiny hair—it is impossible to forget it even for a second...

A cheerful, small, crystalline bell at the head of the bed: 7, rise. To the right and left, through the glass walls—it is as though I am seeing my own self, my room, my clothes, my movements—repeated a thousand times. This is cheering: you see yourself as a part of the vast, powerful whole. And such precise beauty: not a single superfluous gesture, bend, turn.

Yes, without a doubt, this Taylor had been the greatest genius among the ancients. True, he had not thought so far as extending his method to all of life, to every step, to the entire twenty-four hour period—he had not known how to integrate his system from the first hour to the 24th. But all the same: how could they have written whole libraries about some Kant or other there—and hardly take note of Taylor—that prophet who was able to look ten centuries ahead.

Breakfast is over. The Hymn of the United State has been sung in unison. In fours—to the elevators in unison. The barely audible whirring of motors—and quickly down, down, down—the heart skipping a gentle beat...

And then suddenly here for some reason or other that absurd dream again—or some cryptic function or other from that dream. Ah, but of course, yesterday in the aero as well—the descent downwards. However, all of that is finished: period. And a good thing that I was so decisive and abrupt with her.

In a car of the underground railway I was transported to where the exquisite body of the *Integral*, still motionless, still without the breath of fire in it, sparkled on the slip beneath the sun. With eyes closed I was daydreaming with formulae: once again I mentally calculated what initial velocity was required in order to sever the *Integral* from the earth. Every atom of a second—the mass of the *Integral* would change (the blast-off fuel is being expended). The result was a very complicated formula, with transcendent magnitudes.

As though in a dream: here, in the solid numerical world—someone sat down beside me, someone nudged me slightly, said—"Pardon me."

I half-opened my eyes—and at first (an association with the *Integral*) something soaring impetuously into space: a head—and it was soaring because on the sides were pink, protruding wing-ears. And then the curved line of the rounded back of the head—the stooped back—the double-curve—the letter S...

And through the glass walls of my algebraic world—once again the eye-lash—something unpleasant that today I should—

"Not at all, not at all," I smiled to my neighbor, exchanged greetings with him. On his badge flashed: S-4711 (it is understandable why from the very first moment he was connected for me with the letter S: it was an optical impression that did not register on my consciousness). And his eyes sparkled—two sharp, gimlet-eyes, spinning rapidly, drilled deeper and deeper and then in an instant would drill to the very bottom, would see what even I to myself...

Suddenly the eye-lash became perfectly clear to me:—one of them, one of the Guardians, and the simplest of all would be to tell him everything at once, without delay.

"By the way, I was at the Ancient House yesterday..." my voice was strange, hoarse, flat—I tried to clear it with a cough.

"Why, that's excellent. It provides material for very instructive conclusions."

"But, you understand—I was not alone, I accompanied number I-330, and then..."

"I-330? I am glad for you. She is a very interesting, talented woman. She has many admirers."

... But he too—during the walk then—and perhaps he is even registered to her? No, tell him about this—impossible, unthinkable: it is clear.

"Yes, yes! Of course, of course! Quite." I was smiling—more and more broadly, absurdly—and I kept feeling: because of this smile—I was naked, stupid...

The gimlets had reached to the very bottom inside me, then quickly spinning—they drilled their way back into his eyes; S- gave a double-curved smile, nodded to me, slipped off towards the exit.

I hid behind a newspaper (it seemed to me—everyone was looking at me)—and shortly I forgot about the eye-lash, about the gimlets, about everything: I was so upset by what I read. One brief line: "According to reliable information—traces have once again come to light of an organization which has avoided capture up until now and which has set itself the goal of liberation from the beneficent yoke of the State."

Liberation? Amazing: how tenacious criminal instincts are in the human species. I am consciously saying: *criminal*.

Freedom and crime are as inextricably bound together as... well, as the movement of an aero and its speed: the speed of the aero $= 0$, and it does not move; the freedom of man $= 0$, and he does not commit crimes. This is clear. The sole way to rid man of crimes—is to rid him of freedom. And now when we have almost rid ourselves of this (on a cosmic scale, of course, centuries are only an *almost*), suddenly some pitiful half-wits...

No, I do not understand: why, yesterday, I did not go immediately to the Bureau of Guardians. Today after 16—I am going there without fail. . .

At 16:10 I left—and immediately I saw 0- on the corner—all in pink ecstasy over the meeting. ("Now she has a simple, round mind. This is opportune: she will understand and support me". . .) But no: I did not need any support: I had made a firm decision.

The pipes of the Musical Factory harmoniously thundered out the March—that same, daily March. What unspeakable enchantment in this daily, repetitive, mirror-like quality!

O- seized me by the hand.

"A walk?" The round blue eyes were opened wide to me—blue windows to the inside—and I penetrated inside unimpeded: nothing—inside, i.e., nothing alien, extraneous.

"No, not a walk. I have to... " I told her where. And I saw to my amazement: the pink circle of her mouth—formed a pink crescent, with the points downward—as though from something sour. I exploded.

"It seems you female numbers are incurably corrupted with prejudices. You are completely incapable of thinking abstractly. Forgive me, but this is simply dull-wittedness."

"You—are going to the spies... Ugh! And here I was just getting a sprig of lilies-of-the-valley for you at the Botanical Museum... "

"Why *And here I*—why this *And here*! just like a woman." I angrily (I admit) seized her lilies-of-the-valley. "Well here it is, your lily-of-the-valley, well? Have a whiff: good, eh? So have at least this much logic. The lily-of-the-valley smells good: right. But can you really not say of the scent, about the very concept of *scent*, that it is good or bad? Do you find that im-pos-si-ble, now? There is the scent of the lily-of-the-valley—and there is the foul scent of henbane: both are scents. There were spies in the ancient state—and we have our spies now... yes, spies. I am not afraid of the words. But it is indeed clear: there the spy was henbane, here the spy is lily-of-the-valley. Yes, yes, lily-of-the-valley!"

The pink crescent was trembling. Now I understand: it only seemed to me—but then I was certain that she was going to laugh. And I began to shout more and more loudly:

"Yes, lily-of-the-valley. And there's nothing to laugh at, nothing."

The round, smooth spheres of heads kept floating past—and turning around. O- took me tenderly by the hand:

"There's something wrong with you today... Are you ill?" The dream—yellow—the Buddha... Everything immediately became clear to me: I must go to the Medical Bureau.

"Yes, of course, it's true: I am ill," I said quite happily (this was a completely inexplicable contradiction: there was nothing to be happy about).

"Then you must go immediately to the doctor. You do understand: you are obliged to be healthy—it's ridiculous to have to prove that to you."

"Yes, dear O-, yes, of course you are right. Absolutely right!"

I did not go to the Bureau of Guardians: nothing to be done about it, I had to go to the Medical Bureau; I was detained there until 17.

But in the evening (however, it did not matter—in the evening it would already be closed)—in the evening O- came to me. The blinds were not lowered. We solved problems out of an ancient arithmetic workbook: this is very soothing and cleansing for the mind. O-90 sat over the workbook, her head leaning towards her left shoulder and her left cheek puffed out from within by her tongue with the effort. It was so childlike, so enchanting. And everything inside me was so good, precise, simple...

She left. I was alone. I breathed deeply twice (this is very helpful before sleeping). And suddenly some unexpected scent or other—and about something very unpleasant... I soon found what: a sprig of lilies-of-the-valley was hidden in my bed. Suddenly everything emerged in a whirlwind, rose up from the bottom. No, this was simply tactless on her part—to slip these lilies-of-the-valley on me. Well, true: I had not gone, that was so. But after all I was not to blame that I was sick.

Record 8
Synopsis: **An Irrational Root**
                 R-13
                 A Triangle

It was so long ago, during my school years when I came across the square root of -1. I remember so clearly, indelibly: a bright sphere-hall, hundreds of round boyish heads—and Plyapa, our mathematician. We nicknamed him Plyapa: he was already pretty well second-hand, with loose screws, and when the monitor plugged him in from behind, then from the loud-speaker there always came at first: "Ply-plya-plya-tshshsh," and then the lesson would begin. One day Plyapa told us about irrational numbers—and I remember, I wept, I pounded the desk with my fists and wailed: "I don't want the square root of -1! Remove that square root of -1 from me!" This irrational root rooted itself in me like something foreign, alien, strange, it was devouring me—it was impossible to comprehend it, to render it harmless because it was beyond *ratio*.

And now here again was that square root of -1. I looked over my records—and it is clear to me: I was trying to outwit myself, I was lying to myself—so as not to see that square root of -1. This is all nonsense—that I am sick and so forth: I could have gone there; a week ago—I know I would have gone without giving it a thought. But why not now... Why?

For example today. Precisely at 16:10—I was standing in front of the sparkling glass wall. Above me—the golden, sunny, pure radiance of the letters on the sign of the Bureau. In the interior, through the glass, a long line of pale-blue unifs. Like the icon-lamps in an ancient church—their faces were gleaming: they had come in order to perform a great deed, they had come in order to deliver up to the altar of the United State their loved ones, their friends—themselves. And I—longed to join them, to be with them. And I could not: my feet were deeply fused into the glass slabs—I was standing there, gazing dumbly, powerless to move from the spot...

"Hey, mathematician, daydreaming!"

I gave a start. The dark eyes, varnished with laughter, were on me, the thick, negroid lips. The poet R-13, an old friend—and with him the pink O-.

I turned around angrily (I think that if they had not interfered, I might ultimately have torn the square root of -1 out of me with the flesh, I would have gone into the Bureau).

"I am not daydreaming, and if you care to know—I was admiring," I said sharply enough.

"Of course, of course! You shouldn't be a mathematician, old friend, but a poet, yes, a poet! Indeed, join up with us—with the Poets, eh? If you want—I can arrange it in an instant, eh?"

R-13 talks with a sputter, his words seem to gush out of him, and from those thick lips—a spray; every p is a fountain, the *poets* are a fountain.

"I have served and I shall go on serving knowledge." I frowned; I do not care for jokes and I do not understand them, but R-13 has a nasty habit of joking.

"Who cares about that: knowledge! Your knowledge is nothing more than—cowardice. Yes, nothing more: it's true. You simply wish to throw up a wall around infinity, yet you are afraid to take a peep behind the wall. Yes! If you did take a look—you would close your eyes. Yes!"

"Walls—these are the basis of all human... " I began. R-13— showered like a fountain, O-90—was laughing with a pink roundness. I waved my hand: go ahead and laugh, it doesn't matter. I had no time for that. I needed to devour, to stifle that accursed square root of -1

"Listen," I suggested, "let's go and sit a while at my place, we'll solve some arithmetic problems."(I remembered that peaceful hour the day before—perhaps, it would be the same today.)

O- gave R- a glance: she gave me a clear, round glance, almost imperceptibly her cheeks grew flushed with that tender, exciting color of our coupons.

"But today I... Today I have a coupon for him," she nodded to R-, "and he's busy in the evening... So... "

The moist, varnished lips produced a kindly smack:

"That's alright: a half-hour will be sufficient for the two of us. Isn't that right, O-? I'm no lover of those little arithmetic problems of yours, but we can simply—go to my place and sit a while."

I felt eerie about being left alone with myself—or more truthfully, with that new self that was alien to me, whose number only seemed by some strange coincidence to be mine—D-503.

And I went to his place, to R-13's. True, he was not precise, not rhythmic; he had an inverted, mocking kind of logic, but all the same we were friends. It was not by chance that three years ago he and I together chose that darling, pink O-. This bound us somehow more strongly than our school years. Later—in R-13's room. Apparently—everything precisely the same as at my place: the Book of the Hours, the glass of the chairs, the table, the wardrobe, the bed. But no sooner had R- entered—he moved one chair, another,—the planes were altered, everything departed from the established pattern, became non-Euclidean. R-13—he was still the same, still the same. In the classes on Taylor and mathematics—he was always at the tail-end.

We recalled old Plyapa: the way we boys always used to paste little notes of thanks to his glass legs (we were very fond of Plyapa). We recalled the Teacher of Laws.* Our Teacher of Laws had an extraordinarily thunderous voice—so that the air came blasting out of the megaphone— and we, the children, shouted the text out at the top of our lungs after him. And how the desperate R-13 crammed bits of crumpled paper down his mouthpiece: whatever the text—it shot forth crumpled paper. R-, of course, was punished, what he had done—was, of course, bad, but now we were roaring with laughter—our whole triangle—and, admittedly, I too.

"But what if he had been alive—as among the ancients, eh? Then he would have been. . . " (b—a fountain from his thick, smacking lips. . .)

Sun—through the ceiling, the walls; sun from above, from the sides, reflected—downwards. O-90—on R-13's knees, and the minute little drops of sun in her blue eyes. I had somehow warmed up, recovered; the square root of -1 was buried, was not stirring. . .

"Well, then, what about your *Integral*? Will we soon be flying off to enlighten the inhabitants of other planets, eh? Well, hurry, hurry! Otherwise we poets will have scribbled so much for you that not even your *Integral* will be able to take off. Everyday, from 8 to 11. . . " R- shook his head, scratched the back of it: the back of his head—it looked like some kind of quadrangular little valise tied on behind (it recalled an ancient painting—*In the Carriage).*

I livened up:

"So you too are writing for the *Integral*? Well, tell me what about? Just take today for instance."

"Today—nothing. I was busy with something else. . . " (the b showered directly on me).

"With what else?"

R- frowned:

*It goes without saying that we are concerned not with the *Divine Law* of the ancients, but with the law of the United State.

"Just something else! But if you like—a death sentence. I was poeticizing a death sentence. One idiot, from our very own poets... Two years he sat beside me seemingly quite normal. And suddenly—with no warning, he says: 'I am a genius, a genius—I am above the law.' And he made such a mess of things... Well, there you go... Phew!"

The thick lips drooped, the varnished eyes dimmed. R-13 leapt up, turned around and stared somewhere off through the wall. I looked at his firmly locked little valise and thought: what is he picking through there—in his little suitcase.

A minute of awkward, asymetrical silence. It was unclear to me what the matter was, but there was something the matter here.

"Fortunately, the antediluvian times of all those various Shakespeares and Dostoevskys—or whatever they were called then—are past," I said purposely aloud.

R- turned his face to me. The words showered as before, gushed forth out of him, but it seemed to me—the cheerful varnish of his eyes was no longer there.

"Yes, my most dear mathematician, fortunately, fortunately! We are the most fortunate arithmetical mean... As you mathematicians put it: the integration from zero to infinity—from the cretin to Shakespeare... That's how!"

I don't know why—it seems to have been entirely irrelevant—I recalled that other one, her tone, some kind of very fine thread stretched between her and R . (Which thread?) Again the square root of -1 began to squirm. I opened my badge: twenty-five minutes after 16. They had 45 minutes left for their pink coupon.

"Well, time for me to go... " and I kissed O-, shook R-'s hand, went to the elevator.

Out on the avenue, while in the midst of crossing over to the other side, I looked around: in the bright sun-suffused glass monolith of the building—here and there were the grayish-blue, opaque cubicles with lowered blinds—the cubicles of rhythmic, Taylorized happiness. On the seventh floor my eyes found R-13's cubicle: he had already lowered the blinds.

Dear O-... Dear R-... In him there is also (I don't know why *also*—but let it stand as it is)—in him there is also something that is not entirely clear to me. And all the same, I, he and O-90—we are a triangle, even if not an equilateral triangle, but all the same a triangle. We, if one were to speak in the language of our ancestors (perhaps for you, my planetary readers, this language is more intelligible), we are a family. And it is so good to take a rest if only for a short while, to lock oneself up in a simple, strong triangle away from everything that...

Record 9

Synopsis: **Liturgy**
                Iambics and Trochees
                The Cast-Iron Hand

A solemn, bright day. On such a day one forgets about one's weaknesses, imprecisions, illnesses—and everything is crystalline-immutable, eternal—like our new glass...

The Plaza of the Cube. Sixty-six mighty concentric circles: the tribunes. And sixty-six rows: the serene lamps of faces, eyes reflecting the radiance of the heavens—or, perhaps, the radiance of the United State. Flowers crimson like blood: the lips of women. The delicate garlands of children's faces—in the front rows, close to the place of the action. An intensified, stern, gothic silence.

Judging by the descriptions which have come down to us, the ancients experienced something similar during their *services of divine worship*. But they were serving their irrational, unknown God—we serve a rational one and one that is known in a most precise form; their God gave them nothing other than the agony of eternal searchings; their God could not invent anything more clever than self-sacrifice for some unknown reason—but we bear our sacrifice to our God, the United State—a calm, considered, rational sacrifice. Yes, this was a solemn liturgy to the United State, a remembrance of the crusading days and years of the Two Hundred Years' War, a magnificent celebration of the victory of all over one, the sum over the unit...

Now a single one—was standing on the steps of the sun-washed Cube. A white... but not actually—not a white, but rather colorless now—a glass face, glass lips. And there were only the eyes, black, sucking, gulping holes and that eerie peace from which he was but a few minutes away. The yellow badge with the number—had already been removed. The hands were bound with a purple ribbon (an ancient custom: its explanation apparently stems from the fact that in antiquity, when all of this was being performed not in the name of the United State, the condemned understandably felt justified in resisting, and their hands were usually fettered with chains).

Up above, on the Cube, beside the Machine—motionless, as though of metal, was the figure of the one we called the Benefactor. From here, from down below, the face could not be distinguished: one could only see that it was confined to austere, majestic, square features. But then the hands... It is sometimes like that in photographic shots: the hands, placed too close in the foreground—come out enormous, they arrest attention—they overshadow all else. These ponderous hands, for the time being still resting calmly on the knees—it is clear: they are stone, and the knees—barely support their weight...

And suddenly one of these enormous hands was slowly raised—a slow, cast-iron gesture—and from the tribunes, in obedience to the raised hand, a number approached the Cube. It was one of the State Poets to whose lot had fallen the good fortune—of crowning the celebration with his verses. And the divine, brazen iambics thundered forth over the tribunes—about him, the madman, with the glassy eyes who was standing there, on the steps, and awaiting the logical consequences of his mad deeds.

... A conflagration. In the iambics buildings were rocking, they went showering upwards in liquid gold, collapsed. Green trees were writhing, the sap dripped—then there were only the black crosses of the skeletons. But then Prometheus appeared (that was us, of course).

> To steel, to engine harnessed fire,
> And fettered chaos with the law.

Everything was new, of steel: a sun of steel, trees of steel, people of steel. Suddenly some madman—"gave fire freedom from its chains"—and again everything perished...

Unfortunately I have a poor memory for verses, but one thing I do remember: it was impossible to choose more instructive and beautiful images.

Again the slow, ponderous gesture—and on the steps of the Cube a second poet. I even stood up: was it possible?

Yes: his thick, negroid lips, it was him... why had he not said earlier that he was to perform such a high... His lips were trembling, gray. I understood: in the presence of the Benefactor, in the presence of the entire assembly of Guardians—but still: to be so agitated...

Sharp, rapid—like a keen axe—trochees. About an unheard-of crime: about sacrilegious verses, where the Benefactor was called... no, I cannot bring myself to repeat it.

R-13, pale, looking at no one (I had not expected this shyness from him)—descended, sat down. For one infinitesimal differential of a second, I caught a fleeting glimpse of someone's face beside him—a sharp, black triangle—and immediately it was blotted out: my eyes—thousands of eyes—were directed there, up above, to the Machine. There—a third cast-iron gesture of the superhuman hand. And, swayed by an invisible wind,—the criminal was walking, slowly, a step—one more—and then one pace, the final in his life—and facing the sky, with his head thrown back—on his final resting-place.

Ponderous, stony, like fate, the Benefactor walked around the Machine, laid an enormous hand on a lever... Not a rustle, not a breath: all eyes were on that hand. What a fiery, engulfing whirlwind it must be—to be the instrument, to be the equivalent of hundreds of thousands of volts. What a magnificent destiny!

An immeasurable second. The hand was lowered, switching on the current. An unbearably sharp blade of light flashed—a barely audible crackling, like a tremor, in the tubes of the Machine. The outstretched body—all covered in a light, glowing haze—and then before our eyes, melting, melting, dissolving with frightening rapidity. Then—nothing: just a puddle of chemically pure water that only a minute before had been beating red and unrestrained in a heart...

All of this was simple, everyone of us knew this: yes, the dissociation of matter, yes, the splitting of atoms in the human body. And, nontheless, every time it was—like a miracle, it was—like a sign of the superhuman power of the Benefactor.

Up there in front of Him were the glowing faces of ten female numbers, their lips parted in excitement, flowers* swaying in the wind.

According to an old custom—the ten women were decorating with flowers the Benefactor's unif which had not yet dried from the showering. With the majestic stride of a high priest He slowly descended, slowly passed between the tribunes—and in His wake, upward raised, the delicate white branches of women's arms and the uni-millioned tempest of our cheers. And then the very same cheers in honor of the assemblage of Guardians, invisibly present somewhere here in the midst of our ranks. Who knows: perhaps it was precisely they whom the fantasy of ancient man had foreseen in creating his tenderly stern *archangels* who were appointed to each person at birth.

Yes, something of ancient religions, something purifying like a thunderstorm or tempest—was present in all of this solemnity. You, whose lot it will be to read this,—are you familiar with such moments? I feel sorry for you if you are not...

Record 10
Synopsis: **A Letter**
                     The Diaphragm
                     My Shaggy Self

The past day for me has been like that very paper through which chemists filter their solutions: all the suspended particles, everything superfluous, remains on this paper. And in the morning I went downstairs cleanly distilled, transparent.

*Of course, from the Botanical Museum. Personally, I don't see anything beautiful in flowers— the same as I don't in anything that belongs to the wild world banished long ago beyond the Green Wall. Only the rational and useful are beautiful: machines, boots, formulae, food and so forth.

Downstairs, in the vestibule, at a small desk, the female duty clerk, glancing at the clock, was recording the numbers of those entering. Her name is U-... however I had better not mention her number because I am afraid of writing anything bad about her. Although essentially, this is a very respectable, elderly woman. The one thing I do not care for in her—it is that her cheeks droop somewhat—like fish gills (would that seem to matter?)

She scratched with her pen, I saw myself on the page: D-503—and—a blot.

I was just about to call her attention to this when suddenly she raised her head—and spattered me with such an inky little smile:

"Here's a letter. Yes. You'll get it, my dear yes, yes, you will."

I knew: a letter read by her—must still pass through the Bureau of Guardians (I believe it is superfluous to explain this customary procedure), and I would have it not later than 12. But I was confused by that same little smile, the drop of ink had muddied my transparent solution. So much so, that later at the building site of the *Integral*, I could not concentrate in the least—and even on one occasion I made an error in the calculations, something that had never happened to me.

At 12 hours—again the pinkish-brown fish gills, the little smile—and, finally, I had the letter in my hands. Without knowing why, I did not read it right there, but stuffed it in my pocket—and quickly went to my own room. I unfolded it, ran my eyes over it and—sat down... It was an official notification that number I-330 had been registered to me and that today at 21 I must appear at her place—down below, the address...

No: after all that had been, after I had made such an unambiguous display of my attitude towards her. Besides, she did not even know: whether I had been to the Bureau of Guardians,—there was no way she could have known that I was ill—well, that generally I had not been able... And despite all this——

In my head a dynamo was whirling, humming. Buddha—yellow—lilies-of-the-valley—a pink crescent... Yes, and there was this—and there was this as well: today O- wanted to drop in on me. Should I show her this notification—concerning I-330? I don't know: she would not believe (and how could she, in fact, believe it) that I had nothing to do with it, that I completely... And I know: it would be a difficult, absurd, absolutely illogical conversation... No, anything but that. Let it all be decided mechanically: I would send her a copy of the notification.

I was hastily stuffing the notification into my pocket—when I caught sight of that horrible, ape-like hand of mine. I remembered how she, I-330, had taken my hand during that walk, looked at it. Could she really...

And now it was fifteen minutes before 21. A northern white night. Everything was greenish-glass. But this was some other kind of fragile glass—not ours, not the real kind, this was a thin, glass shell, and beneath the shell there was a whirling, soaring, humming... And I would not have been surprised if suddenly the cupolas of the auditoria had risen up in round, slow clouds of smoke, and if the elderly moon had smiled inkily—like that one at the small desk this morning, and if in all the buildings all the blinds were suddenly lowered, and behind the blinds——

A strange sensation: I could feel my ribs—they were like some kind of iron rods and interfered—positively interfered with my heart, it was cramped, not enough room. I stood at the glass door with the gold numbers: I-330. With her back to me, over a desk, I-330 was writing something. I entered...

"Here..." —I handed the pink coupon to her. "I received the notification today and have come."

"How punctual you are! one moment—may I? Take a seat, I'm just finishing."

Again she lowered her eyes to the letter—and what was going on inside her there behind the lowered blinds? What would she say—what was I to do in a second? How to know, how to calculate, when she was so totally—from there, from the wild, ancient land of dreams.

I gazed at her in silence. My ribs—iron rods, cramped... She spoke—her face was like a quick, flashing wheel: you could not make out the individual spokes. But now the wheel was motionless. And I glimpsed a strange combination: dark eyebrows turned up sharply towards the temples—two deep little creases, from the nose to the corners of the mouth—a mocking, sharp triangle with its apex uppermost. And these two triangles seemed to contradict each other, stamped the entire face with that unpleasant, irritating X—like a cross: a face cancelled with a cross.

The wheel began to spin, the spokes merged together... "Then you didn't go to the Bureau of Guardians?"

"I did... But I couldn't: I was ill."

"Yes. Well, that's what I thought as well: something must have prevented you—it hardly matters what (— the sharp teeth, a smile). But now you are in my hands. You remember: 'Every number not reporting to the Bureau within 48 hours is considered'... "

My heart pounded so hard that the rods bent. Like a little boy,—stupidly, like a little boy, I had been caught, I remained stupidly silent. And I sensed: I had become entangled,—tied hand and foot...

She stood up, stretched lazily. She pressed a button, with a faint rustle the blinds fell on all sides. I was cut off from the world—just the two of us.

I-330 was somewhere behind my back, near the wardrobe. Her unif rustled, fell—I listened—listened hard. And I remembered... no: it flashed for one-hundredth of a second...

Recently I had the occasion to calculate the curvature of a new type of street diaphragm (now these diaphragms, exquisitely decorated, record on all the avenues the street conversations for the Bureau of Guardians). And I remember: a concave, pink, quivering membrane—a strange creature, consisting of a single organ—an ear. At that moment I was a diaphragm like that...

Then a button snapped at her collar—at her breast—and still lower. The glassy silk rustled along her shoulders, her knees, onto the floor. I was hearing—and that was even clearer than seeing—how with one foot and then the other she stepped out of the pale-blue, gray silky mound...

The tautly stretched diaphragm trembled and registered the silence. No: sharp, with endless pauses—hammer blows against the rods. And I heard—I saw: behind me, she was thinking a moment.—Then—the doors of the wardrobe, then—some lid banged—and once again silk, silk...

"Now, please."

I turned around. She was in a light, saffron-yellow dress of an ancient design. It was a thousand times more wicked than if she had been dressed in nothing. Two sharp points—through the thin fabric, smouldering pinkly— two embers through the ashes. Two tenderly rounded knees...

She was sitting in a rather low arm chair. On the rectangular little table in front of her was a flask with something poisonously green, two fragile stemmed glasses. At the corner of her mouth something was smoking—in a very thin paper tube, that ancient smoking substance (what it was called—I cannot recall now).

The diaphragm was still trembling. The hammer was pounding there—in my insides—against the red-hot rods. I could hear each blow distinctly and... and what if she could hear it too?

But she kept on producing the smoke calmly, glancing at me calmly and carelessly shaking ashes—on my pink ticket.

As coldbloodedly as possible—I asked:

"Listen, in that case—why did you register for me? And why did you force me to come here?"

It was as though she had not heard. She poured from the flask into a glass, sipped it.

"A charming liqueur. Would you like some?"

It was only then that I understood: alcohol. The events of yesterday flashed before me like lightning: the stone hand of the Benefactor, the unbearable blade of the ray, but especially there: on the Cube—that outstretched body with the head tossed back. I shuddered.

"Listen," I said, "surely you know: all those poisoning themselves with nicotine and especially alcohol—the United State will mercilessly..."

The dark eyebrows—upward towards the temples, the acute mocking triangle:

"To destroy a few quickly is more intelligent than giving many the possibility of ruining themselves—and degeneration—and so forth. This is true to the point of indecency."

"Yes... to the point of indecency."

"A pack of these bald-headed, naked truths—let them loose on the street... No, you could just imagine... well, just take that most unfailing admirer of mine—certainly, you know him,—just imagine him tossing off all that deception of his clothing—and appearing in public in his true form... Oh, my!"

She was laughing. But I could clearly see the lower, mournful triangle: the two deep creases from the corners of her mouth to the nose. And for that reason because of these creases it became clear to me: he, that hunched, winged-eared, double-curved one—he had embraced her—this woman... *He*...

However, now I am trying to convey my—abnormal—impressions at that time. Now, as I am writing this, I am perfectly aware: all of this is as it should be, and he, like any other **honorable number,** has an equal right to various joys—and it would be unjust... Of course, it is clear.

I-330 laughed very strangely and protractedly. Then pierced me with her gaze—deep inside:

"But the main thing—I am completely at ease with you. You are such a dear—oh, I am certain of that,—you wouldn't think of going to the Bureau and informing them that here I am—drinking liqueur, and—smoking. You will be ill—or you will be busy—or something else. Further: I am certain— you will now drink this charming poison with me... "

What an insolent, mocking tone. I had the distinct feeling: now I would hate her once again. However, why *now*? I had hated her all the time.

She tipped the entire glass of green poison into her mouth, stood up and gleaming pinkly through the saffron—she took a few steps—stopped behind my chair...

Suddenly—an arm around my neck—lips on lips... no, somewhere even more deep, more strange... I swear that it was completely unexpected for me, and, perhaps, only because... After all I could not have—now I understand that perfectly clearly—I myself could not have wished for what happened then.

Unbearably-sweet lips (I suppose—it was the taste of the *liqueur*),— and a mouthful of that searing poison was poured into me—and again— and again... I broke loose from earth and like some unattached random planet, in furious revolutions, I plunged down, down—along some incalculable orbit...

The rest I can describe only approximately, only by way of more or less related analogies.

It had never somehow occurred to me earlier—but it was precisely that way: we on earth were walking all the while over a bubbling, crimson sea of fire concealed there—in the bowels of the earth. But we never think of that. And then it is as though all at once the thin shell under our feet has become glass, as though suddenly we perceive...

I became like glass. I saw—inside myself, deep within.

There were two of me. One of me was the former self, D-503, the number D-503, whereas the other... Earlier he had only barely poked his shaggy paws out of the shell, but now he had come crawling out in his entirety, the shell was cracking, any moment now it would shatter into pieces and... and what then?

Clutching with all my strength at a straw—at the arms of the chair—I asked, in order to hear myself—the other one, the former self:

"Where . . . where did you get this . . . this poison?"

"Oh, that! just a doctor, one of my . . ."

"*Of mine*? *Of mine*—who?"

And then this other self—suddenly leaped out and began to yell:

"I won't allow it! I don't want there to be anyone else but me. I will kill anyone who . . . Because it's you I—it's you I——"

I saw: he had seized her roughly in his shaggy paws, tore the fine silk to shreds on her, sank his teeth in—I remember precisely: with his teeth.

I don't know how—I-330 slipped away. And then—her eyes closed up behind those accursed impenetrable blinds—she stood there, leaning back against the wardrobe and listening to me.

I remember: I was on the floor, I was embracing her legs, kissing her knees. And I was begging: "Now—right now—this very minute . . ."

The sharp teeth—the sharp, mocking triangle of her eyebrows. She leaned over, silently unbuttoned my badge.

"Yes! Yes, my dear—my dear." I hastily began to toss off my unif. But I-330—with the same silent manner—raised the watch on my badge right up to my eyes. It was five minutes short of 22 1/2.

I turned cold. I knew what that meant—to show up on the street later than 22 1/2. All my madness—it was as though it were suddenly dispersed. I—was myself. One thing was clear to me: I hated her, I hated her!

Without saying good-bye, without looking back—I tore out of the room. Haphazardly pinning my badge on while on the run, taking the steps two at a time—down the emergency staircase (I was afraid—I might meet someone in the elevator)—I leaped out into the empty avenue.

Everything was as it should be—so simple, ordinary, regular: the glass buildings gleaming with lights, the pale glass sky, the greenish, motionless night. But beneath this quiet, cool glass—something violent, crimson, shaggy was in soundless flight. And gasping, I rushed—so as not to be late.

Suddenly I had a feeling: the badge I had carelessly pinned on—came loose, clattered against the sidewalk. I bent over to pick it up—and in the momentary silence I heard someone's steps behind me. I turned around: something small, hunched, rounded the corner. So, at least, it seemed to me then.

I flew off with all my might—all I heard was the wind whistling in my ears. I halted at the entrance: by my watch it was one minute before 22 1/2. I listened: no one behind. All of that—clearly it had been an absurd fantasy, the effect of the poison.

The night was a torment. The bed beneath me rose, fell and again rose—drifting along a sinusoid. I used auto-suggestion: "At night—the numbers are obliged to sleep; this obligation is the same as work during the day. It is essential in order to work during the day. Not to sleep at night is criminal . . ." And still I could not, I could not.

I am perishing. I am not in any condition to fulfil my obligations before the United State . . . I . . .

Record 11
Synopsis: ...No, I Can't, Leave It Like This Without a Synopsis

Evening. A light mist. The sky overcast with a golden-milky film and one cannot see: what is there—farther on, higher. The ancients knew that up there was their greatest, bored sceptic—God. We know that up there is a crystalline-blue, naked, indecent nothing. I don't know now what is there: I have learned too much. Knowledge, absolutely certain of the fact that it is infallible, is faith. I had a firm faith in myself, I believed that I knew everything in me. And then —

I am before a mirror. And for the first time in my life—yes, exactly: for the first time in my life—I see myself clearly, distinctly, consciously,—with amazement I see myself as the *him* of someone else. Here I am—him, dark brows etched in a straight line; and between them—like a scar—a vertical wrinkle (I don't know: had it been there earlier?). Steel-gray eyes, circled with the shadows of a sleepless night; and behind that steel...it turns out I never knew what was there. And from *there* (this *there* is simultaneously both here and infinitely far away)—from *there* I gaze at myself—at him, and I know firmly: he—with the brows etched in a straight line—he is a stranger, alien to me, I have met him for the first time in my life. Whereas I am the real person, I—not—him...

No: period. All of this is nonsense and all those absurd sensations are a delirium, a result of yesterday's poisoning. With what: with a swallow of the green poison—or with her? It is all the same. I am recording this merely in order to prove how strangely human reason—so precise and sharp—can become confused and go astray. That reason which could make even that infinity palatable which had frightened the ancients—by means of...

The click of the intercom—and the figures: R-13. Let him come, I am even glad: being by myself now would be...

Twenty Minutes Later

On the plane of the paper, in a two-dimensional world—these lines are side by side, but in a different world... I am losing my sensitivity for figures: 20 minutes—that could be 200 or 200,000. And this is so wild: to be recording, calmly, deliberately, pondering every word, what happened with me and R-. It is the same as if you had, with legs crossed, sat down in a chair by your very own bed—and watched with curiosity as you, yes, you,—were writhing on this bed.

When R-13 entered, I was perfectly calm and normal. With a feeling of sincere rapture I began to talk about how magnificently he had succeeded in versifying the death sentence in trochees and it was precisely with those trochees above all else that the madman had been hacked to bits and annihilated.

"... And what's more: if I received an offer to make a schematic draft of the Benefactor's Machine, I would without fail—without fail—add your trochees to the draft," I concluded.

Suddenly I saw: R-13's eyes lose their lustre, his lips turn gray.

"What's the matter with you?"

"What's that? Well ... Well I'm simply fed up: everywhere you look— death sentence, death sentence. I don't want to hear any more about it— that's that. I don't!"

He frowned, rubbed the back of his head—that little valise of his with the baggage that was so strange and incomprehensible to me. A pause. Then he found something in the valise, pulled it out, and unfolding it, laid it out—his eyes grew varnished with laughter, he leaped up.

"Of course, I am composing some verses for your *Integral*... yes, I am! That's what I'm doing!"

His old self: the lips smacked, showered, the words gushed like a fountain.

"You understand—the ancient legend about paradise (the p like a fountain)... It's really about us, about now. Yes! Just think about it. Those two in paradise—were offered a choice: either happiness without freedom—or freedom without happiness; a third one was not given. They, the blockheads, chose freedom and what happened: naturally—for centuries they longed for fetters. For fetters you understand—that is what their world-weariness was all about. Centuries! And only we have figured out again how to bring happiness back... No, you listen—listen some more! The ancient God and we are sitting side-by-side at the same table. Yes! We helped God to finally conquer the devil—of course he was the one who provoked people into breaking the interdict and tasting pernicious freedom, he was the insidious serpent. But we put our big boot on his head—cr-runch! And that was that: paradise once again. And once more we are simple-hearted, innocent like Adam and Eve. None of that muddle about good, evil: everything is very simple, paradisiacally, childishly simple. The Benefactor, the Machine, the Cube, the Gas Bell, the Guardians—all of this is good, all of this is magnificent, beautiful, noble, exalted, crystal-pure. Because this safeguards our non-freedom—that is, our happiness. Here the ancients would have started to make judgments, compare, wrack their brains—ethics, non-ethics... Well, alright, then: in short, how's that for a real little poem about paradise, eh? And a very serious tone all the while... you understand? Nice, eh?"

How could one not understand. I remember that I was thinking: "he has such an absurd, asymmetrical exterior and such a correctly thinking mind." And that is why he is so close to me—to the real me (I still consider my former self—the real one, all this present stuff—this is, of course, only an illness).

R-, apparently, read this on my face, embraced me by the shoulders, burst into laughter.

"Oh, you . . . Adam! Yes, incidentally, about Eve . . ." He rummaged in his pocket, pulled out a notebook, leafed through.

"The day after tomorrow . . . no: in two days—O- has a pink coupon for you. What about you? The same as before? Do you want her to . . ."

"Of course, that's clear."

"Then I'll tell her so. Otherwise she herself, you see, is shy . . . What a business, I tell you! She cares for me only in a pink-coupon fashion, but you she . . . And she won't say who this fourth person is who has crept into our triangle. Who is it—repent—you sinner, well?"

A curtain was raised inside me, and—the rustle of silk, a green flask, lips . . . And for no reason, irrelevantly—I blurted out (if only I had restrained myself!):

"Tell me: have you ever had the opportunity to try nicotine or alcohol?"

R- pursed his lips, looked at me from under his brows. I could hear his thoughts perfectly clearly: "A friend he is—a friend . . . Still . . ." and his response:

"How should I put it? Strictly speaking—no. But I knew one woman . . ."

"I-330," I exclaimed.

"What . . . you—you're also with her?"

He burst into laughter, choked and then began to shower. My mirror was hanging in such a way that one had to look into it over the table: from here in the chair I could only see my forehead and eyebrows.

And then I—the real one—saw the twisted leaping straight line of my eyebrows in the mirror and I, the real one—heard the wild, disgusting cry:

"What *also*? No: what do you mean *also*? No,—I demand . . ."

Widely parted negroid lips. Bulging eyes . . . I—the real I—took a firm grip on this other self by the scruff of the neck—that wild, shaggy, heavily breathing one. I—the real I—said to him, to R-13:

"Forgive me, in the name of the Benefactor. I am quite ill, I haven't been sleeping. I don't know what's the matter with me . . ."

A fleeting smile on the thick lips:

"Yes, yes, yes! I understand—I understand! This is all familiar to me . . . theoretically, of course. Farewell!"

In the doorway he turned around like a small black ball—then came back to the table, tossed a book on the table:

"My most recent one . . . I brought it specially—I almost forgot. Good-bye . . ."—the *b* showered me, he rolled off.

I am alone. Or, rather: face to face with this other me. I am in the chair, and, with legs crossed, I am watching with curiosity from some kind of *there* how I—yes, I myself,—am writhing on the bed.

Why—yes, why for all of three years I and O-90—had lived in such a friendly fashion—and then suddenly now a single word about that one, about I-330... Is it possible that all this madness—love—jealousy—is restricted not only to those idiotic, ancient books? And the main thing— me! Equations, formulae, figures—and... this—I understand nothing! Nothing... Tomorrow I will go to R- and say that —

Not true: I won't go. Not tomorrow, not the day after—I will never go again. I cannot, I do not want to see him. The end! Our triangle—has collapsed.

I am alone. Evening. A light mist. The sky is over-cast with a milky-golden film, if only I knew what is up there—higher? And if only I knew: who am I, which one am I?

Record 12
Synopsis: The Restriction of Infinity
The Angel
Meditations on Poetry

It still seems to me—I will recover, I can recover. I slept beautifully. None of those dreams or other morbid phenomena. Tomorrow, dear O- is coming to me, everything will be simple, correct and restricted like a circle. I am not afraid of this word—"restrictedness": the work of man's highest faculty—reason—leads precisely to the unceasing restriction of infinity, to the fragmentation of infinity into convenient, easily digestable portions— — differentials. Herein lies precisely that divine beauty of my element— mathematics. And an understanding of this very beauty is what is immediately lacking in that female. However this is just an incidental association.

All of this—to the measured, metrical clicking of the wheels of the subway. In my head I was scanning the wheels—and R-13's verses (his book from yesterday). And I had the feeling: from behind, over my shoulder, someone was carefully bending over and peeking at the opened page. Without turning around, only out of the corner of an eye, I saw: the pink, protruding, wing-ears, the double-curve... him! I did not feel like interfering with him—and I pretended that I had not noticed. How he had turned up there—I couldn't say: when I entered the coach—it seemed he was not there.

This occurrence, insignificant in itself, had a particularly good effect on me, I would say: it fortified me. It was so pleasant to feel someone's watchful eye tenderly safeguarding you from the slightest error, the slightest faltering step. Even if it does sound a little sentimental, that same analogy occurred to me once again: the guardian-angels whom the ancients dreamt about. How much of what they could only dream about has materialized in our life.

At that moment when I sensed the guardian-angel behind me, I was enjoying a sonnet entitled "Happiness." I think—I will not be mistaken if I say that this was a thing of rare beauty and depth of thought. Here are the first four lines:

> Two times two, forever in love,
> Union eternal in passionate four,
> Most fervent lovers in the world—
> Indivisibly two times two in love.

And so forth on the same subject: about the wise, eternal happiness of the multiplication tables.

Every genuine poet is unfailingly a Columbus. America existed for centuries before Columbus, but only Columbus managed to discover it. For centuries the multiplication tables existed as well before R-13, but only R-13 managed to find a new Eldorado in that virginal forest of figures. In fact: could there exist anywhere a happiness more wise, more unclouded than in this marvellous world? Steel—rusts; the ancient God—created ancient man, i.e., a man capable of making errors—and consequently, God himself made an error. The multiplication tables are wiser, more absolute than the ancient God: they never—you understand: never—are in error. And there is nothing happier than the figures living according to the harmonious eternal laws of the multiplication tables. No vacillations, no delusions. One truth and one true path; and this truth is two times two, and this true path is four. And would it not be an absurdity if these happily, ideally multiplied two's—began to think about some kind of freedom, i.e., clearly what would be—an error? For me it is an axiom that R-13 managed to grasp the most basic, the most ...

At this point I again felt—first on the back of my head, then on my left ear—the warm, gentle breathing of the guardian-angel. Evidently he had noted that the book on my lap—was now closed and my thoughts were far away. What of it, I was now ready to unfold the pages of my brain before him: it was such a calm, consoling sensation. I remember: I even looked around, I looked insistently, beseechingly into his eyes, but he did not understand—or did not want to understand—he did not ask me about anything... There remains but one thing for me: to relate everything to you, my unknown readers (at this moment you are for me just as dear and close and inaccessible—as he was at that moment).

This is what my path was: from the particular to the whole: the particular is R-13, the majestic whole is our Institute of State Poets and Writers. I was thinking: how could it happen that the entire absurdity of their literature and poetry was not obvious to the ancients. The most enormous, magnificent force of the artistic word was expended to no purpose whatsoever. It is simply ridiculous: each one wrote about whatever entered his head. It is the same ridiculous and absurd thing as the way during the time of the ancients the sea pounded stupidly against the shore around the clock and the millions of kilogram-meters confined in the waves—were expended merely on the warming of lovers' emotions. From the amorous whisper of the waves—we extracted electricity, out of the beast splashing in the violent foam—we made a domestic animal; and in precisely the same way we tamed and harnessed what once was the wild elemental force of poetry. Now poetry is no longer the carefree whistling of the nightingale: poetry is a state service, poetry is utility.

Our distinguished *Mathematical Norms*: without them—could we really have loved the four rules of arithmetic so sincerely and tenderly in school? And *Thorns*—that classical image: the Guardians are the thorns on the rose, safeguarding the tender State Flower from the coarse touch. Whose stone heart will remain indifferent at the sight of the innocent lips of children babbling away like a prayer: "The wicked boy the rose would seize./ But thorn of steel like needle stung,/ the wicked lad, dear me, did sneeze," and so forth? And the *Daily Odes to the Benefactor*? Who, once having read them does not bow piously before the self-denying labor of this Number of Numbers? And the eerie, red *Flowers of Judicial Death Sentences*? And the immortal tragedy *He Who Came Late to Work*? And the indispensable book *Stanzas on Sexual Hygiene*?

All of life in all of its complexity and beauty is minted forever in the gold of words.

Our poets no longer soar in the empyrean: they have descended to earth; they march step for step with us to the austere mechanical march of the Musical Factory; their lyre is the morning rustle of electric tooth brushes and the thunderous crackling of sparks in the Benefactor's Machine, and the majestic echo of the anthem to the United State, and the intimate sound of the crystalline-gleaming night-pot, and the exciting rustle of falling blinds, and the cheerful voices of the latest cookbook, and the barely audible whisper of the street diaphragms.

Our gods are here, down below, with us—in the Bureau, in the kitchen, in the workshop, in the lavatory; the gods have become like us, ergo—we have become like gods. And to you, my unknown planetary readers, we are coming to you in order to make your life divinely rational and precise like ours . . .

Record 13
Synopsis: Mist
            Thou
            A Perfectly Absurd Occurrence

I awoke at dawn,—a pink, solid firmament before my eyes. Everything fine, round. O- would come in the evening. I was undoubtedly well now. I smiled, fell asleep.

The morning bell,—I arose—and it was completely changed: through the glass of the ceiling, walls, everywhere, all over, through and through—mist. Insane clouds, growing more and more ponderous—and then lighter, and nearer, and by now there were no boundaries between the earth and the sky, everything was flying, melting, falling, there was nothing to grasp hold of. There were no longer any buildings: the glass walls melted in the mist like small crystals of salt in water. If one looked up from the sidewalk—the dark figures of people in the buildings—like suspended particles in a delirious, milky solution—were suspended down, below, and, higher up, and still higher—on the tenth floor. And everything was smoking—perhaps some soundlessly raging conflagration.

Precisely at 11:45: I glanced at the clock on purpose at that time—in order to grasp hold of the figures—in order that at least the figures would save me.

At 11:45, before going to the customary physical labor exercises, in accordance with the Book of Hours, I quickly dropped into my room. Suddenly the telephone rang, a voice—a long, slow needle in my heart:

"Aha, you're at home? I am very happy. Wait for me on the corner. You and I will go... well, you'll see where then."

"You know perfectly well: I am going to work now."

"You know perfectly well that you will do what I tell you. Good-bye. In two minutes..."

In two minutes I was standing on the corner. She really had to be shown that I was being run by the United State and not by her. *What I tell you to do* ... And she was certain: you could hear it in her voice. Well, I would shortly have a proper talk with her.

The gray unifs, woven of the damp mist, suddenly materialized for a second near me and suddenly melted again into the mist. I could not tear myself loose from the clock, I was—the sharp, trembling, second hand. Eight, ten minutes... Three minutes before, two minutes before twelve...

Finished. To work—I was already late. How I hated her. But I did have to show...

On the corner in the white mist—blood—the slice of a sharp knife—lips.

"It looks as though I kept you waiting. However, it does not matter. Now you are already too late."

How I hated—however, true: I was already late.

Silently I gazed at her lips. All women are lips, nothing but lips. Those of one were pink, resiliently round: a ring, a tender encirclement from all the world. And these: a moment ago they did not exist and then just now—like a knife—and the sweet blood was still dripping.

Closer—she leaned against my shoulder—and we were one, something was pouring out of her into me—and I knew: this was how it had to be. I knew with every nerve, with every hair, with every painfully sweet heartbeat. And it was such a joy to submit to this *had to be*. Probably a piece of iron has to submit just as joyfully to the inescapable, precise law—and fasten onto a magnet. A stone thrown upwards, wavers for an instant—and then plummets downward, earthward. And man, after an agony, finally must breathe his last—and die.

I remember: I smiled distractedly and said irrelevantly: "Mist ... A lot."

"Thou dost like the mist?"

This ancient, long forgotten *thou*, the *thou* used by the master to the slave—penetrated me slowly, sharply: yes I was a slave, and that too—that was also how it had to be, that also was good.

"Yes, good ..." I said aloud to myself. And then to her: "I hate the mist. I am afraid of the mist."

"It means—thou dost love it. Thou art afraid—because it is more powerful than thou, thou dost hate it—because thou art afraid, thou lovest it—because thou canst not make it submit to thee. After all it is only possible to love that which does not submit ..."

Yes, it was so. And precisely because—precisely because I ...

We walked together—as one. Somewhere far away through the mist the sun was singing almost inaudibly, still burgeoning with resilience, pearl, gold, pink, red. The entire world was a single unembraceable woman, and we were in her very womb, we had not yet been born, we were joyfully ripening. And it was clear to me, indestructibly clear: it was all for—me: the sun, the mist, the pink, the gold—for me ...

I did not question where we were going. It made no difference: as long as we kept going, going, ripening, burgeoning more and more resiliently—

"Well here we are ..." I-330 stopped by the doors. "There just happens to be a person on duty here today ... I was talking about him that time, in the Ancient House."

From afar, with my eyes alone, carefully guarding that ripening something—I read the sign: *Medical Bureau.* I understood everything. A glass room, filled with a golden mist. Glass shelves with colored bottles, jars. Electric wires. Bluish sparks in tubes.

And a small fellow—ever so slender. It was as though he had been entirely cut out of paper and however he turned—he still possessed only a profile, sharply-attenuated: a glittering blade—for a nose; scissors—for lips.

I did not hear what I-330 said to him: I was watching her speak—and I had the feeling: I was smiling unrestrainedly, blissfully. The scissor-lips glittered like a blade, and the doctor said:

"Yes, yes. I understand. A most dangerous illness—I know none more dangerous ..." he laughed, quickly wrote something with an everso slender paper hand, gave the slip to I-330; wrote—and gave one to me.

These were certificates stating that we were ill, that we could not appear at work. I was stealing my work from the United State, I was a thief, I was deserving of the Benefactor's Machine. But to me it seemed—distant, unimportant, as though in a book ... I took the slip, not hesitating for a second; I—my eyes, lips, hands—I knew: that was how it had to be.

On the corner, in the half-empty garage, we took an aero. Again I-330, as the time before, sat at the controls, pressed the starter for "forward," we broke away from the earth, we soared. And everything trailed after us: the pinkish-golden mist; the sun; the slenderest, bladelike profile of the doctor, suddenly so likeable and close. Earlier—everything revolved around the sun; now, I knew, everything was revolving around me—slowly, blissfully, with half-closed eyes ...

The old woman at the gates to the Ancient House. The dear, overgrown mouth with the radiating wrinkles of light. Doubtless it had been overgrown all these days—and only now did it open wide, smile:

"Aha, the mischief-maker! No, you can't work like everyone else ... well, so be it! If anything comes up—then I'll come running and say ..."

The heavy, creaking, opaque door swung shut and my heart opened wide—still wider:—as wide as possible. Her lips—mine, I drank, drank, tore myself loose, silently gazed into those eyes opened wide to me—and again ...

The semi-gloom of the rooms, blue, saffron-yellow, the dark-green morocco, the golden smile of the Buddha, the gleam of mirrors. And—my old dream, such an understandable one now: everything drenched with a golden-pink sap, and suddenly about to overflow the edge, to spurt——

Ripeness was achieved. And inescapably, like iron and a magnet, with sweet submissiveness to a precise, immutable law—I poured into her. There was no pink coupon, there was no reckoning, there was no United State, there was no me. There were only the tenderly-sharp, clenched teeth, there were the golden eyes opened wide to me—and through them I slowly entered inside, ever deeper. And the silence—only in the corner— thousands of miles away drops were dripping into a wash-basin and I was the universe, and from drop to drop—eras, epochs ...

Throwing my unif on, I bent over I-330—and drank her in with my eyes for the last time.

"I knew it ... I knew thee ..." I-330 said very softly. She quickly rose, put on her unif and her customary bite-smile.

"Well, fallen angel. Now you're really ruined. No, you're not afraid? Well, good-bye! You will return alone. Alright?"

She opened the door with the mirror set into the wall of the wardrobe; over her shoulder—at me; she waited. I went out obediently. But I had hardly crossed the threshold—when suddenly I had to have her lean against me with her shoulder—just for a second with her shoulder, nothing more.

I hurtled back—into that room where she (probably) was still buttoning up her unif in front of the mirror, I ran in and stopped. There—I saw it clearly—the antique ring on the key in the door of the wardrobe was still swinging, but there was no I-330. There was nowhere she could have gone to—there was only one exit out of the room—and yet she was gone. I ransacked everything, I even opened the wardrobe and ran my fingers over the motley-colored, ancient dresses there: no one...

I feel somewhat awkward, my planetary readers, telling you about this completely improbable event. But what else can I do if that was precisely what happened. Wasn't it true that the entire day, from first thing in the morning, had been full of improbabilities, wasn't it true that all of this resembled that ancient malady of seeing dreams? And if it is so—then does it make any difference: one absurdity more or less? Besides, I am certain: sooner or later I will succeed in incorporating every absurdity into some kind of syllogism. This consoles me, I hope it will console you as well.

...How full I am! If only you knew: how full I am!

Record 14
Synopsis: **"Mine"**
                It Is Impossible
                A Cold Floor

Still more about yesterday. I was busy during the personal hour before sleep and I could not write up the records yesterday. But inside me all of this is seemingly etched, and hence particularly—surely forever—that unbearably-cold floor...

In the evening O- was supposed to come to me—it was her day. I went downstairs to the duty clerk to get the permit for the blinds.

"What is wrong with you," asked the duty clerk. "Today you seem..."

"I... I'm ill..."

In essence, this was true: I was, of course, ill. All of this was an illness. And then I immediately remembered: but what about the certificate... I felt in my pocket: yes—it rustled. It meant—everything had happened, everything had actually happened...

I handed the piece of paper to the duty clerk. I felt my cheeks start to burn; without looking I could see: the duty clerk was gazing at me in wonder...

And here it was—21 1/2. In the room on the left—the blinds were lowered. In the room on the right—I saw my neighbor: over a book—his bald head and forehead all knobby and bumpy—an enormous, yellow parabola. In agony I paced, paced: how was I to—after everything—with her, with O-? And on the right—I clearly felt the eyes on me, I distinctly saw the wrinkles on the forehead—a series of yellow, indecipherable lines; and for some reason it seemed to me—these lines were about me.

At fifteen before 22 there was a joyful, pink whirlwind in my room, a firm ring of pink arms around my neck. And then I sensed: the ring grew ever weaker, ever weaker—it broke—the arms fell...

"You aren't the same, you aren't like you used to be, you aren't mine!"

"What a wild terminology: *mine*. I have never been..." I faltered: it occurred to me—earlier I had not been, true, but now... After all I was not living now in our rational world, but in an ancient, delirious one, in a world of roots of minus one.

The blinds fell. There, behind the wall to the right, my neighbor dropped a book from the table to the floor, and in that final, fleeting, narrow crack between the blind and the floor—I saw: a yellow hand seizing the book, and inside me: I wanted to seize that hand with all my might...

"I was thinking—I wanted to meet you today during the walk. There's so much I want to—I have so much to say to you..."

Dear, poor O-! The pink mouth—the pink crescent with the horns downward. But I cannot really tell her all that happened—if only for the reason that it would make her an accomplice to my crimes: of course I know she does not have the strength to go to the Bureau of Guardians and, consequently——

O- was lying down. I was kissing her slowly. I was kissing that naive plump fold of skin at her wrist, the blue eyes were closed, the pink crescent slowly blossomed, opened up—and then I was kissing her all over.

Suddenly I clearly felt: to what extent everything was wasted, used up. I could not, it was impossible. I had to—but it was impossible. My lips suddenly grew cold...

The pink crescent began to quiver, faded, writhed. O- threw a blanket over herself, wrapped herself up—with her face in the pillow..

I was sitting on the floor beside the bed—what a desperately-cold floor,—sitting in silence. The agonizing cold from below—ever higher, ever higher. Probably—the same silent cold there, in the blue, mute interplanetary spaces.

"Do understand: I did not want to..." I mumbled... "With all my might I..."

This was true: I, the real I—had not wanted to. And yet: what words could I find to tell her. How could I explain to her that the iron was unwilling, but the law was inescapable, precise——

O- raised her face from the pillows and without opening her eyes said: "Go away," but because of the tears it came out as "o a-ay"—and so this absurd trifle as well was etched into me for some reason.

Chilled right through, rigid, I went out into the corridor. There beyond the glass was a light barely noticeable bank of mist. But by night it would descend again, and everything would be submerged. What kind of night would it be?

O- slipped silently past me, towards the elevator—the door slammed.

"Just a minute," I cried: I was terrified.

But the lift was already humming its way down, down, down...

She had taken R- away from me.

She had taken O- away from me.

And yet, and yet...

Record 15
Synopsis: **The Bell**
                 The Mirror-like Sea
                 I Am to Burn Eternally

I had barely entered the site where the *Integral* was being built—when I was met by the Second Builder. His face looked its usual: round, white, porcelain-like—a plate, and he said—carrying on the plate something so unbearably delicious:

"You chose to get ill and in your absence here, in the absence of authority, yesterday, you might say—something happened."

"Something happened?"

"Yes, it did! The bell rang, work stopped, they began to let everyone off the site—and imagine: the guard caught a man without a number. Just how he managed to get in—I cannot understand. They took him off to Operations. There they'll get it out of him, dear fellow, the how and why..." (a smile—delicious...).

In Operations—worked our best and most experienced doctors, under the immediate direction of the Benefactor himself. Here there were various devices and, principally, the famous Gas bell. It was essentially an ancient school experiment: a mouse was placed under a bell glass; the air in the bell glass is gradually rarified by means of an air pump... Well, and so forth. Only, of course, the Gas Bell is a significantly more sophisticated apparatus—with provision for the use of various gases, and moreover—here, of course there is no longer any humiliation of small, defenseless animals, here we have a lofty purpose—the concern with the security of the United State, in other words—the happiness of millions. About five centuries ago, when work in Operations was only getting organized, there were fools about who compared Operations with the ancient inquisition, but that is really just as absurd as putting on the same level a surgeon performing a tracheotomy, and a highway robber: in both of their hands is, perhaps, the same knife, both do the same thing—cutting a living person's throat. And yet one is a benefactor, the other is a criminal, one has a + sign, the other has a - sign . . .

All of this is overly clear, all of this takes a single second, a single revolution of a logical machine, but then suddenly the teeth in the cogs catch on a minus—and something completely different turns up: the ring was still swaying in the wardrobe. The door, apparently, had only just been slammed shut—but she, I-330, was not there: she had disappeared. There was no way the machine could make this come around. A dream? But even now I can still feel: that incomprehensible sweet pain in my right shoulder—I-330 leaning against my right shoulder—together with me in the mist.

Thou dost love the mist? Yes and the mist . . . I love everything and everything is resilient, new, amazing, everything is fine.

"Everything is fine," I said aloud.

"Fine?" The porcelain eyes bulged roundly. "I mean, what's so fine about this? If this unnumbered fellow contrived . . . it means they are everywhere, all around, all the time, they are here, they are around the *Integral*, they . . ."

"Just who are they?"

"How should I know who. But I sense them—you understand? All the time."

"Have you heard: seems they have invented a new kind of operation— they surgically remove your fantasy?" (The other day, in fact, I had heard something of that sort.)

"Yes, I know. But why bring that up here?"

"For the reason that if I were you—I would go and request this operation for myself."

On the plate there was the distinct appearance of something lemony-sour. The dear fellow—he was offended by the oblique hint that he might possess fantasy . . . However, what of it: a week ago—probably I too would have been offended. But now—not now: because I knew that I had one— that I was ill. And furthermore I knew—I did not have any desire to be cured. I just had no desire, and that was that. We ascended the glass steps. Everything—down below us—as though on the palm of our hand . . .

You who read these records—whoever you might be, the sun is still over your heads. And if you were ever just as ill as I am now—you know what it is like—how it can be—the morning sun, you know that pink, translucent, warm gold. And the very air is slightly pink, and everything is saturated with the tender blood of the sun, everything is alive: alive and soft are the stones; alive and warm is the iron; alive and smiling, every single one of them, are the people. It might happen that in an hour's time—everything will disappear, in an hour's time—the pink blood will be drained out, but for the present it is alive. And I see: something pulsates and overflows in the glassy juices of the *Integral*; I see: the *Integral* is contemplating its great and awesome future, the heavy cargo of inescapable happiness which it will carry up there, to you, to unknown persons, to you, who eternally seek and never find. You will find, you will be happy—you are obliged to be happy and you do not have long to wait.

· The body of the *Integral* is almost ready: the exquisite, elongated ellipsoid of our glass—eternal like gold, flexible like steel. I saw: they were fastening the transverse ribs to the steel body—the frames, the longitudinal supports—the stringers; in the stern they were installing the base for the gigantic rocket engine. Every 3 seconds—an explosive thrust; every 3 seconds the powerful tail-end of the *Integral* would spew flames and gases into universal space—and it would soar, soar—a fiery Tamerlane of happiness...

I saw: in accordance with Taylor, regularly and quickly, in rhythm, like the levers of an enormous machine, bending, straightening, turning, the people down below. In their hands tubes were glittering: they were cutting with fire, they were welding with fire the glass bulkheads, the angle-bars, gussets. I saw the transparent glass monster-cranes rolling slowly along glass rails, and exactly like the people, obediently turning, bending, thrusting their loads inside, into the womb of the *Integral*. And all of this seemed the most exalted, stunning beauty, harmony, music... Faster—down, to them, together with them!

And then—shoulder to shoulder, welded together with them, gripped by the steel rhythm... Measured movements: resilient-round cheeks; mirror-like foreheads unclouded by the insanity of thoughts. I was sailing across a mirror-like sea. I was resting.

And suddenly one of them—turned to me serenely: "Well, now: alright now, better today?"

"What do you mean better?"

"Well—you weren't here yesterday. We were thinking—something serious was wrong with you that..." His forehead gleamed, his smile was childlike, innocent.

The blood rushed into my face. I could not—I could not lie to those eyes. I was silent, drowning...

Up above, a porcelain face gleaming with a round whiteness, poked through a hatchway.

"Hey, D-503! Be good enough to come here! We've got a bad fit with the consoles and the inertial forces are producing a tension which is higher on the square."

Not waiting any longer, I dashed headlong up to him—I was shamefully saving myself by fleeing. I did not have the strength to raise my eyes—I had spots before my eyes from the glittering, glass steps underfoot, and with every step: I felt greater and greater despair: for me, a criminal, a poisoned man—there was no place here. Never again would I be able to melt into that precise, mechanical rhythm, or sail across the mirror-calm sea. I—am to burn eternally, to cast about, to seek out some nook where I might hide my eyes—eternally, until, finally, I find the strength to slip past and——

And an icy spark—right through me: for me—so be it; for me—no matter; but thought would have to be given to her as well, and she too must be . . .

I crawled out through the hatchway onto the deck and stopped: I did not know where to go now, I did not know why I had come here. I looked upward. There the sun, tormented by midday, was rising murkily. Below— was the *Integral*, a glassy-gray lifeless thing. The pink blood had drained out, it was clear to me that all of this had merely been my fantasy, that everything had stayed the way it had been before, and at the very same time it was clear . . .

"What's the matter, 503, have you gone deaf? Here I am calling . . . What's wrong with you?" This was the Second Builder—right above my ear: he must have been shouting for a long while.

What is wrong with me? I have lost control. The motor is whirring at full strength, the aero is quivering and hurtling on, but there is no control,—and I do not know where I am hurtling to: downward—and suddenly into the earth, or upward—and into the sun, into the fire . . .

Record 16
Synopsis: **Yellow**
                   A Two-Dimensional Shadow
                   An Incurable Soul

I made no records for several days. I don't know how many: all the days are alike. All the days are one color—yellow like parched, incandescent sand, and not a shred of shade, not a drop of water, and onward across the yellow sand without end. I can't go on without her—but she, since the time when she disappeared from the Ancient House so mysteriously . . .

Since that time I have seen her only once during a walk. Two, three, four days ago—I don't know: all the days are alike. She flashed past, filled the yellow, empty world for a second. With her, arm-in-arm, shoulder-high to her—was the double-curved S-; and the paper-slender doctor, and some fourth male—I recalled his fingers alone: they were flying out of the sleeves of his unif like fascicles of rays—extraordinarily slender, white, long. I-330 raised her hand, waved to me; I-330—leaned over another head to the one with the finger-rays. I caught the word *Integral*: all four looked around at me; and then were immediately lost in the gray-blue sky, and once again—that yellow, parched road.

She had a pink coupon for me the evening of that same day. I was standing before the intercom—and with tenderness, with hatred, I was begging it to click, to show more quickly in the blank slot: I-330. A door kept banging, emerging from the lift were the pale, the tall, the pink, the swarthy; blinds were falling all around.

She was not there. She did not come.

And, perhaps, precisely at this very minute, at exactly 22, while I am writing this—with eyes closed, she is leaning in the same way against someone with her shoulder and she is saying in the same way to someone: "Thou dost love?" To whom? Who is he? The one with the ray-fingers, or the thick-lipped, showering R-? Or S-?

S-... Why do I hear every day his flat-footed steps accompanying me, squelching as through puddles? Why is he following me every day—like a shadow? In front, on the side, behind, a gray-blue, two-dimensional shadow: people pass right through it, step on it, but it is always just as inalterably here, alongside, attached by an invisible umbilical cord. Perhaps she is this umbilical cord—I-330? I don't know. Or, perhaps, they, the Guardians, are already aware that I...

If you were to be told: your shadow sees you, sees you all the time. Do you understand? And then suddenly—you have a strange sensation: your arms are extraneous, they get in your way, and I catch myself in the absurd situation of swinging my arms not in rhythm to my stride. Or suddenly—I must glance back, but it is impossible to glance back, under any circumstances, my neck is shackled. And I am running, running faster and faster, and with my back I can feel: my shadow running faster after me, no escape from it—nowhere, nowhere...

In my room—finally, alone. But here is something different: the telephone. Again I pick up the receiver: "Yes, I-330, please." And once again in the receiver—a faint noise, someone's steps, in the corridor—past the door of her room, and silence... I throw the receiver down—and I can't, I can't bear it any longer. Over there—to her.

This was yesterday. I ran over there and for a whole hour, from 16 to 17 I wandered around the building where she lived. Passing, in rows, numbers. Thousands of feet were pattering in time, a million-footed leviathan, swaying, floated past. But I was alone, lashed by storms onto an uninhabited island, and I was searching, searching with my eyes in the gray-blue waves.

Anytime now, from somewhere—the sharply-mocking angle of eyebrows upturned to the temples would appear, and the dark windows of eyes, and there, inside—a fireplace would be blazing, someone's shadows would be stirring. And I would go directly there, inside, and I would say to her *thou*—without fail, *thou*: "Thou knowest—I cannot live without thee. So why this?"

But she—would be silent. I suddenly heard the silence, suddenly I heard—the Musical Factory and I understood: it was already after 17, everyone had left long ago, I—was alone, I—was late. All around—a glass desert suffused with the yellow sun. I saw as though in water—in the glassy smooth surfaces, the upside-down, glittering walls, suspended feet-first, and me, upside down, ridiculous, suspended feet-first.

I had to go as quickly as possible, that very same second—to the Medical Bureau to get a certificate that I was ill, otherwise they would take me and—— But perhaps that would be the best. To remain here and calmly wait until I was seen, delivered to Operations—to end everything at once, to atone for everything at once.

A faint rustle, and before me—the double-curved shadow. Without looking I felt the two gray-steeled drills boring into me, I gathered up all my strength to smile and to say—I had to say something:

"I . . . I have to go to the Medical Bureau."

"What's stopping you then? Why are you standing here?" Absurdly upside down, suspended feet-first—I was silent, all ablaze from shame.

"Follow me," S- said severely.

I obediently set out, waving those useless extraneous arms. It was impossible to raise my eyes, all the while I walked in a wild world that was turned on its head: here were some kind of machines with their base uppermost, and people antipodally glued by their feet to the ceiling, and still lower—the sky chained by the thick glass of the pavement. I remember: the most vexing thing of all was that I had seen it this way, for the last time in my life, upside down, not the way it really was. But it was impossible to raise my eyes.

We stopped. Before me—steps. One step—and I would see: figures in white, doctors' gowns, the enormous, mute Bell . . .

Forcefully, with some kind of screw-gear, I finally tore my eyes from the glass underfoot—suddenly the golden letters *Medical* spattered over my face . . . Why he had brought me here, and not to Operations, why he had spared me—I could not even consider in that moment: with a single leap—over the stairs, I slammed the door behind me—and heaved a sigh. It seemed: I had not drawn a breath since morning, my heart had not been beating—and only now did I take a breath for the first time, only now did the sluice open in my chest . . .

Two of them: one—rather squat, with pedestal-legs—tossing patients around on the horns of his eyes; and the other—ever so slender, glittering scissor-lips, a blade-nose . . . That same one.

I rushed to him, as though to some close relative, straight to the blades—something about insomnia, dreams, a shadow, a yellow world. The scissor-lips glittered, smiled.

"Your condition is bad! Apparently a soul has formed in you."

A soul? That strange, ancient, long-forgotten word. Sometimes we say *soulless*, *soul-destroying*, *soul-felt*, but a soul——

"That is... very dangerous," I babbled.

"Incurable," the scissors sliced.

"But... properly speaking, what is it all about? Somehow I can't... I can't conceive of it."

"You see... how can I explain... But you are a mathematician, aren't you?"

"Yes."

"Then look here—a plane, a surface, well take this mirror here. And you and I are on the surface, like this—you see, and we are blinking our eyes from the sun, and this blue electrical spark in a tube, and over there—the shadow of an aero has flashed past. But only on the surface, only for a second. But just imagine—this impenetrable surface has suddenly turned soft from some fire or other, and now nothing will slide over it—everything penetrates inside, to there, into that mirror-world where we peer with curiosity like children,—children are not at all that stupid, I assure you. The surface has become a mass, a body, a world, and all this is inside the mirror—inside you—the sun, and the whirlwind from the propellor of the aero, and your trembling lips and someone else's as well. And you understand: a cold mirror reflects, casts back; but this one—absorbs, and a trace of everything remains—for eternity. Once you saw a barely noticeable wrinkle on someone's face—and it is inside you forever; once you heard: a drop fell in the silence—and you can hear it now..."

"Yes, yes, that's it..." I seized him by the arm. I heard it just now: from—the tap of the washbasin—drops were slowly dripping into the silence. And I knew it was—forever. But still why this soul all of a sudden? None, none before—and all of a sudden... "Why does no one else have it, but I do..."

I fastened more firmly onto that slenderest of arms: I felt eerie about losing my life belt.

"Why? And why don't we have feathers, wings—only shoulder blades—bases for wings? For the reason that wings are no longer necessary—there is the aero, wings would only get in the way. Wings—are for flying, but we no longer have any place to fly to: we—have made our flight—we have made our discovery. Isn't it so?"

I nodded my head distractedly. He looked at me, gave a sharp, lancet-like laugh. He, the other one, had heard; he came clumping out of his office on his pedestal-legs, tossed my ever so slender doctor on the horns of his eyes, tossed me too.

"What's going on? What do you mean: a soul? A soul, you say? What the devil! More of this and we'll soon be back to cholera! I told you (tossing the slender one on his horns)—I told you: everyone's—everyone's fantasy... Have to exterminate fantasy. Just a matter of surgery here, nothing but surgery..."

He stuck on enormous Roentgen spectacles, walked around for a long while and peered through the bones of my skull—into my brain, recorded something in a book.

"Extremely, extremely curious! Listen: would you possibly agree... to be preserved in alcohol? For the United State it would be extremely... it would help us to prevent an epidemic... If, of course, you have no special reasons..."

"But you see," the other said, "number D-503 is the builder of the *Integral*, and I am sure—it would disrupt..."

"Ah," the other one mumbled and clumped back to his office.

We were left alone. The paper hand gently, caressingly, fell on mine, the silhouette-like face leaned over close to me; he whispered:

"I'll tell you a secret—you're not the only one who has this. It's not an accident my colleague is talking about an epidemic. Just try to recall, haven't you yourself noticed something similar in someone else—very similar, very close..." He stared into my face. What was he hinting at—who? Was it possible——

"Listen..." I leaped up from the chair. But he had already begun speaking loudly about something else:

"...As for this insomnia, these dreams of yours—I can only advise you to do one thing: go for more walks. Here, take this, and first thing tomorrow morning take a stroll... say as far as the Ancient House."

He pierced me with his eyes again, gave the slenderest smile. And it seemed to me: I saw with complete clarity the word wrapped up in the thin tissue of that smile—a letter—a name, the one and only name... Or was this fantasy again?

I could hardly wait until he wrote me a certificate of illness for today and for tomorrow. I shook his hand firmly once more in silence and ran outside.

My heart was light, quick, like an aero, and it was soaring, soaring upwards with me. I knew: tomorrow—a kind of joy. What kind?

Record 17
Synopsis: Through the Glass
           I Died
           Corridors

I am utterly perplexed. Yesterday, at that very moment when I was thinking that everything had already been untangled, all the X's found—new unknowns appeared in my equation.

The starting-point for the coordinates in this whole story is, of course, the Ancient House. From this point extend the axials of the X's, Y's, Z's on which for me the entire world has only recently been constructed. Along the axis of the X's (Avenue 59) I was walking to the starting-point of the coordinates. Inside me—yesterday was like a motley-colored whirlwind: upside-down buildings and people, agonizingly-extraneous arms, glittering scissors, sharply-dripping drops from a washbasin—it had been like that, it had been like that once. And all of this—tearing my flesh to shreds was whirling impetuously there—behind that surface melted by fire where the *soul* was.

In order to fulfil the doctor's prescription I purposely chose a route that followed not the hypotenuse, but the two sides of the triangle. And here was the second side already: the circular road at the foot of the Green Wall. Out of the unencompassable green ocean beyond the Wall a wild swell of roots, flowers, branches, leaves came rolling towards me—reared up—and in a moment would overwhelm me, and from a human being—that most delicate and precise of mechanisms—I would be transformed into ...

But, fortunately, between me and the wild green ocean was the glass of the Wall. Oh, the mighty, divinely-restricting wisdom of walls, barriers! This, perhaps, was the greatest of all inventions. Man ceased to be a wild animal only when he built the first wall. Man ceased to be a wild man only when we built the Green Wall, when by means of this Wall we isolated our mechanistic, perfect world—from the irrational, chaotic world of trees, birds, animals ...

Through the glass, looking at me—mistily, obscurely—the dull snout of some kind of beast, yellow eyes, stubbornly repeating one and the same thought uncomprehended by me. For a long while we peered into each other's eyes—through these shafts from the external world into another one beneath the surface. And inside me a thought was hovering: "What if it, the yellow-eyed one—in its absurd, filthy clump of leaves, in its uncalculated life—is happier than we?"

I waved my hand, the yellow eyes blinked, backed off, disappeared into the foliage. Miserable creature! What an absurdity: it—happier than we! Perhaps, happier than me; but then I was only an exception, I was ill. And moreover I ... But then I caught sight of the dark-red walls of the Ancient House—and the dear, overgrown, old lady's mouth—I rushed to the old woman as fast as my feet would carry me:

"Is she here?"

The overgrown mouth slowly opened:

"Just who do you mean—she?"

"Really now, who—who else? I-330, of course ... We were here together that time, she and I—in the aero ..."

"Ah, yes, yes ... Yes-yes-yes ..."

Rays of light—the wrinkles around her lips, cunning rays from her yellow eyes, groping their way inside me—deeper and deeper ... And finally:

"Well, alright, then... she's here, she came not long ago."

Here. I perceived: at the old woman's feet—a bush of silvery-bitter wormwood (the courtyard of the Ancient House—it was just as much a museum, it was painstakingly preserved in its prehistoric form), the wormwood stretched a branch out to the old woman's hand, the old woman was stroking the branch, across her knees—a yellow band from the sun. And for a single instant: I, the sun, the old woman, the wormwood, the yellow eyes—we were all one, we were firmly bound by some kind of veins and through the veins—a single, common, turbulent, magnificent blood...

Now I am ashamed to write about this, but I promised to be frank to the very end in these records. So here I bent over—and kissed that overgrown, soft, mossy mouth. The old woman wiped her mouth and burst into laughter...

Running through familiar, semi-gloomy, echoing rooms—for some reason directly there, to the bedroom. Right at the door I grasped the handle and then suddenly: "But what if she isn't there alone?" I stopped, listened. But I only heard: ticking nearby—not inside me, but somewhere near me—my heart.

I entered. The wide, unrumpled bed. The mirror. The other mirror in the door of the wardrobe, and in the keyhole there—the key with the antique ring. And no one.

I called quietly:

"I-330! Art thou here?"— And still more quietly, my eyes closed, without breathing,—as though I were already kneeling before her: "I-330! Dearest!"

Quiet. Only water was dripping rapidly from the tap into the white washbasin. I could not then explain why, but simply that it displeased me: I gave the tap a firm twist and left. She was not there: it was clear. And, so it meant she was in some other *apartment*.

I ran farther down the wide murky staircase, pulled at one door, another, a third: locked. Everything was locked except that one single apartment of *ours*, and in there—no one...

And all the same—back there, I myself did not know—why. I walked slowly, with difficulty—the soles of my feet had suddenly become cast-iron. I distinctly remember the thought:

"It is an error to think that inertial force is constant. Consequently, all my formulae——"

Then—an explosion: a door slammed way down at the bottom, someone was quickly pounding over the stone slabs. I—once again light, ever so light—rushed to the railing—to lean over, in a single word, in a single cry of *Thou!* to cry out everything...

And I turned cold: down below—inscribed in the dark rectangle of shadow from the window frame, the pink wing-ears flapping, flew the head of S-.

Like lightning—only one naked conclusion, without premises (even now I don't know any premises): "He mustn't—not for anything—see me here."

And on tiptoe, pressing against the wall—I slipped upstairs—towards that one unlocked apartment.

A second by the door. The other one—dully stomping upward, here. If only the door! I implored the door, but it was wooden: it started to creak, it squeaked. Like a passing whirlwind—green, red, the yellow Buddha—I was before the door with the mirror in the wardrobe: my pale face, eyes listening intently, lips... I hear—through the noise of my blood—the door is creaking again... It is him, him.

I grabbed for the key in the door of the wardrobe—and then the ring was swinging. That reminded me of something—again a fleeting, naked conclusion without premises—rather, a fragment: "On that occasion, I-330——." I quickly opened the door into the wardrobe—inside, in the darkness—I banged it firmly shut. A single step—a rocking motion underfoot. Slowly, softly I was floating somewhere downwards, everything grew dark before my eyes, I had died.

* * *

Later, when I had to record all these strange events, I dug through my memory, through books—and now, of course, I understand: this had been a state of temporary death, familiar to the ancients and—as far as I know—completely unknown among us.

I have no conception of how long I was dead, most likely 5 or 10 seconds, but it was only a little while before I came to life again, opened my eyes: it was dark and I had the feeling of—going down, down... I stretched out a hand—made a grab—the rough, rapidly regressing wall scratched me, there was blood on my finger, it was clear—all of this was not the play of my sick fantasy. But what, what was it then?

I heard my punctuated, erratic breathing (I am ashamed to admit it—everything had been so unexpected and incomprehensible).

A minute, two, three—still downwards. Finally—a gentle bump: what had been falling under my feet was now motionless. In the darkness I fumbled until I found a handle, I pushed—the door opened—a murky light. I saw: behind me the small, square platform was flying upwards and away. I rushed—but it was already too late! I was cut off here... where this *here* was—I did not know.

A corridor. A silence weighing a thousand tons. On the round vaults were electric bulbs, an endless, glimmering, trembling dotted line. It resembled a little the *tubes* of our subways, only much narrower and not made of our glass, but out of some other antique material. A memory-flash—about the underground caves where people were supposed to have escaped during the time of the Two Hundred Years' War... It mattered little: I had to go on.

I walked, I suppose, for about twenty minutes. I turned to the right, a wider corridor, brighter bulbs. A kind of vague humming. Perhaps machines, perhaps voices—I only knew that I was by a heavy, opaque door: the hum was from there.

I knocked, again—louder. On the other side of the door—a sudden silence. Something clanged, slowly, heavily, the door swung open.

I don't know which of the two of us was more stunned—in front of me was my blade-nosed, ever so slender doctor.

"You? Here?" And his scissors started clicking so. And I—it was as though I had never known a single human word: I was silent, I looked and comprehended absolutely nothing that he said to me. It must have been—that I had to go away from here; because then with his flat, paper stomach he quickly shoved me to the end of this brighter portion of the corridor—and then gave me a push in the back.

"Excuse me . . . I wanted . . . I thought that she, I-330 . . ." But behind me . . .

"Wait here." The doctor cut me off and disappeared . . . At last! At last, she was nearby, here—and what difference did it make where this *here* was. The familiar saffron-yellow silk, the smile-bite, the eyes covered with blinds . . . My lips were trembling, my hands, my knees—and in my head the stupidest thought:

"Vibrations are sounds. Trembling should have a sound. Why can't it be heard?"

Her eyes opened up to me—to their widest, I went inside . . .

"I couldn't bear it any more! Where were you? Why?"—without tearing my eyes away from her for a second, I talked as though in a delirium—quickly, disconnectedly—perhaps, I only thought I was talking . . . "A shadow—following me . . . I died—out of the closet . . . Because this one of your . . . said with his scissors: I have a soul . . . Incurable . . ."

"An incurable soul! My poor little one!" I-330 burst into laughter—and showered me with her laughter: all the delirium passed, and all around the little particles of laughter were sparkling, ringing, and how—fine everything was.

From behind the corner the doctor unravelled himself—a wonderful, magnificent, ever so slender doctor.

"Well," he stopped beside her.

"Nothing, nothing! I'll tell you later. He came by chance . . . Tell them that I'll return in . . . about fifteen minutes . . ."

The doctor flitted around the corner. She waited. The door made a hollow bang. Then I-330 slowly, slowly, plunging the sharp, sweet needle ever deeper into my heart—leaned against me with her shoulder, her arm, everything—and the two of us started walking together, together,—the two of us—like one . . .

I don't remember where we turned into the darkness—and in the darkness, up some stairs, without end, silently. I did not see, but I knew: she was walking the same as I—with eyes closed, blind, head tossed back, biting her lips—and she listened to the music: my barely audible trembling.

I came to in one of the innumerable secluded corners in the courtyard of the Ancient House: some kind of fence, sticking up out of the earth—the bare, stony ribs and yellow teeth of crumbled walls. She opened her eyes, said:

"The day after tomorrow at 16." She left.

Had all of this taken place in fact? I don't know. I'll know the day after tomorrow. There is one real trace: on the right hand—on the tips of the fingers—the skin is scraped. But today on the *Integral* the Second Builder assured me that he himself had seen me accidentally touch a grinding wheel with those fingers—and that was all there was to it. Well, perhaps that was what happened. It is quite possible. I don't know—I know nothing.

Record 18
Synopsis: Jungles of Logic
**   Wounds and a Plaster**
**   Never Again**

Yesterday I lay down—and immediately sank to the dreamy deeps like a capsized, overloaded vessel. A thick stratum of dense, undulating green water. And then I was slowly floating upwards from the bottom and somewhere in the midst of the deeps I opened my eyes: my room, morning, still green, congealed. On the mirror of the wardrobe door—a sliver of sun—right in my eyes. This was interfering with the precise fulfilment of hours of sleep as stipulated by the Tables. It would have been best of all to open the wardrobe door. But it was as though I were all entangled in a cobweb and there was a cobweb over my eyes, no strength to get up...

All the same I did get up, opened it—and suddenly behind the door with the mirror, disentangling herself from the clothing, all pink—I-330. I had now become so accustomed to the improbable that as far as I could recall—I was not in the least amazed, I did not ask anything: quickly into the wardrobe, I slammed the door with the mirror behind me—and panting, quickly, blindly, greedily became one with I-330. As I see it now: through the crack of the door, in the darkness—a sharp ray of sunlight was being fractured like lightning on the floor, the side of the wardrobe, higher—and then this cruel, glittering blade fell on the upturned, naked neck of I-330... and there was something so terrifying for me in this that I could not restrain myself, I screamed—and once again I opened my eyes.

My room. Still a green, congealed morning. On the door of the wardrobe a sliver of sun. I was in bed. A dream. But my heart was still pounding violently, shuddering, spuming, a dull aching in my fingertips, my knees. This—had undoubtedly happened. And now I could not tell: what was dream—what was wakefulness: irrational values were sprouting up through everything else that was customary, three-dimensional, and instead of the solid, polished planes—all around there was something coarse, shaggy...

Still a long while before the bell sounded. I was lying, thinking—and an extraordinarily strange, logical sequence was unwinding.

For every equation, for every formula in the superficial world there is a corresponding curve or solid body. For irrational formulae, for my square root of -1, we know of no corresponding solids, bodies, we have never seen them... But therein lies the very horror, that these bodies—invisible—do exist, they must, unfailingly, unavoidably, exist: because in mathematics, as though on a screen, their bizzare, prickly shadows pass before us—as the irrational formulae; and mathematics and death—are never mistaken. And if we cannot see these bodies in our world, on the surface, for them there is—inescapably there must be—an entire, enormous world there, beneath the surface ...

I leaped up, without waiting for the bell, and started to run around the room. My mathematics—up until now the single solid and immovable island in my whole disoriented life—had also broken loose, was adrift, going in circles. What, did it mean that this absurd *soul* was just as real as my unif, as my boots—even though I could not see them now (they were behind the wardrobe door with the mirror)? And if the boots were not an illness—why then was the *soul* an illness?

I searched for and could not find an exit from this wild, jungle of logic. These were the same unknown and eerie jungles as those—beyond the Green Wall—and they were also those extraordinary, incomprehensible creatures who spoke without words. I imagined to myself—as though through some kind of thick glass—I was seeing: an infinitely enormous and simultaneously infinitely tiny, scorpion-like square root of -1 with a minus-sign like a stinger that was concealed and could still be sensed... But, perhaps, that was nothing other than my *soul*, resembling the legendary scorpion of the ancients that would sting itself with everything that...

The bell. Daytime. All of this, without dying, without disappearing,— was simply covered over by the light of day; just like visible objects, without dying—were at nighttime covered over by the dark of night. In my head there was a light, vacillating mist. Through the mist—long, glass tables; slowly, silently, sphere-like heads chewing in time. From far away, through the mist a metronome was ticking, and to this customarily-soothing music, I was counting mechanically, together with all the rest, to fifty: fifty statutory chewing motions for each piece. And, mechanically keeping time, I went downstairs, marked my name off in the book for those leaving—like everyone else. But I had the feeling: I was living separately from all the others, alone, enclosed by a soft, sound-absorbing wall, and behind this wall was my world...

But this is the thing: if this world is only mine, why then is it in these records? Why are these absurd *dreams* here, the wardrobes, the endless corridors? It is with regret that I see that instead of a harmonious and austere mathematical poem in honor of the United State—I have produced some kind of fantastic adventure novel. Ah, if only it were in fact merely a novel, and not my present life, filled with X's, the square root of -1 and downfalls.

However—perhaps, it is all for the best. Most likely, you, my unknown readers are children in comparison to us (after all we have been nurtured by the United State—consequently, we have achieved the loftiest heights possible for man). And like children—you will swallow everything bitter that I give you only when it is all carefully coated with the thick syrup of adventure...

* * *

In The Evening:

Are you familiar with this feeling: when you are flashing upward through a blue spiral in an aero, the window open, the whirlwind whistling in your face—there is no earth, you are oblivious of the earth, the earth is just as remote to you as Saturn, Jupiter, Venus? That is how I am living now, a whirlwind in my face, and I have forgotten about the earth, I have forgotten about dear, pink O-. But all the same the earth does exist, sooner or later—plans have to be made for it and I am merely closing my eyes until the day when her name stands in my Sexual Table—the name of O-90...

This evening the distant earth called itself to mind. In order to fulfil the doctor's prescription (I genuinely, genuinely want to be cured)—I wandered along the glass, rectilinear wastelands of avenues for two whole hours. Everyone, in accordance with the Table of Hours, was in the auditoria, and only I alone... This was, in essence, an unnatural spectacle: picture to yourself the human finger, cut off from the rest, from the hand, stooped and bent, skipping and running along the glass pavement. That finger was me. And more strange, more unnatural than all else is the fact that the finger has no desire to be on the hand, to be with the others: either—just alone, like this, or...

What of it, I no longer have anything to conceal: or together with her—with that one, again transfusing all of myself into her through a shoulder, through the intertwined fingers of hands...

I returned home when the sun was already setting. The pink ashes of evening were on the glass of walls, on the gold spire of the Accumulator Tower, on the voices and smiles of the approaching numbers. Isn't it strange: the waning rays of sunlight fall at precisely the same angle as the waxing rays in the morning, but everything is completely different, this pinkness is different—now it is very soft, ever so slightly bitter, but in the morning—once again it will be ringing, sparkling.

And now down below, in the vestibule, from beneath a pile of envelopes covered with pink ashes—U-, the controller, pulled out a letter and handed it to me. I repeat: this is a very respectable woman, and I am certain—she has the very best feelings towards me.

And yet, every time when I see those drooping cheeks resembling fish-gills—I feel unpleasant for some reason.

Holding out the letter to me with her gnarled hand—U- sighed. But this sigh only barely rustled that curtain which separated me from the world: I was totally projected with all my being on the envelope trembling in my hands, where—I had no doubt—there was a letter from I-330.

At this point—a second sigh, so obvious, underlined with two lines, that I tore myself away from the envelope—and saw: between the gills, through the modest jalousies of her lowered eyes—a tender, enveloping, blinding smile. And then:

"You poor, poor fellow," a sigh with three lines and a barely perceptible nod at the letter (naturally she knew the contents of the letter,—it was her duty).

"No, truly I... But why?"

"No, no, my dear fellow: I know you better than you do yourself. I have been keeping an eye on you for a long time—and I see: what you need is someone who has already studied life for many long years to walk hand in hand with you in life..."

I had the feeling: pasted all over with her smile—this was the plaster for those wounds which that trembling letter in my hands was about to cover me with. And finally—through the bashful jalousies—quite softly:

"I'll give it some thought, my dear, I'll give it some thought. And rest assured: If I feel enough strength in me—no-no, first I must still give it some thought..."

Great Benefactor! Am I really fated... Does she really mean to say that——

Before my eyes—spots, thousands of sinusoids, the letter dancing. I went closer to the light, to the wall. There the sun was fading, and from there—on me, on the floor, on my hands, on the letter, dark-pink, melancholy ashes, thicker and thicker.

The envelope was torn open—quickly the signature—and the wound—it was not I-330, not I-330, it was... O-. And another wound: on the sheet down below, in the right corner—a smudged blot,—something had dripped here... I cannot bear a blot—it doesn't matter: whether from ink or from... it doesn't matter from what. And I know—earlier—I simply would have found it unpleasant, unpleasant to the eye—because of this unpleasant blot. But why now did this grayish little spot seem like a cloud, and because of it—everything was more leaden and darker? Or was it again just the *soul*?

The letter:

"You know... or, perhaps, you do not know—I can't write properly—
it doesn't matter: now you know that without you there will never be a
single day, a single morning, a single springtime. Because for me R- is
only... well, that is not important to you. In any case I am very grateful to
him: alone without him all these days—I don't know what I... During
these days and nights I have lived through ten, or, perhaps, twenty years.
And it's as though my room is not four-cornered, but round, and without
end—around, around, and still the same thing, and no doors whatsoever,
anywhere.

I can't go on without you—because I love you. Because I see, I
understand: now you don't need anyone, anyone in the world besides that
one, the other one, and—you understand: precisely because I love you, I
must——

I still need only two or three days more to somehow stick back
together the pieces of myself to some resemblance of the former 0-90—and
then I will go myself and make the application to remove my registration to
you, and it should be better for you, it should be good for you. Never again
will I come,

O-."

Never again. It is better this way, of course: she is right. But why then,
why——

Record 19
Synopsis: **An Infinitesimal of the Third Order**
          Beetle-Browed
          Over the Parapet

There, in that strange corridor with the trembling dotted line of murky
bulbs... or no, no—not there: later, when she and I were already in some
secluded corner in the courtyard of the Ancient House—she said: "The day
after tomorrow." That "day after tomorrow" is today, and everything
has—wings, the day is—flying, and our *Integral* is already winged: the
installation of the rocket engine unit has been completed and today we tried
a test firing. What magnificent, powerful salvoes, and for me, each one of
them is a salute in honor of her, the only one, in honor of today.

At the first go (= firing) about a dozen of the numbers from the site
were caught standing under the exhaust—absolutely nothing was left of
them except for some particles and soot. I am recording here, with pride,
that the rhythm of our work did not falter for a second because of this, no
one flinched; we at our work installations—carried on our rectilinear and
round movement with the very same precision as though nothing had

happened. A dozen numbers—this is hardly one one-hundred-millionth part of the mass of the United State; for practical considerations—this is an infinitesimal quantity of the third order. Only the ancients knew such arithmetically-illiterate pity: to us it is ridiculous.

And it seems ridiculous to me that yesterday I was able to contemplate—and even record on these pages—some pitiful, grayish little spot, some ink-blot. This is still that very same "softening of the surface," which should be diamond-hard—like our walls (the ancient proverb: "like peas against a wall").

Sixteen hours. I did not take the supplementary walk: how can I know that she might not take it into her head to come precisely at this time, when everything is ringing with the sun...

I am almost alone in the building. Through the sun-suffused walls—for a long way to the right, and to the left and down below—suspended in the air, empty, repeating one another: mirror-like rooms. And only along the bluish staircase, lightly delineated with the sun's ink—a gaunt gray shadow was slowly sliding upwards. Then the sound of steps—and through the door I saw—I sensed: the plaster-smile sticking to me—and then passing, along another staircase—down...

The click of the intercom. I dashed headlong to the narrow white slot—and... and some unfamiliar male number (with a consonant for the letter). The elevator hummed, banged. In front of me—a carelessly slanted, overhanging forehead, and the eyes... a very strange impression: as though he were speaking from there, from beneath his beetle-brow, where the eyes were.

"A letter for you from her (—from beneath his beetle-brow, from under the awning)... She asked that without fail—everything, as it says there."

From beneath the beetle-brow, from under the awning—all around.

There's no one, no one here, well, give it here! Looking around once more, he slipped me an envelope, left. I was alone.

No, not alone: out of the envelope—a pink coupon, and—barely perceptible—the scent of her. It was her, she would come, come to me. Quickly—the letter, to read it with my own eyes, to believe it completely...

What? It could not be! I read it once again—skipping lines: "the coupon... and lower the blinds without fail as though I were in actual fact with you... It is essential for me that they think that I... I am very, very sorry..."

The letter—into shreds. In the mirror for a second—my distorted, broken eyebrows. I took the coupon so that it too, like her note——

"She asked that without fail, everything, as it says there."

My hands grew weak, unclenched themselves. The coupon fell from them onto the table. She was stronger than I, and I, it seemed would do as she wished. However... however I don't know: we will see—it's still a long ways to evening... The coupon was lying on the table.

In the mirror my distorted, broken eyebrows. Why didn't I have a doctor's certificate for today as well: I would go for a walk, a walk without end, around the entire Green Wall—and then collapse into bed—to the bottom... But I must go—to No. 13 auditorium, I must screw all of myself up tight, so that for two hours—for two hours, without budging... when I need to scream, to stamp my feet.

The lecture. Very strange that it was not the usual metallic one coming out of the glittering apparatus, but some kind of soft, woolly, mossy voice. A woman's—I have a fleeting impression of her as she must have looked in life at one time: a small, bent over old woman, something like that one—at the Ancient House.

The Ancient House... and everything at once—like a fountain—from down below, and I had to screw myself up with all my might so as not to drown out the entire auditorium with a scream. The soft, woolly words—right through me, and only one thing remains from all of this: something—about children, about child-production. Like a photographic plate: I am printing everything in myself with a kind of alien, detached, senseless precision: a golden scythe—the reflection of light on the loudspeaker; underneath it—a child, a live illustration, reaching for the scythe; the hem of its microscopic unif stuffed in its mouth; a tightly clenched fist with the thumb squeezed inside—a light, plump shadow—the fold of skin at the wrist. Like a photographic plate—I was printing: here now a bare leg—hanging over the edge, the pink fan of toes stepping into air—now any moment, any moment, down onto the floor——

And a woman's scream, a unif fluttered with transparent wings onto the platform, caught the child—her lips—upon the plump little fold at the wrist, moved it to the center of the table, climbed down from the platform. Printing inside me: the pink—with the horns turned down—crescent of the mouth, blue saucer-eyes filled to the brim. It was 0-90. And I, as though during the reading of some kind of harmonious formula—suddenly I sensed the necessity, the naturalness of that insignificant incident.

She sat down just behind me and to the left. I glanced around. She obediently shifted her eyes from the table with the child, and looked—at me, inside me, and once again: she, I and the table on the platform are three points, and through these points lines were drawn, the projections of some kind of unavoidable, yet to come events.

Homeward—along the green, twilight street, now many-eyed from the lights. I heard: I was ticking all over—like a clock. And the clock hands inside me—were about to overstep some figure, I would do something of the sort from which there would be no turning back. She needed to have someone there think: she was with me. But I needed her, and what did I care about her *need*. I did not want to be someone else's blinds—I did not, and that was that.

Behind me—a familiar squelching walk, as though someone were walking through puddles. I was not about to glance back, I knew: S-. He would follow me right up to the door—and then, probably, he would stand down below, on the sidewalk, and with his gimlets drill his way in there, upstairs, into my room—until the blinds fell there, concealing someone's crime...

He, the Guardian Angel, had put a full stop to it. I had made my decision: no. I had made my decision.

When I went up to the room and turned the switch—I did not believe my eyes: beside my desk stood O-90. Or, rather—she was drooping the way an empty, discarded dress droops—beneath her dress it was as though there was not a single spring, the arms, the legs were springless, the drooping voice was springless.

"I came about my letter. Did you receive it? Yes? I have to know the answer, I have to—today."

I shrugged my shoulders. With pleasure—as though she were to blame for everything—I gazed at her blue eyes, filled to the brim with tears—I lingered over my answer. And with pleasure, jabbing her with each word, I said:

"Answer? Well, then... You are right. Completely. About everything."

"So it means... (— the slightest tremble was concealed with a smile, but I saw it). Well, very good! I'll go—I'll go at once."

But she kept drooping over the table. Lowered eyes, legs, arms. The crumpled pink coupon of the other one was still lying on the table. I quickly undid my manuscript WE—and covered the coupon with its pages (perhaps, more from myself than from O-).

"Here—I'm still writing. Already 170 pages... It's turning out quite unexpectedly..."

A voice—the shadow of a voice:

"But do you remember... that time when on the seventh page I... I let a tear fall—and you..."

The blue saucers—brimming over, inaudible, rapid drops—along the cheeks, downward, rapidly brimming over—words:

"I can't bear it, I am going away at once... Never again will I come, and so be it. I don't care. But only I want—I must have a child from you—leave me with a child and I will go away, I will go away!"

I saw: she was trembling all over beneath her unif, and I felt: in just a moment I too—I folded my hands behind my back, smiled:

"What? Do you have some urge for the Benefactor's Machine?"

And at me—the same as before, like streams through weirs—the words:

"I don't care! But at least I shall feel it—I shall feel it inside of me. And even if only for a few days... To see—if only once to see a little fold of skin right here—the way it was there—like on the table. One day!"

Three points: she, I—and there on the table the tiny fist with the plump fold of skin...

Once in my childhood, I remember, we were taken to the Accumulator Tower. On the topmost flight of stairs I leaned over the glass parapet, down below—little people-dots, and my heart was ticking sweetly: "And what if?" Then I merely grasped the railing more firmly; now—I leaped.

"So you want it? Perfectly aware that..."

Closed—as though directly in the face of the sun—her eyes. A moist, radiant smile.

"Yes, yes! I want it!"

I grabbed the pink coupon out from under the manuscript—*from the other one*—and ran downstairs, to the duty clerk. O- seized me by the hand, screamed something, but what—I understood only later when I had returned.

She was sitting on the edge of the bed, her hand tightly clenched in her lap.

"It's... It's her coupon?"

"What difference does it make. Alright—yes, hers." Something cracked. Most likely—O- had simply stirred.

She was sitting, her hands in her lap, silent.

"Well? Quickly..." I squeezed her hand roughly and red spots (tomorrow—black and blue ones) on her wrists, there—where the plump childlike fold of skin was.

This was the last. Then—the switch was turned, thoughts were extinguished, darkness, sparks—and over the parapet and down I went...

Record 20
Synopsis: **Discharge**
The Material of Ideas
The Zero Cliff

A discharge—the most suitable definition. Now I see that this was precisely like an electrical discharge. The pulse-rate of my last few days is becoming more and more dry, more frequent, more intense—the terminals closer and closer—a dry crackling—one millimeter more: an explosion, then—silence.

It is very quiet and empty inside me now—like it is in the building when everyone has left and you are lying alone, sick, and you can hear so clearly the distinct, metallic pounding of your thoughts.

Perhaps this "discharge" has cured me, at last, of my agonizing *soul*—and once again I have become like all of us. At least, now I can mentally see, without the least pain, O-90 on the steps of the Cube, I can see her in the Gas Bell. And if there, in Operations, she names me—I won't care: at the last moment—I shall reverently and thankfully kiss the chastising hand of the Benefactor. In respect to the United State I have this right—to suffer chastisement, and I shall not relinquish this right. None of us numbers should, or dare, renounce this unique—and therefore most valued—right.

... Quietly, metallically-distinctly, my thoughts are pounding; a strange aero is bearing me away into the blue heights of my favorite abstractions. And I see, how here—in the purest, rarified air—with a gentle pop, like a pneumatic tire—my reasoning "about active right" bursts. And I see clearly that this is merely a regurgitation of the absurd prejudice of the ancients— their idea about *right*.

There are ideas of clay—and there are ideas eternally carved in gold or our precious glass. And, in order to define the material of the idea, it is only necessary to drop some strong-acting acid on it. Even the ancients knew one of these such acids: *reductio ad finem*. It seems, that was what they called it; but they were afraid of this poison, they preferred to see at least some kind of heaven, even a clay one, even a toylike one, rather than a blue nothingness. But we—glory be to the Benefactor—we are adults and we have no need of toys.

Now then—what if a drop is applied to the idea of right. Even among the ancients—the more adult knew: the source of right is force, right is a function of force. And so—the two sides of a scale: on one side a gram, on the other a ton, on the one side—*I*, on the other—*We*, the United State. Is it not clear: to assume that *I* might have some *rights* in respect to the State and to assume that a gram might be equal in weight to a ton—that is completely one and the same thing. Consequently, the distribution: to the ton—the rights, to the gram—the obligations and the natural path from insignificance to greatness: to forget that you are a gram and to feel yourself a millionth part of the ton...

You, splendid-bodied, rosy-cheeked Venusians, you Uranians sooty as blacksmiths—I hear your grumbling in my blue silence. But do try to understand: everything great is simple; do try to understand: only the four rules of arithmetic are eternal and immutable. And greatness, immutability, eternity—will abide only in that morality built upon the four rules. This is the ultimate wisdom, this is the pinnacle of that pyramid towards which people—red with sweat, striking out and panting hoarsely,—were scrambling for centuries. And from this pinnacle—there, at the bottom, where like miserable worms something is still crawling about that has survived in us from the savagery of our ancestors—from this pinnacle they are all alike: the illegitimate mother—O-90, and the murderess, and that madman who dared to attack the United State with his verse; and judgment is the same for them all: premature death. This is that very same divine justice about which the stone-house people dreamed, enlightened by the pink, naive rays of history's morning: their *God*—for blasphemy against the Holy Church—chastised them the same as for murder.

You, the Uranians—grim and black, like the ancient Spaniards, wisely knowledgeable in burning at the stake—you are silent, it seems to me, you are with me. But I hear: the pink Venusians—something there about tortures, executions, about a return to barbaric times. My dear fellows: I am sorry for you—you are not capable of philosophical-mathematical thinking.

Human history proceeds upwards in circles—like an aero. There are various circles—gold ones, bloody ones, but they are all equally divided into 360 degrees. And so from zero—forward: 10, 20, 200, 360 degrees—and again zero. Yes we have returned to zero,—yes. But for my mathematically-thinking mind, it is clear: this zero is altogether different, new. We proceeded from zero to the right—we returned to zero from the left and therefore: instead of a plus zero—we have a minus zero. Do you understand?

This Zero I visualize as a kind of silent, enormous, steep knife-sharp cliff. In the ferocious, shaggy darkness, holding our breath, we have cast off from the dark, nocturnal side of the Zero Cliff. For centuries—we, the Columbuses, sailed, sailed, we rounded the entire earth, and finally, hurrah! A salute—and everyone to the masts: before us is the other, hitherto unknown, side of the Zero Cliff, illuminated by the polar radiance of the United State, a blue monolith, sparks of the rainbow, suns—hundreds of suns, billions of rainbows...

What matters it if we are separated from the other black side of the Zero Cliff by the mere thickness of a knife-blade. The knife is the most substantial, the most immortal, the most brilliant of all that man has created. The knife—was a guillotine, the knife is the universal means for solving all knots, and it is along the knife's edge that the path of paradoxes makes its way—the single path worthy of a fearless mind...

Record 21
Synopsis: Authorial Duty
The Ice Swells
The Most Difficult Love

Yesterday was her day, but she—did not come again, and again from her—an incoherent, non-explanatory note. But I am calm, completely calm. If I am still proceeding the way it is dictated in the note, if I am still taking her coupon to the duty clerk and then, after lowering the blinds, sitting in my room alone—then naturally it is not because I do not have the strength to go against her wishes. Ridiculous? Of course not. Simply—

separated by the blinds from all the plaster-sticking smiles, I can calmly write these very pages here, that is the first thing. Secondly: in her, in I-330, I am afraid of losing, perhaps, the sole key to unlocking all the unknowns (the business with the wardrobe, my temporary death and so forth). And to unlock them—I now feel myself duty-bound, simply even as the author of these records, not to mention anything about the fact that the unknown is organically inimical to man, and *homo sapiens* is only a human being in the full sense of that word when there are absolutely no question marks in his grammar, only exclamation marks, commas and periods alone.

And thus, guided, as it seems to me, precisely by authorial duty, at 16 hours today I took an aero and once again made my way to the Ancient House. There was a strong head-wind. With difficulty, the aero forced its way through the dense thicket of air, the transparent branches were whistling and lashing. The city below seemed to be entirely of blue monoliths of ice. Suddenly—a cloud, a swift oblique shadow, the ice turning a leaden color, swelling up as in springtime when you are standing on the shore and waiting: in just another moment everything will crack, surge, swirl and sweep; but minute after minute the ice is still standing, and you begin to swell yourself, your heart is beating more and more uneasily, more and more rapidly (however, why am I writing about this and where are these strange sensations coming from? Because after all there is no such icebreaker as could smash that most transparent and most solid crystal of our life...).

By the entrance to the Ancient House—no one. I walked around it and saw the old woman of a gatekeeper beside the Green Wall: shading her eyes with her hand, she was looking upward. There, above the wall were the sharp, black triangles of some kind of birds: cawing, they were hurling themselves in an assault—breast-first against the solid fence of electrical waves—and then backwards, and once again above the Wall.

I saw: over the dark face overgrown with wrinkles—oblique, swift shadows, a swift glance at me.

"Nobody here, nobody, nobody! Yes! And it's useless coming. Yes..."

What did she mean it was useless? And what kind of strange behavior was that—taking me simply for someone's shadow. But perhaps you yourselves are all my shadows.

Have I not in fact used you to populate these pages—which only a short while ago were rectangular white wastelands. Without me would you really have been seen by all those whom I shall lead behind me along the narrow paths of the lines?

All of this, naturally, I did not say to her; from my personal experience I know: the most agonizing thing—is to plant doubt in a person as to whether he is—a reality, a three-dimensional one—and not any other kind—of reality. I merely remarked drily to her that it was her business to open the door, and she let me into the courtyard.

Empty. Quiet. The wind—there, beyond the walls, distant as on that first day when shoulder-to-shoulder, two-as-one, we emerged from below, out of the corridors—if only that actually took place. I was walking under some stone arches where my footsteps, rebounding against the damp vaults, were falling behind me,—as though all the time someone else were walking at my heels. Yellow walls—with red blotches of brick—were watching me through the dark quadrangular spectacles of their windows, watching me as I opened the melodious doors of barns, as I peered into corners, dead ends, nooks. A wicket in the fence and a wasteland—a monument to the Great Two Hundred Years' War: out of the ground— naked stone ribs, yellow grinning jaw-bones of walls, an ancient stove with its chimney in a vertical line—a forever petrified ship in the midst of yellow stone and red brick waves.

It seemed to me: I had already seen precisely these yellow teeth at one time—unclearly, as though on the bottom, through a layer of water—and I began to search. I kept tumbling into pits, stumbling against stones, rusty paws were grabbing at my unif, down my forehead, into my eyes, crept salt-sharp drops of sweat . . .

Nowhere! Nowhere could I find from that time the exit leading out of the corridors from below—it did not exist. Yet—perhaps it was better that way: a greater probability that all of this—was one of my absurd *dreams*.

Tired, all covered with some kind of cobweb, with dust—I had already opened the wicket—to return to the main courtyard. Suddenly from behind—a rustling, squelching steps and before me—the pink wing-ears, the double curved smile of S-.

Screwing up his eyes, he was drilling into me with his gimlets and he asked:

"Taking a walk?"

I was silent. My arms were getting in the way.

"Well, then, do you feel better now?"

"Yes, thank you. It seems I'm returning to the norm." He set me free— he raised his eyes upwards. His head was tossed back—and for the first time I noticed his adam's apple.

Not very high up above—about 50 meters—aeros were droning. From their slow, low flight, from the lowered black probosces of the observation tubes—I recognized the machinery of the Guardians. But there were not two or three of them, as was usual, but from ten to twelve (unfortunately, I must restrict myself to this approximate figure).

"Why are there so many of them today?" I had the boldness to ask.

"Why? Hm . . . A real doctor—begins treating today the healthy man who might fall ill only tomorrow, the day after tomorrow, in a week's time. Prophylaxis, indeed!"

He nodded, began to squelch off along the stone slabs of the courtyard. Then he turned around—and over his shoulder to me:

"Be careful!"

I am alone. Quiet. Deserted. Far away over the Green Wall birds are dashing about, wind. What did he mean by that?

The aero slipped quickly along with the wind current. Light, heavy shadows from the clouds, down below—the azure cupolas, cubes of glass ice—were turning a leaden color, swelling...

In the Evening:

I opened up my manuscript in order to enter on these pages some of what seemed to me to be useful thoughts (for you, the readers) about the great Day of Unanimity—this day is already close. And I see: I cannot write now. All the time I keep listening to how the wind is banging its dark wings against the glass of the walls, all the time I keep glancing over my shoulder, waiting. For what? I don't know. And when the familiar, brownish-pink fish gills appeared in my room—I was very happy, frankly speaking. She sat down, chastely straightened a fold of her unif that had fallen between her knees, stuck me all over with her smiles—a bit for each of my cracks—and I felt pleasant, tightly bound.

"You understand, when I arrived in class today (— she works at the Child Education Factory)—what should I see but a caricature on the wall. Yes, yes, I assure you! They had depicted me in some form of a fish. Perhaps, in fact, I do..."

"No, no, what are you saying,"— I hastened to say (close up, in fact, it was clear that there was nothing resembling gills, and what had struck me as gills—that was completely out of place).

"Yes, after all—that isn't important. But, you understand: the act itself. Of course, I summoned the Guardians. I love children very much, and I consider that the most difficult and exalted love—that is cruelty,—do you understand?"

Of course! It coincided so closely with my own thoughts. I could not refrain and read her an excerpt from my 20th Record, where it begins: "Softly, metallic-distinctly, my thoughts are pounding..."

Without looking, I saw her brownish-pink cheeks trembling and moving closer and closer to me, and suddenly in my hands—dry, firm, even slightly prickly fingers.

"Give it—give it to me! I will make a recording of it and make the children learn it by heart. Your Venusians don't need it as much as we do, as we do—right now, tomorrow, the day after."

She looked around—and then quite softly: "Did you hear: they are saying that on the Day of Unanimity..."

I leaped up:

"What—what are they saying? What—on the Day of Unanimity?"

The cosy walls were no longer there. I had a fleeting sensation of being cast out there, outside, where the great wind was swooping over the roof-tops, and the oblique, twilight clouds—lower and lower...

U- grasped me around the shoulders resolutely, firmly (although I noted: resonating with my agitation—the small bones of her fingers were trembling).

"Sit down, my dear, don't get upset. What won't people say. . ." And then: "if only you find it necessary—I shall be near you on this day, I shall leave my children from school with someone else—and I shall be with you because after all you, my dear, you too are a child, and you need. . ."

"No, no," I began to wave my arms, "by no means! Then you will, in fact, be thinking that I am some kind of child—that alone I cannot. . . By no means!" (—I confess: I had other plans regarding that day.)

She smiled: the unwritten text of the smile, apparently, was: "Ah, what a stubborn boy!" Then she sat down. Eyes lowered. Hands bashfully straightened the fold of her unif that had once again fallen between her knees—and then about something different:

"I think that I must make a decision. . . for your sake. . . No, I implore you: do not hurry me, I must still give it some thought. . ."

I did not hurry her. Although I understood that I should be happy and that there was no greater honor than to crown someone's twilight years with one's self.

. . .All night—some kind of wings, and I am walking and covering my head with my hands from the wings. And then—a chair. But the chair is not one of ours, a contemporary one, but of an ancient design, out of wood. I am pawing the ground, like a horse (the right front foot—and the left rear one, the left front one and the right rear one), the chair comes running up to my bed, crawls into it—and I love that wooden chair: uncomfortable, painful.

Amazing: is it really impossible to come up with any kind of means for curing this dream-illness or for rationalizing it—perhaps even making it useful?

Record 22
Synopsis: Paralyzed Waves
All Is Becoming Perfect
I Am a Microbe

Picture to you yourself that you are standing on a shore: the waves—rise rhythmically; and having risen—suddenly they stop, they have congealed, become paralyzed. It was just as eerie and unnatural as this—when suddenly our walk, prescribed by the Book of Hours, went awry, grew confused, and came to a halt. The last time something similar happened, as our chronicles state, was 119 years ago when into the very thick of the walk, whistling and smoking, a meteorite plummeted from the sky.

We were walking as always, i.e., the way warriors in the Assyrian monuments are depicted: a thousand heads—two composite, integrated legs, two integrated, swinging arms. At the end of the avenue—there where the Accumulator Tower was whirring threateningly—a rectangle was coming towards us: along the sides, before, after—were guards; in the middle were three of them, on the unifs of these people there were no longer any golden numbers—and everything was eerily clear.

The enormous signboard on the pinnacle of the tower—it was a face: it had bent over out of the clouds, and, spitting its seconds downward, was waiting indifferently. And then precisely at 13 hours and 6 minutes—confusion broke out in the rectangle. All of this was quite close to me, I could see the tiniest details, and I remembered clearly the slender, long neck and on the temple—a tangled nexus of blue veins, like rivers on a map of a small, unknown world, and that unknown world was, apparently a youth. Probably he had noticed someone in our ranks: he raised himself on his toes, stuck out his neck, came to a stop. One of the guards cracked the bluish spark of an electric whip at him; he gave a thin yelp, like a puppy. And then—a distinct crack, approximately every 2 seconds—and a yelp, a crack—a yelp.

We continued walking as before, rhythmically, Assyrian-like—and I, looking at the exquisite zigzags of the sparks, was thinking: "Everything in human society is becoming boundlessly perfect—and it must become perfect. What an ugly instrument the ancient whip was—and now how much beauty there is..."

But then, like a screw-nut that had flown loose under full power, a slender, resiliently flexible female figure tore loose from our ranks and with the cry: "Enough! Don't you dare"—hurtled right there, into the rectangle. It was—like the meteorite—119 years ago: the entire walk froze and our ranks—were the gray crests of the waves chained fast by a sudden frost.

For a second I watched her with detachment, like everyone else: she was no longer a number—she was merely a person, she existed merely as the metaphysical substance of outrage inflicted on the United State. But just a certain motion of hers—as she was twisting, she bent her hips to the left—and it was suddenly clear to me: I knew, I knew that body, flexible like a whip—my eyes, my lips, my hands knew it—at that moment I was perfectly certain of this.

Two of the guards—moved to intercept her. In another moment—at a point on the pavement that was still clear and mirrorlike—their trajectories would intersect—in another moment they would seize her... My heart choked, stopped—and without reasoning: should I, shouldn't I, absurd, rational—I hurtled to that point...

I felt thousands of eyes on me, bulging with horror but that merely gave even more of desperately happy strength to that wild, hairy-handed being that had torn loose out of me, and he ran all the faster. Only two strides more now, she turned around —

Before me was a trembling, freckle-splattered face, red eyebrows...

Not her! Not I-330.

A frenzied, lashing joy. I wanted to shout something like: "She's the one!" "Hold her!"—but I heard only my own whisper. And on my shoulder—already a heavy hand, they were holding me, they led me away, I was trying to explain to them...

"Listen, but you really must understand that I thought that this was..."

But how could I explain all of myself, all of my illness, which is recorded on these pages. And extinguished, I went along submissively... A leaf, torn from a tree by an unexpected blast of wind, falls submissively downwards, but along the way it circles, catches at every familiar branch, fork, twig: thus I was catching at every one of the speechless sphere-heads, at the transparent ice of the walls, at the azure needle of the Accumulator Tower stuck into a cloud.

At that moment, when a dense curtain was ready once and for all to separate all this beautiful world from me, I saw: nearby, flapping his pink arm-wings, a familiar, enormous head was slipping over the mirror of the pavement. And the familiar, flat voice:

"I consider it my duty to testify to the fact that number D-503 is ill and is not in a condition to regulate his emotions. And I am certain that he was inspired by a natural indignation..."

"Yes, yes," I seized upon it. "I even shouted: hold her!"

From behind, at my back:

"You weren't shouting anything."

"Yes, but I wanted to—I swear by the Benefactor, I wanted to."

For one second I was drilled through by the gray, cold, gimlet-eyes. I don't know whether he saw inside me that this was (almost) true, or whether he had some secret purpose in sparing me once again for the time being, but he merely wrote out a note, gave it to one of those holding me,— and I was free again, i.e., rather I was once again locked into the orderly, endless, Assyrian ranks.

The rectangle, and in it the freckled face and the temple with the geographical map of blue veins—disappeared around a corner, forever. We proceeded—a single, million-headed body, and in each of us was that humble joy by which, probably, molecules, atoms, phagocytes live. In the ancient world—this was understood by the Christians, our only (albeit very imperfect) precursors: humility is a virtue, whereas pride is a vice; and *WE* is from God, whereas *I* is from the devil.

There I was—now keeping step with everyone—and all the same separated from everyone. I was still trembling all over from the agitation I had experienced, like a bridge, which an ancient steel train has just gone thundering over. I was aware of myself. But after all an awareness of self, a consciousness of its individuality—that is only for an eye with something in it, an infected finger, an aching tooth: the healthy eye, finger, tooth—it is as if they do not exist. Surely it is clear that personal consciousness is merely an illness.

I, perhaps, am no longer a phagocyte, devouring microbes (those with a blue temple and those with freckles) in a business-like and calm fashion: I, perhaps, am a microbe, and, perhaps, there are already thousands of them among us, still pretending, even as I am, to be phagocytes...

What if today's essentially insignficant occurrence—what if all of this is merely the beginning, merely the first meteorite of a whole series of thundering, burning stones, strewn by infinity on our glass paradise?

Record 23
Synopsis: Flowers
**   Dissolution of a Crystal**
**   If Only**

They say there are flowers which blossom only once in a hundred years. Why not then ones that blossom once in a thousand—in ten thousand years. Perhaps we have not known about this up until now merely because today was precisely that once-in-a-thousand-years.

And thus, blissfully and drunkenly, I am walking down the stairs, to the duty clerk, and rapidly before my eyes, all around me, thousand-year-old buds are soundlessly bursting and chairs are flowering, shoes, golden badges, electrical bulbs, someone's dark, shaggy eyes, the faceted balustrade of the railings, a handkerchief dropped on the steps, the little desk of the duty clerk—the tender-brownish freckled cheeks of U-. Everything was extraordinary, new, tender, pink, moist.

U- took my pink coupon, and over her head—through the glass of the wall—the moon, azure, aromatic,—was hanging from some mysterious branch. Solemnly I pointed to it with my finger and said:

"The moon,—do you understand?"

U- glanced at me, then at the number of the coupon—and I saw that familiar, ever so enchantingly chaste movement of hers: she straightened the folds of her unif between the angles of her knees.

"My dear, you look abnormal, ill—because abnormality and illness are one and the same. You are ruining yourself, and no one will tell you so—no one."

This *no one*—of course, was equated to the number on the coupon: I-330. Dear, wonderful U-! You are right of course: I am imprudent, I am ill, I have a soul, I am a microbe. But isn't blossoming really an illness? Isn't it really painful when a bud bursts? And don't you think that the spermatozoon is the most frightening of all microbes?

I was upstairs, in my room. In the widely-spread calyx of the armchair was I-330. I was on the floor, I was embracing her legs, my head was on her knees, we were silent. Silence, pulse... to illustrate: I am a crystal and I am dissolving in her, in I-330. I feel perfectly clearly how the polished facets limiting me within space are melting, melting—I am disappearing, I am dissolving in her knees, in her, I am becoming ever smaller—and simultaneously ever wider, ever larger, ever more unencompassable. Because she—she is not she, but the universe. And so, for a second, I and this armchair permeated with joy beside the bed—we are one: and the magnificently smiling old woman at the gates of the Ancient House, and the wild jungles beyond the Green Wall, and some kind of ruins, silver against black, slumbering like the old woman, and somewhere, improbably distant, a door banging at this moment—all of this is inside me, together with me, is listening to the beating of my pulse and soaring through that blissful second...

In absurd, confused, overflowing words I was trying to tell her that I am a crystal and therefore there was a door in me, and therefore I feel how happy the chair is. But it came out as such nonsense that I stopped, I am simply embarrassed: I—and suddenly...

"Dear I-330, forgive me! I don't understand in the least: I am speaking such foolishness..."

"Why ever do you think that foolishness is not good? If human foolishness had been cherished and cultivated for centuries in the same way as the mind, perhaps something extraordinarily precious would have resulted from it."

"Yes..." (It seemed to me that she was right,—how could she not be right now?)

"And for that very foolishness of yours—for what you did yesterday during the walk—I love you even more—even more."

"But why then did you torment me, why did you not come, why did you send your coupons, why did you force me..."

"But perhaps I had to torture you? Perhaps I had to know that you would do everything I wanted—that you were already entirely mine?"

"Yes, entirely!"

She took my face—all of me—into her palms, raised my head:

"Well, but what about your obligations to every number? Eh?"

Sweet, sharp, white teeth; a smile. In the unfolded calyx of the armchair she was like a bee: there was both honey and a sting in her.

Yes, obligations... I was mentally leafing through my latest records: in fact, nowhere was there even a thought about what essentially I ought to...

I was silent. I was smiling ecstatically (and probably stupidly), gazing into her pupils, running from one to the other, and in each of them I saw myself: I—minute, millimetric—I was held captive in these minute, rainbow-like prisons. And then again—bees—lips, the sweet pain of blossoming...

In each of us numbers there is something invisible, a quietly ticking metronome, and without looking at a clock, we know the time to within an accuracy of minutes. But at that moment—the metronome inside me had stopped, I did not know how much time had passed, in horror I grabbed my badge with the watch from under the pillow...

Praise be to the Benefactor: still another twenty minutes! But minutes—such absurdly brief, scanty things, they keep running and I must tell her so much—everything, all of me: about the letter from O-, and about that terrible evening when I gave her a child; and for some reason about my childhood years—about the mathematician Plyapa, about the square root of -1, and about the first time I was at the celebration of Unanimity and wept bitterly because on my unif—on a day like that,—a black spot had turned up.

I-330 raised her head, leaned on an elbow. At the corners of her lips— two long, sharp lines—and the dark angle of the upturned brows: a cross.

"Perhaps, on this day..." She stopped and her brows grew yet darker. She took my hand, squeezed it firmly. "Tell me, you won't forget me, you'll always remember me?"

"Why are you talking like that? What do you mean? I-330, dearest?"

I-330 was silent, and her eyes were already looking past me, through me, far away. I suddenly heard the wind beating against the glass with its enormous wings (of course—that had been going on all the while, but I only heard it now), and for some reason I recalled those shrill birds above the top of the Green Wall.

I-330 suddenly shook her head, freed herself from something. Once more, for a second, she touched me with her whole body—the way an aero touches the earth tremblingly before landing.

"Well, give me my stockings! Quickly!"

The stockings had been tossed on my desk, on top of an open page (p. 193) of my records. In my haste I brushed against the manuscript, pages scattered and there was no way I could put them back in order, and the main thing was that even if I did manage, it did not matter—there would be no real order, it did not matter—some kind of rough spots, gaps, X's would still remain.

"I can't go on like this," I said. "Here you are—right here, beside me, and it's as though you're still behind an ancient opaque wall: I hear rustlings, voices through that wall—and I cannot make out the words, I don't know what is there. I can't go on like that. All the time you are leaving something unsaid, you have never once told me where I ended up that time in the Ancient House, and what kind of corridors they were, and why the doctor,—or, perhaps, nothing like this happened?"

I-330 laid her hands on my shoulders, slowly, deeply she penetrated into my eyes.

"Do you want to know everything?"

"Yes, I do. I must."

"And you will not be afraid to follow me anywhere, to the end—wherever I might lead you?"

"Yes, anywhere!"

"Fine. I promise you: when the celebration is finished, if only... Ah, yes: and how is your *Integral*—I keep forgetting to ask,—will it be soon?"

"No: what *if only*? Again? What *if only*?"

She (already at the door):

"You will see for yourself..."

I was alone. All that remained of her was a barely perceptible scent similar to the sweet, dry, yellow pollen of some kind of flowers from beyond the Wall. And in addition: hooklike-questions firmly embedded in me—something like those which the ancients had used for fishing (Prehistoric Museum).

... But why all of a sudden about the *Integral*?

Record 24
Synopsis: The Limits of a Function
Easter
Strike Out Everything

I am like a machine operated at an excessively high number of revolutions: the bearings have become red-hot, one minute more—the melted metal will start to drip, and everything will be ruined. Quickly—some cold water, some logic. I am pouring buckets, but logic only sizzles on the fiery bearings and disperses into the air like elusive white steam.

Yes, of course, it is clear: in order to establish the true value of a function—one must begin with its limits. And it is clear that yesterday's absurd "dissolution in the universe," taken to its extremes, is death. Because death is precisely the utmost dissolution of me in the universe. Hence, if we designate love as "L," and death as "D," then $L = f(D)$, i.e., love and death...

Yes, precisely, precisely. That is the very reason that I am afraid of I-330, why I am struggling against her, why I don't want to. Buy why are "I don't want to" and "I desire" side-by-side in me? The very horror of it is that again I am beginning to desire yesterday's blissful death. The very horror of it is that even now, when the logical function has been integrated, when it is obvious that it secretly contains death in itself, I still desire her with my lips, my arms, my breast, with every millimeter... Tomorrow is the Day of Unanimity. She will be there as well, of course. I will see her, but only from afar. From afar—that will be painful because I have to be, I have an irresistible attraction to be beside her, so that—her arms, her shoulder, her hair... But I even desire this pain—so be it.

Great Benefactor! What an absurdity—to desire pain. Who does not understand that painful things are negative items reducing the sum-total of what we call happiness. And, consequently...

And now—none of that "consequently." Pure and simple.

In the Evening:

Through the glass walls of the building, a windy feverishly-pink, disturbing sunset. I am turning my armchair so that this pinkishness won't be sticking out in front of me, I am leafing through my records—and I see: again I have forgotten that I am writing not for myself, but for you, for strangers whom I love and pity—for you who are still toiling along somewhere in the distant centuries, down below.

Now—about the Day of Unanimity, about this great day. I have always loved it—from childhood years. It seems to me that for us it is something like what *Easter* was for the ancients. I remember, on the eve, I used to compose a little hourly calendar for myself—solemnly each hour was crossed out: an hour closer, one hour less to wait... If I were certain that no one would see—word of honor I would carry that kind of little calendar with me everywhere even today and I would keep track in it how much time was left until tomorrow, when I would see—even if only from afar...

(An interruption: a new unif, fresh from the shop, has been delivered. We are customarily issued new unifs for tomorrow's day. In the corridor—footsteps, joyful exclamations, noise.)

I am continuing. Tomorrow I shall see that spectacle which is repeated year after year and which is always freshly exciting every time: the mighty chalice of accord, the arms raised in reverence. Tomorrow is the day for the annual election of the Benefactor. Tomorrow we shall once again hand the Benefactor the keys to the immutable fortress of our happiness.

Of course, this does not resemble the disorderly, unorganized elections among the ancients when—it is ridiculous to say—the very result of the elections was even unknown beforehand. To build a state on completely uncalculable chance, blindly—what could be more senseless? And, as it turns out, centuries were nonetheless required in order to grasp that.

Need it be said that even here among us, as in all else—there is no place for any chance happenings, there can be no surprises? And the elections themselves have a significance that is more symbolic: to remind us that we are a single, mighty, million-celled organism, that we are—using the words of the "Gospel" of the ancients—the One Church. Because the history of the United State knows of no single instance when on this solemn day even a single voice has dared to violate the majestic unison.

They say that the ancients conducted elections somehow secretly, concealing themselves like thieves; certain of our historians even affirm that they would appear at election celebrations painstakingly masked (I imagine this fantastic sombre spectacle thus: night time, a square, figures stealing along the walls in dark cloaks; the crimson flames of torches dancing up and down in the wind...). What the need was for all of this mystery—has not been thoroughly explained even now; most likely of all, the elections were connected with some kind of mystical, superstitious, perhaps even—criminal rites. But we have nothing to hide or to be ashamed of: we celebrate the elections openly, honorably, in day time. I see all voting for the Benefactor; all see me voting for the Benefactor—and could it be any other way, once all and *I* are the indivisible *WE*. How much more ennobling, sincere, exalted than the cowardly, thievish *mystery* of the ancients. Afterwards: how much more expedient it is. Even if one were to suppose the impossible, i.e., some kind of dissonance in the customary monophony, then after all the invisible Guardians are right here, in our ranks: they can immediately determine the numbers who have fallen into error and save them from further false steps, and save the United State—from those very same people. And finally, one more thing...

Through the wall on the left: before the mirror in the wardrobe door—a woman was hastily unbuttoning her unif. And for a second, vaguely: eyes, lips, two sharp pink buds. Then the blinds fell, all of yesterday passed in a flash inside me, and I do not know what "finally, one more thing" is, and I don't want to know about it, I don't! I want one thing: I-330. I want her to be with me each minute, every minute, always—only with me. And what I was writing just now about Unanimity, this is all unnecessary, not right, I want to strike out everything, tear it up, throw it away. Because I can know (even if it is sacrilege, but it is so) a celebration—only with her, only then if she will be beside me, shoulder to shoulder. And without her—tomorrow's sun will only be a miserable circle of tin, and the sky—blue-painted tin, and I myself...

I seized the telephone receiver:

"I-330, is that you.?"

"Yes, it's me. Why so late?"

"I thought perhaps it wasn't too late. I want to ask you... I want you to be with me tomorrow... dearest..."

Dearest,—I said it very softly. And for some reason what had happened that morning at the building site flashed into my head: as a joke a watch had been placed under a hundred-ton hammer—a swing, the wind in your face—and the gentle, hundred-ton-tender contact with the fragile watch.

A pause. I imagined that I heard there—in I-330's room—someone's whisper. Then her voice:

"No, I can't. After all you do understand: if I could... No I cannot.

Why? You'll see tomorrow."

NIGHT

Record 25
Synopsis: The Descent from Heaven
**   The Greatest Catastrophe in History**
**   The Known Has Ended**

When at the beginning everyone stood up and the Hymn—hundreds of trumpets of the Musical Factory and millions of human voices—began to flutter overhead like a solemn, slow mantle, I forgot everything for a second: I forgot something disturbing that I-330 had said about today's celebration, I forgot, it seemed, even about her. I was now that same boy who at one time on that day had wept because of the minute little spot on his unif that only he noticed. Even if no one else around me saw that I was covered in black, unwashable spots, all the same I myself knew that there was no place for me, a criminal, among these wide-open faces. Ah, if only I could have stood up at that moment and chokingly shouted aloud everything about myself. Even if it then meant the end—even so!—but if only to feel oneself as pure, as untroubled by thought, as this child-blue sky.

All eyes were raised upward: in the immaculate, morning blue, still moist from night's tears, there was a barely noticeable spot, now dark, now clothed in rays of light. Descending to us from heaven, it was He—the new Jehovah in an aero, just as wise and lovingly-cruel as the Jehovah of the ancients. With every minute He came ever closer—and the millions of hearts rose in greeting to Him—and then He saw us. And mentally together with Him I was surveying all from above: the concentric circles of the tribunes marked by a fine azure dotted line—as though the circles of a spider-web strewn with microscopic suns (— the gleam of badges); and in the center of it—a white, wise Spider was about to set down—the Benefactor in white clothing, who had wisely bound us hand and foot in the beneficial nets of happiness.

But now His majestic descent from heaven had come to an end, the brassy hymn fell silent, everyone sat down—and all at once I understood: truly—everything was the most delicate spider-web, it was taut and trembling, and any moment it would tear apart and something improbable would happen...

Standing up slightly, I glanced around—and exchanged glances with lovingly-anxious eyes flitting from face to face. There was one who had raised his hand and barely perceptibly moving his fingers was signalling to another. And then—an answering signal with a finger. And yet another... I understood: they, the Guardians. I understood: they were upset about something, the spider-web was taut and trembling. And inside me—like a radio receiver tuned to the same wave frequency—a reciprocal trembling.

On the platform a poet was reading a pre-election ode, but I did not hear a single word: only the measured swings of the hexametric pendulum, and with every swing of it some designated hour was drawing closer. And I was still feverishly leafing over one face after the other in the rows—like pages—and still I did not see the single one I was seeking and it had to be found quickly because any moment now the pendulum would start ticking and then—

Him—it was him, of course. Down below, past the platform, slipping over the glittering glass, the pink wing-ears were flying past, the running body was reflected as a dark double-curved loop of the letter S—he was rushing somewhere into the intricate passages between the tribunes.

S-, I-330—some kind of thread (for me there has always been some kind of thread between them; I still did not know what kind of one—but I would unravel it at some time). My eyes fastened on him, he was like a little ball rolling away and a thread trailing behind him. Then he stopped, then. . .

Like lightning, a high-voltage discharge: I was transfixed, twisted into a knot. In our row, not more than 40 degrees from me, S- stopped, bent over. I caught sight of I-330, and beside her—the repulsively-negroid, mocking R-13.

My first thought was to dash over there and shout to her: "Why are you with him today? Why didn't you want me to be with you?" But the invisible, beneficent spider-web had firmly entangled my hands and feet; clenching my teeth, I sat like iron, without lowering my eyes. As though it were happening now: that sharp physical pain in my heart, I remember I was thinking: "If there can be physical pain for non-physical reasons, then it is clear that—"

Unfortunately I did not manage to construct any conclusion: I only remember—something fleeting about the *soul*, the senseless ancient saying flashing past—"the soul sinking to his boots." And my soul sank: the hexameter had fallen silent. And now the beginning of. . . What?

There was a five-minute pre-election intermission as established by custom. A pre-election silence established by custom. But this time it was not truly prayerful, reverential, as it usually was: this time it was as among the ancients when they still had no knowledge of our Accumulator Towers, when the untamed sky would still roar with *thunderstorms* from time to time. This time it was as among the ancients before a thunderstorm.

The air was of transparent cast iron. One wanted to breathe with one's mouth wide open. My painfully strained hearing was recording: from somewhere behind came a mouse-nibbling, disquieting whisper. With my eyes downcast I could see all the while those two—I-330 and R-13—side by side, shoulder to shoulder, and in my lap were trembling alien, shaggy hands—my hateful hands.

In everyone's hands were the badges with watches. One. Two. Three...
Five minutes... from the platform—a cast-iron, slow voice:

"Those *for*—I ask you to raise your hands."

If only I could have looked into His eyes as before—directly and
faithfully: "Here I am, all of me. All of me. Take me!" But now I did not
dare. With an effort—as though all my joints were rusted—I raised my
hand.

The rustle of millions of hands. Someone's suppressed "Ah!" And I
felt that something had already begun, was falling headlong, but I did not
understand—what, and I did not have the strength—I did not dare to
look...

"Who is *against*?"

This had always been the most majestic moment of the celebration:
everyone continued to sit motionless, heads joyfully bowed to the
beneficent yoke of the Number of Numbers. But then again I heard with
terror a rustling: ever so light, like a sigh—it was more audible than the
brass trumpets of the hymn had been earlier. The way a man would breathe
his last in life, barely audibly—and all around everyone's face turned
pale—on everyone's forehead were cold drops.

I raised my eyes—and...

It was a hundredth part of a second, a hair-breadth. I saw: thousands
of hands fluttered upwards—*against*—then they fell. I caught sight of the
pale face of I-330, intersected with a cross, her raised hand. Darkness
before my eyes.

Another hair-breadth; a pause; quiet; pulse. Then—as though by the
signal of some insane director—all at once on all the tribunes there was a
crackling sound, cries, a whirlwind of unifs billowing up in flight, the
figures of Guardians dashing hysterically back and forth, someone's heels
in the air right before my very eyes—beside the heels someone's wide-open
mouth straining in an inaudible scream. For some reason this was more
sharply etched than anything else: thousands of soundlessly screaming
mouths—like on a monstrous screen.

And like on a screen—somewhere far away below, before me for a
second, were the blanched lips of O-: pressed against the wall in a passage,
she was standing there, guarding her belly with her crossed arms. And then
she was no longer there—washed away, or I had forgotten about her
because...

This was no longer on the screen—this was inside me myself, in my
contracted heart, in my rapidly pounding temples. Over my head to the left,
on a bench—suddenly R-13 leaped up—showering, red, frenzied. In his
arms was I-330, pale, her unif torn from shoulder to breast, on the white
there was blood. She was firmly holding him around the neck and with
enormous jumps—from bench to bench—repulsive and agile, like a
gorilla—he was carrying her upwards.

Like a conflagration among the ancients—everything became crimson—and there was only one thing left: to jump, catch up to them. I cannot explain to myself now where I got such strength from, but, like a battering ram I broke through the mob—on the shoulders of some—on benches—and then when I was already close, then I grabbed R- by the neck:

"Don't you dare! Don't you dare, I tell you! This very minute..." (fortunately my voice was not audible—everyone was doing their own screaming, everyone was running).

"Who? What's going on? What?" R- turned around, his lips showering, trembling—probably he thought that one of the Guardians had seized him.

"What? I'll tell you what—I don't want this, I won't allow it! Let her go—this very minute!"

But he merely made an angry smacking sound with his lips, tossed his head and started to run farther. And at this point I—I am incredibly ashamed to record this, but it seems to me: I must, I must record everything so that, you my unknown readers, might be able to study the history of my illness to the end—at this point I swung and hit him on the head. You understand—I hit him! I remember this distinctly. And moreover I remember: I felt a kind of liberation, a lightness through my entire body because of this blow.

I-330 quickly slid out of his arms.

"Go away," she screamed at R-, "you can see for yourself: he is... Go away, R-, go away!"

R-, baring his white, negroid teeth, showered my face with some word, dove down, disappeared. And I picked I-330 up in my arms, pressed her firmly to me and started to carry her.

My heart was pounding inside—an enormous heart, and with each stroke it spewed out such a violent, burning, such a joyful wave. And even if something there had been smashed into smithereens—what did it matter! If only I could go on carrying her like this, carrying, carrying...

In the Evening. 22 Hours.

I am holding the pen in my hand with difficulty: such an immeasurable fatigue after all the bewildering events of this morning. Have the salutary, age-old walls of the United State come tumbling down? Are we really once again without shelter, in a wild state of freedom—like our distant ancestors? Is there really no Benefactor? Against... on the Day of Unanimity—against? I am ashamed for them, pained, terrified. However—who are *they*? And who am I myself: they or *we*—do I really—know?

Now: she was sitting on a glass bench hot from the sun—on the uppermost tribune, where I had carried her. Her right shoulder and lower down—the beginning of a marvelous, incalculable curve—were bare; the thinnest little red snake of blood. It was as though she did not notice that there was blood, that her breast was bare... no, rather: she saw all of this—but this was precisely what she needed now, and if her unif had been buttoned up,—she would have torn it apart, she...

"And tomorrow..." she was breathing greedily through clenched, sparkling, white teeth. "And tomorrow—who knows what. Dost thou understand: I don't know, no one knows—the unknown! Dost thou understand that everything that we have known has ended? Now for the new, the improbable, the unforeseen."

There, down below, people were foaming, dashing about, screaming. But this was far away, and even farther away because she was looking at me, she was slowly absorbing me into herself through the narrow golden windows of her pupils. Like this—for a long while, silently. And for some reason I recalled how once, through the Green Wall, I too had gazed into someone's incomprehensible, yellow pupils, and above the Wall birds were circling (or had this been at another time?).

"Listen: if nothing special happens tomorrow—I shall take thee there,—dost thou understand?"

No, I do not understand. But I silently nod my head. I—have dissolved, I am an infinitesimal quantity, I am a point...

After all—there is a logic (contemporary) of its own in this state of being a point: in a point there are more unknowns than in anything else; a point has only to move, to stir—and it can turn into thousands of various curves, hundreds of bodies.

I am terrified of stirring: what will I turn into? And it seems to me—everyone, just like me, is afraid of the minutest movement. Take right now, as I am writing this, everyone is sitting hidden away in their glass cages, and waiting for something. In the corridor the customary humming of the elevator at this hour is not audible, the laughter and footsteps are not audible. At times I see: numbers in twos tip-toeing down the corridor, looking around and whispering...

What will happen tomorrow? What will I turn into tomorrow?

Record 26
Synopsis: **The World Exists**
                A Rash
                41° Centrigrade

Morning. Through the ceiling—the sky was as always, firm, round, red-cheeked. I think—I would have been less amazed if overhead I had seen some kind of extraordinary, rectangular sun, people in motley-colored clothing of animal fur, stone opaque walls. So could it have meant that the world—our world—still existed? Or was this just inertia, the generator was already switched off, but the gears were still rumbling and turning—two revolutions, three revolutions—on the fourth they would come to a standstill...

Are you familiar with this strange state? In the night you have awoken, opened your eyes into the blackness and suddenly you fell—you are lost and faster, faster you begin to fumble around, to search for anything familiar and solid—a wall, a lamp, a chair. That was precisely how I was fumbling, searching in the *United State Gazette*—faster, faster,—and then:

"The Day of Unanimity, long-awaited with impatience by all, took place yesterday. The very same Benefactor, who has repeatedly proven his steadfast wisdom, was unanimously elected for the 48th time. The festivities were marred by a certain disturbance perpetrated by the enemies of happiness who in so doing, naturally, deprived themselves of the right to become the building blocks for yesterday's renewed foundation of the United State. It is clear to everyone that it would have been just as absurd to take their votes into account, as it would be to take for a part of a magnificent, heroic symphony—the coughing of sick people who happen to be present in the concert hall..."

O, Wise One! Can it be that all the same, despite whatever—we are saved? But really, is it, in fact, possible to object to this most crystalline syllogism?

And further on—two more lines:

"Today at 12 a joint meeting will take place of the Administrative Bureau, the Medical Bureau and the Bureau of Guardians. An important State Act will be forthcoming in a few days."

No, the walls are still standing—here they are—I can touch them. And there is no longer any of that strange sensation that I am lost, that I am I know not where, that I have gone astray, and it is not in the least amazing that I see the blue sky, the round sun; and everyone—as usual—is going off to work.

I was walking along the avenue, with an especially firm and resounding step—and it seemed to me, everyone was walking the same way. But then an intersection, a turn around the corner, and I see: everyone is skirting in a strange fashion the corner of a building—as though some pipe had burst there in the wall, showering cold water and making it impossible to pass along the sidewalk.

Another five, ten steps—and then I too was doused with cold water, pitched and swept from the sidewalk... At a height of approximately 2 meters on the wall there was a rectangular sheet of paper and on it were the incomprehensible letters—poisonous-green:

MEPHI

And down below the S-shaped curved back, the wing-ears,

transparently fluttering either from anger or anxiety. With his right arm raised upward and his left helplessly stretched out backwards—like a sick painful, disabled wing, he kept leaping up—to tear the paper away—and he could not do it, missing it by only so much.

Probably each of the passersby had the thought: "If I go up to him, just one of the many—won't he think: I am guilty of something and that is precisely why I want to..."

I admit: I too had the same thought. But I remembered how many times he had been my real guardian-angel, how many times he had saved me—and I went up bravely, stretched out a hand and tore the sheet away.

S- turned around, quickly, quickly the gimlets went into me, to the bottom, fetched something from there. Then he raised his left eyebrow, with the eyebrow he winked at the wall where *Mephi* had been hanging. And I caught the tail-end of his smile—to my amazement, it almost seemed to be cheerful. However, what was there to be amazed at? A doctor always prefers a rash and a forty-degree centigrade fever to the tedious, slowly rising temperature of an incubation period: in the former case, at least, it is clear what kind of illness it is. *Mephi*, which had broken out on the walls today—this was a rash. I understood his smile...*

Descent into the subway—and underfoot, on the immaculate glass of the steps—again a white sheet: *Mephi*. And on the wall down below, on a bench, on a mirror in the coach (apparently, hastily glued on—carelessly, crookedly)—everywhere that same white, eerie rash.

In the silence—the distinct whirring of the wheels, like the noise of inflamed blood. Someone was touched on the shoulder—he started, dropped a bundle of papers. And to the left of me there was another: he was reading in a newspaper over and over again the same line, the same line, the same line, and the newspaper was trembling almost imperceptibly. And I felt how everywhere—in the wheels, the hands, the newspapers, the eyelashes—the pulse was becoming more and more rapid, and, perhaps, today, when I-330 and I ended up in that place—it would be 39, 40, 41 degrees—marked off on the thermometer with a black line...

At the building site it was the same humming silence as a distant, invisible propellor. The work benches were standing silent and frowning. And only the cranes, barely audible, as though on tip-toe, were sliding, bending, seizing the azure blocks of frozen air in their claws and loading them into the lateral tanks of the *Integral*: we were already preparing it for a test flight.

"Well then: will we complete the loading in a week?" This was me—to the Second Builder. His face was porcelain, decorated with sweet azure, tender pink, little flowers (the eyes, the lips), but today they seemed faded, washed-out. We were counting aloud, but I suddenly broke off in mid-

---

*I must admit that I discovered the exact solution to this smile only after many days, which were filled to overflowing with the strangest and most unexpected events.

word and was standing with my mouth gaping; high up under the cupola on an azure block hoisted by the crane—there was a barely noticeable little white square—a small piece of glued paper. And my whole body was shaken—perhaps from laughter—indeed, I heard myself laughing (do you know what it is like when you yourself hear your own laughter?).

"No, listen..." I said. "Imagine to yourself that you are in an ancient aeroplane, altimeter reading 5000 meters, a wing has broken, you are falling like a tumbler-pigeon, and on the way you are figuring out: 'Tomorrow—from 12 to 2... from 2 to 6... at 6 dinner...' Well isn't that ridiculous? And here we are right now—precisely like that!"

The little azure flowers were stirring, bulging. What if I had been glass and he could see that in some three or four hours?...

Record 27
Synopsis: No Synopsis—It Is Impossible

I am alone in the endless corridors—those same ones. A mute sky of concrete. Somewhere water was dripping against rock. A familiar, heavy, opaque door—and a muffled drone coming from there.

She said that she would come out for me at exactly 16. But here it had already passed 16, five minutes, ten, fifteen: no one.

For a second I was my former self who was terrified if this door should open. Five minutes more and if she did not come out —

Somewhere water was dripping against stone. No one. With a sorrowful joy I felt: saved. Slowly I was walking back along the corridor. The quivering dotted line of bulbs on the ceiling was getting more and more murky...

Suddenly from behind—a door was hurriedly slammed, quick footsteps, softly reverberating against the ceiling, the walls—it was she, and flying, slightly breathless from running, breathing through her mouth:

"I knew: thou wouldst be here, thou wouldst come! I knew: thou-thou..."

The lances of her eyelashes were spreading apart, letting me inside and... How can I relate what that ancient, absurd, marvelous rite does to me when her lips touch mine? With what formula can I express that whirlwind which sweeps everything out of my soul except her? Yes, yes, out of my soul—laugh if you wish.

She slowly raised her eyelids with an effort—and slowly, with difficulty, the words:

"No, enough... later; now—let us go."

The door opened. Steps—worn, old. And an unbearably confused racket, whistling, light.

* * *

Almost a whole twenty-four hours have passed since then, everything in me has settled down somewhat—and nonetheless it is extremely difficult for me to give even an approximately exact description. In my head—it is as though a bomb has been exploded, and gaping mouths, wings, screams, leaves, words, stones—they are all side-by-side, in a heap, one after another...

I remember—the first thing that came to me: "Quickly, at breakneck speed, back." Because it is clear to me: while I was waiting there in the corridors—they had somehow blown up or destroyed the Green Wall—and everything had come streaming in from there and swallowed up our city which had been purified of the lower world.

I must have said something of this sort to I-330. She began to laugh:

"Of course not! We have simply gone out on the other side of the Green Wall..."

Then I opened my eyes wide—and face to face with me, in reality, was that very thing which up until then no living person had seen other than a thousand times reduced, weakened, obscured by the murky glass of the Wall.

The sun... it was not our sun, evenly distributed over the mirror-like surface of the pavement: it was made up of some kind of animated splinters, ceaselessly dancing spots which blinded your eyes and made your head swim. And the trees, like candles—up into the very sky; like spiders squatting against the ground on their rough paws; like mute, green fountains... And all of this was crawling, stirring, rustling, some kind of shaggy little ball shied away from underfoot, and I was riveted to the spot, I could not move a single step—because underfoot there was no flat plane—you understand, no flat plane—but something repulsively-soft, yielding, living, green, resilient.

I was stunned by all of this, I choked—this, perhaps, is the most appropriate word. I was standing there, with both hands clutching onto some kind of swaying branch.

"It's alright, it's alright! It's just at first, it will pass. Courage!"

Side-by-side with I-330 there was someone's ever so slender profile, cut from paper, on the green, dizzily bouncing net... no, not someone's, I knew him. I remembered: the doctor,—no, no, I understood everything very clearly. And this I understood as well: they had both grabbed me by the arms and were dragging me forward. My feet were getting entangled, they kept slipping. There, cawing, moss, hummocks, screeching, branches, trunks, wings, leaves, whistling...

And—the trees scattered, a brilliant meadow, in the meadow were people... or I hardly know how to put it: perhaps more correctly—creatures.

Now is the most difficult thing. Because this transcended all limits of probability. And it is clear to me now why I-330 had always kept so stubbornly silent: I would not have believed in any case—even her. It is possible that tomorrow I will not believe even my own self—this very record of mine.

In the meadow, around a bare, skull-like rock—a noise was being created by a crowd of three or four hundred... people,—leave it at *people*, I find it difficult to say otherwise. The same sensation as when in the first moment you are aware only of familiar faces among the general collection in the tribunes, it was true that here at first I perceived only our gray-blue unifs. But a second later—in the midst of the unifs, quite distinctly and simply: raven, reddish, golden, dark-bay, roan, white people,— apparently, people. They were all unclothed and they were all covered with short, glossy hair—of the type that anyone might see on the stuffed model of a horse in the Prehistoric Museum. But the females—they had faces exactly the same—yes, yes, exactly the same,—as our women: tenderly pink and not overgrown with hair, and also free of hair were their breasts— large, firm, of a beautiful geometric form. Among the males, only a portion of the face was without hair—as among our ancestors.

This was incredible to such a degree, to such a degree unexpected, that I stood there calmly—I positively repeat: I stood there calmly and watched. Like scales: overload one of the sides—and then you can place as much there as you wish—the pointer will not move in any event...

Suddenly—alone: I-330 was no longer with me—I didn't know how or where she had disappeared. All around—only these ones, glistening like satin in the sun with their hair. I grasped someone's hot, firm, raven shoulder:

"Listen—in the name of the Benefactor,—didn't you see—where she went? Only just now—just this very minute..."

Looking at me—shaggy, stern brows:

"Sh-sh-sh! Quiet," and they nodded shaggily over there, to the center where the yellow, skull-like rock was.

There, on top, above the heads, above everyone—I saw her. The sun was right in my eyes, from that direction, and because of this—against the blue canvas of the sky—she was sharply defined, coal-black, a coal-black silhouette against the blue. Slightly higher, clouds were flying and... to illustrate: as though not the clouds, but the rock and she herself on the rock, and behind her the crowd, and the meadow,—were soundlessly slipping away, like a ship, and buoyantly—the earth was sailing away underfoot...

"Brothers..." she is speaking. "Brothers! You all know: there beyond the Wall in the city—they are building the *Integral*. And you know: the day has come when we shall destroy this Wall—all walls—so that the green wind will blow from end to end—over the entire earth. But the *Integral* will carry these walls up there, to thousands of other earths, which this night will send their shimmering lights to you through the dark leaves of night..."

Against the rock—waves, foam, wind:

"Down with the *Integral*! Down!"

"No, brothers: not down. Instead the *Integral* should be ours. On that day when it casts off for the first time into the heaven—we shall be on it. Because the Builder of the *Integral* is with us. He abandoned the walls, he came here with me in order to be among you. Hail to the Builder!"

An instant—and I was somewhere up above, beneath me, heads, heads, heads, broadly screaming mouths, hands splashing up and down. It was extraordinarily strange, drunken: I felt myself above everyone, I—was I, a separate world, I ceased to be submerged in the whole, as before, and I had become an individual.

And then—with body rumpled, happy, crumpled as though after love's embraces—I am down below, beside the same rock. The sun, the voices from above—I-330's smile. Some golden-haired woman, satiny-golden all over, smelling of grass. In her hands—a cup, apparently of wood. She sips from it with her red lips—and hands it to me, and greedily, with eyes closed, I drink to drown the fire—I drink the sweet, prickly, cold sparks.

And then—the blood and the whole world inside me—a thousand times faster, the buoyant earth in downy flight. And for me everything was light, simple, clear.

At that moment I see the familiar, enormous letters on the rock: *Mephi*—and for some reason it had to be this way, it was the simple, solid thread that bound everything together. I saw the crude depiction—perhaps as well on that rock: a winged youth, transparent body, and there where the heart should be—a blinding, berry-red smouldering ember. And again: I understood this ember... or rather: I felt it—the same way as without hearing, I felt every word (she was speaking from above, from the rock)—and I felt that everyone was breathing together—and that everyone would fly off somewhere together, like the birds that time above the Wall.

From behind, out of the heavily breathing thicket of bodies a loud voice:

"But this is madness!"

And it seems I—yes, I think that it was none other than I—leaped up onto the rock, and from there the sun, the heads, were a green, toothed saw against the blue, and I shouted:

"Yes, yes, precisely! Everyone must go mad, it is essential for everyone to go mad—the faster the better! That is essential—I know it."

Beside me was I-330; her smile, two dark lines—from the edges of her mouth upwards; and inside me, an ember, and it was fleeting, easy, barely painful, beautiful...

Thereafter—only random slivers still clung to me. Slow, low—a bird. I saw: it was alive, like me, like a person it turned its head to the right, to the left and the black, round eyes were boring into me...

More: a back—with glossy hair the color of old ivory. A dark insect with minute, transparent wings was crawling over the back—the back shuddered to chase the insect away, it shuddered once more...

More: the shade from the leaves was plaited, latticed. They were lying in the shade and chewing something similar to the legendary food of the ancients: a long yellow fruit and a piece of something dark. A woman put it into my hand and it seemed ridiculous to me: I did not know whether I could eat it.

And again a crowd: heads, feet, arms, mouths. Faces flared up for a second—and then disappeared, bursting like bubbles. And for a second— or, perhaps, it only seemed to me—transparent, flying wing-ears.

I clutched I-330's hand with all my might. She looked around:

"What's the matter?"

"He is here... It seemed to me..."

"Who is he?"

"S-... just this moment—in the crowd..."

The coal-black, fine eyebrows were upturned towards the temples: a sharp triangle, a smile. It was not clear to me: why was she smiling—how could she be smiling?

"Thou dost not understand, I-330, thou does not understand what it means if he or anyone else of them is here."

"Ridiculous fellow! Would it really occur to anyone there, on the other side of the Wall, that we are here? Remember: you, for example,— did you really ever think that this would be possible? They are hunting for us there—let them! You are delirious."

She was smiling gently, cheerfully and I was smiling, the earth was drunken, cheerful, light—it was floating on...

Record 28

Synopsis: **Two Women**
Entropy and Energy
The Opaque Part of the Body

Now then: if your world is similar to the world of our distant ancestors, then imagine to yourself that at one time in the ocean you stumbled upon a sixth, a seventh continent of the world—some Atlantis or other, and there are unknown labyrinth-cities, people soaring in the air without the aid of wings or an aero, stones being raised upward through the force of a glance—in a word, such things as could never have entered your mind, even when you are suffering from dream-sickness. This is exactly what happened to me yesterday. Because—do try to understand, none of us had ever been outside the Green Wall since the time of the Two Hundred Years' War—but I have already told you about that.

I know: my duty to you, unknown friends, is to relate in greater detail about this strange and unexpected world which was revealed to me yesterday. But I am not in any condition to return to this for the time being. More and more new things, some kind of downpour of events and there is not enough of me to collect it all: I hold out the folds of my unif, my cupped hands—and still whole bucketfuls stream past, and only drops are falling on these pages...

At first I heard loud voices behind my door—and I recognized her voice, I-330, resilient, metallic,—and another almost inflexible one—like a wooden ruler—the voice of U-. Then the door swung open with a bang and shot both of them into my room. Precisely like that: it shot them.

I-330 put her hand on the back of my armchair and then over her shoulder, the right one—smiled at the other one with her teeth alone. I would not want to stand up to that smile.

"Listen," I-330 said to me, "this woman, it seems, has made it her purpose to guard you from me, like some small child. Is this with your permission?"

And then—the other, shaking her gills:

"Yes, he is a child. Yes! That is why he does not see that all of this between you and him—is only in order to... that all of this is a comedy. Yes! And my duty..."

For an instant in the mirror—the broken, jumping straight line of my eyebrows. I leaped up and with difficulty restraining that other person in me—hairy fists shaking, forcing with difficulty each word through my teeth, I shouted right at her—into those very gills:

"Out of here—this-s very s-second! This very second!" The gills puffed up, brick-red, then collapsed, turned gray. She opened her mouth to say something, and, without saying anything—slammed the door when she left.

I rushed to I-330:

"I'll never forgive myself—I'll never forgive myself for this! She dared—thou? But thou dost not think that I think that... that she... This is all because she wanted to register herself to me, but I..."

"Fortunately she won't have time to register. And even if there were a thousand of those like her: it would be all the same to me. I know—thou wouldst not believe the thousand, but only me. Because after what happened yesterday—I have nothing more to hide from thee, thou seest every last bit, as thou wished. I am in thy hands, thou canst do... at any moment you like..."

"What—at any moment I like?" And all at once I understood—*what*, the blood flooded into my ears, my cheeks, I screamed: "Don't, don't ever speak to me of this! After all thou dost understand that it was that other me, the former one, whereas now..."

"Who knows thee... A person is like a novel: up until the very last page you don't know how it will end. Otherwise it would not even be worthwhile reading it..."

I-330 was stroking my head. I could not see her face, but I heard her voice: she was looking now somewhere very far away, her eyes had become fastened on a cloud, sailing soundlessly, slowly, no one knows where...

Suddenly she pushed me away with her hand—firmly and tenderly:

"Listen: I have come to tell thee that, perhaps—these are already the final days that we... Didst thou know: from this evening all the auditoria have been cancelled."

"Cancelled?"

"Yes, and I walked past—I saw: in the auditoria buildings something is being made ready, some kind of tables, doctors in white."

"But what does it mean?"

"I don't know. For the time being no one knows. And this is the worst of all. I only feel: the current has been switched on, the spark is running—and if not this very day, then tomorrow... But, perhaps, they will not manage in time."

I had already long since ceased to understand: who were they, and who were we. I did not understand what I wanted: that they would manage in time—or that they would not manage in time. Only one thing was clear to me: I-330 was now walking on the very edge,—any moment now...

"But this is madness," I was saying. "You—and the United State. This is the same as closing off the muzzle with your hand—and thinking that they might withhold the shot. This is absolute madness!"

A smile:

"*Everyone must go mad—the sooner the better, go mad.* Someone said that yesterday. Do you remember? There..."

Yes, I have it recorded. And, consequently, it had in fact happened. I looked at her face in silence: particularly clear on her face now was that dark cross.

"I-330, dearest—before it's too late... If thou dost wish—I will give up everything, forget everything—and go away with thee, there, beyond the Wall—to those... I don't know who they are."

She shook her head. Through the dark windows of her eyes—there, inside of her, I saw the stove blazing, the sparks, the tongues of flame leaping upwards, the mountains of dry, pitchy firewood piled high. And it was clear to me: it was already too late, my words were no longer of any avail...

She stood up—she would leave in a moment. Perhaps—already the final days, perhaps—minutes... I seized her by the hand.

"No! just a little longer—please, for the sake of... for the sake..."

She slowly raised my hand upward to the light—my hairy hand that I hated so. I wanted to pull it away, but she held on firmly.

"Thy hand... After all, thou wouldst not know—and few here do know, that it used to happen that women from here, from the city, would make love to those over there. And probably there are a few drops of sunny, forest blood in thee. Perhaps, that is why I really——"

A pause—and how strange it was: because of a pause, the emptiness, because of nothing—the heart would get so carried away. And I was shouting:

"Aha! Not yet! Thou willst not leave yet!—until I know all about them—because thou dost love... them, and I don't even know who they are, where they come from. Who are they? The half which we have lost: H_2 and O, but in order to get H_2O—the springs, the seas, the waterfalls, the waves, the storms,—the halves must be united..."

I distinctly remember each motion of hers. I remember how she took my glass triangle from the table and all the while I was talking, she was pressing the sharp edge to her cheek—a white weal came up on her cheek, then it was suffused with pink and disappeared. And amazingly: I cannot remember her words—particularly at the beginning—only some individual images, colors.

I know: at first it was about the Two Hundred Years' War. And it went thus—the red against the green of the grass, against the dark clay, against the bluishness of the snow—the red puddles that never dried up. Then the yellow, sun-burnt grasses, the naked, yellow, dishevelled people—and the dishevelled dogs—side by side, near the blotted carrion, of a dog, or, perhaps, of a human... This, of course, was beyond the walls: because the city—had already been victorious, in the city there was already our present-day food—petroleum-based food.

And almost from the sky to the earth were black, heavy folds, and the folds were swaying: over the forests, over the villages, slow columns, smoke. A hollow wailing: endless, black files were being driven into the city—in order to save them by force and teach them happiness.

"You knew almost all of this?"

"Yes, almost all."

"But you did not know and only a few did know that a small portion of them still survived and stayed on to live there, beyond the Walls. Naked— they went off into the forests. There they schooled themselves among the trees, the beasts, the birds, the flowers, the sun. They became overgrown with a coat of hair, but nonetheless they preserved their hot, red blood beneath the hair. It was worse for those like you: you became overgrown with mathematical figures, figures are crawling over you like fleas. Everything must be torn off you and you must be chased off naked into the forests. Let them learn how to tremble from terror, from joy, from frenzied wrath, from cold let them worship fire. And we, the Mephi—we want..."

"No, wait—and the *Mephi?* What are the *Mephi?*"

"The Mephi? This is an ancient name, this is the one who... Dost thou remember: there, on the rock a youth was depicted... Or no: better I tell thee in thy own language, then thou willst understand more quickly. Look here: there are two forces in the world—entropy and energy. One leads to blissful tranquillity, to happy equilibrium; the other leads to the destruction of that equilibrium, to an agonizingly-endless movement. Entropy—that is what our, or rather—your ancestors, the Christians, worshipped as God. Whereas we, the anti-Christians, we..."

And at that moment there was a barely audible, whisper-like tap at the door—and into the room leaped that very same flattened person with the beetle-browed awning over his eyes, who had brought me the notes from I-330 more than once.

He ran up to us, stopped, puffing—like an air-pump—and could not say a single word: he must have run with all his might.

"Well, then! What has happened?" I-330 seized him by the hand.

"They are coming—here..." The pump finally puffed out. "Guards... and with them that—whoever he is... kind of hunchbacked..."

"S-?"

"Yes, yes! In the building next door. They'll be here any moment. Faster, faster!"

"Nonsense! There's time..." She laughed, in her eyes were sparks, cheerful little tongues.

This was either absurd, irrational courage—or there was still something I did not understand.

"I-330, for Benefactor's sake! Try to understand—after all this is..."

"For Benefactor's sake," the sharp triangle—a smile. "Well... well for my sake... I beg you."

"Ah, and I still had to talk to you about one thing... Well, it doesn't matter: tomorrow..."

She cheerfully (yes: cheerfully) nodded to me; the other fellow nodded as well—poking out for a second from under his beetle-browed awning. And then I was alone.

Quickly—to the desk. I opened up my records, took a pen—so that *they* would find me at this work for the good of the United State. And suddenly—every hair on my head came alive, separate, bristling: "But what if they take and read even a single page—of these, of the latest ones?"

I was sitting at the desk without moving—and I saw the walls trembling, the pen in my hand trembling, the letters swaying, merging together...

Hide it? But where: everything is glass. Burn it? But from the corridor and the neighboring rooms—they would see. And then I could not do it now, I had not the strength to destroy this agonizing—and perhaps the most valuable of all to me—piece of my own self.

From a distance—in the corridor—already voices, steps. I only had time to seize a stack of sheets, stick them underneath myself—and then I was riveted to the chair that was pulsating with every atom and the floor underfoot was a ship's deck, up and down...

Compressed into a tiny ball, cowering beneath the awning of my forehead—somehow I saw furtively, from under my brow: they were going from room to room, beginning from the right-hand end of the corridor, and getting nearer and nearer. Some were sitting, frozen like me; others—were jumping up to meet them and swinging the doors wide open,—the lucky ones! If only I too...

"The Benefactor—is the most highly perfected disinfectant required for humanity, and, consequently, in the organism of the United State no peristalsis whatsoever is..." I was squeezing out this utter nonsense with my leaping pen, and bent lower and lower over the desk, while in my head there was an insane smithy, and I heard with my back—the handle of the door grated, a puff of wind, the armchair broke into a dance underneath me...

Only then did I tear myself with difficulty away from the page and turn to those who had entered (how difficult it is to perform a comedy... ah, who was talking to me today about a comedy?). S- was in front—gloomy, silent, quickly drilling wells with his eyes in me, in my armchair, in the sheets trembling under my hand. Then for a second—some familiar, everyday faces at the threshold, and now one separated itself from the others—the puffed-out, pink-brown gills...

I remembered everything that had happened in this room a half-hour before, and it was clear to me that she was about to—— My whole being was pounding and pulsating in that (fortunately, opaque) part of the body with which I had concealed the manuscript.

U- came up behind him, behind S-, cautiously touched his sleeve—and quietly said:

"This is D-503, the Builder of the *Integral*. You have probably heard? He is always just like that, at his desk... He does not spare himself in the least!"

...Me? What a marvellous, wonderful woman.

S- slithered towards me, leaned over my shoulder—above the desk. With my elbow I shielded what I had written, but he shouted sternly:

"I ask you to show me at once what you have there!" Burning with shame all over, I gave him the sheet. He read it and I saw a smile slip out of his eyes, flit down his face and barely wiggling its little tail, settle somewhere in the right corner of his mouth...

"Somewhat ambiguous, but still... Well, then, continue: we won't bother you any longer."

He flip-flopped off towards the door—like paddles in the water, and with his every step, my legs, arms, fingers were gradually returning to me—my soul again began to distribute itself evenly throughout my entire body, I was breathing...

The final thing: U- lingered behind in my room, came up to me, bent over to my ear—and in a whisper:

"Lucky for you that I..."

Incomprehensible: what did she mean by that?

In the evening, later, I found out: they took away three people with them. However, no one would talk about this aloud, or about everything that was happening (the educational influence of the Guardians invisibly present in our midst). Conversations were mainly about the rapid fall of the barometer and the change in the weather.

Record 29
Synopsis: Threads on the Face
**   Seedlings**
**   An Unnatural Compression**

Strange: the barometer is going down, but there is still not any wind, silence. There, up above, it has already begun—still inaudible to us—a storm. The clouds are soaring at full strength. Still not many of them—separate, serrated fragments. To illustrate: as though up above some city or other has already been cast down and pieces of the walls and towers are flying downwards, they are growing before one's very eyes with horrifying speed—nearer and nearer—but they still have days left to fly through the azure infinity until they crash against the bottom, where we are, down below.

Down below—silence. In the air—fine, incomprehensible, almost invisible threads. Every autumn they are borne here from there, from beyond the Wall. Slowly they float—and suddenly you feel: something foreign, invisible on your face, you want to brush it away—but no: you cannot, you cannot get rid of it at all...

There are particularly many of these threads—if one goes walking near the Green Wall where I was walking this morning: I-330 had arranged for me to meet her at the Ancient House—in that *apartment* of ours.

I was only a short distance away from the enormous, opaque, rust-red mass of the Ancient House when suddenly from behind I heard someone's small, hasty footsteps, rapid breathing. I glanced around—and I saw: O- was trying to catch up to me.

She was somehow resiliently round all over, more thoroughly so than was usual. Her arms and the cups of her breasts, and her entire body, so familiar to me, had become so rounded out and was stretching her unif taut: any moment now and—it would burst the thin material—and come out into the sun, into the light. I imagined it to myself thus: there, in the green jungles, in the springtime, the seedlings are breaking forth through the earth just as stubbornly—in order to sprout quickly the branches, the leaves, to blossom quickly.

She was silent for a few seconds, she was beaming into my face with a blueness.

"I saw you—then, on the Day of Unanimity."

"I saw you too..." And at that very moment I remembered how she had been standing down below, in the narrow passage, pressed against the wall and covering her belly with her arms. I involuntarily looked at her round belly under the unif.

Evidently she noticed—she became roundly-pink all over, and a pink smile:

"I am so happy—so happy... I am filled—you understand: right to the brim. And here I am—walking around and I hear nothing about me, but I hear everything within, inside me..."

I was silent. On my face—something foreign, it was bothering me— and I could not get rid of it at all. And suddenly unexpectedly, beaming with an even greater blueness, she seized my hand—and I felt her lips on my hand... This was the first time in my life. This was some kind of ancient caress that I had never known before, and it was coming from her—such shame and pain that I (even rudely, if you please) snatched my hand away.

"Listen—you are mad! And not so much this—but in general you... What are you so happy about? Can you really be forgetting what awaits you? If not right now—then all the same in a month, in two months..."

She was extinguished; all the rounded edges—caved in at once, became warped. And in my heart—an unpleasant, even painful compression tied together with a sensation of pity (the heart is nothing other than the ideal pump; compression, contraction—the suction of liquid by a pump—all else is a technical absurdity; hence it is clear: the extent to which all *loves*, all *pities* and so forth, which provoke such a compression, are essentially absurd, unnatural, sick).

Silence. The murky-green glass of the Wall—on the left. The dark-red mass—in front. And these two colors, merging together, gave rise within me to what seemed a brilliant idea in the form of a counter balance.

"Wait! I know how to save you. I will spare you from this: from only glimpsing your child—and then dying. You will be able to feed it—you understand,—you will watch it growing in your arms, getting rounder, swelling, like fruit..."

She began to shake so all over and fastened onto me so.

"So you remember that woman... well, from, a long time ago, during the walk. Listen then: she is here right now, in the Ancient House. Let's go to her and I swear: I will arrange everything immediately."

I was already seeing how the three of us, including I-330, would go together with her through the corridors—and then she would already be there, among the flowers, the grasses, the leaves... But she backed away from me, the little horns of her crescent were trembling and bending downwards.

"That is that same one," she said.

"Well..." for some reason I was embarrassed. "Well, yes: that same one."

"And you want me to go to her—to beg her—so that I... Don't you dare ever speak of that again to me!"

Hunching over she quickly went away from me. As though she had just remembered something else—she turned and screamed:

"And I shall die—yes, I don't care! And it's none of your business—what difference does it make to you?"

Silence. Falling from above, with terrifying speed and growing before my eyes—pieces of blue towers and walls, but they still had hours more—perhaps days—to fly through infinity; the invisible threads are slowly floating, settling on my face—and there is no way to brush them away, no way to get rid of them.

I walked slowly towards the Ancient House. In my heart, an absurd, agonizing compression...

Record 30
Synopsis:　　The Final Number
Galileo's Error
Would It Not Be Better?

Here is my conversation with I-330—there, yesterday, in the Ancient House, in the midst of that motley noise of reds, greens, bronze-yellows, whites, oranges, that drown out the logical procession of thoughts... And all the while—beneath the smile, frozen in marble, of a snub-nosed ancient poet.

I shall reproduce this conversation word for word—because it seems to me, it will have an enormous, decisive significance for the fate of the United State—and, moreover: for the universe. And later—here, you, my unknown readers, perhaps will find a certain justification for me...

Immediately, without any preparation, I-330 brought everything down on my head:

"I know: the day after tomorrow the first test flight of the *Integral* will take place. On that day—we shall seize it with our hands."

"What? The day after tomorrow?"

"Yes. Sit down, don't get upset. We cannot lose a single minute. Among the hundreds taken at random yesterday by the Guardians—there happened to have been 12 Mephi. If two or three days are allowed to slip past—they will perish."

I was silent.

"In order to observe the test run—they must be sending electro-technicians, mechanics, doctors, meteorologists. And precisely at 12—remember that—when the bell rings for lunch and everyone goes into the dining hall, we will remain in the corridor, lock everyone in the dining hall—and the *Integral* is ours... Understand: this is necessary, whatever might happen. The *Integral* in our hands—that will be the weapon which will enable us to end everything immediately, quickly, without pain. Their aeros... ha! That will simply be an insignificant swarm of midges against a falcon. And then: if it will really be inevitable—the engine exhausts can be directed downwards and with their work alone..."

I jumped up.

"This is unthinkable! This is absurd! Is it really not clear to thee: what thou art provoking—is a revolution?"

"Yes, a revolution! And why is this absurd?"

"Absurd—because there can be no revolution. Because ours—thou dost not believe it, but I am saying this—our revolution was the final one. And there cannot be any more revolutions. Everyone knows that..."

The mocking, sharp triangle of her brows:

"My dearest: thou art a mathematician. Even more: thou art a philosopher—because of thy mathematics. So here: name me the final number."

"Meaning what? I... I don't understand: which final one?"

"Well—the final one, the highest, the biggest."

"But I-330—this is quite absurd. Since the number of numbers is infinite, what final one dost thou want?"

"And just what final revolution dost thou want? There is no final one, revolutions are infinite. The final one, that's for children: children are frightened by infinity, and it's necessary—so that children can sleep peacefully at night..."

"But what sense—just what sense is there in all of this—for Benefactor's sake? What sense, since everyone is already happy?"

"Let's suppose... Well, fine: even if it is so. And what then?"

"Ridiculous! A completely childish question. Tell some story to children—right to the very end, and still they will invariably ask: but then what, but why?"

"Children are the only daring philosophers. And daring philosophers are invariably children. One should always be precisely like children and ask: but then what?"

"Nothing more then! Period. Everywhere in the universe everything is uniformly distributed..."

"Aha: uniformly, everywhere! Here it is once again—entropy, psychological entropy. To thee, a mathematician—can it not be clear that only differences—differences—of temperatures, only in thermal contrasts—only in them is there life. And if everywhere, throughout the entire universe, there are only uniformly warm—or uniformly cold bodies... They must be given a jolt—so that there will be fire, explosion, Gehenna. And we—we shall give them a jolt."

"But I-330,—do try, do try to understand: our ancestors—during the time of the Two Hundred Years' War—that is precisely what they did..."

"Oh, and they were right—a thousand times right. They only made one error: later they believed that they were the final number—which does not exist in nature, which does not exist. Their error was Galileo's error: he was correct about the world moving around the sun, but he did not know that the entire solar system—is moving around yet another center, he did not know that the real, not the relative, orbit of the earth is not at all a naive circle..."

"What about you others?"

"And we—for the time being we know there is no final number. Perhaps we will forget. No: it is quite probable—we will forget, when we grow older—just as everything else invariably grows older. And then we—yes, we too must inevitably fall down—just as the leaves do from the trees in autumn—just as the day after tomorrow the rest of you... No, no, dearest—not thou. Thou art with us, thou art with us!"

Ablaze, stormy, flashing—I had never seen her like that before—she embraced me with herself, all of herself. I disappeared...

The last thing—gazing firmly, forcefully into my eyes: "So remember then: at 12."

And I said:

"Yes, I'll remember."

She went away. I was alone—amid the violent, discordant uproar—of blues, reds, greens, bronze-yellows, oranges...

Yes, at 12...—and suddenly an absurd sensation of something foreign settling on my face—of something that cannot be brushed away. Suddenly—yesterday morning, U-,—and what she had been shouting into I-330's face then... Why? What an absurdity.

I hastened to go outside—and quickly home, home... Somewhere from behind I heard the piercing chirping of birds over the Wall. And in front, in the setting sun—of berry-red, crystallized fire—the spheres of cupolas, the enormous, blazing cube-buildings, and like congealed lightning in the sky—the spire of the Accumulator Tower. And all of this—all this impeccable, geometric beauty—I would have to do it with my own hands... Was there really no way out, no other way?

Past some sort of auditorium (I don't remember the number). Inside—benches piled in a heap; in the center—tables covered with sheets of snow-white glass; against the white a spot of pink sunny blood. And there is something unknown concealed in all of this—that's why it's eerie—tomorrow. This is unnatural: for a thinking—perceiving being to live in the midst of irregularities, of unknowns, of X's. Then it would have been as though your eyes had been blindfolded and you had been forced to walk around like that, groping, stumbling, and you knew that somewhere here very close by—is the edge, one step more—and all that would remain of you is a flattened, ruined piece of flesh. Is it really not exactly the same?

...And what if without waiting for it to happen—you yourself take the headlong plunge? Wouldn't that be the single and correct thing which would resolve everything at once?

Record 31
Synopsis: The Great Operation
I Forgave Everything
A Collision of Trains

Saved! At the very last moment when it already seemed—there was nothing to grasp onto, when it seemed—everything was already finished...

To illustrate: as though you had already mounted the stairs to the stern Machine of the Benefactor, and with a heavy clank the glass bell had enclosed you, and for the final time in life,—quickly—swallow the blue sky with your eyes...

And suddenly: all of this is only a *dream*. The sun is pink and cheerful, and the wall—such joy to stroke the cold wall with your hand—and the pillow—to revel endlessly in the depression made by your head in the white pillow...

This was, approximately, what I experienced when I read the *State Gazette* this morning. It had been a terrible dream and now it was ended. And I, fainthearted, I, non-believing,—I had been thinking already about a self-inflicted death. Now I am ashamed to read the last lines written yesterday. But all the same: let them stand, let them stand as the memory of that incredible business that could have happened—which no longer will... yes, it will not!..

Gleaming on the first page of the *State Gazette:*

Rejoice:

For henceforth you are perfect! Up until this day your own offspring, mechanisms,—were more perfect than you.

How?

Every spark of the dynamo is a spark of purest reason; every turn of a piston is an immaculate syllogism. But is not that very same infallible reason in you as well?

The philosophy of cranes, presses and pumps is as complete and clear as a circular circle. But is your philosophy any less circular?

The beauty of a mechanism is in its undeviating and accurate rhythm, like a pendulum. But you who have been nurtured on Taylor's system from childhood—have you not become pendulum-accurate?

But there is only one thing:

A mechanism has no fantasy.

Have you ever seen spreading over the physiognomy of a pump cylinder during operation—a far-away, senselessly-dreamy smile? Have you ever heard cranes in the night, during the hours designated for rest, tossing, turning and sighing restlessly?

No!

But among you—you should blush!—the Guardians have been seeing these smiles and sighs more and more often. And—you should hide your eyes!—the historians of the United State are asking to resign so they will not have to record the shameful events.

But this is not your fault—you are ill. The name of this illness is:

Fantasy.

This is the worm which is gnawing the dark wrinkles on foreheads. This is the fever which drives you to keep running ever farther—even if this *farther* began there where happiness ends. It is the final barricade on the road to happiness.

And rejoice: the barricade has already been blasted.

The road is free.

The latest discovery of State Science: the **Center of Fantasy** is a miserable little cerebral nodule in the region of the Varolo Bridge. A thrice-repeated cauterization of this nodule with X-rays—and you are cured of fantasy—

Once And For All

You are perfect, you are machine-equal, the road to one-hundred-per-cent happiness is free. Hurry, one and all—old and young—hurry to undergo the Great Operation. Hurry to the auditoria where the Great Operation is being performed. Hail to the Great Operation! Hail to the United State, hail to the Benefactor!

... You—if you were reading all of this not in these records of mine which resemble some kind of ancient, fanciful novel—if, instead, a newspaper page, still smelling of the ink, were trembling in your hands as it is in mine—if you knew, as I do, that all of this is the most genuine reality for tomorrow if not today,—would you not in fact be feeling the very same thing as me? Wouldn't your head—like mine is now—be swimming? Wouldn't these eerie, sweet, icy needles be running up and down your back and arms? Wouldn't it seem to you that you were a giant, an Atlas—and if you were to straighten up, then you would unfailingly strike your head against the glass ceiling?

I grabbed the telephone receiver:

"I-330... Yes, yes: 330—" and then choking, I shouted: "are you home, yes? Did you read—are you reading it? This is really, this is... This is astounding!"

"Yes..." A long, dark silence. The receiver was buzzing almost inaudibly, she was thinking about something... "I must see you without fail today. Yes, in my room after 16. Without fail."

Dearest! What a dear she is! *Without fail*... I felt: I was smiling—and I could not stop at all, and so I would be carrying this smile through the street—like a lantern, high above my head...

There, outside, the wind came swooping down on me. It swirled, whistled, whipped. But I merely became even more cheerful. Howl, scream—it doesn't matter: you won't be knocking over any walls now. And overhead the cast-iron, flying clouds were tumbling down—let them: you won't be eclipsing the sun—we have fastened it forever with a chain to its zenith—we, the Joshuas, the sons of Nun.

Standing on the corner—a tight little group of Joshuas—Sons-of-Nun, their foreheads pasted to the glass of the wall. Inside, there was already one lying on a blindingly-white table. The naked soles of the feet could be seen sticking out at a yellowish angle from under the whiteness, doctors in white—were bent over the forehead, a white hand—passed a syringe filled with something to another hand.

"What about you—why aren't you going?" I asked—of no one, or rather, of everyone.

"What about you?" someone's sphere turned to me.

"I will—later. First I still have to..." Somewhat embarrassed, I moved away. I really did have to see her, I-330, first. But why *first*—I could not answer myself...

The launching site. The *Integral* was glittering, scintillating with a pale icy-blue. In the engine room the dynamo was humming—tenderly, repeating endlessly some single word or other—as though a familiar word of my own. I bent down, stroked the long, cold engine tube. Darling... what a darling you are. Tomorrow thou willst come to life, tomorrow—for the first time in life thou willst shudder from the fiery, burning discharge in thy womb...

How differently might I have been looking at this mighty, glass monster if all had but remained as it was the day before? If I had known that tomorrow at 12—I would betray it... yes, betray...

Cautiously—a touch on my elbow from behind. I turned around: the plate-like, flat face of the Second Builder.

"You know already," he said.

"What? The Operation? Yes, it's true, isn't it? How—everything, everything—suddenly is..."

"Why no, not that: the test flight has been cancelled until the day after tomorrow. All because of this operation... All the hurry and effort for nothing..."

All because of the Operation... A ridiculous, limited person. He can see nothing beyond his own plate. If he knew that if it weren't for the Operation—at 12 tomorrow he would be sitting locked up in a glass cubicle, dashing about and climbing the wall...

In my room, at 15 1/2. I entered—and saw U-. She was sitting at my desk,—boney, straight, firm—her right cheek supported on her hand. She must already have been waiting for a long time: because when she jumped up to greet me—five little depressions from her fingers still remained on her cheek.

For one second inside me—that most unfortunate morning, and right here, right by the desk—— she beside I-330, in a fury... But only for a second—and then immediately washed away by today's sun. The same way it happens if on a brilliant day, upon entering a room you turn the switch absentmindedly—the bulb is lit up, but it is as though it does not exist—it is so ridiculous, poor, unnecessary...

Without a second's thought I held out my hand to her, I had forgiven everything—she seized both of mine, firmly, with a tight prickly squeeze, and with her sagging cheeks quivering excitedly, like ancient ornaments,— she said:

"I was waiting... I just came for a minute... I only wanted to say: how overjoyed, how happy I am for you! You understand: tomorrow or the day after tomorrow—you will be perfectly healthy, you will be reborn anew..."

I caught sight of a sheet on the table—the final two pages of my record from yesterday: they were still lying there the way I had left them from the evening. If she had seen what I had been writing there... However it did not matter: now this was only history, now this was as ridiculous in its remoteness as looking through reversed binoculars...

"Yes," I said, "and you know: I was just walking this minute along the avenue, and in front of me was a fellow, and there was a shadow from him on the pavement. And you understand:—the shadow—it was shining. And it seems to me—in fact, I am certain,—tomorrow there will be no shadows at all, not from a single person, not from a single thing, the sun—through everything..."

She—tenderly and sternly:

"You are a fantaseur! The children in my school—I wouldn't allow them to talk like that..."

And something about children and how she had taken all of them at once, in a body, to the Operation, and how it had been necessary to tie them up there, that "love must be merciless, yes merciless" and that she, it seemed, would finally make the decision...

She straightened the gray-blue fabric between her knees, silently, quickly—and stuck me all over with her smile, then left.

And—fortunately, the sun had not come to a halt today, the sun was running, and here it was already 16, I was knocking on the door—my heart was knocking...

"Come in!"

Onto the floor—beside her armchair, embracing her legs, head tossed back, gazing into her eyes—each in turn, first the one and then the other—and in each one seeing myself—in wonderful captivity...

But there, beyond the wall, a storm, there, the clouds more and more like cast iron: let them be! My head swarming, impetuous—brimming over—words, and I in resounding flight somewhere together with the sun... no, *now* we already knew where—and behind me the planets—the planets showering flames and populated with fiery, singing flowers—mute, blue planets where rational stones were united into organized societies—planets like our earth that had achieved the pinnacle of an absolute, one-hundred-per-cent happiness...

And suddenly—from above:

"But don't you think that the pinnacle is nothing more than stones united into an organized society?"

And the triangle ever sharper and ever darker: "And happiness... What of it? After all desires are agonizing, aren't they? And it is clear: happiness is when there are no longer any desires, not a single one... What an error, what an absurd prejudice that up until now in front of happiness—we have placed a plus sign, in front of absolute happiness—there should be a minus—a divine minus."

I—I remember—I muttered absentmindedly: "Absolute minus is 273°..."

"Minus 273—precisely. A bit chilly, but that in itself does not really prove that we are at the pinnacle."

Like then, long before—she was speaking somehow for me, through me—developing my thoughts to the end. But there was something so eerie in this—I could not—and only with an effort did I extract from myself a *no*.

"No," I said. "Thou... thou art joking..."

She began to laugh, loudly—too loudly. Quickly, in a second, she had laughed herself up to some kind of edge—another step back—and down... A pause.

She stood up. She put her hands on my shoulders. For a long while, slowly she looked. Then she drew me to herself—and there was nothing: just her sharp, burning lips.

"Farewell!"

This—from afar, from above, and it came to me only slowly—perhaps in a minute, in two.

"But why *farewell*?"

"But thou art ill, committing crimes because of me,—has it really not been agony for thee? But now the Operation—and thou willst be cured of me. And this is farewell."

"No," I began to shout.

A mercilessly-sharp, black triangle against white: "What? Thou dost not want happiness?"

My head was racing, two logical trains had collided, crawled up on each other, had been wrecked, shattered...

"Well, what then, I'm waiting—choose: the Operation and one-hundred-per-cent happiness—or..."

"I can't live without you, I need you"—I said or merely thought it—I don't know; but I-330 had heard.

"Yes, I know," she answered me. And then—still keeping her hands on my shoulders and not releasing my eyes from hers:

"Then—until tomorrow. Tomorrow—at 12: you remember?"

"No. It has been postponed for one day. The day after tomorrow."

"So much the better for us. At 12—the day after tomorrow..."

I was walking alone—along the twilight street.

The wind swept me around, carried me, chased me—like a piece of paper, the fragments of the cast-iron sky were flying, flying—they still had a day or two to fly through eternity... The unifs coming towards me brushed against me—but I went on walking alone. It was clear to me: all were saved, but there was no salvation for me any longer, *I did not want salvation...*

Record 32
Synopsis: **I Do Not Believe**
              Tractors
              A Small Human Splinter

Do you believe in the fact that you will *die*? Yes, a human is mortal, I am a human: consequently... No, that's not it: I know that you know this. But I am asking this: have you ever happened to *believe* in this, to believe once and for all, to believe not with your mind, but with your *body,* to feel that at some time the fingers which are holding this very page here—will be yellow, icy...

No: of course you don't believe it—and that is why up until now you have not leaped from the tenth floor to the pavement, that is why up until now you go on eating, turning the page, shaving, smiling, writing. . .

It is the very same—yes, precisely the very same—with me today. I know that this small black hand on the clock will shortly come sliding here, down below, then towards midnight, again slowly rise upwards, overtake some final demarcation or other—and an improbable tomorrow will arrive. I know this, but still I somehow *do not believe it*—or, perhaps, it seems to me that twenty-four hours—those are twenty-four years. And that is why I can still do something, rush off somewhere, answer questions, clamber up the companion-way to the *Integral*. I still feel it rocking on the water, and I understand—that I must grasp onto the handrail—and beneath my hand is the cold glass. I see the transparent, life-like cranes, their bird-like necks bent, claws outstretched, lovingly and tenderly feeding the *Integral* with the terrifying explosive food for its engines. And down below the river—I see clearly the blue veins, the nodes, swelling under the wind. But it is as though: all of this is very isolated from me, alien, flat—like a schematic drawing on a sheet of paper. And it was strange that the flat, schematic face of the Second Builder—was suddenly speaking:

"So then: how much fuel are we taking on for the engines? If we calculate three. . . well three and a half hours. . ."

Before me—in projection, on a schematic drawing—my hand with the calculator, the logarithmic dial, the figure 15.

"Fifteen tons. But better take. . . yes: take a hundred. . ."

This was because I knew all the same that tomorrow—

And out of the corner of my eye I saw—my hand with the logarithmic dial starting to tremble just perceptibly.

"A hundred? But why such an incredible amount like that? Why that's enough for a week. What am I saying—a week: it's more!"

"All sorts of things might come up. . . who knows. . ."

"I know. . ."

The wind was whistling, all the air was crammed to the top with something invisible. It was difficult for me to breathe, difficult to walk—and with difficulty, slowly, not stopping for even a second—the hand on the clock of the Accumulator Tower, there at the end of the avenue, was creeping along. The spire of the tower—in the clouds—was hazy, blue and howling with a dull sound: sucking up electricity. The tubes of the Musical Factory were howling.

As usual—in ranks, four abreast. But the rows are somehow unstable, and perhaps, because of the wind—they are wavering, bending. Then more and more. Then suddenly they had struck against something on the corner, washed back and now were in a tight, frozen, compact, heavy breathing ball, and at once all of them had long, goose-like necks.

"Look! No, look—over there, quickly!"

"Them! It's them!"

". . . Not me—not for anything! Not for anything—better to stick your head in the Machine..."

"Quiet! You madman..."

On the corner, in the auditorium—the door was wide open, and from there—a slow, sluggish column, of about fifty people. However, *people*—was not quite right: not feet—but some kind of heavy, forged wheels being turned by an invisible drive-mechanism; not people—but some kind of humanoid tractors. Over their heads, flapping in the wind, was a white banner with a golden embroidered sun—and inside the rays was the inscription: "We are the first! We have had our operation! Everyone follow us!"

Slowly, irresistibly, they plowed their way through the crowd—and it is clear that if there were walls, a tree, a building in their way instead of us—without stopping they would still have plowed through the wall, the tree, the building. Then—they were already in the center of the avenue. Screwing themselves together, arm in arm—they stretched out into a chain, facing us. And we—this tense ball with heads bristling—we were waiting. Necks outstretched, goose-like. Clouds. The wind whistling.

Suddenly the wings of the chain, on the right and left, quickly began to bend in—and straight at us—faster and faster—like a heavy machine going downhill—they closed in a ring—and then towards the wide open doors, through the doors, inside...

Someone's piercing scream:

"They're rounding us up! Run!"

Everything broke loose. Right by the wall there was still a narrow, living gateway, everyone made for there, headfirst—the heads momentarily became sharpened into wedges, and sharp elbows, ribs, shoulders, sides. Like a stream of water, constricted by a firehose, they came bursting forth fan-like, and with stamping feet, waving arms, unifs were being strewn all around. Out of somewhere my eyes caught for an instant—the double-curved body, like the letter S, the transparent wing-ears—and suddenly it was gone, disappeared into the ground—and I was alone—among the second-hand arms, legs—I was running.

Stop to catch my breath in some doorway—my back pressed firmly against the doors—and suddenly, a small human sliver was driven as though by the wind, right up against me.

"I was all the time... I was behind you... I don't want to—do you understand—I don't want to. I am ready to..."

The round, tiny hands on my sleeve, the round blue eyes: it was her, O-. And then all of her was somehow slipping down the wall and settling on the ground. She bent over in a little ball there, down below, on the cold steps, and I, standing over her, I was stroking her head, her face—my hands were wet. It seemed: as though I was very big and she was quite small,—a small part of my own self. This was completely different than with I-330, and I immediately imagined: something similar could have happened among the ancients in respect to their own personal children.

Down below—through hands covering her face—barely audibly:

"Every night I... I can't bear it—if they cure me... Every night alone, in the darkness, I am thinking about him—what he'll be like, how I will... There won't be anything for me to live for then—do you understand? And you must—you must..."

An absurd feeling—but in fact I was certain: yes, I had to. Absurd—because this duty of mine was yet another crime. Absurd—because white cannot be black at the same time, duty and crime—cannot coincide. Or there is neither black nor white in life, color depends only on the basic logical premise. And if as the premise there was the fact that I had illegally given her a child...

"Well, fine—only don't, just don't..." I was saying. "You understand: I must take you to I-330—as I suggested then—so that she..."

"Yes," (—quietly, without taking her hands from her face).

I helped her to get up. And silently, each deep in his own thoughts—or, perhaps, deep in the very same thoughts—we went along the darkening street, amid the mute leaden buildings, through the springy branches of the wind...

At some transparent, tense point—I caught from behind the sound through the wind's whistle of familiar steps squelching as though through puddles. At a turning I looked back—amid the upside-down soaring clouds reflected in the murky glass of the pavement—I saw S-. Immediately my arms became extraneous, swinging out of rhythm, and then I was telling O- in a loud voice—that tomorrow... yes, tomorrow—would be the first flight of the *Integral,* it would be something completely unprecedented wonderful, eerie.

O-90—amazed, round, blue-eyed, looked at me, at my loud, senselessly swinging arms. But I did not let her speak a word—I kept talking and talking. Yet inside, separately,—only I could hear it—the thought was pounding and buzzing feverishly: "I must not... somehow or other I have to... I must not lead him to I-330."

Instead of turning to the left—I turned to the right. The bridge offered its submissively, slavishly bent back to the three of us: me, O-90—and him, S-, behind. From the illuminated buildings on the other bank lights were being strewn into the water, shattering into thousands of feverishly dancing sparks spattered by the frenzied white foam. The wind was droning—like a taut cable-bass string somewhere low overhead. And through the bass—behind all the while——

The building where I lived. O- stopped at the door, was starting to say something like:

"No! But you promised me..."

But I did not let her finish, I hurriedly pushed her through the door—and we were inside, in the vestibule. Above the controller's desk—the familiar, excitedly-quivering, sagging cheeks; all around—a thick little crowd of numbers—some kind of argument, heads hanging over the second-floor railing—one by one running downstairs. But about this—later, later... Immediately I drew O- hurriedly off into the opposite corner, sat down with my back to the wall (there, on the other side of the wall I saw: the dark, large-headed shadow sliding back and forth along the sidewalk), and pulled out a note-pad.

O-90—slowly collapsed into her armchair—as though her body were evaporating, melting under her unif, and all that remained were an empty dress and empty eyes sucking in a blue emptiness. Tiredly:

"Why did you bring me here? Were you deceiving me?"

"No... Quiet! Look there: do you see—on the other side of the wall?"

"Yes. A shadow."

"He is following me all the time... I can't now. Do you understand—I mustn't. I'll write a few words in a moment—you take it and go alone. I know: he will stay here."

Under the unif—the replenished body began to stir again, the belly grew everso slightly more rounded, on her cheeks, a barely noticeable dawn, a morning glow.

I slipped the note into her cold fingers, squeezed her hand firmly, for the last time I scooped from her blue eyes with my own eyes.

"Farewell! Perhaps, sometime again..."

She withdrew her hand. Hunched over, she slowly left—two steps—turned about quickly—and then was once more beside me.

The lips were stirring—with her eyes, her lips—all of her—over and over again saying some word or other to me, the same word—and that smile, what pain...

And then a hunched over human sliver in the doorway, a tiny shadow on the other side of the wall—not looking around, quickly—more and more quickly...

I went up to U-'s desk. Puffing up her cheeks anxiously and indignantly, she said to me:

"You understand—everyone seems to have gone mad! This number here assures me that he himself has seen around the Ancient House some fellow or other—naked and all covered with hair..."

Out of the vacuous group bristling with heads—a voice.

"Yes! And I'm repeating it once more: I saw it, yes."

"Well, how do you like that, eh? What kind of delirium is this!"

And she was so convinced, so inflexible about this *delirium* that I asked myself: "Isn't all of this a delirium, in fact, that has been happening to me and around me recently?"

But I glanced at my hairy hands—I remembered: "There is in you, apparently, a drop of forest blood... Perhaps that's the reason why I..."

No: fortunately, it was no delirium. No: unfortunately—it was no delirium.

Record 33
Synopsis: (This Is In a Hurry Without a Synopsis, the FinalOne)

That day—has arrived.

Quickly to the newspaper: perhaps—there... I am reading the newspaper with my eyes (precisely like that: my eyes now are like a pen, like a calculator that you hold, you feel, in your hands—they are something alien, they are an instrument).

There—in large type, all over the front page:

> The enemies of peace do not slumber.
> Hang on to happiness with both hands!
> Tomorrow all work will be suspended—all numbers will present themselves for the Operation. Those who do not appear are subject to the Machine of the Benefactor.

Tomorrow! Is it really possible—can there really be some kind of tomorrow?

From daily inertia, I reached out my hand (an instrument) to the bookshelf—inserted today's *Gazette* with the others in the gold ornamented binding. And in the midst of this:

"What for? What difference does it make? After all I won't ever be coming back here again, into this room..."

And from my hands the newspaper—onto the floor. And I stood and took in all, all, all of the room with a glance around, I was hastily gathering up everything with me—feverishly stuffing everything into an invisible suitcase that I was sorry to leave here.

The table. The books. The armchair. I-330 had been sitting in that armchair at that time—and I was down there, on the floor... The bed...

Then for a minute, two—I was absurdly waiting for some kind of miracle, perhaps—the telephone would ring, perhaps she would say that...

No. No miracle...

I am leaving—for the unknown. These are my final lines.

Farewell—you, my unknown ones, you, my beloved ones, with whom I have lived through so many pages, to whom I, who have fallen ill with a soul—have revealed all of myself, to the very last ruined little screw, to the very last broken spring...

I am leaving.

Record 34
Synopsis: **Freedmen**
A Sunny Night
A Radio-Valkyrie

Oh, if I had actually smashed myself and everyone else into smithereens, if I had actually—together with her—ended up somewhere on the other side of the Wall, among those beasts baring their yellow fangs, if I had actually never returned here again. A thousand—a million times easier. And now—what? Go and throttle that—— But would that really help anything?

No, no, no! Get a grip on yourself, D-503. Set yourself on a firm, logical axis—if only for a short while, lean with all your might on the lever—and, like an ancient slave, turn the millstones of syllogisms—until you have recorded, have interpreted everything that happened...

When I boarded the *Integral*—everyone was already assembled, everyone was at his station, all the cells of the giant, glass beehive were filled. Through the glass of the decks—the tiny, ant-like people down below— by the telegraphs, the dynamo, the transformers, the altimeters, the valves, the switches, the engines, the pumps, the tubes. In the ward-room—various people over tabulations and instruments—probably commissioned by the Science Bureau. And beside them—the Second Builder with two of his assistants.

All three heads were withdrawn into their shoulders like turtles, the faces were gray, autumnal, rayless.

"Well, then?" I asked.

"It's... sort of awful..." One of them gave a gray, rayless smile. "Might have to land who knows where. And in general—a lot of unknowns..."

It was unbearable for me to look at them,—those, whom I would, with these very hands of mine, in one hour's time, cast out of the comfortable figures of the Table of Hours forever, tear away from the maternal breast of the United State for ever. They reminded me of the tragic figures of *The Three Freedmen*—whose story was known to any schoolboy among us. This story is about how three numbers, by way of an experiment,were released from work for a month: do what you will, go where you will.* The poor wretches loitered about their usual place of labor and would peer inside with hungry eyes; they would stop at the plazas—and for hours on end they would go through those motions which at a specific time of the day had already become a physical need for their bodies: they sawed and planed the air, with invisible sledges they pounded and hammered the ingots. And,

---

*This was a long time ago, still in the third century after the Table of Hours.

finally, on the tenth day they could not bear it any longer: taking each other by the hand they walked into the water and to the sounds of the March they immersed themselves deeper and deeper, until the water put an end to their agonies...

I repeat: it was painful for me to look at them, I hastened to leave.

"I'm just going to check in the engine room," I said, "and then, we're away."

I was being asked about something—what voltage to apply for the blast-off, how much water ballast in the lateral tank. Inside me there was some kind of gramophone: it answered all the questions quickly and accurately, whereas I, unceasingly, inside, was deep in my own thoughts.

And suddenly in the narrow gang-way—something suddenly penetrated there, deep inside me—and from that moment, in essence, it began.

In the narrow gang-way gray unifs were flitting past, gray faces, and for a second there was one face in their midst: the hair in a low awning, the eyes under the beetle-brow—that same one. I understood: they were here and there was nowhere for me to go away from all of this, and only minutes remained—some dozens of minutes... A minute, molecular tremor through my whole body (subsequently it did not cease until the very end)— as though an enormous motor had been installed and the housing of my body—was too light, and thus all the walls, the bulkheads, the cables, the beams, the lights, everything was trembling...

I still did not know: whether she was there. But now there was no longer any time—I had been sent for to go quickly above, to the control cabin: time to take off... Where to?

Gray, rayless faces. The tense blue veins down below, on the water. The heavy, cast-iron strata in the sky. And just as cast-iron heavy for me to raise my hand, take the receiver of the control cabin telephone.

"Up—at 45°!"

A muffled blast—a jolt—a frenzied, white-green mountain of water at the stern—the deck underfoot was moving—soft, rubber-like—and everything down below, all of life, forever... For a second—falling ever deeper into some kind of crater, everything was shrinking all around—the convex, icy-blue scheme of the city, the round bubbles of the cupolas, the solitary, leaden finger of the Accumulator Tower. Then—the momentary cotton-batten curtain of clouds—we were through them—and the sun, the blue sky. Seconds, minutes, miles: the blue was quickly hardening, filling with darkness, stars were emerging like drops of a cold, silvery sweat...

And then—an eerie, unbearably-brilliant, black, starry, sunny night. As though you had suddenly gone deaf: you still see the tubes roaring, but you are only seeing it: the tubes are mute, silence. Such was the sun—mute.

This was natural, this had to be expected. We had emerged from the earth's atmosphere. But somehow so quickly, by surprise—that everyone around was overawed, silenced. And to me—to me it seemed even easier under this fantastic mute sun: as though having held back cowering for the last time, I had finally crossed over that inevitable threshold—and my body was somewhere there, down below, whereas I was soaring in a new world where everything was supposed to be unlikely, upside down...

"Hold it like that," I shouted into the receiver—rather, not me, but that same gramophone inside me—and with a mechanical, hinged hand I handed the command telephone to the Second Builder. And totally enveloped in the finest, molecular tremor which only I could sense—I ran down below, to look for...

The door to the wardroom—that very door: in an hour it would creak heavily and be locked... Beside the door—some unfamiliar, squat fellow, with a face like a hundred, a thousand others that would disappear in a crowd, and only the arms were extraordinarily long, down to his knees: as though by mistake they had been carelessly taken from a different human assemblage.

A long arm stretched out, barred the way:

"Where are you going?"

It was clear to me: he did not know that I knew everything. So be it: perhaps—it had to be that way. And from above him I said with intentional abruptness: "I am the builder of the *Integral*. And I am directing the tests. Understood?"

The arm disappeared.

The wardroom. Over instruments, maps—heads criss-crossed with gray bristle—and heads that were yellow, bald, ripe. Quickly all of them were taken in—with a single glance—and then back, along the gang-way, the companion-way, down, into the engine-room. There the heat and rumble from the red-hot combustion tubes, the glittering levers in an unceasing, drunken desperate dance, in the barely noticeable tremor that did not cease for a second—the indicators in the dials...

And there—at last,—beside the tachometer—him, the one with the beetle-brow bent over a notebook...

"Listen..." (the roar: one had to shout right into the ear). "Is she here? Where is she?"

In the shadow—of the brow—a smile: "She? There. In the radio-telephone compartment..." And I made for there. There were three of them there.

All of them in wing-like receiving helmets. And she seemed to be a head higher than usual, winged, glittering, flying—like the ancient valkyries, and there seemed to be enormous, blue sparks up above, on the radio-antenna—coming from her—a light, lightning-like ozone odor.

"Somebody... no, it may as well be you..." I said to her, panting (from having run). "I have to transmit down below, to the earth, the launching site... Come, I'll dictate..."

Beside the apparatus was a small box-like cabin. At the table, side by side. I found and firmly squeezed her hand:

"Well, then? What will happen?"

"I don't know. Dost thou understand how marvellous this is: without knowing—flying—it doesn't matter where... And it will soon be 12—and who knows what? And the night... where will thou and I be during the night? Perhaps—on the grass, on dry leaves..."

From her came blue sparks and the scent of lightning, and inside me the tremor grew more rapid.

"Record it," I said loudly and still puffing (from having run). "Time 11:30. Speed: 6800..."

And she—from under the winged helmet, without tearing her eyes from the paper, softly:

"... Yesterday evening she came to me with your note... I know—I know everything: don't speak. After all, the child is yours? I sent her off—she is already there, beyond the wall. She will live.. "

I was back again in the control room. Again—a night delirious with the black, starry heaven and the dazzling sun; slowly from one minute to the next the limping hand of the clock on the wall; and everything as though in a mist, clothed in the slightest, barely noticeable (only to me) tremor.

For some reason it seemed: better if all of this took place not here but somewhere down below, closer to earth.

"Stop," I shouted into the apparatus.

Still forward—from inertia—but more and more slowly. And then next the *Integral* had caught on the hair-breadth of a second, hung motionless for an instant, whereupon the hair broke—and the *Integral*, like a stone, downward—and faster and faster. Thus in silence, for minutes, for dozens of minutes—an audible pulse—before one's eyes the clock hand ever closer to 12. And it was clear to me: I was this stone, I-330 was the earth, and I was a stone thrown by someone—and there was an irresistible need for the stone to fall, to crash against the earth into smithereens... And what if...—down below there was already the solid, blue haze of the clouds...—and what if...

But the gramophone inside me—picked up the receiver in a precise, hinge-like motion and gave the command for "slow ahead"—the stone stopped falling. And then only four tubes were snorting tiredly—two stern tubes and two forward ones—just enough to paralyze the weight of the *Integral* and the *Integral*, barely trembling, held firm as though on an anchor—came to a stop in the air, at a kilometer or so from the earth.

Everyone spilled out onto the deck (it was now 12, the bell rang for lunch) and leaning over the glass railing, were hastily gulping up in mouthfuls the unknown world beyond the Wall—there, down below. Amber, green, blue: an autumnal forest, meadows, a lake. At the end of a small blue dish were some kind of yellow, bone-like ruins, a yellow dessicated finger was threatening—it must have been a tower of an ancient church that had survived by some miracle.

"Look, look! Over there—more to the right!" There—across a green empty space—some kind of quick spot was flying like a brown shadow. I had binoculars in my hands, I raised them mechanically to my eyes: up to their chest in the grass fluttering their tails, a herd of brown horses was galloping along, and on their backs were those ones, the dark-bay ones, the white, the raven-coloured...

From behind me:

"And I'm telling you:—I saw—a face."

"Go on! Tell that to someone else!"

"Well go on, you take the binoculars..."

But they had already disappeared. An endless green empty expanse...

And in the empty expanse—filling all of it, as well as all of me and all the others—the piercing tremor of the bell: lunch, in one minute—12.

The world was shattered into fleeting, disconnected fragments. On the steps—the clear ringing sound of someone's golden badge—and little did it matter to me: it had just crunched under my heel. A voice: "But I'm telling you—a face!" A dark rectangle: the open door of the wardroom. Clenched, white, sharply-smiling teeth...

And at that moment when with infinite slowness, holding my breath from one stroke to the next, the clock began to strike, and the front rows had already begun to move—the rectangle of the door was suddenly crossed out by two familiar, unnaturally-long arms:

"Stop!"

Fingers bit deeply into my palm   it was I-330, it was she beside me:

"Who is it? Dost thou know him?"

"But isn't he, isn't he really one of..."

He was on someone's shoulders. Above a hundred faces was his face alone, that one face like a hundred or thousand other faces:

"In the name of the Guardians... You—to whom I am speaking, the ones whom I mean can hear me, each of you can hear me—I am telling you: we know. We still don't know your numbers—but we know everything. The *Integral* will not be yours! This test will be carried out to the end, whereas you—you will not dare to make a move now,—you, yourselves, with your own hands, will carry it out. And later... However, I have finished..."

Silence. The glass slabs underfoot were soft, like cotton-batten, and my legs were soft, like cotton-batten. Beside me she had a perfectly white smile, frenzied blue sparks. Through her teeth—into my ear:

"And, was it you? Did you *fulfill your duty*? Well, what of it..."

The hand—was wrenched out of mine, the valkyrie-like, wrathfully-winged helmet was somewhere far away in front of me. Alone, I walked frozenly, silently, like everyone else, into the wardroom...

"But after all it wasn't me—not me! I never said anything about it to anyone, except these white, mute pages..."

Inside me—inaudibly, desperately, loudly—I was shouting this to her. She was sitting across the table, opposite, and she never once laid her eyes on me. Beside her—someone's ripe-yellow bald head. I could hear (it was I-330):

"*Nobility*? But, my dearest professor, after all even a simple philological analysis of this word—shows that it is a prejudice, a remnant of ancient, feudal eras. Whereas we..."

I felt: I was turning pale—and everyone would see it in just a moment... But the gramophone inside me was performing the established 50 chewing motions for each piece, I was locked up inside myself, like in an ancient, opaque house—I had piled up the door with stones, I had curtained off the windows...

Then—the control telephone was in my hands and the flight as well—in icy, final grief—through the clouds—into the icy, starry, sunny night. Minutes, hours. And, apparently, inside me all the while, feverishly, at full speed—that logical motor that not even I could hear. Because suddenly at some point or other in the blue expanse: my desk, over it—the fish-gill cheeks of U-, the forgotten sheet of my records. And it was clear to me: no one but she,—all was clear to me...

Ah, if only—if only I could reach the radio... Winged helmets, the odor of blue lightning... I remember—I said something loud to her, and I remember—she looking through me, as though I were made of glass—from afar:

"I am busy: I am receiving from down below. Dictate it to her there..."

In the minute box-like cabin, having pondered for a minute, I firmly dictated:

"Time—14:40. Down! Stop engines. Everything is finished."

The control cabin. The machine heart of the *Integral* had stopped, we were falling and my heart—could not keep up with the rate of fall, it was lagging behind, rising ever higher into my throat. Clouds—and then far away a green patch—growing greener, growing more distinct—rushing towards us like a whirlwind—the end in just a moment——

The porcelain-white, distorted face of the Second Builder. Probably it was he who pushed me with all his might, I struck my head against something and as I was falling and everything was turning dark—I heard through the mist:

"Stern engines—full power!"

An abrupt leap upwards... I remember nothing more.

Record 35
Synopsis: **In A Hoop**
A Carrot
A Murder

I did not sleep all night. The same thing—all night...

My head is tightly bandaged after what happened yesterday. To illustrate: as though these are not bandages, but a hoop: a merciless hoop of glass steel has been riveted about my head, and inside that same forged circle I have one thought: to kill U-. To kill U-,—and then to go to the other one and say: "Now—do you believe me?" The most disgusting thing of all is that killing is somehow filthy, ancient, to smash somebody's skull in with something—leaves a strange sensation of something revoltingly sweet in my mouth, and I cannot swallow my saliva, I keep spitting it out in my handkerchief, my mouth is dry.

Lying in my closet was a heavy piston rod that had broken after casting (I had had to examine the structure of the break under a microscope). I rolled my records up into a tube (let her read all of me— right to the last word), slipped the broken piston rod inside it and went downstairs. The staircase was endless, the steps were somehow disgustingly slippery, liquid, all the while—wiping my mouth with a handkerchief...

Downstairs. My heart was pounding. I stopped, pulled out the piston rod—and up to the controller's desk——

But U- was not there: an empty, icy desk-top. I remembered: today— all work was cancelled; everyone had to go to the operation, and understandably: there was no need for her, there was no one to register here...

On the street. Wind. A sky of soaring cast-iron slabs. And exactly as it had happened at some given moment yesterday: the whole world was shattered into individual, sharp, independent pieces, and each of them, falling headlong, was arrested for a second, suspended before me in the air—and then evaporated without a trace.

As though the black, precise letters on this page—suddenly shifted, scattered terrified in all directions—and not a single word left, only utter nonsense: sca—rif—dir—. On the street—the crowd was just as scattered, not in ranks—forwards, backwards, sideways, crosswise.

And then no one. And frozen for a second, in a headlong flight: over there, on the second floor, in a glass cubicle suspended in the air—a man and a woman—standing in a kiss—she with her whole body bent brokenly backwards. This was forever, the final time...

On some corner or other—a swaying prickly bush of heads. Above the heads—independently, in the air—a banner, the words: "Down with

Machines! Down with the Operation!" And independently (from me)—was that self who was thinking for a second: "Is it possible that each person has the kind of pain which can be removed from within—only together with the heart, and each person must do something before——" And for a second, nothing in the entire world except for (my) beastly hand with the cast-iron heavy rolled-up bundle...

Then—a boy: all of him straining forward, underneath the lower lip—a shadow. The lower lip—turned out like the cuff of a rolled-up sleeve—his whole face turned out—he was howling—and running from someone as fast as his legs would carry him—behind him, pounding feet...

Because of the boy: "Yes, U- must be in school now, I must hurry." I ran to the nearest subway entrance.

At the entrance someone hurrying:

"They're not running! The trains are not running today! There—" I went down. There—utter delirium. The gleam of faceted, crystal suns. The platform solidly jammed with heads. An empty, frozen train.

And in the silence—a voice. I could not see her, but I knew, I knew that voice, resilient, flexible, lashing like a whip—and somewhere there the sharp triangle of the brows turned up towards the temples... I started to shout:

"Let me through! Let me through to there! I must —" But people's claws on me—my hands, my shoulders, like nails. And in the silence—a voice:

"...No: run back up there! There they'll cure you, there they'll feed you with fancy happiness until you're stuffed, and you, the sated ones, you will sleep peacefully, organized, snoring in rhythm,—can't you hear that mighty symphony of snores? Ridiculous people: they want to liberate you from the question marks that writhe like worms, that gnaw at you agonizingly like worms. And here you are standing and listening to me. Hurry—upstairs—to the Mighty Operation! What business is it of yours if I stay here alone? What business is it of yours—if I don't want what others wish for me, but that I want what I myself wish,—if I want the impossible..."

Another voice—slow, heavy:

"Aha! The impossible? Does that mean—go chase after your foolish fantasies while they twirl their little tail in front of your nose? No: we take them by the tail, and put them under us and then..."

"And then—gobble them up and start to snore—and then you need a new tail before your nose. They say the ancients had a kind of animal: a donkey. In order to force him to keep going forward and forward—they tied a carrot to the shaft in front of his snout so that he could not reach it. And if he reached it, he gobbled it up..."

Suddenly the claws released me, I dashed to the middle where she was speaking—and at that very moment everything broke loose and there was a crush—from behind, a cry:

"Here, they're coming here!" The light danced and then went out—someone had cut the wire—and an avalanche, screams, groans, heads, fingers. . .

I don't know how long we rolled about like this in the subway tube. Finally: stairs—twilight—growing lighter—and once again we were in the street fanning out in various directions. . .

And then I was alone. Wind, the gray low shadows of twilight, right overhead. On the damp glass of the sidewalk—very deep down—upside-down lights, walls, moving figures, feet uppermost. And the incredibly heavy rolled-up bundle in my hand—pulling me into the depths, to the bottom.

Downstairs, at the small desk, still no U-, and her room was empty, dark.

I went upstairs to my room, turned on the light. My temples, tightly bandaged in the hoop, were pounding, I paced,—still chained in one and the same circle: the table, on the table the white bundle. . . In the room on the left the blinds were lowered. On the right: over a book—the lumpy bald head, and the forehead,—an enormous yellow parabola. The wrinkles on the forehead—a series of yellow indecipherable lines. Sometimes our eyes met—and then I felt: these yellow lines were about me.

. . .It happened precisely at 21. U- came—herself. Only one thing has remained distinct in my memory: I was breathing so loudly that I could hear myself breathing, and I kept wanting to do it more quietly somehow—and I couldn't.

She sat down, straightened the unif on her knees. The pink-brown gills were quivering.

"Ah, my dear fellow—so it's true, you are wounded? I only just found out—just this moment. . ."

The piston rod was on the table in front of me. I leapt up, breathing even more loudly. She heard it, stopped in mid-word, and for some reason stood up as well. I already had my eyes on that spot on her head, a repulsively-sweet taste in my mouth. . . a handkerchief, but there was none—I spat on the floor.

The one behind the wall on the right—the yellow, staring wrinkles—about me. I had to do it so that he would not see, it would have been more disgusting if he were watching. . . I pushed the button—what did it matter that I did not have any permission, was it not all the same now,—the blinds fell.

Apparently, she sensed, she understood, she dashed for the door. But I cut her off there—and breathing loudly, not for a second taking my eyes from that spot on her head. . .

"You. . . you've gone mad! You don't dare. . ." she backed away—sat down, rather she fell on the bed—trembling, she stuck the clasped palms of her hands between her knees. All coiled, still holding her tightly on a leash with my eyes, I slowly reached out my hand to the table—only a single hand was moving—and seized the piston rod.

"I implore you! A day—just one day! Tomorrow—yes, tomorrow—I shall go and do everything..."

What was she talking about? I swung——

And I believe: I killed her. Yes, you, my unknown readers, you have the right to call me a murderer. I know that I would have brought the piston rod down on her head if she had not shouted:

"For the sake of... for the sake of... I agree—I'll do it right away."

With shaking hands she tore the unif from herself—the expansive, yellow, sagging body toppled over on the bed... And only then did I understand: she had thought that the blinds had been—it had been done so that—that I wanted...

It was so unexpected, so stupid, that I burst into laughter. And immediately the tightly coiled spring inside me—burst, my hand weakened, the piston rod crashed to the floor. At that moment I perceived from my own personal experience that laughter is the most terrifying weapon: everything can be killed with laughter—even murder.

I was sitting at the table and laughing—a desperate, final laughter—and I did not see any way out of this entire absurd situation. I don't know how all of this would have ended if it had followed its natural course—but then suddenly a new, external factor: the phone began to ring.

I dashed over, seized the receiver: maybe her? And then someone's unfamiliar voice in the receiver:

"Just a moment."

A tedious, endless buzzing. From off in the distance—heavy footsteps, getting closer, more resounding, more and more cast-iron—and then...

"D-503? Ahem... This is the Benefactor speaking to you. Come here at once!"

Ding,—the receiver hung up,—ding.

U- was still lying on the bed, her eyes closed, the gills puffed out in a broad smile. I scooped her dress from the floor, threw it at her—and through my teeth:

"Well! Quickly—quickly!"

She raised herself on one elbow, her breasts splashed over on the side, eyes round, she had turned to wax all over.

"Why?"

"Because. Well—just get dressed!"

All in a knot, clutching her dress tightly, her voice flattened:

"Turn around..."

I turned around, leaned against the glass with my forehead. Lights, figures, sparks were trembling on the black, wet mirror. No: this was me, this was inside me... Why did He want me? Could He already know about her, about me, about everything?

U-, already dressed, was at the door. Two steps towards her—I grasped her hands as tightly as though it were precisely from those hands that I was about to squeeze out drop by drop what I needed:

"Listen... Her name—you know who I mean—did you give her name? No? Only the truth—I have to know... it doesn't matter to me now—only the truth..."

"No."

"No? But why—if you had already gone there and informed..."

Her lower lip was suddenly turned inside-out, like that boy earlier—and out of her cheeks, down the cheeks, drops...

"Because I... I was afraid that if they... that because of that you might... you would stop lov... Oh, I can't—I just couldn't have!"

I understood: this was the truth. The absurd, ridiculous, human truth! I opened the door.

Record 36
Synopsis: **Empty Pages**
                The Christian God
                About My Mother

It seemed strange then—it was like an empty white page in my head: how I went there, how I waited (I know that I waited)—I remember nothing, not a single sound, not a single face, not a single gesture. As though all the wires between me and the world had been severed.

I came to—when I was already standing before Him, and it was terrifying for me to raise my eyes: I saw only His enormous cast-iron hands—on His knees. These hands weighed even on Him, bent His knees. His fingers slowly stirred. His face was somewhere up high in a mist and it was as though it were only because His voice reached me from such a height that it did not roll like thunder, did not deafen me, but was still similar to an ordinary human voice.

"So—you too? You—the Builder of the *Integral?* You—whose fortune it was to have been the greatest conquistador. You—whose name was to have begun a new, brilliant chapter in the history of the United State ... You?"

The blood splashed into my head, my cheeks—again a white page: only the pulse in my temples, and the hollow voice up above, but not a single word. Only when He became silent did I come to, I perceived: the hand, ton-heavy, was moving—slowly it crawled—and a finger was pointed at me.

"Well? Why are you silent? Is it true or not? Am I the Executioner?"

"Yes."—I answered submissively. And thereafter I clearly heard every word of His.

"What? Do you think—I am afraid of that word? But have you ever tried stripping the shell from it to take a look at what is inside? I will show you right now. Remember: the blue hill, the cross, the mob. Some are up on top, spattered with blood, they are nailing a body to a cross; others are down below, spattered with tears, they are looking. Does it not seem to you that the role of those ones up at the top is the most difficult, the most important. Indeed if it were not for them, would all of this majestic tragedy have been staged? They were hissed at by the ignorant mob: but after all, for this, the author of the tragedy—God—must reward them even more generously. And that Christian, most merciful God Himself, slowly burning all the unrepentant in the infernal fire—is He really not an executioner? And was the number of those burned by the Christians at the stake really any fewer than the Christians who themselves were burned? And all the same—try to understand this—all the same this God was glorified for centuries as the God of Love. An absurdity? No, on the contrary: it is a testament, written in blood, to the ineradicable wisdom of man. Even at that time—wild, shaggy—he understood: true, algebraic love for humanity is indispensible, inhuman, and the indispensible sign of truth is its cruelty. Just as with fire the indispensible sign is the fact that it burns. Show me a non-burning fire? Well,—go ahead and prove it, dispute it!"

How could I dispute it? How could I dispute it when these had been (earlier) my very thoughts—only I had never been able to array them in such gleaming, forged armor. I was silent.

"If this means that you agree with me—then let's talk like adults when the children have gone to bed: everything to the very end. I ask: what have people—right from the very cradle—prayed for, tormented themselves for, dreamed about? So that someone would tell them once and for all what happiness is—and then chain them to this happiness. And what else are we doing right now if not this? The ancient dream of paradise... Remember: in paradise they no longer know desires, they do not know pity, they do not know love, there they are blessed, their fantasy has been operated on (that is the only reason they are blessed)—they are angels, servants of God... And now, at that very moment when we have already caught up to this dream, when we have seized it like this (— His hand closed: if a stone had been in it—juice would have squirted out), when all that remains now is merely to skin the prey and distribute it in pieces—at that very moment you—you..."

The cast-iron rumble suddenly ceased. I was all red, like a piece of iron on an anvil beneath a pounding sledge. The sledge was silently hanging suspended, and to wait for it,—this was even... more ter...

Suddenly:

"How old are you?"

"Thirty-two."

"And you are exactly twice sixteen naive! Listen: has it never once in fact entered your head that they—we still do not know their names, but I am certain that we will learn from you,—that they needed you only because you were the Builder of the *Integral*—only because, through you. . ."

"Don't! Don't!" I screamed.

. . .It was the same as shouting at and trying to ward off a bullet with your hands: you can still hear your absurd don't, but the bullet—has already burned through you and you are already writhing on the floor.

Yes, yes: the Builder of the *Integral*. . . Yes, yes. . . and then suddenly: the furious face of U- with the quivering brick-red gills—that morning when they were both in my room. . .

I remember very clearly: I started to laugh—I raised my eyes. Before me sat a bald, Socratically-bald, man and on his bald head were minute drops of sweat.

How simple everything was. How majestically-banal and absurdly simple it all was.

I was suffocating with laughter, I was bursting in puffs of air. I stuffed my mouth with my palm and dashed headlong away from there.

Stairs, the wind, wet, dancing fragments of lights, faces, and while I was running: "No! I must see her! I must see her at least once more!"

At this point—again an empty, white page. I remember only: feet. Not people, but precisely—feet: pounding unrhythmically, hundreds of feet falling onto the pavement from somewhere up above, a heavy rain of feet. And some kind of cheerful, mischievous song, and a scream—probably for me: "Hey! Hey! Over here, join us!"

Then—a deserted plaza, crammed to the top with a compressed wind. In the middle—the murky, ponderous, awesome mass: the Machine of the Benefactor. And because of it—a somehow unexpected echo inside me: a brilliantly-white pillow: on the pillow, a head tossed back and eyes half-closed; a sharp, sweet stripe of teeth. . . And all of this somehow absurdly, terrifyingly connected with the Machine—I know how, but I still don't want to see how, to say it out loud—I don't want to, I don't have to.

I closed my eyes, sat down on the stairs leading up to the Machine. It must have been raining: my face was wet. Somewhere far away, muffled—screams. But no one heard, no one heard me screaming: save me from this—save me:

If only I had a mother—like the ancients did: my very own—that's it precisely—a mother. So that for her—I would not be the Builder of the *Integral*, and not the number D-503, and not a molecule of the United State, but a simple piece of humanity—a piece of her own self—trampled, crushed, cast out. . . And whether I was driving the nails in or they were being driven into me—perhaps it's one and the same—if only she could hear what no one else hears, if only her old-woman's lips, overgrown with wrinkles could—

Record 37
Synopsis: **Infusoria**
                   Doomsday
                   Her Room

Morning in the cafeteria—the neighbor on my left whispered fearfully to me:

"Go ahead and eat! People are looking at you!" With all my might—I smiled. And I felt as though it were some kind of crack on my face: I was smiling—the edges of the crack were creeping apart farther and farther—and it was becoming more and more painful for me...

Next—like this: I had barely managed to take a small cube on my fork when suddenly the fork shook in my hand and clattered against the plate—and the tables, the walls, the dishes, the air began to reverberate, and outside there was some kind of enormous, round iron rumbling reaching up to the sky—over the heads, over the houses—and then it died out far away like barely noticeable, minute ripples in the water.

I caught sight of faces that had faded and blanched in an instant, of mouths braked in mid-action, forks frozen in the air.

Then everything became confused, jumped from the centuries-old rails, everyone leaped up from their places (without having sung the Hymn)—every which way, out of rhythm, still chewing, pushing, grabbing on to one another: "What? What happened? What?" And—the chaotic fragments of the once orderly mighty Machine—all went spilling downstairs to the elevators—down the staircase—stairs—stamping feet—snatches of words—like the scraps of a letter ripped and swept in circles by the wind...

They were spewing out of all the neighboring buildings in the same way, and in a minute the avenue was like a drop of water under a microscope: the infusoria locked in the glassy-transparent drop were darting distractedly sideways, upwards, downwards.

"Aha," someone's triumphant voice—before me was the back of a head and a finger aimed at the sky—I remember quite distinctly the yellowish-pink finger nail and at the bottom of the nail—the white half-moon as though it had just crawled up from behind the horizon. And it was like a compass: a hundred eyes, following this finger, turned up toward the sky.

There, escaping from some kind of invisible pursuit, clouds were flitting past, crushing, leaping over one another—and there, too, decorated with the clouds, the dark aeros of the Guardians with the dangling black prosbosces of their tubes—and yet farther away—there, in the west, something resembling —

At first no one understood what it was—not even I understood, to whom (unfortunately) more was revealed than to all the others. It looked like an enormous swarm of black aeros: somewhere up at an incredible height—barely discernible swift dots. Closer and closer: from up above, hoarse, throaty drops—finally, the birds were over our heads. They filled the sky with sharp, black, piercing, diving triangles, they were beaten down by the windstorm, they settled on the cupolas, on the roof-tops, on pillars, on balconies.

"Aha-a," the triumphant back of a head turned—I saw him, that one with the beetle-brow. But now only some kind of classification label remained of the former person, somehow he had totally crawled out from under that eternal beetle-brow of his, and on his face—around the eyes, around the lips—rays had sprouted like fascicles of hair, he was smiling.

"You understand," through the whistling of the wind, of the wings, of the cawing,—he shouted to me.—"You understand: the Wall—they have blown up the Wall! Un-der-stand?"

Passing by, somewhere in the background, flitting figures—heads outstretched—were running quickly inside, into the buildings. In the middle of the sidewalk—a quick, and yet almost seemingly slow (from weight) avalanche of those who had been operated on, marching off there—to the west.

. . . The hairy fascicles of rays around the lips, the eyes. I seized him by the arm:

"Listen: where is she—where is I-330? There, behind, the Wall—or. . . I have to know,—you hear? Right this minute, I can't. . ."

"Here," he shouted at me drunkenly, cheerfully—strong, yellow teeth. . . "She is here, in the city, she has begun. Oho—we have begun!"

Who is this we? Who am I?

Around him—were about half a hundred exactly like him—ones who had crawled out from under their dark brows, loud, cheerful, strong-toothed people. Gulping the storm down with wide-open mouths, waving electrocutors (where had they gotten them from?) that looked so harmless and innocent,—they moved off in the same direction, to the west, following the ones who had been operated on, but in a flanking movement—along the parallel-running 48th avenue. . .

I stumbled against the tense cables woven by the wind and ran to her. What for? I don't know. I kept stumbling, empty streets, an alien, wild city, the incessant, triumphant din of birds, doomsday. Through the glass of the walls—in several buildings I saw (it's engraved in me): female and male numbers in shameless copulation—the blinds had not even been lowered, without any coupons, in broad daylight. . .

A building—her building. The perplexed door was wide open. Downstairs, at the controller's desk—empty. The lift was stuck in the middle of the shaft. Puffing, I ran up the endless staircase. The corridor. Quickly—like wheel-spokes—the numbers on the doors: 320, 326, 330. . . I-330, yes!

And through the glass door: everything was strewn about, confused, crumpled. A hastily overturned chair—face down, all four legs sticking up—like a dead cow. The bed—somehow absurdly, had been moved away from the wall, at an angle. On the floor—the strewn, trampled petals of pink coupons.

I bent over, picked one up, a second, a third: on all of them was D-503—! was on all of them—drops of me, melted, splashing over the brim. And this was all that remained...

Somehow or other it was impossible to leave them like that on the floor and to have everyone walking over them. I grabbed another fistful, laid them on the table, carefully smoothed them out, looked—and... began to laugh.

I did not know it earlier—but now I know, and you know it: laughter can be of different colors. It is merely the distant echo of the explosion inside you: perhaps—festive, red, blue, gold rockets, perhaps—scraps of a human body blown to bits... I caught a fleeting glimpse of a completely unfamiliar name on the coupons. I did not remember the number—only the letter: F. I swept all the coupons from the table onto the floor, stamped on them—on myself, with my heel—there, take that—and I left...

I was sitting in the corridor on the window-ledge opposite the door—I was still waiting for something, dully, interminably. On the left the flapping sound of steps. An old man: his face was like a punctured, empty bladder sagging in folds—and out of a puncture something transparent was still oozing, flowing slowly downwards. Slowly, hazily I understood: tears. And only when the old man was already far away—I gave a start and called out to him:

"Listen—listen, do you know: number I-330..." The old man turned around, waved his hand despairingly and hobbled off...

In the gloom I returned home, to my room. In the west the sky was twitching every second in a pale-blue convulsion—and there was a deep, muffled rumble coming from there. The roof-tops were strewn with black, smouldering brands: birds.

I lay down on the bed—and immediately sleep collapsed on me like a beast and smothered me...

Record 38
Synopsis: **(I Don't Know What Synopsis. Perhaps the Entire Synopsis Is Only: A Discarded Cigarette)**

I came to—a brilliant light, painful to look. I squinted with my eyes. In my head was some kind of caustic blue haze, everything was in a mist. And through the mist:

"But I didn't turn the light on—how did..."

I leaped up—at the desk, chin resting on her hand, I-330 looking at me with a mocking smile...

I am writing at that very same desk right now. These ten or fifteen minutes, cruelly coiled into the tautest spring, are already behind. But it seems to me that the door has only just closed behind her, and I could still catch up to her, grab her by the hand—and perhaps she would laugh and say...

I-330 was sitting at the desk. I dashed over to her: "Thou, thou! I was—I saw thy room—I thought thou—"

But half way I stumbled against the sharp, immovable lances of her eyelashes, I halted. I remembered: that was how she had looked at me then, in the *Integral*. And this very instant, in a single second, I would have to find a way of telling her everything—so that she would believe me—otherwise there would never be...

"Listen, I-330,—I must... I must tell you everything... No, no, in a minute—I'll just drink some water..."

It was dry in my mouth, as though it were all lined with blotting paper. I was trying to pour the water—and I could not: I set the glass on the table and took hold of the carafe with both hands.

Then I saw: the blue haze—it was from a cigarette.—She raised it to her lips, drew on it, greedily swallowed the smoke—the same as I had done with the water, and said:

"No need. Keep quiet. It doesn't matter—you see: I came anyway. There, downstairs—they're waiting for me. And do you want that these last minutes of ours together..."

She tossed the cigarette on the floor, leaned back over the arm of the chair (the button was there in the wall, and it was difficult to reach it)—and I remembered how the armchair rocked and two of its feet lifted from the floor. Then the blinds fell.

She came over, embraced me tightly. Her knees through the dress—a slow, tender, hot, poison that enveloped everything...

And suddenly... At times it happens: you have already plunged totally into a sweet and warm sleep—suddenly something stabs you, you shudder, and again your eyes are wide open... So it was then: on the floor in her room the trampled pink coupons and on one of them: the letter F- and some figures... Inside me they had contracted into a single clump and now I could not even say what kind of a feeling it was, but I clasped her so tightly that she cried out from pain...

Still one minute left—of those ten or fifteen, on the brilliantly-white pillow—a head tossed back with half-closed eyes; a sharp, sweet stripe of teeth. And all the while this was persistently, absurdly, agonizingly reminding me of something, about something it must not, about something now that was unnecessary.

And I kept squeezing her more tenderly, more cruelly—the blue marks from my fingers became darker. . .

She said (without opening her eyes—I noticed this): "They say thou were at the Benefactor's yesterday? Is it true?"

"Yes, it's true."

And then the eyes flew open—and I watched with pleasure how quickly her face turned pale, faded and disappeared: only the eyes.

I told her everything. And only—I don't know why. . . no, it's not true, I know—I kept silent only about one thing—about what He said at the very end, about the fact that they needed me only. . .

Gradually, like a photograph in developing fluid, her face emerged: the cheeks, the white stripe of teeth, the lips. She stood up, went up to the mirror in the wardrobe door.

Again my mouth was dry. I poured some water, but it was disgusting to drink—I set the glass on the table and asked:

"Is this why thou came—because thou had to find out?" From the mirror—the sharp, mocking triangle of her brows turned upwards, towards the temples. She turned around to say something to me, but said nothing.

No need. I know.

Say good-bye to her? I moved my—foreign—legs, bumped against the table,—it fell face down, dead, like there—in her room. Her lips were cold—at one time the floor had been that cold, right here, in my room beside the bed.

And when she had left—I sat down on the floor, bent over her discarded cigarette —

I can't write any more—I don't want to any more!

Record 39
Synopsis: The End

All of this was like the final grain of salt thrown into a saturated solution: quickly, bristling with needles, the crystals started to creep, hardening, congealing. And it was clear to me: everything had been decided—and tomorrow morning *I would do it*. It was the same thing as killing oneself—but, perhaps, only then would I be resurrected. Because after all only what has been killed can be resurrected.

In the west, the sky was twitching every second in a blue convulsion. My head was burning and pounding. I sat like that through the entire night and fell asleep only around seven o'clock in the morning, when the darkness had already begun to thin, grow green and the roof-tops, strewn with birds, became visible. . .

I awoke: already ten (apparently, there was no bell today). On the table—still from yesterday—stood the glass of water. I greedily emptied it in gulps and ran off: I had to do all of this quickly, as quickly as possible.

The sky was empty, azure, picked clean by the storm. Prickly angles of shadows, everything sharply cut out of the blue, autumn air—everything so delicate—one was afraid to touch it: it might shatter at any moment, disintegrate into a glassy dust. And inside me—such: I must not think, no need to think, no need to think, otherwise —

And I was not thinking, perhaps even was not seeing properly, but merely registering. There on the pavement—branches from somewhere, the leaves on them green, amber, berry-red. There, up above—birds and aeros criss-crossing, swooping. There—heads, mouths wide open, hands waving branches. Probably all of this was yelling, cawing, buzzing...

Then—empty streets, as though swept clean by some plague or other. I remember: I stumbled against something unbearably soft, yielding and yet immovable. I bent over: a corpse. He was lying on his back, the bent legs spread wide, like a woman. The face...

I recognized the thick, negroid lips that even now seemed still to be showering with laughter. With eyes squinting intensely, he was laughing in my face. In a second—I stepped over him and started to run—because I could no longer bear it, I had to do everything quickly, otherwise—I felt—I would break, collapse like an overloaded rail...

Fortunately—it was only about twenty steps to the sign—the golden letters *Bureau* of *Guardians*. I stopped on the threshold, swallowed some air, as much as I could—and went in.

Inside, in the corridor—like an endless chain, numbers were standing front to back, with sheets of paper, with thick notebooks in their hands. Slowly they moved forward a step or two at a time and again they would stop.

I dashed along the line, my head bobbing in all directions; I was clutching at their sleeves, I was begging them—like a sick man begs you to give him quickly anything that would sever everything at once with a second's sharp torment.

Some woman, tight-waisted with a belt over her unif, the two dorsal hemispheres bulging out distinctly, and all the while she was moving them from side to side as though her eyes were there. She snorted at me:

"He has a stomach ache! Take him to the toilet—over there, the second door on the right..."

And they laughed—at me: and this laughter made something rise in my throat and any moment now I would start to scream or... or...

Suddenly, somebody grabbed me by the elbow from behind. I turned around: transparent winged ears. However they were not pink as usual, but crimson: the adam's apple on his neck was bobbing up and down—any moment now it might tear through the thin slip-cover.

"Why are you here?" he asked, quickly drilling into me. I just seized hold of him:

"Quickly—to your office... I must tell everything—this very minute! It's good that it'll be precisely to you... It's terrible, perhaps, that it will be precisely to you, but it's good, it's good..."

He also knew *her*, and therefore it was all the more agonizing for me, but, perhaps, he too would shudder, when he heard, and then we would be doing the killing together, I would not be alone in that final second of mine...

The door slammed. I remember: down under the door some small piece of paper had got stuck and scraped against the floor when the door was being closed, but then, we were enveloped in some kind of special, airless silence as though by a bell glass. If he had said even a single word— no matter what—the most trifling word, I would have blurted out everything at once. But he was silent.

And so straining all over to the point where my ears started buzzing—I said (without looking):

"It seems to me—I always hated her, from the very beginning. I struggled... But yet—no, no, don't believe me: I could not and I did not want to be saved, I wanted to perish, but that she... And even right now— even right now, when I already know everything... Do you know, do you know that the Benefactor summoned me?"

"Yes, I know."

"But what He said to me... Try to understand—it is the same thing as though the floor were to be pulled out from under you at this very moment—and you, together with everything here on the table—the paper, the ink... the ink would splash out and everything would turn into an ink spot..."

"Go on, go on! And hurry. Others are waiting there." And then— stuttering and confused—everything that happened, everything that is recorded here. About my real self and my shaggy self, and what she had said that time about my hands—yes that was precisely where it had all begun—and how then I did not want to fulfill my duty and how I was deceiving myself, and how she had obtained false certificates, and how I grew rusty from day to day, and the corridors underground, and how there—beyond the Wall...

All of this—in clumsy lumps, scraps—I was stuttering, I couldn't find the words. The crooked, double-curved lips grinningly fed me the necessary words—I kept nodding thankfully: yes, yes... And then (what was happening?)—then he was already doing the speaking for me, and I was merely listening: "Yes, and then... That's precisely how it was, yes, yes!"

I felt: it was starting to grow cold, right here, around my collar, as though from ether, and I asked with effort:

"But how can it be—but there's nowhere you could have..."

A mocking smile on his face—silently—more and more crooked... And then:

"But you know—you wanted to conceal something from me, you've just listed all of those whom you noticed there on the other side of the Wall, but you forgot one of them. You say—no? But don't you remember that there, fleetingly, for a second—there you saw... me? Yes, yes: me."

A pause.

And suddenly—like lightning, from head to foot, it became shamelessly clear to me: he—he too was one of them... And all of myself, all my agonies, all of what I had brought here, exhausted and with my final strength, as a great feat—all of this was simply ridiculous, like the ancient tale about Abraham and Isaac. Abraham—all in a cold sweat—had already raised the knife above his son—above himself—and suddenly from above a voice: "Don't bother! I was just joking..."

Without tearing my eyes from that smile which kept growing more and more crooked, I leaned with my hands against the edge of the table, slowly, slowly pushed myself backwards together with the chair, then suddenly—I grabbed all of myself together—and out past the screams, the stairs, the mouths—headlong.

I don't remember how I came to be down below, in one of the public lavatories in a subway station. There, up above, everything was perishing, the greatest and most rational civilization in all of history was collapsing, while here—by virtue of someone's irony—everything remained in its former beautiful condition. And to think: all of this was doomed, all of this would be overgrown with grass, about all of this—there would only be *myths*...

I began to moan loudly. And at that very moment I felt—someone stroking me lovingly on the shoulder.

It was my neighbor occupying the seat on the left. The forehead—an enormous bald parabola, yellow, indecipherable lines of wrinkles on the forehead. And those lines were about me.

"I understand you, I understand completely," he said. "But still, calm yourself: no need for that. All of this will return, it will inevitably return. The only important thing is for everyone to learn about my discovery. You're the first one I'm telling about it: I have calculated that there is no infinity!"

I gave him a wild look.

"Yes, yes, I'm telling you: there is no infinity. If the world is infinite—then the average density of matter in it must be equal to zero. But since it is not zero—this we know—then, consequently, the universe is finite, it is of a spherical shape and the square of the universal radius, $y^2 =$ average density, multiplied by... All I have to do right now is calculate the numerical coefficient and then... You understand: everything is finite, everything is simple, everything is calculable; and then we shall be victorious in a philosophical way,—do you understand? But you, esteemed sir, are preventing me from completing the calculation, you are screaming..."

I don't know what I was more astounded by: his discovery or his steadfastness in that apocalyptic hour: in his hands (I only perceived that now) was a notebook and a logarithmic dial. And I understood: even if everything perished, my duty (before you, my unknown, beloved ones) was to leave you my records in a completed form.

I asked him for some paper—and thereupon I recorded these final lines...

I just wanted to put a period down—the way the ancients put a cross over the pits where they tossed the dead, but suddenly the pencil started to shake and fell out of my fingers...

"Listen," I tugged at my neighbor, "Just listen, I'm telling you! You must—you must answer me: and there where your finite universe comes to an end? What's there—further?"

He did not have time to answer; from up above—down the stairs—feet trampling——

Record 40
Synopsis: **Facts**
                 The Bell
                 I Am Certain

Day. Clear. Barometer 760.

Did I, D-503, actually write these two hundred and twenty pages? Did I at some time actually feel—or imagine that I felt this?

The handwriting is mine. And what follows is in the very same handwriting, but—fortunately, only the handwriting. No delirium at all, no absurd metaphors, no feelings: only facts. Because I am healthy, I am completely, absolutely healthy. I am smiling—I cannot do other than smile: they have pulled some kind of splinter out of my head, in my head it is light, empty. Rather: not empty, but there is nothing extraneous to prevent smiling (a smile—is the normal state of a normal person).

The facts are these. That evening my neighbor, who had discovered the finiteness of the universe, I, and everyone who was with us, were arrested for not having the Certificate of Operation and we were led off to the nearest auditorium (the number of the auditorium is for some reason familiar: 112). Here we were tied to the tables and subjected to the Great Operation.

The following day, I, D-503, appeared before the Benefactor and related to Him everything that was known to me about the enemies of happiness. How could this have seemed difficult to me earlier? Incomprehensible. The sole explanation: my former illness (a soul).

In the evening of that same day—at the same table with Him, the

Benefactor—I was sitting (for the first time) in the famous Gas Room. They brought that woman. In my presence she was supposed to give her testimony. This woman remained stubbornly silent and smiling. I noticed that she had sharp and very white teeth and that this was beautiful.

Then she was put under the Gas Bell. Her face became very white, and since her eyes were dark and large—then this was very beautiful. When they started to pump out the air—she flung back her head, half-closed her eyes, lips compressed—this reminded me of something. She was looking at me, gripping the arms of the chair strongly—she looked until her eyes closed completely. Then she was dragged out, quickly revived with electrodes and once again seated under the Gas Bell. This was repeated three times—and still she did not say a single word. The others who had been brought together with this woman, proved to be more honest: many of them began to talk the very first time. Tomorrow they will all ascend the steps of the Benefactor's Machine.

No postponement is possible—because in the western quarters—there is still chaos, tumult, corpses, beasts and—unfortunately—a significant quantity of numbers who have betrayed reason.

But on the transverse-running 40th avenue they have succeeded in constructing a temporary wall out of high-voltage waves. And I am hoping—we will be victorious. More than that: I am certain—we will be victorious. Because reason must be victorious.

Translated by Samuel Cioran   *1920*

The Serapion Brothers.

VENIAMIN KAVERIN

Veniamin Kaverin (Zilberg, 1902-) was born in Pskov. While at school in Petrograd, he studied with Zamyatin and became a member of the Serapion Brothers. He managed to produce works of some merit throughout his career, but there is little doubt that his best work was done during the 1920s, culminating in his major novel, *Artist Unknown.* Kaverin continued to be a liberal force in Soviet literary politics throughout his life.

"Shields and Candles" is from the 1923 collection *Masters and Apprentices,* and is very representative of the "western" group within the Serapions. Heavily influenced by E. T. A. Hoffmann, Poe, and western adventure novels, this work demonstrates the concern with formal techniques and the inclination toward the grotesque and the mysterious typical of early Kaverin.

SHIELDS AND CANDLES

> The game is not worth the candle.
>
> *Famous saying.*

I

All three preserved silence or spoke briefly.

The cobbler's workroom—small, square, with a little oblong window looking out on a yard—was lit by a candle. The candle burned and crackled. Shadows crept behind it, and in its light three faces appeared in sharp outline: the first with a low brow and a heavy chin, the second redbearded and blunt, and the third the face of Birheim the cobbler.

They were playing.

The jack of diamonds was expending his worthless fate in an unequal squabble with the queen and king of clubs. The hearts calmly followed the course of the battle.

"There's the shadow," said Birheim. "There's the shadow of your head, carpenter."

The carpenter glanced at the cards, smiled in his beard and spoke:

"Keep your mind on the game, Birheim."

"There is no sorrow in the world," said Birheim again. "Carpenter, do you agree with me? There is no sorrow in the world."

"Maybe so," answered the carpenter. "I'm discarding the jack of spades, what do you say to that?"

And so the game continued. But late that night, after a fixed period of time had elapsed, Birheim arose, removed the decree from the table drawer and said:

"Lay down your cards."

And he threw his own down on the table.

The mute lowered his hand and carefully mixed up his cards, but the carpenter only glanced at Birheim.

"Silence," repeated Birheim. Then he placed a tabouret on the table and sat down on it, stretching out his long and bony legs.

The mute removed the snuff from the candle, walked off and leaned against the wall, folding his arms.

Birheim read:

> The decree of Landsknecht, the ancient game invented in Germany.
>
> We, the game of Landsknecht, bearing in mind both honor and faith, hereby inform our faithful servants: preserve our merits.
>
> By edict of the king and the heretics, We, Landsknecht, are henceforth outlawed on penalty of death. Our servants are beset by unexampled persecutions. Many have paid with their lives for opposing this edict.
>
> Yielding to the protracted prayers of Our faithful subjects and wishing to safeguard the life of Our people, We direct:
>
> To change the symbols and names of the suits in the deck: hearts are shields, diamonds—banners, spades—lances, and clubs— swords.

"So then," said Birheim, "listen, mute and carpenter."

"Someone's knocking," answered the carpenter. "Birheim, listen."

> In order that the new suits be fixed in the hearts of Our subjects, We deem it appropriate to institute and effect a game on the night of Saturday, month of August, year of 17--, using the new suits. But since the masters, as yet unaware of Our edict, were unable to print the aforesaid, the carpenter, mute and Birheim will serve as the suits for Our game.

"You are lances," said Birheim to the carpenter, "I am swords and the mute is banners, the merry suit."

"Listen," said the carpenter, "someone's knocking. Do you hear it? Or are you deaf, Birheim?"

"Someone's knocking," answered Birheim, "but in the edict there is no fourth person for hearts. The game cannot take place; there are only three of us, carpenter."

He continued reading:

At the conclusion of the game to notify us how the game was effected and in what way it ended.

Proclaimed in the year 17--, month of August, on the 7th day.

Signed on the original in His Majesty's own hand:

Landsknecht

"Birheim, you have been mad from the day of your birth," laughed the carpenter. "But I will obey the edict."

"Shut up," answered Birheim, "we lack the fourth suit."

"Night will pass quickly and we will fail to enact the king's edict."

The mute mumbled indistinctly. His eyes blazed, while he himself, firmly clasping both elbows, shook from the terrible strain.

"An awl will serve as a sword," said Birheim, "needles as lances, scraps of leather as banners. But where will we get the shields?"

"When did you write that decree?" asked the carpenter. "After all, I spent the whole day with you."

The skin on Birheim's forehead gathered into creases and his eyebrows rose up toward his knotted hair.

"Someone's knocking," said the carpenter again, "I'll open the door."

He took a knife from the table and held it near the candle.

The light slid along the sparkling blade, formed a point and disappeared behind the folds of clothing.

The carpenter went to the door.

"Who knocks?" he asked, raising his hand to the bolt.

No one answered.

"Silence," said Birheim and tossed back his head, baring to the light a chin overgrown with stiff hairs.

The carpenter ran the tip of his finger along the blade and began to unfasten the bolt. The door flung open.

The flame of the candle tossed to the left, to the right, and again to the left.

The wind coursed through the room, and the mute, freeing his firmly clinched arms, breathed deeply and noisily.

A man stepped slowly through the door. The carpenter closed it and refastened the bolt.

"Who here is Birheim the cobbler?" asked the man. "The Jew Birheim, damn his soul!"

"His Majesty, the King," announced Birheim. "Landsknecht, I see. The fourth suit is shields."

He pursed his lips slyly and raised a finger to his brow.

"The Jew Birheim," repeated the soldier, sitting down at the table. "Hell's spawn. Are you Birheim, you with the red beard?"

The carpenter remained silent.

"We will enact the king's edict," screamed Birheim, and laughed:

"Four suits: swords, lances, banners, shields—and the heretics will not touch us."

"He abducted my sister," said the soldier wearily. "Which one of you is Birheim, speak up."

The mute walked up close to him and raised his hands to the level of his shoulders. But then as if fearing something, he pressed his lips tightly and hurried back.

"Sister?" said Birheim, trying to recollect. "Your sister, Landsknecht? My memory has been rather vague of late."

The Jew Birheim abducted her," repeated the soldier. "And stop calling me by that blasted name. I must kill him and return my sister to our home. Our home is burned down and destroyed."

"The devils dance on its ruins," said the carpenter sympathetically. "You are too late to return."

"Night fell long ago," observed Birheim. "Time to start the game."

His hands flicked away the cards and they landed on the table in a disordered heap.

The mute removed a bundle of candles from his pocket and began to light them slowly, one by one.

The room splintered into sharp angles under Birheim's unwavering gaze.

He lifted his eyelids with his fingers and looked around smiling: the window grating had weaved into iron fingers and the gloomy night had fused into one mass behind the window.

"Where is my sister?" repeated the soldier. "I cannot find her anywhere."

"Birheim is anxious," said Birheim, placing his hand over his heart. "It is time to begin the game."

"Let us begin," prompted the carpenter, and the mute nodded in approval.

And they began.

II

"May I have your attention," said Birheim, raising his hand. "May I have your attention. Ching-Tsze-Tung says that our game was created in 1120 and that its origin is divine."

"I do not remember," answered the carpenter, "are the diamonds banners, or the clubs? The decree was vague on that point. And if I am lances, why don't you give me a shoe needle?"

"I will give you a needle," said Birheim, "and the mute a scrap of leather."

He separated the four suits from a deck of colored cards and threw one suit before each player. The black fell to the carpenter and Birheim; the mute and the soldier got red.

"Landsknecht, Your Majesty," said Birheim, "pick up your cards, you are delaying the game."

The soldier stood up and rattled his weapons. Instantly the mute's eyes blackened and his eyelids slightly flared. The carpenter fingered the knife in his pocket.

"Just a minute," said the soldier hoarsely and wearily, "I do not wish anyone ill. The Jew Birheim abducted my sister. I wish only to kill him. Nothing more."

"Fine," replied Birheim, "but you are delaying the game. Please begin, Your Majesty."

The soldier sat down and moved the cards to the center of the table.

The jack of lances and the ten and ace of banners were dealt Birheim.

He threw down the ace and gathered in the low cards. The soldier calmly discarded the queen of shields.

Landsknecht, the king of banners, was still far away.

"Your beret is crumpled," said the queen of clubs to the jack, "and your face reveals expectation."

"Silence," rustled the jack, bending over in the hands of the soldier. "The people are in a peculiar mood today. The hands of that one sitting at the end of the table are trembling."

"Trembling?" repeated the queen derisively. "They are exchanging frayed pieces of paper, and the hands of the one who is losing them are beginning to tremble."

"The hands of the hook-nosed man are trembling," answered the jack. "But don't you love it when they play with those round pieces of yellow and white? They ring gloriously when they fall and it's so pleasant to cover them with a jack's clothing."

"Their minutes are centuries to us," rustled the king of spades. "The senate must be convened; we will perish this night."

"That cannot be done until a new game begins," responded the jack. "Your Majesty, we will take every measure to safeguard your precious life. Take care, Your Majesty, not to scratch the dotted line on the uneven surface of the table."

"Seven years ago you left her a marvelous maiden," said Birheim. "But now you have not found her and you have not even found your own home."

"Home is burned down," answered the soldier. "Enough said about that. I recall with perfect clarity that her tresses were fair."

"The sister of His Majesty, King Landsknecht, cannot disappear without a trace," said Birheim again. "You need only intensify your search and you will find her. But you have forgotten her face."

"Birheim killed the maiden," said the carpenter, beginning to tremble, but the mute squeezed his arm firmly and he fell silent.

"In the course of seven years I have forgotten her face," said the soldier. "Nothing wrong with that. But why do you keep calling me by the name of a king?"

And he threw down the ace of shields. The carpenter and mute—low cards, Birheim—jack of banners.

The first hand was coming to an end. The candles had burned down half-way and long streams of bright wax had poured down from the flames.

Landsknecht, the king of banners, a fair-haired man in a blue beret with a sceptre in his hands, lay on top of the deck.

The insignia of the game, the sign of Landsknecht, had been cut by Birheim into blue ribbon which was strung across his shoulder.

He fell to the soldier, who noisily pushed away the tabouret and stood up.

"Landsknecht?" said Birheim, glancing at the soldier's cards. "His Majesty, the King. Just look, Carpenter, how pale his face is."

"Noble senate and loyal subjects," said the soldier, standing up to full height and raising his hand, "we have summoned you here today in order to discuss in the most sagacious manner the many difficulties which we have encountered at the very source of our lofty responsibilities."

"Madness, madness," screamed the carpenter, covering his face with his hands. "Birheim killed the maiden. Why play on any further?"

The soldier rose up from behind the table and waved his hands furiously.

"Play!"

They played.

III

"In the name of our King Landsknecht," announced the king of clubs, when all the kings had gathered in the center of the deck, "I declare this session of the senate open. The following questions require deliberation: First, an attack on His Imperial Majesty by those persons commonly termed people."

All present started and reached for their swords.

"Second," continued the king of clubs, "the replacement of our sacred suits by others. And third, the threat to the whole happy family of our subjects presented by the distressing condition of those persons who direct our fate."

"People are our fate," grumbled the king of spades with contempt, "and we are the fate of people. Who can make sense out of it?"

"I request a guard at the doors of the senate," he said loudly. "A crowd is rumbling at the windows. The fires on the squares have gone out."

"As regards the first question, it behooves me to state the following," said the third king, raising his sceptre: "From whom came the information of the assassination attempt? In my domain all is quiet."

"The information came to us from the province of diamonds," answered the king of clubs. "During the last hand the mood of the people became unusually alarming."

"I have every basis," declared the king of hearts, arising from his place and holding high his sceptre, "to confirm the aforesaid information. Our firm decision, taken in a recent session of the senate...."

"I beg your forgiveness, Your Majesty," interrupted the king of clubs, "the guard has snapped to attention. It appears that the king is approaching the senate chamber."

The doors flung open and Landsknecht entered, jangling his weapons. His face twitched with a virulent spasm, his lips trembled.

"Who among you is Birheim the cobbler?" he screamed, going up to the table and casting his weary eyes about. "Home is burned down. My sister has vanished."

The kings glanced around in confusion.

"Your Majesty is ill," prompted the king of clubs, bowing low and blanching, "the events of recent days have taken a heavy toll on Your Majesty's health."

"Nonsense," answered King Landsknecht, breathing heavily and attempting to draw his sword, "disloyalty pursues me, death snaps at my heels."

"He's falling, my God, he's falling," screamed the king of clubs, extending his arms.

Night passed and the quick rays of dawn glimmered in a chink of the window.

"It seems to me," said the soldier, after the second hand had ended, "that games of chance were outlawed by an edict of the king. I will play no more."

"One more hand," answered Birheim. "Landsknecht, pick up your cards, we will continue the game."

"No," said the soldier again. "I will play no more. Night has passed. I came here to kill Birheim.

"You will kill him at the end of the game," insisted Birheim. "I beg you to pick up your cards."

"Nonsense," said the soldier, arising. "You see that morning has come, it is time to snuff the candles."

The mute pushed away the tabouret and stood up. Then he began to snuff the candles.

"He is executing the king's order," laughed the carpenter. "His

Majesty gives orders."

"I will not play," repeated the soldier, breathing heavily and drawing the shiny steel of a cutlass from its scabbard. "You have a hooked nose. Are you Birheim, tell the truth?"

"Indeed I am," said Birheim, "you are not mistaken. But look at your shadow. Does it not seem to be falling?"

All the candles but one had gone out. And this last one rested in the hands of the mute.

He walked slowly from one man to the next. Coming up to Birheim, he stopped and peered into his eyes.

"The maiden was killed by me," said Birheim. "Night has passed, the candles have gone out, it is time to end the game."

And all three threw themselves on the soldier. He tried to lean forward and swing his cutlass but suddenly fell and lay still.

"We shall continue the game without the fourth suit," said Birheim. "We shall enact the king's edict."

And he wrappd a white rag around the teeth marks on his hand and outlined the soldier's profile with an awl on the edge of the table.

Translated by Gary Kern   *January 1922*

Vsevolod Ivanov.

VSEVOLOD IVANOV

Vsevolod Ivanov (1895-1963) was born in the Semipalatinsk region of Siberia, the setting of the majority of his prose works. The son of a drunken schoolteacher, Ivanov at the age of 15 ran away to join the circus, an experience that forms the background of his autobiographical novel, *The Adventures of a Fakir* (1934-35). During the Civil War he fought in the Red Guard against the Czechs, in the White Army against the Reds and, lastly, after he had renounced his White sympathies when threatened with execution, he fought in the Red Army in Siberia.

Ivanov made his literary debut in 1915. In 1921 he joined both the Serapion Brotherhood and the group of proletarian writers known as the Cosmists—an action characteristic of Ivanov's mixed allegiances during this period. Ivanov's *Partisans* appeared in the first issue of Voronsky's new journal *Red Virgin Soil* (1921). The publication was mutually beneficial for contributor and journal, since both were acknowledged as forces to be reckoned with. Ivanov's best-known work, *Armored Train 14-69,* was published the following year and to this day remains one of the classic tales of the Civil War. Though Ivanov continued to write and publish for the remainder of his long career, all of his most influential works were written by the end of the 1920s. The novels *U* and *Uzhginsky Kremlin* were not published until the 1980s.

Armored Train was adapted for the stage by the Moscow Art Theater in 1927. Ivanov, in an attempt to tone down the impressionism of the narrative and make it more consonant with the ever-changing political climate, reworked the novel a number of times. (The translation here is from the original, journal publication of the work.) *Armored Train* exhibits some characteristics of the ornamentalism of the 1920s, most notably with its incorporation of Siberian regionalisms, but never at the expense of plot and action which are primary in Ivanov's tale.

ARMORED TRAIN 14-69

Chapter One

I

Armored train No. 14-69, "Polar," was guarding the railroad line against the partisans.

The remnants of Kolchak's[1] army were retreating from Lake Baikal: into Manchuria, along the Amur River toward Vladivostok.

Captain Nezelasov, commander of the armored train, was sitting in his compartment of the railroad car smoking one Manchurian cigarette after another, flicking his ashes into the split-open stomach of a cast-iron Buddha.

Captain Nezelasov said, "We're oozing out...like pus from a wound...to the outskirts, eh? And after that into the sea, right?"

With his head tilted, Ensign Obab examined Nezelasov's distorted face and answered slowly, "You need medical help."

Ensign Obab was one of the brown-nose volunteers from Kolchak's army and he would say, "He needs medical help," about almost all the regular officers.

He respected Captain Nezelasov, and therefore he repeated, "Without medical help you're going to be bad off."

Nezelasov was wide, but flat, like a piece of paper: from the side—a piece of thread, from the front—a mile wide. The captain hastily pulled out a new cigarette and answered, "You're riveted up tight, Obab!.. Nothing gets through to you!.."

And quickly flicking off his ashes he began to speak shrilly, "What would it take to get through to you even just a little!.. It's misery, Obab, misery! Our motherland...has tossed us out! We all thought—we were necessary, very necessary, desperately necessary, and suddenly we got fired!... And not even fired, but we got the axe... the axe!.. the axe!.."

And the captain, coughing and sputtering spit and smoke, raised his voice, "Oh careless and stupid slaves!.. Stupid!.."

· Obab extended his long arm toward the captain, who was leaning over. As if supporting a falling tree he said with an effort, "The bastards are rebelling. They should be shot. And the dumber ones—should be flogged!"

"That's not the way, Obab, it's not the way!"

"It's a sickness."

"My insides have dried up...vodka doesn't go down, it doesn't!..

From tobacco—scum and stink. . . My head feels like that of a setting hen, one who's sitting on 300 eggs!. . She's hatching them. Ah!. . Warmth, steam. . . Something warm and slimy is swarming around, I'm afraid. . . it's going to crawl out. I must overcome something, but what I don't know, and I can't."

"You need a woman. Has it been a long time since you've had a woman?"

Obab looked dully at the captain. He repeated, "You need a woman without fail. With such work—once a month. I'm healthy—every two weeks. Better than quinine."

"Maybe, maybe. . . I'll try, why shouldn't I give it a try?"

"You can get one fast, there's a lot of refugees here. . . Real flowers!" Nezelasov raised the window.

It began to smell of coal and hot earth. The station, crammed full of people, was sweating like a jar of worms. Its walls glistened damply, the windows were wide open, a small bell was near the doors.

People bore the mark of flight.

A clean teacher resembling a steel pen was walking along, but a dirty rag fluttered on his shoulder. There were uncombed young women with one cheek wrinkled and red; the pillows must be hard, or perhaps there weren't any pillows—just a bag under the head.

"People are getting worse," thought Obab. He felt like getting married. . . He spit into his handkerchief and said, "Nonsense."

Refugees always examined the steel armor of the train with a bit of embarrassment and it seemed to Nezelasov that they were examining him naked. Naked, Nezelasov was dried up, bony, and resembled a crumpled can: angles and smooth gray skin.

He looked the car over and said to Obab, "Give orders to take on water. . .without fail, immediately. We'll take off in the evening."

"In sight? Again?"

"Who?"

"The partisans?"

Obab slapped his thighs with his arms, long and even like a rope, "I like it!"

Noticing the mellow pupil of Nezelasov's eye upon himself, the ensign said, "But as for deaths! Don't kill them. Just so the body moves around. Be calm, as long as their meat looks rusty. . ."

Obab smiled constrainedly. He was narrow-eyed, with prominent cheekbones similar to pieces of zwieback. His sigh was slow—like that of a peasant.

Closing his dreary eyelids, Nezelasov hurriedly asked, "Ensign, who is our immediate commander?"

"General Smirnov."

"Where is he?"

"The partisans have hanged him."

"That means the next in command is our immediate commander?"

"Yes."

"Who?"

"Lieutenant General Sakharov."

"And where is he?"

"I don't know."

"Where's the commander of the army?"

"I don't know."

The captain stepped over to the window. He quietly rapped on the glass. "Who are we to obey, ensign? What are we waiting for?"

Obab looked at the cast-iron Buddha, tried to catch some thought in his head, but missed. "I don't know. It's not my duty to think."

And Obab left, his riding breeches flapping like a goose with wings not yet grown out.

II

A scrawny-looking soldier in light blue French puttees, and wearing large boots, holding onto a dagger with his left hand, hastily saluted the captain who had just left his car.

Nezelasov didn't feel like walking along the train platform. Skirting the steelplated cars of the train, he started walking among the boxcars of the evacuated refugees.

"Unnecessary Russia," he thought with shame and blushed.

"Well, so you are in this Russia too!"

A woman with cheeks painted red and a fat rear that looked like she had two sacks under her skirt triggered Obab's suggestion in his head.

"Fool!" the captain said loudly.

The woman looked around. She had sad dimmed eyes under a small deeply wrinkled forehead.

Nezelasov turned away.

The boxcars were covered with boards which had grown brown. Faded moss stuck out from the grooves. Doors with straps on them instead of handles were banging. Meat, birds, and fish in woven twine sacks were hanging on nails on the sides of the dirty doors.

Pine branches were hung over some doors, and from these cars a young feminine voice could be heard.

From the wagons came the smell of sick sweat and diapers, and the trampled excrement beside the wagons smelled heavily of ammonia.

The feeling of shame and of distant anger which was hiding somewhere deep in his legs did not leave him.

A straightbacked old man, wearily lifting a heavy axe, was cutting a half-rotten railroad tie.

"Are you from far away?" asked Nezelasov.

"From Syzran," the old man answered.

"Where are you going?"

He dropped his axe. Shuffling his bare foot with gray cracked nails, he answered dejectedly, "Wherever they take me."

His Adam's apple was large, about the size of a child's fist. It was covered with flabby wrinkles which separated when he talked and exposed clean white strips of skin.

"It's obvious...he rarely has a chance to talk," thought Nezelasov.

"I have land there in Syzran," uttered the old man tenderly, "The 'most best' type of black soil. It's not land, but real gold—you can mint coins with it!.. And now, just imagine I've given it up."

"Are you sorry?"

"Certainly I am. But I left it. Now I'll have to go back."

"It's a long way to go back...very long..."

"That's what I say—I might die along the way."

"Don't you like it here?"

"They're not our people here. Our people are always tender, but here they don't even know how to talk. The Chinese, well they don't even understand Russian. And God only knows how they live! They live falsely. If I get wormy here, I'll go back. I'll give up everything and go back. The Bolsheviks are people too, aren't they?"

"I don't know," answered the captain, walking further along.

III

In the evening the station was covered with smoke.

A forest was burning.

The smoke was light and warm.

A bluish foam enveloped the brick buildings of the station, the pumphouse which looked like a clay mug,the Chinese huts, and the yellow fields of sorghum. People immediately turned pale.

Ensign Obab was laughing, "Ventriloquists!.."

And as if catching the laughter, his long arms fluttered greedily in the air.

A consumptive, sallow-complexioned refugee woman in a chestnut-colored mantle belted up with a piece of twine used to tie up sugar was running around the station in small steps and saying in a whisper, "The partisans...the partisans...they've set fire to the taiga...and they're shooting people..."

She was seen at once in all twelve trains. Her velvet mantle became covered with ashes; her shallow temples began to sweat. Everyone felt a dull languor, similar to hunger.

The superintendent of the station—the soldiers called him "four-storied"—huge-headed, with a gray transparent moustache like icicles, was calming people down, "Observe mental chastity. Don't get excited!"

"Chita has been taken."

"Nothing of the sort! Your ears are much too big. We still have communications with Chita. Just now they were looking for General Knox's nurse by telegraph!"

And disrespectfully chuckling in his throat, he said clearly "General Knox has lost his nurse. He's looking for her. They've promised a reward. A diplomatic nurse, devil take it, and suddenly some partisan will rape her."

A young curlyhaired blond fellow, who looked like a blooming cherry tree, pasted posters and war communiques from headquarters onto the cars of the train. And, although nobody knew where headquarters was and who was fighting with the Bolsheviks,they all perked up.

Warm streams of water started hurriedly flowing onto the earth. Thunder struck. The taiga started to howl.

The smoke went away. But when the downpour stopped and a rainbow rose into the sky, clouds of smoke again descended and again it became hot and difficult to breathe. The sticky mud glued people's feet to the earth.

The damp pastures smelled, and the moist sorghum stalks behind the Chinese huts rustled with a soft resonance.

All of a sudden two Cossacks brought the corpse of a sergeant-major onto the platform from behind the pumphouse. The forehead of the sergeant-major was smashed, and the grey matter of his brain jiggled like jello on his nose and on his reddish moustache, which was covered with dark red clots of coagulated blood.

"The partisans got him..." whispered the refugee woman in the mantle belted with twine.

In the brown cars of the trains people began stirring and whispering, "The partisans...the partisans..."

Captain Nezelasov walked through his train.

The refugee woman wearing the chestnut-colored mantle was standing by the stairwell of one car and hastily asking the soldiers, "Your train won't leave us here, will it?"

"Don't interfere," Nezelasov said to her, and suddenly he started to hate this thin-nosed woman. "No talking is allowed."

"But they'll butcher us one by one, captain. You know..."

Captain Nezelasov slammed the door and shouted, "Go to hell! To hell. To hell!.." he shouted shrilly, couching his orders in four-letter words.

Somewhere inside there grew the desire to see, to feel with one's own hands the anxiety which was crossing over to the armored train No. 14-69 from the trains of the refugees.

Captain Nezelasov ran around inside the train waving his revolver threateningly, and he wanted to shout still louder, so that his shout would tear through the walls of the cars insulated with felt and plated with steel. More than this he didn't understand why he needed to shout.

Dirty soldiers stuck out their heads, and let the icy air freeze their four-cornered faces. Unnecessary rags of clothing made it difficult for them to move about the steel artillery.

Ensign Obab quickly and quietly followed Nezelasov.

The bumpers clanked. The conductor gave an incomprehensibly short whistle. An iron bucket on the bench began to rattle.

Bending the rails to the earth and scattering behind stations, cabins of switchmen, the smoke-covered forest, and the granites of mountains, the heavy steel box-like cars, which carried hundreds of human bodies filled with anguish and anger, were flooded with a warm and damp wind, were falling but couldn't fall, were flying into the darkness.

IV

At this time Chinaman Sin-Bin-U was lying on the grass in the shade of a cork tree, and his slanted eyes closed, was singing about how the Red Dragon attacked the girl Chen-Hua.

The girl's face was the color of a ginseng root, and her food was *u-vej-tsy*, cock's combs; *ma-zhu*, mushrooms the size of the pupil of an eye; *chzhen-tszaj-tsaj*. There was a lot of this, and all of it was very tasty.

But the Red Dragon took the gates of life from Chen-Hua and then the rebellious Russian was born.

The partisans were sitting a short distance away, and Pentefly Znobov was shouting, joyously letting words of unshakable faith break across his teeth which were jumping up and down. "They're on the run, brothers, on the run. We've got to the quick of them, they're hitting the ground, fluttering. But our job is not to fall asleep, and the city, o-oh. . .is it strong. It'll take everything!"

It smelled of rocks and the sea. Dry grasses rustled on the sand.

Chapter Two

I

For the sixth day the body felt the hot stone, the trees which were languishing in the oppressive heat, the crackling grass which was ready to be made into hay, and the limpid wind.

And their bodies were like the granite of the hills, like the trees, like the grass; hot and dry they rolled along the narrowly dug-out mountain paths.

The smalls of their backs hurt sharply from the guns which were pressing on their shoulders.

Their legs ached, as if put into very cold water, and their heads were like the inside of a dead reed—empty, juiceless.

This was the sixth day that the partisans had been heading for the mountains.

Cossack mounted patrols attacked the partisan patrols now and then. At such times shots which sounded like bursting bean pods were heard.

And behind them—along the railroad line—and deeper: in the fields and forests—the Cossacks, Czechs, Japanese and still other people of unknown lands were burning peasant villages and overrunning pastures.

On the sixth day, with short rest breaks similar to prayer breaks, two hundred partisans protecting the string of carts which was travelling ahead with families and utensils, were walking wearily along the black paths. They were bored by the road, and often turning off the paths among the stones and breaking off branches, they would walk straight ahead toward mountains which resembled huge ant hills.

II

The Chinaman, Sin-Bin-U, pressing himself flat against the cliff, let the detachment pass him and said to every man maliciously, "You should have beat the hell out of the Japs... o-oh, how you should have!"

And spreading his arms widely, he showed how they should have beat the Japanese.

Vershinin stopped and said to Vaska Okorok, "A Jap is worse than a tiger for us. Before devouring a Chink the tiger will pull off his clothes, let him air out. But a Jap won't stop to take stock—he'll devour you boots and all."

The Chinaman liked this conversation about himself and started walking beside Vershinin and the others.

Nikita Vershinin, chairman of the partisan revolutionary staff, was walking with Vaska Okorok, the paymaster, at the rear of the detachment. His wide—like a flour sack—dark blue velveteen *sharovary*[2] fit tightly around his knees, which were as large as horses' hooves. His face, with wind-burned spots from the sea, had a frown on it.

Looking at Vershinin's beard wearily and dreamily, Vaska Okorok spoke in a drawl, as if talking about a rest, "Nikita Egorich, they're going to build the Tower of Babel in Russia for sure. And for sure they're going to drive us away, just as a hawk does its chicks! So that we won't recognize each other. I'll tell you this: Nikita Egorich, you want some vodka? And you, foreigner, you can act like a Jap! And this Sin-Bin-U—sock him in the nose, and he'll start singing Russian. Eh?.."

Vaska used to work in mines and always talked as though he had hit upon a vein of ore and trusted neither himself nor others. His head is covered with curly hair; he shakes it lazily. It looks just like it's melting in the warm, tired wind which is blowing from the sea, in the hot, anguish-filled odor of the earth and trees.

Vershinin threw his rifle over his right shoulder and answered, "What makes you want to, Vaska? Haven't we suffered enough?"

Quickly overcoming his weariness, Okorok suddenly burst into laughter, "So you don't like it!"

"You're ruining your own property. Your pasture, let's say, your wheat, your houses. You won't get by with this. You're going to have to pay for it, for sure."

"We've got to get the Japs the hell out of here, Nikita Egorich. Stuff their bellies with earth—and into the sea."

"The Japs are short people, and what can you ask from a short guy? They're cheap people. It's something like a *papirosa*³—on the one hand it's something to smoke, it gives off smoke, but on the other hand—it's nothing. But a pipe now, that's a different story."

With soft weary snores bubbling streams of people, cattle, carts, and iron were pouring into the channels of paths leading into the forest and hills. In the rocks above cedars loomed gloomily. The heat was drying out their hearts like broken branches; their feet, as if walking through a fire, could not find a place to rest.

Again shots resounded behind them.

Several partisans dropped behind the detachment and prepared to return fire.

Okorok smiled widely, "Today I rode with the carts. That was fun!.."

"Well?"

"A rooster was crowing. They're taking their chickens and mules to the hills. I say to them, 'Eat 'em up. You'll have to get rid of them anyhow.'"

"'Impossible,' they say, 'Man can't live without animals. Without animals he loses everything there is to worry about. All the weight from his soul...'."

Sin-Bin-U said loudly, "The Cossacks are bad! The Japs are scoundlels, they lape women... That's not good. The Cossacks are bad! The 'Russ' are good..."

Tightening his lips, he flung a gob of spit through his teeth; his face, the color of the sand of gold mines, with little narrow slits like melon seeds for eyes, broke into a joyful smile, "It's good!.."

As a sign of approval Sin-Bin-U stuck up his thumb.

But, as usual, he didn't hear the laughter of the partisans and said sadly, "It's bad..."

And he looked back wistfully.

The partisans, like a herd of wild boar that have abandoned their lair because of a forest fire, were rushing into the mountains in confusion and anger.

And the mother earth clasped her sons with delight—it was difficult to walk. The horses would look back and neigh lightly, with a crying sound. The dogs had forgotten how to bark and ran along silently. The last dust and the last tar of the homeland was flying off the wheels.

To the right, in the ravines, loomed an oak tree; an ash tree shone palely.

To the left—it was impossible to get away from it—the calm, dark green sea—redolent of sand and waterplants.

The forest was like the sea, and the sea like the forest, only the forest was a bit darker, almost dark blue. The partisans looked steadily westward, and in the west the rose-colored granites of the mountains gleamed like gold; and the peasants let their eyes drift there through the clear spaces between the trees; and then they sighed, and from these sighs the horses of the train moved their ears and twitched their bodies, as if sensing wolves.

But it seemed to Sin-Bin-U that the men wanted to see something else, something which they expected behind the rose-colored granites in the west.

The Chinaman felt like singing.

III

Nikita Vershinin was a fisherman of many generations.

Without the sea he was unhappy—for him life was the water, and his five fingers—the small holes of a net: they would always catch something.

They caught a woman, fat and soft, like a burbot. She bore him five children—one each year, five autumns—when the herring were running upstream, and perhaps because of this his children grew up blond-headed—silvery-scaled.

On fishing trips he was always lucky, and the saying about him, "Vershinin's luck," travelled throughout the whole *okrug,*[4] and when his *volost*[5] decided to go against the Japanese and Semyonov's men—Nikita Egorich was elected head of the revolutionary staff.

The carts left from the *volost* were now being used to take the children and their mothers into the mountains. Now they had to put their lives together anew—as their great-grandfathers had put together their huts when they arrived here (God only knows when) in this wild region from Perm.

A lot of things were incomprehensible—and his wife didn't want to have a child, as she had when they were young.

It was difficult to think; you wanted to turn back and shoot at the Japs, the Americans, Semyonov's men, at this satisfied sea which was sending from its islands people who knew only how to kill.

At the base of the steep bank a rock pile blocked the road, and a wicker suspension bridge had been attached to the cliff like a balcony. The main force of the current burst onto the rocks, and further down the river the foam from the strongest part of the current was splashing up and down on the rocks as though in an epileptic fit.

"Should we make camp?" asked Vershinin after crossing the suspension bridge.

The peasants stopped, and they lit up their cigarettes.

They decided not to make camp, to get through the village of Davya, and the mountains weren't far off and they could rest there for the night.

By the fence of the pasture outside the village of Davya a barefooted peasant with a cloth wrapped around his head galloped up to them bareback on his palomino and said, "We had a battle here, Nikita Egorich."

"Who'd you have the battle with?"

"In the settlement the Japs fought with our people. Who knows what's going to happen tomorrow. The Japs left—we beat them off, but we expect that they'll come back tomorrow. So we're packing up our junk and thinking of going up to the mountains with you."

"Who are 'our people'?"

"Don't know, young man. Not from our *volost*. Christians too. They have machine guns, good machine guns. Do they ever shoot. From the mountains, too!"

"We'll see you! Good-bye."

Carts, corpses of people and cattle were scattered about on the wide streets of the settlement. A Japanese, his neck pierced with a bayonet, lay on a Russian. The Russian's dark blue eye had dropped out onto his cheek. Flies were crawling around on his field shirt, which was covered with blood.

Four Japanese lay by a fence with their faces down, as if ashamed of something. The backs of their heads were shattered. Pieces of skin with their coarse black hair stuck to the backs of their neat little uniforms and their yellow spats were carefully cleaned, as if the Japanese intended to take a walk on the streets of Vladivostok.

"You should bury them," said Okorok, "It's shameful."

People were packing their belongings into carts. Little boys were driving out the cattle. Everyone's face was the same as always—calm and businesslike.

Only a little white dog which had lost its mind was running around in circles from yard to yard among the corpses.

An old man with a face like a well-worn sheepskin coat came up to the partisans. Where clumps of fur had fallen out, the skin of his cheeks and forehead shone red.

"Are you warring?" he asked Vershinin in a whining voice.

"We've got to, old man."

"That's what I'd say too—sickening to the people. We ain't never had such a dumb war. Before, the Tsar would call us to fight, but now—damn it to hell, everyhody's fighting each other."

"It's just like we've been riding and riding, and now our cart—has gone smash! It turns out that it rotted out a long time ago; now we've got to make a new one."

"Eh?"

The old man bent his head to the earth and, as if listening to a noise under his feet, repeated, "I can't understand... Eh?.."

"I say the cart has fallen apart!"

And the old man, as if shaking water from his hands, walked away mumbling, "Well, that's the kind of carts they make nowadays. The Antichrist has been born, so don't expect any good carts."

Vershinin rubbed his aching back and looked around.

The little dog still hadn't stopped screeching.

One of the partisans took out his carbine and shot it. The little dog turned into a ball, then it extended its whole body, as if waking up and stretching. It croaked.

IV

The peasant with the bandaged head galloped away again, but in a few minutes he reappeared, madly driving his palomino out of an alley.

His body stuck to the horse's flat back, his face was dancing, his fists shook, and his throat joyously shouted, "They've caught an American, brothers!.."

Okorok shouted, "Oho, oho, ho!.."

Three peasants with rifles appeared in the alley.

Between them, slightly limping, dressed in a summer flannel uniform, walked an American soldier.

His face was shaved, young. His open lips quivered with fright, and a muscle was twitching on his right cheek by his cheekbone.

The long-legged, gray-haired peasant who was accompanying the American asked, "Who's in charge here?"

"Why do you want to know?" Vershinin called back.

"He's in command, him," shouted Okorok. "Nikita Egorich Vershinin. Now tell us how you caught him!"

The peasant spit, and patting the American soldier on the shoulder as if he himself had just appeared, started telling about it with all the enthusiasm of an old man.

"We brought him to you, Nikita Egorich. We're from the Voznesensk *volost*. Our detachment went a long way after the Japs."

"From what villages?"

"We went as one village. Maybe you've heard of the village Penino?"

"I've heard they've burned it down."

"The people are bastards. You're right, they burnt down the whole village, that's why we've left for the mountains."

The partisans gathered around and started talking, "All we do is suffer, understand?"

The grey-haired peasant continued, "Two of them were travelling together, Americans. They were transporting milk in large metal cans. Stupid people, they come here to fight a war and they feed their faces with chocolate and milk. We knocked one off, but this one surrendered. So we brought him here; we wanted to give him to the person in charge, but there is a whole group here."

The American stood straight, like a soldier, and did not take his eyes off Vershinin, as if he were a judge.

The peasants crowded around.

The American caught the smell of tobacco and pungent peasant bread. The closely crowded bodies there exuded a heat which made the head swim, and a dry feverish anger rose through the entire body.

The peasants started hooting, "What's the matter?"

"Shoot him down, the bastard!"

"Get him!"

"Finish him off!"

"And that's that!"

The American soldier hunched his shoulders a little bit and fearfully pulled his head into his shoulders; from this movement the anger overflowed in their bodies even more violently.

"They're burning everything, the bastards!"

"They're running things!!"

"As if they were back in America!.."

"See how far they've come..."

"As if they were asked to!.."

Someone started screeching piercingly, "Beat him!!."

At this time Pentefly Znobov, who had earlier worked on the Vladivostok docks, climbed up into a cart and as if pointing at something lost started shouting, "Hold on!.."

And he added, "Comrades!.."

The partisans looked at his moustache, shaggy like a fox's tail, and the unbuttoned fly of his pants and grew quiet.

"We can always kill him. It's very simple. It doesn't cost anything to kill. Look how many of them have been dumped out onto the street. In my opinion, comrades,—indoctrinate him with our propaganda—then let him go. Let him get a whiff of 'Bolshik' truth. That's what I suggest..."

Suddenly a deep laugh poured out of the peasants, like millet from a sack, "Ho-ho-ha!..."

"He-e-e!.."

"Ho-o!.."

"Button up your fly, you old devil!"

"Go on, Pentya, go to it..."

"Give him a good whack on the back of the head!"

"He's a human being too!.."

"Even a stone can be chiseled."

"Thrash him!.."

Gathering up her straw-colored skirts, strongbodied Avdotya Seshchenkova leaned forward and shoved the American with her shoulder, "Try and understand, you fool, they wish you well!"

The American soldier examined the hairy reddish-bronze faces of the peasants, Znobov's unbuttoned fly, listened to the incomprehensible language, and politely wrinkled up his shaven face in a smile.

The peasants walked around him excitedly and moved him about in the crowd like a leaf in water; they shouted loudly, as if at a deaf person, and shook hands.

The American, squinting frequently as if from smoke, raised his head up, smiled, and did not understand anything.

Okorok shouted at the American at the top of his lungs, "Explain to them back at home in detail. What you're doing is bad."

"Why should you meddle in our affairs!"

"They are forcing you to go against your brother!"

Vershinin said seriously, "All people are good, they ought to understand. Let's say that they're the same kind of peasants, like us, you till the land and all of that. But the Jap—what does he do, stuffs his face with rice, and you've got to talk to him differently."

Znobov started stomping his feet heavily in front of the American and stroking his moustache said, "We're not robbing anyone, we're only straightening out things here! I'm afraid your people across the sea don't know this; it's too far away; and then again you've got the soul of a strange land..."

Peoples' voices rose and grew deeper.

The American looked around helplessly and muttered, "I don't understand!"

The peasants fell silent all together.

Vaska Okorok said, "He doesn't understand! That's poverty, not to know Russian."

The peasants walked away from the American slowly, as if guilty of something.

Vershinin felt embarrassed. "Send him to the pack train, why screw around with him here?" he said to Znobov.

Znobov didn't agree and stubbornly insisted, "He'll understand... You've only gotta... he'll understand!.."

Znobov was thinking.

The American, bending one leg a bit and slightly rocking back and forth, stood there and hardly noticeably, like a light wind across a haystack, anguish stirred across his face.

Sin-Bin-U lay down on the ground beside the American. Covering his eyes with the palm of his hand, he sang a slow, piercing Chinese song.

"Oh, what misery," said Vershinin drearily.

"Maybe a book of some sort?" said Vaska Okorok half-heartedly.

But all the books they found were in Russian.

"They're only good for making cigarettes," said Znobov, "if they only had pictures."

Avdotya went forward to the carts which were standing by the cattle pen, rummaged around in her trunks, and finally brought them a worn-out book with torn corners. It was a religious primer for village schools. "Maybe we can teach him from this?" she asked.

Znobov opened the book and said somewhat perplexedly, "They're all religious pictures. We're not going to convert him. We're not preachers."

"Well, try," Vaska suggested.

"How? I'm afraid he won't get it."

"Maybe he will. Go ahead!"

"Hey, comrade, come on over here!" called Znobov.

The American came over. The peasants gathered together again; again it smelled of bread and tobacco.

"Lenin!" said Znobov loudly and firmly, and somehow, as if unwillingly stumbling, he smiled.

The American's whole body started; his eyes shone, and he answered joyfully, "There's a chap!"

Znobov pounded his chest with his fist and patted the peasants on their backs and shoulders and for some reason said in broken Russian, "Sovet Respublik!"

The American held his hand out to the peasants; his cheeks started jumping and he shouted excitedly, "That is pretty indeed!"

The peasants began to laugh joyfully.

"He understands, the bastard!"

"There's a real son of a bitch for you, eh?"

"And Pentya. Our Pentya can curse in English!"

"Tell these bourgeois pigs what their mothers do, Pentya!"

Znobov hurriedly opened up the church primer, and sticking his finger onto the picture where Abraham was delivering Isaac as a sacrifice and God was up in the clouds, he began to explain, "This one, with the knife, is a bourgeois. See how fat his stomach hangs out. All he needs is a watch and chain. And here, on the boards, lies a proletarian. Understand? Pro-le-tar-i-an."

The American pointed at his chest with his hand and in a drawling stammer pronounced happily and proudly, "Pro-le-tar-i-an... We!..."

The peasants hugged the American, felt his clothing, and squeezed his hands and shoulders as hard as they could.

Grabbing him by the head and looking into his eyes, Vaska Okorok shouted gleefully, "Boy, you tell them there, across the sea!..."

"That's enough, windbag," said Vershinin amiably.

Znobov continued, "He's lying there, the proletarian, on the logs, and the bourgeois is cutting his throat. And up in the clouds are sitting the Japs, American women, English women—all the scum of Imperialism is sitting up there."

The American tore his cap from his head and howled, "Imperialism away!"

Znobov hurled the book to the ground with bitterness. "To hell with Imperialism and the bourgeoisie!"

Sin-Bin-U jumped over to the American, and holding up his pants which were falling down, said hurriedly, "Lussia is a lepublic, China is a lepublic, Amelica is bad lepublic. The Japanese ale all bad, we need a Led Lepublic."

And looking around, he stood on his tiptoes, stuck up his thumb slowly, and said, "Good."

"We've got to feed him. And then take him to the road and let him go," ordered Vershinin.

The old man who was an escort asked, "Should we blindfold him? How should we take him? He won't bring them back here, will he?"

"It's not necessary. He won't betray us!" decided the peasants.

V

Laughing and whistling, the partisans threw their guns on their shoulders.

Okorok began to shake his curly red head and then suddenly, with a voice thin like a spiderweb, started singing:

> I'll sow sadness and anguish about the green field,
> Come on up my grief, as green, green grass,
> And don't dry up, don't fade, but open up in blossoms...

And someone's quick and happy voice joined in after Vaska's:

> After sowing I went into the green garden—
> There are cherries, grapes, and pears aplenty in the garden.

And then a hundred peasant voices, hoarse, jerky, like the wind on the sea, broke out, rose, and carried the song into the paths, the forest, and the mountains.

> After sowing I went into the green garden,
> Ekh, I went, I went!..

The partisans, as if at a wedding, moved on toward the hills with howls, laughs, and whistling.

The sixth day was fading.

An enervating and joyous odor rose from the evening trees.

Chapter Three

I

The story of why Sin-Bin-U hated the Japanese is a long one. Sin-Bin-U had a wife from the family E, a strong, good, well-built hut, and in the hut they had warm painted plank beds and behind the hut yellow fields of sorghum and millet.

And one day, after the geese had flown south, all of this disappeared.

Only his cheek turned out to be pierced by a bayonet.

Sin-Bin-U used to read Shi-tszin, weave mats which he sold in town, but then he threw Shi-tszin into the well, forgot about his mats, and left with the Russians along the road of the red banner and revolution.

Sin-Bin-U was resting on the sand by the sea. Warmth from below, warmth from above, as if the sun were burning through his body and making the sand white hot.

His legs are splashing in the sea; when the waves, as warm as fresh milk, creep up his pants and shirt, he pulls up his legs and curses, "Mothe Fucke!.."

Sin-Bin-U wasn't listening to what the thick-moustached and aquiline-nosed Russian was saying. Sin-Bin-U had killed three Japanese, and for now the Chinese did not want anything, he was content.

The peasants' beards are matted and yellowish green, like swamp algae, from the sun and the damp wind: they smell of cattle and grass.

By the carts are machine-guns with shields that look like green plates, belts of ammunition, and rifles.

A wounded man covered with a torn tarpaulin was rolling around in a cart with a low detachable front. Avdotya Seshchenkova was encouraging him, "Don't moan, it'll go away!"

The sweaty crowd tightly filled in the space between the carts. And it seemed that the carts, squeezed by the raging human flesh, also started to sweat. Lips which had grown out of the beards in dull red stripes glistened in the sun as they dripped with spit.

"O-o-o-u-u-u!."

With his body aching as though this wordless cry were tossing him up and down on bayonets, Vershinin gave a deafening shout from his insides.

"Don't let the Ja-aps have the land!.. We'll take everything back! Don't let them!"

And he just couldn't quit yelling. Nothing seemed enough to him. No other words came to him. "Don't le-et the-em!..." he screamed.

"A-a-a!.." shouted the crowd after him.

And then the crowd quieted down for a second. It took a deep breath.

The wind carried away the sour smell of sweat.

The partisans were having a political meeting.

Vaska Okorok's face, red as a sunflower, jumped wildly about in the crowd, and his lips, cracked by the heat, whispered, "There are.... There are millions of people, comrades!.."

Tall and fleshy, looking like a rearing horse, Nikita Vershinin shouted from a stump, "The main thing is not to let them!.. The army will soon arrive here...the Red Army...but don't let them...old man!.."

And as a fish caught in a net gets tightly thrown into the middle part, everyone jumped on the words, "Do-o-n't le-e-et them!!"

And it seemed that at any second now a word would come falling down, would break in half, and something incomprehensible and malicious, like a typhoon, would appear.

At this point a scrawny pock-marked peasant in a silk raspberry-colored shirt, pressing his arms to his stomach, reassured them in a piercing voice, "It's the truth!.."

"Peter has fallen to its... knees... because of us!.. and all the foreign lands as well! There's nothing to be afraid of... The Japs?—What's a Jap?—A Jap is light... A piece of muslin!.."

"True, young fellow, true!" screeched the scrawny peasant.

The dense sweaty multitude trampled down his scream, "Tru-u-e..."

"Don't le-e-t them!.."

"Let them ha-a-ve it!.."

"O-o-o-u-u-u!!!"

"O-o!!!"

II

After the meeting Nikita Vershinin drank a ladle of homemade vodka and set out toward the sea. He sat down on a rock next to the Chinaman and said, "Pull up your legs, you'll get your pants all wet. Why didn't you go to the meeting, Senka?"

"That all light," sid Sin-Bin-U, "I no need it... I knowee all that... knowee all... too much well."

"Pull up your legs, come on!"

"That all light. Sun is walm. That all light-eh?.."

Vershinin frowned and sternly looking somewhere besides the Chinaman, said in a deliberate tone, "There's a lot of disorder. A lot of people are dying, and it's all for nothing. My soul, Senka, is whining like a kitten thrown out into the cold... Yeah... We'll blow up this bridge, and then we'll have to build it again."

Vershinin pulled in his stomach so that his ribs stretched under his shirt like the roots of willow trees under dried-up silt. He leaned over to the Chinaman and with a darkened face he asked questioningly, "And you... What do you think? Huh? Why all this, huh?..."

Sin-Bin-U, quickly putting the loops on the wooden buttons of his jacket, timidly crawled away, "I no knowee, Kita. It just misely!.. I no knowee!.."

Vershinin, bending toward the Chinaman, who was crawling away, was deeply sinking into the sand with his heavy boots like those of a statue; drearily, and not hoping for an answer, he asked, "Are you saying nothing for some reason or other?... Well?.."

It seemed to the Chinaman that it was best not to get up and he babbled "I no knowee nothing!.. Nothing!.."

Vershinin felt his body getting weak and sat down on a stone.

"Well, to hell with you!.. Nobody knows anything, nobody understands anything... They got waked up and started running, and after that, what?.."

And sitting tightly against the rock like a wood spirit, he wearily said to Okorok, who had just come up to him, "Either people's minds have grown scanty, either I..."

"What?" asked Okorok.

"People are just begging for death."

"For what?"

"They want to take the armored train. A lot of people are going to die. And even then people rush to death like snow to an open hole in the ice."

Giving a whistle, Okorok stuck out his lower lip, "Are you sorry for them?"

Znobov came up to them; he was holding his cap with some papers under his arms. "Sign these orders!"

Vershinin traced a thick letter V on the paper and next to it a long heavy line. "Before I'd puff and sweat, scarcely be able to write my name. It dawned on me, thank goodness, to write just one letter and a line—and they know what it is."

Okorok repeated, "Aren't you sorry for them?"

"Huh?" asked Znobov.

"People are dropping dead."

Znobov stuck the papers into the folder and said, "You're talking nonsense. Why feel sorry for the people? A new generation will grow up."

Vershinin answered hoarsely, "If there were only the real key. But what if we have to open the doors with a different key?"

"Then why are you going along with us?"

"I feel sorry for the land. The Japs'll take it."

Okorok laughed crudely, "And you, the protectors of the land, rich and green!"

"What are you snorting for?" said Vershinin, with restrained anger. "There are those who are for the land and those who are for the sea. The land is firmer, boy. I'm from a family of fishermen myself..."

"Well, a prophet!"

"I'm going to quit fishing now."

"Why?"

"I've suffered too much to go back to sea again. I'm going to be a farmer. The city only deceives you. It's a soap bubble; you can't put it in your pocket."

Znobov recalled the city, the chairman of the revolutionary committee, the bright spots on the wharf—the people, the streetcars, the houses,—and said with indignation, "We don't need your land, Blockhead, we will take the land from all the planets and then—working masses sign for it!..."

Okorok stretched out on the sand beside the Chinaman, and kicking the earth up with his feet he said, "And if they're going to shoot the Japanese mikado, then the bastard will start screeching. Real fun!.. I'll bet you he's not waiting for this to happen, huh, Senka? What do you think, Egorich?"

"They know better," answered Vershinin half-heartedly.

Above the sands were cliff-like shores; further in the distance—mountains. An oak. A larch.

High on a rock stood a little man in yellow—like a piece of sap on the trunk of a tree—a watchman, a guard.

Stepping heavily, Vershinin started walking among the carts.

Sin-Bin-U said, "He little sad in healt, huh?"

"It'll pass," sid Okorok, calming him and lighting a cigarette.

Sin-Bin-U agreed, "It all light."

III

The scrawny pock-marked peasant in the raspberry-colored shirt caught Vershinin by the flap of his jacket and taking a few steps to the side mysteriously began to whisper, "I understand you. You think I'm a complete fool. Pound it into their heads, and they'll believe and will follow!.. The main thing is to believe in a person... And what about the 'Internashunal'?"

He winked and added quietly, "You see, I know—there ain't nothing in it. You'll never find anything good in back of such a fancy word. A word should be simple—let's say like 'field.' A good word.... That's a good word."

"I'm tired of good words."

"You're lying! You were just using them and you will again. Beat it into their heads. And then you can hide whatever's left over... That's how it's always done... Every man wants the hugest measure possible—that's human nature... Say that you deserve a square mile of land, but he, the bastard, won't even measure you out a square inch... And let him, let him measure as he wants to... At least you know what you deserve!.. He-he-he!.."

The scrawny peasant slapped Vershinin on the shoulder in a familiar way.

Vershinin's body contracted and burned. He lay down under a cart and tried to fall asleep, but couldn't.

He jumped up, buckled his belt tightly around his stomach, washed up with heated water from an iron hand basin, and went to round up the young fellows.

"Up with you! Drill time! On the double!.."

The fellows, their faces murky and quivering like jello, gathered obediently.

Vershinin lined them up and commanded, "Ten-hut!.."

And from this shout he started to feel like a soldier in the power of machines which resembled people.

"Eyes ri-i-ght..."

Vershinin drove the fellows until late evening.

The men sweated as they went through their drills angrily, looking at the sun from time to time.

"Left ha-a-acc!.. Careful. We're going after the Japs!"

One of the fellows smiled plaintively.

"What's with you?"

Blinking his eyelashes, which had become lighter from the sea salt, the young fellow said timidly, "Why for after the Japs? We should worry about the Whites. They say the Japs have the sea... And their water is steaming hot, a Christian can't drink it."

"Aren't they the same people, stupid?"

"Then why are they yellow? From the hotwater, they say."

The fellows began to laugh.

Vershinin walked through their line and commanded sternly, "Company, fi-i-ire..."

The fellows clicked their bolts.

A peasant lying under a cart raised his hand and said, "He's training them. A reliable man, Vershinin..."

Another answered him sleepily, "He's a rock, a cliff... He's going to be a big commissar."

"Him? Sure is."

IV

Three days later a sailor from the city arrived in a small buggy woven out of reeds.

His face was burning, one cheek was bruised, and on his chest dangled a red ribbon.

"There's a rebellion in the city," shouted the sailor from the buggy, "they're rebelling, comrades... Captain Nezelasov has been ordered to bring the armored train there in order to put it down. You can have it.Go get it... And I'll organize the militia..."

And the sailor left.

Chapter Four

I

On wide mats woven out of sorghum stalks lay heaps of flounder, eels that looked like wet strings, and thick layers of other kinds of fish. The sky and the stones of the houses were reflected on the scales of the fish; their fins still preserved the tender colors of the sea—sapphire gold, bright yellow, and dense orange.

The Chinaman looked at the piles of meat indifferently, as if looking at the ground, and shouted piercingly, as if giving birth, "You wantee some fish, Lussian captain? Clabs?... Fish?... I have plenty sell!.. Eh?.."

Pentefly Znobov, spattered with yellow mud which smelled of silt, was sitting in a boat by the steps of the seawall and saying with dissatisfaction, "That Chink is really shouting, and yet all he's doing is pushing fish."

"And what do you have to offer, fellow?"

"Our task is to destroy everything! Yes. Destroy and destroy, I'm tired of it. When are we going to build? Ekh, if I could find a literate Jap."

The sailor let his legs down to the water and played with the waves with the soles of his feet. "What do you need a Jap for?" he asked.

The sailor's head was round and smooth as an egg, and it had dirty ears sticking out. The sea was splashing him all over as it splashes a boat: his shirt, his wide pants, his flowing sleeves. All of it was splashing and floating.

"A happy guy," thought Znobov, "I *can* find a Jap. I'll find one. There're a lot of them here..."

Znobov got out of the boat, bent over to the sailor, and looking over his shoulder at the crowd, which was as motley as the patches in a quilt, at the clanging streetcars and at the plain bluish-green short jackets,—the tunics of the Chinese, he said in a whisper, "We need a special Jap, not a local one. To circulate a proclamation. To print it and post it all over town. Also so that their soldiers get to read it."

He imagined a yellow sheet of paper completely covered with incomprehensible figures and smiled tenderly, "They'll understand. Man, we have already reduced an American to tears. He cried just like he had busted his water tank!..."

"He might have been crying from fear, too."

"Don't talk nonsense. The main thing is that you have to explain life to people. Without an explanation, what can you ask of him, you blockhead?"

"It's hard to find a Jap like that."

"That's what I'm saying. Most likely you'd have to bump into one."

The sailor got up on his tiptoes and looked at the crowd. "See how many people there are. Maybe there is a good Jap here, and how are you going to find him?"

Znobov sighed, "It's hard to find one. Especially for me. I don't see any people at all. My head right now feels like the choir loft of a church. Our own people will come in, sing, and the rest of the public only has to listen. It's like having a shroud over your eyes."

"Now there's a lot of people like that..."

"No other way. You're going along the path, if you don't concentrate on one spot, then your head'll start spinning—you'll crash into the ravine. Try drying your bones off after that!"

Well-dresed Canadians passed by laughing loudly; Japanese resembling little figures carved out of rutabagas went by silently. The spurs of Ataman Semyonov's Cossacks in silver-gallooned trousers were singing.

The sea pressed wearily against the granite. The wind, damp as foam and smelling of fish, skipped across the waves. The gray lilac ships, the white-headed Chinese schooners, and the boats of the fishermen in the bay looked like flowers woven on chintz.

"This is a whorehouse, and not Russia!"

The sailor bounced about and burst out laughing, "Just wait—we'll make their necks sore. The Whites, that is."

"Shall we go?" asked Znobov.

"Let's get the hell out of here!"

They were walking uphill on Peking Street.

From the doors of the houses it smelled of roast meat, garlic, and grease.

Two Chinese deliverymen, adjusting heaps of material tightly wrapped with belts on their shoulders, looked at the Russians and laughed impudently.

Znobov said, "They're laughing, the devils. And my belly feels like somebody's building a new house in it. And now it's up and crashed."

The sailor moved his body under the shell of his shirt and coughed, "To each his own!"

It looked like the large maritime city was living its usual everyday life.

But already the anguishing depression of the defeats had put ulcers on the faces of people, animals, houses, and even the sea.

One could see officers wrapped up in service jackets hastily drinking cognac behind the gleaming windows of a cafe, as if they were piercing themselves with glasses. Their shoulders were bent wearily, and often their thin exasperated eyelids would drop onto their eyes.

Horses, starved by the retreats, thin as aspen brushwood, limping weakly, were pulling carts full of dirty linen. It had been evacuated from Omsk by mistake instead of shells and arms. And it seemed to everyone that this linen was from corpses.

Splotches of houses half destroyed during the uprising ate into the eyes like a soap solution. Actually there weren't so many, but everyone was saying for some reason that the whole city had been razed by shells.

And different, with another face than usual, the sea splashed on.

And the green ocean wind, in another way, from behind the distant horizon, thin and jingling like a steel wire, touched the city with its song.

The sailor saluted unhurriedly and a bit foppishly. "Aren't you afraid of spies?" he asked Znobov. "They'll kill you."

Znobov thought about the Japs, and stroking his hand as though combing out thoughts which had fallen deeply, answered a bit hastily, "Not at all! I'm worried about something else. At first I was afraid, but then I got used to it. Now they're waiting for the Bolsheviks. They're afraid of revenge. They know us and won't betray us."

He grinned, "How we've scared the hell out of people. They won't get over it in ten years."

"And we weren't spared either."

"Right... Any of you been arrested?"

"They've taken three."

"Really?.. Come with us to the mountains."

"The stone, forest. I don't like it...it's boring."

"That's true. You can throw up a lot of good houses using stone like this. You could make an America. But lying around with nothing to do, nothing to eat, or for a pillow. It's all right for a peasant, but it bores me, too. We'll have to go to the city."

"Right."

II

The head of the underground revolutionary committee, comrade Peklevanov, a small freckly man in tortoise-shell glasses, was sharpening his pencil with a penknife. The sun played sharply on the lenses of his glasses, like the blade of a knife sharpening his eyes, and his eyes sparkled in a new way.

"You come a bit often, comrade Znobov," said Peklevanov.

Znobov laid his hand, cracked from the wind and water, on the table and said, "The people want to work."

"Well?"

"No one gives them any work to do. They're furious... They're pressing me... It's awkward for me, as if I'm persuading a rich fiancee."

"We'll let you know."

"We're bored with waiting. It's worse than vomit. Shoot at trains, burn, fight Cossacks..."

"It'll pass."

"We know. Just so what we're giving our lives for doesn't pass. They want to blow up a bridge."

"Excellent."

"We need explosives and an explosives man too. We need a dynamite man."

"We'll send you one."

They were silent for a bit. "You don't have any discipline," said Peklevanov.

"Among us?"

"No, inside youselves."

"Well, nobody has that type of discipline now."

The chairman of the revolutionary committee scratched his sharp elbow, which had begun to itch. The skin on his face was unhealthy, as if he had not slept all his life, but joy was lashing out somewhere deep inside and its jolts burned his cheeks with red spots.

The sailor extended his hand to him, shook it as if squeezing the juice out of it, and left the room.

Znobov moved a bit closer and asked quietly, "All the peasants are talking about the uprising, what do you think? In case of something or other we'll give you three thousand from the village. They fought with the Germans; they're experienced soldiers. Is there a plan?"

He spread his arms apart as though embracing the table and whispered wearily, "And you—get out a proclamation against the Japs. So it burns through their hearts..."

Peklevanov had a sunken chest, and he spoke with a weak voice. "Of course, we're thinking... We're taking measures."

All of a sudden Znobov felt sorry for him. "As a person you're all right, but...as far as being chairman, you're...," he thought, and he wanted to see a healthy, shaven man, somehow with a completely bald head, as chairman.

On the table lay a large newspaper, and on it gloomy black bread and thinly sliced pieces of salami. A little further away on a dark blue saucer were two potatoes and next to the saucer the skin from the salami.

"Bird food," thought Znobov with dissatisfaction.

Peklevanov rubbed his unshaven cheek with his shoulders—from the bottom up.

"At the appointed time of the uprising, rebelling workers and soldiers who have joined them will appear in the trams from all parts of the city. They will cut telegraph lines and seize institutions."

Peklevanov talked as though he were reading a telegram, and Znobov was happy. He shook his moustache and said quickly:

"Well?.."

"The Revcom will do everything else. In the future it will be in charge of operations."

Znobov put his hands, bulging with strength, onto the table and said, "Is that all?"

"For the time being, yes."

"That's not enough, comrade!"

Peklevanov's fingers ran along the buttons of his jacket, and his freckled face became covered with spots. He seemed to be hurt.

Znobov muttered, "You shouldn't abandon the peasants in such a way. You should call them. It turns out that we have been sitting in the mountains for nothing, like a hen on rotten eggs. There are a lot of us, comrade... thousands..."

"There are forty thousand Japs."

"That's true, they can squeeze us like lice. But the peasants will go anyhow."

"Who?"

"Everybody, the peasants want it."

"You have a lot of Social Revolutionary spirit in you, comrade Znobov. You smell of the earth."

"And you of salami."

Peklevanov started laughing a motley laugh.

"I'll give you some vodka, do you want some?" he offered. "Only don't sit too long and don't curse the government. They watch us!"

"We'll do it so no one will hear," answered Znobov.

After drinking a glass of vodka Znobov broke into a sweat, and wiping his face with a towel said, hiccupping drunkenly, "Don't you get angry, man—take it easy. And if you want to know, I didn't like you at first."

"Have you changed your mind now?"

"Now it's all right. We'll blow up the bridge, brother, and then there's this armored train there."

"Where?"

Znobov spread out his arms. "It goes back and forth. . . along the train line, it has No. 14 and some other numbers. It's called. . . It's ruined a lot of people. It's probably already cut down a million poeple. So we'll. . .get it. . ."

"Into the water?"

"Why into the water? We want to be just. It's government property, so we'll take it."

"It's armed."

"Again, that doesn't mean anything. What we'll do, we'll do, what the hell. . ." Znobov shook his head sluggishly. "Your vodka is strong. My body is like the earth,—it doesn't hear human words. It's doing what it wants to." He raised his leg to the threshold and said, "Farewell, you're a person of the past, honest to God!"

Peklevanov cut off a piece of salami, drank some vodka, and looking at the wall which was spotted with flies, said, "Yes, a person of the past."

He smiled gaily, took a piece of paper, and strongly squeaking his pen, began writing a draft of instructions to the military units that had already rebelled.

Outside on the street by the front garden Znobov caught sight of a Japanese soldier wearing a uniform cap with a red band and yellow spats. The soldier was carrying a long enamel bowl. The Japanese had a small stiff mouth and a thin moustache which looked like the wings of a dragonfly.

"Wait a second!" said Znobov, grabbing him by the sleeve.

The Japanese pulled his arm away sharply and asked strictly, "Well? What?"

Znobov screwed up his face and mimicked him, "Oink! You're a pig, you fat louse! I'm being nice to you and all I get from you is 'oink.' Do you believe in God?"

The Japanese squinted his eyes, and from under his turned up eyelashes which resembled the corners of the roofs of a pagoda he examined Znobov crossways—from shoulder to shoulder; then he examined his boots, and noticing dried up yellow mud on them he screwed up his mouth and said hoarsely, "Lussian scum! So?.."

And squeezing his bowl to his ribs he walked away unhurriedly.

Znobov looked after him, at the lively shining plates of his belt, and said with sadness, "You're a fool, I'll tell you that!"

Chapter Five

I

The Cossack answered exhaustedly, "Yes sir...with papers..."

The peasant stood with his body thrown back, and his beard, which resembled a red scarf, was pressed directly against the chest.

The Cossack, who was handing over the envelope said, "They found him in back of a log-pile!"

The young, large-eyed commander of the station, weakly leaning on a low little table, began to interrogate the young partisan. "Whose band are you from?.. Vershinin's?.."

In the commander's room Captain Nezelasov was shaking from the cold and suppressing his irritation. With the palm of his hand he was rubbing a bench which smelled dirty, like a soldier's footcloth. He wanted to leave, but the clanging telegraph apparatus in the next room wouldn't let him. "Maybe there'll be an order...maybe..."

The commander, shifting about dully shining squares of papers asked in an exhausted voice, "How many... What?.. Where?.."

Whenever the front door slammed pieces of plaster fell off the walls. It seemed to Nezelasov that the commander was pretending to be calm. "He wants to please me...the armored train...that is to say, ours..."

And on the inside he had such pain, like the pain a bear feels when it swallows a piece of ice with a whale's whisker rolled up in it. The piece of ice melts, the spring straightens out, tears the insides, first one intestine, then the other...

The peasant talked in a stiff deathly voice, and only at the words, "They say the city was taken by our men," did he look sternly around, but again enveloped in anguish, he hid his eyes.

A woman's rosy face appeared in the window. "Mr. Commander, they don't answer from the city."

The commander said, "I hear that they don't shoot you—they use sticks."

"What?" asked the rosy-cheeked face.

"Work. What are you worried about? You shouldn't care! Did you hear, Captain?"

"Perhaps... anything is possible... but, you see, I think..."

"What?"

"The partisans have cut the lines. Yes, cut them, only..."

"No, I don't think so. However!"

When the captain went out onto the station platform, the commander wearily putting his body on the windowsill, said loudly, "Bring along the arrested man."

The red-bearded peasant was still sitting on the train. All his blood had left him; his face and hands had become clammy, like moist gray clay.

When they were shooting him it seemed to the soldiers that they were shooting a corpse. That's probably why one soldier ordered, before the execution, "Take his boots off now, you can fuss around later."

The peasant pulled off his boots with a habitual motion.

Later it was revolting to see his blood slowly lash out of his wounds. Obab brought a puppy into the train compartment—a small bundle of weak body. The bundle rolled uncertainly across the ensign's wide palm onto the bed and started to whine.

"What do you want that for?" asked Nezelasov.

Obab smiled somehow not in his usual way, "It's something alive. In our village—we have cattle. I'm from Barnaul."

"You shouldn't do that...it's useless, Ensign."

"What?"

"Who cares about your district here. You... here... Ensign Obab, have gold epaulettes and... an enemy of the revolution. No districts are necessary."

"So?" blurted Obab harshly.

And as though wiping away his barely noticeable delight, the captain said, "As such...as an enemy of the revolution... that means you are subject to liquidation."

Obab looked dimly at his knees and the wide knotty fingers of his hand, which resembled dry roots. "Nonsense," he said in a dull syrupy voice, "We'll cut them up into noodles!"

It was exhaustingly stuffy in the armored train while it was in motion. One's body sweated profusely, and one's hands stuck to the walls and benches.

Only when they took the peasant with the red beard out and shot him did a puny, sick wind weakly enter the car and slightly freshen their faces. A piece of the steel sky and shreds of torn leaves from maple trees flashed by.

The puppy squeaked sadly.

Captain Nezelasov hurriedly walked through the cars and cursed shrilly like a woman. The soldiers' long faces were inert, and the captain was sputtering words. "Shut up, louse eggs. No talking, shut up!.."

The soldiers stuck out their cheekbones even more so and were frightened of their inflamed thoughts. At the captain's shouts it seemed to them that someone who didn't accept discipline was quietly scowling by the machine-guns and other weapons.

They looked around quickly.

The steel plates which covered the crisp wooden boards were being carried along the rails, as even as matches, toward the east, toward the city, toward the sea.

II

Sin-Bin-U was sent out as a scout.

He sprinkled a basket woven from willow twigs full of roasted sunflower seeds, placed a revolver on the bottom, and as he was selling the sunflower seeds he smiled slyly and joyfully.

An officer in black riding breeches with two-striped silver galloons, noticing the joyfully exhausted face of the Chinaman, bent over to his face and asked quickly, "Do you have any cocaine?"

Sin-Bin-U tightly closed the cowls of his eyelids which were as thin as silk and answered, as if regretting it, "No!"

The officer straightened up sternly. "Well, what do you have?"

"Sunflowel seeds."

"You've sold yourself to the Jews," said the officer, walking away. "You should all be hanged!"

A thin-chested little soldier in blue puttees and in a greatcoat that looked like a dirty hospital robe was sitting right next to Sin-Bin-U and saying, "In our Semipalatinsk Province, brother Chinaman, we have a special sort of watermelon—a Chinese melon's a far cry from ours."

"Good," agreed Sin-Bin-U.

"I want to go home, but they're taking me to the sea."

"Go."

"Where."

"Home."

"I'm tired. If they take me, I'll go—I don't have the strength to go by myself."

"I got lots sunflowel seeds."

"What?"

Sin-Bin-U shook his basket. The sunflower seeds rustled dryly and emitted the smell of warm ashes. "Lot of sunflowel seed fol Lussian heads. Ukh...they lustle..."

"What's rustling?"

"Sunflowel seeds, gleen..."

"What do you want, a stone or something in their heads?"

Sin-Bin-U moved his lips approvingly and pointing at a wide but flat officer who was walking by in a gray field coat asked, "Who?"

"Captain Nezelasov, you Chink, boss of the armored train. The train has been called to town, it's leaving! Do you think the partisans will knock us off?"

"Good."

"For you everything is good; but we have to figure everything out here!" A brown-eyed young man carrying a sack with sparse chicken down sticking out stopped in front of the Chinaman and shouted gaily, "Have you sold enough?"

The Chinaman jumped up quickly and took off after the fellow.

The armored train left on track one. The evacuees looked after it greedily and sadly from the platform and began whispering to each other fearfully. The Cossack walked past in exhaustion. A gray, longbearded old man was sobbing beside the faucet for drinking water, and while he was wiping his tears one could see—his hands were small and clean. A soldier passed by and glanced around with curiosity and hidden joy; he looked into a barrel filled with rotten smelling water that looked like tarnished copper.

"What a life!" he said lovingly.

III

In the early morning they were ready to suffocate. In thick insurmountable waves the stifling heat rushed in from the dark cast-iron fields and from the forests, running across the lips like warm water, and with each breath the chest swelled with grief as heavy as damp clay.

Twilight here was as short as a madman's span of thought. Immediately—darkness. The sky is covered with sparks. Sparks race after the locomotive, the locomotive tears up the rails and the darkness, and emits pitiful impotent sobs. Behind fly the mountains, the forest. They'll fly up and squash you, as a sheep does a beetle.

At moments such as this Ensign Obab always ate. He was hurriedly grabbing eggs out of a canvas sack, ripping off the shell, sticking bread, butter and meat into his mouth. He loved half-raw meat, chewed it with his front teeth, dropping spit as sticky as honey onto the blanket. But inside, as before, there was still fever and hunger.

The soldier-orderly would dilute his grain alcohol with tea, and at train stops he would bring in baskets of food and report awkwardly, "Mr. Ensign, there aren't any communications with the city."

Obab wouldn't say anything, and grabbing the basket with his knotty fingers, he would tear the bread out; and if he couldn't eat any more he would squeeze it and roll it voluptuously and then fling it away.

Letting the puppy down onto the floor and watching it, with slow, dull eyes, Obab lay motionless. Perspiration broke out on his body. It was particularly unpleasant when his hair sweated.

The puppy, also sweaty, was whining. The axle bones were whining. The steel was roaring—as if being riveted.

Blazing up briefly and pitifully, like a match in the wind, Nezelasov was in his compartment muttering, "We'll get through... to hell with it!.. We don't need any commands... We don't give a damn!.." But as the day before, the armored train hurriedly and greedily, as Obab did his food, grabbed up mile after mile—and did not get its fill. Switchmens' booths flashed by in the same way and in the same way cut off up by the fields, the wind and the sea, the city lived at the other end of the rails— incomprehensible and terrifying in its silence.

"We'll get through," coughed up the captain, and he ran to the engineer.

The engineer, dark-faced, impetuous, and waving his whole body, shouted at Nezelasov, "Go away!.. Go away!.."

The captain, grimacing on the sly, enmeshed him in words, "Don't you worry... there aren't any partisans here... We'll get through, yes, without fail... and you, hurry up... And... We, nevertheless..."

The engineer was a volunteer from Ufa, and he was ashamed of his cowardice.

The stoker, jabbing his finger into the darkness, said, "There by the red line... do you see?.."

The captain looked at the sooty eye of the engineer and thought feverishly of the "red line." Behind it the locomotive would blow up, it would lose its mind.[6] "All of us... yes... in the locomotive."

It smelled bad from coal and grease. It brought to mind the rebelling workers.

Nezelasov suddenly jumped out of the locomotive and ran through the cars shouting, "Shoot!.."

Buckling up their belts for some reason or other, the soldiers assumed position by the machine-guns and fired bullets out into the darkness. They were sick to their stomachs from the familiar working of the machine-guns.

Obab appeared. His lips were greasy, his face gleaming with sweat, and he asked the same thing over and over again, "Are they firing, are they firing?"

"As you were!" ordered the captain.

"Go to sleep, Captain!"

Everything in the train was running around and shouting—things and people. And the gray puppy in Ensign Obab's compartment was also squealing.

The captain hurried to light up a cigarette, "Go... to hell!.. Eat...all you want...we'll get along without you."

And he drawled out shrilly, "Ensign!.."

"Yes, sir," said the ensign. "What do you want? Are you searching?"

"We'll get through... I say—we'll get through!.."

"It's clear. There's enough of everything."

The captain lowered his voice. "Nothing. We've lost!... We have a yoke... But neither cups... nor weights. Who are we going to hang and with what?.."

"We? I'll... their mothers."

The captain left for his compartment, muttering along the way, "Ah, the ground is here...outside, behind the windows... While you... here... while... it curses... you, eh?.."

"Why are you dragging it out so long? I don't like it. Shorter."

"Ensign, we are the corpses... of tomorrow. Both you and I, and everyone in the train—we're all ashes... Today we buried... a man, and tomorrow... the shovel is for us... yes."

"You need medical help."

The captain went up to Obab, and quickly sucking in a gulp of air he whispered, "You don't heal steel, you have to reforge it. It is that... it moves if it works... But if it's gotten rusty... All my life, all my life I have been convinced of something, but... It turns out that I've been mistaken... It's good to realize your mistake on your deathbed... But I'm 30 years old, Obab. Thirty, and I have a child—Valka... And his nails are pink, aren't they, Obab?"

Obab's thoughts, dull as the toe of an American boot, scattered in incomprehensible directions. He lagged behind, returned to his compartment, took a cigarette, and then, not yet smoking, started spitting,—at first on the blanket, and when his mouth had gone dry he sat down on his bed and stared dully at the wet live bundle squealing on the floor.

"Worm!.."

IV

At dawn the captain ran into Obab's compartment.

Obab was lying with his face down, his shoulders raised as if he were covering his head with them.

"Listen," the captain said indecisively, pulling Obab by the sleeve.

Obab turned over, quickly moving his back away as one takes away the torn lining of a dress.

"Are they shooting? The partisans?"

"No... Listen!.."

Obab's eyelids were swollen and damp from the stifling heat and he stared up with dull and haggard eyes that looked like tears in a dress.

"But I don't really have a place... among people. I want to... get a letter... From home, well!.."

Obab said hoarsely, "Leave me alone, I have to sleep!"

"I want to get from home... They don't write me...I don't know anything. If you would only write it for me... Ensign!.."

The captain giggled shamefully. "Well. It can happen in this way, unexpectedly... Hm?"

Obab jumped up, pulled on his large boots with trembling hands and then began to shout hoarsely, "Talk to me about army business, but don't dare speak to me this way! I have my own... In Barnaul..."

The ensign drew himself up as if at parade.

"Maybe the guns aren't cleaned? Maybe I should order it to be done. The soldiers are drunk and here you... You don't have the right..."

He began waving his hands; and pulling in his stomach said, "What business do I have with you? I don't want to feel sorry for you, I don't want to!"

"It's misery, Ensign... And you... still!.."

"Your life is wretched. You yourself are wretched... Masturbation in childhood and... you wanted affection..."

"Understand... Obab."

"It has nothing to do with my work."

"Please..."

The ensign started shouting, "I don't wa-a-ant to!.."

And he repeated this several times and with each repetition the words lost their color; something huge, hoarse and fearsome, like a running army tore out from his throat, "O-o-a-e-g-g-t-y!.."

Not listening to each other, they shouted frenziedly, until they were hoarse, until their voices dried up.

The captain sat wearily on the bunk, took the puppy onto his knees, and said with bitterness, "I thought... a rock. About you?.. But here—a fruit drop... melted in the heat!.."

Obab flung the window open and jumping up to the captain sharply grabbed the puppy by the back of the neck.

The captain hung onto his arm and shouted, "Don't you dare!.. don't dare throw him out!..."

The puppy started whining.

"Let me!.." Obab drew out thickly and wickedly. "Let me-e-e..."

"I won't let you, I'm telling you!.."

"Let me-e-e!..."

"Stop!.. I!.."

Obab took his hand away, and stomping his feet hard as if intentionally, he went out.

The puppy yelped quietly as it moved its gray paws uncertainly about on the floor, on the gray blanket. It looked like a damp crawling spot.

"Poor thing," muttered Nezelasov and suddenly his throat began gurgling. He felt a viscous dampness in his nose. He started to cry.

V

The bell in the compartment was ringing—the armored train's engineer was summoning Nezelasov.

Nezelasov wearily called out, "Obab?"

Obab walked in behind him and was dissatisfied with the small steps of the captain.

Obab said, "There aren't any blown-up bridges here. What do they have? They've taken up the ties... Partisans... And nothing from the city. Nonsense!"

Nezelasov said guiltily, "It's great... the way we're living, isn't it? Up to this moment I... don't know your first name... or your patronymic, but... Obab and Obab?.. Excuse me, it's just like a dog's name..."

"My name is Semyon Avdeich. Sounds like a good solid name."

The engineer, as always, was standing at the levers. Dried up, veiny, with a copper-colored moustache and eyes which looked as if they were covered with soot.

Pointing forward he blurted, "There's a man lying there."

Nezelasov didn't understand. The engineer repeated, "There's a man on the tracks!"

Obab stuck his head out. The engineer quickly moved some levers.

The wind tore at Obab's hair. "There's a man on the tracks, Captain, sir!"

The ensign's calm voice irritated Nezelasov and he said sharply, "Stop the train!"

"I can't," said the engineer.

"It's an order!"

"It's impossible," repeated the engineer. "You came too late. We'll run him over and then stop."

"But it's a man!"

"According to instructions I cannot stop. Otherwise there'll be a wreck."

Obab burst into laughter, "There's no reason at all to stop. We've killed all kinds of people. If we're going to stop because of each one, then we wouldn't have gotten farther than Novo-Nikolaevsk."

The captain said irritatedly, "Will you please not tell me what to do. Stop after running him over."

"Yes, sir, Captain, sir," answered Obab.

This answer, rude and curt, made the captain still angrier, and he said, "And you, Ensign Obab, go quickly and see to it that I get a report on what kind of corpse that is on the tracks."

"Yes, sir," answered Obab.

The engineer speeded up the train.

The cars gave a tense start. The whistle piercingly flooded the air.

The person on the rails lay immobile. The dark blue spot of his shirt was already visible on the yellow ties.

The platforms between the cars convulsed like shovels of iron.

"Of course," said the engineer, "Right now. I'll stop and we'll take a look."

Unbuttoning the collar of his shirt so that the wind would fan his sweaty body, Obab jumped from the upper landing directly onto the ground. The engineer jumped after him.

Soldiers appeared in the doors. Nezelasov put on his cap and went to the exit too.

But at this moment the forest shot at the armored train—with a booming rifle volley. And a little bit later, still one more stray rifle shot.

Ensign Obab stretched out his hands in front of himself as though getting ready for a dive into water, and suddenly he started rolling heavily

nostrils with your gods. Just think.... If there were a life—they think up gods..."

"Don't blaspheme, you Herod, don't blaspheme!.."

"Sock the bastard in the teeth, Egorich! The cheap provocateurs!" said Okorok maliciously.

Jumping up on his pacer, Okorok started to shout, smoothing out his words, "Well, how about it, comrades?.. Should we vote maybe?...."

"Vote!" someone in the crowd answered timidly.

The peasants started raising a din, "Go ahead!.."

"Why think about it!.."

"Go to it, Vaska!"

After they had already voted and decided to attack the armored train, to the left, far above the forest, they heard an uneven boom that sounded like part of a cliff breaking off. The smoke thrown up into the sky looked like a huge shaggy broom.

The fat secretary took off his cap and said to the peasants in an official manner, "This is what the staff has decreed—our men have blown up the bridge over Mulenka. That means the train won't get to the city, anyhow. I'm afraid five of our men were lost..."

The peasants took off their caps and crossed themselves so that the dead might rest in peace. They set out through the forest toward the railroad embankment to entrench themselves.

Vershinin walked through the bushes to the embankment, climbed up it, and planting his feet firmly into the earth between the ties, looked west for a long time into the horizon of shining steel strips.

"What are you up to?" asked Znobov.

Vershinin turned around, and climbing down from the embankment said, "And after us are people really going to live well?"

"Well?"

"That's all."

Znobov parted his moustache with his fingers and said with pleasure, "That's their business."

II

The shaved short-legged man lay down on the table on his chest—it looked as if his legs couldn't hold him—and said hoarsely, "You shouldn't do that, Comrade Peklevanov: your Revcom refuses to regard the opinion of the Council of Unions. Your attack is premature."

One of the workers who was sitting on a chair in the corner said biliously, "The Japanese have announced that they're going to maintain their neutrality. But we're not going to wait until they take off to their islands. Power should be in our hands, then they'll leave sooner."

The short-legged man argued, "The Council of Unions doesn't bear you malice, perhaps you should wait, comrades..."

"Then the Japs will put someone else forward."

"Will they set out again to calm down the peasants?"

"We've waited long enough!"

The meeting was getting agitated. Peklevanov, sipping his tea, calmed them, "And you, comrades, be more quiet."

The short-legged representative of the Council of Unions protested, "You're not taking the momentum of everything into consideration. It's true the peasants are in a fanatic mood, but... You've already sent agitators about the area, the peasants are coming toward the city; the Japanese are maintaining their neutrality... True!.. Let Vershinin delay the armored train even, we're still not going to have an uprising."

"Show him!.."

"This is demagogy!.."

"May I speak!.."

"Comrades!"

Peklevanov rose, pulled a paper out of his briefcase, and read, blushing "Permit me to announce the following: 'According to the directive of the Coucil of the People's Commissars of Siberia—the uprising is set for 12 o'clock noon, September 16, 1919. The starting point for the uprising is the Artillery division barracks... On signal... The Council of the People's...'"

When he was leaving, the short-legged man said to Peklevanov, "They're watching us! You be more careful... And you sent the sailor into that area in vain."

"How come?"

"He's a high-strung person: God only knows what he might say! Right now you must choose people carefully."

"He knows the peasants well," said Peklevanov.

"No one knows the peasants. He's a flighty person, and flightiness really acts on them, right? Nevertheless... Are you going to the meeting?"

"Where?"

"At the shipbuilding factory. The workers want to see you."

Peklevanov blushed.

The short-legged man went right up to him and said to him quietly, straight to his face, "I feel sorry for you. And they don't want to act without you. They don't believe words, but they want to believe a person. They're watched... counterintelligence... They're shot when they're caught—but nonetheless they want to see you. To see if you're with them. You're starting all this in vain."

Peklevanov wiped his sweaty, freckled forehead, stuck his small hands into the pockets of his short jacket and walked about the room. The short-legged man watched all his movements from his concave glasses.

"Sentimentality," said Peklevanov, "Nothing's going to happen!"

The short-legged man sighed, "As you wish. So you want us to come and get you."

"When?"

Peklevanov blushed more deeply and thought, "He's afraid for himself." And he was completely taken aback by this thought; even his hands started to tremble. "But it's all the same to me. Whenever you want!"

That evening the short-legged man drove up to the front garden and waited... His straw hat and moustache, which was yellowish and trimmed so that it resembled a toothbrush, were visible through the shrubbery. His horse was snorting.

Peklevanov's wife was crying. She had sharp teeth and a very rosy face. There shouldn't have been any tears on it; it wasn't pleasant to see them on her rosy cheeks and soft chin. "You've worn me out. Every day I wait—they'll arrest you... God only knows what next... Just do one thing for me!.."

She ran about the room, then jumped to the door and grabbing it by the handle pleaded, "I won't let you... Who is going to return you to me after they shoot you. The Party? The revolutionary committee? I don't give a damn about all of those idiots!"

"Manya! Semyonov is waiting."

"He's a scoundrel. That's all he is. I won't let you go, I'm telling you—I don't want to! Well?.."

Peklevanov looked around and then went up to the door. His wife bent her body over like a thin board under the wind; the tendons tightened under the damp skin on her arm.

Peklevanov stepped over to the window in embarrassment, "I don't understand you!.."

"Don't you love anyone... Not me, not yourself, Vasenka?.. Don't go!.."

The short-legged man called hoarsely from the cab, "Soon, Vasily Maximych? Otherwise it will get dark. They'll lock the stores."

Peklevanov said quietly, "Shame, Manya. What am I going to have to do? Jump out the window like Podkolesin?[10] You know I can't say no—they'll say I've become a coward."

"But you're going to your death. I won't let you."

Peklevanov stroked his short, thin hair. "I'll have to..."

After rummaging in the pockets of his narrow-breasted jacket and smiling crookedly, he began to crawl onto the windowsill. "Such nonsense... You shouldn't make me do this..."

His wife covered her face with her hands and ran out of the room loudly, as if crying on purpose.

"Shall we go," asked the short-legged man. He sighed.

Peklevanov thought that he heard weeping in his house. He awkwardly stuck his hands into his pockets, but there was no cigarette case. He was ashamed to return home. "Do you have any cigarettes?" he asked.

III

On a large-bellied horse that was shaggy like a huge hunting dog, Nikita Vershinin rode around the bushes by the railroad embankment.

Peasants lay in the bushes, smoking and preparing to wait long and firmly. Motley spots of shirts—dozens of them, hundreds of them—spread on both sides of the embankment between the spurs, almost for ten miles.

The horse was lazy, instead of a saddle—only a bag. Vershinin's legs dangled and his boot painfully rubbed his heel through the badly wrapped footcloth.

"Just so there aren't any women," he said.

The heads of the divisions stuck up their heads in a "soldierly manner" and as if calming themselves by their military bearing asked glibly, "Haven't you heard anything from the city, Nikita Egorich?"

"The rebellion's on."

"And what're the results? Military?"

Vershinin kicked his horse in the stomach with his heel and, feeling the tiredness of sleep in his body, rode away. "We've had good results, fellow. The main thing is for us not to make a mess out of it!"

The peasants, as though at a hay cutting, lined up along the railroad embankment. They were waiting.

The embankment looked unfamiliar and strangely deserted. For the last few days trains with evacuees and Japanese, American and Russian soldiers had been leaving for the East one after another.

Somewhere the thread was broken and people were pushed in the other direction. It was said that the peasants who had come from the mountains were robbing the evacuees and people were envious. Only Armored Train No. 14-69 traveled between the stations, preventing soldiers from abandoning everything and escaping.

Partisan headquarters was holding a meeting in the switchman's booth. The switchman was standing wearily at the telephone and asking the station, "Is the armored train coming soon?"

A partisan with a revolver was sitting next to him with a calm face and looking into his mouth.

Vaska Okorok was kidding the switchman. "We'll make you our cook. Don't be afraid!"

And pointing at the telephone he said, "They say in Petersburg the educated Bolsheviks are talking with the moon?"

"If that's true you can't do anything about it."

The peasants sighed and looked at the embankment.

"The truth will even climb onto the stars."

The staff were waiting for the armored train. They had sent 500 peasants to the bridge and had brought logs to the embankment on Russian carts so that the armored train couldn't go backwards. Crowbars were lying near the ties to tear up the rails.

Znobov said with dissatisfaction, "It's all true, yes, true! And we ourselves don't know what all this is for. Why do you want to talk to the moon, Vaska?"

"But it's remarkable, anyhow! Maybe we'll want to create a peasant on the moon."

The peasants began to laugh, "Nonsense."

"Okorok!"

"We should be concerned with not wasting extra people, and here he is talking about the moon. Are we going to take the train, you devil?"

"We'll take it!"

"It's not a squirrel that you can shoot off a tree."

At that moment Vershinin arrived. He entered, breathing with effort, put his hat down on the table heavily and said to Znobov, "Will it be soon?"

The switchman at the telephone said, "They don't answer."

The peasant sat silently. One started to talk about hunting. Znobov mentioned the head of the Revcom in the town.

"That one, the tow-headed guy?" asked the peasant who was talking about hunting, and immediately began to tell lies about Peklevanov—that his face was whiter than white flour and that women jumped all over him like frogs in a swamp, that an American cabinet member had offered him seven hundred billion to convert to the American religion, and Peklevanov answered proudly, "We wouldn't take you into ours—for any amount."

"There's a real bastard for you," said the peasants exuberantly. For some reason or other Znobov liked listening to these lies and wanted to say something. Vershinin took off his boots and began to put other shoes on.

All of a sudden the switchman asked timidly, "At what time? Five-twenty?"

And turning to the peasants he said, "It's coming!"

And true, the train was already at the booth—everyone ran out, and throwing their rifles on their shoulders they crawled into their carts and set off to the east toward the blown-up bridge.

"We'll make it in time!" said Okorok.

They sent a special express messenger ahead.

They looked at the rails which were dully shining among the trees.

"We should tear up the rails and leave it at that."

"It's impossible that way. And who's going to pick them up?"

"Us, brother, right on the train!"

"We'll roll them into the city!"

"And gather them up here."

Okorok shouted, "But brothers, they have people for that!"

"Where?"

"Nezelasov's. There are men who repair rails?"

"You're stupid, Vaska. What if we kill them off? All of them?"

And getting excited about the work they all agreed.

"Anything is possible... We'll shoot them all down!.."

"No, there'd be no one to gather up the ties."

They kept looking back to see if the armored train was coming. They were hiding in the forest—because people on the tracks were unusual now—the train would rush past and shoot at them. Their hearts were pounding fearfully, they beat their horses, drove them as though shelter were waiting for them at the bridge.

About two miles from the switchman's house they saw a man on horseback on the embankment.

"He's ours!" shouted Znobov.

Vaska took aim at him. "Should I knock him off?"

"What the hell do you mean 'ours'? If he were ours he wouldn't aim."

Sin-Bin-U, who was sitting next to Vaska, held him back, "Wait, Vaska!.."

"Wait!" shouted Znobov.

The man on the horse galloped up closer. It was the peasant with the bandaged cheek who had brought the American to them.

"Is Nikita Egorich here?"

"Well?"

The peasant shouted gladly, "We got there, and there were Cossacks there. Around the bridge! We fired for a bit and then turned back."

"From where?"

Vershinin rode up to the peasant and examining him asked, "Did you kill them all?"

"All of them, Nikita Egorich. Five of them—God rest their souls!.."

"And where were the Cossacks from?"

The peasant slapped his horse on the mane, "But the bridge, Nikita Egorich, we didn't raise it."

The peasants began to shout.

"What do you mean?.."

"Trouble-maker!"

"Sock him in the mug!"

The little peasant hastily crossed himself. "Honest to God—they didn't raise it. They blew themselves up in the rocks, about 600 yards from the bridge. They must have gotten it into their heads to test the dynamite. We only found a pants leg with meat in it, and all the rest... Disappeared..."

The peasants were silent. They set out again. But they stopped suddenly. With his face distorted Vaska yelled, "Brothers, the armored train's going to slip by! To the city! Brothers!.."

The crowd of peasants sent ahead burst out of the forest.

One of them said, "There are logs all piled up by the bridge, Nikita Egorich, on the embankment. The Cossacks are shooting back. Well. There aren't too many of them."

"Should we go over to the bridge?" asked Znobov.

Here for some unknown reason everyone looked around at once.

Smoke was thinly stretching out across the forest.

"It's coming!" said Okorok.

Hitting his horse with his whip violently, Znobov repeated, "It's coming..."

The peasants repeated, "It's coming!"

"Comrades," twanged Okorok, "we've got to stop it!.."

They bounced off the cart. Grabbing their rifles they rushed to the embankment. The horses went into the high grasses, and shaking their bridles, they nibbled at the grass.

The peasants ran up to the embankment. They lay on the ties. They put in their cartridge clips. They got ready.

The rails were moaning softly—the armored train was coming.

Znobov said softly, "It'll run them over—that's all. They won't even waste any bullets, not for anything!"

And sensing this, they all suddenly crawled quietly from the tracks into the bushes, and again left the embankment bare.

The smoke was getting thicker; the wind was tearing at it, but it was steadily creeping across the forest.

"It's coming!.. It's coming!.." The peasants were running to Vershinin and shouting.

Vershinin and the whole staff lay in the bushes, wet and disturbed. Vaska Okorok was angrily beating his fist on the ground. Sin-Bin-U was squatting on his heels and pulling up grass.

Znobov said quickly, with fright in his voice, "If we only had a dead person."

"What for?"

"Well, you see, according to the law—if they run over a dead person, then the train stops. In order to make up a report... A certificate and all that!.."

"Well?"

"Well, if we had a corpse, we could lay it out. They'd run over it and stop, and then the engineer—when he comes out, we could shoot him. We could take..."

The smoke got thicker. A whistle blasted.

Vershinin jumped up and shouted, "Who wants to...to get on the rails, comrades, so that the train will run him over!.. We're going to die sooner or later. Well?.. And we'll knock off the engineer from the train! But it's more likely to stop without reaching the person."

The peasants raised their bodies and looked at the embankment which resembled a burial mound.

"Comrades!" shouted Vershinin.

The peasants were silent.

Vaska threw down his rifle and climbed onto the embankment.

"Where?" shouted Znobov.

Vaska angrily snapped back, "To hell with you!.. Bastards!.."

And stretching his arms alongside his body, he lay across the rails.

The trees were already breathing and moaning, and the yellowish crimson smoke rose into the sky and jumped about on the tops of the trees like foam.

Vaska turned over on his stomach. The rails smelled of tar. Vaska sprinkled a handful of sand onto the tie and put his cheek down on it.

Like wind in the foliage, the peasants in the bushes talked unintelligibly. The earth in the forest hummed...

Vaska raised his head, and turned to the bushes and asked softly, "Is there any vodka?.. I'm burning!.."

A peasant with a beard the color of straw crawled up on all fours with a ladle of vodka. Vaska drank up and put the ladle beside himself.

Then he raised his head, and wiping the sand from his cheek with his hand, looked toward the rumble: the blue trees were humming, the blue ties were ringing.

He raised himself up on his elbows. His face stretched into one yellow wrinkle, his eyes like two crimson tears... "I can't do it!.. My soul!"

The peasants were silent.

Sin-Bin-U threw down his rifle and crawled up to the embankment. "Where you going?" shouted Znobov.

Without turning around, Sin-Bin-U said, "Vaska lonely thele by self!"

And he lay down beside Vaska.

His yellow face wrinkled and turned as dark as an autumn leaf. The tie was crying. Sin-Bin-U didn't know, didn't see whether it was a man crawling down the slope, the bushes there receiving someone....

"I can't!..fellows!.." sobbed Vaska, crawling down.

The grass dripped spit, the sky dripped spit...

Sin-Bin-U was alone....

His head, flat and emerald-eyed like that of a cobra, felt the ties, tore itself off of them, and wavering, lifted itself up above the rails... It looked around.

Silent peasant heads with hungry, waiting eyes raised the bushes. Sin-Bin-U lay down again.

And once again the emerald-eyed cobra stretched upward—and again a few hundred heads rustled the bushes and looked at it.

Sin-Bin-U lay down again.

The pockmarked little peasant with the staw-like beard shouted at him, "Throw the ladle over here, Chink!.. And you could also leave your revolver here. What do you need it for?.. Eh!.. But I can use it!.."

Sin-Bin-U took out the revolver and without lifting his head, waved his hand, as though wishing to throw it into the bushes, and suddenly he shot himself in the back of the neck.

The body of the Chinaman stuck to the rails tightly.

The pines ejected the armored train. It was gray, square, and the pupils of the locomotive shone a malicious crimson. The sky was covered with a gray mold, the trees were like blue cloth...

And the corpse of the Chinaman, Sin-Bin-U, sticking tightly to the earth, listened to the resonant ringing of the rails...

Chapter Seven

I

Ensign Obab remained lying by the embankment, in the grass.

Captain Nezelasov was in the compartment, in the engine cab, in the cars. And it seemed to everyone that he was in a hurry, although he said, swallowing his words, "Go on!.. Go on!.."

The engineer's assistant came running to replace him. Muddling with the levers and wiping his hands on his oil-covered coat, he said, "Right away... one shouldn't...time to look!.."

The water lines started to boil.

While looking for a chisel in the locomotive, the narrow-necked man bruised his head and suddenly started to shout, but not from pain.

Bending over, Nezelasov ran away, "Well, to hell with you...to hell!"

The train was rushing toward the bridge, but there on the rails, for three miles, lay logs, an enormous larch. And for some reason it seemed that the bridge had been blown up.

Clanging its bumpers, the armored train jumped back and with a screech sped off for the station. But at the turn in the forest where Obab was killed, the ties had been taken up...

And on the straight portion of the track—from the bridge to the switch-man's booth it was six miles—Captain Nezelasov rushed back and forth like a huge pendulum.

Machine-guns were firing, the train cars were firing machine-guns, the machine-guns were hot, like blood... Like blood...

One could see badly wounded partisans jumping up out of the bushes. Now they weren't afraid to show their faces.

But those who were alive couldn't be seen, and in the same way the golden gray bushes bent over, and the cedars shone darkly. At times it seemed that only the armored train was firing.

Nezelasov could not make out the faces of the soldiers in the train. The lamps shone dimly and their faces seemed brighter than the yellow wicks of the lamps.

Nezelasov's body obeyed him submissively, his throat shouted clearly, a bit sharply, and his left hand was grasping at something in the air.

He wanted to shout some words of comfort to the soldiers, but he thought, "They know it themselves!"

And again he felt anger at Ensign Obab.

At night the partisans lit campfires. They burned with a huge milky-yellow flame, and since it was dangerous to go up and throw wood into the fire they threw it from afar, and it seemed that the fires were wide, about the size of a peasant's hut.

The armored train ran through these fires and the guns and the machine-guns intensified their fire.

Thus fires burned on both sides of the track and no one was visible, but the shots from the taiga resembled the crackling of burning green logs.

It seemed to the captain that his heavy body was being drawn to one end of the train, and he ran to the center and thought that the engineer would defect to the partisans and that the soldiers in the engineer's box behind him were uncoupling the cars while the train was in motion.

The captain, trying to seem strict, said, "The cartridges... shoot them all... don't spare them!.."

And consoling himself, he shouted to the engineer, "I'm speaking... Can't you hear when you're spoken to?.. Don't spare the cartridges!.."

The captain grabbed a rifle and tried to shoot into the darkness himself, but remembered that the commander is necessary as an administrator, not as a military unit. He felt his shaved chin and thought quickly, "And what am I good for?"

But then he thought, "It would be a good idea for the captain to fall in love... with a beard half a yard long!.. A general's daughter... a career... Don't dare!.."

The captain started running to the center part of the train, "Don't you dare, not without orders!"

Without the captain's orders the armored train was rushing back and forth from the bridge—a small wooden bridge across the river which the partisans for some reason or other couldn't blow up—to the switchman's booth, but already growing closer and closer—like the heads of two screws, logs were crawling along the rails, and behind the logs—peasants.

Bullets struck the logs, the peasants shot back at them.

Blind, afraid of stumbling, the armored train went directly into the bullets, and behind its steel walls the soldiers were already running from car to car, changing places, working guns not their own, and wiping off their sweaty chests and saying, "Forgive us, God!"

Nezelasov was afraid to show himself to the engineer. And as if behind steel walls, his thoughts ran from place to place, and when he had to say something necessary, the captain would shout, "Bastards!.."

And the necessary word beat around for a long time in his legs and elbows, covered with goosebumps.

The captain ran into his compartment. The brown puppy was sleeping in a bundle on the bed.

The captain started waving his arm. "I said... neither shells!..nor pity!.. And here the bastards... bastards!.."

He stomped about in one place, struck the pillow with the palm of his hand; the puppy jumped back, opened his mouth, and quietly began to whimper. The captain bent over toward it and listened.

"I-i-i!.." whined the puppy.

The captain grabbed it and stuck it under his arm and started running up and down the cars with it.

The soldiers did not look around at the captain. His familiar, wide but flat figure, which right now was somehow transparent, like bad cigarette paper, was running around with a quiet whining. And the fact that the captain was whining did not surprise them.

But the puppy was whining and weakly scratching the captain's field jacket with its soft paws.

For the seventh hour in a row without stopping the machine-guns were firing non-stop at the grass, trees, darkness, and at the stones lighted up by the fire; and it was incomprehensible why the partisans were firing at the train's steel armor, because they knew the bullets would not pierce it.

When he reached up to his head, the captain felt weariness. His boots, dry and hard, as if made of wood, pressed his legs tightly.

The roof was whirling, the walls bending, it smelled of burned meat—from where and why? And the steam engine hummed without stopping, "A-w-o-e-e-e-i."

More and more peasants were arriving. They left the carts with their wives in the forest, and with rifles on their shoulders they walked along the paths to the clearing. From there they crawled to the railroad embankment and entrenched themselves.

The women, lamenting, met the wounded and took them home. The wounded men who were a bit stronger cursed the women with vile language, and those who were seriously wounded, hopped around on roots, exposing their hollow pieces of flesh to the air and to the falling yellow leaves. Leaves stuck to the blood of the spattered carts.

A small pock-marked woman with a ladle of holy water was walking around the clearing, sprinkling those who were going past her with a piece of coal. They were crawling and turning toward her, then they crawled by quietly, like a herd of satisfied sheep returning from the field.

In a cart behind the switchman's booth, Vershinin was listening to reports which a fat secretary was reading to him.

Vaska Okorok whispered fearfully, "Is it terrible, Nikita Egorich?"

"What?" asked Vershinin hoarsely.

"There's such a mass of people here."

"What does it have to do with you—you're not a horse-thief. What do you expect, the whole village commune came out!.."

Since Sin-Bin-U's death, Vaska had been walking around with his shoulders hunched and his head drawn into them and looking at everyone's face with a dull, guilty little smile.

"They're coming quietly, Nikita Egorich. I don't feel right inside."

"Keep quiet and it will pass!"

Znobov said, "I don't know how many nights we haven't slept, and you, Vaska, are red-headed, and a red-head should have feathers."

Vaska sighed quietly, "In one country, they say, they don't take red-heads as soldiers. But I've been honored to serve seven years for the Tsar—four years active service and three years during the German war."

"It's a good thing that we didn't blow up the bridge. . ." said Znobov.

"What?" asked Vaska.

"How would we take the armored train to the city? They didn't even want to take up the ties, and we should try to get them to blow up the bridge? Gloom! . . ."

Vaska drew his curly head into his shoulders and raised his collar.

"I really feel sorry for the Chinaman, Znobov! I think he'll go to heaven—he suffered for the Christian faith."

"And you're a fool, Vaska."

"What?"

"You believe in God."

"And you don't?"

"Not at all! . ."

"You're a bastard, Znobov. However, that's your business brother. Now we have freedom, you can lick whoever you want. Only I can't live without religion—my whole family has always been schismatic, Old Believers."

"Some believers! . ." Znobov broke out laughing. Vaska sighed in anguish.

"Let me go, Nikita Egorich, at least I can shoot a bit!"

"That's impossible. If you're staff, then sit in the staff room."

"But the carts."

The glass in the booth began to rattle and fell with a soft ring. A shell fell next to them.

All of a sudden Vershinin became really angry and pushed the secretary. "Stay here. And when night comes—let them light the fire. Otherwise they'll get off the train and run into the forest, or the devil only knows what they might get into their heads."

Vershinin drove his horse along the railroad line after the departing armored train. "You won't get away, whore!"

His little horse, shaggy as a dog, shook its stomach, large as a barrel. His cart jumped up and down. Vershinin jumped to his feet and gave the reins a pull, "Go-o! . ."

The little horse tightened his legs up, started whipping its tail, and took off. Znobov, galloping up, held firmly onto the end of the cart with his heavy body and tried to dissuade Vershinin, "Don't chase them, you won't catch up with them! And if they get a chance to kill you for nothing they will."

"It's not going to get anywhere. Get going!"

He lashed the horse's sweaty back with his whip.

Vaska shouted, "Go ahead! The whole staff is examining the soldiers! To hell with the captain and his train. Take off, Egorich! Go!"

The carts ran past the entrenched peasants. The peasants got up on their knees and silently accompanied the men standing on the cart with their eyes: then they took up their guns and waited for the train which would be rushing past in order to shoot at it.

The armored train was charging at them with shots and a thundering roar.

Vaska screwed up his eyes.

"They're aiming too high," said Znobov, "see they're not hitting. They must have gone mad, they can't see a thing!"

"Nothing at all!" shouted Vaska furiously, and grabbed a switch and started to beat his horse.

Vershinin was huge; his eyebrows tore across his wet face.

"Don't let them get me, comrades!"

"Cover him!" shouted Vaska at the top of his voice.

The cart was rattling; a board was beating on the wheels; the jolts were throwing the hay under the seat onto the ground. The peasants in the bushes answered in an unsoldierly-like manner, "That's all right!.."

And this seemed powerful and understandable, and even Znobov jumped onto his knees and waving his gun shouted, "Come on, let's go. If we perish, we perish!"

The armored train, no longer terrifying, was again tearing towards them and Vaska was threatening with his fist, "We'll get to it!"

Among the lights of the quiet fires the gray boxes of the cars rumbled and rushed swiftly back and forth in the darkness.

And the hairy man on the cart was giving orders. The peasants were dragging logs to the embankment, and they crawled slowly, pushing them in front of themselves as they crawled. The armored train was approaching and shooting point-blank.

The logs were like corpses and the corpses like logs—branches and hands were crackling; both the trees and the men had young and healthy bodies.

The sky was dark and heavy, forged out of iron, and the locomotive's hollow howl roared above.

The peasants were crossing themselves, loading their rifles, and pushing the logs. The logs smelled of sap and the peasants of sweat. The pines were like spears and broke brittlely on the armor of the approaching train.

Bending over in the cart, Vaska laughed, "You're not drinking, you bastard. We'll get to you, brother. You won't jump away. We didn't give you the Chinaman for nothing."

Znobov was calculating, "Tomorrow their water will run out. We'll take it. That's for sure."

Vershinin said, "We have to go help the town."

People were falling and kissing the earth with last mortal kisses—as ripe fruits are blown down in the wind.

Their hands could hold no longer, and their bodies fell softly and weren't hurt anymore—the earth pitied them. At first there were dozens of them. Women cried quietly at the edge of the forest by a clearing. Then hundreds of them—and the howling grew higher and higher. There was no one to carry them away and the corpses kept them from pushing more logs up to the tracks.

The peasants kept on crawling and crawling.

The armored train continued to eat up the tracks without tiring, and as if losing its way in the smoke from the empty campfires, it made its steps from the switchman's booth to the wooden bridge across the river smaller and smaller.

Then it stopped.

The peasants started attacking long before Vershinin's shout, "Let's go!.. Comrades!.."

Pieces of lead and copper ricocheted off the steel walls into bodies; they tore into open chests, buttoning them and death into one buttonhole forever.

The peasants howled, "O-a-a-a-o!!"

Grass crawled along their chests, stomachs. Their faces caught on the branches of the bushes and their beards were torn and their lips stuck out from behind the sweaty hair "O-o-e-a-ai-i-!!!"

The campfires remained behind them, and not far away the dark cars stood like barns; and there was no way to get the people who were hiding behind the steel walls in terror.

A partisan threw a grenade at the wheels. It exploded, hitting everyone in the chest.

The peasants retreated.

It was getting light.

When they saw the corpses in the light, they started shouting loudly, as if someone had scraped the skin from their backs; and again they started crawling to the train cars.

Vershinin took off his boots and walked barefoot. Znobov, often squatting, was crawling cautiously, almost on all fours—for some reason going around the bushes. Vaska Okorok looked at Vershinin with glee and shouted, "And you, Nikita Egorich, are Eruslan!"[8]

Vaska's face was happy; but tears were shining in his eyes.

The armored train was whistling.

"Stuff something down its throat," shouted Okorok piercingly, and suddenly he got up from his knees and grasping his chest said in a thin voice, as hurt children do, "My God... and me, too!.."

He fell.

Not looking at Vaska, the partisans were crawling toward the high yellow embankment, which looked like a huge coffin.

His whole body jerking convulsively, as if hurrying somewhere, Vaska died.

The partisans retreated again.

III

The soldiers, wet from sweat and clanging their water cans, were cooling off their machine-guns by the embrasures. And, as if ashamed, the movements of their scratched hands were timidly swift.

The train was quivering in a slight quick tremor, hot all over, like a person sick with typhoid fever.

The dark crimson gloom filled the head of Captain Nezelasov with quivering clots of blood. A hot chilling shiver went like an upside-down barbed triangle from his temples downward, settling in his heart, jarring his whole body.

"The bastards!" shouted the captain.

He didn't know how it got there, but there was a cavalry carbine in his hands; its lock bolt was surprisingly warm and soft. Hitting the doors with the butt of the rifle, Nezelasov was running through the cars, "The bastards!" he shouted shrilly. "The bastards!..."

It was a pity that he could not find a word that would sound like an order, and cursing seemed to him the most appropriate and easiest thing he could do.

The peasants were attacking the train. Through the patches of light in the embrasures one could see hunched backs running among the bushes, which resembled matted yellow wool with rifles like little boards flashing at their sides.

The forests and the always surprisingly fat, dark green mountains which resembled breasts were beyond the bushes. But more frightening than these large mountains were the backs, like pieces of bark, which were running swiftly back and forth among the bushes.

And the soldiers felt this terror, and in order to drown out the incomprehensible cry from the bushes, they deafened it with machine-guns.

The machine-guns shot at the bushes—tirelessly, comparable to nothing and no one.

Captain Nezelasov ran past his compartment several times. For some reason or other it was frightening to go in there. A lithographed picture of Kolchak, the plan of the European war theater, and the cast-iron Buddha which took the place of an ashtray were visible through the door. The captain felt that if he went into the compartment, he would start crying and not leave, he would hide somewhere in a corner like the whining puppy who was whining Gods knows where.

The peasants were attacking.

It was shameful to confess, but he did not know how many attacks there had been, and it was impossible to ask the soldiers, their eyes were filled with such malice. They would not lift them from the locks of the rifles and machine-gun belts, and it was impossible to tear away these eyes without punishment—they would kill. The captain ran about among them, and the carbine which was hitting the top of his boot was as light as a reed cane.

The armored train was already going off into the night, and the darkness unwillingly let the heavy steel boxes pass. The captain thought in snatches, what if he were to hear the noise of the wind in the forest... The soldiers morosely shot their rifles and machine-guns into the darkness. It seemed as if the machine-guns were cutting a huge, violently screaming body.

A pale-haired soldier was pouring kerosine into a lamp. The kerosine had been flowing on his knees for a long time already, and the captain, standing beside him, sensed the light smell of apples.

"The puppy... should be given water!.." said Nezelasov hurriedly.

The pale-haired soldier obediently stuck out his lips and called, "N'akh... n'akh... n'akh!.."

Another one with thin but awfully short arms was changing his boots, and holding up his footcloth, he smelled it for a long time and said to the captain, "Kerosine, your excellency. In our village it costs twenty to forty rubles per pound..."

* * *

... There were an awful lot of them... All of them for some reason had to die and lie near the armored train in the brush which looked like yellow matted wool.

They lit the fires. They burned like candles, evenly, hardly flickering and one could not see who was adding the wood. The mountains were burning.

"Stone doesn't burn!.."

"It burns!.."

"It burns!.."

Another attack.

Someone runs to the train and falls. He runs back and again runs to the train.

"Is this an attack?"

"Nonsense."

"They'll lie there for a little while—those in the bushes, then get up, run back, and then come again."

... They started running! ..

* * *

A cry, thick as stone, charged across the machine-guns past the small ringing barrels and fell into the cars, "Oo-u-oe! .."

And thinly, thinly, "Oi! .. Oi! .."

A soldier with sunken gray cheeks said, "They're wailing... there in the taiga... the women, for them! .."

And he sank onto the bench.

A bullet hit him in the ear and tore a hole as large as a fist in the other side of his head.

"Why is everything visible in the darkness?" said Nezelasov. "There are fires there, but it should be dark here."

"The fires in the darkness, behind them the cry of women. Perhaps the mountains are wailing? ..."

"Nonsense! .. The mountains are burning! .."

"No, that's nonsense too, it's the fires burning! .."

The machine-gunner burned his side and started crying like a little boy.

An old volunteer, bearded like a priest, shot him with his revolver.

The captain wanted to shout, but for some reason or other stayed silent and only touched his thin eyelids, which were as dry as paper.

* * *

The carbine was getting heavy, but for some reason he had to drag it around.

Captain Nezelasov had soft white skin, and on it, like a flower on silk—his eyes.

Night was already passing. Soon the sun would rise.

The pale-haired soldier was sleeping at his machine-gun and another one, still sleepy, was shooting. However, perhaps it was not his gun that was shooting, but his neighbor's. Or the neighbor's gun was sleeping and his neighbor was shouting, "Over there! .. Over there! .."

* * *

The pain stretched from his throat to his chin, as if his skin were being scratched off by a nail. And now Nezelasov saw before his face: his thin hands with their long dirty fingernails were shaking.

Then he forgot about this. He forgot a lot that night... It's necessary to forget some things, because it is hard to bear everything...hard...

And suddenly silence...

There, outside the doors of the cars, in the bushes.

You've got to fall asleep. It seems like morning, but perhaps it's evening. You shouldn't remember every day...

They're not shooting there, in the mountains. Calm, blood-spattered peasants lie by the embankment. Of course, it's not comfortable for them to lie there.

And here before your eyes—darkness. The captain had gone blind. "This is from the silence..."

Both his eyes and his soul had gone blind. It even seemed like fun.

But now everyone felt, at first lightly, but then as if being scorched—that they couldn't bear this silence.

The pale-haired soldier, raising his arms, ran to the doors. Darkness. In the darkness his raised arms were invisible.

And the captain sensed it right away: now men were rushing to the doors in all seven cars. On the sand it's easier to stand firmly, and it's possible to escape somewhere...

* * *

He got sick to his stomach for a second. He felt sick not only in his stomach, but also in his legs, arms, and shoulders. But his shoulder suddenly grew weak, and under his foot the captain felt grass, and his knees gave way.

In front of him the captain saw a bearded shirt, an epaulet on a bayonet, and a piece of meat...

...His, Captain Nezelasov's meat...

Pork cutlets... The Olympia restaurant... A Mexican Negro is directing a Rumanian... An aspen... Autumn...

* * *

The train is not on the embankment. That means it is night... He felt under his arm—human hair covered with sweat. Half of a torn-off ear, like cloth; a tear, torn by a nail, he tore it with a nail...

...In his hand—bushes, but he does not feel the other hand. You can break off the bush calmly and even shove it into your mouth. That is not an ear.

And the carbine is across his boot, so it left the train too.

Nezelasov rejoiced. He could not remember where this belt with cartridges on his field jacket had come from.

He believed something.

He burst out laughing and perhaps roared.

The bushes smelled swampy from the warm blood. A black piercing wind blew from the mountains; it blew the long wet branches. Perhaps wet from blood...

Then Obab crawled past with the puppy under his arm. His riding breeches looked like the wheel of a cart.

The pale-haired soldier stuck his head out and announced quietly, "Do you order us to leave?"

"Go to hell!"

The refugee in the brown mantle whispered into his ear, "They're coming!...they're coming!.."

Even Captain Nezelasov himself knew that they were coming. He had to get into an advantageous position. Climbing up on the sill he raised his carbine and fired.

But one hand, it turns out, is missing. It's awkward with one hand. But you could put it on your knee. You can't see the sight from your knee... Why didn't he shoot from the train, for here...

He is alone here, but look how many of them are crawling, bearded ones, the bastards are falling to the earth, otherwise...

Thus Captain Nezelasov fired quickly into the darkness until he used up all his cartridges.

Then he put aside the carbine, crawled from the hill into the brush, and burying his face in the grass—died.

Chapter Eight

I

The sorghum rustled copiously in the rich dark fields.

The copper Chinese dragon is striking his yellow jangling rings in the forest, and in the rings square steel boxes are rolling, ringing, and rumbling...

On the yellow scales of the dragon are smoke, ashes, sparks...

Steel is ringing on steel, it is being forged!...

Smoke. Sparks. Sorghum. Fertile fields.

Maybe the Chinese dragon is from the mountains, maybe the forest...

Yellow leaves, yellow sky, yellow embankment.

Sorghum.

* * *

By the door of the compartment a bald-faced little old man, trying on Ensign Obab's wide, wide blue riding breeches, was shouting in a perky, boyish voice, "*Vot xalipa!*.. It's just like a skirt, and knees as bare as can be: like a cucumber!.."

Ashes on the table. Smoke tearing through the window.

Windows wide open. Doors wide open. Trunks wide open.

The Chinese Buddha is on the floor, covered with spit, smirking sorrowfully. A funny little eccentric...

On the other side of the embankment—another god crawls from the mountains; yellow, it rings with forged bells...

Rich sorghum, black!

Man has a rich look, full and satisfied.

"Oh-ho-ho!..."

"The end of the devils!.."

"That's enough!..."

The peasants have grabbed onto the locomotive, they are moving around the steel with their hot intoxicated bodies.

One in a red shirt threatens with his fist, "We'll show you!"

"Who, what?"

"I don't know!"

"But you've always got to threaten!"

A red shirt, like a red ribbon, on a gray overcoat.

Ribbon!

"O-o-o-o!.."

"Come on Gavrila!.."

"A-a-a!.."

Ribbon!..

Armored train "Polar," No. 14-69 is under the red flag.

On the red-headed dragon from the hills—on the red one—a ribbon!..

* * *

Here a wheel would travel two miles a minute. Now the rails are quiet, they are not humming, they are frightened...

What?

The puny little soldier in the light blue French puttees, with his dagger, "Cantaloupe grow badly on the Irtysh...there are more sunflowers and watermelons. The people are neither mean nor affectionate... I don't know—what they are."

"Who knows about the people?"

"God Himself gave up on them..."

"Oh-oh!.."

"Well, he says, to hell with you!.."

"Oh-oh!..."

"Lithographed Kolchak" is on the floor of the toilet; the orders are on the floor; newspapers are on the floor...

People do not notice the floor. They walk around—not feeling...

"A-a-a!.."

"Polar" is under the red flag...

What?

Huge, sedate—the train swims along in the wind—a piece of red material. Bloody, alive, shouting, "O-o-!.."

The glasses on Peklevanov's nose are trying to jump, but they don't succeed; he himself is trying to jump somewhere with his body and the words, "In America—any day now!"

Znobov shouts, "I know... I myself carried out propaganda with an American bourgeois!.."

"They learned it!.."

"In England, comrades!.. 'Arise, you branded by the curse.' "

"Oh-oh-oh!.."

The glasses on his nose jumped up. His eyes saw: smoke, tobacco, machine-guns on the floor, rifles, cartridges like grain, peasants' hair, greasy and drunken eyes.

"The Revcom, comrades, having as its task..."

"We know!.."

"That's enough... I want to shout myself!.. 'Nightingale, nightingale, little bird, little canary!'"

Vershinin is on the bed; he is breathing deeply and regularly, he is burning only on the inside—the air is heavy in the compartment from his breathing. Even though the doors are wide open. The air is earthy, heavy, it smells of peasants.

Next to him is a woman. Wherever she came from, she came with her breasts thrust forward; she is quivering all over.

Znobov shouts, "Did you find him? He's a good fellow!.."

Someone is crying drunkenly behind the doors, "Vaska... the bastards, Vaska—they killed him...I'll rip open the guts of five of them—for Vaska and the Chinaman... Bastards..."

"To hell with them... Dogs..."

"I'll get them...for Vaska!.."

II

That night his wife came again; she breathed heavily, panted, fell silent. Her white teeth could be seen in the moonlight—teeth, cold and cooling the body, and the body was like the teeth, only warm and trembling.

She spoke the same words as before, childish, and there was

something childish in her; but in her hands was a strength not hers, strange—earthy.

And in her legs, too...

"A-ta-ta-ta! Akh!.. Akh!.."

It's the armored train—going toward the city, toward the sea.

The people are going too...

Perhaps to the same place, perhaps even further...

They have to go further, that is because they are the people...

* * *

"I say, I—"

We turn into beasts at night, beasts!!

I know—and I rejoice... I believe...

The earth smells—you can smell it from behind the steel, although the doors are wide open, the soul is wide open. It smells of autumn grasses, subtly, joyfully, and approvingly.

The tender evening forests are going toward man, they tremble and rejoice—he is the master.

I know!

I believe!

Man trembles—he too is a leaf on a huge and beautiful tree. His is the sky and his is the earth, and he is the sky and the earth.

It is good, good—to believe everything, to know and to love everything. Everything is as it should be and will be—always and in every heart.

* * *

"Oh-oh-oh!.."

"Senka, Styopka... Monster!.."

"Well!"

These people have a greasy roar—they are wearing steel clothes; they are rejoicing at them; perhaps the steel leaves bend; the huge locomotive shudders and the darkness spreads out in an oily rumbling.

"U-a-u-a... u-u-u!.."

The Armored Train, "Polar..."

The whole line knows, the city knows, all of Russia... At Lake Baikal, and most likely on the Ob...

So!..

* * *

A station.

A Japanese officer came out of the crowd and with an even, strange gait, walked up to the armored train. An alien force hiding in the darkness behind him could be sensed and therefore should have been gay, somewhat cold and terrible.

Znobov went to meet him. At first there was a crowd of Znobovs—shaggy, thick-haired, and then one separated from them.

The officer extended his hand quickly and adroitly and said in purposely broken Russian, "We—neutlal!.."

And raising his voice, he started talking clearly and authoritatively in Japanese. There was contempt and some sort of incomprehensible boredom in his voice. And Znobov said:

"Neutrality, that's all right. But are there a lot of you?.."

"Twenty thousand..." said the Japanese, and turning around in a military fashion he went away, unnecessary and again completely strange.

Znobov stood there a moment, then he turned around too, and said to himself in a whisper, "But there's a million of us, you bastard!.."

And he explained to the partisans, "They're cowards. Neutrality, he says, and we want to go to the islands—to grow rice... We don't give a damn about you—go ahead."

And he spit into the palm of his hand angrily, "And he even shakes my hand, the bastard!.."

"There's only one thing to do—hang them," decided the partisans.

* * *

They were leading a crying officer with a rosy girlish face. His eyes and lips were also crying girlishly.

A lame peasant with an empty dirty sack thrown across his arm went up to the officer and with his free hand hit him in the bridge of the nose. "Don't sing!.."

Then the escort, as if having remembered something, swung his arms apart and jumping up as if at drill, stuck a bayonet between the officer's shoulder blades.

A station.

A yellow lantern, yellow faces, and black earth.

Night.

* * *

Night.

A woman was on the cot in the compartment. Next to her black clothes.

Vershinin got up and went to the office.

He explained to the fat clerk, "Write this..."

The clerk was drunk and didn't understand, "What?"

And Vershinin himself didn't know what to write. He stood there for a moment and thought. "We have to do something, for someone, somehow..."

"Write this..."

The drunken clerk wrote in handwriting as thick as himself, "Order, according to the resolution..."

"Don't," said Vershinin, "don't, boy."

The clerk agreed with him and fell asleep, putting his fat head on the fragile little table.

* * *

The puny little soldier in the light blue puttees was saying, "I've covered a lot of land and seen a lot of all kinds of people..."

Znobov's golden eyes and golden moustache were hungry and tender. They said, "Where are you from?"

The soldier spun a merry story and they didn't believe him and he himself didn't believe it. But everyone was having a good time.

There were machine-gun ribbons on the floor. The cartridges looked like grain, and the partisans' pants were drying on the machine-guns. On the barrels there was dried blood which looked like rotted darkened silk.

"Once the Persian Shah was traveling through the Turkmen lands and he meets the Queen of England..."

III

The city met them calmly.

Already at the switch station the watchman was saying apprehensively, "I haven't heard about any uprisings. But could be there are some. We're railroad men. Our salary is small, so, well..."

His beard was grayish, like rotten manure, and he smelled like a chicken coop.

At the train station officers tearing off their epaulets were apprehensively rushing around the commander's office. By the train platform drivers shouted joyously from their trucks. Workers were going from the depot.

Peklevanov was fussing around next to Vershinin, "We've got to start, Nikita Egorich."

Partisans with machine-guns and rifles were jumping out of the cars. Almost all of them were without caps and had drunken narrow eyes.

"There's nothing?.."

"Set up the machine-gun..."

"Give us a car, come on!.."

Trucks were approaching. In the commander's room broken glass and revolver shots were ringing. Some pale young girls were putting up a tattered red banner in the first-class buffet.

The workers were shouting "hurrah." Znobov was shouting something incomprehensible. Peklevanov was sitting in a truck and smiling vaguely through his glasses.

The dead were taken past in a cart.

And an old lady in a rose-colored dress was crying. An arrested priest was brought by. The priest was telling something funny and his escorts were laughing.

A clean-shaven American jumped up onto a pile of railroad ties and snapped his Kodak several times in a row.

* * *

They didn't know anything in General Somov's staff.

Fluffy-haired girls were pounding on typewriters.

Officers with yellow stripes on their trousers were running up and down staircases and around halls as resonant as violins. A canary in a cage was singing in the entrance hall and the man on duty was sleeping on a wooden couch.

Immediately the trucks jumped out from around the corner. The crowd gave a deafening moan as it surged into the gates. The streetcars started to clang, the horns of the cars started blowing, and the partisans ran up the staircases. Again on the floor there were papers, typewriters, people who were maimed, perhaps killed.

The gray-haired general with pink ears was brought down the staircase. They killed him on the last step and dragged him to the couch where the man on duty was slumbering.

Holding his stomach up with his hand, a partisan was running down the staircase. His face was gray and after running halfway downstairs he started shouting shrilly and suddenly wrinkled up his face.

A woman started screaming.

The canary in the cage kept giving a rolling whistle.

A crowd of officers was brought into the basement. Not a single one of them noticed the corpse of the general lying by the staircase.

The little soldier in the light blue puttees was standing guard by the entrance of the basement in which the arrested soldiers were locked up.

In his hands was an English grenade—it was ordered, just in case, toss the grenade down there, to hell with them.

A small square window shone blue in the door of the basement, and in it there was an angular lower jaw covered with black hair, with a moist eye blinking frequently. Behind the door people were frequently mumbling incomprehensibly, as though praying...

The soldier thought wearily, "And when I throw the thing, will he jump back from the window or not?..."

* * *

The streetcars weren't ringing. The crowd on the pavement wasn't ringing. A yellow and heavy heat exhausted the town like the breathing of a typhoon. And like the rocks on the mountains, the houses stood around the bay motionless and gloomy.

And a Japanese mine-bearer stood silently in the bay, rocking lightly and freely on the greenish-blue water.

In the entrance hall of the headquarters the canary was singing sharply and trilling, and somewhere, as always, people were crying.

The stout secretary of the revolutionary staff, smiling with one cheek, was writing an order on a bench, even though all the tables were empty.

Four partisans ran by quietly talking about something excitedly. It started to smell of damp skin, tar...

The secretary of the revolutionary staff was looking for the stamp, but Vershinin had left with the stamp; the secretary lifted up the ink bottle and wanted to call someone...

...In the distance—at the edge of town, there was a shot. The shot was booming, as if not from a gun—it was huge and heavy; it shook the whole body...

Then closer to the main streets of town, tearing the heart with joy, machine-guns, rifles, and streetcars struck the streets...the wharf began to roar...

The uprising had begun...

And then—two hours later, a warm and damp dark green wind started blowing from the sea.

* * *

...Miners in wide, pleated *sharovary* and in dark-blue canvas shirts were passing by. They had bony faces with gray hair that looked like moss. And only their rounded eyes, which were accustomed to stone, shone incomprehensibly like unknown mines...

Long-armed—lower than the knees—to the calves of their legs—fishermen from the Zeyski lakes were passing by. They were wearing trousers from burbot skins and had long hair, thick as spring grass, which smelled of fish...

And more—shepherds from the mountain ridge Sikhote Alin with Chinese-looking, narrow-eyed faces and with the long-barreled rifles of their great-grandfathers passed by in tempered stony step.

And still more—thick-lipped men from the River Khor, wide-chested fishermen, accustomed to the ocean winds, fishermen from the Bay of St. Olga who were suffocating in the reeds of the mainland...

Vershinin and his wife were riding in a car in front. His wife's strong and large body, wrapped in bright material, was burning under her dress. Her cracked lips bled, and her strong stomach stuck out, raising her dress. They sat motionless, not looking around, and only the wind, the same as in the mountains, taut, smelling of the sea, rocks, and seaweed, stirred her dress...

An American correspondent scribbling in his notebook, stood on a post which braced a streetlight. He was clean and smooth and looked the demonstration over quickly, like a mouse.

And opposite him, across the street, stood the frail little soldier wearing the overcoat that looked like a hospital robe and the light blue puttees and English boots. He was looking over the passers-by at the American (he was tired and was accustomed to demonstrations) and was trying to fix the American in his memory. But the American was smooth, slippery, elusive, like a fish in water.

...And he did not know whether he was ashamed for himself, for the American, for Russia or for Europe.

Translated by Frank Miller   *1922*

Notes

1. White army general in Siberia, killed by the Bolsheviks.
2. Pantaloons, tucked in at boots, usually worn by Cossacks.
3. A cigarette with one inch of tobacco and a cardboard tube some two inches long.
4. A medium-sized administrative unit, smaller than a "region" *(oblast')*.
5. Several villages united into one administrative unit.
6. *Soiti s uma.* A play on *soiti s rel'sov* which is used for both people and trains.
7. Main character of Gogol's play *The Marriage,* who avoids marriage by jumping out a window.
8. Eruslan (Lazarevich) is the hero of a common Russian tale, a warrior of untold strength.

Rodchenko's photomontage for Mayakovsky's book *Pro eto*, a montage which was not included in the book.

Isaac Babel.

ISAAC BABEL

Isaac Babel (1894-1941), a young Jewish intellectual from Odessa, arrived in St. Petersburg in 1915 to make his literary career. Gorky published two of Babel's stories in his journal *The Chronicle,* but according to Babel's somewhat embroidered autobiography, Gorky sent his protégé out into the world to acquire experience. During the years 1917-20 Babel held a number of positions both civilian and military, including in the Cheka (the secret police), but it is the campaign in the Ukraine and Poland in Budyonny's cavalry army that is of greatest interest to the reader of Babel's fiction. Babel returned to Odessa at the end of 1920 and began to write the stories based on his Civil War experiences that became *Red Cavalry.*

Babel intended from the beginning that the *Red Cavalry* stories should form a cycle. The book is organized chronologically by the campaign, opening with the army's entrance into Poland and closing with the retreat. Babel uses the Civil War theme—a major subject in the 1920s—not for the glorification of heroes or documentary reportage. Instead, the stories are primarily plotless and anecdotal in nature. The majority of the stories are narrated in the first person by a Jewish intellectual, Lyutov, who is confronted with the alien and cruel world of the Cossacks as in the story "My First Goose."

Red Cavalry brought Babel a fame that would never be repeated. At the First Congress of the Union of Writers in 1934 Babel declared that he was working in a new genre—silence. Babel's other main collection, *The Odessa Tales,* was written concurrently with *Red Cavalry.* He had not stopped writing, but found publication increasingly difficult. Babel was arrested in May 1939 and died in 1941.

Babel wrote sketches and journalism throughout his career. The two sketches "In the Rest Home" and "Without a Homeland" are representative of this work by one of the great stylists of the twentieth century.

IN THE REST HOME

Beyond the veranda is night, full of slow sounds and grandiloquent darkness. An inexhaustible rain stands watch over the lilac gashes of the mountains; the gray rustling silk of its watery walls hangs over the cool and menacing dusk of the gorges. Amid the tireless murmur of the pouring water, the blue flame of our candle flickers like a distant star, playing vaguely across wrinkled faces hewn by the heavy and expressive chisel of labor.

Three old tailors, as humble as nursemaids, the enchanting M., who had lost an eye at his workbench not long before, and I, worn out and troubled by the bitter and troubled dust of our cities—we sit on the veranda staring into the night, into the limitless and aromatic night.... An indescribable peace soothes our nervous and broken muscles with its maternal palms, and we drink tea, slowly and pensively—three humble tailors, the enchanting M., and I, an exhausted and enraptured old workhorse.

Petit bourgeoisie who built yourselves these "little dachas," untalented and hopeless as a shopkeeper's paunch, if only you could see us resting in them now.... If only you could see how faces chewed to bits by the steel jaws of machines grow fresh....

In this manly and silent kingdom of rest, in these mediocre dachas, transformed into workers' houses of rest by the miraculous power of events, here abides the elusive and noble substance of vivifying idleness, peaceful, prudent, and quiet.... O, this inimitable gesture of the resting worker's hand is modestly economical and wisely calculated! I follow it, this directed, jerky black hand, accustomed to the unwearying and complex spirit of motors, with intent delight. This obedient, quiet, and carefully thought-out immobility of the fatigued body was taken from them alone. Philosophy of respite, teaching of the restoration of spent energy—how much I have learned about you on this clear, noisy evening, when the tailors and metal workers drank their endless patriarchal cooling tea on the terrace of the workers' home in Mtskhet.

Getting intoxicated by the tea, the bracing champagne of the poor, we perspire gradually and earnestly, fondly exchanging soft words; and we recall the story of the development of these rest homes.

They are still in their first year. It was just in February of the present year that a commission of the Georgian Trade Union went out to Mtskhet for the initial procurements. The dachas were found in terrible shape— unlivable, filthy, dilapidated. This business was pursued with unflagging energy, and the bourgeoisie came to the aid of the Trade Union in this blessed undertaking, to the limit of their modest powers. As is well known, fines which the Trade Union has imposed on shopkeepers of every stripe for obstructing rules which protect labor reached the comfortable sum of six million rubles. And so, a hundred and fifty million of this money was spent to transform the half-ruined dachas into workers' homes—from which it clearly follows that the bourgeoisie's bloody money (from the word "blood") supports the first health resorts for workers in Georgia, for which great thanks. There exists the firm conviction that on the strength of the particular qualities inherent in that species, the influx of forced donations will not cease and will provide the Trade Union a chance to spread a model workers' town across the blooming hills of Mtskhet in place of the present dachas. Unfortunately, the scientific arsenal of compliments mentioned above cannot be poisoned by the memory of those wonderful and heroic efforts which the owners of the dachas made in the battle with the Trade Union. They threatened to go to the "government." And they went. The road was long, and paved with the subtle poison of judicial pettifoggery. But "government" (in the new orthography "The All-Russian Central Executive Committee") was quick and just. The petitioners left with a velocity inversely proportional to the slowness of their arrival. They were born about twenty years too late—that's the moral which the dacha owners derived from this matter, in their unflagging search for truth. A moral not without some acuity.

The dachas are meant for sixty people. The Labor Protection Division intends to increase their capacity to a thousand or fifteen-hundred persons per season, figuring two weeks per person. In some cases the period can be increased to a month. We must have certain reservations, though, for in the great majority of cases two weeks is not enough for the exhausted bodies of our workers.

The period of construction and reconstruction of the Mtskhet dachas is still going on. For that reason, certain advice, dictated by good feeling and love, will not be superfluous here. The food, which is generally healthful and plentiful, should be increased in the mornings and evenings. And another thing—it would be good to destroy the sacramental and sickening dormitory aspects of the Trade Union houses. These make the ill sick and us wanderers through furnished rooms, chancelries, barracks. What we need during those two happy weeks when we stretch our worn-out and wheezing chests is a corner that is absolutely clean, cosy, and filled with solitude.

A library is already in operation. That's good. Next week concerts for the vacationers will start in the evenings. But meantime we subsist on "durachok." But, lords, with what unspent ebullience and fervor this dear endless game goes on, as heated as a grandfather's jacket. I cannot forget the simple and radiant faces bent over the fingerworn and bedraggled cards, and long shall I bear with me the memories of the gay and restrained laughter heard under the sound of the dwindling rain and mountain winds.

Translated by Nicholas Stroud   *1922*

WITHOUT A HOMELAND

(A Letter from Batum)

... And it turned out that we caught the thief. The thief's "collar" turned out to be spacious. Two cargo and passenger ships had fit inside it. "The presumptuous usurpers' flag" descended dejectedly, and a different flag soared to the summit of the mast, a flag colored by the blood of battle and the purple of victory. Speeches were made and cannon salutes were fired. Someone was gnashing his teeth at the time. Let him gnash....

And now further. Once upon a time there were three oil tankers plying the Black Sea—the Ray, the Light, and the Glitter. The Light died a natural death, but the Ray and Glitter fell into that very same starched "collar." And it happened that we pulled the Ray out of it about three days ago; that's now the Lady Eleanor—a solid ship with three masts, carrying two thousand tons of oil, glittering with the crystal of its cabins, the blackness of its powerful hulls, the red veins of its oil pipes, and the polished silver of its cylinders. A very useful Lady. We may assume that she will be able to provide Soviet oil for the dimmed furnaces of the Soviet shores.

The Lady is already berthed at the Black Sea Transport dock, right where the Shaumian was brought before. Some gentlemen in lilac suspenders and lacquered shoes are still roaming her flat deck. Their dry and shaven faces are weighed down by grimaces of weariness and dissatisfaction. Dressing cases and cages with canaries are brought to them from the cabins. The gentlemen curse each other in hoarse voices and listen to car horns, carried through the rain and fog....

The pale flame of crimson roses.... The gray of silk-clad little legs.... The chatter of foreign speech.... The mackintoshes of sturdy men and the steel creases of their pressed pants.... The piercing and cheerful scream of motors....

The canaries, dressing cases and gentlemen are packed into cars and disappear. But the rain remains, the invincible Batum rain, murmuring on the surface of the darkened waters, clouding the leaden swelling of the sky, rustling under the wharf like millions of angry mice. And there also remains an assembled cluster of people by the coal holds of the Lady Eleanor. A dumb and gloomy drift of wilting blue blouses, extinguished cigarettes, toil-hardened fingers and joyless silence. These are the ones that no one will have anything to do with....

The Russian consul in Batum told the former crew of the ships we had taken:

"You call yourselves Russians, but I don't know you. Where were you when Russia was exhausted by the unbearable burdens of unequal battle? You want to remain in your former positions, but wasn't it you who got up the steam, raised anchor and hung out the sailing lamps in those terrible hours when enemies and mercenaries deprived the impoverished Soviet ports of their last property? Being a citizen of a workers' country is an honor which must be earned. You have not earned it."

And here they are, sitting by the coal holds of the Lady Eleanor, locked in a cage of rain and loneliness, these people without a homeland.

"It's strange," an old stoker says to me, "who are we? We're Russians, but we're not citizens. Here they don't receive us, and there they throw us out. A Russian doesn't recognize me, and an Englishman never knew me. Where can I go, and what do I start with? In New York there are four thousand ships standing empty, and in Marseilles three hundred. They all tell me to go back to where I came from... But thirty years ago I came from the Ryazan District."

"You didn't have to run away," I tell him. "You senseless stoker, who did you run from?"

"I know," the old man answers me, "now I know everything...."

And that evening, in a sad herd, they went into the port with their duffel bags, in order to embark on a foreign steamer leaving for Constantinople. At the gangway they were pushed around and the bags of overblown women and gray mackintoshes were thrown away. A crimson-faced captain with gold braid on his cap yelled at them from the bridge:

"Get away, you rascals. I've had it with you free-loading riff-raff. . . Get aside. Let the public pass. . . ."

Then they were dumped on a pile of cables in the stern. Then the cables were needed, and they were chased to the other end of the ship. They loafed around the deck, stunned, frightened, noiseless, with their dirty shirts and orphan-like little bundles. And when the ship gave its farewell whistle and the women aboard started to throw flowers to those who were seeing them off, the old stoker, who had come up to the gate, shouted to me in despair:

"If we were someplace's citizens, he wouldn't be able to bully us this way, the bald dog."

Translated by Nicholas Stroud   *1922*

MY FIRST GOOSE

Savitsky, commander of the sixth division, stood up when he saw me, and I was surprised by the beauty of his gigantic body. He stood up and the purple of his breeches, the crimson of his hat, tilted to one side, the medals pinned to his chest, cleaved the hut in half as a standard cleaves the sky. He smelled of scent and the cloying, fresh smell of soap. His long legs were like girls sheathed to their shoulders in polished riding boots.

He smiled at me, struck the table with his whip and drew toward him the order that had just been dictated by the staff commander. It was an order for Ivan Chesnokov to advance with the regiment under his command in the direction of Chugunov-Dobryvodka and, after making contact with the enemy, to annihilate the same. . .

"For which annihilation," the commander began to write and smeared the whole sheet, "I am making entirely responsible the same Chesnokov, whom I will strike down on the spot, of which you, Comrade Chesnokov, who have been working with me at the front for some months, can have no doubt."

The commander of the sixth division signed the order with a flourish, tossed it to the orderlies and turned on me his gray eyes, dancing with gaiety; I gave him the paper that ordered my appointment to the division staff.

"Register the order!" said the commander. "Register the order and sign him up for any amusement except the front. Can you read and write?"

"Yes," I answered, envying the iron and flower of this youth. "I have a law degree from Petersburg University..."

"So you're one of those scholar-kids," he shouted, smiling, "and glasses on your nose too. What a mangy specimen!.. They send you without asking, but here you could get killed for those glasses. Going to make it with us?"

"I'll make it," I answered and left for the village with the quartermaster to find lodgings for the night.

The quartermaster carried my trunk on his shoulders, the village street extended before us, the dying sun, round and yellow as a pumpkin, breathed its last rosy ray on the sky.

We approached a hut decorated with painted wreaths; the quartermaster stopped and said suddenly with a guilty smile:

"It's a bad business here with glasses, and nobody can put a stop to it. No place here for a distinguished fellow. But you go and bed down some lady, a nice upright lady, then the boys'll be good to you..."

He hesitated with my trunk on his shoulders, came up close to me, then jumped back in despair and ran to the nearest yard. Cossacks were sitting there on hay and were shaving each other.

"Here, soldiers," the quartermaster said and put my trunk down on the ground. "According to Comrade Savitsky's orders you have to take this fellow in and without any fooling around, because this fellow's got a lot of learning."

The quartermaster turned purple in the face and left without turning back. I raised my hand and tipped my hat to the Cossacks. A young fellow with long, flaxen hair and a handsome Ryazan face went up to my trunk and threw it over the gate. Then he turned his back to me and with surprising skill he began to emit shameful noises.

"Weapon No. Zero-Zero," shouted an older Cossack to him and then began to laugh. "Rapid fire..."

The fellow exhausted his unsubtle talents and walked away. Then, crawling on the ground, I started to collect the manuscripts and my old clothes, full of holes, that had fallen out of the trunk. I collected and carried them to the other end of the yard. By the hut, on a stove made of bricks, was a pot of cooking pork; it smoked as my far-away home in the country smoked, and hunger became confused with my unparalleled loneliness. I covered my trunk with hay, made a pillow of it and lay down on the ground to read Lenin's speech at the Second Congress of the Comintern in *Pravda*. The sun fell upon me from behind the jagged hillocks, the Cossacks stepped on my feet, the same young fellow did not tire of making fun at my expense, the beloved lines were approaching me along the thorny path but were unable to reach me. I then put the newspaper aside and went to see the landlady who was spinning on the porch.

"Landlady," I said, "I need to eat..."

The old woman raised the spreading whites of her half-blind eyes and again lowered them.

"Comrade," she said after her silence, "all of this makes me want to go and hang myself."

"By God I'll strangle you, woman," I muttered irritably and shoved the old woman with my fist to her chest. "I'm supposed to explain it to you..."

And, when I turned around I saw somebody's sword lying around not far away. A tyrannical goose was waddling around the yard and was serenely preening its feathers. I caught up with it and pushed it down to the ground, the goose's head cracked under my boot, snapped, and blood began to flow. The white neck lay in the dung and the wings began to flap over the dead body.

"By God, I'll strangle you, woman!" I said, rooting in the goose with my sword. "Landlady, cook it for me."

The old woman, sparkling with her blindness and glasses, picked the bird up, wrapped it in her apron and carried it to the kitchen.

In the yard the Cossacks were already sitting around their pot. They were sitting motionlessly, erect, like priests, and didn't look at the goose.

"The fellow's okay," one of them said about me, winked and ladled the cabbage soup.

The Cossacks began eating with the restrained elegance of peasants who respect each other, and I cleaned the sword with sand, walked out through the gate and came back again, weary. The moon hung over the yard like a cheap earring.

"Hey," Surovkov, the eldest of the Cossacks, said to me suddenly, "come and have some grub with us until your goose is done."

He pulled an extra spoon out of his boot and gave it to me. We guzzled down the homemade cabbage soup and ate the pork.

"Anything in the newspaper?" the fellow with the flaxen hair asked and he made room for me.

"Lenin writes in the newspaper," I said, pulling out *Pravda*, "Lenin writes that there's shortages of everything..."

And loudly, like an exultant blind man, I read Lenin's speech to the Cossacks.

Evening wrapped me in the intoxicating liquor of its twilight sheets, evening put its maternal palms to my enflamed forehead.

I read and rejoiced and was on the watch, while rejoicing, for the secret curve in Lenin's straight line.

"Truth tickles everybody's nose," Surovkov said when I had finished, "but the problem is picking it out of the heap, but he hits on it right away, like a chicken with a piece of grain."

That's what Surovkov, the platoon commander of the staff squadron, said about Lenin, and then we went to bed in the hayloft. The six of us slept there, sharing our warmth with each other, our legs entangled, under the roof, full of holes, which let the stars in.

I dreamed and saw women in my dreams, and only my heart, stained with the blood of the killing, creaked and bled.

Translated by Ronald Meyer   *1924*

MIKHAIL BULGAKOV

Mikhail Bulgakov (1891-1940) was born in Kiev to the family of a Professor of Theology. During his lifetime he was known as the author of the incredibly popular play *The Days of the Turbins.* Although his shorter prose works, such as *The Fatal Eggs* were justly admired for their brilliance, they were published in journals and books of such small editions that the general public was largely ignorant of them. Bulgakov was the victim of censorship fairly early—after 1925 this story was torn out of the collection which contained it. By the end of the 1920s, Bulgakov, like so many other writers, was hounded in print and had his plays banned. After a letter to Stalin, he was able to make a living as a theatrical consultant. However, he had only one play produced for the rest of his life, and nothing published. It was not until 1966 that the Russian public learned of Bulgakov's masterpiece, *The Master and Margarita.*

The Fatal Eggs was published in the Moscow journal *Nedra* in 1925. It attracted the notice of many literary figures, including Gorky and Zamyatin. Using a plot idea taken from H. G. Wells, and combining it with aspects of the Faust theme and a suspicion of allegory on the Revolution, Bulgakov parodies futuristic conceits of every kind—his future, however, is only a few years ahead. The targets of the satire are brash journalists, ignorant Party workers, and pseudo-science. To what degree this work may be profitably interpreted as being about the Revolution depends on the reader—some have seen Lenin in Persikov and his red ray. Stylistically, this work is a catalogue of the devices of the mid-twenties, and demonstrates Bulgakov's cinematic ability to describe the unimaginable, as he does again in his last novel.

Mikhail Bulgakov.

THE FATAL EGGS [1]

I

Professor Persikov's Curriculum Vitae

On April 16, 1928, in the evening, Persikov,[2] professor of Zoology at the Fourth State University and director of the Zoological Institute in Moscow, entered his office at the Zoological Institute on Herzen Street. The professor switched on the frosted globe overhead and looked around.

The beginning of the terrifying catastrophe must be set precisely on that ill-fated evening, and just as precisely, Professor Vladimir Ipatievich Persikov must be considered the prime cause of this catastrophe.

He was exactly fifty-eight years old. A remarkable head shaped like a pestle, bald, with tufts of yellowish hair standing out on the sides. A smooth-shaven face with a protruding lower lip. Because of this Persikov always had a somewhat pouting expression on his face. Small, old-fashioned spectacles in a silver frame on a red nose; small, glittering eyes; tall, stoop-shouldered. He spoke in a high, squeaky voice, and among his other idiosyncrasies was this: whenever he spoke of anything emphatically and with assurance, he screwed up his eyes and curled the index finger of his right hand into a hook. And since he always spoke with assurance, for his erudition in his field was utterly phenomenal, the hook appeared very often before the eyes of Professor Persikov's listeners. As for any topics outside his field, i.e., zoology, embryology, anatomy, botany, and geography, Professor Persikov almost never spoke of them.

The professor did not read newspapers and did not go to the theater, and the professor's wife ran away from him in 1913 with a tenor from the Zimin Opera, leaving him the following note: "Your frogs make me shudder with intolerable loathing. I will be unhappy for the rest of my life because of them."

The professor never remarried and had no children. He was very short-tempered, but he cooled off quickly; he liked tea with raspberries; and he lived on Prechistenka in a five-room apartment, one room of which was occupied by his housekeeper Marya Stepanovna, a shriveled little old woman who looked after the professor like a nanny.

In 1919 the government requisitioned three of his five rooms. Then he declared to Marya Stepanovna: "If they don't cease these outrages, Marya Stepanovna, I will emigrate."

There is no doubt that had the professor realized this plan, he could easily have got settled in the department of zoology at any university in the world, since he was an absolutely first-rate scientist; and with the exception of Professors William Weccle of Cambridge and Giacomo Bartolommeo Beccari of Rome, he had no equals in the field bearing in one way or another on amphibians. Professor Persikov could lecture in four languages besides Russian, and he spoke French and German as fluently as Russian. Persikov did not carry out his intention to emigrate, and 1920 turned out to be even worse than 1919. Events kept happening one after the other. Great Nikitskaya was renamed Herzen Street. Then the clock built into the building on the corner of Herzen and Mokhovaya stopped at a quarter past eleven, and finally, in the terraria at the Zoological Institute, unable to endure the perturbations of that famous year, first eight splendid specimens of the tree frog died, then fifteen ordinary toads, followed, finally, by a most remarkable specimen of the Surinam toad.

Immediately after the toads, whose deaths decimated the population of the first order of amphibians, which is properly known as tailless, the institute's permanent watchman, old Vlas, who did not belong to the class of amphibians, moved on into a better world. The cause of his death, however, was the same as that of the poor animals, and Persikov diagnosed it at once: "Lack of feed."

The scientist was absolutely right: Vlas had to be fed with flour, and the toads with mealworms, but since the former had disappeared, the latter had also vanished. Persikov tried to shift the remaining twenty specimens of the tree frog to a diet of cockroaches, but the cockroaches had also disappeared somewhere, thus demonstrating their malicious attitude toward War Communism. And so, even the last specimens had to be tossed out into the garbage pits in the institute's courtyard.

The effect of the deaths, especially that of the Surinam toad, on Persikov is beyond description. For some reason he put the whole blame for the deaths on the current People's Commissar of Education.

Standing in his hat and galoshes in the corridor of the chilly institute, Persikov spoke to his assistant, Ivanov, a most elegant gentleman with a pointed blond beard. "Why, killing him is not enough for this, Peter Stepanovich! Just what are they doing? Why, they'll ruin the institute! Eh? A singular male, an extraordinary specimen of *Pipa americana,* thirteen centimeters long..."

As time went on things got worse. After Vlas died, the windows of the institute froze right through, and patterned ice covered the inner surface of the glass. The rabbits died, then the foxes, wolves, fish, and every last one of the garter snakes. Persikov started going around in silence for whole days through; then he caught pneumonia, but did not die. When he recovered he went to the institute twice a week, and in the amphitheater, where the temperature for some reason never changed from its constant five degrees below freezing regardless of the temperature outside, wearing his galoshes, a hat with earflaps, and a woolen muffler, exhaling clouds of white steam, he read a series of lectures on "The Reptilia of the Torrid Zone" to eight students. Persikov spent the rest of his time at his place on Prechistenka, covered with a plaid shawl, lying on the sofa in his room, which was crammed to the ceiling with books, coughing, staring into the open maw of the fiery stove which Marya Stepanovna fed gilded chairs, and thinking about the Surinam toad.

But everything in this world comes to an end. Nineteen twenty and 1921 ended, and in 1922 a kind of reverse trend began. First, Pankrat appeared, to replace the late Vlas; he was still young for a zoological guard, but he showed great promise; the institute building was now beginning to be heated a little. And in the summer Persikov managed, with Pankrat's help, to catch fourteen specimens of the common toad in the Klyazma River. The terraria once again teemed with life... In 1923 Persikov was already lecturing eight times a week—three at the institute and five at the university; in 1924 it was thirteen times a week, including the workers' schools, and in the spring of 1925 he gained notoriety by flunking seventy-six students, all of them on amphibians.

"What? How is it you don't know how amphibians differ from reptiles?" Persikov would ask. "It's simply ridiculous, young man. Amphibians have no pelvic buds. None. So, sir, you ought to be ashamed. You are a Marxist, probably?"

"Yes, a Marxist," the flunked student would answer, wilting.

"Very well, come back in the fall, please," Persikov would say politely, and then shout briskly to Pankrat, "Give me the next one!"

As amphibians come back to life after the first heavy rain following a long drought, so Professor Persikov came back to life in 1926 when the united Russo-American Company built fifteen fifteen-storey houses in the center of Moscow, starting at the corner of Gazetny Lane and Tverskaya, and 300 eight-apartment cottages for workers on the outskirts of town, ending once and for all the terrible and ridiculous housing crisis which had so tormented Muscovites in the years 1919 to 1925.

In general, it was a remarkable summer in Persikov's life, and sometimes he rubbed his hands with a quiet and contented chuckle, recalling how he and Marya Stepanovna had been squeezed into two rooms. Now the professor had gotten all five rooms back; he had spread out, arranged his 2,500 books, his stuffed animals, diagrams, and specimens in their places, and lit the green lamp on the desk in his study.

The institute was unrecognizable too: it had been covered with a coat of cream-colored paint, water was conducted to the reptile room by a special pipeline, all ordinary glass was replaced by plate glass, five new microscopes had been sent to the institute, as had glass-topped dissecting tables, 2,000-watt lamps with indirect lighting, reflectors, and cases for the museum.

Persikov came to life, and the whole world unexpectedly learned of it in December 1926, with the publication of his pamphlet: *More on the Problem of the Propagation of the Gastropods,* 126 pp., "Bulletin of the Fourth University."

And in the fall of 1927 his major opus, 350 pages long, later translated into six languages, including Japanese: *The Embryology of the Pipidae, Spadefoot Toads, and Frogs,* State Publishing House : price, three rubles.

But in the summer of 1928 the incredible, horrible events took place...

II

The Colored Spiral

And so, the professor turned on the globe and looked around. He switched on the reflector on the long experiment table, donned a white smock, and tinkled with some instruments on the table...

Many of the thirty thousand mechanical vehicles which sped through Moscow in 1928 darted along Herzen Street, wheels humming on the smooth paving stones; and every few minutes a trolley marked 16 or 22 or 48 or 53 rolled, grinding and clattering, from Herzen Street toward Mokhovaya. Reflections of varicolored lights were thrown on the plate-glass windows of the office, and far and high above, next to the dark, heavy cap of the Cathedral of Christ, one could see the misty, pale lunar sickle.

But neither the moon nor Moscow's springtime noises interested Professor Persikov in the slightest. He sat on a three-legged revolving stool and with fingers stained brown from tobacco, he turned the adjustment screw of the magnificent Zeiss microscope under which an ordinary undyed culture of fresh amoebas had been placed. At the moment that Persikov was shifting the magnification from five to ten thousand, the door opened slightly, a pointed little beard and a leather apron appeared, and his assistant called, "Vladimir Ipatievich, the mesentery is set up—would you like to take a look?"

Persikov nimbly slid off the stool, leaving the adjustment screw turned halfway, and slowly turning a cigarette in his fingers, he went into his assistant's office. There, on a glass table, a semi-chloroformed frog, fainting with terror and pain, was crucified on a cork plate, its translucent viscera pulled out of its bloody abdomen into the microscope.

"Very good," said Persikov, bending down to the eyepiece of the microscope.

Apparently one could see something very interesting in the frog's mesentery, where as clearly as if on one's hand living blood corpuscles were running briskly along the rivers of the vessels. Persikov forgot his amoebas and for the next hour and a half took turns with Ivanov at the microscope lens. As they were doing this both scientists kept exchanging animated comments incomprehensible to ordinary mortals.

Finally, Persikov leaned back from the microscope, announcing, "The blood is clotting, that's all there is to that."

The frog moved its head heavily, and its dimming eyes were clearly saying, "You're rotten bastards, that's what..."

Stretching his benumbed legs, Persikov rose, returned to his office, yawned, rubbed his permanently inflamed eyelids with his fingers, and sitting down on his stool, he glanced into the microscope, put his fingers on the adjustment screw intending to turn it—but did not turn it. With his right eye Persikov saw a blurred white disk, and in it some faint, pale amoebas—but in the middle of the disk there was a colored spiral resembling a woman's curl. Persikov himself and hundreds of his students had seen this spiral very many times, and no one had ever taken any interest in it, nor, indeed, was there any reason to. The colored swirl of light merely interfered with observation and showed that the culture was not in focus. Therefore it was ruthlessly eliminated with a single turn of the knob, illuminating the whole field with an even white light.

The zoologist's long fingers already lay firmly on the knob, but suddenly they quivered and fell off. The reason for this was Persikov's right eye; it had suddenly become intent, amazed, and flooded with excitement. To the woe of the Republic, this was no talentless mediocrity sitting at the microscope. No, this was Professor Persikov! His entire life, all of his intellect, became concentrated in his right eye. For some five minutes of stony silence the higher creature observed the lower one, tormenting and straining his eye over the part of the culture which was outside of focus, Everything around was silent. Pankrat had already fallen asleep in his room off the vestibule, and only once the glass doors of the cabinets rang musically and delicately in the distance: that was Ivanov locking his office as he left. The front door groaned behind him. And it was only later that the professor's voice was heard. He was asking, no one knows whom, "What is this? I simply don't understand."

A last truck passed by on Herzen Street, shaking the old walls of the institute. The flat glass bowl with forceps in it tinkled on the table. The professor turned pale and raised his hands over the microscope like a mother over an infant who is being threatened by danger. Now there could be no question of Persikov turning the knob, oh no, he was afraid that some outside force might push what he had seen out of the field of vision.

It was bright morning with a gold strip slanting across the cream-colored entrance to the institute when the professor left the microscope and walked up to the window on his numb feet. With trembling fingers he pressed a button, and the thick black shades shut out the morning, and the wise, learned night came back to life in the study. The sallow and inspired Persikov spread his feet wide apart, and staring at the parquet with tearing eyes, he started talking: "But how can this be? Why, it's monstrous!... It's monstrous, gentlemen," he repeated, addressing the toads in the terrarium—but the toads were sleeping and did not answer.

He was silent for a moment, then walked to the switch, raised the shades, turned off all the lights, and peered into the microscope. His face got tense, and his bushy yellow eyebrows came together. "Uhmmm, uhmmm," he muttered. "Gone. I see. I see-e-e-e," he drawled, looking at the extinguished globe overhead madly and inspiredly. "It's very simple." And again he lowered the swishing shades, and again he lit the globe. Having glanced into the microscope, he grinned gleefully, and almost rapaciously. "I'll catch it," he said solemnly and gravely, raising his finger in the air. "I'll catch it. Maybe it's from the sun."

Again the shades rolled up. Now the sun was out. It poured across the institute walls and lay in slanting planes across the paving stones of Herzen Street. The professor looked out the window, calculating what the position of the sun would be during the day. He stepped away and returned again and again, dancing slightly, and finally he leaned over the windowsill on his stomach.

He got started on some important and mysterious work. He covered the microscope with a glass bell. Melting a chunk of sealing wax over the bluish flame of a Bunsen burner, he sealed the edges of the bell to the table, pressing down the lumps of wax with his thumb. He turned off the gas and went out, and he locked the office door with an English lock.

The institute corridors were in semidarkness. The professor made his way to Pankrat's room and knocked for a long time with no result. At last there was a sound behind the door something like the growling of a chained dog, hoarse coughing and muttering, and Pankrat appeared in a spot of light wearing striped underpants tied at his ankles. His eyes fixed wildly on the scientist; he was still groaning somewhat from sleep.

"Pankrat," said the professor, looking at him over his spectacles. "Forgive me for waking you up. Listen, my friend, don't go into my office this morning. I left some work out which must not be moved. Understand?"

"U-hm-m, I understand," Pankrat replied, understanding nothing. He was swaying back and forth and grumbling.

"No, listen, wake up, Pankrat," said the zoologist, and he poked Pankrat lightly in the ribs, which brought a frightened look into his face and a certain shadow of awareness into his eyes. "I locked the office," continued Persikov. "So you shouldn't clean up before my return. Understand ?"

"Yes, sir-r," gurgled Pankrat.

"Now that's excellent, go back to bed."

Pankrat turned, vanished behind the door, and immediately crashed back into bed, while the professor began to put his things on in the vestibule. He put on his gray summer coat and floppy hat. Then, recalling the picture in the microscope, he fixed his eyes on his galoshes and stared at them for several seconds, as if he were seeing them for the first time. Then he put on the left galosh and tried to put the right one over it, but it would not go on.

"What a fantastic accident it was that he called me," said the scientist, "otherwise I would never have noticed it. But what does it lead to? . . . Why, the devil only knows what it can lead to!"

The professor grinned, frowned at his galoshes, removed the left galosh, and put on the right one. "My God! Why, one can't even imagine all the consequences." The professor contemptuously kicked away the left galosh, which annoyed him by refusing to fit over the right, and went to the exit wearing one galosh. At that point he dropped his handkerchief and walked out, slamming the heavy door. On the stairs he took a long time looking for matches in his pockets, patting his sides; then he found them and headed down the street with an unlit cigarette in his lips.

Not a single person did the scientist meet all the way to the cathedral. There the professor tilted his head back and gaped at the golden cupola. The sun was sweetly licking it on one side.

"How is it I have never seen it before, such a coincidence? . . . Phooey, what an idiot." The professor bent down and fell into thought, looking at his differently shod feet. "Hm . . . what should I do? Return to Pankrat? No, there's no waking him up. It'd be a shame to throw it away, the vile thing. I'll have to carry it." He took off the galosh and carried it in his hand with disgust.

Three people in an ancient automobile turned the corner from Prechistenka. Two tipsy men with a garishly painted woman in silk pajamas of the latest 1928 style sitting on their knees.

"Hey, popsy!" she cried in a low, rather hoarse voice. "Did 'ja drink up the other galosh!"

"The old boy must have loaded up at the Alcazar," howled the drunk on the left, while the one on the right leaned out of the car and shouted, "Is the all-night tavern on Volkhonka open, buddy? We're headed there!"

The professor looked at them sternly above his spectacles, dropped the cigarette from his lips, and immediately forgot their existence. Slanting rays of sunshine appeared, cutting across Prechistensky Boulevard, and the helmet on the Cathedral of Christ began to flame. The sun had risen.

III

Persikov Caught It

The facts of the matter were as follows. When the professor had brought his eye of genius to that eyepiece, for the first time in his life he had paid attention to the fact that one particularly vivid and thick ray stood out in the multicolored spiral. This ray was a bright red color and it emerged from the spiral in a little sharp point, like a needle, let us say.

It is simply very bad luck that this ray fixed the skilful eye of the virtuoso for several seconds.

In it, in this ray, the professor caught sight of something which was a thousand times more significant and important than the ray itself, that fragile offshoot born accidentally of the movement of the microscope's lens and mirror. Thanks to the fact that his assistant had called the professor away, the amoebas lay about for an hour and a half subject to the action of the ray, and the result was this: while the granular amoebas outside the ray lay about limp and helpless, strange phenomena were taking place within the area where the pointed red sword lay. The red strip teemed with life. The gray amoebas, stretching out their pseudopods, strove with all their might toward the red strip, and in it they would come to life as if by sorcery. Some force infused them with the spirit of life. They crawled in flocks and fought each other for a place in the ray. Within it a frenzied (no other word can properly describe it) process of multiplication went on. Smashing and overturning all the laws that Persikov knew as well as he knew his own five fingers, the amoebas budded before his eyes with lightning speed. In the ray they split apart, and two seconds later each part became a new, fresh organism. In a few seconds these organisms attained full growth and maturity, only to immediately produce new generations in their turn. The red strip and the entire disk quickly became overcrowded, and the inevitable struggle began. The newborn ones attacked each other furiously, tearing each other to shreds and swallowing them up. Among the newly born lay corpses of those which had perished in the battle for existence. The best and strongest were victorious. And the best ones were terrifying. First, they were approximately twice the size of ordinary amoebas, and second, they were distinguished by some sort of special viciousness and motility. Their movements were speedy, their pseudopods much longer than normal, and they used them, without exaggeration, as an octopus uses its tentacles.

The next evening, the professor, drawn and pale, studied the new generation of amoebas—without eating, keeping himself going only by smoking thick, roll-your-own cigarettes. On the third day, he shifted to the prime source—the red ray.

The gas hissed softly in the burner, again the traffic whizzed along the street, and the professor, poisoned by his hundredth cigarette, his eyes half-shut, threw himself back in his revolving chair. "Yes, everything is clear now. The ray brought them to life. It is a new ray, unresearched by anyone, undiscovered by anyone. The first thing to be clarified is whether it is produced only by electric light or by the sun as well," Persikov muttered to himself.

In the course of one more night this was clarified. He captured three rays in three microscopes, he obtained none from the sun, and he expressed himself thus: "We must hypothesize that it does not exist in the sun's spectrum... hmmm... in short, we must hypothesize that it can be obtained only from electric light." He looked lovingly at the frosted globe above him, thought for a moment, inspired, and invited Ivanov into his office. He told him everything and showed him the amoebas.

Assistant Professor Ivanov was astounded, completely crushed; how was it that such a simple thing as this slender arrow had never been noticed before! By anyone, dammit. Not even by him, Ivanov, himself, and this really was monstrous! "You just look!... Just look, Vladimir Ipatievich!" cried Ivanov, his eye gluing itself to the eyepiece in horror. "What is happening?... They're growing before my very eyes... Look, look!"

"I have been watching them for three days," Persikov replied animatedly.

Then there was a conversation between the two scientists, the idea of which may be summed up as follows: Assistant Professor Ivanov undertakes to construct a chamber with the aid of lenses and mirrors in which this ray will be produced in magnified form—and outside the microscope. Ivanov hopes—indeed, he is absolutely sure that this is quite simple. He will produce the ray, Vladimir Ipatievich cannot doubt that. Here there was a slight pause.

"When I publish my work, Peter Stepanovich, I will write that the chambers were constructed by you," Persikov put in, feeling that the pause needed to be resolved.

"Oh, that's not important... Still, of course..."

And the pause was instantly resolved. From that moment on, the ray utterly absorbed Ivanov too. While Persikov, losing weight and getting exhausted, was sitting all day and half the night over the microscope, Ivanov bustled around the brilliantly-lit physics laboratory combining lenses and mirrors. A technician assisted him.

After a request was sent through the Commissariat of Education, Persikov received from Germany three parcels containing mirrors and polished lenses—biconvex, biconcave, and even convex-concave. This all ended with Ivanov finishing the construction of a chamber and actually capturing the red ray in it. And in all justice, it really was an expert job: the ray came out thick—almost four centimeters in diameter—sharp and powerful.

On the first of June, the chamber was installed in Persikov's office, and he avidly began experiments with frog roe exposed to the ray. The results of these experiments were staggering. Within two days thousands of tadpoles hatched from the roe. But that is the least of it—within twenty-four hours, growing at a fantastic rate, the tadpoles developed into frogs, and they were so vicious and voracious that half of them immediately devoured the other half. Then the survivors began to spawn, ignoring all normal time rules, and in another two days they had produced a new generation, this time without the ray, which was absolutely numberless. The devil only knows what had started in the scientist's office: the tadpoles were crawling out of the office and spreading all over the institute, in the terraria, and on the floor, from every nook and cranny, stentorian choruses began to croak as if it were a bog. Pankrat, who had always feared Persikov like fire anyway, was now experiencing only one feeling for him—mortal terror. After a week, the scientist himself began to feel he was going crazy. The institute was pervaded with the odors of ether and prussic acid, which almost poisoned Pankrat, who had taken off his mask at the wrong time. They finally managed to exterminate the teeming swamp population with poisons, and the rooms were thoroughly aired out.

Persikov said the following to Ivanov: "You know, Peter Stepanovich, the ray's effect on the deutoplasm and the ovum in general is quite remarkable."

Ivanov, who was a cool and reserved gentleman, interrupted the professor in an unusual tone. "Vladimir Ipatych, why are you discussing petty details, deutoplasm? Let's be frank—you have discovered something unprecedented!" Though it cost him obvious great effort, still Ivanov squeezed out the words: "Professor Persikov, you have discovered the ray of life!"

A faint color appeared on Persikov's pale, unshaven cheekbones. "Now, now, now," he muttered.

"You," continued Ivanov, "you will make such a name... It makes my head spin. Do you understand," he continued passionately, "Vladimir Ipatych, the heroes of H. G. Wells are simply nonsense compared to you... And I had always thought his stories were fairy tales.... Do you remember his *The Food of the Gods?*"[3]

"Oh, a novel," replied Persikov.

"Why yes, good Lord, a famous one!"

"I have forgotten it," said Persikov. "I remember now, I did read it, but I've forgotten it."

"How can you not remember, why, just look..." From the glass-topped table Ivanov picked up a dead frog of incredible size with a bloated belly and held it up by the leg. Even after death it had a malevolent expression on its face. "Why, this is monstrous!"

IV

Deaconess Drozdova

God knows how it happened, whether Ivanov was to blame for it or sensational news transmits itself through the air, but everyone in gigantic, seething Moscow suddenly started talking about the ray of Professor Persikov. True, this talk was casual and very vague. The news of the miraculous discovery hopped through the glittering capital like a wounded bird, sometimes disappearing, sometimes fluttering up again, until the middle of July when a brief notice treating the ray appeared on the twentieth page of the newspaper *Izvestia,* under the heading: "News of Science and Technology." It was said distantly that a well-known professor of the Fourth State University had invented a ray which greatly accelerated the vital processes of lower organisms and that this ray required further study. The name, of course, was garbled and printed as "Pepsikov."

Ivanov brought in the newspaper and showed the notice to Persikov.

"Pepsikov," grumbled Persikov, puttering around with the chamber in his office, "where do these blabbermouths learn everything?"

Alas, the garbled name did not save the professor from events, and they began the very next day, immediately upsetting Persikov's whole life.

After a preliminary knock, Pankrat entered the office and handed Persikov a magnificent satiny calling card. "He's out there," Pankrat added timidly.

Printed on the card in exquisite type was:

Alfred Arkadievich
Bronsky

Contributor to the Moscow
Journals *Red Spark, Red Pepper,* and
Red Projector and the newspaper
Red Evening Moscow

"Tell him to go to hell," Persikov said in a monotone, and he threw the card under the table.

Pankrat turned, walked out, and five minutes later he came back with a long-suffering face and a second specimen of the same card.

"Are you making fun of me, or what?" Persikov croaked, and he looked terrifying.

"From the GPU,[4] the man says," answered Pankrat, turning pale.

Persikov grabbed the card with one hand, almost tearing it in half, and with the other hand he threw a pair of pincers onto the table. On the card there was a note written in curlicued handwriting: "I beg sincerely, with apologies, most esteemed professor, for you to receive me for three minutes in connection with a public matter of the press; I am also a contributor to the satirical journal *The Red Raven,* published by the GPU."

"Call him in," said Persikov, and he breathed out heavily.

Immediately a young man with a smooth-shaven, oily face bobbed up behind Pankrat's back. The face struck one with its permanently raised eyebrows, like a Chinaman's, and the little agate eyes beneath them, which never for a second met the eyes of his interlocutor. The young man was dressed quite impeccably and fashionably: a long narrow jacket down to the knees, the widest of bell-bottomed trousers, and preternaturally wide patent-leather shoes with toes like hooves. In his hands the young man held a cane, a hat with a sharply pointed crown, and a notebook.

"What do you want?" asked Persikov in a voice that made Pankrat step back behind the door immediately. "You *were* told I am busy."

Instead of answering, the young man bowed to the professor twice, once to the left and once to the right—and then his eyes wheeled all over the room, and immediately the young man made a mark in his notebook.

"I'm busy," said the professor, looking with revulsion into the guest's little eyes, but he had no effect, since the eyes were impossible to catch.

"A thousand apologies, esteemed professor," the young man began in a high-pitched voice, "for breaking in on you and taking up your precious time, but the news of your earth-shaking discovery—which has created a sensation all over the world—compels our journal to ask you for whatever explanations..."

"What kind of explanations all over the world ?" Persikov whined squeakily, turning yellow. "I'm not obliged to give you any explanations or anything of the sort... I'm busy... terribly busy."

"What exactly is it you are working on?" the young man asked sweetly, making another mark in his notebook.

"Oh, I... why do you ask ? Do you intend to publish something?"

"Yes," answered the young man, and suddenly he started scribbling furiously in his notebook.

"First of all, I have no intention of publishing anything until I complete my work—particularly in these papers of yours... Secondly, how do you know all this ?" And Persikov suddenly felt that he was losing control.

"Is the news that you have invented a ray of new life accurate?"

"What new life?" the professor snapped angrily. "What kind of rubbish are you babbling? The ray I am working on has not yet been investigated very much, and generally nothing is known about it as yet! It is possible that it may accelerate the vital processes of protoplasm."

"How much?" the young man inquired quickly.

Persikov completely lost control. What a character! The devil only knows what this means! "What sort of philistine questions are these? Suppose I said, oh, a thousand times..."

Rapacious joy flashed through the little eyes of the young man. "It produces giant organisms ?"

"Nothing of the sort! Well, true, the organisms I have obtained are larger than normal... Well, they do possess certain new characteristics... But, of course, the main thing is not the size, but the incredible speed of reproduction," said Persikov to his misfortune, and he was immediately horrified by what he had said. The young man covered a page with his writing, turned it, and scribbled on.

"But don't you write that!" Persikov said hoarsely, in desperation, already surrendering and feeling that he was in the young man's hands. "What are you writing there?"

"Is it true that in forty-eight hours you can obtain two million tadpoles from frog roe?"

"What quantity of roe?" Persikov shouted, again infuriated. "Have you ever seen a grain of roe... well, let's say, of a tree frog?"

"From half a pound?" the young man asked, undaunted.

Persikov turned purple.

"Who measures it like that? Ugh! What are you talking about? Well, of course, if you took half a pound of frog roe, then... perhaps... well, hell, perhaps about that number or maybe even many more."

Diamonds began to sparkle in the young man's eyes, and in a single swoop he scratched out another page. "Is it true that this will cause a world revolution in animal husbandry ?"

"What kind of newspaper question is that?" howled Persikov. "And, generally, I'm not giving you permission to write rubbish. I can see by your face that you're writing some sort of rotten trash!"

"Your photograph, professor, I beg you urgently," the young man said, slamming his notebook shut.

"What? My photograph ? For your stupid little journals ? To go with that devilish garbage you're scribbling there? No, no, no!... And I'm busy. I'll ask you to... "

"Even if it's an old one. And we'll return it to you instantly."

"Pankrat!" the professor shouted in a rage.

"My compliments," the young man said and vanished.

Instead of Pankrat, Persikov heard the strange rhythmic creaking of some machine behind the door, a metallic tapping across the floor, and in his office appeared a man of extraordinary bulk, dressed in a blouse and trousers made of blanket material. His left leg, a mechanical one, screaked and scropped, and in his hands he held a briefcase. His round shaven face, filled with yellowish gelatine, offered an amiable smile. He bowed to the professor in military fashion and straightened up, causing his leg to twang like a spring. Persikov went numb.

"Mr. Professor," began the stranger in a pleasant, somewhat husky voice, "forgive an ordinary mortal for breaking in on your privacy."

"Are you a reporter?" asked Persikov. "Pankrat!"

"Not at all, Mr. Professor," replied the fat man. "Permit me to introduce myself: sea captain and contributor to the newspaper *Industrial News,* published by the Council of People's Commissars."

"Pankrat!" Persikov shouted hysterically, and at that instant the telephone in the corner flashed a red signal and rang softly. "Pankrat!" repeated the professor. "Hello, what is it?"

"*Verzeihen Sie, bitte, Herr Professor,*" croaked the telephone in German, "*dass ich störe. Ich bin ein Mitarbeiter des Berliner Tageblatts.*"

"Pankrat!" The professor shouted into the receiver, "*Bin momentan sehr beschäftigt und kann Sie deshalb jetzt nicht empfangen!*... Pankrat!"

And in the meantime the bell at the front entrance of the institute was starting to ring constantly.

"Nightmarish murder on Bronny Street!" howled unnatural hoarse voices twisting in and out of the thicket of lights among wheels and flashing headlights on the warm June pavement. "Nightmarish outbreak of chicken plague in the yard of Deacon Drozdov's widow, with her portrait!... Nightmarish discovery of Professor Persikov's ray of life!"

Persikov jumped so violently that he nearly fell under the wheels of a car on Mokhovaya, and he furiously grabbed the newspaper.

"Three kopeks, citizen!" shrieked the boy, and squeezing himself into the crowd on the sidewalk, he again started howling, "*Red Evening Moscow,* discovery of x-ray."

The stunned Persikov opened the newspaper and leaned against a lamppost. From a smudged frame in the left corner of the second page there stared at him a bald-headed man with mad, unseeing eyes and a drooping jaw—the fruit of Alfred Bronsky's artistic endeavors. "V. I. Persikov, who discovered the mysterious red ray," announced the caption under the drawing. Below it, under the heading, "World Riddle," the article began with the words: "'Sit down, please,' the venerable scientist Persikov said to us amiably..."

Under the article was a prominent signature: "Alfred Bronsky (Alonso)."

A greenish light flared up over the roof of the university, the fiery words *Speaking Newspaper* leapt across the sky, and a crowd immediately jammed Mokhovaya.

"'Sit down, please!!!'" a most unpleasant high-pitched voice, exactly like the voice of Alfred Bronsky, magnified a thousand times, suddenly boomed from the roof across the way, "the venerable scientist Persikov said to us amiably. 'I have long desired to acquaint the proletariat of Moscow with the results of my discovery!...'"

Persikov heard a quiet mechanical screaking behind his back, and someone tugged at his sleeve. Turning around, he saw the round yellow face of the mechanical leg's owner. His eyes were wet with tears and his lips were shaking. "Me, Mr. Professor, me you refused to acquaint with the results of your amazing discovery, professor," he said sadly, and he sighed heavily, "you made me lose two smackers."

He looked gloomily at the roof of the university where the invisible Alfred was ranting in the black maw of the speaker. For some reason, Persikov suddenly felt sorry for the fat man. "I didn't say any 'sit down, please' to him!" he muttered, catching the words from the sky with hatred. He is simply a brazen scalawag, an extraordinary type! Forgive me, please, but really now—when you're working and people break in... I don't mean you, of course..."

"Perhaps, Mr. Professor, you would give me at least a description of your chamber?" the mechanical man said ingratiatingly and mournfully. "After all, it makes no difference to you now..."

"In three days, such a quantity of tadpoles hatches out of half a pound of roe that it's utterly impossible to count them!" roared the invisible man in the loudspeaker.

"Too-too," shouted the cars on Mokhovaya hollowly.

"Ho, ho, ho... How about that! Ho, ho, ho," murmured the crowd, heads tilted back.

"What a scoundrel! Eh?" Persikov hissed to the mechanical man, trembling with indignation. "How do you like that? Why I'm going to lodge a complaint against him!"

"Outrageous," agreed the fat man.

A most dazzling violet ray struck the professor's eyes, and everything around flared up—the lamppost, a strip of block pavement, a yellow wall, curious faces.

"It's for you, professor," the fat man whispered ecstatically and hung on to the professor's sleeve like a lead weight. Something clicked rapidly in the air.

"To the devil with all of them!" Persikov exclaimed despondently, ripping through the crowd with his lead weight. "Hey, taxi! To Prechistenka!"

The beat-up old car, vintage 1924, clattered to a halt at the curb, and the professor began to climb into the landau while trying to shake loose from the fat man. "You're in my way," he hissed, covering his face with his fists against the violet light.

"Did you read it? What are they yelling about?... Professor Persikov and his children were found on Little Bronnaya with their throats slit!..." voices shouted around the crowd.

"I haven't got *any* children, the sons of bitches," Persikov bellowed and suddenly found himself in the focus of a black camera, which was shooting him in profile with an open mouth and furious eyes.

"Krch... too... krch... too," shrieked the taxi, and it lanced into the thicket of traffic.

The fat man was already sitting in the landau warming the professor's side.

V

A Chicken Tale

In a tiny provincial town, formerly called Troitsk and currently Steklovsk, in the Steklov district of the Kostroma province, onto the steps of a little house on the street formerly[5] called Cathedral, and currently Personal, came out a woman wearing a kerchief and a gray dress with calico bouquets on it—and she began to sob. This woman, the widow of the former Archpriest Drozdov of the former cathedral, sobbed so loudly that soon another woman's head, in a downy woolen shawl, was stuck out the window of the house across the street, and it cried out, "What is it, Stepanovna? Another one?"

"The seventeenth!" dissolving in sobs the former Drozdova answered.

"Oh, deary, oh dear," the woman in the shawl whimpered, and she shook her head. "Why, what is this anyway. Truly, it's the Lord in His wrath! Is she dead?"

"Just look, look, Matryona," muttered the deaconess, sobbing loudly and heavily. "Look what's happening to her!"

The gray, tilting gate slammed, a woman's bare feet padded across the dusty bumps in the street, and the deaconess, wet with tears, led Matryona to her poultry yard.

It must be said that the widow of Father Savvaty Drozdov, who had passed away in 1926 of anti-religious woes, did not give up, but started some most remarkable chicken breeding. As soon as the widow's affairs started to go uphill, such a tax was slapped on her that her chicken breeding was on the verge of terminating, had it not been for kind people. They advised the widow to inform the local authorities that she was founding a workers' cooperative chicken farm. The membership of the cooperative consisted of Drozdova herself, her faithful servant Matryoshka, and the widow's deaf niece. The widow's tax was revoked, and the chicken breeding flourished so much that by 1928 the population of the widow's dusty yard, flanked by rows of chicken coops, had increased to 250 hens, including some Cochin Chinas. The widow's eggs appeared in the Steklovsk market every Sunday; the widow's eggs were sold in Tambov, and sometimes they even appeared in the glass showcases of the store that was formerly known as "Chichkin's Cheese and Butter, Moscow."

And now a precious Brahmaputra, by count the seventeenth that morning, her tufted baby, was walking around the yard vomiting. "Er... rr... url... url... ho-ho-ho," the tufted hen glugged, rolling her melancholy eyes to the sun as if she were seeing it for the last time. Cooperative member Matryoshka, was dancing before the hen in a squatting position, a cup of water in her hand.

"Here, tufted baby... cheep-cheep-cheep... drink a little water," Matryoshka pleaded, chasing the hen's beak with her cup; but the hen did not want to drink. She opened her beak wide and stretched her neck toward the sky. Then she began to vomit blood.

"Holy Jesus!" cried the guest, slapping herself on the thighs. "What's going on ? Nothing but gushing blood! I've *never,* may I drop on the spot, I've never seen a chicken with a stomach ache like a human."

And these were the last words heard by the departing tufted baby. She suddenly keeled over on her side, helplessly pecked the dust a few times, and turned up her eyes. Then she rolled over on her back, lifted both feet upwards, and remained motionless. Spilling the water in the cup, Matryoshka burst into a baritone wail, as did the deaconess herself, the chairman of the cooperative, and the guest leaned over to her ear and whispered, "Stepanovna, may I eat dirt, but someone's ruined your chickens. Who's ever seen anything like it before? Why, this ain't no chicken sickness! It's that somebody's bewitched your chickens."

"The enemies of my life!" the deaconess cried out to the heavens. "Do they want to run me off the earth?"

A loud roosterish crow answered her words, after which a wiry bedraggled rooster tore out of a chicken coop sort of sideways, like a boisterous drunk out of a tavern. He rolled his eyes back wildly at them, stamped up and down in place, spread his wings like an eagle, but did not fly off anywhere—he began to run in circles around the yard like a horse on a rope. On the third circle he stopped, overwhelmed by nausea, because he then began to cough and croak, spat bloody spots all around him, fell over, and his claws aimed toward the sun like masts. Feminine wailing filled the yard. And it was echoed by a troubled clucking, flapping, and fussing in the chicken coops.

"Well, ain't it the evil eye?" the guest asked victoriously. "Call Father Sergei; let him hold a service."

At six in the evening, when the sun lay low like a fiery face among the faces of the young sunflowers, Father Sergei, the prior of the Cathedral Church, was climbing out of his vestments after finishing the prayer service at the chicken coops. People's curious heads were stuck out over the ancient collapsing fence and peering through the cracks. The sorrowful deaconess, kissing the cross, soaked the torn canary-yellow ruble note with tears and handed it to Father Sergei, in response to which, sighing, he remarked something about, well, see how the Lord's shown us His wrath. As he was saying this, Father Sergei wore an expression which indicated that he knew very well precisely why the Lord had shown His wrath, but that he was just not saying.

After that, the crowd dispersed from the street, and since hens retire early, nobody knew that three hens and a rooster had died at the same time in the hen house of Drozdova's next-door neighbor. They vomited just like the Drozdov hens, and the only difference was that their deaths took place quietly in a locked hen house. The rooster tumbled off his perch head down and died in that position. As for the widow's hens, they died off immediately after the prayer service, and by evening her hen houses were deadly quiet—the birds lay around in heaps, stiff and cold.

When the town got up the next morning, it was stunned as if by thunder, for the affair had assumed strange and monstrous proportions. By noon only three hens were still alive on Personal Street, and those were in the last house, where the district financial inspector lived, but even they were dead by one o'clock. And by evening the town of Steklovsk was humming and buzzing like a beehive, and the dread word "plague" was sweeping through it. Drozdova's name landed in the local newspaper, *The*

Red Warrior, in an article headlined "Can It Be Chicken Plague?" and from there it was carried to Moscow.

Professor Persikov's life took on a strange, restless, and disturbing character. In a word, working under such circumstances was simply impossible. The day after he had gotten rid of Alfred Bronsky, he had to disconnect his office telephone at the institute by taking the receiver off the hook, and in the evening, as he was riding the trolley home along Okhotny Row, the professor beheld himself on the roof of a huge building with a black sign on it: *WORKERS' GAZETTE.* Crumbling and turning green and flickering, he, the professor, climbed into a landau, and behind him, clutching at his sleeve, climbed a mechanical ball wearing a blanket. The professor on the white screen on the roof covered his face with his fists against a violet ray. Then a golden legend leaped out: "Professor Persikov in a car explaining his discovery to our famous reporter Captain Stepanov." And, indeed, the wavering car flicked past the Cathedral of Christ along Volkhonka, and in it the professor struggled helplessly, his physiognomy like that of a wolf at bay.

"They are some sort of devils, not men," the zoologist muttered through his teeth as he rode past.

That same day, in the evening, when he returned to his place on Prechistenka, the housekeeper, Marya Stepanovna, handed the zoologist seventeen notes with telephone numbers that had called while he was gone, along with Marya Stepanovna's verbal declaration that she was exhausted. The professor was getting ready to tear up the notes, but stopped, because opposite one of the numbers he saw the notation "People's Commissar of Public Health."

"What's this ?" the learned eccentric asked in honest bewilderment. "What has happened to them?"

At a quarter past ten the same evening the doorbell rang, and the professor was obliged to converse with a certain citizen in dazzling attire. The professor had received him because of a calling card, which stated (without first name or surname), "Plenipotentiary Chief of the Trade Departments of Foreign Embassies to the Soviet Republic."

"Why doesn't he go to hell?" growled Persikov, throwing down his magnifying glass and some diagrams on the green cloth of the table and saying to Marya Stepanovna, "Ask him here into the study, this plenipotentiary."

"What can I do for you?" Persikov asked in a tone that made the Chief wince a bit. Persikov transferred his spectacles to his forehead from the bridge of his nose, then back, and he peered at his visitor. He glittered all over with patent leather and precious stones, and a monocle rested in his right eye. "What a vile mug," Persikov thought to himself for some reason.

The guest began in a roundabout way, asked specific permission to light his cigar, in consequence of which Persikov with the greatest of reluctance invited him to sit down. The guest proceeded to make extended apologies for coming so late.

"But... the professor is quite impossible to catch... hee-hee... pardon... to find during the day." (when laughing the guest cachinnated like a hyena).

"Yes, I'm busy!" Persikov answered so abruptly that the guest twitched a second time.

"Nevertheless, he permitted himself to disturb the famous scientist. Time is money, as they say... Is the cigar annoying the professor?"

"Mur-mur-mur," answered Persikov, "he permitted. . . "

"The professor *has* discovered the ray of life, hasn't he?"

"For goodness sake, what sort of life! It's all the fantasies of cheap reporters!" Persikov got excited.

"Oh no, hee-hee-hee.... He understands perfectly the modesty which is the true adornment of all real scientists... But why fool around... There were telegrams today... In world capitals such as Warsaw and Riga everything about the ray is already known. Professor Persikov's name is being repeated all over the world. The world is watching Professor Persikov's work with bated breath... But everybody knows perfectly well the difficult position of scientists in Soviet Russia. *Entre nous soit dit...* There are no strangers here?.... Alas, in this country they do not know how to appreciate scientific work, and so he would like to talk things over with the professor... A certain foreign state is quite unselfishly offering Professor Persikov help with his laboratory work. Why cast pearls here, as the Holy Scripture says? The said state knows how hard it was for the professor during 1919 and 1920, during this... hee-hee... revolution. Well, of course, in the strictest secrecy... the professor would acquaint this state with the results of his work, and in exchange it would finance the professor. For example, he constructed a chamber—now it would be interesting to become acquainted with the blueprints for this chamber... "

At this point the visitor drew from the inside pocket of his jacket a snow-white stack of banknotes.

"The professor can have a trifling advance, say, five thousand rubles, at this very moment... and there is no need to mention a receipt... the Plenipotentiary Trade Chief would even feel offended if the professor so much as mentioned a receipt."

"Out!!" Persikov suddenly roared so terrifyingly that the piano in the living room made a sound with its high keys.

The visitor vanished so quickly that Persikov, shaking with rage, himself began to doubt whether he had been there, or if it had been a hallucination.

"His galoshes?" Persikov howled a minute later from the hallway. "The gentleman forgot them," replied the trembling Marya Stepanovna.

"Throw them out!"

"Where can I throw them? He'll come back for them."

"Take them to the house committee. Get a receipt. I don't want a trace of those galoshes! To the committee! Let them have the spy's galoshes!..."

Crossing herself, Marya Stepanovna picked up the magnificent leather galoshes and carried them out to the back stairs. There she stood behind the door for a few moments, and then hid the galoshes in the pantry.

"Did you turn them in?" Persikov raged.

"I did."

"Give me the receipt!"

"But, Vladimir Ipatych. But the chairman is illiterate!"

"This. Very Instant. I. Want. The. Receipt. Here! Let some literate son of a bitch sign for him!"

Marya Stepanovna just shook her head, went out, and came back fifteen minutes later with a note: "Received from Prof. Persikov 1 (one) pair galo. Kolesov."

"And what's this?"

"A tag, sir."

Persikov stomped all over the tag, and hid the receipt under the blotter. Then some idea darkened his sloping forehead. He rushed to the telephone, roused Pankrat at the institute, and asked him: "Is everything in order?" Pankrat growled something into the receiver, from which one could conclude that everything, in his opinion, was in order.

But Persikov calmed down only for a minute. Frowning, he clutched the telephone and jabbered into the receiver: "Give me ... oh, whatever you call it ... Lubyanka[6] ... *Merci* ... Which of you there should be told about this? ... I have suspicious characters hanging around here in galoshes, yes ... Professor Persikov of the Fourth University ..."

Suddenly the conversation was abruptly disconnected and Persikov walked away, muttering some sort of swear words through his teeth.

"Are you going to have some tea, Vladimir Ipatych?" Marya Stepanovna inquired timidly, looking into the study.

"I'm not going to have any tea ... mur-mur-mur ... and to hell with them all ... they've gone mad ... I don't care."

Exactly ten minutes later the professor was receiving new guests in his study. One of them, amiable, rotund, and very polite, was wearing a modest khaki military field jacket and riding breeches. On his nose, like a crystal butterfly, perched a pince-nez. Generally, he looked like an angel in patent leather boots. The second, short and terribly gloomy, was wearing civilian clothes, but they fit in such a way that they seemed to constrain him. The third guest behaved in a peculiar manner; he did not enter the professor's study but remained in the semidark hallway. From there he had a full view of the well-lit study which was filled with billows of tobacco smoke. The face of this third visitor, who was also wearing civilian clothes, was graced with a dark pince-nez.

The two in the study wore Persikov out completely, carefully examining the calling card and interrogating him about the five thousand, and making him keep describing the earlier visitor.

"The devil only knows," grumbled Persikov. "A repulsive physiognomy. A degenerate."

"He didn't have a glass eye, did he?" the short one asked hoarsely.

"The devil only knows. But no, it isn't glass; his eyes keep darting around."

"Rubenstein?" the angel said to the short civilian softly and interrogatively. But the latter shook his head darkly.

"Rubenstein wouldn't give any money without a receipt, never," he mumbled. "This is not Rubenstein's work. This is someone bigger."

The story of the galoshes provoked a burst of the keenest interest from the guests. The angel uttered a few words into the telephone of the house office: "The State Political Administration invites the secretary of the house committee Kolesov to report at Professor Persikov's apartment with the galoshes," and Kolesov appeared in the study instantly, pale, holding the galoshes in his hands.

"Vasenka!" the angel called softly to the man who was sitting in the hall. The latter rose limply and moved into the study like an unwinding toy. His smoky glasses swallowed up his eyes.

"Well?" he asked tersely and sleepily.

"The galoshes."

The smoky eyes slid over the galoshes, and as this happened it seemed to Persikov that they were not at all sleepy; on the contrary, the eyes that flashed askance for a moment from behind the glasses were amazingly sharp. But they immediately faded out.

"Well, Vasenka ?"

The man they addressed as Vasenka replied in a languid voice, "Well, what's the problem? They're Pelenzhkovsky's galoshes."

The house committee instantly lost Professor Persikov's gift. The galoshes disappeared into a newspaper. The extremely overjoyed angel in the military jacket got up, began to shake the professor's hand, and even made a little speech, the content of which boiled down to the following: "This does the professor honor.... The professor may rest assured ... no one will bother him again, either at the institute or at home ... steps will be taken ... his chambers are quite safe."

"Could you shoot the reporters while you're at it?" Persikov asked, looking at him over his spectacles.

His question provoked a burst of merriment among his guests.

Not only the gloomy short one, but even the smoky one smiled in the hall. The angel, sparkling and glowing, explained that this was not possible.

"And who was that scalawag who came here?"

At this everyone stopped smiling, and the angel answered evasively that it was nobody, a petty swindler, not worth any attention... but nevertheless, he urged citizen professor to keep the evening's events in strictest secrecy, and the guests departed.

Persikov returned to his study and diagrams, but he still did not get to do any work. A fiery dot appeared on the telephone, and a female voice offered the professor a seven-room apartment if he would like to marry an interesting and hot-blooded widow. Persikov bawled into the receiver, "I advise you to go to Professor Rossolimo for treatment!" and then the telephone rang a second time.

Here Persikov was somewhat abashed because a rather well-known personage from the Kremlin was calling; he questioned Persikov sympathetically and at great length about his work and made known his wish to visit the laboratory. As he started to leave the phone, Persikov mopped his forehead, and took the receiver off the hook. At that moment there was a sudden blare of trumpets in the upstairs apartment, followed by the shrieking of the Valkyries: the director of the Woolen Fabrics Trust had tuned his radio to a Wagner concert from the Bolshoi Theater. Over the howling and crashing pouring down from the ceiling, Persikov shouted to Marya Stepanovna that he was going to take the director to court, that he was going to smash that radio, that he was going to get the hell out of Moscow, because obviously people had made it their goal to drive him out of it.   He broke his magnifying glass and went to bed on the couch in his study, and he fell asleep to the gentle runs of a famous pianist that came wafting from the Bolshoi.

The surprises continued the next day too. When he got to the institute on the trolley, Persikov found an unknown citizen in a stylish green derby waiting at the entrance. He looked Persikov over closely, but addressed no questions to him, and therefore Persikov ignored him. But in the foyer, Persikov, in addition to the bewildered Pankrat, was met by a second derby which rose and greeted him courteously. "Hello there, Citizen Professor."

"What do you want?" Persikov asked menacingly, pulling off his overcoat with Pankrat's help. But the derby quickly pacified Persikov, whispering in the tenderest voice that the professor had no cause to be upset. He, the derby, was there for precisely the purpose of protecting the professor from any importunate visitors; the professor could set his mind at ease with regard not only to the doors of his study, but even to the windows. Upon which the stranger turned over the lapel of his suit coat for a moment and showed the professor a certain badge.

"Hm... how about that, you've really got things well set up," Persikov mumbled, and added naively, "and what will you eat here ?"

At this the derby grinned and explained that he would be relieved.

The three days after this went by splendidly. The professor had two visits from the Kremlin, and one from students whom he gave examinations. Every last one of the students flunked, and from their faces it was clear that Persikov now inspired only superstitious awe in them.

"Go get jobs as trolleycar conductors! You aren't fit to study zoology," came from the office.

"Strict, eh?" the derby asked Pankrat.

"Ooh, a holy terror," answered Pankrat, "even if someone passes, he comes out reeling, poor soul. He'll be dripping with sweat. And he heads straight for a beer hall..."

Engrossed in these minor chores, the professor did not notice the three days pass; but on the fourth day he was recalled to reality again, and the cause of this was a thin, squeaky voice from the street.

"Vladimir Ipatievich!" the voice screeched from Herzen Street into the open window of the office.

The voice was in luck: the last few days had exhausted Persikov. Just at the moment he was resting in his armchair, smoking, and staring languidly and feebly with his red-circled eyes. He could not go on. And therefore it was even with some curiosity that he looked out the window and saw Alfred Bronsky on the sidewalk. The professor immediately recognized the titled owner of the calling card by his pointed hat and notebook. Bronsky bowed to the window tenderly and deferentially.

"Oh, is it you?" the professor asked. He did not have enough energy left to get angry, and he was even curious to see what would happen next. Protected by the window, he felt safe from Alfred. The ever-present derby in the street instantly cocked an ear toward Bronsky. A most disarming smile blossomed on the latter's face.

"Just a pair of minutes, dear professor," Bronsky said, straining his voice from the sidewalk. "Only one small question, a purely zoological one. May I ask it?"

"Ask it," Persikov replied laconically and ironically, and he thought to himself, "After all, there is something American in this rascal."

"What do you have to say as for the hens, dear professor?" shouted Bronsky, folding his hands into a trumpet.

Persikov was nonplussed. He sat down on the windowsill, then got up, pressed a button, and shouted, poking his finger toward the window, "Pankrat, let that fellow on the sidewalk in."

When Bronsky appeared in the office Persikov extended his amiability to the extent of barking, "Sit down!" at him.

And Bronsky, smiling ecstatically, sat down on the revolving stool.

"Please explain something to me," began Persikov. "Do you write there—for those papers of yours?"

"Yes, sir," Alfred replied deferentially.

"Well, it's incomprehensible to me, how you can write when you don't even know how to speak Russian correctly. What is this 'a pair of minutes' and 'as for the hens'? You probably meant to ask 'about the hens'?"

Bronsky burst out into a thin and respectful laugh. "Valentin Petrovich corrects it."

"Who's this Valentin Petrovich ?"

"The head of the literary department."

"Well, all right. Besides, I am not a philologist. Let's forget your Petrovich. What is it specifically that you wish to know about hens?"

"In general everything you have to tell, professor."

Here Bronsky armed himself with a pencil. Triumphant sparks flickered in Persikov's eyes.

"You come to me in vain; I am not a specialist on the feathered beasts. You would be best off to go to Emelyan Ivanovich Portugalov of the First University. I myself know extremely little."

Bronsky smiled ecstatically, giving him to understand that he understood the dear professor's joke. "Joke: little," he jotted in his notebook.

"However, if it interests you, very well. Hens, or pectinates... Order, *Gallinae.* Of the pheasant family... " Persikov began in a loud voice, looking not at Bronsky, but somewhere beyond him, where a thousand people were presumably listening, "of the pheasant family, *Phasianidae.* They are birds with fleshy combs and two lobes under the lower jaw... hm... although sometimes there is only one in the center of the chin... Well, what else? Wings, short and rounded. Tails of medium length, somewhat serrated, even, I would say, denticulated, the middle feathers crescent shaped... Pankrat, bring me Model No. 705 from the model cabinet—a cock in cross section... but no, you have no need of that? Pankrat, don't bring the model... I reiterate to you, I am not a specialist— go to Portugalov. Well, I personally am acquainted with six species of wild hens—hm... Portugalov knows more—in India and the Malay Archipelago. For example, the Banki rooster, or Kazintu, found in the foothills of the Himalayas, all over India, in Assam and Burma... Then there's the swallow-tailed rooster, or *Gallus varius,* of Lombok, Sumbawa, and Flores. On the island of Java there is a remarkable rooster, *Gallus eneus;* in southeast India, I can recommend the very beautiful *Gallus souneratti* to you. As for Ceylon, there we meet the Stanley rooster, not found anywhere else."

Bronsky sat there, his eyes bulging, scribbling.

"Anything else I can tell you?"

"I would like to know something about chicken diseases," Alfred whispered very softly.

"Hm, I'm not a specialist, you ask Portugalov... Still, and all... well, there are tapeworms, flukes, scab mites, red mange, chicken mites, poultry lice or *Mallophaga,* fleas, chicken cholera, croupous-diphtheritic inflammation of the mucous membranes... pneumonomycosis, tuberculosis, chicken mange—there are all sorts of diseases." There were sparks leaping in Persikov's eyes. "There can be poisoning, tumors, rickets, jaundice, rheumatism, the *Achorion schoenleinii* fungus...a quite interesting disease. When it breaks out little spots resembling mold form on the comb."

Bronsky wiped the sweat from his forehead with a colored handkerchief. "And what, professor, in your opinion is the cause of the present catastrophe?"

"What catastrophe?"

"What, you mean you haven't read it, professor?" Bronsky cried with surprise, and pulled out a crumpled page of *Izvestia* from his briefcase.

"I don't read newspapers," answered Persikov, grimacing.

"But why, professor?" Alfred asked tenderly.

"Because they write gibberish," Persikov answered, without thinking.

"But how about this, professor?" Bronsky whispered softly, and he unfolded the newspaper.

"What's this?" asked Persikov, and he got up from his place. Now the sparks began to leap in Bronsky's eyes. With a pointed lacquered nail he underlined a headline of incredible magnitude across the entire page:

CHICKEN PLAGUE IN THE REPUBLIC

"What?" Persikov asked, pushing his spectacles onto his forehead.

VI

Moscow in June of 1928

She gleamed brightly, her lights danced, blinked, and flared on again. The white headlights of buses and the green lights of trolleys circled around Theater Square; over the former Muir and Merilis, above the tenth floor built up over it, a multicolored electric woman was jumping up and down, making up multicolored words letter by letter: WORKERS CREDIT. In the square opposite the Bolshoi, around the multicolored fountain shooting up sprays all night, a crowd was milling and rumbling. And over the Bolshoi a giant loudspeaker was booming: "The anti-chicken vaccinations at the Lefort Veterinary Institute have produced excellent results. The number...of chicken deaths for the day declined by half."

Then the loudspeaker changed its timbre, something rumbled in it; over the theater a green stream flashed on and off, and the loudspeaker complained in a deep bass: "Special commission set up to combat chicken plague, consisting of the People's Commissar of Public Health, the People's Commissar of Agriculture, the Chief of Animal Husbandry, Comrade Avis-Hamska, Professors Persikov and Portugalov, and Comrade Rabinovich!...New attempts at intervention," the speaker cachinnated and wept like a jackal, "in connection with the chicken plague!"

Theater Lane, Neglinny Prospect, and the Lubyanka flamed with white and violet streaks, spraying shafts of light, howling with horns, and whirling with dust. Crowds of people pressed against the wall by the huge pages of advertisements lit by garish red reflectors.

"Under threat of the most severe penalties, the populace is forbidden to employ chicken meat or eggs as food. Private tradesmen who attempt to sell these in the markets will be subject to criminal prosecution and confiscation of all property. All citizens who own eggs must immediately surrender them at their local police precincts."

On the roof of *The Worker's Gazette* chickens were piled skyhigh on the screen, and greenish firemen, quivering and sparkling, were pouring kerosene on them with long hoses. Then red waves swept across the screen; unreal smoke billowed, tossed about like rags, and crept along in streams, and fiery words leaped out: "BURNING OF CHICKEN CORPSES ON THE KHODYNKA."

Among the wildly blazing show windows of the stores which worked until three in the morning (with breaks for lunch and supper) gaped the blind holes of windows boarded up under their signs; "Egg Store. Quality Guaranteed." Very often, screaming alarmingly, passing lumbering buses, hissing cars marked "MOSHEALDEPART FIRST AID" swept past the traffic policemen.

"Someone else has stuffed himself with rotten eggs," the crowd murmured.

On the Petrovsky Lines the world-renowned Empire Restaurant glittered with its green and orange lights, and on its tables, next to the portable telephones, stood cardboard signs stained with liqueurs: "By decree—no omelettes. Fresh oysters have been received."

At the Ermitage, where tiny Chinese lanterns, like beads, glowed mournfully amid the artificial, cozy greenery, the singers Shrams and Karmanchikov on the eye-shattering, dazzling stage sang ditties composed by the poets Ardo and Arguiev:

Oh, Mamma, what will I do without eggs?

while their feet thundered out a tap dance.

Over the theater of the late Vsevolod Meyerhold, who died, as everyone knows, in 1927, during the staging of Pushkin's *Boris Godunov*[7] when a platform full of naked boyars collapsed on him, there flashed a moving multicolored neon sign promulgating the writer Erendorg's play, *Chicken Croak,* produced by Meyerhold's disciple, Honored Director of the Republic Kukhterman. Next door, at the Aquarium Restaurant, scintillating with neon signs and flashing with half-naked female bodies to thunderous applause, the writer Lazer's review entitled *The Hen's Children* was being played amid the greenery of the stage. And down Tverskaya, with lanterns on either side of their heads, marched a procession of circus donkeys carrying gleaming placards. Rostand's *Chantecler* was being revived at the Korsh Theater.

Little newsboys were howling and screaming among the wheels of the automobiles: "Nightmarish discovery in a cave! Poland preparing for nightmarish war! Professor Persikov's nightmarish experiments!"

At the circus of the former Nikitin, in the greasy brown arena that smelled pleasantly of manure, the dead-white clown Bom was saying to Bim, who was dressed in a huge checkered sack, "I know why you're so sad!"

"Vhy-y?" squeaked Bim.

"You buried your eggs in the ground, and the police from the fifteenth precinct found them."

"Ha, ha, ha, ha," the circus laughed, so that the blood stopped in the veins joyfully and anguishingly—and the trapezes and the cobwebs under the shabby cupola swayed dizzily.

"Oop!" the clowns cried piercingly, and a sleek white horse carried out on its back a woman of incredible beauty, with shapely legs in scarlet tights.

Looking at no one, noticing no one, not responding to the nudging and soft and tender enticements of prostitutes, Persikov, inspired and lonely, crowned with sudden fame, was making his way along Mokhovaya toward the fiery clock at the Manège. Here, without looking around at all, engrossed in his thoughts, he bumped into a strange, old-fashioned man, painfully jamming his fingers directly against the wooden holster of a revolver hanging from the man's belt.

"Oh, damn!" squeaked Persikov. "Excuse me."

"Of course," answered the stranger in an unpleasant voice, and somehow they disentangled themselves in the middle of this human logjam. And heading for Prechistenka the professor instantly forgot the collision.

VII

Feyt

It is not known whether the Lefort Veterinary Institute's inoculations really were any good, whether the Samara roadblock detachments were skillful, whether the stringent measures taken with regard to the egg salesmen in Kaluga and Voronezh were successful, or whether the Extraordinary Commission in Moscow worked efficiently, but it is well known that two weeks after Persikov's last interview with Alfred, in a chicken way things had already been completely cleaned up in the Union of Republics. Here and there forlorn feathers still lay about in the backyards of district towns, bringing tears to the eyes of the onlookers, and in hospitals the last of the greedy people were still finishing the last spasms of bloody diarrhea and vomiting. Fortunately, human deaths were no more than a thousand in the entire Republic. Nor did any serious disorders ensue. True, a prophet had appeared briefly in Volokolamsk, proclaiming that the chicken plague had been caused by none other than the commissars, but he had no special success. In the Volokolamsk marketplace several policemen who had been confiscating chickens from the market women were beaten up, and some windows were broken in the local post and telegraph office. Luckily, the efficient Volokolamsk authorities quickly took the necessary measures as a result of which, first, the prophet ceased his activities, and second, the post office's broken windows were replaced.

Having reached Archangel and Syumkin village in the North, the plague stopped by itself, for the reason that there was nowhere for it to go—as everybody knows, there are no hens in the White Sea. It also stopped at Vladivostok, for there only the ocean is beyond that. In the far South it disappeared, petering out somewhere in the parched expanses of Ordubat, Dzhulfa, and Karabulak; and in the West it halted in an astonishing way exactly on the Polish and Rumanian borders. Perhaps the climate of these countries is different or perhaps the quarantine measures taken by the neighboring governments worked, but the fact remains that the plague went no further. The foreign press noisily and avidly discussed the unprecedented losses, while the government of the Soviet Republics, without any noise, was working tirelessly. The Special Commission to Fight the Chicken Plague was renamed the Special Commission for the Revival and Reestablishment of Chicken Breeding in the Republic and was augmented by a new Special Troika, made up of sixteen members. A "Goodpoul" office was set up, with Persikov and Portugalov as honorary assistants to the chairman. Their pictures appeared in the newspapers over titles such as "Mass Purchase of Eggs Abroad"and "Mr. Hughes Wants to Undermine the Egg Campaign." All Moscow read the stinging feuilleton by the journalist Kolechkin, which closed with the words, "Don't whet your teeth on our eggs, Mr. Hughes—you have your own!"

Professor Persikov was completely exhausted from overworking himself for the last three weeks. The chicken events disrupted his routine and put a double burden upon him. Every evening he had to work at conferences of chicken commissions, and from time to time he was obliged to endure long interviews either with Alfred Bronsky or with the mechanical fat man. He had to work with Professor Portugalov and Assistant Professors Ivanov and Bornhart, dissecting and microscoping chickens in search of the plague bacillus, and he even had to write up a hasty pamphlet "On the Changes in Chicken Kidneys as a Result of the Plague" in three evenings.

Persikov worked in the chicken field with no special enthusiasm, and understandably so—his whole mind was filled with something else which was fundamental and important—the problem from which he had been diverted by the chicken catastrophe, i.e., the red ray. Straining still further his already shaken health, stealing hours from sleep and meals, sometimes falling asleep on the oilcloth couch in his institute office, instead of going home to Prechistenka, Persikov spent whole nights puttering with his chamber and his microscope.

By the end of July the race let up a little. The work of the renamed commission fell into a normal groove, and Persikov returned to his interrupted work. The microscopes were loaded with new cultures, and under the ray in the chamber fish and frog roe matured with fantastic speed. Specially ordered glass was brought from Königsberg by plane, and during the last days of July mechanics laboring under Ivanov's supervision constructed two large new chambers in which the ray reached the width of a cigarette pack at its source and at its widest point—a full meter. Persikov joyfully rubbed his hands and started to prepare for some sort of mysterious and complicated experiments. To start with he talked to the People's Commission of Education on the telephone, and the receiver quacked out the warmest assurances of all possible cooperation, and then Persikov telephoned Comrade Avis-Hamska, the director of the Animal Husbandry Department of the Supreme Commission. Persikov received Avis-Hamska's warmest attention. The matter involved a large order abroad for Professor Persikov. Avis said into the telephone that he would immediately wire Berlin and New York. After this there was an inquiry from the Kremlin about how Persikov's work was progressing, and an important and affable voice asked whether Persikov needed an automobile.

"No, thank you, I prefer to ride the trolley," replied Persikov.

"But why?" the mysterious voice asked, laughing condescendingly.

In general everybody spoke to Persikov either with respect and terror, or laughing indulgently, as though he were a small, though overgrown, child.

"It's faster," Persikov replied, to which the resonant bass replied into the telephone, "Well, as you wish."

Another week passed, during which Persikov, withdrawing still further from the receding chicken problems, engrossed himself completely in the study of the ray. From the sleepless nights and overexertion his head felt light, as if it were transparent and weightless. The red circles never left his eyes now, and Persikov spent almost every night at the institute. Once he abandoned his zoological retreat to give a lecture at the huge Tsekubu Hall on Prechistenka—about his ray and its effect on the egg cell. It was a tremendous triumph for the eccentric zoologist. The applause was so thunderous that something crumbled and dropped down from the ceilings of the colonnaded hall; hissing arc lights poured light over the black dinner jackets of the Tsekubu members and the white gowns of the ladies. On the stage, on a glass-topped table next to the lectern, a moist frog as big as a cat sat on a platter, gray and breathing heavily. Many notes were thrown onto the stage. They included seven declarations of love, and Persikov tore them up. The Tsekubu chairman dragged him forcibly onto the the stage to bow to the audience. Persikov bowed irritably; his hands were sweaty, and the knot of his black tie rested not beneath his chin, but behind his left ear. There amid the sounds of respiration and the mist before him were hundreds of yellow faces and white shirtfronts, and suddenly the yellow holster of a revolver flashed and disappeared somewhere behind a white column. Persikov dimly perceived it, and forgot it. But as he was departing after the lecture, walking down the raspberry-colored carpet of the staircase, he suddenly felt sick. For a moment the dazzling chandelier in the vestibule turned black, and Persikov felt faint and nauseated... He thought he smelled something burning; it seemed to him that blood was dripping, sticky and hot, down his neck... And with a shaky hand the professor caught at the handrail.

"Are you sick, Vladimir Ipatych?" anxious voices flew at him from all sides.

"No, no," replied Persikov, recovering. "I am just overtired... yes... May I have a glass of water?"

It was a very sunny August day. That bothered the professor, so the shades were lowered. A reflector on a flexible stand threw a sharp beam of light onto a glass table piled with instruments and slides. Leaning against the backrest of the revolving chair in exhaustion, Persikov smoked, and his eyes, dead tired but satisfied, looked through the billows of smoke at the partly open door of the chamber where, faintly warming the already close and impure air of the office, the red sheaf of his ray lay quietly.

Someone knocked on the door.

"Well?" asked Persikov.

The door creaked softly, and Pankrat entered. He put his arms stiffly at his sides, and blanching with fear before the divinity, he said, "Mr. Professor, out there Feyt has come to you."

A semblance of a smile appeared on the scientist's cheeks. He narrowed his eyes and said, "That's interesting. But I'm busy."

"He says he has an official paper from the Kremlin."

"Fate with a paper? A rare combination," uttered Persikov, adding, "oh, well, get him in here."

"Yes, sir," said Pankrat, and he disappeared through the door like an eel.

A minute later it creaked again and a man appeared on the threshold. Persikov squeaked around on his swivel chair, and, above his spectacles, fixed his eyes on the visitor over his shoulder. Persikov was very remote from life—he was not interested in it—but even Persikov was struck by the predominant, the salient characteristic of the man who had entered: he was peculiarly old-fashioned. In 1919 the man would have been entirely in place in the streets of the capital; he would have passed in 1924, in the beginning of the year—but in 1928 he was odd. At a time when even the most backward section of the proletariat—the bakers—wore ordinary jackets, and the military service jacket was a rarity in Moscow—an old-fashioned outfit irrevocably discarded by the end of 1924—the man who had entered was wearing a double-breasted leather coat, olive-green trousers, puttees, and gaiters on his legs, and at his hip a huge Mauser of antiquated make in a cracked yellow holster. His face produced the same kind of impression on Persikov that it did on everyone else—an extremely unpleasant impression. His little eyes looked at the whole world with surprise, but at the same time with assurance; there was something bumptious in the short legs with their flat feet. His face was blue from close shaving. Persikov immediately frowned. He squeaked the screw of his chair mercilessly, and looking at the man no longer over his spectacles but through them, he asked, "You have some paper ? Where is it?"

The visitor was apparently overwhelmed by what he saw. Generally he had little capacity for being taken aback, but here he was taken aback. Judging by his tiny eyes, he was struck most of all by the twelve-shelved bookcase, which reached to the ceiling and was crammed with books. Then, of course, there were the chambers, in which—as though in hell—the scarlet ray flickered, diffused and magnified through the glass. And Persikov himself in the penumbra beside the sharp needle of light emitted by the reflector was sufficiently strange and majestic in his revolving chair. The visitor fixed on the professor a glance in which sparks of deference were clearly leaping through the self-assurance. He presented no paper, but said, "I am Alexander Semyonovich Feyt!"[8]

"Well? So what?"

"I have been appointed director of the model Sovkhoz[9]—the 'Red Ray' Sovkhoz," explained the visitor.

"And?"

"And so I've come to see you, comrade, with a secret memorandum."

"Interesting to learn. Make it short, if you can."

The visitor unbuttoned the lapel of his coat and pulled out an order printed on magnificent thick paper. He held it out to Persikov. Then, without invitation, he sat down on a revolving stool.

"Don't jiggle the table," Persikov said with hatred.

The visitor looked around at the table in fright—at the far end, in a moist dark aperture, some sort of eyes gleamed lifelessly like emeralds. They exuded a chill.

No sooner had Persikov read the paper than he rose from his stool and rushed to the telephone. Within a few seconds he was already speaking hurriedly and with an extreme degree of irritation. "Excuse me . . . I cannot understand . . . How can this be? I . . . without my consent or advice . . . Why, the devil only knows what he'll do with it!"

Here the stranger turned on his stool, extremely insulted. "Pardon me," he began, "I am the direc . . ."

But Persikov waved him away with his hooked index finger and continued: "Excuse me, I can't understand ... And finally, I categorically refuse. I will not sanction any experiments with eggs ... Until I try them myself ...."

Something squawked and clicked in the receiver, and even from a distance one could understand that the condescending voice in the receiver was speaking to a small child. It ended with crimson Persikov slamming down the receiver and saying past it into the wall, "I wash my hands of this!"

He returned to the table, took the paper from it, read it once from top to bottom above his spectacles, then from bottom to top through them, and suddenly he yelled, "Pankrat!"

Pankrat appeared in the door as though rising up through a trap door at the opera. Persikov glanced at him and ejaculated, "Get out, Pankrat!"

And without showing the least surprise, Pankrat disappeared.

Then Persikov turned to his guest and began, "All right, sir ... I submit. It's none of my business. And I'm not even interested."

The professor not so much offended as amazed his guest. "But pardon me," he began, "you *are* a comrade? ..."

"Comrade ... comrade.... Is that all you know how to say?" Persikov grumbled, and fell silent.

"Well!" was written on Feyt's face.

"Pard ..."

"Now, sir, if you please," interrupted Persikov. "This is the arc light. From it you obtain, by manipulating the ocular," Persikov snapped the lid of the chamber, which resembled a camera, "a cluster which you can gather by adjusting object-lens No. 1, here, and mirror No. 2." Persikov turned off the ray, turned it on again—aimed at the floor of the asbestos chamber. "And on the floor you can place whatever you please in the ray and conduct experiments. Extremely simple, don't you think?"

Persikov meant to show irony and contempt, but his visitor did not notice, peering intently into the chamber with his glittering little eyes.

"But I warn you," Persikov went on, "one should not put one's hands in the ray, because, according to my observations, it causes growth of the epithelium—and I unfortunately have not yet been able to establish whether it is malignant or not."

Here the visitor nimbly hid his hands behind his back, dropping his leather cap, and he looked at the professor's hands. They were covered with iodine stains, and his right wrist was bandaged.

"And how do you do it, professor?"

"You can buy rubber gloves at Schwab's on Kuznetsky," the professor replied irritably. "I'm not obliged to worry about that."

Here Persikov looked up at his visitor, as though studying him through a magnifying glass. "Where are you from? Why you? In general, why you ?"

Feyt was finally deeply offended, "Pard . . ."

"After all, one has to know what it's all about... Why have you latched on to my ray? . . ."

"Because it's a matter of utmost importance."

"Oh. The utmost? In that case—Pankrat!"

And when Pankrat appeared: "Wait, I'll think it over."

And Pankrat obediently disappeared.

"I cannot understand one thing," said Persikov. "Why is such rushing and secrecy necessary?"

"You have already got me muddled, professor," Feyt answered. "You know that every last chicken has died off?"

"Well, what about it?" shrieked Persikov. "Do you want to resurrect them instantly, or what? And why use a ray that has still been insufficiently studied?"

"Comrade Professor," replied Feyt, "I must say, you do mix me up. I am telling you that it is essential for us to reestablish chicken breeding, because they're writing all kinds of nasty things about us abroad. Yes."

"Let them write."

"Well, you know!" Feyt responded mysteriously, shaking his head.

"I'd like to know who got the idea of breeding chickens from eggs ."

"I did," answered Feyt.

"Uhmmm ... So ... And why, may I inquire? Where did you hear about the characteristics of this ray?"

"I attended your lecture, professor."

"I haven't done anything with eggs yet! I am just getting ready to!"

"It'll work, I swear it will," Feyt said suddenly with conviction and enthusiasm. "Your ray is so famous, you could hatch elephants with it, let alone chickens."

"Tell me," uttered Persikov. "You aren't a zoologist, are you? No? A pity... you'd make a very bold experimenter... Yes, but you are risking failure. And you are just taking up my time . . ."

"We'll return your chambers."

"When?"

"Well, as soon as I breed the first group."

"How confidently you say that! Very well, sir. Pankrat!"

"I have men with me," said Feyt. "And guards . . ."

By that evening Persikov's office had been desolated... The tables were bare. Feyt's men had carried off the three large chambers, leaving the professor only the first, his own little one with which he had begun the experiments.

July twilight was settling over the institute; grayness filled it and flowed along the corridors. From the study came the sound of monotonous footsteps—this was Persikov pacing the large room from window to door without turning on the light. It was a strange thing: that evening an inexplicably dismal mood overcame both the people who inhabited the institute and the animals. The toads for some reason raised a particularly dismal concert, twittering ominously, premonitorily. Pankrat had to chase along the corridors after a garter snake that had escaped from its cage, and when he caught it, the snake looked as though it had decided to flee wherever its eyes would lead it, if only to get away.

In the deep twilight the bell rang from Persikov's office. Pankrat appeared on the threshold and he saw a strange sight. The scientist was standing solitarily in the center of the room, looking at the tables. Pankrat coughed once and stood still.

"There, Pankrat," said Persikov, and he pointed to the bare table.

Pankrat was horrified. It seemed to him that the professor's eyes were tear-stained in the twilight. It was so extraordinary and so terrible.

"Yes, sir," Pankrat answered lugubriously, thinking, "It'd be better if you'd yell at me."

"There," repeated Persikov, and his lips quivered like a child's when his favorite toy has suddenly, for no reason, been taken away from it. "You know, my good Pankrat," Persikov went on, turning away to the window, "my wife... who left me fifteen years ago—she joined an operetta... and now it turns out she is dead... What a story, my dear Pankrat... I was sent a letter."

The toads screamed plaintively, and twilight enveloped the professor. There it is... night. Moscow... here and there outside the windows some sort of white globes began to light up... Pankrat, confused and in anguish, held his hands straight down his sides, stiff with fear...

"Go, Pankrat," the professor murmured heavily, waving his hand. "Go to bed, my dear, kind Pankrat."

And night came. For some reason Pankrat ran out of the office on his tiptoes, hurried to his cranny, rummaged through the rags in the corner, pulled out a half-full bottle of Russian vodka, and gulped down almost a regular glassful in one breath. He chased it with some bread and salt, and his eyes cheered up a bit.

Later in the evening, close to midnight now, Pankrat was sitting barefoot on a bench in the dimly lit vestibule, talking to the sleepless derby on duty, and scratching his chest under the calico shirt. "It'd be better if he'd kill me, I swear... "

"He really was crying?" inquired the derby with curiosity.

"I swear . . ." Pankrat assured him.

"A great scientist," agreed the derby. "Obviously no frog can take the place of a wife."

"Absolutely," Pankrat agreed. Then he thought a bit and added, "I'm thinking of getting my woman permission to come out here[10]... why should she sit there in the village? Only she can't stand them snakes no how... "

"Sure, they're terribly nasty," agreed the derby.

From the scientist's office not a sound could be heard. And there was no light in it. No strip under the door.

VIII

Events at the Sovkhoz

There is absolutely no time of year more beautiful than mid-August in, let us say, the Smolensk province. The summer of 1928, as is well known, was one of the finest ever, with spring rains which had come at precisely the right time, a full hot sun, and a fine harvest... The apples were ripening in the former Sheremetiev estate... the woods stood green, the fields lay in yellow squares. A man becomes better in the bosom of nature. And Alexander Semyonovich would not have seemed as unpleasant here as in the city. And he no longer wore that obnoxious coat. His face had a coppery tan, his unbuttoned calico shirt betrayed a chest overgrown with the thickest black hair, his legs were clad in canvas trousers. And his eyes had grown calmer and kinder.

Alexander Semyonovich ran briskly down the stairs from the becolumned porch over which a sign was nailed, under a star: THE "RED RAY" SOVKHOZ. And he went straight to meet the pickup truck which had brought him three black chambers under guard.

All day Alexander Semyonovich bustled around with his helpers, setting up the chambers in the former winter garden—the Sheremetiev greenhouse... By evening all was in readiness. A frosted white globe glowed under the glass ceiling, the chambers were arranged on bricks, and the mechanic who had come with the chambers, clicking and turning the shiny knobs, turned the mysterious red ray onto the asbestos floor of the black boxes.

Alexander Semyonovich bustled around, and even climbed the ladder himself to check out the wiring.

On the following day, the same pickup returned from the station and disgorged three crates made of magnificent smooth plywood and plastered all over with labels and warnings in white letters on black backgrounds : "*Vorsicht: Eier!* Handle with care: Eggs."

"But why did they send so few?" wondered Alexander Semyonovich—however, he immediately started bustling around and unpacking the eggs. The unpacking was done in the same greenhouse with the participation of: Alexander Semyonovich himself; his wife Manya, a woman of extraordinary bulk; the one-eyed former gardener of the former Sheremetievs, currently working on the sovkhoz in the universal capacity of watchman; the guard, now condemned to life on the sovkhoz; and Dunya, the cleaning woman. This was not Moscow, and so the nature of everything here was simpler, friendlier, and more homely. Alexander Semyonovich supervised, glancing affectionately at the crates, which looked like a really sturdy, compact present under the soft sunset light coming through the upper windows of the greenhouse. The guard, whose rifle rested peacefully by the door, broke open the clamps and metal bindings with a pair of pliers. Crackling filled the room. Dust flew. Flopping along in his sandals, Alexander Semyonovich fussed around the crates.

"Take it easy," he said to the guard. "Careful. Don't you see it's eggs?"

"Don't worry," the provincial warrior grunted, drilling away. "Just a second." T-r-r-r... and the dust flew.

The eggs turned out to be exceedingly well packed: under the wooden lid there was a layer of wax paper, then absorbent paper, then a solid layer of wood shavings, and then sawdust, in which the white tips of the eggs gleamed.

"Foreign packing," Alexander Semyonovich said lovingly digging into the sawdust. "Not the way we do things here. Manya, careful, you'll break them."

"You've gotten silly, Alexander Semyonovich," replied his wife. "Imagine, such gold. Do you think I've never seen eggs before?... Oy! What big ones!"

"Europe," said Alexander Semyonovich, "Did you expect our crummy little Russian peasant eggs?... They must all be Brahmaputras, the devil take 'em! German . . ."

"Sure they are," confirmed the guard, admiring the eggs.

"Only I don't understand why they're dirty," Alexander Semyonovich said reflectively... "Manya, you look after things. Have them go on with the unloading, and I'm going to make a telephone call."

And Alexander Semyonovich set off for the telephone in the sovkhoz office across the yard.

That evening the telephone cracked in the office of the Zoological Institute. Professor Persikov ruffled his hair and went to the phone. "Well?" he asked.

"The provinces calling, just a minute," the receiver replied with a soft hiss in a woman's voice.

"Well, I'm listening," Persikov said fastidiously into the black mouth of the phone.

Something clicked in it, and then a distant masculine voice anxiously spoke in his ear. "Should the eggs be washed, professor?"

"What? What is it? What are you asking?" Persikov got irritated. "Where are you calling from?"

"From Nikolsky, Smolensk province," the receiver answered.

"I don't understand any of this. I don't know any Nikolsky. Who is this?"

"Feyt," said the receiver sternly.

"What Feyt? Oh, yes... it's you... so what is it you're asking?"

"Should they be washed?... I was sent a batch of chicken eggs from abroad . . ."

"Well?"

"They seem slimy somehow . . ."

"You're mixing something up . . . How can they be 'slimy' as you put it? Well, of course, there can be a little . . . perhaps some droppings stuck on . . . or something else . . ."

"So they shouldn't be washed?"

"Of course not . . . What are you doing—are you all ready to load the chambers with the eggs?"

"I am. Yes," replied the receiver.

"Harumph," Persikov snorted.

"So long," the receiver clicked and went silent.

"So long," Persikov repeated with hatred to Assistant Professor Ivanov. "How do you like that character, Peter Stepanovich?"

Ivanov laughed. "Was that him? I can imagine what he'll cook up with those eggs out there."

"The id . . . id . . . idiot," Persikov stuttered furiously. "Just imagine, Peter Stepanovich. Fine, it is quite possible that the ray will have the same effect on the deutoplasm of the chicken egg that it did on the plasm of the amphibians. It is quite possible that the hens will hatch. But neither you nor I can say what sort of hens they will be . . . Maybe they won't be good for a damned thing. Maybe they'll die in a day or two. Maybe they'll be inedible! Can I guarantee that they'll be able to stand on their feet? Maybe their bones will be brittle." Persikov got all excited and waved his hands, crooking his index fingers.

"Absolutely right," agreed Ivanov.

"Can you guarantee, Peter Stepanovich, that they'll produce another generation? Maybe this character will breed sterile hens. He'll drive them up to the size of a dog, and then you can wait until the second coming before they'll have any progeny."

"No one can guarantee it," agreed Ivanov.

"And what bumptiousness!" Persikov got himself even more distraught. "What insolence! And, note this, I have been ordered to instruct this scoundrel." Persikov pointed to the paper delivered by Feyt (it lay on the experiment table). "How am I to instruct this ignoramus, when I myself cannot say anything on the problem?"

"But was it impossible to refuse?" asked Ivanov.

Persikov turned crimson, picked up the paper, and showed it to Ivanov. The latter read it and smiled ironically.

"Um, yes," he said very significantly.

"And then, note this . . . I've been waiting for my order for two months—and there's neither hide nor hair of it. While that one is sent the eggs instantly, and generally gets all kinds of cooperation."

"He won't get a damned thing out of it, Vladimir Ipatych. And it will just end by their returning the chambers to you."

"If only they don't take too long doing it, otherwise they're holding up my experiments."

"That's what's really rotten. I have everything ready."

"Did you get the diving suits?"

"Yes, today."

Persikov calmed down somewhat, and livened up. "Hhmmm... I think we'll do it this way. We can seal the doors of the operating room tight and open the window ..."

"Of course," agreed Ivanov.

"Three helmets ?"

"Three. Yes."

"Well, so... That means you, I, and possibly one of the students. We'll give him the third helmet."

"Greenmut's possible."

"The one who's working on the salamanders with you now? Hmmm, he's not bad... although, wait, last spring he couldn't describe the structure of the air bladder of the Gymnodontes," Persikov added rancorously.

"No, he's not bad... He's a good student," interceded Ivanov.

"We will have to go without sleep for one night," Persikov went on. "And one more thing, Peter Stepanovich, you check the gas—otherwise the devil only knows about these so-called Goodchems—they'll send some sort of trash."

"No, no," Ivanov waved his hands. "I already tested it yesterday. We must give them their due, Vladimir Ipatych, it's excellent gas."

"On whom did you try it?"

"On ordinary toads. You let out a little stream and they die instantly. Oh, yes, Vladimir Ipatych, we'll also do this—you write a request to the GPU, asking them to send an electric revolver."

"But I don't know how to use it."

"I'll take that on myself," answered Ivanov. "We used to practice with one on the Klyazma, just for fun ... there was a GPU man living next door to me. A remarkable thing. Quite extraordinary. Noiseless, kills outright from a hundred paces. We used to shoot crows ... I don't think we even need the gas."

"Hmmm, that's a clever idea ... Very." Persikov went to the corner of the room, picked up the receiver, and croaked, "Let me have that, oh, what d'you call it . . . Lubyanka..."

The days got unbearably hot. One could clearly see the dense transparent heat shimmering over the fields. But the nights were mar- velous, deceptive, green. The moon shone brightly, casting such beauty on the former Sheremetiev estate that it is impossible to express it in words. The sovkhoz palace gleamed as though made of sugar, the shadows trembled in the park, and the ponds were cleft into two colors—a slanting shaft of moonlight across it, and the rest, bottomless darkness. In the patches of moonlight you could easily read *Izvestia,* except for the chess column, which is printed in tiny nonpareil. But, naturally, nobody read *Izvestia* on nights like these . . . Dunya, the cleaning woman, turned up in the copse behind the sovkhoz, and as a result of some coincidence, the red-moustachioed driver of a battered sovkhoz pickup turned up there too. What they did there—remains unknown. They took shelter in the melting shadow of an elm, right on the driver's outspread leather jacket. A lamp burned in the kitchen where two gardeners were having their supper, and Madame Feyt, wearing a white robe, was sitting on the becolumned veranda and dreaming as she gazed at the beautiful moon.

At ten in the evening when all of the sounds had subsided in the village of Kontsovka, situated behind the sovkhoz, the idyllic landscape was filled with the charming, delicate sounds of a flute. It is unthinkable to try to express how this suited the copses and former columns of the Sheremetiev palace. Fragile Liza from *The Queen of Spades*[11] mingled her voice in a duet with the voice of the passionate Polina, and the melody swept up into the moonlit heights like the ghost of an old regime—old, but infinitely lovely, enchanting to the point of tears.

"Waning . . . waning...," the flute sang, warbling and sighing.

The copses fell silent, and Dunya, fatal as a wood nymph, listened, her cheek pressed to the prickly, reddish masculine cheek of the driver.

"He blows good, the son of a bitch," said the driver, encircling Dunya's waist with his manly arm.

Playing the flute was none other than the sovkhoz director himself, Alexander Semyonovich Feyt, and we must give him his due, he played extremely well. The fact is that at one time the flute had been Alexander Semyonovich's specialty. Right up until 1917 he had been a member of Maestro Petukhov's well-known concert ensemble, whose harmonic sounds rang out every night in the lobby of the cozy Magic Dreams Cinema in the city of Yekaterinoslav. The great year of 1917, which had broken the careers of many people, had turned Alexander Semyonovich onto new roads too. He abandoned the Magic Dreams and the dusty star-spangled satin in the lobby and dove into the open sea of war and revolution, exchanging his flute for a deadly Mauser. For a long time he was tossed on the waves, which cast him up now in the Crimea, now in Moscow, now in Turkestan, and even in Vladivostok. It took a revolution to bring Alexander Semyonovich fully into his own. The man's true greatness was revealed, and naturally he was not meant to sit around the lobby of the Dreams. Without getting into great detail, let us say that late 1927 and early 1928 found Alexander Semyonovich in Turkestan where he had, first, edited a huge newspaper and, next, as the local member of the Supreme Agricultural Commission, covered himself with glory through his remarkable work in irrigating the Turkestan territory. In 1928 Feyt arrived in Moscow and got a well-deserved rest. The highest committee of the organization whose card the provincial-looking, old-fashioned man carried in his pocket with honor showed its appreciation and appointed

him to a quiet and honorable post. Alas! Alas! To the misfortune of the
Republic, the seething brain of Alexander Semyonovich was not cooled
off; in Moscow Feyt ran across Persikov's discovery, and in his room at the
Red Paris Hotel on Tverskaya, Alexander Semyonovich conceived the
idea of using Persikov's ray to replenish the chicken population of the
Republic in one month. Feyt's plan was heard out by the Commission on
Animal Husbandry, they agreed with him, and Feyt went with the thick
sheet of paper to the eccentric zoologist.

The concert over the glassy waters and copses and park was already
drawing to a close when suddenly something happened that interrupted it
ahead of time. Namely, the dogs in Kontsovka, who should have been
asleep at that hour, suddenly burst out into an incredible fit of barking
which gradually turned into a general and very anguished howling. The
howling, increasing in volume, flew across the fields, and this howling was
suddenly answered by a chattering, million-voiced concert of frogs in all
the ponds. All of this was so uncanny that for a minute it even seemed that
the mysterious, witching night had grown dim.

Alexander Semyonovich laid down his flute and went out onto the
veranda, "Manya! Do you hear that? Those damned dogs... What do you
think is making them so wild?"

"How should I know?" replied Manya, staring at the moon.

"You know what, Manechka, let's go and take a look at the eggs,"
suggested Alexander Semyonovich.

"By God, Alexander Semyonovich, you've gone completely nuts with
your eggs and chickens. Take a little rest!"

"No, Manechka, let's go."

A bright bulb was burning in the greenhouse. Dunya also came in,
face flushed and eyes flashing. Alexander Semyonovich gently opened the
observation panes, and everyone started peering inside the chambers. On
the white asbestos floor the spotted bright-red eggs lay in even rows; the
chambers were silent, and the 15,000 watt bulb overhead was hissing
quietly.

"Oh, what chicks I'll hatch out of here!" Alexander Semyonovich said
enthusiastically, looking now into the observation slits in the side walls of
the chambers, now into the wide air vents above. "You'll see.   What?
Won't I?"

"You know, Alexander Semyonovich," said Dunya, smiling, "the
peasants in Kontsovka are saying you're the Anti-Christ. Them are
devilish eggs, they say. It's a sin to hatch eggs by machine. They wanted to
murder you."

Alexander Semyonovich shuddered and turned to his wife. His face
had turned yellow. "Well, how do you like that? Such people! What can
you do with people like that? Eh? Manechka, we'll have to arrange a
meeting for them. Tomorrow I'll call some Party workers from the district.
I'll make a speech myself. In general we'll have to do some work here... It's

some sort of wild country. . ."

"Dark minds," said the guard, reposing on his coat at the greenhouse door.

The next day was marked by the strangest and most inexplicable events. In the morning, at the first flash of the sun, the copses, which usually greeted the luminary with a mighty and ceaseless twittering of birds, met it in total silence. This was noticed by absolutely everyone. As though before a storm. But there was not the slightest hint of a storm. Conversations in the sovkhoz assumed a strange, ambiguous tone, very disturbing to Alexander Semyonovich, especially because from the words of the old Kontsovka peasant nicknamed Goat's Goiter, a notorious troublemaker and smart aleck, it got spread around that, supposedly, all the birds had gathered into flocks and cleared out of Sheremetievka at dawn, heading north—which was all simply stupid. Alexander Semyonovich was very upset and wasted the whole day telephoning the town of Grachevka. From there he was promised two speakers would be sent to the sovkhoz in a day or two with two topics—the international situation and the question of the "Goodpoul" Trust.

Neither was the evening without its surprises. Whether or not in the morning the woods had gone silent, demonstrating with utmost clarity how unpleasant and ominous absence of sound is in a forest, and whether or not all of the sparrows had cleared out of the sovkhoz yards by midday, heading somewhere else—by evening the pond in Sheremetievka *had* gone silent. This was truly astounding, since the famous croaking of the Sheremetievka frogs was quite well known to everyone for forty versts around. But now all of the frogs seemed to have died out. Not a single voice came from the pond, and the sedge was soundless. It must be admitted that Alexander Semyonovich completely lost his composure. All of these events began to cause talk, and talk of a very unpleasant kind, i.e., it was behind Alexander Semyonovich's back.

"It's really strange," Alexander Semyonovich said to his wife at lunch. "I can't understand why those birds had to fly away."

"How should I know?" answered Manya. "Maybe from your ray?"

"Manya, you're just a plain fool," said Alexander Semyonovich, throwing down his spoon. "You're like the peasants. What has the ray got to do with it?"

"Well, I don't know. Leave me alone."

That evening the third surprise happened—the dogs at Kontsovka again started howling—and how they howled! The moonlit fields were filled with ceaseless wailing, and anguished, angry moans.

To some extent Alexander Semyonovich felt rewarded by yet another surprise—a pleasant one in the greenhouse. An uninterrupted tapping began to come from the red eggs in the chambers. "Tap... tap... tap... tap". . . came tapping from first one egg, then another, then yet another.

The tapping in the eggs was a triumphant tapping for Alexander

Semyonovich. The strange events in the woods and the pond were instantly forgotten. Everyone gathered in the greenhouse: Manya, Dunya, the watchman, and the guard, who left his rifle at the door.

"Well? What do you have to say about that?" Alexander Semyonovich asked victoriously. They all pressed their ears curiously to the doors of the first chamber. "It's the chicks—tapping, with their beaks," Alexander Semyonovich continued, beaming. "You say I won't hatch any chicks? Not so, my friends." And in an excess of emotion he slapped the guard on the back. "I'll hatch out such chicks you'll ooh and ah. Now I have to look sharp," he added sternly. "As soon as they begin to break through, let me know immediately."

"Right," the watchman, Dunya, and the guard answered in chorus.

"Tap... tap... tap." The tapping started again, now in one, now in another egg in the first chamber. Indeed, the picture of new life being born before your eyes within the thin, translucent casings was so interesting that this whole group sat on for a long while on the empty overturned crates, watching the raspberry-colored eggs ripen in the mysterious flickering light. They broke up to go to bed rather late, after the greenish night had poured light over the sovkhoz and the surrounding countryside. It was an eerie night, one might even say terrifying, perhaps because its utter silence was broken now and then by outbursts of causeless, plaintive, and heart-rending howling from the dogs in Kontsovka. What made those damned dogs go mad was absolutely unknown.

In the morning a new unpleasantness awaited Alexander Semyonovich. The guard was extremely embarrassed, put his hand over his heart, swore and made God his witness that he had not fallen asleep, but that he had noticed nothing. "It's a queer thing," the guard insisted. "I'm not to blame, Comrade Feyt."

"Thank you, my heartfelt thanks," Alexander Semyonovich began the roasting, "What are you thinking about, comrade? Why were you put here? To watch! So you tell me where they've disappeared to! They've hatched, haven't they? That means they've escaped. That means you left the door open and went away to your room. I want those chicks back here—or else!"

"There's nowhere for me to go. Don't I know my job?" The warrior finally took offense. "You're blaming me for nothing, Comrade Feyt!"

"Where've they gone to?"

"Well, how should I know?" the warrior got infuriated at last. "Am I supposed to be guarding them? Why am I posted here? To see that nobody filches the chambers, and I'm doing my job. Here are your chambers. But I'm not obliged by the law to go chasing after your chickens. Who knows what kind of chicks you'll hatch out of there; you probably couldn't catch them on a bicycle, maybe!"

Alexander Semyonovich was somewhat taken aback, grumbled a bit more, then fell into a state of astonishment. It was indeed a strange thing.

In the first chamber, which had been loaded before the others, the two eggs lying closest to the base of the ray turned out to be broken. And one of them had even rolled off to the side. The shell was scattered on the asbestos floor under the ray.

"What the devil?" muttered Alexander Semyonovich. "The windows are shut—they couldn't have flown out through the roof!" He tilted his head back and looked up where there were several wide holes in the glass transom of the roof.

"What's wrong with you, Alexander Semyonovich," Dunya cried extremely surprised. "All we need is flying chicks. They're here somewhere. Cheep... cheep... cheep," she began to call, looking in the corners of the greenhouse where there were dusty flowerpots, boards, and other rubbish. But no chicks responded anywhere.

All of the personnel ran about the sovkhoz yard for two hours, searching for the nimble chicks, but no one found anything anywhere. The day went by in extreme agitation. The guard over the chambers was increased by one watchman, and he had been given the strictest order to look through the windows of the chambers every fifteen minutes and call Alexander Semyonovich the second anything happened. The guard sat by the door, sulking, holding his rifle between his knees. Alexander Semyonovich was snowed under with chores, and he did not have his lunch until almost two in the afternoon. After lunch he took an hour-long nap in the cool shade on the former ottoman of Prince Sheremetiev, drank some sovkhoz kvass, dropped by the greenhouse and made sure that everything was in perfect order there now. The old watchman was sprawled on his belly on a piece of burlap and staring, blinking, into the observation window of the first chamber. The guard was sitting alertly without leaving the door.

But there was also something new: the eggs in the third chamber, loaded last of all, began to make a gulping and clucking sound, as if someone were sobbing inside.

"Oh, they're ripening," said Alexander Semyonovich. "Getting ripe, I see it now.   Did you see?" he addressed the watchman ...

"Yes, it's a marvel," the latter replied in a completely ambiguous tone, shaking his head.

Alexander Semyonovich sat by the chambers for a while, but nothing hatched in his presence; he got up, stretched, and declared that he would not leave the estate that day, he would just go down to the pond for a swim, and if anything started to happen, he was to be called immediately. He ran over to the palace to his bedroom, where two narrow spring beds with crumpled linen stood, and on the floor there was a pile of green apples and heaps of millet, prepared for the coming fledglings. He armed himself with a fluffy towel, and after a moment's thought he picked up his flute, intending to play at leisure over the unruffled waters. He walked out of the palace briskly, cut across the sovkhoz yard, and headed down the small willow avenue toward the pond. He strode along briskly, swinging the towel and carrying the flute under his arm. The sky was pouring down heat through the willows, and his body ached and begged for water. On his right hand began a thicket of burdocks, into which he spat as he passed by; and immediately there was a rustling in the tangle of broad leaves, as though someone had started dragging a log. Feeling an unpleasant fleeting twinge in his heart, Alexander Semyonovich turned his head toward the thicket and looked at it with wonder. The pond had reverberated with no sounds of any kind for two days now. The rustling ceased; the unruffled surface of the pond and the gray roof of the bathhouse flashed invitingly beyond the burdocks. Several dragonflies darted past in front of Alexander Semyonovich. He was just about to turn to the wooden planks leading down to the water when the rustle in the greenery was repeated, and it was accompanied by a short hiss, as if a locomotive were discharging steam and oil. Alexander Semyonovich got on guard and peered into the dense wall of weeds.

"Alexander Semyonovich," his wife's voice called at that moment, and her white blouse flashed, disappeared, and flashed again in the raspberry patch. "Wait, I'll go for a swim too."

His wife hastened toward the pond, but Alexander Semyonovich made no answer, all attention was riveted on the burdocks. A grayish and olive-colored log began to rise from the thicket, growing before his eyes. The log, it seemed to Alexander Semyonovich, was splotched with some sort of moist yellowish spots. It began to stretch, flexing and undulating, and it stretched so high that it was above the scrubby little willow . . . Then the top of the log broke, leaned over somewhat, and over Alexander Semyonovich loomed something like a Moscow electric pole in height. But this something was about three times thicker than a pole and far more beautiful, thanks to the scaly tattoo. Still comprehending nothing, but his blood running cold, Alexander Semyonovich looked at the summit of the terrifying pole, and his heart stopped beating for several seconds. It seemed to him that a frost had suddenly struck the August day, and it turned dim, as though he were looking at the sun through a pair of summer pants.

There turned out to be a head on the upper end of the log. It was flat, pointed, and adorned with a spherical yellow spot on an olive-green background. Lidless, open, icy, narrow eyes sat on the top of the head, and in these eyes gleamed utterly infinite malice. The head made a movement, as though pecking the air, then the pole plunged back into the burdock, and only the eyes remained, staring unblinkingly at Alexander Semyonovich. The latter, bathed in sticky sweat, uttered four completely incredulous words and evoked only by terror bordering on insanity. So beautiful were those eyes among the leaves!

"What sort of joke . . . "

Then he recalled that the fakirs . . . yes . . . yes . . . India . . . a woven basket and a picture . . . They charm . . .

The head arched up again, and the body began to emerge too. Alexander Semyonovich lifted the flute to his lips, squeaked hoarsely, and gasping for breath every second, he began to play the waltz from *Eugene Onegin.*[12] The eyes in the foliage instantly began to smolder with implacable hate for the opera.

"Have you lost your mind, playing in this heat?" Manya's merry voice resounded, and out of the corner of his eye Alexander Semyonovich caught sight of a white spot.

Then a sickening scream pierced through the whole sovkhoz, expanded and flew up into the sky, while the waltz hopped up and down as if it had a broken leg. The head in the thicket shot forward—its eyes left Alexander Semyonovich, abandoning his soul to repentance. A snake approximately fifteen yards long and as thick as a man leaped out of the burdock like a steel spring. A cloud of dust whirled from the road and the waltz was over. The snake swept past the sovkhoz manager straight toward the white blouse down the road. Feyt saw it all quite distinctly: Manya turned yellow-white, and her long hair stood up like wire a half-yard over her head. Before Feyt's eyes the snake opened its maw for a moment, something like a fork flicked out of it, and as she was sinking to the dust its teeth caught Manya by the shoulder and jerked her a yard above the earth. Manya repeated her piercing death scream. The snake coiled itself into a huge screw, its tail churning up a sandstorm, and it began to crush Manya. She did not utter another sound, and Feyt just heard her bones snapping. Manya's head swept up high over the earth, tenderly pressed to the snake's cheek. Blood splashed from Manya's mouth, a broken arm flipped out, and little fountains of blood spurted from under her fingernails. Then, dislocating its jaws, the snake opened its maw, slipped its head over Manya's all at once, and began to pull itself over her like a glove over a finger. Such hot breath spread all around the snake that it touched Feyt's face, and its tail almost swept him off the road in the acrid dust. It was then that Feyt turned gray. First the left, then the right half of his jet-black hair was covered with silver. In mortal nausea he finally tore away from the road, and seeing and hearing nothing, making the countryside resound with wild howls, he took off running...

IX

A Living Mass

Shchukin, the agent of the State Political Administration (GPU) at the Dugino Station, was a very brave man. He said thoughtfully to his assistant, redheaded Polaitis, "Oh, well, let's go. Eh? Get the motorcycle." Then he was silent for a moment, and added, turning to the man who was sitting on the bench, "Put down the flute."

But the trembling, gray-haired man on the bench in the office of the Dugino GPU did not put his flute down—he began to cry and mumble. Then Shchukin and Polaitis realized that the flute would have to be taken from him. His fingers seemed frozen to it. Shchukin, who possessed enormous strength, almost that of a circus performer, began to unbend one finger after the other, and he unbent them all. Then he put the flute on the table.

This was in the early, sunny morning the day following Manya's death.

"You will come with us," said Shchukin, addressing Alexander Semyonovich. "You will show us what happened where." But Feyt moved away from him in horror and covered his face with his hands in defense against a terrible vision.

"You must show us," Polaitis added sternly.

"No, let him alone. Don't you see, that man is not himself."

"Send me to Moscow," Alexander Semyonovich begged, crying.

"You mean you won't return to the sovkhoz at all?"

But instead of answering, Feyt again put out his hands as if to ward them off, and horror poured from his eyes.

"Well, all right," decided Shchukin. "You really aren't up to it . . . I see. The express will be arriving soon, you go ahead and take it."

Then, while the station guard was plying Alexander Semyonovich with water, and the latter's teeth chattered on the blue, cracked cup, Shchukin and Polaitis held a conference. Polaitis felt that, generally, none of this had happened, and that Feyt was simply mentally ill and had had a terrifying hallucination. But Shchukin tended to think that a boa constrictor had escaped from the circus which was currently performing in the town of Grachevka. Hearing their skeptical whispers, Alexander Semyonovich stood up. He came to his senses somewhat, and stretching out his arms like a Biblical prophet, he said, "Listen to me. Listen. Why don't you believe me? It was there. Where do you think my wife is?"

Shchukin became silent and serious and immediately sent some sort of telegram to Grachevka. At Shchukin's order a third agent was to stay with Alexander Semyonovich constantly and was to accompany him to Moscow. Meanwhile, Shchukin and Polaitis started getting ready for the expedition. All they had was one electric revolver, but just that was quite good protection. The 1927 fifty-round model, the pride of French technology, for close-range fighting, had a range of only one hundred paces, but it covered a field two meters in diameter and killed everything alive in this field. It was hard to miss. Shchukin strapped on the shiny electric toy, and Polaitis armed himself with an ordinary, twenty-five-round submachine gun, took some cartridge belts, and on a single motorcycle they rolled off toward the sovkhoz through the morning dew and chill. The motorcycle clattered off the twenty versts between the station and the sovkhoz in fifteen minutes (Feyt had walked all night, crouching now and then in the roadside shrubbery in spasms of mortal terror) and the sun was really beginning to bake when the sugar-white becolumned palace flashed through the greenery on the rise—at the bottom of which meandered the Top River. Dead silence reigned all around. Near the entrance to the sovkhoz the agents passed a peasant in a cart. He was ambling slowly along, loaded with sacks, and soon he was left behind. The motorcycle swept across the bridge, and Polaitis blew the horn to call someone out. But no one responded anywhere, except for the frenzied Kontsovka dogs in the distance. Slowing down, the motorcycle drove up to the gates with their green lions. The dust-covered agents in yellow leggings jumped off, fastened the machine to the iron railing with a chain lock, and entered the yard. They were struck by the silence.

"Hey, anyone here ?" Shchukin called loudly.

No one responded to his bass. The agents walked around the yard, getting more and more astonished. Polaitis frowned. Shchukin began to look more and more serious, knitting his fair eyebrows more and more. They looked through the closed window into the kitchen and saw that no one was there, but that the entire floor was strewn with white fragments of broken china.

"You know, something really has happened here. I see that now. A catastrophe," said Polaitis.

"Hey, anyone in there? Hey!" called Shchukin, but the only response was an echo from under the kitchen eaves. "What the hell," grumbled Shchukin, "it couldn't have gobbled all of them up at once. Unless they ran off. Let's go into the house."

The door to the palace with the columned porch was wide open, and inside it was completely empty. The agents even went up to the mezzanine, knocking on and opening all of the doors, but they found absolutely nothing, and they went back out to the courtyard across the deserted porch.

"Let's walk around back. To the greenhouses," decided Shchukin. "We'll go over the whole place, and we can telephone from there."

The agents walked down the brick path past the flowerbeds to the backyard, crossed it, and saw the gleaming windows of the greenhouse.

"Wait just a minute," Shchukin noted in a whisper, unsnapping the pistol from his belt. Polaitis got on his guard and unslung his submachine gun. A strange and very resonant sound came from the greenhouse and from behind it. It was like the hissing of a locomotive somewhere. "Z-zau-zau ... z-zau-zau ... ss-s-s-s-s," the greenhouse hissed.

"Careful now," whispered Shchukin, and trying not to make noise with their heels, the agents tiptoed right up to the windows and peered into the greenhouse.

Polaitis instantly jumped back, and his face turned pale. Shchukin opened his mouth and froze with the pistol in his hand.

The whole greenhouse was alive like a pile of worms. Coiling and uncoiling in knots, hissing and stretching, slithering and swaying their heads, huge snakes were crawling all over the greenhouse floor. Broken eggshells were strewn across the floor, crunching under their bodies. Overhead burned an electric bulb of huge wattage, illuminating the entire interior of the greenhouse in an eery cinematic light. On the floor lay three dark boxes that looked like huge cameras; two of them, leaning askew, had gone out, but in the third a small, densely scarlet spot of light was still burning. Snakes of all sizes were crawling along the cables, climbing up the window frames, and twisting out through the openings in the roof. From the electric bulb itself hung a jet-black spotted snake several yards long, its head swaying near the bulb like a pendulum. Some sort of rattling clicked through the hissing sound; the greenhouse diffused a weird and rotten smell, like a pond. And the agents could just barely make out the piles of white eggs scattered in the dusty corners, and the terrible, giant, long-legged bird lying motionless near the chambers, and the corpse of a man in gray near the door, beside a rifle.

"Get back," cried Shchukin, and he started to retreat, pushing Polaitis back with his left hand and raising the pistol with his right. He managed to fire about nine times, his gun hissing and flicking greenish lightning around the greenhouse. The sounds within rose terribly in answer to Shchukin's fire; the whole greenhouse became a mass of frenzied movement, and flat heads darted through every aperture. Thunderclaps immediately began to crash over the whole sovkhoz, flashes playing on the walls. "Chakhchakh-chakh-takh," Polaitis fired, backing away. A strange quadruped was heard behind him, and Polaitis suddenly gave a terrified scream and tumbled backwards. A creature with splayed paws, a brownish-green color, a massive pointed snout, and a ridged tail resembling a lizard of terrifying dimensions, had slithered around the corner of the barn, and viciously biting through Polaitis' foot, it threw him to the ground.

"Help!" cried Polaitis, and immediately his left hand was crunched in the maw. Vainly attempting to raise his right hand, he dragged his gun along the ground. Shchukin whirled around and started dashing from side to side. He managed to fire once, but aimed wide of the mark, because he was afraid of killing his comrade. The second time he fired in the direction of the greenhouse, because a huge olive-colored snake head had appeared there among the small ones, and its body sprang straight in his direction. The shot killed the gigantic snake, and again, jumping and circling around Polaitis, already half-dead in the crocodile's maw, Shchukin was trying to aim so as to kill the terrible reptile without hitting the agent. Finally he succeeded. The electric pistol fired twice, throwing a greenish light on everything around, and the crocodile leaped, stretched out, stiffened, and released Polaitis. Blood was flowing from his sleeve, flowing from his mouth, and leaning on his sound right arm, he dragged his broken left leg along. His eyes were going dim. "Run... Shchukin," he murmured, sobbing.

Shchukin fired several times in the direction of the greenhouse, and several of its windows flew out. But a huge spring, olive-colored and sinuous, sprang from the basement window behind him, slithered across the yard, filling it with its enormous body, and in an instant coiled around Shchukin's legs. He was knocked to the ground, and the shiny pistol bounced to one side. Shchukin cried out mightily, then gasped for air, and then the rings covered him completely except for his head. A coil passed over his head once, tearing off his scalp, and his head cracked. No more shots were heard in the sovkhoz. Everything was drowned out by an overlying hissing sound. And in reply to it, the wind brought in the distant howling from Kontsovka, but now it was no longer possible to tell what kind of howling it was—canine or human.

X

Catastrophe

Bulbs were burning brightly in the office of *Izvestia*, and the fat editor at the lead table was making up the second page, using dispatch-telegrams "Around the Union of Republics." One galley caught his eye; he examined it through his pince-nez and burst out laughing. He called the proofreaders from the proof room and the makeup man and he showed them all the galley. On the narrow strip of paper was printed:

Grachevka, Smolensk province.
A hen which is as large as a
horse and kicks like a stallion
has been seen in the district.
Instead of a tail, it has a
bourgeois lady's feathers.

The compositors roared with laughter.

"In my day," said the editor, guffawing expansively, "when I was working for Vanya Sytin on *Russkoe Slovo*,[13] some of the men would get so smashed they'd see elephants. That's the truth. But now, it seems, they're seeing ostriches."

The proofreaders roared.

"That's probably right, it's an ostrich," said the makeup man. "Should we use it, Ivan Vonifatievich?"

"Are you crazy?" answered the editor. "I'm amazed that the secretary let it past—it's simply a drunken telegram."

"It must have been quite a bender," the compositors agreed, and the makeup man removed the communication about the ostrich from the table.

Therefore *Izvestia* came out the next day containing, as usual, a mass of interesting material, but not a hint of the Grachevka ostrich.

Assistant Professor Ivanov, who read *Izvestia* quite punctiliously, folded the paper in his office, yawned, commented, "Nothing interesting," and started putting his white smock on. A bit later the burners went on in his office and the frogs began to croak. But Professor Persikov's office was in confusion. The frightened Pankrat was standing at attention.

"I understand... Yes, sir," he said.

Persikov handed him an envelope sealed with wax and said, "You go directly to the Department of Animal Husbandry to that director Avis, and you tell him right out that he is a swine. Tell him that I, Professor Persikov, said so. And give him the envelope."

A fine thing, thought the pale Pankrat, and he took off with the envelope.

Persikov was raging.

"The devil only knows what's going on," he whimpered, pacing the office and rubbing his gloved hands. "It's unprecedented mockery of me and of zoology. They've been bringing piles of these damned chicken eggs, but I haven't been able to get anything essential for two months. As if it were so far to America! Eternal confusion, eternal outrage!" He began to count on his fingers: "Let's say, ten days at most to locate them... very well, fifteen... even twenty... then two days for air freight across the ocean, a day from London to Berlin... From Berlin to us... six hours. It's some kind of outrageous bungling!"

He attacked the telephone furiously and started to call someone. In his office everything was ready for some mysterious and highly dangerous experiments; on the table lay strips of cut paper prepared for sealing the doors, diving helmets with air hoses, and several cylinders, shiny as quicksilver, labeled: "Goodchem Trust" and "Do Not Touch." And with drawings of a skull and crossbones.

It took at least three hours for the professor to calm down and get to some minor tasks. That is what he did. He worked at the institute until eleven in the evening, and therefore he did not know anything about what was happening outside the cream-colored walls. Neither the absurd rumor that had spread through Moscow about some strange snakes nor the strange dispatch in the evening papers, shouted by newsboys, had reached him, because Assistant Professor Ivanov was at the Art Theater watching *Tsar Fyodor Ioannovich,*[14] and therefore, there was no one to inform the professor of the news.

Around midnight Persikov came home to Prechistenka and went to bed. Before going to sleep he read in bed an English article in the magazine *News of Zoology* which he received from London. He slept and all of Moscow, which seethes until late at night, slept—and only the huge gray building in a courtyard off Tverskaya Boulevard did not sleep. The whole building was shaken by the terrific roaring and humming of *Izvestia's* printing presses. The editor's office was in a state of incredible pandemonium. The editor, quite furious, red eyed, rushed about not knowing what to do and sending everyone to the devil's mother. The makeup man was following him around, breathing wine fumes, and saying, "Oh, well, it's not so bad, Ivan Vonifatievich, let's publish a special supplement tomorrow. We can't pull the whole issue out of the presses, you know!"

The compositors did not go home, but walked around in bunches, gathered in groups and read the telegrams that were now coming in every fifteen minutes all night long, each more peculiar and terrifying than the last. Alfred Bronsky's peaked hat flicked about in the blinding pink light flooding the press room, and the Mechanical fat man screaked and limped, appearing here, there, and everywhere. The entrance doors slammed incessantly, and reporters kept appearing all night long. All twelve telephones in the press room rang constantly, and the switchboard almost automatically answered every mysterious call with "busy, busy," and the signal horns sang and sang in front of the sleepless young ladies at the switchboard.

The compositors clustered around the mechanical fat man, and the sea captain was saying to them, "They'll have to send in airplanes with gas."

"No other way," answered the compositors. "God knows what's going on out there."

Then terrible Oedipal oaths shook the air, and someone's squeaky voice screamed, "That Persikov should be shot!"

"What has Persikov to do with it?" someone answered in the crowd. "That son of a bitch on the sovkhoz—he's the one should be shot!"

"They should have posted a guard!" someone exclaimed.

"But maybe it's not the eggs at all!"

The whole building shook and hummed from the rolling presses, and the impression was created that the unprepossessing gray edifice was blazing with an electric fire.

The new day did not stop it. On the contrary, it only intensified it, even though the electricity went out. Motorcycles rolled into the asphalt yard one after the other, alternating with cars. All Moscow had awakened, and the white sheets of newspaper spread over it like birds. The sheets rustled in everyone's hands, and by eleven in the morning the newsboys had run out of papers, in spite of the fact that *Izvestia* was coming out in editions of one and a half million that month. Professor Persikov left Prechistenka by bus and arrived at the institute. There something new awaited him. In the vestibule stood wooden boxes, three in number, neatly bound with metal straps and plastered with foreign labels in German—and the labels were dominated by a single Russian inscription in chalk: "Careful—Eggs."

The professor was overwhelmed with joy. "At last!" he exclaimed. "Pankrat, break open the crates immediately and carefully, so none are crushed. They go into my office."

Pankrat immediately carried out the order, and within fifteen minutes the professor's voice began to rage in his office, which was strewn with sawdust and scraps of paper.

"What are they up to ? Making fun of me, or what?" the professor howled, shaking his fists and turning the eggs in his hands. "He's some kind of animal, not an Avis. I won't allow him to laugh at me. What is this, Pankrat?"

"Eggs, sir," Pankrat answered dolefully.

"Chicken eggs, you understand, chicken eggs, the devil take them! What to hell do I need them for? Let them send them to that scalawag on his sovkhoz!"

Persikov rushed to the telephone in the corner, but he did not have time to call.

"Vladimir Ipatych! Vladimir Ipatych!" Ivanov's voice thundered from the institute corridor.

Persikov tore himself away from the phone, and Pankrat dashed aside, making way for the assistant professor. Contrary to his gentlemanly custom, the latter ran into the room without removing his gray hat, which was sitting on the back of his head. He had a newspaper in his hands.

"Do you know what's happened, Vladimir Ipatych?" he cried, waving in front of Persikov's face a sheet of paper headed *Special Supplement* and graced in the center with a brightly colored picture.

"No, but listen to what they've done!" Persikov shouted in reply, without listening. "They've decided to surprise me with chicken eggs. This Avis is an utter idiot, just look!"

Ivanov was completely dumbfounded. He stared at the opened crates in horror, then at the newspaper, and his eyes almost jumped out of his head. "So that's it! he muttered, gasping, "Now I see... No, Vladimir Ipatych, just take a look." He unfolded the newspaper in a flash and pointed to the colored picture with trembling fingers. It showed an olive-colored, yellow-spotted snake, coiling like a terrifying fire hose against a strange green background. It had been taken from above, from a light plane which had cautiously dived over the snake. "What would you say that is, Vladimir Ipatych?"

Persikov pushed his spectacles up onto his forehead, then slipped them over his eyes, studied the picture, and said with extreme astonishment, "What the devil! It's... why, it's an anaconda, a water boa!"

Ivanov threw down his hat, sat down heavily on a chair, and said, punctuating every word with a bang of his fist on the table, "Vladimir Ipatych, this anaconda is from the Smolensk province. It's something monstrous! Do you understand, that good-for-nothing has hatched snakes instead of chickens, and, do you understand, they have had progeny at the same phenomenal rate as the frogs!"

"What?" Persikov screamed, and his face turned purple. "You're joking, Peter Stepanovich . . . Where from?"

Ivanov was speechless for a moment, then he recovered his voice, and jabbing his finger at the open crate, where the tips of the white eggs gleamed in the yellow sawdust, he said, "That's where from."

"Wha-a-t!" howled Persikov, beginning to understand.

Ivanov shook both of his clenched fists quite confidently and exclaimed, "You can be sure. They sent your order for snake and ostrich eggs to the sovkhoz and the chicken eggs to you by mistake."

"My God ... my God," Persikov repeated, and turning green in the face, he began to sink onto the revolving stool.

Pankrat stood utterly dumbfounded at the door, turned pale, and was speechless.

Ivanov jumped up, grabbed the paper, and underscoring a line with a sharp nail, he shouted into the professor's ears, "Well, they're going to have fun now. Vladimir Ipatych, you look." And he bellowed out loud, reading the first passage that caught his eye on the crumpled page, "The snakes are moving in hordes toward Mozhaisk ... laying incredible quantities of eggs. Eggs have been seen in the Dukhovsk district ... Crocodiles and ostriches have appeared. Special troop units ... and detachments of the GPU halted the panic in Vyazma after setting fire to the woods outside the town to stop the onslaught of the reptiles ..."

Persikov, turning all colors, bluish-white, with insane eyes, rose from his stool and began to scream, gasping for breath, "Anaconda ... anaconda ... water boa! My God!" Neither Ivanov nor Pankrat had ever seen him in such a state.

The professor tore off his tie in one swoop, ripped the buttons from his shirt, turned a terrible livid purple like a man having a stroke, and staggering, with utterly glazed, glassy eyes, he dashed out somewhere. His shouts resounded under the stone archways of the institute. "Anaconda ... anaconda," thundered the echo.

"Catch the professor!" Ivanov shrieked to Pankrat, who was dancing up and down in place with terror. "Get him some water! He's having a stroke!"

XI

Battle and Death

The frenzied electric night was ablaze in Moscow. Every light was on, and there was not a place in any apartment where there were no lamps on with their shades removed. Not a single person slept in a single apartment anywhere in Moscow, which had a population of four million, except the youngest children. In every apartment people ate and drank whatever was at hand; in every apartment people were crying out; and every minute distorted faces looked out the windows from all floors, gazing up at the sky which was crisscrossed from all directions with search lights. Every now and then white lights flared up in the sky, casting pale, melting cones over Moscow, and they would fade and vanish. The sky hummed steadily with the drone of low-flying planes. It was especially terrible on Tverskaya-Yamskaya Street. Every ten minutes trains arrived at the Alexander Station, made up helter-skelter of freight and passenger cars of every class and even of tank cars, all covered with fear-crazed people who then rushed down Tverskaya-Yamskaya in a dense mass, riding buses, riding on the roofs of trolleys, crushing one another, and falling under the wheels. At the station, rattling, disquieting bursts of gunfire banged out every now and then over the heads of the crowd: the troops were trying to stop the panic of the demented running along the railway tracks from the Smolensk province to Moscow. Now and then the station windows flew out with a crazy light gulping sound, and all the locomotives were howling. All of the streets were strewn with discarded and trampled placards, and the same placards—under fiery red reflectors—stared down from the walls. All of them were already known to everyone, so nobody read them. They proclaimed martial law in Moscow. They threatened penalties for panic and reported that unit after unit of the Red army, armed with gas, was departing for Smolensk province. But the placards could not stop the howling night. In their apartments people were dropping and breaking dishes and flowerpots; they were running around, knocking against corners; they were packing and unpacking bundles and valises in the vain hope of making their way to Kalancha Square, to the Yaroslavl or Nikolaev stations. Alas, all stations leading to the north and east had been cordoned off by the heaviest line of infantry, and huge trucks with rocking and clanging chains, loaded to the top with crates on which sat soldiers in peaked helmets, with bayonets bristling in all directions, were carrying off the gold reserves from the cellars of the People's Commissariat of Finance and huge boxes marked "Handle with Care. Tretyakov Art Gallery." Automobiles were roaring and running all over Moscow.

Far on the horizon the sky trembled with the reflection of fires, and the thick August blackness was shaken by the continuous booming of howitzers.

Toward morning a serpent of cavalry passed through utterly sleepless Moscow, which had not put out a single light. Its thousands of hooves clattered on the pavement as it moved up Tverskaya, sweeping everything out of its path, squeezing everything else into doorways and show windows, breaking out the windows as they did so. The ends of its scarlet cowls dangled on the gray backs, and the tips of its lances pierced the sky. The milling, screaming crowd seemed to recover immediately at the sight of the serried ranks pushing forward, splitting apart the seething ocean of madness. People in the crowds on the sidewalks began to roar encouragingly:

"Long live the cavalry!" cried frenzied female voices.

"Long live!" echoed the men.

"They'll crush me! They are crushing me!..." someone howled somewhere.

"Help!" was shouted from the sidewalks.

Packs of cigarettes, silver coins, and watches began to fly into the ranks from the sidewalks; some women hopped down onto the pavement and risking their bones they trudged along beside the mounted columns, clutching at the stirrups and kissing them. Occasionally the voices of platoon leaders rose over the continuous clatter of hooves: "Shorten up on the reins!"

Somewhere someone began a gay and rollicking song, and the faces under the dashing scarlet caps swayed over the horses in the flickering light of neon signs. Now and then, interrupting the columns of horsemen with their uncovered faces, came strange mounted figures in strange hooded helmets, with hoses flung over their shoulders and cylinders fastened to straps across their backs. Behind them crept huge tank trucks with the longest sleeves and hoses, like fire engines, and heavy, pavement-crushing caterpillar tanks, hermetically sealed and their narrow firing slits gleaming. Also interrupting the mounted columns were cars which rolled along, solidly encased in gray armor, with the same kind of tubes protruding and with white skulls painted on their sides, inscribed: "Gas" and "Goodchem."

"Save us, brother!" the people cried from the sidewalks.

"Beat the snakes!... Save Moscow!"

"The mothers...The mothers...,"curses rippled through the ranks. Cigarette packs leaped through the illuminated night air, and white teeth grinned at the demented people from atop the horses. A hollow, heart-rending song began to spread through the ranks:

> ... no ace, no queen, no jack,
> We'll beat the reptiles; without doubt,
> Four cards are plenty for this pack. . .

Rolling peals of "hurrah" rose up over this whole mass, because the rumor had spread that at the head of all the columns, on a horse, rode the aging, graying commander of the huge cavalry who had become legendary ten years before. The crowd howled and the roars of "hurrah!" "hurrah!" swept up into the sky, somewhat calming frantic hearts.

The institute was sparsely lit. Events reached it only as vague, fragmentary, distant echoes. Once a volley of shots burst fanlike under the fiery clock near the Manège: soldiers were shooting on the spot some looters who had tried to rob an apartment on Volkhonka. There was little automobile traffic on this street—it was all massing toward the railway stations. In the professor's study, where a single lamp burned dimly, casting light on the table, Persikov sat with his head in his hands, silent. Layers of smoke were floating around him. The ray in the box had gone dark. The frogs in the terraria were silent because they were already asleep. The professor was not reading or working. At one side, on a narrow strip of paper under his left elbow, lay the evening edition of news dispatches reporting that all of Smolensk was in flames, and that the artillery was shelling the Mozhaisk forest all over, sector by sector, to destroy the heaps of crocodile eggs piled in all the damp ravines. It was reported that a squadron of planes had been extremely successful near Vyazma, flooding almost the entire district with gas, but that the number of human victims in the area was incalculable, because instead of abandoning the district following the rules for orderly evacuation, the people had panicked and rushed around in divided groups in all directions, at their own risk and terror. It was reported that a separate Caucasus cavalry division near Mozhaisk had won a brilliant victory over flocks of ostriches, hacking them all to pieces and destroying huge caches of ostrich eggs. In doing this the division itself had sustained insignificant losses. It was reported by the government that in case it proved impossible to halt the reptiles within two hundred versts of the capital, the latter would be evacuated in complete order. Workers and employees should maintain complete calm. The government would take the sternest measures to prevent a repetition of the Smolensk events. There, thanks to panic caused by the unexpected attack of rattlesnakes—several thousand of which appeared—the people had started hopeless, wholesale exit, leaving burning stoves—and the city began to catch fire everywhere. It was reported that Moscow had enough provisions to last for at least six months and that the Council of the Commander-in-Chief was undertaking prompt measures to fortify all apartments in order to conduct the battle with the snakes in the very streets of the capital in the event that the Red armies and air forces failed to halt the advance of the reptiles.

The professor read none of this; he stared ahead, glassy-eyed, and smoked. Besides him, there were only two other people at the institute—Pankrat and the housekeeper, Marya Stepanovna, who every now and then would break into tears. The old woman had not slept for three nights, spending them in the professor's office, where he adamantly refused to leave his only remaining, now extinguished chamber. Now Marya Stepanovna was huddled on the oilcloth couch in a shadow in the corner, and she was keeping silent in sorrowful meditation, watching the kettle with some tea for the professor coming to a boil on the tripod over the gas burner. The institute was silent, and everything happened abruptly.

From the sidewalk there was suddenly such an outburst of rancorous shouts that Marya Stepanovna started and cried out. Flashlights flickered in the street, and Pankrat's voice was heard in the vestibule. The professor was hardly aware of this noise. He raised his head for a second and muttered, "Ooh... they're going crazy... What can I do now?" And he again fell into his stupor. But it was rudely broken. The iron doors of the institute on Herzen Street began a terrible clangor, and all of the walls began to shake. Then the solid mirrored wall in the adjoining office crashed. The glass in the professor's office began to tinkle and fly to pieces, and a gray brick bounced through the window smashing the glass table. The frogs scuttled around in their terraria and set up a cry. Marya Stepanovna ran around shrieking, rushed to the professor, seized him by the hands, and shouted, "Run, Vladimir Ipatych, run!"

The professor rose from his revolving stool, straightened himself up, and curled his index finger into a little hook, his eyes recovering for an instant the old sharp glitter reminiscent of the old, inspired Persikov. "I'm not going anywhere," he pronounced. "This is simply stupidity. They are rushing around like lunatics... And if all Moscow has gone insane, then where can I go? And please stop screaming. What do I have to do with this? Pankrat!" he called, pressing a button.

He probably wanted Pankrat to stop all the commotion, something which generally he had never liked. But Pankrat could no longer do anything. The banging had ended with the institute doors flying open and a distant popping of shots; and then the whole stone institute shook with the thunder of running feet, shouts, and crashing windows. Marya Stepanovna clutched at Persikov's sleeve and began to drag him back; but he pushed her away, drew himself up to his full height, and just as he was, in his white lab coat, he walked out into the corridor. "Well?" he asked. The doors swung open, and the first thing to appear in them was the back of a military uniform with a red chevron and a star on the left sleeve. He was retreating from the door, through which a furious mob was surging forward, and he was firing his revolver. Then he started to run past Persikov, shouting to him, "Save yourself, professor! I can't do anything else!"

His words were answered by a shriek from Marya Stepanovna. The officer shot past Persikov, who was standing there like a white statue, and vanished in the darkness of the winding corridors at the opposite end.

People flew through the door, howling.

"Beat him! Kill him!"

"Public enemy!"

"You let the snakes loose!"

Distorted faces and ripped clothing jumped through the corridors, and someone fired a shot. Sticks flashed. Persikov stepped back a little, barring the door to his office, where Marya Stepanovna was kneeling on the floor in terror; and he spread out his arms, as one crucified... he did not want to let the mob in, and he yelled irascibly, "This is utter lunacy... You are absolute wild animals. What do you want?" And he bellowed, "Get out of here!" and completed his speech with a shrill, familiar cry,

"Pankrat, throw them out!"

But Pankrat could no longer throw anyone out. Pankrat, trampled and torn, his skull crushed, lay motionless in the vestibule, while more and more crowds tore past him, paying no attention to the fire of the police in the street.

A short man with crooked, apelike legs, wearing a torn jacket and a torn shirt twisted to one side, dashed out ahead of the others, leaped toward Persikov, and with a terrible blow from his stick he split open Persikov's skull. Persikov tottered and began to collapse sideways. His last words were, "Pankrat... Pankrat..."

Marya Stepanovna, who was guilty of nothing, was killed and torn to pieces in the office; the chamber in which the ray had gone out was smashed to bits, the terraria were smashed to bits, and the crazed frogs were flailed with sticks and trampled underfoot. The glass tables were dashed to pieces, the reflectors were dashed to pieces, and an hour later the institute was a mass of flames. Corpses were strewn around, cordoned off by a line of troops armed with electric pistols; and fire engines, pumping water from the hydrants, were pouring streams through all the windows, from which long, roaring tongues of flame were bursting.

XII

A Frosty Deus ex Machina

On the night of August 19 to 20 an unprecedented frost fell on the country, unlike anything any of its oldest inhabitants had ever seen. It came and lasted two days and two nights, bringing the thermometer down to eleven degrees below zero. Frenzied Moscow locked all doors, all windows. Only toward the end of the third day did the populace realize that the frost had saved the capital, and the boundless expanses which it governed, and on which the terrible catastrophe of 1928 had fallen. The cavalry at Mozhaisk had lost three-quarters of its complement and was near prostration, and the gas squadrons had not been able to stop the onslaught of the vile reptiles, which were moving toward Moscow in a semicircle from the West, Southwest, and South.

The frost killed them. Two days and two nights at eleven below zero had proved too much for the abominable herds, and when the frost lifted after the 20th of August, leaving nothing but dampness and wetness, leaving the air dank, leaving all the greenery blasted by the unexpected cold, there was no longer anything left to fight. The calamity was over. Woods, fields, and infinite bogs were still piled high with multicolored eggs, often covered with the strange, unearthly, unique pattern that Feyt— who had vanished without a trace—had once mistaken for mud, but now these eggs were quite harmless. They were dead, the embryos within lifeless.

For a long time the infinite expanses of land were still putrescent with numberless corpses of crocodiles and snakes which had been called to life by the mysterious ray born under the eyes of genius on Herzen Street—but they were no longer dangerous; the fragile creatures of the putrescent, hot, tropical bogs had perished in two days, leaving a terrible stench, disintegration, and decay throughout the territory of three provinces.

There were long epidemics; there were widespread diseases for a long time, caused by the corpses of snakes and men; and for a long time the army combed the land, no longer equipped with gases, but with sapper gear, kerosene tanks and hoses, clearing the earth. It cleared the earth, and everything was over toward the spring of 1929.

And in the spring of 1929 Moscow again began to dance, glitter, and flash lights; and again, as before, the mechanical carriages rolled through the traffic, and the lunar sickle hung as if on a fine thread over the helmet of the Cathedral of Christ; and on the site of the two-storey institute that had burned down in August 1928, a new zoological palace rose, and Assistant Professor Ivanov directed it, but Persikov was no longer there. Never again did the persuasively hooked index finger rise before anyone's eyes, and never again was the squeaking, croaking voice heard by anyone. The ray and the catastrophe of 1928 were long talked and written about by the whole world, but then the name of Professor Vladimir Ipatievich Persikov was shrouded in mist and sank into darkness, as did the red ray he had discovered on that April night. The ray itself was never again captured, although the elegant gentleman and now full professor, Peter Stepanovich Ivanov, had occasionally made attempts. The raging mob had smashed the first chamber on the night of Persikov's murder. Three chambers were burned up in the Nikolsky sovkhoz, the "Red Ray," during the first battle of an air squadron with the reptiles, and no one succeeded in reconstructing them. No matter how simple the combination of lenses and mirrored clusters of light had been, the combination was never achieved again, in spite of Ivanov's efforts. Evidently this required something special, besides knowledge, something which was possessed by only one man in the world—the late Professor Vladimir Ipatievich Persikov.

Translated by Carl R. Proffer   *Moscow, October 1924*

Notes

1. "The Fatal Eggs" was first published in *Nedra,* No. 6 (Moscow, 1925), pp. 79-148. A slightly censored version (with descriptions which might be seen as anti-religious cut) was published in Riga and later by the Chekhov Publishing House in M. Bulgakov, *Sbornik rasskazov* (New York, 1952). The full text can be found in in M. Bulgakov *Sobranie sochinenii,* vol. 3 (Ann Arbor: Ardis, 1983).

2. Persikov derives from *persik,* "peach."

3. H. G. Wells' *The Food of the Gods* was written in 1904.

4. *Gosudarstvennoe politicheskoe upravlenie*—"State Political Administration," one of the many names over the years for the secret police.

5. After the Revolution one's "former" position became all-important. It could determine job, living quarters, and food ration. Streets, professions, and even people became "former."

6. Moscow's most notorious political prison.

7. Vsevolod Meyerhold, who was still quite alive when this story was written, was already famous for his unorthodox, "futuristic" productions of Russian classics. He and Bulgakov, who was a more traditional playwright, were enemies for years, partly because of the friction between Bulgakov and Mayakovsky, Meyerhold's close collaborator.

8. In Russian his name is Rokk, and *rok* means "fate."

9. A state collective farm.

10. One had to get police permission for changes of residence.

11. Tchaikovsky's romantic opera based on Pushkin's short story of the same title.

12. Tchaikovsky's romantic opera based on Pushkin's novel in verse of the same title.

13. A prerevolutionary newspaper, *The Russian Word.*

14. Stanislavsky's Moscow Art Theater doing A. K. Tolstoi's verse drama *Tsar Fyodor Ioannovich* (1868).

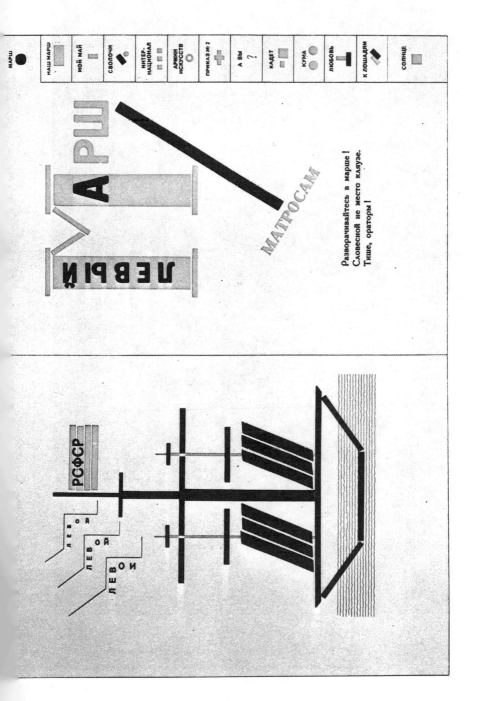

A two page spread designed by El Lissitzky for Mayakovsky's book, *Dlia golosa*.

Mikhail Zoshchenko.

MIKHAIL ZOSHCHENKO

Mikhail Zoshchenko (1895-1958) was born in Poltava to the family of a Ukrainian painter. Raised in Petersburg, he fought in World War I, and then joined the Red Army. His first book came out in 1921, bringing him immediate fame. Zoshchenko's ironical humor, use of the language of the man on the street, and eye for detail made him the most popular comic writer in Russia. He was a member of the Serapion Brothers, and was artistically very serious about his comedy. His language and narrative style (featuring skaz) were brilliantly employed, and he gradually allowed his philistine characters tell their own stories, which permitted him to make many satiric points without answering for them. Zoshchenko always focuses on the specifics of Soviet existence, and lets the seemingly minor detail imply the larger picture.

In the 1930s even this most popular of writers had to bend to prevailing political winds, and he wrote a number of talentless works, such as the stories for children about Lenin. However, as was typical of him, he still managed to publish a number of stunningly "subjective" works, such as *Youth Restored* (1933), and *Before Sunrise* (1943), the latter an examination of his life-long case of melancholia. After Zhdanov attacked him and Akhmatova in 1946 as a warning to other writers, Zoshchenko appears to have ceased writing.

THE BATHHOUSE

I've heard, comrades, that bathhouses in America are mighty excellent.

There, for example, a citizen can simply come, shed his clothes into a special box, then wash to his heart's content. He doesn't have a worry in the world, like having his things stolen or lost. He doesn't even bother with claim checks.

Okay, maybe some jittery American will say to the attendant:

"Goodbyeski, Mac. Keep an eye on my stuff, will you?"

And that's all.

So this American goes to wash. And when he returns, he gets his underwear back whiter than snow—all washed and ironed. I bet they put brand new cardboard in his shoes to cover up the holes. Even his shorts'll be mended and patched up. That's the life!

Our bathhouses are all right too, but they aren't quite in the same league. Still, they do give you a chance to wash up.

One problem we have is claim checks. Last Saturday I went to the bathhouse—"Can't very well go to America," I said to myself. They gave me two tags, one for the coat and hat, the other for all the rest.

And what's a naked man supposed to do with those tags? Tie them to his beard? All I could see was my belly and my legs, and they don't come with pockets. They were a pain in the neck, those tags.

Okay, so I tied a tag to each leg—that way I wouldn't lose them both at once—and in I went to bathe.

Now the tags kept slapping at my legs. That took all the fun out of walking. Yet I had to walk because I needed a tub. What kind of washing would it be without a tub? A pain in the neck.

So, I set out to look for a tub. Soon I found some citizen washing in three tubs. One he was using to stand in, the other one to lather his noggin, and the third one he clenched with his left hand so nobody would swipe it.

I tried to pull that third tub away, thinking, kind of, of taking it for myself, but the citizen wouldn't let go.

"What's the idea," he said, "stealing other people's tubs? I'll give you a tub," he said, "right between the eyes. That'll learn you."

"This isn't tsarist Russia," I said, "to go around smacking people with tubs. Talk about selfishness," I said. "Other people too would like to wash. Show business," I said, "this isn't."

But he just turned away, bent over, and went on washing.

"It's no use standing here," I thought, "breathing down his neck. Now, just to be ornery," I thought, "he'll take three days to finish washing."

So I went on.

An hour later I saw some geezer slip up: he took his hands off his tub. Maybe he was reaching for his soap, maybe he took to daydreaming, who knows? All I know is, I took that tub for myself.

Okay, now I got myself a tub of my own, but there was no place to sit down. And what kind of washing would it be standing up? A pain in the neck.

Well, anyway. So I stayed standing up on my feet, holding the tub in one hand, and began washing.

In the meantime, people all around me had gone into the laundry business. Holy cow! Here was one man washing his pants; there another scrubbing his shorts; a third one was also messing around with something or other. And they all splattered, damn their hides. No sooner would I get some part of me clean—splash! and it was dirty again. And the noise they made with all that rub-a-dub-dubbing! It took all the fun out of washing. Couldn't hear myself think what to soap up next. A pain in the neck, that's what it was.

"They can all go jump in a swamp," I thought. "I'll finish my washing at home."

So I went to the locker room. In exchange for one of the tags, they gave me my clothes. Right away I saw that almost everything was mine—only the pants weren't.

"Citizens," I said, "my pants had a hole right about here. These have one way over there."

The attendant said:

"I ain't paid," he said, "to keep track of holes. Show business," he said, "this ain't."

Okay. I put on these pants and went to get my coat. They wouldn't give it to me—not without a tag. And the tag's on my leg where I left it. Now I had to undress. I took off my pants, looked up and down my leg, found the string, but the paper tag with the number on it was gone. Down the drain.

I offered the attendant my string, but he didn't want it.

"I don't issue nothing for string," he said. "Any citizen," he said, "could show up with a bunch of string. Where'd I get that many coats? Wait around till the other customers go home," he said. "Then I'll give you what's left."

I said:

"Oh, come on, buddy, what if some old rag's left? This isn't show business," I said. "I'll describe the article to you," I said. "There's a hole in one pocket," I said, "the other one's long gone. As regards buttons," I said, "the top one is still there," I said, "all the rest are missing in action."

He gave me the coat after all. Without taking the string even.

I got dressed and walked out in the street. Then I remembered—I'd left my soap behind.

Back I went once again. They wouldn't let me in with my coat on.

"Take it off," they said.

I said:

"Fellow citizens, I can't spend my life getting dressed and undressed," I said. "This isn't show business. Why don't you give me at least what the soap cost?"

The wouldn't.

I didn't care any more. I went home without the soap.

Of course, a curious reader may want to know—which bathhouse was this? Where is it? What's the address?

Which bathouse you ask? Any old bathhouse. Take your pick.

Translated by Serge Shishkoff   *1924*

WHAT THE NIGHTINGALE SANG

I

They'll have quite a laugh at us some 300 years from now, won't they? What a strange life those miserable people lived, they'll say. They had something called money, they'll say, passports. Something called vital statistics and square meters of living space...

Well, it's okay by me, let 'em laugh.

One thing bothers me, though: half of it they won't understand, the bastards. And how could they understand? They'll be living the kind of life we don't dream about, probably, in our wildest dreams.

The author doesn't know and doesn't intend to venture guesses about the kind of life they'll have. Why should the author frazzle his nerves and upset his health for no good reason, since he will never set foot in that wonderful life?

And anyway, it's not at all certain that it will be wonderful. The author expects, for his own peace of mind, that there will be a lot of junk and nonsense there too.

Still—it's possible the nonsense will be of the small variety. Let's say, if you'll pardon my paucity of speculation, someone's bald spot gets spat on from a dirigible. Or the folks at the crematorium get the orders mixed up, so that instead of the dearly departed's ashes, they'll hand out someone else's inferior remains.

This, of course, can't be helped—there'll always be these small-scale annoyances on the petty level of everyday existence. The rest of that life to come, though, will most likely be splendid and outstanding.

It's even possible there will be no such thing as money. Maybe everything will be free, gratis. Maybe they'll try to give away fur coats or foulards at department stores...

"Here, take this excellent fur coat, citizen," they'll say.

And you just walk on by. Your pulse won't even quicken.

"Forget it, dear comrades," you'll say. "What the hell do I want your fur coat for? I've got six already."

Hot damn! How cheerful and attractive the author visualizes this future life to be!

But here we must stop and reflect. If you do rid life of its penny-ante money matters and mercenary motivations, what wondrous shapes life itself will assume! What excellent qualities human relationships will immediately acquire! And, for example, love. How splendidly, I bet, will this flower of human emotions bloom!

My goodness, what a life it will be, what a life! With what sweet joy the author contemplates it even from afar, even without the slightest guarantee that he'll be around to see any of it. But there it is—love...

About love in particular we must say a few things. After all, many scientists and Party people in general have a tendency to downgrade this feeling. Come on, they say, what do you mean—love? There's no such thing as love. And there never was. And, anyway, it's just a trivial matter of vital statistics, something like a funeral.

Now this is something the author cannot accept.

The author has no desire to make confessions to chance readers, nor does he wish to expose his intimate life to some critics he finds particularly unpleasant. Still, as he looks back and tries to sort things out, he remembers a girl from his teenage days. She had a sort of cute, milky-white dumb face, tiny hands, pitiful shoulders. Into what starry-eyed raptures did the author go over her! What emotional moments did the author experience when, brimming with noble sentiments, he fell to his knees and, like a fool, kissed the ground she had walked on.

Fifteen years have gone by and, at a time when the author's hair is turning gray due to various illnesses, the vicissitudes of life, and worries about the daily bread, when the author simply does not wish to tell lies, nor is there any reason for him to lie, and, finally, when the author wants to see life as it is, without any falsehood or embellishments, he still maintains, without fear of appearing a laughable leftover from the last century, that scientific and Party circles are making a big mistake in this matter.

The author has a sure thing in forecasting the merciless dressing-down that these lines about love will elicit from public figures.

"Your own sorry personality, comrade," they'll say, "is no example. Stop shoving our noses," they'll say, "into your amorous fooling around. Your personality," they'll say, "isn't consonant with the epoch and, now that you mention it, it's a sheer accident that it has survived to this day."

"D'you hear that? Sheer accident! Well, now, if I may beg to inquire, what do you mean 'sheer accident'? Are you suggesting I should throw myself under the wheels of a streetcar?"

"That's entirely up to you," they'll say. "Under the wheels or off a bridge, only it's a fact that your existence has no rational basis. Take a look," they'll say, "at simple, untouched people, and you'll see that they don't think the way you do at all."

Ha!—Forgive me, reader, this insignificant laugh. Recently the author read in *Pravda* about some minor tradesman, an apprentice barber, who bit off a female citizen's nose out of jealousy.

That's not love! Are you going to say this is something insignificant, like a fly turd? Are you going to say the nose was bitten off in pursuit of a taste sensation? Well, then go to hell! The author doesn't want to get upset and give himself ulcers. He still has to finish the story, make a trip to Moscow, and what's more, visit certain literary critics—something the author isn't looking forward to at all—begging them not to overexert themselves writing critical essays and reviews of this story.

And so, love.

Let everyone think whatever he wants to about this refined feeling. As to this author, while fully recognizing his own nonentity and inability to live and even, if you insist, damn it, let there be a streetcar lying in wait for him, this author still stands firm in his opinion.

All the author wants to do is tell the readers about a minor love episode which unfolded against the backdrop of our time. What, again, they'll say, minor episodes? Again, trifles from a dime novel? What's the matter with you, young man, they'll say, have you gone crazy? Who needs it, they'll say, on a cosmic scale?

The author openly and honestly asks:

"Don't interfere, comrades! Let a man express himself—for the sake of discussion, if nothing else."

II

Phew! How tough it is to write literature!

You sweat buckets while trying to hack your way through an impenetrable jungle.

And for what? For the sake of some love story concerning citizen Preseedkin. This man in no skin off the author's nose. The author didn't borrow money from him, and does not even share the same ideology.

To tell the truth, the author has a profoundly indifferent attitude toward him. And the author does not feel like depicting him in brilliant colors. What's more, the author doesn't even remember the face of this Preseedkin, Vassily Vassilevich, all that well.

As to the other characters involved one way or another in this tale, well, these other characters also attracted little notice as they passed through the author's field of vision. Except, I suppose, Lisochka Kupbordov, whom the author remembers for very special and, so to speak, subjective reasons.

But Mishka Kupbordov, her kid brother, member of the Komsomol, him I remember less well. He was a fresh young lout and a bully. As to his looks, he was rather blondish and somewhat fat-faced.

The author does not feel like dwelling on those looks of his either. The kid is a teenager. I'll describe him and, by the time the book comes out, the son of a bitch will have grown a few inches—then go figure out which is the real Mishka Kupbordov. And where did that moustache come from if, at the time these events unfolded, he had none?

As to the old lady herself—Ma Kupbordov, so to speak, the reader is not likely to complain if we refrain from describing her altogether. Particularly since it's so hard to describe old ladies artistically. You've seen one old lady, you've seen them all. Who the devil can figure out what kind of old lady she is? And, anyway, who on earth needs a description of her, say, nose? A nose is a nose is a nose. And my detailed description of it will not make the reader's sojourn on this planet any easier.

Of course, the author would not have undertaken to write an artistic story if he possessed only scant and irrelevant information about the heroes. No, the author has sufficient information. For instance, the author can visualize their whole way of life quite vividly. The crummy little Kupbordov house—kind of dark, one story. On the wall facing the street it says "22". Above this number is a board on which an ax is painted. This is a fire-fighting provision. Should a fire break out in the neighborhood, the pictures tell who is supposed to bring what. The Kupbordovs are supposed to bring the ax. Only, do they have an ax? Bet you they don't ... Anyway, it's not the business of artistic literature to look into this and perhaps draw the attention of the county administration to it.

But the author can picture the entire inside of their house and its material inventory, furniture-wise, in pretty vivid detail... Three not too large rooms. Uneven floors. A Becker piano. A rather frightful one at that. But still playable. Furniture on the mangy side. A sofa. A cat of undetermined gender on the sofa. A cheap clock under a glass bell on the mantelpiece. Dust on the bell. A dishonest murky mirror above it—it lies to your face. An enormous trunk smelling of moth balls and dead flies.

Metropolitan citizens, I bet, would find no fun at all in living in these rooms!

I bet it would be no fun at all for a metropolitan citizen to walk into that kitchen of theirs, where wet laundry hangs on a cord. And the old lady fixes dinner at the stove. She might, for instance, be peeling potatoes, the peel curling up under her knife like a ribbon.

But the author doesn't want the reader to think that he is describing all these trifling trifles with affection and admiration. No way! There's nothing sweet or romantic in these trifling memories. The author knows such houses and kitchens only too well. He's seen them. And lived in them. For all you know, he still does. And there's nothing good to be said about them—it's misery, nothing but misery. Every time you walk into a kitchen like that, some wet piece of laundry slaps you in the kisser—it never misses. And you should be grateful if it is a respectable piece of apparel, for it could be, heaven forbid, a wet stocking or something. Having your face wiped with a wet stocking is rather repulsive, wouldn't you say? Yech! How nauseating!

Anyway, for reasons of no concern to artistic literature, this author had been in the Kupbordov house on several occasions. And the author was always amazed that in such dust, must, and banality there lived such an outstanding young lady—such a, if I may say so, lily of the valley and nasturtium as Lisochka Kupbordov.

The author is not all that impressed with humans. It is time, citizens, to renounce our senseless self-glorification. The author believes that if a slug can learn to live amid wet slime, why shouldn't a human being get used to living among damp laundry?

Still, the author always felt profoundly sorry for Lisochka Kupbordov.

About her, however, we will speak at length and in some detail at the proper time. Right now the author is compelled to say a few things about citizen Vassily Vassilevich Preseedkin. Whether he is politically sound. What his relation to the Kupbordovs is. And whether he's a relative of theirs or what.

No, he isn't; he just stumbled into their lives by accident.

The author has already warned the reader that this Preseedkin's face didn't stick in his memory all that well. Although, at the same time, when he closes his eyes, the author can see citizen Preseedkin as if in the flesh.

This Preseedkin always walked slowly, even thoughtfully. He kept his hands behind him. He blinked his eyelashes at an unbelievable rate. Furthermore, his posture was somewhat stooped, as if this Preseedkin were weighted down by the vicissitudes of life. As regards the heels of his shoes, Preseedkin tended to wear them all the way down, towards the inside of his feet.

As far as his education is concerned, he had the appearance of someone who had no less than eight years of pre-revolutionary schooling.

His social background—unknown.

The man arrived from Moscow while the revolution was in full swing and he preferred to keep mum about himself.

And what he came for is not clear either. Was it because the chances for eating were better in the provinces? Or did he get restless sitting in one place and felt the lure of faraway exciting places and adventures? Who in hell can figure out how his mind worked. You can't crawl into every psychology.

But his feeling that chances of eating would be better in the provinces is the more likely reason. Therefore, Preseedkin at first kept walking around farmers' markets casting hungry glances at fresh loaves of bread and mountains of every kind of produce.

But, by the way, how he managed to eat at all remains for the author an unclear mystery. He might even have panhandled. Or, perhaps, he might even have collected stoppers from soda-pop and mineral water bottles. And afterwards sold them. There were, you know, desperate profiteers of this sort in town.

It was, however, obvious that the man had had a wretched life. Everything about him looked worn out, and he had begun to lose his hair. And he walked around apprehensively, looking over his shoulder all the time and dragging his feet. Eventually he even stopped blinking his eyes and gazed at the world with a fixed and joyless stare.

But later, due to some unelucidated cause, he started going uphill. And by the time the present love story unfolded, Preseedkin had a solid social standing, state employment, and a seventh rank salary plus bonuses.

And by now, Preseedkin had rounded out his figure to some extent, having replenished, so to speak, his depleted system with the sap of life and again, often and annoyingly, he began to blink his eyes as he had of old.

And he walked through the streets with the somewhat heavy tread of a man percolating with life to the core and having a right to live, the tread of a man who knows his full worth.

And indeed, at the time of the about-to-be narrated events, he cut an impressive figure of a man just under 32 years of age.

He took long and frequent strolls in the streets and, swinging his cane, he lopped off flowers, seeds, and even leaves along the way.

Sometimes he sat down on a bench on the avenue and smiled happily as he energetically filled his chest with air.

What he thought about and what exceptional ideas illuminated his brain at such moments—no one knows. Maybe he didn't think about anything. Maybe he was busy imbuing himself with the delight occasioned by his lawful existence. Or, most likely, he was thinking that he absolutely had to find another apartment.

And indeed: he lived at Hirsutov's. Hirsutov was a deacon of the Living Church, and Preseedkin, in view of his official position, was greatly worried about living in the home of a person politically contaminated to such an extent.

He had asked many times if anyone knew, for God's sake, of any apartment or room, be it ever so lousy, as he just couldn't stand to live any longer in the home of the practitioner of a certain cult

And finally someone, out of the kindness of his heart, cooked up a deal for him concerning a small room—about 10 square yards. This happened to be precisely in the house of the excellent Kupbordovs.

Preseedkin moved in without delay. One day he looked the room over, the next morning, bright and early, he started moving, having hired Nikita the water carrier for logistic purposes.

The reverend deacon had no use whatsoever for this Preseedkin; nevertheless, apparently wounded in some unspecified but no doubt noble sentiments of his, he cursed something awful and even threatened to punch Preseedkin in the nose if he ever got the chance. And while Preseedkin was piling his stuff on the cart, the deacon stood at the window laughing a loud and phony laugh, wishing to express his total unconcern with the departure.

The deacon's better half, on the other hand, ran out from time to time and, tossing some article into the cart, yelled:

"Nobody's keeping you. Get lost. Good riddance to bad rubbish."

The assembled onlookers and neighbors enjoyed a good laugh as they hinted broadly at the love relations which were thought to exist between these two. The author isn't going to stick his neck out on this. He doesn't know. Nor does he wish to spread any unnecessary gossip in fine literature.

III

The old lady Darya Vassilevna Kupbordov had no pecuniary motivation or even any particular need to rent the room to Preseedkin, Vassily Vassilevich. It was rather that she feared that the authorities, striving for a more efficient use of square footage in view of the critical housing shortage, might decide to squeeze the Kupbordov family by putting some uncouth and undesirable element in to live with them.

Preseedkin even took some little advantage of the situation. And, as he walked by the Becker piano, he looked at it askance and with displeasure commented that this instrument, generally speaking, was not at all needed and that he, Preseedkin, was himself a quiet man shaken by the vicissitudes of life, who had been at two fronts and been shelled by heavy artillery and hence could not stand unnecessary petit-bourgeois noise-makers.

The old lady, offended, said that this dear little piano had been with them for forty years and that just to cater to Preseedkinian whims, they couldn't break it to pieces or pull the strings and pedals out of it, particularly since Lisochka Kupbordov was studying to play the instrument and that the pursuit of such studies might be, for all he knows, Lisochka's main goal in life.

Preseedkin brushed the old lady off brusquely and announced that his comment had been made in the form of a tactful request and not at all in the manner of a strict order.

In reply to which the old lady, now extremely offended, burst into tears and was about to refuse him the room altogether, but then she reflected on the possibility of their square footage being invaded from another quarter.

Preseedkin moved in the next morning and spent the day late into that night groaning in his room as he set up and arranged everything to suit his metropolitan tastes.

Two or three days went by quietly and without any changes in his routine.

Preseedkin went to work, returned late, and for a long time shuffled around his room in his felt slippers. In the evening he would munch on something and, eventuallly, go to sleep, snoring slightly and making chirping noises through his nose.

Lisochka Kupbordov walked around these two days in a somewhat subdued state and many times questioned her mother, as well as Mishka Kupbordov, about what kind of person Preseedkin was in their opinion— did he smoke a pipe, for example, and did he ever in his life have anything to do with the Commissariat of the Navy.

Finally, on the third day, she saw Preseedkin for herself.

This happened early in the morning. Preseedkin, as usual, was getting ready to go to work.

He was walking in the hallway wearing a nightshirt with the collar unbuttoned. Suspenders dangled behind from his pants, flapping from side to side. He was walking slowly, holding a towel and some aromatic soap in one hand, while with the other he was smoothing down his hair, which had gotten mussed during the night.

She was standing in the kitchen tending to her household chores, starting up the samovar or chipping kindling off a dry log.

She gave a gentle cry when she saw him, and darted to one side, embarrassed at being seen in her untidy morning garb.

But Preseedkin, standing in the doorway, examined the young lady with some surprise and even ecstasy.

And he was right: that morning she looked very good indeed.

That youthful freshness of her slightly sleepy face. That careless cascade of blond hair. Her gently turned-up nose. And her bright eyes. And her not too tall, but pleasingly plump figure. All of this made her unusually attractive.

This was the captivating casualness—I might even say sloppiness—of a Russian woman who hops up from her bed in the morning and, without taking the time to wash, wearing felt slippers on her bare feet, starts doing her work around the house.

The author, as a matter of fact, rather likes such women. He has no complaints about such women.

If you come right down to it, there is really nothing good about these overweight women with their lazy bedroom eyes. There is no liveliness in them, no vividness of temperament, and, finally, no coquetry in their manner. Take a look at one—she doesn't move much, wears soft slippers, her hair is uncombed... As a matter of fact, I guess they are pretty repulsive, all things considered. And yet...

It is a strange thing, reader!

Some doll-like cutie pie, one of those inventions of bourgeois Western culture, so to speak, doesn't at all fill the author's bill. She has this kind of hairdo, who in hell knows what kind, Greek or something—look, but don't touch. And if you do, there'll be no end of kicking and yelling. Her dress is something unreal—again, don't you dare touch it. You might rip it or soil it. Tell me, who needs this? What is the big attraction and how can one find existential joy in this?

When our kind of girl sits down, for instance, everyone can plainly see that it is a girl sitting there and not a butterfly stuck on a pin. That's what those others are like—butterflies on a pin. Who needs it?

The author admires many things in foreign cultures; with respect to women, however, the author will cling to his national opinion.

It would seem that this is the kind of woman Preseedkin liked too.

In any event, he now stood in front of Lisochka Kupbordov and, with his mouth slightly agape from ecstasy, and without gathering in his dangling suspenders, he looked at her in joyful surprise.

But this lasted only a moment. Lisochka Kupbordov softly said, "oh!", scurried about the kitchen in a panic, then left, arranging her clothes and tousled hair along the way.

Towards evening, when Preseedkin came back from work, he walked to his room slowly, expecting to meet Lisochka in the hallway. But he didn't.

Even farther towards evening, therefore, Preseedkin made five or six trips to the kitchen and finally met Lisochka Kupbordov, whom he then greeted with an exceedingly respectful and courtly bow, tilting his head to one side and making with his hands a certain indefinite gesture which by convention shows rapture and unmitigated agreeableness.

Several days of such meetings in the hallway and in the kitchen drew them considerably closer.

Preseedkin nowadays returned home and, listening to Lisochka playing some plinkety-plunk on the piano, begged her to interpret more and more mushy tunes.

And she would play something like chopsticks or a Charleston, or strike a few bouncy chords from the Second, Third, or—who the hell can tell them apart?—even the Fourth of Liszt's rhapsodies.

And he, Preseedkin, who had twice been to all the fronts and been shelled by heavy artillery, listened to the clinking sounds of the Becker piano as if for the first time. And, sitting in his room, he dreamily leaned back in his armchair, thinking about the charms of human existence.

Mishka Kupbordov began living a life of great opulence. Twice Preseedkin gave him ten kopecks and another time fifteen with the request that Mishka whistle softly between his fingers when the old lady was in her kitchen and Lisochka alone in the room.

Why Preseedkin felt he needed to do this is extremely unclear to the author. The old lady looked on the love birds with perfect delight, calculating that she'd have them wed no later than fall and get Lisochka off her hands.

Mishka Kupbordov didn't go into the intricacies of Preseedkin's psychology either and whistled for all he was worth as many as six times a day, inviting Preseedkin to drift now into this room, now into that.

And Preseedkin duly went to that room, sat next to Lisochka, exchanged at first insignificant phrases with her, then asked her to play one of her very favorite pieces on the instrument. And there, by the piano, when Lisochka stopped playing, Preseedkin placed the gnarled fingers of a man in a philosophical mood—one who was seething with life and had been shelled by heavy artillery—on Lisochka's white hands and asked the young lady to tell him about her life, being eagerly interested in the details of her former existence. Sometimes, however, he would ask her whether she had ever felt the flutterings of true love before, or was this the first time.

And the young lady would smile enigmatically and, as she ran her fingers over the keyboard, she would say:

"I don't know..."

IV

They fell passionately and dreamily in love.

Tears and trepidations marked their every meeting.

And each time they saw each other, they experienced afresh a new onrush of exalted joy.

Preseedkin, though, was even somewhat frightened as he peered into his soul and realized with amazement that he, who had twice been on all the fronts and who had earned the right to existence with such incredible difficulty, would now readily give up that life for one insignificant whim of this relatively cute young lady.

And, as he reviewed in his mind the women who had come into his life, including even the last one, the deaconess with whom he had, after all, had a romance (the author is completely convinced of it), Preseedkin thought with complete confidence that it was only now, in his thirty-second year that he had discovered true love and the genuine fluttering of that feeling.

Whether it was that Preseedkin was filled to the point of bursting with the sap of life or whether a human being has a predisposition and penchant for abstract romantic emotions remains for the time being a mystery of nature.

Be that as it may, Preseedkin could see that he was now a different man than he had been before, and that the composition of his blood had changed, and that all of life was laughable and insignificant before such extraordinary intensity of love.

And Preseedkin, this slightly cynical man, seething with life, who had been stunned by shells and who had more than once looked death in the face—well, this frightful Preseedkin even took a modest fling at poetry and wrote a dozen poems of various kinds and one ballad.

The author is not too familiar with his verse efforts but one poem, entitled "For Her, for That One...," which Preseedkin sent off to the *Dictatorship of Labor* and which was rejected by the editorial board as not being consonant with the socialist epoch, accidentally and thanks to the kindness of the technical secretary, Ivan Abramovich Krantz, was made known to the author.

The author has his own definite opinions about rhyme-mongering and amateur poetry and so the author will not burden the readers and typesetters with the entire and rather lengthy poem. The author submits to the attention of the typesetters only a couple of the last, most resounding stanzas:

His flaming heart was eager to embrace
Great love, for love and progress he equated.

The lovely image of your dainty face
Adoringly he always contemplated.

Oh, Lisa, in the book of fates it's written
The fellow who is hopelessly thus smitten
                        None other is but I.

From the point of view of the Formal Method, these verses may appear to be not all that bad. But, all things considered, these are pretty crummy verses and, indeed, are neither consonant nor co-rhythmical with the epoch.

Subsequently, Preseedkin lost interest in poetry and did not follow the thorny path of the poet. Preseedkin, always somewhat prone to Americanism, soon abandoned his literary achievements and buried his talents in his backyard without any regrets, and returned to his former life without projecting any more mad thoughts onto paper.

Preseedkin and Lisochka, who now met every evening, would leave the house and wander through the empty streets and boulevards well into the night. Sometimes they would go down to the river and there sit at the edge of a sandy cliff and watch with deep and silent joy the rapid waters of the Grasshopper River. At other times, however, holding each other by the hand, they softly uttered exclamations of delight and engaged in ecstasies spawned by the unbelievable colors of nature or a whispy airy cloud racing across the sky.

All this was new to them, charming and—most important—it seemed to them that they were seeing everything for the first time.

Sometimes the couple went to the country and walked in the woods. And there, holding one another by a finger, they walked around all mushy-eyed and, stopping in front of some pine tree or fir, they looked at it in wonderment, sincerely amazed at the daring and fanciful tricks of nature, which had produced from under the ground a tree so useful to man.

And then Vassily Preseedkin, shaken to the core by the unusualness of his existence on this earth, with its amazing laws, and overtaken by an excess of emotion, fell to his knees in front of the young lady and kissed the ground around her feet.

All the while everywhere around them, there was the moon, the mysteriousness of the night, grass, fireflies chirping, the silent forest, frogs and bugs. All around there was some sort of sweetness and appeasement in the air. All around was this kind of simple existence, which the author does not quite wish to renounce and therefore he cannot, in any shape or form, accept the notion that he is a superfluous figure on the stage of the new life at its sunrise. The author, just like every insignificant Boris, Ivan, or Sergei, thought himself well within his right to live out his life, however miserably, in spite of all the jeering of his severe and impatient critics.

And so, Preseedkin and Lisochka liked these out-of-town strolls best of all.

But during one such charming stroll, on a damp night one assumes, the careless Preseedkin got badly chilled and was soon quite ill. A disease akin to mumps forced him to stay in bed.

In the evening after the walk, Preseedkin felt a slight shiver and a piercing pain in this throat. Later that night his face began to balloon.

Crying softly, Lisa would come to his room and, her hair down, wearing soft slippers, she rushed from the bed to the table, not knowing how to proceed or what to do, wondering how to alleviate the lot of the patient.

Even Ma Kupbordov herself trundled into the room several times a day asking whether the patient would like some stewed rhubarb, which is supposedly unsurpassed for cases of infectious disease.

Two days later, when Preseedkin's kisser was bloated beyond all recognition, Lisochka fetched a doctor.

After examining the patient and prescribing some medicines, the doctor left, apparently cursing in his heart because he had been paid in small change.

Lisochka Kupbordov ran after the doctor, caught up with him in the street and, wringing her hands, began babbling and asking—Tell me the truth, doctor, is there any hope? And she let the physician know that she couldn't survive the loss of this man.

Thereupon the physician, accustomed by reason of his profession to such scenes, said with indifference that mumps is nothing but mumps and it seldom happens, unfortunately, that people die of it.

Somewhat peeved by the insignificance of the danger, Lisochka sadly returned home and began self-sacrificingly to look after the patient, not sparing her health or her feeble efforts, not even fearing to catch this disease that makes one look like a hog.

The first few days Preseedkin was afraid to lift his head from the pillow and, feeling his swollen neck with his gnarled fingers, kept asking whether Lisochka Kupbordov would stop loving him after his illness, which had made it possible for her to see him in such a disfigured and repulsive state.

But the young lady, begging him not to worry, kept saying that, in her view, he had become an even more imposing representative of his sex than he had been before.

And Preseedkin laughed softly and said gratefully that this illness had more than anything else, tested the endurance of their love.

V

It was an absolutely extraordinary love.

Furthermore, ever since he got up from his bed of pain, and his head and neck had once again assumed their former shapes, he began to believe that Lisochka Kupbordov had saved him from certain death.

Because of this, to their love relationship was now added a certain solemnity and even generosity.

One day, very soon after his illness, Preseedkin took Lisochka by the hand and in the voice of a man who has come to a decision about something, asked her to hear him out without asking any unnecessary questions for the time being, and without butting in with any of her silly lines.

Preseedkin made a long and solemn speech about the fact that he knew to perfection what life was and he knew how difficult it was to exist on earth and that before, when he was still a wet-eared youth, his attitude toward life had been criminally frivolous, something that caused him a lot of suffering at one time, but now that he had gone over the high-water mark of thirty and had been wisened up by life's experiences, he knew how to live and knew the unforgiving and unshakeable laws of life. And that, having thought all this over, he expected to introduce certain changes into the draft of his future life.

In a word, Preseedkin made Lisochka Kupbordov a formal proposal of marriage, insisting that she need not worry about her future wellbeing, even if Lisochka Kupbordov persisted in being unemployed and would not be in any position to contribute her fair share to the modest Preseedkin family kettle.

After hemming and hawing a little and talking about free love for the sake of gilding the lily or in order to give this heartfelt moment a tinge of elegance, Lisochka nevertheless accepted the proposal, adding that she'd been waiting for it for a long time and that had he not made it, he would have been the worst scoundrel and bum. As to free relations, they too are fine and excellent at the proper time but it's not at all the same thing and one was definitely not the other.

With this happy news, Lisochka Kupbordov ran at once to her Ma and also to the neighbors, asking them to come to the nuptials which would take place within a very short period of time and would be endowed with a modest and family character.

The neighbors warmly congratulated her, saying that it was high time, and that she had certainly endured the hopelessness of her existence long enough.

Ma Kupbordov, of course, shed a few tears and went to look for Preseedkin to confirm for herself the reliability of these facts.

And Preseedkin reassured the old lady by solemnly asking for permission to henceforth call her "Ma." The old lady, crying and blowing her nose into her apron, said that she'd been living in this world for fifty-three years but that this day was the happiest day of her life. And, in turn, she asked to call him Vassya. Preseedkin generously gave his consent to this.

As far as Mishka Kupbordov is concerned, Mishka took the change in the life of his sister rather indifferently and presently was running through the streets somewhere at a breakneck speed, like a bat out of hell.

Now the love birds didn't go out of town any more. Most of the time they stayed at home and, prattling late into the night, discussed plans for their future life.

During one such conversation, Preseedkin, pencil in hand, began to draw on paper the layout of their future rooms, which would constitute something like a separate small, but cozy, little apartment.

Arguing themselves out of breath, they tried to prove to each other what the best place for the bed was, and where the table should be, and where they should put the dresser.

Preseedkin was trying to convince Lisochka not to be so stupid as to put the dresser in a corner.

"Putting the dresser in a corner is extremely lower middle class," he said. "Every Miss Nobody puts it there. It's infinitely better and more monumental to put the chest of drawers in the corner and cover it with a lace scarf which Ma, I trust, won't begrudge to give us."

"Having a chest of drawers in the corner is extremely low middle class too," said Lisochka, almost in tears. "Besides, the chest of drawers is Ma's, and whether she'll let us have it or not is still a question to be asked and answered."

"Baloney," said Preseedkin, "what do you mean, 'she won't let us have it?' We can't keep our linen on window sills, can we? It's obvious nonsense."

"You, Vassya, talk to Ma about it," Lisochka said sternly. "Simply talk to her as if she were your own mother. Say—'Give us the chest of drawers, Mommy dear.' "

"Nonsense," said Preseedkin. "On the other hand, I can go right now and see the old lady if that's what you want."

And Preseedkin went to the old lady's room.

It was now pretty late. The old lady was asleep.

Preseedkin shook her for a long time, but she just kicked in her sleep and refused to wake up and understand what was expected of her.

"Come on, Ma, wake up," Preseedkin said sternly. "Can't Lisochka and I, after all, expect some little comfort? We can't have our linen gathering dust on window sills, now can we?"

Barely understanding what was going on, the old lady launched into a spiel to the effect that the chest had been standing in its rightful place for fifty-one years and that now, in the fifty-second year, she had no intention of dragging it around this way and that and tossing it at the first person who came along. Also, she didn't make chests of drawers herself. And it was a bit late for her, in her old age, to start learning the carpenter's craft. It was about time people understood this and quit making an old lady miserable.

Preseedkin set about to shame Ma, saying that, as a person who'd been at all the fronts and had been shelled twice by heavy artillery, he should be able, shouldn't he, to expect, at last, a peaceful life.

"Shame on you, Ma!" Preseedkin said. "You're being stingy about that chest of drawers. And you can't take it to the grave, you know. I want you to realize that."

"I won't give up my chest of drawers!" the old lady said in her high-pitched voice. When I die, you can take every stick of furniture for all I care."

"Yeah, sure. When you die!" said Preseedkin indignantly. "I should live so long!"

Seeing that things were taking a serious turn, the old lady wasted no time going into a fit of wailing and whimpering, but still managed to say that, all things considered, the last word should come out of the babe's mouth belonging to her innocent child Mishka Kupbordov, particularly since he was the only male representative of the Kupbordov clan and the chest of drawers belonged by rights to him, not to Lisochka.

Mishka Kupbordov, after being awakened, was extremely unwilling to give up the chest of drawers.

"Yeah," said Mishka. "He shells out a lousy ten kopecks and now he wants the chest of drawers. Chests of drawers are worth money, you know."

Preseedkin then slammed the door and went back to his room where he bitterly upbraided Lisochka, saying that being without a chest of drawers is like being without a right arm and that he, a man tempered in battles, knew what life was like and would not retreat from his ideals one single step.

Lisochka literally bounced from Preseedkin to her mother and then back again, imploring them to come to some kind of agreement and suggesting that every once in a while the chest of drawers be shuttled from one room to the other.

Then, asking Lisochka to quit bouncing back and forth, Preseedkin suggested that she go to bed and gather her strength the better to tackle this life-or-death problem the next morning.

The morning brought nothing good.

Many a bitter and insulting truth was uttered on all sides.

The angered old lady said with desperate resoluteness that she had him, Vassily Vassilevich Preseedkin, figured out up one side and down the other and that while today he was demanding the chest of drawers, tomorrow he'd make mincemeat pie out of her and eat it along with his vegetables. That's the kind of man he was!

Preseedkin shouted that he'd swear out a complaint to the police and have her arrested for maliciously disseminating false and slanderous rumors.

Lisochka, shrieking softly, scurried from one to the other, beseeching them to quit yelling already and try to examine the problem calmly.

The old lady then said that she had outgrown the age when people yell and that she could, without yelling, tell all and sundry that Preseedkin had, during this time, had dinner with them three times and hadn't even bothered, as a good-will gesture, to offer any compensation whatsoever for even one of those dinners.

Terribly excited, Preseedkin acidly said that in exchange he had, while walking with Lisochka, many times bought her caramels and gumdrops and twice a bouquet of flowers and nonetheless, he was submitting no bills to Ma Kupbordov. To which Lisochka, biting her lips, said that he should not lie so shamelessly, that there had been no gumdrops, just a couple of fruit lozenges and a small bunch of violets not worth half a kopeck, which, to boot, withered the very next day.

After saying this, Lisochka left the room crying, leaving everything in the hands of fate.

Preseedkin wanted to run after her and apologize for supplying inaccurate information but, again locking horns with the old lady, he called her "Ma Hellhound" and, after giving her a raspberry, ran out of the house.

For two days Preseedkin was gone no one knew where. And when he reappeared, he announced in a formal tone of voice that he no longer deemed it possible to reside in the Kupbordov house.

Two days later, Preseedkin moved to an apartment in the Skinsky house. All four days Lisochka made it a point to stay in her room.

The author doesn't know the details of Preseedkin's moving, nor does he know what bitter moments Lisochka experienced. Nor, indeed, that she experienced any at all. Nor whether Preseedkin was sorry about the whole thing or whether he had acted with full awareness and determination.

The author has only gathered that Preseedkin, after moving, kept on visiting Lisochka Kupbordov for a long time, having, it is true, married Marussya Skinsky in the meantime. And the two of them, still reeling from their misfortune, sat side by side exchanging insignificant words. At times, however, as they sifted through their memories and came up with a particularly happy episode or occurrence from the past, they talked about it with sad and pitiful smiles, holding back tears.

Occasionally Lisochka's mother came into the room and then all three of them deplored their fate together.

Eventually Preseedkin stopped visiting the Kupbordovs. And, when he met Lisochka in the street, he greeted her correctly and with reserve and then continued on his way...

VI

That's how this love ended.

At another time, of course, maybe some three hundred years into the future, this love story would not have ended this way. It would have bloomed, my dear reader, splendidly and extraordinarily. But each lifetime imposes its own rules.

To conclude this narrative, the author wants to say that as he was unfolding this uncomplicated story of love, he was caught up in the emotional upheavals of his heroes and completely lost sight of the nightingale which was mentioned so mysteriously in the title.

The author fears that the honest reader or typesetter, or maybe even a hopeless critic, might be upset after reading this story.

"Wait a minute," he'll say, "what about the nightingale? What's the idea, trying to hornswoggle your readers," he'll say, "and entice them with a frivolous title?"

It would, of course, be absurd to start the story of this love all over again. This is not at all what the author is trying to do. The author only wants to recall certain details.

This occurred when the flame of their feeling was burning at its brightest, when it had reached its highest point—at the time Preseedkin and the young lady went out of town and strolled through the woods until after dark. And there, as they listened to the chirping of bugs or the singing of a nightingale, they would stand motionlessly transported for a long time. And then Lisochka, wringing her hands, asked many a time:

"Vassya, what do you think this nightingale is singing about?"

To which Vassya Preseedkin replied without undue sentimentality:

"His belly's empty, so he sings."

And only later, when he had familiarized himself a little with the young lady's psychology, Preseedkin answered in greater detail and more vaguely. He suggested that the bird was singing about some future many-splendored life.

That's precisely what the author thinks. The nightingale was singing about a wonderful future life maybe some three hundred years from now, or, perhaps, even less.

Yes, reader, let those three hundred years pass by quickly, like a dream, and then we'll really start to live!

If, however, things are bad then too, the author, his heart cold and empty, will agree to consider himself a superfluous figure on the backdrop of the rising life.

Then he won't mind throwing himself under the wheels of a streetcar.

Translated by Serge Shishkoff   *1926*

YURY OLESHA

Yury Karlovich Olesha (1899-1960) is a major Soviet writer, best known for his novels *Envy* and *The Three Fat Men,* many short stories and the play "A List of Blessings." Both of his novels became popular and were successfully adapted for the stage. The son of Polish Catholics, Olesha grew up in Odessa and broke with his family to support the Revolution. In the 1920s he worked for the journal *The Whistle (Gudok)* together with Bulgakov, Ilf and Petrov, Babel and Kataev. Olesha began a long period of creative silence in the early thirties, a response to the controls that had been placed on literature; he lived off of translations and film scenarios during the Stalinist period. In 1965 *No Day without a Line*, a collection of autobiographical fragments, was published posthumously.

Envy, a characteristic work of the 1920s, sets a bourgeois, romantic, solipsistic artist against the new Soviet man—a technocrat, athlete, pragmatic man of action. The future belongs to the new man—he gets the girl, but the reader's sympathies are with the artist, even though Olesha clearly shows his weaknesses and limitations. The themes of old vs. new, artist-dreamer vs. scientist-pragmatist, the alienation of the romantic, imaginative artist in the modern technological era are present in Olesha's short stories as well. Central to his art is the device of *ostranenie* (making things strange), a practice clearly evident in "The Chain." The world is made strange—and more real—through the perspective of an artist, or child, or man in love. In this way art distorts our familiar perceptions and brings new vision to life.

THE CHAIN

The student Orlov was courting my sister Vera.

He would ride up to the summer cottage on a bicycle. The bicycle stood by the flowerbed, leaning on its side against the veranda. The handlebars looked like cows' horns.

From his ankles the student took off some glittering clips, something like spurs except they didn't clink, and threw them on the wooden table. Then the student took off his cap with the light-blue band and wiped his forehead with his handkerchief. His face was brown, his forehead white, his head was closely shaven, iridescent, with bumps on it. The student didn't see me. I saw everything. He didn't say a word to me.

The wooden table had wrinkles on it, on the table stood a pot of flowers, the student blew on the flowers, and the flowers turned away. The student looked off into the distance and saw the light-blue band of the sea.

"Bleriot's flown the English Channel," I said. I was still at that age when a person has to swallow his saliva before uttering a sentence.

"So he has," said the student.

And again there is silence.

I do not have the right to participate in the goings-on of the world. I am even ashamed to sound so smart: Bleriot...English channel...

From the flower pot the student pulls out a stem on which are two carnation blossoms and a bud. He bites off the bud. The bud is tightly closed, shiny, cylindrical, like a bullet. The student pulls in his cheeks and fires the bud. It hits the bicycle, one of the spokes. The wheel makes a sound like a harp.

"Do airplanes have bicycle wheels?" I ask.

They are like bicycle wheels—I know that perfectly well. But the student seems stupid to me. I'm sure that I'm much more well-versed than he in the field of aviation. But it is awkward for me to recognize this, and I consider it necessary to give the student a chance to appear more knowledgeable.

"Yes," says the student.

There is a triangle here: the bicycle, the student, and I.

I blush: I keep wanting to talk about the bicycle; I feel this is shameful, the blush flows to my face. He's a blockhead, this student—I know that. I can see through him.

"Your Seva is a goose," Papa said to Vera.

Seva really is a goose. But what can I do? He owns a bicycle. And I act affected, play the hypocrite. I feel feverish in his presence.

I want to say:

Vsevolod Vasilyevich, let me ride it. Not far, just along the path. Then I'll turn around at the gate. It's a level surface there. I'll ride carefully. Or I don't even have to go as far as the gate. Along the path will be enough."

That's what I want to say. Even my eyebrows move up from shame. Leaning my elbows on the table, I lower my eyebrows with the help of my fingers.

Yesterday I was allowed to ride it. I shouldn't ask so often. I'll ask tomorrow. Or even the day after tomorrow.

I look at the bicycle. At any minute the student might notice where I'm looking. Then I'll lift my gaze just a little, imperceptibly, in a straight line, and I'll look at a vine. There's a cat hanging on it. In complete silence it hangs among the leaves—a small, white cat, a Persian, fluffy—oh, almost feathery!—the representative of a distinguished species, who has become a tramp.

The student noticed the cat.

"Hey, you scrawny thing!" he said. "It's eating the grapes."

Cats never eat grapes. And these are wild grapes. But the student gets up—and I don't protest. On the contrary, I jump up. The student tears the cat from the vine-covered wall and flings it over the top.

The student goes down into the garden. In a minute Vera will come back from swimming. And she'll appear on the other side of the wire fence. She'll quicken her step, once she's seen her goose; she'll run. Now they've met, she folds up her pink parasol.

The student says:

"Go ahead!"

From a leather bag fastened beneath the seat, I got a monkey-wrench. I turned a screw and lowered the seat. How cool the grips on the handlebars are! I wheel the bicycle along the steps to the garden. It bobs up and down and jingles. It nods its light. I turn it around. On the front of the frame, the green trademark flashes. Motion—and the trademark vanishes like a lizard.

I'm riding.

The gravel crunches; under my gaze the tire runs along above it; the gate tries to get below my shoulder like a crutch; some kind of screw, furry with rust, is lying on the road—so begins my journey!

The movement occurs as if along the bisector between the swiftly narrowing sides of a corner.

A gnat got in my eye. Oh, why did that happen? It's such a huge expanse I'm rushing through, and my movement is so fast—and this had to happen. It just had to come about that two completely uncoordinated lines of motion—mine and the insect's—should collide in such a small place as my eye!

My field of vision becomes bitter. I squeeze my eye shut so hard that my eyebrow touches my cheek. I can't let go of the handlebars—I try to raise my eyelid, it trembles... I brake, get off, the bicycle lies there, the pedal is still turning; I open my eye with my fingers—my eyeball is turned downward, and I see the scarlet bed of my eyelid.

Why does the insect which has fallen in my eye perish so quickly? Do I really secrete poisonous juices?

And I ride off again.

A bird flies out from under the very wheel—at the very last second. It's not afraid. It's a tiny bird. But the pigeon doesn't even fly away. The pigeon just walks off to the side, without even glancing at the cyclist.

The movement of the bicycle is accompanied by a sound like something being fired. Sometimes it's as if a fire cracker is exploding. But this isn't important. These are details which you can pile up as many of as you like. You could say about cows that their skeletons make them burst open from inside and they remind one of tents. Or that cows wear white suede masks. What is important is that I lost the gear chain. Without it you can't ride the bicycle. The chain flew off at full speed, and I noticed it too late.

It's lying on the road. I have to turn around and pick it up. That's not so bad. That's not so bad at all. I walk back, leading the bicycle by its handle-grip. The pedal nudges me below the knee. Three little boys, three boys I don't know are running along the edge of the gully. They're running off, gilded by the sun. A blissful weakness rises in me below my stomach. I understand: the boys have found the chain. They're boys I don't know, street kids. And they're already running into the depths of the landscape.

That's how the misfortune came about.

And I imagine—

—I return to the cottage as if nothing had happened. I walk up with the bicycle which is out of commission and lean it against the side of the veranda. They are drinking tea: Papa, Mama, Vera, and the student Orlov. There's a plum pie with the tea. It's a flat purple circle. We sit opposite each other: the student Orlov and I. The situation is this: the student had a bicycle, and I damaged that bicycle. You could intensify it: the student had a wife, and I poked out her eye. Evening comes. I imagine the following: evening comes, they bring out a lamp, on Mama's chest, on her glass beads. a path of moonlight forms. The student gets up, says:

"I'd better be going."

He walks to the bicycle.

Then there is a deathly silence.

No, not a silence... Actually, Vera is saying something, Mama is talking too, but in my consciousness the silence already exists. The student bends over the bicycle, and I have the feeling that now his head is turning in my direction—and a silence already stretches between the student and me.

"Where's the chain?" the student asks.

"What chain?" I ask.

"What do you mean 'what chain?' "

"What chain?"

"Did you lose it?"

"There wasn't any chain," I say. "I rode without a chain. Was there a chain?"

"He's gone crazy," says Papa. "Look, he's sitting there with his tongue sticking out."

Silence. I sit there with my tongue sticking out.

That's how I imagine it. You can't extricate yourself from misfortune by means of the lawful route. One way remains: to break the law. I decide to act as in a dream. And from the depths of my memory comes a terrible dream that recurs from time to time: I kill Mama. I get up. Vera covers her face with her hands. Mama seems to turn gray all over, she becomes fatter, her neck disappears.

That's how I imagine it.

I cannot return home.

Soon they'll notice I'm gone.

I set off for the Gurfinkels' cottage. Grisha Gurfinkel, who is in the same class with me, he'll help me. I'll cry: the famous surgeon, Professor Gurfinkel, will feel sorry for me. The anemic little boy will cry and writhe about in the presence of the great doctor. Anyway, how much can a chain cost? They'll give it to me... We'll buy a chain.

And off I went. A strange woman with an eye poked out was shuffling behind me. We glanced back: hadn't the pursuit begun?

But the Gurfinkels weren't there, they had gone out. They had gone to Chabeau for grapes. I leave. Near the shop where they sell soft drinks, a crowd had gathered. And I hear the word "Utochkin."

An automobile stands there. A terrifying automobile. I have already seen it once before. It was flying along Langeronovsky Street, making a din like shooting, giving off smoke... It didn't roll along, but tore past as if with little jumps.

This automobile, which has no hood over the motor, is dirty, shining with grease that drips from it, there's a hissing in it.

Utochkin is drinking a soft drink in the shop. The crowd is talking about the great racedriver. "Utochkin," they say. "Redhead," they say and remember that he stutters.

The crowd makes way. The great race driver comes out. Without a cap. And there are some other people with him. Also redheads. He walks in front. On the race track he had beat Peterson, Bader.

(He is considered an eccentric. Their attitude toward him is one of amusement. I don't know why. He was one of the first to start riding a bicycle, a motorcycle, driving an automobile, one of the first to start flying. They laughed. He crashed on a Moscow-Petersburg flight and hurt himself badly. They laughed. He was a champion, but in Odessa they thought he was the village idiot.)

I look at Utochkin.

He is wearing something reminiscent of a sack, dirty, shiny, slit open at the top. He is finishing a cream puff. There are leather gloves on his hands. There is pastry scattered on his gloves like lilac. Persian lilac on his lips, his cheeks. They start up the motor, which begins to backfire like a cannon, the whole place trembles, a whirlwind rises. The bicycle and I fall down. I grab at the spokes. The terrible automobile reminds me of some letter—either a G or a B, lying on its back.

Utochkin picks me up.

Amidst the chaos there occurs a quiet, sentimental scene: I grasp the hand in the cuffed glove, tell about everything that happened to me—about the student, about the bicycle, about the disaster...

Then they put my bicycle crosswise in the automobile. The terrible car has gotten a transparent ornament. Five people, with me among them, sit in the belly of the letter B. Oh, industrial story! I don't remember anything! I don't know anything! I only remember: our trip was accompanied by all the dogs along the road, who stood up on their hind legs.

I, of course, will not die, I will go on living—even after today, tomorrow, and for a long, long time. Nothing has changed, I will be a little boy like before, the student Orlov will be there, and the tragedy of the chain will not end easily and painlessly... But now... Now I am impudent, arrogant, and cruel. Where am I rushing to? I'm rushing to punish Mama, Papa, Vera, the student... If they died now before my eyes, I would laughingly exclaim: "Look, Utochkin! Ha-ha-ha! They're dying... we're in a car, a black one... Who said: 'love, obedience, compassion'? We don't know, we don't know, we have cylinders, gasoline, tires... We are men. And this is a great man: Utochkin! The man is going to punish Papa."

We stop at the gate. We go in. Utochkin walks in front. I run behind with the bicycle. The motor keeps firing. In distant cottages people run to their gates and listen to the far-off cannonade.

Utochkin and the student meet face to face.

The people around them don't understand anything.

I had ridden off with tender good-byes. How meek and obedient I was! I asked permission. They gave it to me. That was an hour ago! And suddenly I have appeared with thunder and lightning and an apparition. Audacious! Indomitable!

"You shouldn't insult the kid," Utochkin said to the student, stuttering and wrinkling up his face. "Why did you insult the kid? Be a nice guy, give him back the chain."

And it ends up that the automobile jumps away from the cottage and the student Orlov shouts after the storm flying off.

"Pig! Fraud! Crazy man!"

This is a story about the distant past.

My dream was to have a bicycle. Well, now I'm a grown-up. And now, grown-up, I say to myself, the schoolboy:

"Go ahead, now you can demand. Now I can avenge myself. Tell me your most cherished desires."

And nobody answers me.

Then I say again:

"Look at me, how far away I've gotten from you—and already, look at me: swollen, much too fat... You were the same age as the century. Remember? Bleriot flew the English Channel? Now I've fallen behind, look how I've fallen behind, I mince along—a fat man on short little legs... See how hard it is for me to run, but I run even though I gasp for breath, even though my feet get stuck—I run after the thundering storm of the century!"

Translated by Aimee Anderson   *1928*

BORIS PILNYAK

Boris Pilnyak (pseudonym of Boris Vogau, 1894-1937?) was one of the most influential and popular Soviet prose writers in the early 1920s. His novel *The Naked Year* brought him quick fame and many imitators. By 1929, however, the year *Mahogany* was published in Berlin (it was never published in the Soviet Union), Pilnyak's work had already become the target of a savage smear campaign. He was expelled from the Writers' Union and in 1937 became one of the first prominent writers to be arrested and to die during the purges. The exact date of his death is not known.

Pilnyak grew up in "Old Russia"—in provincial towns near Moscow. Rural Russia came to play a major role in his fiction in both setting and theme. When Pilnyak first began to publish in 1915, primitivism was a popular current in the arts, and his early works reflect an interest in the intuitive and irrational side of man, in man's sexual drives and in the elemental forces in nature. Pilnyak's outlook was romantic and was also influenced by the ideas of the Eurasians; certain dialectical polarities in his thinking were already present by the time of the 1917 Revolution—instinct/reason, nature/civilization, country/city, Asia/Europe, Slavic Russia/European civilization. When the Revolution came, Pilnyak saw it and accepted it as a peasant revolt, a surge of elemental forces, a sexual release, a cleansing upheaval. From this point on the fate of Russia and Revolution in Russia became his major theme.

Pilnyak was also a literary experimenter. He learned from the ornamental prose writers, especially Bely and Remizov, and through Pilnyak their devices became acceptable and popular in Soviet prose. *Mahogany* is typical of Pilnyak's works in its collage-like structure, long and disjointed sentences, catalogues, sound play, and mixture of stylistic levels. It has a more coherent plot than some of his earlier works since after 1924 Pilnyak tried to write in a somewhat more traditional realistic vein.

Mahogany ("Red tree" in Russian) pictures the Revolution during the period of the New Economic Policy in the provincial town of Uglich (never named in the story). The town, its bells, and its surroundings are as important as the characters. It is clear why *Mahogany* upset the critics: the true Revolution, the struggle for brotherhood and love for one's fellow man, has been stopped and lives on only in the drunken dreams of a group of outcasts—fools whom Pilnyak compares to the holy fools of Russia's past. The Trotskyite Akim, another true believer in the Revolution, has missed the train of history, yet he is presented favorably compared with the other characters. Pilnyak also criticizes Soviet bureaucracy and especially the disastrous agricultural policy; yet the story is not anti-Communist, but anti-regime. Entropy has set in. The Bezdetov brothers are portrayed as emotionless NEP men, speculators who are indifferent to the destruction of the past and to human suffering. "Bezdetov" means "without children"; the brothers are contrasted with Rimma, the sister who has acted out of love and given birth. The brothers are also contrasted with the creative craftsmen of the past who lived for their work and took pride in it. Pilnyak does not romanticize the pre-Revolutionary past: it is criticized and satirized as well as the present, but on the whole *Mahogany* is a lament for the lost crafts and creative spirit of the past and especially for the lost ideals of love and brotherhood that the once-creative Revolution had promised.

Boris Pilnyak

MAHOGANY

Chapter One

Beggars, seers, tramps, mendicants, wailing alms seekers, pilgrims, male and female, cripples, false saints, blind singers, prophets, idiots, fools, holy fools—these synonymous names are like *krendeli*—the twisted sweet rolls of everyday life in Holy Russia; the beggars in Holy Russia, the wandering singers, the cripples in Christ, the holy fools of Holy Russia—these *krendeli* have embellished daily life since the days of Russia's rise, from the first Tsar Ivans, the daily life of a thousand years of Russia. All Russian historians, ethnographers and writers have dipped their quills to write about the blessed. These madmen or rogues—mendicants, false saints, prophets—were considered to be the Church's embellishments, Christ's brothers, supplicants for the world, as they were called in classical Russian history and literature.

A famous Muscovite holy fool, Ivan Yakovlevich, a failed seminary student who lived in Moscow in the middle of the nineteenth century, died in the Preobrazhensky Hospital. Reporters, poets and historians wrote about his funeral. One poet wrote in *The News:*

> What celebration is the Yellow House[1] preparing?
> Why are waves of people flowing there
> In carts and landaus, in carriages and on foot,
> And why is every heart full of dark foreboding?
> A mournful voice is heard from time to time among them
> Full of heartfelt, heavy grief:
> "Ivan Yakovlevich has died before his time!
> Expired hath the prophet, worthy of a better fate!"

The chronicler Skavronsky relates in his *Moscow Sketches* that in the five days before the corpse was buried more than two hundred funeral requiems were sung around it.[2] Many people spent the night outside the church. N. Barkov, the author of a study entitled "Twenty-six Muscovite False Prophets, False-Holy Fools, and Male and Female Idiots," who was an eyewitness at the funeral, relates that Ivan Yakovlevich was to have been buried on Sunday, "as was announced in *The Police News,* and on that day, at the crack of dawn, his admirers began to gather, but the interment did not take place because of the arguments that arose about exactly where he was to be buried. It did not quite come to blows, but there were words, and strong ones at that. Some wanted to take him to Smolensk, his birthplace;

others went about trying to have him buried in the Pokrovsky Monastery where a grave had even been made for him in the church; others imploringly begged that his remains be given to the Alexeevsky Convent; still others, seizing hold of the coffin, were hauling it off to the village of Cherkizovo.... They feared that Ivan Yakovlevich's body might be stolen." The historian writes: "It rained this whole time and the mud was terrible, but despite this, as the body was carried from the lodgings to the chapel, from the chapel to the church, and from the church to the cemetery, women, girls, young ladies in crinolines prostrated themselves and crawled beneath the coffin." Ivan Yakovlevich—when he was alive—used to relieve himself on the spot: "it ran out of him (as the historian writes) and the attendants were ordered to throw sand on the floor. And this sand, urinated upon by Ivan Yakovlevich, was gathered by his admirers and taken home, and the sand began to display curative properties. If a baby got sick with a tummy-ache, his mother would mix half a teaspoon of the sand into his cereal and the child would get better. The cotton with which the deceased's ears and nose were plugged was divided up into tiny pieces after the funeral service for distribution among the faithful. Many approached the coffin carrying little vials and collected in them the moisture that flowed out of the coffin on account of the fact that the deceased had died from dropsy. The shirt in which Ivan Yakovlevich had died was torn into little pieces... And when it came time for him to be carried out of the church, freaks, holy fools, hypocrites and male and female pilgrims had gathered. They did not go into the church because it was so crowded; they stood on the streets. And right there, in broad daylight, among those assembled, sermons were delivered before the people, visions were summoned and wonders performed, prophesies and denunciations were uttered, money was collected, and ominous roarings were emitted." In the last years of his life Ivan Yakovlevich had ordered his followers to drink the water in which he had washed himself: they drank it. Ivan Yakovlevich made not only spoken prophesies, but also written ones, which have been preserved for historical investigation. People would write to him and ask, "Should so-and-so marry?" and he would reply, "No pains—no gains."

Chinatown in Moscow was the cheese in which the holy fool-maggots lived. Some wrote poetry, others sang like roosters, peacocks or bullfinches, others heaped abuse on everyone in the name of the Lord, still others knew only one of the simple sayings which were considered prophetic and which gave the prophets their names—for example,— "man's life is a fairy tale, the coffin a carriage, the ride is smooth!" There were devotees of dog barking, who prophesized God's will through barks. In this estate of beggars, seers, tramps, mendicants, wailing alms seekers, false saints—the cripples of all Holy Russia—there were peasants, townspeople, nobles, and merchants—children, old men, robust male peasants, and fertile peasant women. They were all drunk. The onion-domed, light-blue calm of the Asiatic tsardom of Russia sheltered them all; they were bitter, like cheese and onions, for the onion domes on the churches are, of course, a symbol of the onionish Russian life.

And in Moscow, in Petersburg, in other large Russian towns there are other eccentrics. Their genealogy is imperial, not tsarist. The art of Russian furniture-making, begun by Peter, developed in the reign of Elizabeth. No written history of this peasant art exists and the names of its craftsmen have been destroyed by time. This art was the work of solitary men, in cellars in the towns, in the closet-sized backrooms of servants' huts on country estates. This art was fueled on bitter vodka and cruelty. Jacob and Boulle were its teachers. Peasant youths were sent to Moscow and Saint Petersburg, to Paris, and to Vienna—in these places they learned the craft. Then they returned—from Paris to the cellars of Saint Petersburg, from Saint Petersburg to the cramped back rooms of huts—and they created. A single craftsman would work for decades on one great sofa or dressing table, or on a bureau or book cabinet—he would work, drink and die, leaving his art work to his nephew, for it wasn't the custom for craftsmen to have children, and the nephew would either copy his uncle's art or develop it. The craftsmen would die, but the objects would live on for a century or more on the estates of landowners and in their townhouses; in such surroundings people made love; they died on the great sofas; they hid secret notes in concealed bureau drawers; brides examined their youth in the mirrors of dressing tables, and old women their age. Elizabeth—Catherine—rococo, baroque—bronze, scrolls, rosewoods, ebony, Karelian birch, Persian walnut. Paul is austere; Paul—a knight of Malta; Paul's time saw military lines, austere calm, dark polished mahogany, green leather, black lions and griffins. Alexander is Empire, classic lines, Hellas. Nicholas—another Paul, crushed by the grandeur of his brother Alexander. Thus have epochs left their marks on mahogany. In 1861 serfdom was abolished. The peasant craftsmen were replaced by furniture factories—Levinson, Thonet, Viennese furniture. But the craftsmen's nephews survived—thanks to vodka. These craftsmen no longer make anything, they restore antiques, but they have retained all the skills and traditions of their uncles. They are solitary and silent. They take pride in their work, like philosophers, and they love it, like poets. They live in cellars as before. You can't send off such a craftsman to a furniture factory; you can't force him to restore anything made after the time of Nicholas I. He is an antique dealer, a restorer. In the attic of a Moscow home or in the barn of an estate which has not been burned down, he will find a table, a three-leaved mirror, or a sofa—dating back to Catherine, Paul or Alexander—and for months on end he will fuss over it in his cellar, smoking, thinking, sizing it up, in order to restore life to a dead object. He will love this thing. Who knows?—he might find a yellowed packet of letters in the secret drawer of a small bureau. He is a restorer, he looks back to the time these things were made. He is sure to be an eccentric, and in an eccentric way he will sell the restored object to some equally eccentric collector, with whom, on sealing the bargain, he will drink brandy poured from an ordinary bottle into a decanter from Catherine's time; they will drink from glasses which were once part of the diamond-studded service of the Imperial Family.

Chapter Two

The year 1928.

The town is a medieval Russian Bruges and imperial Russia's Kamakura.[3] Three hundred years ago in this town the last tsarevich of Rurik's dynasty was murdered. On the day of the murder the boyar Tuchkov's children were playing with the tsarevich—and the Tuchkov line lives on in the town to this day, as do the monasteries and many other families of less illustrious lineage ... Ancient Russia, the Russian provinces, the upper reaches of the Volga, forests, marshes, villages, monasteries, landowners' estates—a chain of towns—Tver, Uglich, Yaroslavl, Rostov the Great. The town is a monastic Bruges of medieval Russia, with narrow streets overgrown with medicinal camomile and with stone monuments commemorating murders and centuries. It's two hundred versts from Moscow, and the railroad is fifty versts away.[4]

Here lie stranded ruins of estates and of mahogany. The curator of the museum of antiquities here walks about in a top hat, a cape and checked trousers; he has let his sideburns grow like Pushkin's; in the pockets of his cape are kept the keys to the museum and monasteries; he drinks tea in the tavern and vodka when alone—in his pantry; his house is piled with Bibles, icons, archimandrital cowls and mitres, surplices, stoles, cuffs, cassocks, chasubles, patens, palls, altar cloths—of the thirteenth, fifteenth and seventeenth centuries; there is mahogany furniture in his study that once belonged to the Karazins; on the desk is an ashtray—shaped like a nobleman's cap with a red band and white crown.

Squire Karazin Vyacheslav Pavlovich, served at one time in the cavalry and resigned about twenty-five years before the Revolution on a point of honor—a colleague of his was caught stealing, he was sent to investigate, he reported the truth to his superior officers, the superior officers covered up for the thief—this was too much for Squire Karazin to take and he submitted a second report—he resigned—and settled down on his estate, riding forth to his district town once a week to buy goods; he travelled with two footmen in a heavy, unwieldy carriage; he would motion to the clerk with his white glove to wrap up half a pound of the highest-grade caviar, three-quarters of sturgeon fillet, and a whole sturgeon; one footman would settle the account, another would pick up the purchases;

one day the merchant was just about to proffer the squire his hand, but the squire made no move to extend his, explaining this refusal with a curt "no need for that!" Squire Karazin walked about in a nobleman's cap and an overcoat in the style of Nicholas I; the Revolution had uprooted him from his estate into the town, but had left him his cap and greatcoat; the squire, wearing his nobleman's cap, would now stand in line preceded by his wife instead of the footmen.

Squire Karazin lived off the sale of his antiques; on such business he would drop in to see the museum keeper; at the musuem keeper's place he would see things which had been confiscated from his estate by the will of the Revolution and he would look at them with disdain. But one day on the museum keeper's table he saw an ashtray shaped like a nobleman's cap.

"Remove it," he said curtly.

"Why?" asked the musuem keeper.

"The cap of a Russian nobleman cannot be used as a spittoon," answered Squire Karazin.

The two connoisseurs of antiques argued. Squire Karazin walked off in anger. Never again did he cross the museum keeper's threshold. In the town lived a saddlemaker who gratefully remembered how Squire Karazin—when the saddlemaker was very young and lived at the Squire's as a boy servant—how with one blow of his left hand the squire had knocked out seven of his teeth because he had been too slow at something.

Over the town a dense silence congealed, which, out of anxious boredom, broke out twice a day into the wails of steamboat whistles and ringing from the ancient heights of church belfries—until 1928, for in 1928 the bells in many churches were dismantled for the State Ore and Metal Trust. High up in their towers, by means of pullies, beams and hempen ropes, the bells were removed from their belfries; they hung over the town, then were thrown down. And as the bells inched along the ropes, they sang an age-old lament—and this lament hovered over the ancient foundations of the town. The bells fell with a roar and a crash and sank a good three yards into the ground.

In the days when this tale took place the town was moaning with the moans of these same bells of old.

The most essential thing in the town was a trade-union card; there were two lines in the shops—one for cardholders, the other for non-cardholders; to hire a boat on the Volga cost cardholders ten kopecks, and others forty kopecks an hour; cinema tickets for the non-cardholders were twenty-five, forty and sixty kopecks, for cardholders—five, ten and fifteen. The union card, if one had it, together with the bread card, were the most important things in the house; and as for bread cards—and therefore bread—these were only distributed to those who had the vote,[5] four hundred grams per person per day; those without the vote and their children were not given any bread. The cinema was located in a heated barn in the trade-union park; no bells had been assigned the cinema—instead the electric power station signaled the whole town at once: the first signal meant—finish drinking your tea; the second—get dressed and be on your way. The power station worked until 1:00 a.m., but on namesdays, *oktiabriny,*[6] and other unofficial celebrations at the houses of the Executive Committee chairman or the Industrial Combine chairman, or of other bosses, the electricity was not shut off until much later, sometimes all night, and the remainder of the population adjusted their own celebrations to fall on these nights. One day in the cinema a representative of the Ministry of Domestic Trade, one Satz or perhaps Katz, in a completely sober condition accidentally bumped against the Executive Committee chairman's wife; full of contempt she uttered the words—"I am Kuvarzina"; Representative Satz, ignorant of the power of this name, excused himself in a somewhat surpised manner—and as a result of his surprise he was banished from the district. The local higher-ups lived as a tightly-knit group, keeping a watchful eye, out of inborn suspiciousness, on the rest of the population; they substituted petty quarrels for constructive social activity, and reelected each other every year to one important district post after another, depending on the alignment of the quarrelers, on the principle of robbing Peter to pay Paul. The economy was managed on the same principle of robbing Peter to pay Paul. The Combine organized everything (the Combine came into being the same year that Ivan Ozhogov—the hero of this story—went off to join the *okhlomons*).[7] The board of the Combine consisted of the chairman of the Executive Committee Kuvarzin (the husband of the wife) and the representative of the Workers' and Peasants' Inspectorate Presnukhin; Nedosugov acted as chairman. They presided over the gradual draining of prerevolutionary resources with stupid bungling and loving care. The oil mill operated at a loss; the sawmill also at a loss; the tannery—without a loss but without profit and without paying off its debts. In the winter a new boiler for the tannery had been hauled about fifty versts through the snow by forty-five horses and half the population of the district; they dragged it there and then left it because it was the wrong kind—they entered the cost in the profit-and-loss account; next they bought a bark crusher—and abandoned that too—because of its unsuitability, entering the cost in the profit-and-loss account; then they bought a chaff-cutter to crush the bark—and abandoned it, since bark is not chaff—that too was entered in the account. They tried to improve the workers' living conditions with a building project: they bought a two-storied wooden house, transported it to the tannery and—sawed it up for firewood (they sawed up five cubic meters in all), as it turned out that the house was rotten; only thirteen of the beams proved to be sound and to these thirteen beams they added nine thousand rubles and built a house—and just at the time that the tannery was shut down because, although it didn't incur a loss like the other undertakings, neither did it make a profit; the new house remained empty. The Combine covered its losses by selling equipment from enterprises that had been out of business since before the Revolution, and also by maneuvers such as the following: Chairman Kuvarzin sold some timber to boardmember Kuvarzin at controlled prices with a discount of 50 percent—for twenty-five thousand rubles; boardmember Kuvarzin sold the same timber to the public, and to Chairman Kuvarzin in particular, at controlled prices without the discount—for some fifty thousand. By 1927 the board wanted to rest on its laurels: they presented Kuvarzin with a briefcase—the money for the briefcase was taken from public funds—and then in order to raise money to return to the treasury they ran around the populace with a subscription list. In view of the secrecy surrounding their interests and lives which were spent in seclusion from the rest of the population, the higher-ups are of no interest whatsoever to this story. In the town only two kinds of alcohol were sold—vodka and Communion wine; that was all. Vodka was in great demand, as was Communion wine—to a lesser degree, but still great—both for Christ's blood and for warmth. The cigarettes on sale in the town were "Cannon," at eleven kopecks a pack, and "Boxer," at fourteen; there was nothing else. As for vodka, so were there lines for cigarettes—one for union members and one for non-union members. Twice a day steamers called and in the restaurant one could buy "Sappho" cigarettes, port and rowanberry vodka; "Sappho" smokers were obvious embezzlers, as there was no private enterprise in the town and budgets were not calculated to include "Sapphos." The townspeople looked forward to the day when the town would lose its status as an administrative center; in the meantime they helped each other with vegetable gardens and mutual support.

Near the Skudrin Bridge stood the Skudrin house, and in this house lived Yakov Karpovich Skudrin, an agent for peasant affairs, a man of eighty-five; besides Yakov Karpovich Skudrin there lived in the town, but not under the same roof as Yakov Karpovich, his two much younger sisters, Kapitolina and Rimma, and his *okhlomon* brother Ivan, who had changed his surname to Ozhogov—more on them later.

For the last forty years or so Yakov Karpovich had suffered from a hernia, and when he walked he would support this hernia of his with his right hand through a slit in his trousers—his hands were swollen and greenish—he salted his bread from the communal salt dish in ample amounts, rubbing the salt between his fingers, and thriftily returning any remaining salt to the dish. For the last thirty years Yakov Karpovich had lost the habit of normal sleep; he would wake up at night and stay awake over his Bible until dawn, then sleep until noon; at noon he would always go off to the public reading room to read the newspapers: newspapers were not sold in the town—there wasn't enough money for subscriptions—newspapers were read in reading rooms. Yakov Karpovich was obese, completely gray and bald; his eyes watered and he wheezed and puffed when preparing to speak. The Skudrin house had once belonged to the landowner Vereisky who, after the abolition of serfdom, had gone bankrupt as an elected Justice of the Peace: Yakov Karpovich, having served in the pre-reform army, worked as a clerk for Vereisky; he became proficient at legal skulduggery, and when Vereisky went bankrupt, he bought up his home and position. The house had stood untouched since Catherine's time; during the century and a half of its existence it had darkened like the mahogany within; its windows had turned green. Yakov Karpovich remembered serfdom. The old man remembered everything— as far back as the squire of his serf village, as far back as the recruiting for Sevastopol; for the last fifty years he could remember all the names, patronymics and surnames of all the Russian ministers and people's commissars, all the ambassadors to the Imperial Russian Court and the Soviet Central Executive Committee, all the foreign ministers of the great powers, all the prime ministers, kings, emperors and Popes. The old man had lost count of the years and would say:

"I've outlived Nikolai Pavlovich, Alexander Nikolaevich, Alexander Alexandrovich, Nikolai Alexandrovich, Vladimir Ilych—and I'll outlive Alexei Ivanovich!"

The old man had a nasty little smile, servile and spiteful at the same time; his whitish eyes watered whenever he smiled. The old man was stern as were the sons who took after him. The eldest son, Alexander, long before 1905, was sent to the steamer landing with an urgent letter and, having missed the steamer, received a box on the ears from his father with the words: "Get out, you good-for-nothing!" This box on the ears was the last straw—the boy was fourteen years old—the boy turned around, walked out of the house—and came back home—but only six years later, a student of the Academy of Fine Arts. During those years the father once sent his son a letter in which he ordered the son to return and vowed to deprive him of his paternal blessing, cursing him forever: on the very same letter, just beneath the father's signature, the son wrote: "To hell with your paternal blessing"—and returned the letter to his father. When, six years after walking out, Alexander walked into the drawing room one sunny spring day, his father came to meet him with a joyous smile and an arm raised to strike his son: with a cheerful grin the son grabbed his father's wrists with both hands, and smiled again—his smile radiated strength and happiness; his father's hands were held tightly; the son forced his father to sit down, applying slight pressure to his wrists, in an armchair near the table, and the son said:

"Hello, papa; why are you getting upset, papa? Sit down, papa!"

The father began wheezing, giggling, snuffling; malevolent kindliness spread over his face; the old man shouted to his wife:

"Maryushka, yes, hee-hee, a drop of vodka, bring us some vodka, my dear, nice and cold, from the cellar, and something cold to go with it—he's grown up, our boy, he's grown up; he's come back to plague us, the son of a bitch!

The sons went their ways: artist, priest, ballet dancer, doctor, engineer. Two younger brothers took after the oldest—the artist—and their father; two younger ones left home, like the oldest, and the youngest of all became a Communist, the engineer Akim Yakovlevich, and he never returned to his father's home; on those occasions when he passed through the town of his birth, he stayed with his aunts Kapitolina and Rimma. By 1928 Yakov's oldest grandsons were married, but his younger daughter was only twenty years old. She was his only daughter, and in the thunder of the Revolution she was never given any education.

In the house lived the old man, his wife Maria Klimovna, and the daughter Katerina. Half the house and the attic went unheated in winter. The house lived the way people used to live long before Catherine, and even before Peter, despite the fact that the house's silence was furnished with mahogany of Catherine's time. The old folks lived off their garden. Industrial life had brought only matches, kerosene and salt to the house: the matches, kerosene and salt were handed out by the father. Maria Klimovna, Katerina, and the old man slaved away from spring to autumn at the cabbages, beetroots, turnips, cucumbers, carrots and licorice, which took the place of sugar. In summer one could meet the old man at dawn—in his nightclothes, barefoot, his right hand thrust through a slit, a switch in his left hand—grazing the cows in the dew and mist beyond the outskirts of the town. In winter the old man lit the lamp only when he was up—the rest of the time the mother and daughter sat in dark. At noon the old man would go off to the reading room to read the newspapers, absorbing the names and the news of the Communist revolution. —Katerina would then sit at the harpsichord and practice Kostalsky's hymns;[8] she sang in the church choir. The old man came home at dusk, ate, and went to bed. The home sank into women's whispering and darkness. Katerina would then go to the cathedral for choir practice. The father would wake up at midnight, light the lamp, eat and immerse himself in the Bible, reciting it aloud by heart. At about six o'clock the old man would nod off again. The old man had lost a sense of time, having ceased to fear death, having forgotten how to fear life. The mother and daughter were silent in the old man's presence. The mother made porridge and cabbage soup, baked pies, baked and curdled the milk, prepared pigs'-feet jelly (hiding the knuckle bones for the grandchildren)—in short, she lived as Russians had lived in the fifteenth and also in the seventeenth centuries, and she prepared food in the manner of the fifteenth- and seventeenth-centuries. Maria Klimovna, a dried-up old woman, was a wonderful woman, the kind of woman who is still preserved in the Russian villages together with the ancient icons of the Virgin Mother. The cruel will of her husband, who fifty years ago, on the day after their wedding, when she had put on her raspberry-colored, velvet bodice, had asked her, "What's that for?" (she didn't understand the question at first)—"What's that for?" her husband asked again, "take it off!"—"I know you without your finery on, and there's no need for others to stare!"—then, spitting on his thumb, the husband painfully showed his wife how to pull her hair back at the temples—the cruel will of the husband, which forced the wife to pack away her velvet bodice forever in a trunk, and which banished her to the kitchen—had it broken his wife's will, or was she hardened by subjugation? The wife stayed forever submissive, dignified, taciturn, and sad, but she was never devious. Her world did not extend beyond the garden gate—and there was but one path beyond the gate—certain as the grave, the path to the church. She sang Kostalsky's psalms with her daughter; she was sixty-nine years old. Pre-Petrine Russia had congealed in the house. At night the old man recited the Bible by heart, having ceased to fear life. Very rarely, once every few months, in the silent hours of the night, the old man would walk over to the wife's bed—he would then whisper,

"Yes, Maryushka, hem, h'mm!...yes, hem, Maryushka, it's life, Maryushka."

His hands would hold a candle, his eyes would water and laugh, his hands would shake.

"Maryushka, h'mm, here I am, yes, this is life, Maryushka, hem!"

Maria Klimovna would cross herself.

"Shame on you, Yakov Karpovich!.."

Yakov Karpovich would put out the light.

Their daughter, Katerina, had little yellow eyes which seemed unable to move from endless sleep. Freckles multiplied around her swollen eyelids all year round. Her arms and legs were like logs, her breasts were huge, like the udders of Swiss cows.

...The town is a medieval Russian Bruges, imperial Russia's Kamakura.

Chapter Three

...Moscow rumbled with truckloads of activities, beginnings, accomplishments. Automobiles and houses rushed about—into heights and open spaces. Posters proclaimed Gorky's State Publishing House, movies and congresses. The noises of tramcars, buses and taxis asserted the capital from one end to the other.

The train departed from Moscow into a night black as soot. The feverish glows and thunders of Moscow were fading, and they perished very quickly. The fields were lying in black silence and this silence settled in the car. In a double compartment of a first-class car sat two men—the two Bezdetov brothers, Pavel Fyodorovich and Stepan Fyodorovich, mahogany specialists and restorers. They both looked strange, dressed in European frockcoats as they were, like merchants of Ostrovsky's time, but with Russian overcoats over them—their faces, although shaven, preserved the Slavic features of Yaroslavl; the eyes of both were vacant and shrewd. The train was dragging time away into the black expanses of fields. The car smelled of tanned hide and hemp. Pavel Fyodorovich took a bottle of brandy and a small silver tumbler from his suitcase; he poured and drank; he poured, and silently handed it to his brother. The brother drank and returned the tumbler. Pavel Fyodorovich put the bottle and the tumbler back in the suitcase.

"Are we buying beads?" asked Stepan.

"Certainly," answered Pavel.

Half an hour passed in silence. The train dragged time along, stopping it at stations. Pavel took out the bottle and tumbler, took a drink, poured one for his brother, and put them away.

"Are we treating the girls? Shall we buy porcelain?" asked Stepan Fyodorovich.

"Certainly," answered Pavel Fyodorovich.

And after another half hour of silence the brothers each drank another glass.

"Shall we take any so-called Russian Gobelins?" asked Stepan.

"Certainly," answered Pavel.

At midnight the train reached the Volga, at a village famed throughout Russia for its handicraft boot industry. The smell of leather grew stronger and stronger. Pavel poured them each a last glass.

"We won't take anything after Alexander?" asked Stepan.

"Out of the question," answered Pavel Fyodorovich.

Mounds of Russian boots were piled up at the station—not the expression of a philosophy, but a concrete confirmation of the state of Russian roads. The handmade goods smelled of pitch. The darkness was thick, like the pitch that it smelled of. Bootmakers were running about the station. Around the station everything was sinking into mud. Pavel Fyodorovich quietly hired a cart to the steamer landing for forty kopecks. In the darkness the drivers were swearing at each other like bootmakers.[9] Damp rolled in from the vast black Volga. The far bank glowed with the electric lights of the cobbling trade. In the steamer's buffet a group of Jewish buyers was getting drunk; a young woman in a monkey-fur wrap acted as the party's hostess and poured the vodka; the group left after the third whistle. The steamer dimmed its lights. The wind began to explore the expanses of the Volga; dampness crept into the cabins. While serving the Bezdetovs, a buxom waitress was making up beds on the tables in the restaurant and talking about her boyfriend, who had stolen a hundred and twenty-two rubles from her. The steamer was transporting the smells of boot leather. Deck passengers were singing bandit songs to keep away the cold. In the gray dross of morning landscapes appeared—not of the fourteenth, but of some prehistoric century—banks untouched by man, pines, firs, birches, boulders, clay, water—according to European chronology the fourteenth century manifested itself in rafts, ferries, villages. By noon the steamer had arrived in the seventeenth-eighteenth century of the Russian Bruges; the town sloped down to the Volga with churches, its kremlin and the ruins left by the fire of 1920. (At that time, in 1920, a good half—the central part—of the town was burned down. The fire had broken out in the headquarters of the District Food Committee—the fire should have been extinguished—but instead the townfolk began to round up the bourgeoisie and put them in jail as hostages—they rounded up bourgeoisie for three days, exactly as long as the town burned, and stopped rounding them up when the fire had burned itself out without any interference from fire hoses or the public.) At the very time the antique dealers were disembarking, crazed flocks of jackdaws were flying over the town, and the town was moaning with the strange moan of bells being pulled down from the belltowers. Above the town rain was getting ready to drizzle.

Pavel Fyodorovich—silently—hired a carriage to Skudrin Bridge—to the house of Yakov Karpovich Skudrin. The driver rattled off on the camomile-covered ancient road, told them the news about the town's bells, explained that many people in the town had suffered nervous disorders while waiting for the bells to fall and expecting the thunderous noise, just as inexperienced gunners often screw up their eyes while anticipating a shot. The Bezdetovs met Yakov Karpovich outside; the old man was chopping kindling for the stove. Maria Klimova was clearing manure out of the cowshed. Yakov Karpovich did not immediately recognize the Bezdetovs—when he did, he was overjoyed—he broke into smiles, began snorting and snuffling, and said:

"Aah, the buyers!... I've thought up a theory about the proletariat for you!"

Maria Klimovna made a deep bow to the guests, tucking her hands beneath her apron, and sang out hospitably:

"Dear guests, welcome to you, long-awaited guests!"

Katerina, in a skirt hitched up to her thighs, and covered in dirt, rushed headlong into the house—to change her clothes. Over the roofs of the houses, the sound of a falling bell rang out, startling the flocks of crows—Maria Klimovna crossed herself—the bell boomed louder than a cannon, the glass rattled in the windows facing the yard—it was, indeed, enough to shatter the nerves.

They all went into the house. Maria Klimovna went over to her stove, the samovar began to hum at her feet. Katerina came out to the guests like a young lady and curtsied. The old man removed his felt boots, walked around the guests barefoot, cooing like a pigeon. The antique dealers washed up from the journey and sat down at the table side by side, in silence. The guests' eyes were vacant, like those of the dead. Maria Klimovna inquired after their health and spread the table with dishes of the seventeenth century. The guests set a bottle of brandy on the table. At the table only Yakov Karpovich spoke, giggling and grunting; he told them where they should look for antiques, those places he had taken mental note of for the Bezdetov brothers' sake.

Pavel Fyodorovich asked:

"But you're going to hold out, are you?—You're not selling?"

The old man began to fidget and titter, and answered in a whining voice:

"Yes, yes, that's right. I can't, no, I can't. What's mine is mine, I'll need it myself—time will tell, yes, hem. I'd better tell you my theory...I'll outlive you yet!"

After the meal the guests went to lie down—they shut the squeaking doors, lay down on the feather beds and without saying a word drank brandy out of antique silver. By evening the guests were completely drunk. All day long Katerina sang hymns. Yakov Karpovich hovered around the doors to the guests' room, waiting for the guests to come out or begin to speak—so that he could go in and have a chat with them. The crows carried the day away; all through sunset the crows were disturbed, stealing the day bit by bit. Dusk came with the water carts. When the guests came out to tea, their eyes were utterly dead, stupefied, unblinking. The guests sat down at the table side by side, without speaking. Yakov Karpovich squeezed in behind them to be closer to their ears. The guests drank tea from the saucers and laced their brandy with tea, having unbuttoned their frock coats. A torchère from Catherine's time was smoking near the table. The dinner table was round, made of mahogany.

Yakov Karpovich choked as he spoke, hurrying to have his say:

"I've an idea ready for you, ahem! an idea... Marx's theory on the proletariat is bound to be forgotten soon, because the proletariat itself will have to disappear—there, that's my idea!—and so the whole revolution was for nothing, h'mmm! a mistake of history. By virtue of the fact, yes, that another two or three generations and the proletariat will disappear— first of all in the United States, in England, in Germany. Marx wrote his theory in the epoch of the blossoming of muscle labor. Now machine labor is replacing muscles. There, that's my idea. Soon only engineers will remain around machines, and the proletariat will disappear; the whole proletariat will turn into engineers. There, hem, that's my idea. And an engineer is no proletarian, because the more cultured a man is, the fewer arrogant demands he makes, and the more content he is to live according to the same material standards as everyone else, to spread material well-being evenly in order to set thought free, yes—take the English, rich and poor alike—all sleep in jackets and live in the same kind of houses, three-storied; but with us—compare a merchant with a peasant in the old days—the merchant dressed up like a priest and lived in a mansion. But I can walk about barefoot and be none the worse for it. You'll say, h'mmm, won't you, that exploitation will remain? Well, how can it remain? The peasant who can be exploited, because he's like a wild beast—he won't be allowed near a machine, he'll break it, and it's worth millions. A machine costs too much for you to try to save a few kopecks on the man who works it—a man must know his machine, machines need men who understand them—and there'll be only one man needed in place of the previous hundred. Such a man will be cherished. That'll be the end of the proletariat!.."

The guests drank tea and listened with unblinking eyes. Yakov Karpovich snorted, hacked, and hurried on—but there was not time for him to develop his idea to the end: for Ivan Karpovich arrived, his brother—the *okhlomon,* who had changed his name from Skudrin to Ozhogov. Neatly dressed in complete rags, his hair neatly trimmed, galoshes on his bare feet—he bowed respectfully to all and sat off to the side in silence. Nobody acknowledged his bow. His face was the face of a madman. Yakov Karpovich began to fidget and grew uneasy.

Maria Klimovna said sorrowfully:

"And just what have you come for, brother?"

The *okhlomon* answered:

"To view aspects of the counter-revolution, sister dear."

"And what counter-revolution is there here, brother?"

"As far as you are concerned, sister dear, your life is the everyday counter-revolution," the *okhlomon* Ozhogov began in a quiet and mad voice. "But you have been crying over me—that means that you have the seeds of Communism in you. Brother Yakov has never wept, and I very much regret that I didn't put him up against the wall and shoot him when I had the chance."

Maria Klimovna sighed, shook her head, and said:

"How's your boy?"

"My son," the *okhlomon* proudly answered, "my son is finishing the university and doesn't forget me, he visits my domain during vacations, warms himself by the stove, and I compose revolutionary verses for him."

"And your wife?"

"We never meet. She manages the Women's Division. Do you know how many managers we have for every two production workers?"

"No."

"Seven. Too many cooks spoil the broth. As for your guests—they are the historical counter-revolution."

The guests, leaden-eyed, drank their tea. Yakov Karpovich flushed with crimson rage; he began to resemble a beet. He went up to his brother, tittered with politeness, began to twist his hands, and rubbed them together vigorously, as one does in a frost.

"You know what, brother," Yakov Karpovich began to say, began to whisper hoarsely—very politely—"You can get the hell out of here. I'm asking you straight out!.."

"Beg pardon, brother Yakov—I didn't come to see you; I came to look at the historical counter-revolution and to have a chat with it," answered Ivan.

"And I'm asking you—to get the hell out of here!"

"And I'm not going!"

Pavel Fyodorovich Bezdetov slowly glanced at his brother with his leaden left eye, and said:

"We can't be bothered with fools—if you don't leave, I'll order Stepan to throw you out on your neck."

Stepan glanced the same way as his brother, and sat up in his chair. Maria Klimovna pressed her hands to her cheeks and sighed. The *okhlomon* sat silently. Stepan Fyodorovich half-heartedly got up from the table and walked over to the *okhlomon*. The *okhlomon* rose apprehensively and backed towards the door. Maria Klimovna let out another sigh. Yakov Karpovich giggled. Stepan stopped in the middle of the room—the *okhlomon*, grimacing, stopped at the door. Stepan stepped towards the *okhlomon*—the *okhlomon* went out the door. From behind the door he pleaded:

"In that case give me a ruble twenty-five for vodka."

Stepan looked at Pavel. Pavel said:

"Slip him enough for a half-bottle."

The *okhlomon* left. Maria Klimovna walked out beyond the gate to see him off, and handed him a piece of pie. Beyond the gate the night was black and still. The *okhlomon* Ozhogov walked towards the Volga by way of dark alleys, past monasteries, through vacant lots, on paths known to him alone. The night was very black. Ivan kept talking to himself, mumbling unintelligibly. He walked down to the Combine brick works; there he climbed through a hole in the fence, and made his way across the clay pits. In the midst of the pits a kiln glowed. Ivan crawled down, beneath the ground, into the kiln pit—there it was very warm and stuffy; a red glow shone through cracks in the kiln door. Here on the ground sprawled a ragged bunch of men with long and matted hair, Ivan Ozhogov's Communists, men who had a tacit agreement with the Industrial Combine: they stoked the brick kiln for free—the kiln whose fire was used to bake the bricks—and they lived by the kiln for nothing, these people for whom time had come to a standstill during the period of War Communism, and who had chosen Ivan Ozhogov as their chairman. On the straw near a plank that served as a table lay three ragged men taking a rest. Ozhogov squatted down next to them; while warming himself up, he shivered at first, the way people shiver when thawing out; he put the money and the piece of pie on the table.

"They didn't cry?" asked one of the outcasts.

"No, they didn't cry," Ozhogov answered.

They fell silent.

"It's your turn to go, Comrade Ognyov," said Ozhogov.

Into the clay of the cave crawled two more men with matted beards and moustaches, dressed in beggars' rags; they lay down next to the others and put money and bread on the plank. A man of about forty, already an old man, who had been lying in the very darkest heat—Ognyov—crawled over to the plank, counted the money—and started to climb up out of the cave. The others continued to sit and lie in silence—one of the men who had just come said only that the next morning they would have to start loading the barge with firewood. Ognyov soon returned with bottles of vodka. The *okhlomons* then moved closer to the plank, picked up their mugs, and sat down in a circle. Comrade Ognyov poured everyone some vodka, they clinked mugs, and emptied them in silence.

"Now I shall speak," said Ozhogov. "Once there were brothers named Wright; they decided to fly in the sky, and they perished when they crashed to the ground after falling from the sky. They perished, but people did not abandon their work: people took hold of the sky—and people are flying, comrades, they are flying above the earth like birds, like eagles! Comrade Lenin is dead, like the Wright brothers—I was the first chairman of the Executive Committee in our town. In 1921 everything came to an end. We are the only real Communists in the whole town, and now the only place left for us is this cave. I was the first Communist here, and I shall remain one as long as I live. Our ideas will not perish. What ideas they were!—now nobody remembers, comrades, except us. We are like the Wright brothers!.."

Comrade Ognyov poured everyone a second round of vodka. And Ognyov interrupted Ozhogov:

"Now I shall speak, Comrade Chairman! What deeds we did! How we fought! I commanded a detachment of partisans. We pushed through the woods by day, and at night, and for another day and another night. And then suddenly at dawn we heard—machine guns..."

Pozharov interrupted Ognyov; he asked him:

"How do you slash? How do you hold your thumb when you slash— bent or straight? Show us!"

"On the blade. Straight," answered Ognyov.

"Everyone holds it on the blade. Show us. Here, show us with the knife!"

Ognyov picked up the cobbler's knife that the *okhlomons* used to cut bread, and showed how he placed his thumb on the blade.

"You're slashing the wrong way!" Pozharov shouted. "I don't hold my saber like that when I slash; I slice with it like a razor. Here, let me show you!—you're slashing the wrong way!"

"Comrades!" Ozhogov said quietly, and his face was contorted with terrible pain—"today we must talk about ideas, about great ideas, not about slashing!"

Ozhogov was interrupted by a fourth man, who shouted:

"Comrade Ognyov! You were in the third division, and I was in the second—do you remember how you missed the crossing near the village of Shinki!?.."

"We missed it! No, it was you who missed it, not us!"

"Comrades!" Ozhogov said again in a quiet, insane voice, "we must talk about ideas!"

By midnight the men in the cave were asleep near the kiln, these ragged outcasts who had gained themselves the right to live in a cave in the kiln pit of a brick works. They slept slumped together in a heap, the head of one on the knees of another, covered by their rags. The last to sleep was their chairman Ivan Ozhogov—he lay for a long time by the mouth of the kiln, a sheet of paper in front of him. He was lying on his stomach with the paper spread out on the ground. He sucked on the pencil; he wanted to write a poem. "We have raised a world-wide," he wrote and then crossed it out. "We have lit a world-wide," he wrote and crossed out. "You who warm your thieving hands," he wrote and crossed out. "You—either lackeys or idiots," he wrote and crossed out. Words would not come to him. He fell asleep with his head on the scribbled over sheet of paper. Here slept Communists who had been called up during the period of War Communism and demobilized in 1921, men of fixed ideas, madmen and drunkards, men who while living together in a cave and working together at unloading barges and sawing firewood had created the strongest brotherhood, the most strict communism, having nothing private, not money, not things, not wives—incidentally, their wives had left them, their dreams, their madness, and alcohol. In the cave it was very stuffy, very warm, very destitute.

Midnight, as inert and dark as the history of these parts, watched over the town.

At midnight the younger of the restorers, Stepan Fyodorovich, stopped Katerina on the staircase to the attic, touched her shoulders, strong as a horse's, felt them with a drunken hand, and said quietly:

"You, there, tell your . . . sisters . . . We'll fix another time. Tell them to find a place . . ."

Katerina stood there obediently and obediently whispered:

"All right, I'll tell them."

Downstairs at that moment Yakov Karpovich was expounding his theories of civilization to Pavel Fyodorovich. On a round table in the drawing room stood a frigate of glass and bronze that was made to pour alcohol—so that through the alcohol, poured from a little tap on the frigate, and from glasses into men's throats—through the alcohol one could journey on this frigate from fantasy to fantasy. This frigate was an eighteenth-century piece. The frigate was filled with brandy. Pavel Fyodorovich sat in silence. Yakov Karpovich fussed around Pavel Fyodorovich; he hopped about like a little pigeon, holding his hernia through the slit in his pants.

"Yes, hem," he said. "What do you think it is that moves the world, civilization, science, steamboats. Well, what?"

"Well, what?" Pavel Fyodorovich asked.

"What do you think it is? Labor? Knowledge? Hunger? Love? No! Civilization is moved by memory! Just imagine that tomorrow people lose their memory—their instincts and reason remain, but their memory is gone. I wake up in bed—and I fall from the bed because it's through memory that I know about space, and once memory is gone, I don't know about it. My trousers are lying on the chair and I am cold, but I don't know what to do with the trousers. I don't know how to walk—on my hands or on all fours. I can't remember the previous day—that means I'm not afraid of death because I don't know anything about it. The engineer has forgotten all his higher mathematics, and all the tramcars and steamers have come to a standstill. Priests cannot find their way to church, and also do not remember anything about Jesus Christ. Yes, h'mmm!.. I still have my instincts, though they are also a kind of memory, but let's say I have them—and I don't know what to eat, the chair or the bread that was left on the chair the night before—and when I see a woman, I could mistake my own daughter for my wife."

Like a northeaster, the alcohol frigate on the table cleared Yakov Karpovich's thoughts: besides the frigate the eighteenth century had left behind a Russian Voltaire in the mahogany drawing-room. Beyond the windows of the eighteenth century passed a Soviet provincial night.

An hour later the Skudrin house was asleep. And then in the sour silence of the bedroom Yakov Karpovich's slippers began to shuffle towards Maria Klimovna's bed. Maria Klimovna, an old, old woman, was asleep. The candle in Yakov Karpovich's hand was flickering. Yakov Karpovich tittered. Yakov Karpovich touched Maria Klimovna's parchment shoulder; his eyes began to water with pleasure. He whispered:

"Maryushka, Maryushka, it's life, life, Maryushka."

The eighteenth century sank into Voltairian darkness.

In the morning the bells were dying over the city, howling as they were shattered into shreds. The Bezdetov brothers woke up early, but Maria Klimovna was up even earlier, and with tea there were hot pies with mushrooms and onions. Yakov Karpovich slept. Katerina was half-asleep. Tea was drunk in silence. The day came on gray and slow. After tea the Bezdetov brothers set off for work. On a piece of paper Pavel Fyodorovich had composed a list of houses and families that they had to visit. The streets lay in a silence of provincial roads, stone walls, weeds under the walls, elders on ruins left by a fire, churches, and bell towers—and sank into an even deeper silence when the bells began to whine, and screamed in silence when the bells howled as they fell.

The Bezdetovs would enter a house silently, side by side, and look around with empty eyes.

1. On Old Rostov Street stood a house which leaned slightly to one side. In this house the widow Myshkina was dying, the widow was an old woman of seventy. The house stood with one corner to the street, as it was built before streets existed; and the house was not built with sawed wood, but with hewn wood, because it rose before the time that Russian carpenters began to use saws—when they only used axes to build—that is, before the time of Peter. At that time the house belonged to a boyar. The

house preserved a tiled stove and tiled ledge from those days; the tiles were adorned with sheep and boyars, and glazed with ocher.

The Bezdetovs walked through the gate without knocking. The old woman Myshkina was sitting on an earthen ledge in front of the pigs' trough; a pig ate steamed nettles from the trough. The Bezdetovs bowed to the old woman and silently sat down beside her. The old woman acknowledged the bow, embarrassed, pleased, and frightened. She was wearing torn felt boots, a calico skirt, and a Persian shawl of many colors.

"Well, are you selling?" asked Pavel Bezdetov.

The old woman hid her hands beneath the shawl and lowered her gaze to the ground in the direction of the pig—Pavel and Stepan Fyodorovich looked at each other, and Stepan winked—she'll sell. The old woman wiped the corners of her mouth with her bony, lilac-nailed hand, and her hand shook.

"Well, I don't know what to do," the old woman said, and glanced guiltily at the brothers, "our grandfathers lived here and left it to us, and our great-grandfathers, and further back than anyone can remember... And when my lodger—God rest his soul—died, times got to be hard—he used to pay three rubles a month for his room, he bought the kerosene, I had plenty... And here my mother and father both died on this stove ledge... What should I do? God rest his soul, my lodger was a quiet one, he payed three rubles, and died in my arms... Well, I've thought and thought, how many nights I've stayed awake—you've broken my peace of mind."

Pavel Fyodorovich spoke.

"There are about a hundred and twenty tiles on the stove and ledge. As we agreed, twenty-five kopecks a tile. That makes thirty rubles we owe you right away. You'll have enough for the rest of your life. We'll send the stove setter; he'll take them out and put bricks in their place and whitewash them. And all at our expense."

"I'm not talking about the price," said the old woman, "you're giving a good price. Nobody around here pays prices like that... And who needs them, anyway, except me? If it just weren't that my parents... I'm all alone..."

The old woman started to think. She thought for a long time—or was she thinking at all? Her eyes became unseeing, they sank into their sockets. The pig had eaten up the nettles and was poking at one of the old woman's felt boots with its snout. The Bezdetov brothers were looking at the old woman in a stern, business-like manner. Again the old woman wiped the corners of her mouth with a trembling hand. Then she smiled guiltily, guiltily glanced all around—at the lopsided fence of the yard and the garden—then guiltily lowered her eyes before the Bezdetovs.

"Well, so be it! and God bless you!" said the old woman, and held out her hand to Pavel Fyodorovich, feeling awkward and embarrassed, but in the manner required by this time-honored trading practice—the tiles were passed from hand to hand.

2. In the cathedral square in the basement apartment of what used to be their own house lived a family of landowners—the Tuchkovs. Their former estate had been converted into a dairy. Here in the basement lived two adults and six children; there were two women—the old woman Tuchkova and her daughter-in-law, whose husband, a former officer, had shot himself in 1925, when he was on the verge of dying from tuberculosis. The old colonel had been killed in 1915 in the Carpathians. Four of the children belonged to Olga Pavlovna, as the daughter-in-law was called; the two others belonged to the younger Tuchkov, who had been shot for counter-revolutionary activities. Olga Pavlovna was a wet-nurse and played the piano in the cinema in the evenings. And, at thirty, she looked like an old woman.

When the Bezdetov brothers arrived, the basement was unlocked, as in all poor homes. They were met by Olga Pavlovna. She nodded, inviting them inside—she ran on ahead into what was called the dining room to cover the bed so that the strangers would not see that there was no bed linen under the blanket. Olga Pavlovna looked at herself in the triple mirror of a mahogany dressing table made in the Alexandrian Empire style. The brothers were business-like and efficient. Stepan turned the chairs upside down, moved the sofa away from the wall, lifted up the mattress on the bed, pulled drawers out of the commode—examining the mahogany. Pavel sorted through miniatures, beads, and porcelain. The young, aged woman, Olga Pavlovna, still possessed the lightness of a girl's movements and an ability to be embarrassed. The restorers silently ransacked the rooms, dragging filth and poverty out of the corners. The six children, curious about the strange event, clung to their mother's skirt; the two oldest were ready to take part in the havoc. The mother was embarrassed for her children; the younger ones were sniveling as they hung by her skirt, distracting her from making apologies. Pavel put three chairs and an armchair to one side, and said:

"It's not a set, not a suite."

"What did you say?" asked Olga Pavlovna, and cried helplessly to the children. "Children, please, leave! This is no place for you, please!"

"It's not a complete set," Stepan Fyodorovich said. "There are three chairs, but only one armchair. I don't deny that the pieces are of good quality, but they need a considerable amount of repair work. You can see for yourself—you're living in a damp place. And a complete set has to be collected.

The children quieted down when the restorer began to speak.

"Yes," said Olga Pavlovna, blushing, "they all used to be here, but the set could scarcely be put together now. Part was left on the estate when we left, part was split up among the peasants, part got broken by the children, and—then there's the damp—I carried into the barn..."

"I suppose they ordered you out within twenty-four hours?" asked Stepan Fyodorovich.

"Yes, we left at night, without waiting for the order. We foresaw…"

Pavel Fyodorovich entered in the conversation; he asked Olga Pavlovna:

"Do you understand French and English?"

"Oh yes," answered Olga Pavlovna, "I speak…"

"The miniatures wouldn't be—Boucher and Cosway?"

"Oh yes, those miniatures…"

Looking at his brother, Pavel Fyodorovich said:

"We can give you twenty-five for each."

Stepan Fyodorovich firmly interrupted his brother:

"If you can gather up even half a set of furniture, I'll buy all your furniture. If, as you say, the peasants have some, you could go see them."

"Oh, yes," answered Olga Pavlovna, "if half a set… It's thirteen versts to our village… only a bit more than a stroll… I can get half a set together. I'll walk to the village today and give you an answer tomorrow. But—if some things are broken…"

"That doesn't matter, we'll lower the price. Don't bother about an answer, just bring them direct so that we can pick them up and get them packed. Sofas are fifteen rubles, armchairs seven fifty, chairs five apiece. We'll see to the packing."

"Oh, yes, I'll walk over there today, it's only thirteen versts to our village, that's almost a stroll… I'll set out right away."

The eldest boy said:

"Maman, then will you buy me some shoes?"

Beyond the windows the day was gray, beyond the town lay the Russian country roads.

3. Squire Vyacheslav Pavlovich Karazin was lying on the sofa in the dining room, covered with a squirrel jacket that was almost worn through. The dining room which belonged to him and his wife as well as their study-bedroom made up a museum of curios stuck into the apartment of a mail-coach driver. The Bezdetov brothers stood at the threshold and bowed. Squire Karazin stared at them for a long time, and then barked:

"Clear off, you r-rogues! Get out of here!"

The brothers did not move.

The blood rushed to Squire Karazin's face, and he barked again:

"Out of my sight, you scoundrels!"

His wife came out when she heard the shouting. The Bezdetov brothers bowed to Karazina and stepped back behind the door.

"Nadine, I can't stand the sight of those scum!" Squire Karazin said to his wife.

"All right, Vyacheslav, go to the study, I'll talk to them. Oh, you know how things are, Vyacheslav!" Squire Karazin's wife replied.

"They've interrupted my rest. All right, I'll go into the study. Only, please, don't be courteous to those slaves."

Squire Karazin left the room, trailing his jacket behind him; the

Bezdetov brothers entered the room as he left; again they bowed politely.

"Be so kind as to show us your Russian Gobelins, and also give us a price for the small bureau," said Pavel Fyodorovich.

"Please have a seat, gentlemen," said Madame Karazina.

The door of the study burst open, the squire stuck his head out the door. Squire Karazin gave a shout, glancing to the side, toward the windows, lest he should accidentally see the Bezdetov brothers.

"Nadine, don't let them sit down! How can they appreciate the beauties of art! Don't let them choose!—sell them what we have to sell. Sell them the porcelain, the porcelain clock, and the bronze!"

"We can leave, if you want," said Pavel Fyodorovich.

"Ah, wait a minute, gentlemen, let Vyacheslav Pavlovich calm down, he's quite ill," said Karazina, and then helplessly sat down at the table. "We have to sell a few things. Ah, gentlemen, . . . Vyacheslav Pavlovich, I beg you, shut the the door, don't listen to us—go for a walk . . ."

4—5—7

Towards evening, after the jackdaws had torn up the day and the bells had stopped howling, the Bezdetov brothers returned home and ate their dinner. After dinner Yakov Karpovich Skudrin equipped himself for a trip. His pockets contained the Bezdetovs' money and their list. The old man put on a wide-brimmed felt hat and a short sheepskin coat; on his feet were worn-out boots. He went to see the carpenter and the carter, to get ropes and bast matting, and to arrange for the purchases to be packed and transported to the steamer jetty for dispatch to Moscow. The old man went about his business, and said as he left:

"We should have left the job of transporting and packing to the *okhlomons;* they are completely honest people, even if they are fools. But it wouldn't be possible. Brother Ivan wouldn't let them—their most important revolutionary wouldn't let them work for the counter-revolution, ha-ha . . .!"

The Bezdetov brothers settled down in the drawing room for a rest. The earth followed suit for the night. All evening people were stealthily knocking at Maria Klimovna's windows: Katerina went out to them, and the people, ingratiating themselves like beggars, offered: "they say you've guests staying with you, and that they buy all kinds of old things"—old rubles and kopecks, broken lamps, old samovars, books and candleholders; these people did not understand the art of the past—they were poor in every respect. Katerina did not let them in with their copper lamps to see her guests; she suggested that they leave the things until the morning when the guests, having rested, would take a look at them. The evening was dark. At dusk the wind began to blow, bringing storm clouds, and rain began to drizzle with autumnal persistence; through the woods, through the mud of country roads (the very ones on which Akim Skudrin was soon to get stuck), walked Olga Pavlovna, the woman with an old woman's face and movements as light as a girl's. The woods made noises in the wind, in the woods it was frightening. In girlish terror of the woods this woman walked to her village in order to buy from the peasants armchairs for which peasants have no need.

At about eight o'clock in the evening Katerina got her mother's permission to go—first to choir practice and then to see her friend; she got all dressed up and left. Half an hour later Stepan and Pavel Fyodorovich went out into the rain. Katerina was waiting for them by the bridge. Stepan Fyodorovich took Katerina by the arm. In pitch blackness they took a path that ran along the ravine towards the outskirts of the town. There lived the old Skudrin aunts. Katerina and the Bezdetovs snuck into the yard like thieves, like thieves they crept into the garden. At the end of the garden stood a dark bathhouse.

Katerina knocked, and the door opened slightly. A light was burning in the bathhouse; three girls were waiting for the guests. The girls had drawn the curtains to deaden any sound and moved a table up to the steps leading to the sweat shelf. The girls wore their party dresses; they greeted the guests very politely.

The Bezdetov brothers took from their pockets bottles of brandy and port which they had brought from Moscow.

The girls spread out on the table—on paper—cooked sausages, sprats, sweets, tomatoes, and apples. The oldest girl in the group—Klavdia—took out a bottle of vodka from behind the stove. They all spoke in whispers. The Bezdetov brothers sat down side by side on the steps to the sweat shelf. An iron lamp was burning on the shelf.

Within an hour the girls were drunk—nevertheless they still spoke in whispers. Drunken people, and drunken women—in particular, when they are very drunk—keep the expressions created by the alcohol fixed on their faces for a very long time. Klavdia was sitting at the table, propping up her head with her fist, the way men do, her teeth bared, and her lips frozen in contempt; sometimes her head slipped off her fist and then she tugged at her cropped hair, feeling no pain; she was smoking one cigarette after another and drinking brandy; she was very flushed and hideously beautiful. She said with disgust:

"Am I drunk? Yes, I'm drunk. So what? Tomorrow I'll go to school and teach again . . . and what do I know? What am I teaching? And at six o'clock I'll attend the parents' meeting that I called. Here's my notebook, everything is written down here . . . I'm drinking, so what?—and here I am, drunk. And what are you? What relation are you to me? You buy mahogany? Antiques? And you want to buy us with your wine! You think I don't know what life's all about? I know—soon I'm having a baby, but who the father is, I don't know.—So what, what do I care ?"

Klavdia's teeth were bared, and her eyes did not move. Pavel kept pestering Zina, the youngest—she was a short-legged, giggly girl with curly blond hair; she sat on a block of wood, apart from the rest, legs spread apart, hands resting on her hips. Pavel Fyodorovich said:

"I bet you won't take your blouse off, Zina. You won't undo your bra, you don't dare!"

Zina covered her mouth to keep herself from laughing out loud; she burst out laughing and said:

"Yes, I do! I'll show you!"

"No you won't! You don't dare!"

Klavdia contemptuously said:

"She will. Zinka, show them your breasts, let them have a look. I'll show mine, if you want. You think I'm a drunk? No, the last time I was drunk was when you were here. And today I came with the aim of getting drunk—dead drunk—understand?—dead drunk! So what! Zinka, show them your breasts! You show them to your Kolya, don't you?.. Do you want to see mine?"

Klavdia tore at the neck of her blouse. The girls rushed to her. Katerina said sobermindedly:

"Klavdia, don't tear your clothes or they'll find out at home."

Zina was hardly able to stand; she caught Klavdia's hands and embraced her. Klavdia gave Zina a kiss.

"Don't tear them?" she asked. "Well, okay, I won't... But you show them... Let them have a look. We're not inhibited by old-fashioned prejudices! Do you buy mahogany?"

"Okay, I'll show them," Zina said submissively, and she began to undo her blouse in a business-like manner.

The fourth girl left the bathhouse; she felt sick. Of course, the Bezdetovs saw themselves as buyers—buying was the only thing they knew.

Outside the bathhouse it was raining and the trees rustled in the wind. At that hour Olga Pavlovna had reached her village, and, happy and grateful to Granddad Nazar for selling her an armchair and some chairs, she was falling asleep on the straw in Nazar's hut. Squire Karazin at that hour was in the throes of a fit of senile hysteria. At that hour in the kiln pit the *okhlomons,* with the eyes and voices of madmen, were affirming the year 1919, when everything was common property—both bread and labor—when nothing lay behind them, and ahead lay ideas, and there was no money because there was no need for it.—And within another hour the bathhouse was empty. The drunken women and the Bezdetov brothers had gone to their homes; the drunken girls silently crept through their houses to their beds. The notebook was left lying on the floor of the bathhouse. In the notebook was written: "Call a parents' meeting at 6 o'clock on the 7th." "At the meeting of the local trade-union committee suggest that people subscribe to the Industrialization Loan in an amount equal to one month's wages." "Recommend that Alexander Alexeevich go over the *ABC of Communism* again."[10]

In the morning the bells moaned again and in the morning cartloads of mahogany—Catherines, Pauls, Alexanders—were hauled to the steamer jetty under the direction of Yakov Karpovich. The Bezdetov brothers slept until noon. By that time a crowd of people had gathered in the kitchen to await the fate of their old rubles, lamps, and candleholders.

The town is a Russian Bruges.

Chapter Four

And at about the same time, two days later than the Bezdetov brothers, the engineer Akim Skudrin, Yakov Skudrin's youngest son, arrived in the town. The son did not go to his father's house, but stayed with his aunts Kapitolina and Rimma. The engineer Akim did not come on business—he just had a week off.

...Kapitolina Karpovna walks to the window. The provinces. A crumbling red brick wall has one corner set against an ochred house with a belvedere, the other corner leans against a church. It is raining. A pig is sniffing at a puddle. A watercart rounds the corner.—Klavdia goes out the gate, wearing greased boots, a black coat that hangs down to her boot tops, and a blue scarf on her head; she lowers her head, crosses the street, walks along the ruins of the wall, and turns the corner to the square. Kapitolina Karpovna's eyes are bright—she watches Klavdia for a long time. Behind the wall Rimma Karpovna is feeding her granddaughter, the daughter of her oldest, Varvara. The room is very bare and very clean and tidy—unchanged for decades, as one would expect an old maid's room to be—an elderly virgin's room—with a narrow bed, a worktable, a sewing machine, a dressmaker's dummy, curtains. Kapitolina Karpovna goes into her dining room.

"Rimma, dear, let me feed your granddaughter. I saw Klavdia leave. Did Varya leave too?"

These two old women, Kapitolina Karpovna and Rimma Karpovna, were descended from a line of respectable, well-established seamstresses and dressmakers in the town. Their lives were simple, like the lifelines on their left palms. The sisters had been born within a year of each other— Kapitolina was the oldest. And Kapitolina's life had been filled with the virtues of middle-class morality. Her whole life had been put on display for the whole town's eyes and lived according to the town's rules. She was a respected middle-class citizen. And not only the whole town but she herself knew that all her Saturdays were spent at church services, that all her days were spent crouched over hemstitching and embroidery on blouses and shirts—thousands of shirts—and that not once had any man from outside the family kissed her—but only she knew those thoughts that knit the heart, the pain of the soured wine of life. In her life there had been youth and youthfulness and Indian summer, but not once in her life had she been loved or had she known secret sins. She remained a model of obedience to the town's rules, a virgin, an old woman, who had soured her life with chastity, God, tradition.—Rimma Karpovna's life had turned out differently. Twenty-eight years earlier it had happened, it lasted for three years—three years of shame, a shame that was to remain for her whole life. It happened at a time when Rimma's years had rolled on past thirty, when they had taken away her youth and had already sown hopelessness. In the town lived a treasury official, an amateur actor—handsome and a rogue. He was married, had children, and was a drunkard. Rimma fell in love with him, and Rimma did not resist her love. Everything about it was shameful. This love had everything that could shame a woman in the eyes of provincial morality, and everything went wrong. All around stood a forest in which the secret might have been kept hidden—but she gave herself to this man at night on a street; she was ashamed to take home her torn and bloodstained (pure blood, in truth) panties; she stuck them in the bushes. The following morning some boys found them for everyone to see—and not once during the three years of her shame did she meet her lover under a roof; they met in the woods and on streets, in the shambles of houses, on deserted barges, even during the fall and winter. Her brother Yakov Karpovich renounced his sister and drove her from the house—even her sister Kapitolina turned against her. In the streets people pointed at her and treated her as an outcast. The lawful wife of the treasury-department actor came round to give Rimma a beating and urged on the local boys to beat her as well; the town and its laws were on the side of the legal wife. Rimma gave birth to a daughter, Varvara, who was both witness to her shame and her shame. Rimma gave birth to a second daughter, Klavdia, and Klavdia was the second witness to her shame. Her treasury-department lover left town. Rimma was left alone with two children, in stark poverty and shame, a woman who at the time was already well past thirty. Since that time almost thirty more years have passed. The older daughter Varvara is happily married, and she already has two children. Rimma Karpovna has two grandchildren. Varvara's husband is in government service. Varvara is in government service. Rimma Karpovna runs a large household; she is the founder of a family line. And Rimma Karpovna—a kindly old woman—is content with her life. Old age has shortened her, contentment has filled her out. The eyes of this short, plump old woman are very kind and full of life. And now Kapitolina Karpovna has but one concern: the life of Rimma, Varvara, Klavdia, and the grandchildren—her own chastity and honorable reputation in the town have proven to be worthless. Kapitolina Karpovna has no life of her own.

Kapitolina Karpovna says:

"Rimma, dear, let me feed your granddaughter. I saw Klava leave. Did Varya leave too?"

Beyond the windows lie the provinces, the fall, the rain.—And then in the hallway the door hinge squeaks, men's boots stamp on the floor to shake off the wet and the mud—and into the room comes a man who looks around helplessly, as all nearsighted people do when they take off their glasses. It is the engineer Akim Yakovlevich Skudrin, the spit and image of his father fifty years earlier. He has come—nobody knows why.

"Greetings, dear aunts!" says Akim and kisses his aunt Rimma first.

The provinces, the rain, the fall, a Russian samovar... The engineer Akim has not come for any real business. His aunts welcomed him with the samovar, freshly made flatcakes and the warm hospitality of the Russian provinces. Akim did not visit his father or the authorities. Over the town the dying bells whined, the streets bloomed with camomile. Akim spent a day and a night, and then left, having decided that he had no use for his birthplace: the town did not accept him. He spent the day with his aunts, in the memory's journeys through time, in the futility of memory, in the cruel poverty of his aunts, their affairs, their thoughts, their dreams. Things in the house stood just as they had twenty, twenty-five years before, and the dressmaker's dummy, which was so frightening in his childhood, did not scare him now. Towards dusk Klavdia returned from school. They both sat down on the sofa, cousins ten years apart in age.

"How's life?" asked Akim.

They talked about trivial matters, and then Klavdia began to talk about the most important thing for her. She spoke very simply. She was very beautiful and very calm. Dusk tarried and darkened.

"I want to ask your advice," Klavdia said. "I'm about to have a baby. I don't know what I should do. I don't know who the father is."

"You don't know who the father is?"

"I'm twenty-four," said Klavdia. "In the spring I decided it was time for me to become a woman, and I became one."

"But have you a boyfriend?"

"No, I haven't. There were several. I was curious. I did it out of curiosity, and—it was time, I'm twenty-four."

Akim was at a loss what to ask next.

"My attention was not centered on love for somebody else but on my own experiences. I picked out some men, different ones, in order to find out everything. I didn't intend to get pregnant, sex is a joy—I didn't think about a child. But I got pregnant and I have decided not to have an abortion."

"And you don't know who the man is?"

"I can't be certain. But it doesn't matter. I'm a mother. I'll cope, and the state will help me, but morality... I don't know what morality is. I've been taught to forget it. Or perhaps I have my own morality. I'm answerable only to myself and with myself. Why is it immoral to give oneself?—I do what I want and I'm beholden to no one. The man? I don't want to burden him in any way; men are only good when I need them and when they are not tied down in any way. I don't need a man in bedroom slippers to get pregnant by. People will help me—I believe in people. People love the proud and those who are not a burden on them. And the state will help. I slept with men I liked and because I liked it. I'll have a son or a daughter. I'm not sleeping with anyone now—I don't need to. Yesterday I got completely drunk—for the last time. But I'm thinking out loud to you. It disgusts me that I got drunk yesterday.—But perhaps the child will need a father. You abandoned your father—and I was born without a father and never heard anything except dirty stories about him; in childhood I was hurt by this and I was angry at my mother. But all the same I've decided not to have an abortion. My whole womb is filled with child. This is an even greater joy than... I am strong and young."

Akim couldn't collect his thoughts. On the floor before his eyes lay runners made of rags, paths of poverty and philistinism. Klavdia was calm, beautiful, strong, very healthy and very beautiful. Outside the windows the rain was drizzling. The Communist Akim wanted to believe that a new way of life was coming—the present way of life was ancient. Klavdia's morals were both unusual and new to him—but weren't they correct, if Klavdia saw things that way?

Akim said:

"Have the child."

Klavdia leaned against him, put her head on his shoulders, tucked in her feet beneath her, grew cozy and helpless:

"I'm very physical," she said—"I like to eat, I like to wash myself, I like to do exercises, I like it when our dog Sharik licks my hands and feet. I like to scratch my knees until they bleed... But life is big, it's all around and I can't fathom it; I can't fathom the Revolution—but I believe in these things—in life, the sun and the Revolution, and I'm at peace with myself. I understand only what concerns me. The rest doesn't even interest me."

A cat walked along the runner towards the sofa and, as was its habit, jumped onto Klavdia's lap. It had grown dark outside the windows. On the other side of the partition a lamp was lit and the sewing machine started up. Peace came into the darkness.

In the evening Akim went to see Uncle Ivan, who had changed his name from Skudrin to Ozhogov. The *okhlomon* Ozhogov came out of the kiln pit to see his nephew. For some reason the earth is always dug up around brick works, and the roofs of brick sheds are long and low—brick works always resemble places of destruction and mystery. The *okhlomon* was drunk. It was impossible to talk to him, but he was very glad, very happy that his nephew had come to see him. The *okhlomon* could hardly stand and he was trembling all over like a dog.

The *okhlomon* led his nephew under the roof of the brick shed.

"You've come, you've come," he whispered, pressing his trembling hands to his trembling chest.

He turned a wheelbarrow upside down and sat his nephew down on it.

"Did they throw you out yet?" he asked happily.

"Out of where?" Akim asked.

"Out of the Party," said Ivan Karpovich.

"No."

"No? They didn't throw you out?" Ivan asked again and in his voice there rose a certain sadness—but he finished in a cheerful manner: "Well, not yet, but later on they'll throw you out, they'll throw out all the Leninists and Trotskyites."

After this Ivan Karpovich grew delirious—in his delirium he talked about his commune, how he was the first chairman of the Executive Committee, what those years were like and how they had been lost, those terrible years, how he had been driven from the Revolution and now went among the people, to make them cry, remember, love—he told again about his commune, about its equality and brotherhood—he affirmed that Communism first and foremost is love, the intense regard of man for man, friendship, comradeship, working together—Communism means the renunciation of things, and genuine Communism first of all requires love, respect for man—people. The neat little old man trembled in the wind, fingering his jacket collar with his trembling bony hands. The yard of the brick works attested to ruin. The engineer Akim Skudrin was the flesh of Ivan Ozhogov's flesh. Beggars, tramps, seers, mendicant minstrels, wailing alms seekers, pilgrims, cripples, blind singers, prophets, holy fools—these were the *krendeli* of everyday life in Holy Russia, the holy fools in Christ's name of Holy Russia. They were an adornment of daily life, the brotherhood of Christ, supplicants for the world.—Before the engineer Akim stood—a beggar-tramp, a holy fool-wailing alms seeker—a fool of Soviet Russia in justice's name, a supplicant for the world and Communism. Uncle Ivan must have been a schizophrenic; he had his own program: he would walk around the town, call on acquaintances and strangers and ask them to weep; he would deliver fiery and insane speeches about Communism, and many people in the marketplaces wept over his speeches; he made the rounds of government offices—and a rumor spread through the town that some political leaders were rubbing their eyes with onion in order to gain some much-needed popularity in the town through the *okhlomons*. Ivan was afraid of churches, and he cursed the priests, not afraid of them. Ivan's slogans were the most left-wing in town. Ivan was revered in the town in the same way that people in Russia throughout the centuries had come to revere holy fools—fools through whose mouths the truth is spoken and who, for the sake of truth, are ready to go to their deaths. Ivan drank, destroying himself with alcohol. He gathered about him men like himself who had been cast out by the Revolution that had created them. They found a place for themselves in the cave; they enjoyed genuine Communism, brotherhood, equality, friendship—and each possessed his own kind of madness: one had a program to correspond with people on Mars; another suggested catching all the fully grown fish in the Volga and using money from the sale of the fish to build iron bridges over the Volga; a third dreamt of building a streetcar system in the town.

"Weep!" Ivan said.

Tearing himself away from his own thoughts, Akim did not immediately understand Ivan.

"What did you say?" he asked.

"Weep, Akim, weep here and now for Communism lost!" shouted Ivan, pressing his hands against his chest and bowing his head, as do people at prayer.

"Yes, yes, I'm weeping, Uncle Ivan," answered Akim.

Akim was strong, tall, and massive. He stood up next to Ivan. Akim kissed his uncle.

The rain beat down. The gloom of the brick works attested to ruin.

Akim was returning from the *okhlomons* through the town, across the marketplace. In a lone window a light burned. This was the house of the town's eccentric, the museum keeper. Akim walked up to the window— once he had rummaged about in the cellars of the Kremlin with this museum keeper. He was about to knock but saw something strange and stopped. The room was piled high with surplices, stoles, chasubles, and cassocks. In the middle of the room sat two men: the museum keeper poured vodka from a three-liter bottle and raised the glass to the lips of a naked man—the latter didn't move a muscle. On the head of the naked man was a crown. And then Akim realized that the museum keeper was drinking vodka by himself—with a wooden statue of a seated Christ. The Christ was carved of wood and was life-size. Akim remembered—as a boy he had seen this Christ in the Divny Monastery; this Christ was a work of the seventeenth century. The museum keeper was drinking vodka with Christ, raising the glass to the lips of the wooden Christ. The museum keeper unfastened his Pushkin-style frockcoat, his side whiskers were tousled. The naked Christ in his crown of thorns seemed alive to Akim.

Late at night Akim's mother, Maria Klimovna, came to see him. The aunts left the room. His mother had come in her everyday house dress; she had thrown a shawl over her shoulders and come running. On her eyes his mother wore a pair of glasses held together by thread—so that she could get a better look at her son. And his mother was solemn, as at Communion. The mother embraced her son, the mother pressed her wizened breast to her son's chest, the mother ran her bony fingers through her son's hair, the mother pressed her head to her son's neck. The mother didn't even cry. She was very serious. Not trusting her eyes, she kept touching her son all over with her fingers. And she blessed him.

"Won't you come, won't you come to see us, son?" his mother asked.

The son did not answer.

"What—oh what have I lived my life for, then?"

The son knew that his father would beat his mother if he found out that she had been to see her son. The son knew that his mother sat for long hours in the darkness, when his father was asleep, thinking about him, about her son. The son knew that his mother would hide nothing from him and would say nothing at all new—the past was cursed—but a mother is a mother!—the most unique, the most wonderful, the most beautiful thing—

his mother, an ascetic, a martyr, and dear to him all her life. And the son didn't answer his mother; he said nothing to her.

The next morning the engineer Akim left. The steamer didn't leave until evening—he had to travel fifty versts by carriage in order to catch the night train. He was given a carriage and a pair of bays. The day was uncertain—one minute rain, the next sun and blue sky. The route followed the Moscow road. Mud reached the axles of the wheels and the horses' knees. They rode through dense forests; the forests were gloomy, wet, and silent. The old and taciturn coachman was perched on the box. The horses moved at a walk. Halfway along the road, when Akim had already begun to worry that he might be late for the train, they stopped to feed the horses. In the cooperative tearoom they were told that vodka was not sold there, but they got vodka from the tavern keeper across the street, the secretary of the village soviet. The coachman got a bit tight and started to talk. He tediously told the story of his life—about how he had worked for thirty years, as he put it, in the meat trade, but dropped it after the Revolution as it was no longer needed. When the coachman was completely drunk, he began to show his astonishment at the authorities: "Well, now, there you have it, how do you like that, God help us—I was thirty years in the meat trade and a commissar comes and wraps the whole thing up in three weeks, and three weeks later he cans my brother, who was in the flour trade, and my brother had specialized in his trade for thirty years too!" And it was impossible to tell if the coachman was really expressing bewilderment or if he was being derisive.—They fed the horses, set off on their way, and again were silent.

The engineer Akim was a Trotskyite, his faction had been crushed. His birthplace, his town, had become useless to him: he had set aside this week for reflection. He ought to have been thinking of the fate of the Revolution and his Party, about his own fate as a revolutionary—but these were not his thoughts now. He looked at the forest, and thought about the forest, the thickets, the marshes. He looked at the sky—and thought about the sky, the clouds, the open spaces. The horses' ribs had long been covered with foam, the horses' bellies heaved with heavy breathing. The mud on the road was impassable; lakes had collected on the road precisely because a road was there. Dusk was already falling. The forest was silent. From his thoughts about the forest, about country roads stretching thousands of versts, Akim's thoughts turned to his aunts Kapitolina and Rimma—and for the thousandth time Akim justified the Revolution. Aunt Kapitolina had led what was considered an honorable life—not a single crime in the eyes of the town, nor any sin against the town's morals—and her life had turned out to be empty and of no use to anyone. In Rimma's passport would always be—as would have been in the Virgin Mary's passport had she lived in Russia before the Revolution—the word "spinster" and "has two children": Rimma's children were her shame and her grief. But her grief became her joy, her virtue; her life was full, fulfilled . . . she, Aunt Rimma, was happy, and Aunt Kapitolina lived on the happiness of her sister, not having a life of her own. You must not fear anything, you must act—every deed, even if bitter, is happiness, but nothing—remains nothing. And Klavdia—was she not happier than her mother?—because she does not know who the father of her child is and her mother knew that she had loved a scoundrel. Akim remembered his father: it would have been better not to have known him! And then Akim suddenly realized that when thinking about his father, about Klavdia, about his aunts, he was not thinking about them but about the Revolution. And the Revolution was the beginning of life for him, and life, and its end.

The forests and roads grew dark. They came out into fields. The west had long been dying, covered in the red wounds of the sunset. They rode through fields—the same as they were five hundred years earlier. They drove into a village, trudged through the mud of the seventeenth century. Beyond the village the road led to a ravine; they crossed a bridge—beyond the bridge was a huge puddle of water that proved to be impassable. They drove into the puddle. The horses shied and came to a halt. The coachman beat the horses with his whip—the horses strained but could not move. Impassable mud lay all around—the carriage settled in the middle of the puddle, its front wheel had sunk in above the linchpin. The driver steadied himself on the box and gave the shaft horse a kick in the rear. The horse strained forward and fell, thrusting the shaft beneath him, then sank up to its halter in mud. The coachman whipped the horses until he realized that the shaft horse could not get up; then he climbed down into the mud to unharness the horse. He took a step and his leg sank knee-deep into mud—he took a step with his other foot, got stuck, couldn't pull out his leg, and his feet slipped out of his boots—his boots were left in the mud. The old man lost his balance and sat down in the puddle. And the old man burst into tears—into bitter, hysterical, helpless tears of anger and despair—this man, a specialist in the slaughter of cows and bulls.

The Trotskyite Akim missed the train, as he had missed the train of the times.

Chapter Five

The art of mahogany was an anonymous art, an art of objects. The master craftsmen became drunkards and died, but the things they made remained alive and lived on: in their presence people loved and died, in them were kept the secrets of griefs, loves, business affairs, joys. Elizabeth, Catherine—rococo, baroque. Paul is a Knight of Malta, Paul is austere, austere calm, serenity, darkly polished mahogany, green leather, black lions, griffins, gryphons. Alexander is Empire, classical, Hellas. People die, but things live on—and from the things of the past come "fluids" of antiquity, of epochs gone by. In 1928 in Moscow, in Leningrad, in provincial towns antique shops sprang up in which antiques were bought and sold—by pawnbrokers, by the State Export and Import Office, by the State Museum Fund, by museums: in 1928 there were many people who collected "fluids." The people who bought antiques after the thunders of Revolution—favoring things from the past in their own homes– inhaled the living life of dead objects. And Paul—the Knight of Malta—was highly esteemed—straight and austere, without bronze or scrolls.

The Bezdetov brothers lived in Moscow on Vladimir Dolgorukov Street—in the Zhivodyorka, as Vladimir Dolgorukov Street was called in the old days. They were antique dealers, restorers—and they were eccentrics, of course. Such people are always solitary and taciturn. They take pride in their work, like philosopers. The Bezdetov brothers lived in a cellar; they were eccentrics. They restored Pauls, Catherines, Alexanders, Nicholasses—and eccentric collectors came to them to see their antiques and their work, to talk about the past and craftsmanship, to inhale antiquity, to select something and to purchase it. If the eccentric collectors bought anything, then the purchase was celebrated with brandy poured into a decanter of Catherine's time and drunk out of glasses from the former imperial diamond service.

... Back at Skudrin Bridge nothing is happening.

The town is a medieval Russian Bruges, imperial Russia's Kamakura.

Yakov Karpovich would wake towards midnight, light the lamp, eat and read from the Bible, aloud, by heart, as he had done for the last forty years. In the morning the old man was visited by friends and petitioners—peasants—for Yakov Karpovich was a petitioner for the peasants. In those years the peasants were bewildered by the following "problematical dilemma"—as Yakov Karpovich put it—which they could not comprehend. In their failure to comprehend the problem the peasants were divided about fifty-fifty. Fifty percent of the peasants got up at three o'clock in the morning and went to bed at eleven at night, and every one of them, young and old alike, worked their fingers to the bone: if they wanted to buy a calf, they would give it a thorough going-over ten times before they bought; they dragged home any brushwood they found lying on the road; their huts, like their carts, were well kept, their cattle well fed and well cared for, just as they themselves were well fed and up to their ears in work; their taxes-in-kind and other debts were paid to the State on time; they feared the authorities—and they were thought of as enemies of the Revolution— no more and no less than that. The other fifty percent of the peasants each had a hut that the winds would blast, a scrawny cow, and a mangy sheep— they had nothing else. In spring they were given a State seed loan from the town: they ate half the seed loan since they had no grain of their own; they scattered the other half so that the ears were shouting distance apart—and

thus in the fall there was no harvest; they justified the poor crop to the
authorities by the lack of manure from their scrawny cows and mangy
sheep; the State relieved them of taxes-in-kind and the seed loan
repayments—and they were considered friends of the Revolution. The
"enemy" peasants asserted that about thirty-five percent of the "friends"
were drunkards (and here, of course, it is difficult to establish whether
poverty resulted from drunkenness or drunkenness from poverty), about
five percent had bad luck (or perhaps didn't get help!), and about sixty
percent were loafers, blabbermouths, philosophers, idlers, good-for-
nothings. Throughout the village the "enemies" were pressured in every
possible way in an attempt to convert them into "friends" and at the same
time deprive them of their ability to pay the taxes-in-kind, while converting
their huts into such a state that the winds would blast through. Yakov
Karpovich wrote moving, ineffective petitions. One of Yakov Karpovich's
visitors was Vasily Vasilievich, an enemy of the Fatherland, a man who had
gone mad. Before the Revolution Vasily Vasilievich had been a clerk of the
District Council; he had read every book on agronomy that he could lay his
hands on. In 1920 he went to work on the land. He was given one
desyatina[11] of land: he went to his land, a man of forty, with only bare
hands and an ardent heart. In 1923 at the All-Russian Agricultural
Exhibition he won a gold medal on paper and words of praise from the
People's Commissar of Agriculture for his cow and milk and for his work
as chairman of the dairy collective; in the spring of 1924 he was offered
forty *desyatins* of land on which to build a model farm—he took twenty—
and by 1926 he had seventeen cows; then he hired a farmhand and that was
the end of him—he had become a *kulak*;[12] by 1927 he was left with only five
desyatins and three cows—the rest he had paid out in assessments, loans
and taxes. In the fall of 1928 he gave it all up and decided to return to town
to his job as a clerk, despite the fact that in the fall of 1928—on rafts
crossing the Volga, on country roads, in taverns and in marketplaces the
peasants talked figures: if you sold a pood of rye at the cooperative, you'd
get one ruble eighty kopecks; if you bought a pood of rye at the same
cooperative—with a coupon—it was three rubles sixty kopecks; and if you
sold the pood at the street market, you got six rubles. Vasily Vasilievich
returned to town and went mad, not having the strength to break away
from a *kulak* way of life. In these parts villages and hamlets are sparse—
there are mainly forests and marshes.

Yakov Karpovich had lost his sense of time and his fear of life. Apart
from petitions that nobody had any use for he wrote proclamations and
philosophical treatises. Yakov Karpovich was depressingly, nauseatingly
vile.

The town is a medieval Russian Bruges and imperial Russia's
Kamakura. In this town Tsarevich Dmitri was murdered in the sixteenth
century. It was then that Boris Godunov took down the bell from the
Church of the Savior in the Kremlin, the same bell that the priest Ogurets

had struck to announce the murder. Boris Godunov had the bell sentenced to death—he tore out its ear and tongue and had it flogged in the town square along with other townspeople, and he exiled it to Siberia, to Tobolsk. Today the bells are dying above the town.

Yakov Karpovich Skudrin is alive—nothing happens in his life.

In 1744 the leader of a caravan to China, Gerasim Kirillovich Lobradovsky, upon arriving at the Kyakhta outpost, took into the caravan a certain silversmith, Andrei Kursin, a native of the town of Yaransk. Kursin, on Lobradovsky's orders, journeyed to Peking where he was to learn from the Chinese the secret of making china—*portselen,* as it was called in those days. In Peking with the help of Russian "apprentices of ensign rank" Kursin bribed a master craftsman from the Chinese Emperor's porcelain works for a thousand *lan,* that is, two thousand Russian rubles of the time. This Chinese demonstrated the art of making porcelain to Kursin in abandoned shrines thirty-five *li* from Peking. On his return to St. Petersburg Gerasim Kirillovich Lobradovsky brought Kursin with him, and wrote a report to the Empress about the secrets of porcelain-making that he had brought from China. An imperial edict ensued, presented to Baron Cherkassov by Count Razumovsky, which commanded that the new arrivals be sent to Tsarskoe Selo. Kursin received great honors, but his trickery did him no good, for it became clear that in fact the Chinese had deceived Andrei Kursin, had "acted perfidiously," as it was reported at the time in a secret memorandum. Kursin returned home to Yaranksk, fearing a flogging.—At the same time, on February 1, 1744, Baron Korf concluded a secret agreement with Christoph Konrad Hunger, a master craftsman in porcelain, who had served his apprenticeship, so he said, and mastered the craft at the Meissen Works in Saxony. Hunger concluded a deal with Baron Korf and secretly came to Russia, to St. Petersburg, on a Russian frigate. Hunger began building a porcelain factory, which subsequently became the Imperial Porcelain Works; he conducted experiments, at the same time indulging in drunken brawls and cudgel fights together with his Russian assistant Vinogradov. He continued this fruitless activity until 1748, when he was banished from Russia for charlatanry and incompetence. Hunger was replaced by a Russian mining engineer—Peter's protege—Dmitri Ivanovich Vinogradov, a dissolute drunkard and a man of great talent; and it was he who built up the Russian porcelain industry in such a way that Russian porcelain was not copied from anywhere but was the invention of Vinogradov. Nevertheless, Andrei Kursin of Yaransk, who was roundly deceived by the Chinese, and the German Christoph Hunger, who roundly deceived everyone with his Europe, must be considered the fathers of Russian porcelain. And Russian porcelain had its golden age. The masters—of the Imperial Works, of the works of Old Gardner, of *les vieux*—Popov, Batenin, Miklashevsky,

Yusupov, Kornilov, Safronov, Sabanin—flourished during serfdom in the golden age. And, in the tradition of Dmitri Vinogradov, the business of porcelain-making attracted amateurs and eccentrics, drunkards and misers; the factories were run by the princes Yusupov, the Vsevolozhskys, a family of ancient lineage, and the eccentric Bogorodsky merchant, Nikita Khrapunov, who was flogged on the orders of Alexander I for making a statuette which depicted a monk bent under the weight of a wheat sheaf, in which was hidden a young peasant girl. All the masters stole secrets from each other—Yusupov, from the Imperial Works; Kiselev, from Popov; and Safronov spied on secret processes late at night, through a hole in an attic, like a thief. These masters and eccentrics created beautiful objects. Russian porcelain is a marvelous art, an adornment to the Earthly Globe.

Translated by A. R. Tulloch   *Yamskoe Pole—the Volkov House*
                                                  15 January 1929

Notes

1. A euphemism for an insane asylum.

2. The fool Ivan Yakovlevich Koreisha did live in a Moscow asylum for many years. The scholarly works referred to are fictitious.

3. Kamakura, a religious center in Japan in medieval times, was severely damaged by an earthquake in 1923.

4. One verst equals 3500 feet; the distances mentioned here are approximately 135 and 35 miles.

5. Former members of certain so-called "exploiter" classes, such as landlords and capitalists, were deprived of the right to vote after the Revolution.

6. A secular ceremony introduced after the Revolution which was to replace Baptism.

7. Pilnyak coined this word. Vera Reck suggests that *okhlomon* is derived from the Greek *ochlos* (mob) and *monos* (alone); thus, "alone from the mob," or "outcast."

8. A. D. Kastalsky (1856-1926), composer, folklorist, historian of Russian choral music.

9. A proverbial expression.

10. A study widely used in the mid 1920s.

11. 2.7 acres.

12. A name given to peasants who in the opinion of the Bolsheviks were prosperous enough to be classified as "village capitalists."

ANDREI PLATONOV

Andrei Platonov (Klimentov, 1899-1951) was born in Voronezh to the family of a metalworker. He was inclined toward both engineering and literature from an early age, and published both poetry and journalistic pieces while still young. He joined the Party in 1920, left it in 1921, and spent the first part of his life as a specialiast in irrigation and land reclamation, playing an important part in the trade unions. His experiences in Tambov province showed him how a backward area could easily defeat—or pervert—science, and his time there provided him with much material for his works, in which science is often portrayed as a double-edged sword.

His first major collection of stories, *The Epiphany Locks* (1927), revealed both an unusual style and ideology, although a kinship with both Pilnyak and Zamyatin may be seen. One of Platonov's constant themes is how language can determine consciousness and vice-versa. The degradation of the Russian language is a major concern, as semi-literate characters try to speak the language of "building socialism," to the point where they lose humanity. The men of science, on the other hand, are often seen as supermen who have no humanity to begin with.

In 1929 Platonov was attacked by RAPP for the story "Makar the Doubtful." He was silenced for a time, then managed to publish off and on through the thirties, although his major works, *Chevengur* (begun 1929) and *The Foundation Pit* (c. 1930) were published only in the West, some twenty years after his death. The collections of Platonov stories which then appeared in the Soviet Union were a revelation to the new generation, and he quickly became a major influence on young writers.

MAKAR THE DOUBTFUL

Amidst the rest of the laboring masses there lived two citizens of the State: an ordinary peasant, Makar Ganushkin, and a more distinguished one, Comrade Lev Chumovoi, who was smarter by far than anyone else in the village and because of his intelligence he supervised the progress of the people forward in a straight line towards the communal weal. As a result the entire population of the village would say of Lev Chumovoi whenever he was passing by anywhere, "There goes our leader; see him walking. There'll be measures of some sort taken tomorrow—you just wait . . . A real smart head he has; it's only that his hands are hollow. He lives by his bare brain . . ."

Makar, on the other hand, just as any other peasant, liked migrant jobs better than plowing and was concerned with spectacles rather than bread, because he had, according to Comrade Chumovoi, an empty head.

Without obtaining Comrade Chumovoi's permission, Makar once organized a public spectacle—a merry-go-round pushed round about itself by the might of the wind. The public swarmed to Makar's merry-go-round like a dense thundercloud and awaited the storm which might start the

Andrei Platonov.

merry-go-round turning. The storm, however, seemed to be long in coming, the people stood about doing nothing, and in the meantime Chumovoi's colt ran off into the meadows and got lost there in the damp grounds. If the village community had been at leisure, it would have caught Chumovoi's colt at once and would not have allowed Chumovoi to undergo a material loss, but Makar had distracted the community and thus helped inflict a loss on Chumovoi's property.

Chumovoi himself did not chase the colt but approached Makar, who was silently pining for his storm, and said, "Here you are distracting people, and I haven't got anybody to retrieve my colt..."

Makar awoke from his reverie because something dawned on him. He was unable to think, having an empty head above clever hands, but on the other hand he could immediately sense things.

"Don't be sad," said Makar to Comrade Chumovoi, "I will make you a self-driving machine."

"How?" asked Chumovoi, because he did not know how to make a self-driving machine with his hollow hands.

"From hoops and ropes," answered Makar, not thinking, but sensing the pulling power and the rotation of those ropes and hoops to be.

"Then do it quickly," said Chumovoi, "or else I'll make you legally responsible for illegal spectacles."

But Makar was not thinking of the fine he'd have to pay—being unable to think—instead he was recalling where it was that he had seen iron, and could not remember where, since the whole village was put together from superficial materials: clay, straw, wood and hemp.

No storm came, the merry-go-round did not move, and Makar returned home.

At home Makar drank some water to drown his sorrow and felt the hard taste of that water.

"That must be the reason why we have no iron," surmised Makar, "it's because we drink it all down with the water."

At night Makar climbed down into a dry well which had fallen into disuse, and lived inside it for a day and a night looking for iron under the moist sand. On the second day the peasants dragged Makar up under the direction of Chumovoi, who was afraid that a citizen might perish outside the front line of socialist construction. Makar was difficult to lift—it turned out that he was holding brown chunks of iron ore in his hands. The men lifted him out and cursed him for the heavy weight while Comrade Chumovoi promised to lay an additional fine on Makar for creating a public disturbance.

Makar, however, ignored him, and in a week's time made iron from the ore, using the stove after his woman had finished baking bread loaves in it. How he managed to melt the ore nobody knows, because Makar acted with his clever hands and his taciturn head. A day later Makar fashioned an iron wheel and then another iron wheel, but neither wheel turned by itself—

one had to roll them with one's own hands.

Chumovoi came to Makar and asked him, "Have you made a self-driving machine to replace my colt?"

"No," said Makar, "I was thinking that they would roll by themselves, but they don't."

"What did you deceive me for, you elemental head!" exlaimed Chumovoi in an official voice. "In that case—make me a colt!"

I don't have any flesh, or I'd make one," declined Makar.

"Oh, and how did you make iron out of clay?" remembered Chumovoi.

"I don't know," replied Makar, "I don't have any memory."

Here Chumovoi took offense.

"Oh, so you're going to conceal a discovery of national economic significance, you scoundrel of an individualist! You're not a man, you're a private property owner! I'm going to fine you head to toe—that'll teach you how to think!"

Makar became submissive, "But I don't think at all, Comrade Chumovoi, I'm an empty-headed man."

"Then keep your hands in check, don't make things you don't realize," Comrade Chumovoi reproached Makar.

"If I could have a head like yours, Comrade Chumovoi, then I would think too," confessed Makar.

"That's exactly right!" confirmed Chumovoi. "But there's only one such head in the whole village and you have to obey me."

And here Chumovoi fined Makar from head to toe, so that Makar was forced to set out for Moscow to earn some money to pay this fine, leaving the merry-go-round and his farm belongings to the zealous solicitude of Comrade Chumovoi.

* * *

Makar had last gone train-riding nine years ago, in 1919. At that time they let him ride for free because Makar immediately struck them as a hired field-hand, and they did not even ask him for any documents. "Ride on," the proletarian guard used to say to him, "we like you, because you don't have a stitch."

This time Makar got into the train just as he did nine years ago, without asking anybody's leave. The scarcity of people and the number of open doors surprised him. Nevertheless Makar did not sit inside the train, but between the cars, so as to watch the work of the wheels in motion. The wheels started to turn and the train set out for the core of the nation—for Moscow.

The train was going faster than any average horse. The prairie plains kept running toward the train and would not stop coming.

"They're going to work the machine to death this way," said Makar, feeling sorry for the wheels. "Indeed, what a lot of things there are in this world since there is so much space and emptiness in it!"

Makar's hands were resting, their free clever strength flowing into his empty, spacious head, and he began to think. Makar sat between the cars and thought as well as he could. However, Makar did not sit there long. An unarmed guard went by and asked him for his ticket. Makar had no ticket with him since, as he supposed, a firm Soviet rule had been established and was now giving free rides to all the needy. The controller-guard told Makar to avoid trouble and get off the train at the next railway station, which would have a cafeteria, so that, heaven forbid, Makar should not die of hunger in some deserted spot in the middle of nowhere. Makar saw that the government was disposed to take good care of him, since it did not simply kick him off, but offered him a cafeteria, and he thanked the train official.

All the same, Makar did not get off at the small-town station, although the train stopped there to unload envelopes and post-cards from the mail car. Makar remembered a certain technical concept and stayed on the train in order to help it on its way.

"The heavier a thing is," compared Makar, imagining stone and feathers, "the farther it flies when you fling it; in the same way, I will be like an extra brick on the train, so that the train might rush to Moscow."

Not wishing to offend the train guard, Makar climbed all the way into the bowels of the machine, underneath the car, and there he lay down to rest, listening to the quivering speed of the wheels. From the tranquility and the sight of the railroad sand Makar fell into a deep sleep and dreamed that he was torn away from the ground and was flying along with the cold wind. This luxurious sensation made him pity the people who had remained back on earth.

"Seryozhka! You're not supposed to throw bolts while they're hot!"

Makar woke up from these words and touched his neck to check whether his body and all his innermost life were safe and sound.

"It's all right!" yelled Seryozhka from afar. "It's not far to Moscow: it won't burn!"

The train was standing at a station. Workers were checking the car axles and swearing under their breath.

Makar climbed out from under the car and saw in the distance the very center of the whole nation—the capital city of Moscow.

"Now I will make it on foot just as well!" Makar realized. "Chances are the train will manage to get there without the extra weight!"

And Makar set out in the direction of the towers, the churches and the awe-inspiring buildings—into the city of scientific and technological miracles in pursuit of a living for himself.

* * *

Having unloaded himself from the train, Makar set out toward the visible Moscow, feeling an interest in that central city. So as not to lose his way, Makar walked along the railroad tracks and was surprised at the numerous station platforms. Near the platforms grew woods of pine and fir and in the woods stood small wooden houses. The trees were sparse and underneath them candy wrappers, wine bottles, sausage skins and other wasted products lay scattered. Grass did not grow here, being oppressed by man, and the trees for the most part also suffered, growing very little. Makar's understanding of this kind of nature was vague, "Maybe some special scoundrels live here, for even the plants die from being near them! This is extremely sad, that man should live and create a desert around himself! What happened to science and technology?"

Stroking his chest with regret, Makar walked on. On another station platform they were unloading empty milkcans from the train and putting milk-filled cans into the train. Makar stopped, arrested by a thought, "Again there's no technology!" said Makar, defining the situation out loud. "It is right to carry the milk-filled containers, since there are also children in the city who await their milk. But why use the machine to carry empty cans? That's just a needless waste of technology and those containers take up a lot of room!"

Makar walked up to the manager who was in charge of the cans and advised him to build a milk-pipe from here all the way to Moscow, in order not to waste train-power on empty milk containers.

The milk manager heard Makar out—he respected people who represented the masses—however, he advised Makar to apply to Moscow: that's where all the wisest people are, and they are in charge of all the remedies.

Makar became annoyed, "But it's you, not they, who does the carrying of the milk! They only drink it, they cannot see how extra technology is being wasted needlessly!"

The manager explained, "My business is to assign loads: I am an executive, not an inventor of pipes."

Then Makar left him alone and walked, doubtful, all the way up to Moscow.

In Moscow it was late morning. Tens of thousands of people rushed along the streets like peasants hurrying to gather the harvest.

"What kind of work are they going to do?" Makar stood thinking in the thick of the crowd. "They must have mighty factories here which clothe all the far-off villagers and provide them with shoes!"

Makar glanced at his boots and said "Thank you!" to the running people; without them he would have been barefoot and undressed. Almost all of the people were carrying leather bags under their arms—that's probably where they kept the shoe-nails and cobbler's thread.

"Only why are they running, wasting strength?" puzzled Makar. "Better that they should work at home and food could be carted around to their houses on a moving platform!"

However, the people continued running, climbing into tram-cars which were so overloaded that they sagged, and they did not spare their bodies for the sake of useful labor. This satisfied Makar altogether. "These are good people," he thought, "it's very hard for them to make their way to the workshops, and yet they want to get to work so badly!"

Makar was pleased with the tram-cars because they moved by themselves and because the driver in the front car sat very lightly, as if he were not driving a thing. Makar also got into a tram-car without any effort, being pushed inside by the hasty people from behind. The car moved smoothly, the invisible power of the engine growling beneath the floor; and Makar listened to it and sympathized with it.

"The poor hard-working thing!" thought Makar of the engine. "How it pulls the car and strains itself. But it's good that it carries useful people to one spot, thereby preserving live feet!"

A woman—the tram-car hostess—was passing out coupons to the people, but Makar, not wishing to trouble the hostess-woman, refused to take one. "It's all right!" said Makar, and walked by.

People yelled to the hostess, asking her for something or other "on demand" and she would agree. Wishing to check what was being handed out here, Makar also spoke up, "Hostess, give me something on demand too!"

The hostess pulled a cord and the tram instantly stopped in place.

"Get out; here you are on demand!" said the citizens to Makar, and they forced him out by their pressure.

Makar came out into the open air.

It was the kind of air proper for a capital city: it smelled of seething gasoline fumes and dust from cast-iron tram-brakes.

"Where do you have the very central spot of the whole nation around here?" Makar asked a chance passerby.

The man pointed with his hand and threw his cigarette into a street garbage can. Makar approached the can and also spat into it in order to have the right to use everything there was in the city.

The houses were so bulky and towering that Makar felt sorry for the Soviet government: it must be very difficult maintaining such a housing enterprise.

At a crossing a policeman raised a red stick while making a fist with his left hand towards a wagoner who was driving a load of rye flour.

"They have no respect for rye flour hereabouts," concluded Makar, "here they feed on white buns."

"Where's the center around here?" he asked the policeman.

The policeman pointed towards a slope and informed Makar, "Near the Bolshoi Theater, in the ravine."

Makar walked down the hill and found himself between two lawns with flower beds. On one edge of the square stood a wall and on the other— a house with pillars. These pillars were holding up four cast-iron horses, and the pillars could have been made a bit thinner because the horses were not that heavy.

Makar began looking about the square for some kind of a rod with a red flag, which would signify the middle of the central city and the very core of the nation itself, but there was no such rod anywhere: instead there was a stone with an inscription. Makar leaned on the stone so that he might stand in the very center and fill himself with respectful feelings towards himself and his country. Makar sighed happily and felt hungry. Then he walked toward the river and saw the construction site of an enormous building.

"What are they building here?" he asked a passerby.

"An eternal building out of iron, concrete, steel and bright glass!" replied the passerby.

Makar decided to visit it so that he might work awhile on the construction and get something to eat.

A guard stood at the gate. The guardsman asked, "Whad-duya want, fella?"

"I'd like to do some work; I've grown so skinny," announced Makar.

"How can you work here when you've come without any employment coupon?" asked the guardsman sadly.

At this a stone-mason came up and stopped to listen to Makar.

"Go to our barracks and to the communal mess; the guys will feed you there," said the mason helpfully to Makar. "As for working here, you cannot join us right away: you're living free, and that means you're nobody. First you have to register in a workers' union and go through class-background investigation."

And so Makar went to the barracks to eat from the communal pot in order to sustain life in himself for a better fortune in the future.

* * *

Makar settled down nicely at the construction site of that Moscow building which had been called eternal by the chance passerby. First he ate his fill of black and nourishing mush in the workers' barracks and then went out to take a good look at the construction work. The earth was indeed stricken with pits everywhere, people were bustling about, machines whose names Makar did not know were battering piles into the ground. Concrete mush was pouring out through a trough and other industrial events were also taking place right before one's eyes. It was evident that a house was being built, though there was no knowing for whom. Makar was not even interested in knowing who would get what—he was interested in technology as the future well-being for all people. The boss of Makar's native village, Comrade Lev Chumovoi, would naturally be interested in the assignment of housing space in the future building instead of becoming wrapped up in a cast-iron pile hammer, but then Makar only had learning in his hands, none in his head, so all he could think of was doing something.

Makar walked all about the construction area and saw that the work was going quickly and well. However, something inside Makar was surging dismally though he did not know what it was yet. He walked into the middle of the construction work and surveyed the whole scene of labor: there was obviously something lacking, something was missing, but he could not define it. It was just that a certain conscientious workingman's sorrow was growing inside Makar's chest. From sorrow, and from having had a full meal, Makar found a quiet spot and went to sleep there. In his dreams Makar saw a lake, some birds, a forgotten village copse, but the necessary thing, the thing which was lacking at the construction site—that Makar did not see. Then Makar woke and suddenly discovered the deficiency at the construction site: the workers were packing the concrete into iron casts to make a wall. But there is no technology in that, only senseless labor! To do it according to technology one must send the concrete up in pipes, while the worker merely holds the pipe in place without tiring, thus not allowing the festive force of the mind to escape into the common hands of unskilled labor.

Makar at once went to look for the chief Moscow office of scientific technology. Such an office was located in a sturdy fireproof building which stood in one of the city's dales. There Makar found a young lad standing at the door and told him that he had invented a construction hose. The fellow heard him out and even asked about some things which Makar himself did not know and then sent Makar up the stairs to a chief clerk. This clerk was an educated engineer, yet for some reason he had chosen to write on paper without touching construction work with his hands. Makar told him about the hose too.

"Buildings should not be built, they should be cast," said Makar to the learned clerk.

The clerk listened to him and concluded, "And by what means will you prove, Comrade Inventor, that your hose is more economical than the usual method of concrete construction?"

"By the means that I feel it very clearly," asserted Makar.

The clerk pondered something in secret and sent Makar to the end of the corridor, "There indigent inventors are given a ruble for food and a train ticket back home."

Makar received the ruble but refused to accept the ticket because he had decided to live forward, without turning back.

In another room Makar was given a document for the workers' union so that he might get special assistance there as a man from the masses and a hose-inventor. Makar thought that at the union they would at once give him money for making the hose and so joyfully went there.

The workers' union was situated in an even more enormous building than the technological office. For about two hours Makar roamed in its caverns in search of the manager in charge of the massive people, as was laid down in his document, but the manager was not to be found in his working place—he was off somewhere taking care of the other laboring masses. As the sun was setting the manager came, ate some fried eggs and read Makar's document through the help of his assistant—a rather nice-looking, modern-type young girl with a long braid. This young girl went to the cashier and brought one more ruble for Makar, and Makar signed a receipt for it as an unemployed unskilled laborer. They gave Makar back his document. There was now written on it among other letters: "Comrade Lopin, help this member of our union to arrange his hose invention in an industrial way."

Makar remained pleased with this and the next day he went to look for the industrial way on which he expected to see Comrade Lopin. Neither the policeman nor any of the passersby knew anything about such a way and Makar decided to find it independently. Posters and red satin cloths were hung out on the streets, displaying the name of the very institution that Makar needed. It was clearly stated on the posters that the whole proletariat must stand firmly on the way to industrial development. This enlightened Makar at once: first he must find the proletariat, underneath the proletariat would be the way, and Comrade Lopin ought to be found somewhere nearby.

"Comrade policeman," demanded Makar, "show me the road to the proletariat."

The policeman took out a book, found the proletariat's address in it, and told grateful Makar what that address was.

* * *

Makar walked across Moscow towards the proletariat and wondered at the city's power, running in busses, tram-cars, and in the live feet of the crowd.

"You need lots of grub to feed such bodily movement!" reasoned Makar inside his head, which knew how to think when his hands were not occupied.

Puzzled and saddened, Makar finally reached the house, the location of which the policeman had pointed out to him. This house turned out to be a free night lodginghouse where the poor class lay down its head during the night. Before, in pre-revolutionary days, the poor class simply lay down its head on the ground, and the rains fell on it, the moon shone over it, the stars passed, the winds blew, while the head lay, grew chill and slept, being tired. But nowadays the head of the poor class reclined on a pillow beneath a ceiling and the iron covering of a roof, and the night wind of nature no longer disturbed the hair on the head of the poor man who had once upon a time lain right on the surface of the terrestrial ball.

Makar saw several neat new houses and remained pleased with the Soviet authority.

"Not a bad power!" appraised Makar. "Only it must not get out of hand, because it is ours!"

There was an office in the night lodginghouse, as there was in every Moscow residential house. Without an office, apparently, the end of the world would set in at once, while the office clerks gave a slow but accurate rhythm to the life process. Makar had a respect even for clerks.

"Let them live!" decided Makar on the subject of clerks. "They must be doing some sort of thinking since they get a salary, and since they are thinking because of duty, they will probably become intelligent people, and those are the kind of people we need!"

"What do you want?" the lodginghouse official asked Makar.

"I need the proletariat," Makar informed him.

"Which layer?" the official inquired.

Makar did not start to ponder—he already knew what he wanted.

"The lower," said Makar, "The lower level is the thickest, it has more people; that's where the real mass is!"

"Aha!" understood the official. "In that case you have to wait for the evening: you'll go spend the night with the largest bunch that comes—that will be either the seasonal workers..."

"I'd like to go with the ones who are building socialism itself," pleaded Makar.

"Aha!" said the official, again understanding. "Then you want the ones who are building the new buildings?"

But this time Makar grew doubtful.

"Why, before, when there wasn't any Lenin, they used to build buildings too. What kind of socialism is there in an empty building?"

The official also grew thoughtful, all the more because he himself did not know for certain in what guise socialism should appear—would an amazing joy come with socialism, and what would it be like?

"They did build buildings before," the official conceded. "Only then scoundrels used to live in them, while now I am giving you a coupon for spending the night in a new building."

"Right," Makar agreed happily. "That means you're a true helper of the Soviet power."

Makar took the coupon and sat down on a heap of bricks which had been left over from some construction job and lay homeless.

"And look here..." Makar reasoned, "there's this brick lying under me, it was the proletariat who made this same brick and labored hard over it—Soviet rule is too limited if it can't watch its own property!"

Makar sat on the bricks until evening and watched things happening in sequence: the sun fading away, the lights coming on, the sparrows abandoning the manure pile and going to their rest.

Finally the proletarians began appearing: some with bread, others without it, some sick, some tired, but all nice-looking from long toil and kind with that kindness which comes from extreme weariness.

Makar waited until the proletariat had made itself comfortable on the government cots and had a chance to catch its breath after the day's construction work. Then Makar walked boldly into the sleeping hall, and taking a position in the middle of the room, announced, "Comrade laboring workers! You are living here in our own city of Moscow, amid the very central force of the State, but meanwhile you have disorder and waste of valuable material going on here..."

The proletariat stirred on its cots.

"Mitry!" said someone's broad voise hoarsely. "Give that guy a bit of a shove to make him normal..."

Makar was not offended, because it was the proletariat and not some hostile force that lay before him.

"Not everything has been invented here yet," Makar went on. "Milk cans are being transported in valuable train-cars when the cans are empty, when the milk has already been drunk. For this a pipe and a piston pump would have been enough... The same goes for building houses and barns—they should be cast whole by means of a hose, and you build them bit by bit... I've thought up this hose and I'm giving it to you free so that socialism and other good arrangements might come about sooner..."

"What hose?" uttered the same hoarse voice of the unseen proletariat.

"My own hose," affirmed Makar.

The proletariat was silent at first but then someone's clear voice cried out certain words from the far corner and Makar heard them like the wind, "It isn't force that matters to us—we'll build buildings the hard way, so what, it's the soul which we care about. If you're a man, the important thing is heart, not buildings. All of us here work on accounts, we conserve labor, we belong to trade unions, we have recreation in clubs, but we pay no attention to each other—we do not take care of each other—we've left that up to the law... If you're an inventor, why don't you make some invention for the soul?"

Makar's spirits fell at once. He had invented all kinds of things, but had never touched upon the soul, and now it appeared that this was the most necessary invention of all for the people who lived here. Makar lay down on a government bunk and grew still from doubt that all his life had been spent on nonproletarian work.

Makar did not sleep long, because in his sleep he began feeling tormented. And then his torment turned into a dream: he dreamed of a mountain or a height on which there stood a scientific man. Meanwhile, Makar lay at the foot of that mountain like a drowsy fool and stared at the scientific man, waiting for either a word or a deed from him. But that man stood motionless and silent, not seeing the grief-stricken Makar and thinking only about the overall scheme, not about the individual man Makar. The face of the most learned man was illuminated by the glow of a distant life for the masses which was spread out far before him, and his eyes were horrible and dead from standing on the elevation and staring too far into the distance. The scientific man remained silent while Makar lay in his sleep and grieved.

"What must I do in life to be useful both to myself and to others?" asked Makar, and grew still from horror.

The scientific man was as mute and unresponsive as before and millions of living fates were reflected in his dead eyes.

Then in astonishment Makar began crawling up the slope over the dead stony ground. Three times fear before the motionlessly-scientific one seized him and three times the fear was conquered by curiosity. If Makar had been an intelligent man, he would not have gone clambering up that slope, but he was a backward person, having only a pair of inquisitive hands beneath an imponderable head. Thus by the force of his inquisitive foolishness Makar climbed all the way up to the highly educated one and lightly touched his obese, enormous body. Under his touch the strange body stirred as if it were alive, and then at once fell down on Makar, because it was dead.

Makar woke up from a blow and saw the lodginghouse overseer standing over him and touching him on the head with a kettle to wake him up.

Makar sat up on his cot and saw a pock-marked proletarian washing himself out of a saucer without letting a single drop of water go to waste. Makar was surprised at this method of washing oneself thoroughly with a handful of water and asked the pockmarked one, "Everyone has left for work—how is it you're standing there alone and washing yourself?"

The pitted one rubbed his wet face in the pillow, dried off, and replied, "There are lots of proletarians who work, but only a few of those who think—I have assigned myself to think for everyone. Did you understand what I said, or are you silent from being stupid and oppressed?"

"From being sad and doubtful," answered Makar.

"Aha, in that case let's go: come with me and we'll think for everyone's sake," declared the pitted one, figuring it all out.

And Makar got up to accompany the pockmarked man, whose name was Peter, in order to find his vocation.

Toward Makar and Peter walked a great variety of women, dressed in tight clothing, which indicated that the women would prefer to be naked: there were also men, but they used a more comfortable covering for their bodies. Great thousands of other men and women, careful of their flesh, were riding in cars and carriages, and also in barely budging tram-cars which squeaked from the live human weight, but suffered patiently. Both the riding and the walking people were pressing urgently forward with scientific expressions on their faces, which made them basically similar to that gigantic and powerful man whom Makar had contemplated from afar in his dream. As a result of observing exclusively scientific and literate individuals, Makar experienced a sinking in his inner feelings. He glanced at Peter for help; what if Peter too was only a scientific man with his gaze set into the distance?

"I bet you know all the sciences and you see everything too far ahead?" asked Makar timidly.

Peter concentrated his consciousness.

"Me? I strain myself to be something like Ilych—Lenin: I look far and near and wide and deep and high."

"Oh, yes, that's it!" said Makar, relieved. "Because the other day I saw a huge scientific man: he doesn't look anywhere except far off while next to him—about two yards away—one individual person is lying and suffering without help."

"No wonder!" uttered Peter intellectually. "That man stands on a slope, that's why it seems to him that everything is far off and not a damn thing close by! While at the same time another man looks only beneath his feet, scared of stubbing his toes on a lump and killing himself and considering himself righteous, while the masses are not interested in living at a slow pace. We're not afraid of lumpy ground, brother!"

"Our people are pretty well shod nowadays!" confirmed Makar.

But Peter continued with his own thoughts, refusing to be distracted by anything.

"Have you ever seen the Communist Party?"

"No, Comrade Peter, nobody's ever shown it to me! I've seen Comrade Chumovoi in the village, though!"

"We've got a full collection of Chumovoi's kind here as well. No, I'm telling you about the pure Party, which looks clear and straight, right into the heart of things. When I find myself at a meeting of the Party, I always feel like a fool."

"Why so, Comrade Peter? You look almost like a scientific man yourself."

"It's because my mind eats up my body. I want food, and the Party says, 'Let's build some factories first, because bread grows poorly without iron.' Do you understand me, what this is all about?"

"I understand," replied Makar.

Those who build machines and factories—he understood them at once just as if he were a scientist. Makar had observed clay-and-straw villages from the day of his birth and had no faith whatsoever in their future without fiery engines.

"See then," announced Peter. "And you say you didn't like that man the other day! We don't like him either, the Party and I: he was created by stupid capitalism, and we're pushing suchlike and similar persons gradually down the slope!"

"I feel something too, only I don't know what it is!" said Makar, expressing himself.

"Well, since you don't know what it is, then follow my directions in life; otherwise you're sure to take a nose dive off the narrow line."

Makar let his gaze wander, and watching the Moscow people, thought, "The people here are well-fed; they all have clean, neat faces, they live in plenty—by rights they ought to be multiplying, and yet there don't seem to be many children about."

Makar mentioned this to Peter.

"Over here, instead of nature they have culture," explained Peter. "Here people live in families without multiplying, here they eat without producing labor..."

"How is that?" said Makar in surprise.

"Just like that," the knowledgeable Peter told him. "Sometimes a man will write out a single thought on a certificate-paper, and for that he and his entire family get fed for a whole year and a half... And someone else doesn't even write anything, just exists as an example for others."

Makar and Peter walked about until evening; they inspected the Moscow River, the streets, the textile stores, and a desire to eat grew in them.

"Let's have dinner at the police station," said Peter.

Makar went along; he figured that one gets fed at police stations.

"I'll do the talking while you keep quiet and act somewhat pained," said Peter, warning Makar beforehand.

At the station there were burglars, vagrants, people-beasts, and nameless miserable persons. Facing them all sat an officer on duty and received people squarely head-on. Some of them he sent to the jailhouse, some of them to the hospital, and others he rejected and sent away.

When it was Peter and Makar's turn, Peter said, "Comrade superior, I've caught you a loony on the street and brought him here by the hand."

"What kind of a loony is he?" inquired the officer on duty. "What has he disrupted in a public place?"

"Nothing," said Peter candidly, "he's just walking around agitatedly, but then one day he'll go and kill somebody. The bringing him to law won't be much use... Prevention is the best method of combatting criminal activity. So here I have prevented a crime."

"That makes sense!" agreed the officer. "I'll refer him to the psychopathic institute for a general examination..."

The policeman wrote out the certificate and grew depressed, "But there's nobody to take you there—all the men are out..."

"Let me lead him there," suggested Peter. "I'm a normal man myself, it's he who is the loony one."

"Get going!" said the policeman, cheering up, and handed the piece of paper to Peter.

Peter and Makar got to the institute for the mentally ill in an hour's time. Peter said that he was assigned by the police to accompany a dangerous fool and could not leave him for a single moment, and that the fool had not had anything to eat and would turn violent any minute.

"Go to the kitchen, they'll give you something to eat there," the kind caretaker-nurse directed them.

"He eats a lot," Peter demurred. "He needs a pot of cabbage soup and two bowls of mush. Better have it brought over here, or he might belch into the common cauldron."

The nurse gave official instructions. A triple serving of tasty food was brought for Makar, and Peter had his fill along with Makar.

In a short while a doctor received Makar and began questioning him about such circumspect ideas that Makar, having led an ignorant life, answered the doctor's questions like a madman. At that the doctor examined and found that there was surplus blood swelling in his heart.

"We'll have to keep him here for a check-up," decided the doctor.

So Makar and Peter remained in the mental hospital for the night. In the evening they went to the reading room and Peter began reading Lenin's books aloud to Makar. "Our administrative offices are crap," read Peter from the works of Lenin, while Makar listened, amazed at the accuracy of Lenin's mind. "Our laws are crap. We're good at giving instructions, but bad at carrying them out. In our administrative offices are people who are hostile to us, while some of our comrades have turned into pompous courtiers and are doing their work like nincompoops..."

The other mentally disturbed persons also listened avidly to Lenin— they had not known until then that Lenin knew everything.

"That's right!" assented the workers and peasants whose souls were sick.

"We must have more workers and peasants in our institutions," the pock-marked Peter read on. "Socialism must be built by the hands of the man from the masses, not by the bureaucratic pieces of paper issued by our administrative offices. And I do not lose hope that one day we shall be most deservedly hanged for all this..."

"You see?" said Peter to Makar. "Bureaucratic institutions could tire out even Lenin, and all we do is walk and lie around. Here's the whole Revolution for you written down live... I am going to steal this book from here, because this is an institution, and tomorrow you and I will go to any office and say that we are workers and peasants. You and I will sit down in some administrative office and start thinking for the good of the nation."

After reading this, Makar and Peter lay down to sleep, so as to rest from the cares of the day in the madhouse. Especially since on the morrow they were both supposed to go and struggle for the cause of Lenin and all the poor people.

* * *

Peter knew just the place to go: the RKI, where they like plaintiffs and all kinds of oppressed people. Opening the first door in the top corridor of the RKI building they saw an absence of people. Over the second door hung a curt poster: "Who's stronger?"—and Peter and Makar went inside. There was no one in the room except Comrade Lev Chumovoi, who was sitting there and administrating something or other, having abandoned his village to the mercy of poverty.

Makar did not get scared of Chumovoi and said to Peter, "Well, since it's said 'Who's stronger?', let's show him..."

"No," said the experienced Peter, rejecting this idea, "we have a government here, not a free-for-all. Let's go further up."

Further up they were received because there was a great thirst for people and for genuine laboring-class intelligence there.

"We are members of the working class," Peter said to the highest official. "We have an accumulation of brains, give us power over the oppressive bureaucratic bastards."

"Take it. It is yours," said the high official and gave the power into their hands.

From then on Makar and Peter sat at desks across from Lev Chumovoi and began talking to the poor people who came there and decided all the cases in their heads—on the basis of sympathy for the poor. Soon people stopped coming to Makar's and Peter's office because their way of thinking was so simple that the poor themselves were able to think and decide the same way, and so the working people began thinking for themselves in their own apartments.

Lev Chumovoi was left alone in the office, since no one recalled him by means of a written notice. And he remained there until the time when a commission was appointed for the liquidation of the State. Comrade Chumovoi worked in this commission for forty-four years and died in the midst of oblivion and official affairs, those with which his precious administrative mentality had been invested.

Translated by Alexey A. Kiselev   *1929*

El Lissitzky cover for the magazine *Veshch*.

ILF AND PETROV

Ilya Ilf (Fainzilberg, 1897-1937) and Evgeny Petrov (Kataev, 1903-1942) were the most popular satiric team of the 1920s and 1930s. Best known for the novels *The Twelve Chairs* and *The Little Golden Calf,* about the comic adventures of NEP manipulators, they were the authors of many popular stories and feuilletons. This story continues to be cited as completely contemporary by Soviet writers.

HOW ROBINSON WAS CREATED

The editorial board of the illustrated bi-weekly *Affairs of Adventure* felt the lack of artistic works capable of attracting young readers.

There were some manuscripts around, but none of them was right. There was just too much drivelling seriousness in them. To tell the truth, rather than attracting young readers, they depressed their spirits. And the editors wanted to attract them.

In the end they decided to commission a serial novel.

The editorial errand-boy rushed off with a note to the writer Moldavantsev, and the very next day Moldavantsev was sitting on the bourgeois couch in the editor's office.

"You understand," droned the editor, "it should be entertaining and fresh, full of interesting adventures. In general, we need a Soviet *Robinson Crusoe.* Something that the reader can't put down."

"A *Robinson*—can do," said the writer laconically.

"Not just a *Robinson,* but a *Soviet Robinson.*"

"What else! Not a Rumanian one, for example!"

The writer was not loquacious. Obviously, he was a man of action.

And, indeed, the novel was ready on the agreed-upon date. Moldavantsev didn't stray too far from the great original. They wanted a *Robinson,* they got a *Robinson.*

A Soviet youth suffers a shipwreck. A wave carries him to a deserted island. He's alone, defenseless in the face of mighty nature. Dangers are everywhere: beasts, lianas, the approaching rainy season. But the Soviet Robinson, full of energy, conquers all the obstacles which appear so unconquerable. Three years later a Soviet expedition finds him flourishing. He's dominated nature, built a little house, surrounded it with a green ring of gardens, raised rabbits, has sewn himself a Russian shirt from gorilla tails, and has taught a parrot to wake him in the morning with the words: "Attention! Take off the blanket, take off the blanket! We're starting morning exercises!"

"Very good," said the editor, "the stuff about the rabbits is just superb. Completely contemporary. But, you know, the basic idea of the work isn't quite clear to me."

"Struggle of man with nature," reported Moldavantsev with his usual brevity.

"But there's nothing Soviet in it."

"But what about the parrot? He replaces the radio. An experienced announcer."

"The parrot's good. And the ring of gardens is good. But one gets no sense of Soviet public spirit here. Where, for example, is the local committee? The leading role of the unions?"

"How can there be a local committee? The island's supposed to be deserted."

"Yes, quite true, deserted. But there must be a local committee. I'm not an artist of the word, but if I were you I'd put one in. As a Soviet element."

"But the whole plot is based on the idea that the island is deserted..."

At this point Moldavantsev happened to glance into the editor's eyes and stopped cold. Those eyes were so spring-like, one even sensed in them the empty blueness of March, and he decided to compromise.

"Actually, you're right," he said, raising his finger. "Of course, why didn't I see it right away? Two people survive the shipwreck: our Robinson and the head of the local committee."

"And also two regular members," said the editor coolly.

"Oy," squeaked Moldavantsev.

"Nothing to oy about. Two regular members and one woman activist, who collects dues."

"Why a dues collector too? Who's she going to collect dues from?"

"From Robinson."

"The committee head can collect Robinson's dues. That's all right for him."

"In that you are mistaken, Comrade Moldavantsev. That's absolutely objectionable. The head of the local committee should not be misused for such trivial things as running around collecting dues. We are trying to combat just such things. He should spend his time on serious leadership work."

"Well, then there can be a dues collector. That's even better. She'll marry either the committee head or Robinson. More entertaining to read."

"Not worth it. Don't lapse into trashiness, into unhealthy eroticism. Let her collect the dues and keep them in a fire-proof safe."

Moldavantsev squirmed on the couch.

"With all respect, a fire-proof safe can't be on a desert island!"

The editor gave it some thought.

"Wait a minute," he said, "you've got a terrific section in the first chapter. The wave washes up various things along with Robinson and the local committee."

"An axe, a rifle, a compass, a barrel of rum and a bottle of anti-scurvy medicine," recited the writer.

"Cross out the rum," said the editor quickly, "and then what's the point of the scurvy medicine? Who needs that? Better to have it be a bottle of ink! A fire-proof safe is vital."

"You're crazy on the subject of that safe! The membership dues can just be kept in the hollow of the baobab tree. Who's going to steal them?"

"What do you mean, who? What about Robinson? The head of the committee? The regular members? The store commission?"

"The store commission also survives?" asked Moldavantsev cravenly.

"They survive."

Silence ensued.

"Maybe the wave also washes up a meeting table?!"

"Pos-i-tively! We have to create the conditions for people to work in. Give them a pitcher of water, a bell, a table cloth. The wave can wash up whatever kind of table cloth you like. Either red or green. I'm not interfering with creativity. But the first thing you've got to do, old man, is show the masses. A broad cross-section of working people."

"The waves can't wash up the masses," said Moldavantsev obstinately. "That goes completely against the plot. Just think a minute! The waves suddenly wash up several thousand people! We'd be laughingstocks."

"But actually, a little healthy, cheerful, life-loving laughter never hurts," added the editor.

"No! A wave can't do that."

"Who needs a wave?" said the editor in sudden amazement.

"How else are the masses to land on the island? It's a deserted island, you know."

"Who says it's deserted? You're getting me mixed up. It's clear. There's an island, better—a peninsula. That way it's calmer. And on it occur a series of entertaining, fresh, interesting adventures. Union work is being carried on, sometimes badly. The activist exposes a series of defects, for example, in the area of dues collection. The broad cross-section helps her. And the repentant committee head. At the end you can show a general assembly. That will be really effective artistically. There, that's it."

"What about Robinson?" gibbered Moldavantsev.

"Yes. Good you reminded me. Robinson bothers me. Throw him out completely. An absurd, completely unjustified sniveller."

"Now everything's understood," said Moldavantsev in a funereal tone, "everything will be ready tomorrow."

"That's all. Go create. By the way, you have that shipwreck at the start of the novel. You don't need it, you know. Do it without the shipwreck. It'll be more riveting that way. Right? Good. Good-bye."

When he was alone, the editor began to laugh happily.

"Finally," he said, "I'll have a work that's both a real adventure and a genuine work of art as well."

Translated by Ellendea Proffer   *1932*

ALEXANDER BLOK

Alexander Alexandrovich Blok (1880-1921), poet and playwright, was the most revered poet of the St. Petersburg Symbolists. His book of lyrics *Verses on a Beautiful Lady* (1904) was hailed by young poets. The image of the Beautiful Lady, a muse inspired by mystical currents of the time, dominated Blok's early work. Over the years this image changed from an object of love, vague and holy, to a city whore in a destructive urban world. Though Blok remained a poet of "old world" culture he was to write what became *the* poem of the Revolution as well as his most famous work—*The Twelve*. Soviet critics see the work as Blok's praise of Bolshevism: he did hail the Revolution at first, though he soon became disillusioned. But *The Twelve* can also be seen as a poetic continuation and summation of Blok's earlier themes, rather than marking a break, and as a religious-moral tragedy that poses irresolvable questions and is satiric as well as positive in its treatment of the Revolution. The poem is written in twelve different stanzaic forms, corresponding to the twelve Apostle-Red Guards, and uses the rhythms of popular songs and urban speech, thus marking a break with the past in form and style.

1
Black evening.
White snow.
Wind, wind!
Man can't stand it.
Wind, wind—
All over God's world.

The wind whirls
The white snowflakes.
Under the coat of snow, there's ice.
It's slippery, it's hard going.
Everyone skidding—
Oops!—Oh, pour soul!

They've stretched a rope
Across the street,
And on it's a banner:
"All Power to the Constituent Assembly!"
The old woman's crying her heart out,
Can't think what it's all about,
What such a banner's for,
Such a huge piece of stuff?
So many foot-rags there for the boys,
All of them wanting clothes, and boots!

Alexander and Lyubov Blok.

Like a hen, any-old-how,
She's scrambled up and over the snowbank.
   —Och, Mother of God, pray for us!
   —These Bolsheviks, they'll drive us to the grave!

     The wind's like a whip,
     And there's frost to follow up!
     The bourgeois at the crossroads
     Tucks his nose into his coat.

And who's that?—with the long hair,
Muttering beneath his breath:
     —Traitors! he says,
     Russia's done for!
Must be a writer—
     An orator...

And there's that fellow in the cassock—
Behind the snowbank, sneaking past...
Hey, what's eating you today,
     Comrade priest?

Remember how it used to be,
How you sailed about, all belly,
With your cross, and how it shone,
Your belly, on the people?..

And over there, in her astrakhan,
Madame swept up to a friend:
—Oh how we cried and cried... But then
     She slipped
And—bam!—went sprawling!

      My, my!
     Up she comes—heave!

     The gay wind's
     Both glad and angry,
     Twists skirts,
     Cuts people down
     And tears and crumples and drags about
     The enormous banner:
"All Power to the Constituent Assembly!"..
     And whispers these words:

...We too had a meeting...
...In this very building...
     ...We've discussed,
     And we've decided:
A short time, ten; twenty-five for the night...
     ...And nothing less from anyone...
      ...Let's get some sleep...

Late evening.
The street's soon empty.
Only a tramp,
Hunched up,
And the wind whistling...

Hey you, you poor bugger!
   Come over here—
Come and give us a hug...

Bread! Yes—
But what's ahead for us?
   Go on, get off with you!

Black, black sky.

Hatred, sad hatred
   Boils in the breast...
Black hatred, holy hatred...

Comrade!
   Watch out!

                2
The wind whirls off, the snow dances down,
And twelve men go marching out.

Black slings to their rifles,
Lights, and lights, and lights... all round them...

Fags in their teeth, and crumpled caps,
They want broad-arrows on their backs!

   Liberty, liberty,
ay! Ay, and without the Cross!

   Tra-ta-ta!

It's cold, comrades—it's cold!

—Vanya's with Katya there in the pub...
—'Er stockings are stuffed with Kerensky rubles!

—He's rich himself now, is old Vanya...
—He was one of us, and now he's a soldier!

—C'mon Vanya, you sonofabitch, you bourgeois,
You try and kiss my girl, I dare you!

   Liberty, liberty,
ay! Ay, and without the Cross!
Katya's busy with Vanya.—How,
How's she busy?

Tra-ta-ta!

Around them, lights, and lights, and lights...
Over their shoulders, rifle-slings...

For the Revolution, keep in step!
The tireless enemy's never asleep!

Come on, get a grip on your rifle, comrade!
Let's shoot off a bullet into Holy Russia—

Good, sound
Peasant stock,
With her fat backside!

Ay, ay, and without the Cross!

3

That's the way the boys went off,
Off to serve in the Red Guard—
Off to serve in the Red Guard—
Mad-keen to get their heads shot off!

Ach, and a sorry life it is,
The only life we've got!
With an Austrian rifle
And a torn old coat!

Won't we make the bourgeois sorry
When we fan the world to fire,
Fan the world afire with blood—
Bless us Thou the work O Lord!

4

Whirling snow, the driver yelling,
Vanya, Katya, off and racing—
There's the electric lantern
Twinkling on the shafts...
Ready, steady—go!..

In a military greatcoat,
With a dopey-looking mug,
He keeps on twirling his moustache,
Twisting it, and twirling it,
Cracking jokes, cracking jokes...

Look at Vanya—look at those shoulders!
Look at him—he's full of blarney!
Hugs that dummy Katya now,
Chats her up a treat...

Back she lies, she smiles at him.
Her pretty teeth like shining pearls,
That's my Katya, that's my own
Wee cuddlesome Katya...

5
The knife-scar on your neck
Hasn't healed yet, Katya.
That scratch beneath your breast,
That's fresh too, Katya!

Hey, hey, do a dance for us!
Let's see those pretty legs of yours!

Once you had lace underwear—
So wear it, keep wearing it!
You whored around with officers—
So whore away, get on with it!

Hey, hey, get on with it!
My heart leaps when I think of it!

The officer, Katya—remember him?
He didn't escape the knife...
Or don't you think of him now, you bitch?
Isn't that memory fresh?

Hey, hey, don't you forget!
Put me down for a night of it!

Once you'd fancy spats to wear,
Liqueur creams to guzzle on,
Once you went with the officers—
Now you've got around to men?

Hey, hey, screw away!
It doesn't matter a damn to me!

6
The cabby gallops back again,
Screeching, yelling out to them...

Stop, stop! Andryukha, give us a hand!
Petrukha, you get round behind!..

Trakh-tararakh-takh-takh-takh-takh!
The snow spun up in the air like dust!

The cabby's off—and Vanya with him...
Once again now! Pull the trigger!..

Trakh-tarakh! I'll see you learn
. . . .
To play around with another man's girl!..

Got away, the rat! You wait, though,
I'll get even with you tomorrow!

But where's Katya?—Dead as dead!
Shot, shot right through the head!

Happy, Katya?—Not a cheep!
Lying on the snow in a heap!

For the Revolution, keep in step!
The tireless enemy's never asleep!

7

And again the twelve march on,
At their shoulders their rifles swing.
Only the poor murderer's face
Looks blank, featureless...

Faster now, and faster still.
He goes striding on ahead.
He's wrapped his scarf around his neck—
He just can't snap out of it...

—And what's eating you, comrade?
—What's struck you dumb, old man?
—Petrukha, what's made you so sour?
You feeling sorry for Katya now?

—Oh my friends, dear friends,
I did love that girl...
Drunk with our love, we were, those nights
I used to spend with her...

—All for the reckless bravery
That flashed in her eyes like fire,
All for the sake of the scarlet mole
By her right shoulder there,
I've killed her now, and in anger—Oh!

—What d'you know, the bastard's whining!
What are you, Petya, a girl, or what?
—So now he wants to turn his soul
Inside out for us? So what!
—Hitch up your dignity!
—Take care to keep yourself in control!

—My dear comrade, don't depend
On us to nurse you now.
In times like these you're going to find
We've bigger jobs to do!

And Petrukha slows
His hasty stride...

Hi-ho!
It's no sin to have fun!

Lock up your flats!
There's looting tonight!

Open the cellars—
The gang's on the town tonight.

8

Now I know what grief is,
    The emptiness,
        Like death, it is!

        So, for now,
        To pass the time...

        To pass the time,
        I'll scratch my head...

        Sunflower seeds
        I'll crack and spit...

        And take my knife
        And slash, and slit...

Yes, bourgeois, you fly away, like a sparrow!
        I'll drink your blood,
        For that girl that I loved,
        Those dark eyes she had...

Lord, have mercy on her soul...

        The emptiness!

9

Not an echo now of the city's roar,
By the tower on the Neva silence reigns,
And no policeman any more—
So live it up, boys, without your wine!

The bourgeois stands at the crossroads
And into his collar he's tucked his nose,
And the scabby cur cringing at his side
Tucks in its tail and presses close.

The bourgeois like a question stands there
Silent, hungry as the dog,
And like a stray the old world stands
Behind him, tail between its legs.

10

    The blizzard's gone beserk,
        Hey blizzard, blizzard hey!
    Can't see the other blokes
        Even four steps away!

The snow spun like a funnel...
The snow rose like a pillar...

—Och Savior, what a storm it is!
—Hey Petya, steady on with your lies!
Tell men, when's your precious savior
Ever done any good?
You're not being sensible about it,
You stop and think, and get things straight—
Wasn't it Katya's love that caused
Your hands to be so stained with blood?
—Keep your step, for the Revolution!
The tireless enemy is not far off!

    On, on, on
      Workers, march on!

      11
...And on they march, without God blessing,
    On, and on, all twelve of them.
      Ready for anything,
      Sorry for nothing...

Their steel rifles trained
On the invisible foe...
Into silent alleyways
Where only the storm whisks up the snow...
And into drifts like feather-beds
That won't let your boot go...

    Again the red flag
    Strikes the eye.

    The measured tread
    Resounds, resounds.

    Look out! The deadly
    Enemy stirs...

But the blizzard fills their eyes
    Nights and days
    Ceaselessly...

On, onward
Workers, on!

      12
    ...With sovereign tread they march away.
    —Who's that there? You come out!
    That's the demented wind there playing
    With the red flag out in front...

Out in front, there's a cold snowdrift.
—Who's in the snowdrift? Out of there!..
Only that beggar limping after
At their heels, the hungry cur...

—Get out of there, you scabby creature,
I'll tickle you with my bayonet!
Get lost, like the mangy hound you are,
You old world—or I'll beat you up!

It bares its teeth like a hungry wolf,
Tucks in its tail, won't let them go—
The cold, homeless mongrel brute...
—Who goes there? Hey, speak up, you!

—Who's there, that's waving the red flag?
—You try and see—how dark it is!
—Who goes there, like a fugitive,
Hiding behind every house?

—Wait and see, I'm going to get you,
Better give yourself up alive!
—Hey, comrade, you'll regret it,
Come on out, or we'll open fire!

Trakh-takh-takh!—But only the echo
Answers from the houses now...
Only the blizzard with its gigantic
Laughter pealing through the snow...

    Trakh-takh-takh!
    Trakh-takh-takh...

   ...So they march with sovereign tread—
    At their heels, the hungry dog,
At their head—with a bloody flag,
    And unseeen behind the storm,
    Among the bullets free from harm,
As softly walking upon the blizzard
As snowy pearls roll lightly scattered,
    His brow with white roses wreathed—
    At their head, goes Jesus Christ.

1918
Translated by Natasha Templeton

NIKOLAI GUMILYOV

The Acmeist poet, critic and theoretician Nikolai Gumilyov (1886-1921) attended the famous Tsarskoe Selo Lyceum, then under the directorship of Innokenty Annensky, whom Gumilyov acknowledged as his mentor. Gumilyov studied at the Sorbonne in 1907-8 after which he returned to St. Petersburg. In 1910 he married Anna Akhmatova, a resident of Tsarskoe Selo and another pupil of Annensky. (Akhmatova divorced him in 1918.) Shortly after his marriage Gumilyov embarked on two journeys to Africa, an experience reflected in his poetry. In 1912, together with Sergei Gorodetsky, Gumilyov organized the Poet's Guild as an alternative to Vyacheslav Ivanov's Academy of Verse. Gumilyov served in the Imperial Army during World War I, returning to Petersburg after the war to resume his literary career. He was arrested in 1921 on the false charge of conspiracy and shot. His literary rehabilitation did not take place in the Soviet Union until 1986.

Gumilyov is often, unfortunately, best remembered as a poet of romantic adventure, that is, for the early poetry in the manner of "The Captains" (1908). His mature and best work, however, was published in the final years of the young poet's short life and has little of the romantic exoticism and bravado that is associated with the earlier poetry. The poems below, all from Gumilyov's last book, *Pillar of Fire* (published posthumously in 1921), show another side of Gumilyov with their intimate, philosophical, sometimes fantastic or grotesque, lyricism.

Memory

Only snakes cast off the skins they're wearing,
So that souls may grow as skin is shed.
But alas, there can be no comparing
Us and snakes. We change our souls instead.

Memory, with your huge hand you lead me
Like a bridled horse my whole life through
And describe those you have seen precede me
In this body—souls known just to you.

Thin and unattractive was the very
First. A child of magic, he preferred
Gloomy woods and fallen leaves strewn there; he
Often stopped the raindrops with a word.

'Twas a tree and red-haired dog he took for
Friends. O, Memory, as years go by
You will never find the sign you look for,
Nor convince the world that this was I.

And the second loved the south wind's sighing,
In each sound he heard a lyre play.
And the world was like a carpet lying
Under foot. Life was his friend, he'd say.

Toward this one I can no fondness show; it
Seemed he saw himself as godlike or
As a tsar. He hung the sign of poet
In my silent house above the door.

Him I love who valued freedom dearly,
Rifleman and swimmer in the sea.
Ah, to him the waters sang so clearly,
As the clouds themselves watched jealously.

Straight into the sky arose his lofty
Tent, and strong mules frolicked on their own,
Here he drank, like wine, the sweet air wafting
Gently o'er a land to him unknown.

Memory, your powers now have faded;
As the years have passed, you've grown less bright.
Which of these two souls was it who traded
Your gay freedom for a holy fight?

With both thirst and hunger well acquainted,
He knew endless paths, nights without rest,
But the holy bullet of the sainted
George twice entered his yet untouched breast.

I, a sternly structured temple, tower,
Breaking through the mist, immovable.
I was jealous of the Father's power,
Glory of which heav'n and earth are full.

In my heart a fire will burn, not ending
Till the day when I can clearly see
On my native plains the walls ascending
Of the New Jerusalem to be.

And it's then a strange wind will start blowing—
And the sky will be filled with awesome light,
Suddenly the Milky Way is glowing,
Lit by dazzling planets in the night.

Then a traveler will appear; I'll find him
Standing there before me, face concealed,
Eagle overhead, lion behind him,
And to me will all things be revealed.

I'll cry out... that my soul may not perish,
On whom can I count to give me aid?

Only snakes cast off the skins they're wearing,
But it's in our souls that change is made.

1921
Translated by Jamie Fuller

The Sixth Sense

Beautiful is wine in love with us,
And good bread put into the oven for us,
And the woman who, after tortuous resistance,
Gives herself for our pleasure.

But what are we to do with the rosy sunset
Over skies which grow cold,
Where there is silence and unearthly peace,
What are we to do with immortal verses?

Not eat them, nor drink them, nor kiss them.
Inexorably the moment rushes,
And we wring our hands, but again
We're condemned to keep on, keep on moving past.

As a young boy who forgets his games
Sometimes spies on bathing girls,
And ignorant in every way of love,
Is still tormented by mysterious desire,

As once upon a time 'mid tangled ferns
A slimy creature, of his impotence aware,
Roared when sensing on his shoulders
Wings which had not yet appeared,

So age after age—will it be soon, O Lord?—
Beneath the scalpel of nature and art,
Our spirit screams, our flesh depletes itself,
Giving birth to an organ for the sixth sense.

1921
Translated by Carl R. Proffer

A Baby Elephant

Right now my love for you is a baby elephant
Born in Berlin or in Paris,
And treading with its cushioned feet
Around the zoo director's house.

Do not offer it French pastries,
Do not offer it cabbage heads,
It can eat only sections of tangerine,
Or lumps of sugar and pieces of candy.

Don't cry, my sweet, because it will be put
Into a narrow cage, become a joke for mobs,
When salesmen blow cigar smoke into its trunk
To the cackles of their girlfriends.

Don't imagine, my dear, that the day will come
When, infuriated, it will snap its chains
And rush along the streets
Crushing howling people like a bus.

No, may you dream of it at dawn,
Clad in bronze and brocade and ostrich feathers,
Like that Magnificent beast which once
Bore Hannibal to trembling Rome.

1921
Translated by Carl R. Proffer

The Streetcar Gone Astray

I was walking along an unfamiliar street,
And suddenly heard a cawing of crows,
And resonant lutes, and distant rumbling,
—Before me a streetcar flew.

How I leapt to its platform
Was a riddle to me,
Even in the light of day
It left a fiery trail in the air.

Rushing ahead like a dark-winged storm,
It went astray in the abyss of Time...
"Stop, conductor,
Stop the car right now!"

Too late. We had already passed the wall,
We leapt through the grove of palms,
Across the Neva, the Nile, the Seine,
We boomed across three bridges.

And flashing past the window's frame,
Casting a searching glance after us was
An old man—of course, the same one
Who died in Beirut a year ago.

Where am I? So languid and anxious,
My heart hammers in answer:
"Do you see that station where one
Can buy a ticket to the India of the Spirit?"

A sign...letters poured from blood
Announce—"Vegetables." I know this is where,
Instead of cabbages, instead of rutabagas,
Corpses' heads are being sold.

Clad in red shirt, with a face like an udder,
The executioner cleaves my head too,
It was lying here with the others,
On the very bottom in a slippery box.

And in an alley—a board fence,
A three-windowed house with gray grass.
"Stop, conductor,
Stop the car right now!"

Mashenka, here you lived, and here you sang,
You wove a rug for me, your love.
Where are your voice and body now,
Can it be that you are dead!

How you sobbed in your chamber,
But I with powdered queue
Was going to present myself to the Empress,
And never again did we meet.

Now I understood: our freedom
Is only light which strikes from there,
Humans and shades are standing at the gate
To the zoological garden of the planets.

And suddenly a sweet, familiar wind
And across the bridge, flying toward me—
The iron-gloved hand of the Horseman
And the two hooves of his steed.

That faithful bulwark of Orthodoxy,
St. Isaac's is chiseled into the sky,
There I'll have some prayers for Mashenka's
Health, and a requiem mass for myself.

And still my heart is dark forever,
And it's hard to breathe, and pain to live...
Mashenka, I never believed
It possible to love and grieve like this.

1921
Translated by Carl R. Proffer

Anna Akhmatova.

ANNA AKHMATOVA

Anna Andreevna Akhmatova (born Anna Gorenko, 1889-1966) is one of the major twentieth-century Russian poets. She was born near Odessa, and grew up in Tsarskoe Selo and St. Petersburg. She joined the Guild of Poets and the Acmeist movement together with her husband, the poet Nikolai Gumilyov. Akhmatova's first book of poems was *Evening* (1912); *Rosary* (1914) brought her fame and many imitators among women poets. By 1922 three more of her books came out, but between 1922-40 no new works were published because her work was considered too apolitical to fit the new Soviet literature. Her poems from the 1920s included here give some idea of Akhmatova's unique poetic voice. She wrote short, highly condensed lyrics which formed a poetic self-portrait. The poems are psychologically precise, written with a clarity and accuracy that was classical and in the tradition of Pushkin. During the long period of poetic silence in the late 20s and 30s, Akhmatova translated and wrote critical studies on Pushkin. In the late 30s the arrests of her son, Lev Gumilyov, and husband, N. Punin, inspired one of her major works, *Requiem,* which went unpublished. Her troubles with the regime were not over after the war ended. Akhmatova and Zoshchenko were attacked by the Party and expelled from the Writers' Union. It was not until the thaw that followed Stalin's death that she was published again. In the 1960s Akhmatova was at last given some official recognition in her own country and won international acclaim as well.

It is nighttime. The twenty-first. Monday.
The lines of the city fog-furled.
Some young ne'erdowell improvised one day
That there's something called love in the world.

And from slackness or out of frustration,
All believed it and now follow suit:
Make assignments and dread separation
And go caroling love-songs to boot.

But the truth of the matter will surface
For some in a speechless spell . . .
I chanced on it, quite without purpose,
And ever since haven't been well.

1917
Translated by Walter Arndt

On the crest of a hard-frozen snow ridge
To my white and mysterious home,
So hushed, you and I, by our knowledge,
In intimate silence we come.

To me this fulfillment is sweeter
Than all I have thought of to sing—
And the branches we brush, and their teeter,
And your spurs with their delicate ring.

January 1917
Translated by Walter Arndt

So you thought me the standard romantic,
To be dropped and forgotten, of course;
That I'd fling myself, sobbing and frantic,
To the hooves of a runaway horse.

Or I'd go to a wise-woman peasant
For persuading decoctions of wort,
And would send you a frightening present,
Like my kerchief all perfumed with hurt.

Be accursed, then. Nor moaning nor gazes
To the reprobate soul will I turn,
But I swear by the shrine's sacred hazes,
By the grove where the angels sojourn,
By the fume of our sensuous blazes—
I have gone and shall never return.

July 1921
Translated by Walter Arndt

I am free now. And, keeping my fun up,
In the nighttime the Muse wings me cheer,
And ambition lopes round with the sun-up
And goes rattling its beads in my ear.

It's not worth it to pray for me even,
Or look back as you go on your way.
The black wind will assuage me on leaving,
And the gold of the fall make my day.

I'll count riddance a gift of good fortune,
And oblivion a generous boon.
Tell me, though, dare you visit that torture
Of the damned on another girl soon?

August 1921
Translated by Walter Arndt

Bezhetsk

There white churches nestle, and resonant, sparkling ice gleams,
There I see the cornflower-blue eyes of my dear son blossom.
And over the old town stretch diamond nights, beautifully awesome;
More golden than honey from lime trees the sky's crescent seems.
From fields past the river the dry gusty snowstorms arise,
On God's Day, like angels, men join in a glad celebration,
The lamps in the tidied front room lend soft illumination,
And there on an old oaken table the Holy Book lies.
There memory, stern and more miserly now than before,
Gave me a low bow, the small rooms in her attic revealing;
But I didn't enter and slammed shut the terrible door;
The city was filled with the gay sound of Christmas bells pealing.

26 December 1921
Translated by Jamie Fuller

It is fine here: all rustle and creak,
With each morning the frost only grows,
Flaming white hangs a bush, frozen sleek,
In a dazzle of rose upon rose.
Down this holiday glory of snow
Runs a ski-track, as if it would try
To recall that dim ages ago
We went walking this way, you and I.

1922
Translated by Walter Arndt

A New Year's Ballad

And the moon, bored in its cloudy darkness,
Cast a wan glance at the room.
There stand six glasses on the table
And only one glass is empty.

It's my husband, and I, and my friends
Meeting the New Year.
Why do my fingers seem to be bloody,
And the wine burn like poison?

The host, lifting a full glass,
Was grave and motionless:
"I drink to the land of our native plains
In which we all lie!"

And a friend, glancing at my face,
And recalling God knows what,
Exclaimed: "And I drink to her songs
In which we all live!"

But the third, who knew nothing
When he left this world,
Uttered in answer to my
Thoughts: "We should drink to the one
Who is not yet with us."

1923
Translated by Carl R. Proffer

Lot's Wife

> *But his wife looked back from behind him,*
> *and she became a pillar of salt.*   Genesis

The just man strode after God's messenger proudly,
Prodigious and bright, along mountains of black.
But aching unease to his lady spoke loudly:
There's time yet—it wasn't too late to look back.

On the stately red towers of the Sodom she fled now,
The court of her singing, the hall where she span,
The goodly high mansion, its window-gaps dead now,
Wherein she gave birth for the love of a man.

She looked—and by lethal oblivion assaulted,
Her eyes lost the art to take in any more;
To luminous rock-salt her body was altered,
Her nimble feet merged with the quartz of the tor.

Who weeps for the woman, who thinks to regret her?
Who does not account her the less for her lack?
My own heart alone cannot ever forget her,
Who laid down her life for a single glance back.

1922-24
Translated by Walter Arndt

The Muse

When nights I wait for her epiphany,
Life seems suspended by a hair, and moot.
What's honors, being young, and feeling free,
Before this dear guest with her shepherd's flute.

And here she was. She gazed at me and waited
Attentively, her veil tossed overhead.
I ask her: "Was it you then who dictated
The script of Hell to Dante?" "I," she said.

1924
Translated by Walter Arndt

This is where Pushkin's exile was begun,
This is where that of Lermontov was ended.
The highland herbs up here are lightly scented,
And it was but a single time I won
A glimpse into the shore's deep plane-tree cover,
And on that westering and ruthless hour
Saw the indomitable glinting glower,
The eye-light of Tamara's deathless lover.

Kislovodsk, 1927
Translated by Walter Arndt

When the bane of the moon is at work,
Town is steeped in its venomous potion.
No illusions of sleep still lurk,
And I see through the lurid murk
Not my childhood, and not the ocean,
Not the butterflies' wedding swarm, once
Over snowy-white daffodils vaulted,
Was it nineteen-sixteen, perchance,
But the cypresses' choral dance
On your grave-mound, forever halted.

1928
Translated by Walter Arndt

Osip Mandelstam.

OSIP MANDELSTAM

Osip Emilievich Mandelstam (1891-1938) is generally regarded as one of the greatest Russian poets. He was born in Warsaw but grew up in the cultural world of the St. Petersburg intelligentsia. In 1911 he joined Gumilyov's Guild of Poets and became an active member of the Acmeist group. The elegantly crafted poems in his first book *Stone* (1913) reveal what was important to this new literary movement that sought to replace the once-dominant Symbolist art. The Acmeists believed that aesthetic rather than philosophical or religious values were most important for art; they called for a return to the traditions of classicism and humanism and stressed that man and the things of this world should be the concern of artists. Above all, perhaps, they believed in art as a craft; the good poet was a fine craftsman. Of the works published during Mandelstam's lifetime *Tristia* (1922) is most important, but much of his work went unpublished. It became increasingly difficult for Mandelstam to write and publish in the 1920s because of his ideological incompatibility with the regime. He was arrested and exiled in the 1930s and died in a labor camp in Siberia in 1938. His unpublished poems were preserved for many years by his widow, Nadezhda, and were first published in the West decades later. Mandelstam's poems of the 1920s and later reflect his anguish over what he saw as the disintegration of culture. He also wrote several fine works of prose and many essays.

Tristia

The science of parting I have studied well
In night complaints with open spread-out hair.
The oxen chew their cuds. The long slow wait,
Last hour of city vigils, drags on and on.
I honor the rite of that same rooster night,
When tear-stained eyes were gazing far beyond,
Lifting the heavy load of travel's grief,
And women's weeping joined the Muses' song.

And who can ever know at the word "parting"
What kind of separation lies in wait?
Or what the rooster's outcry promises,
When fire burns in the Acropolis,
And at the dawn of some kind of new life,
When lazily the ox chews in the hall,
Why does the rooster, herald of new life,
Beat with his wing upon the city wall?

And spinning is a custom that I love:
The shuttle scurries and the spindle hums.
O look! As lightly as the down from swans,
Already barefoot Delia floats this way!
And O how very poor joy's language is,
That meagre bare foundation of our life!
It all was long ago and shall repeat,
And recognition's flash alone is sweet.

And so, let it be thus: a shape transparent
Is lying on a clean flat plate of clay.
And like a squirrel's flattened, spread-out skin,
Bent over the wax, a girl directs her gaze.
We're not to guess about the Greek Erebus,
For women wax is what for men is bronze.
Only in battles can *our* lot be cast,
Their fate it is to die while guessing fortunes.

1918
Translated by Margaret Troupin

We shall gather again in Petersburg
As though we'd buried the sun there
And newly speak the blissful,
Meaningless word. In black velvet
Soviet night, the velvet of universal
Emptiness they sing—the kindred eyes
Of blessed blissful matrons.
And deathless flowers bloom.

The city humps its catback bridges
Where sentries come to a halt,
And a single angry motorcar
Goes cuckooing into the gloom.
I have no need of a night pass
For I've no fear of sentries—
I'll bless in the Soviet night
The meaningless, blissful word.

At the theater I hear
A gentle rustling and a girlish "oh"
And Venus holds an armful
Of deathless roses. Bored
We warm ourselves by the bonfire.
Perhaps the centuries will pass
And blessed matrons' kindred hands
Will gather in the gentle ash.

Somewhere sweet choirs of Orpheus sound,
The singers' kindred pupils darkly shine.
Playbill doves come fluttering down
From gallery to stalls. So go ahead
And snuff our candles out.
In the world's black velvet emptiness
Blissful matrons' sloping shoulders sing.
And the night sun glows unnoticed.

November 25, 1920
Translated by Alexander Kovitz

O, take this gift for joy's sake from my palms,
A little honey and a little sun,
As ordered by the bees of Proserpine.

An unbound boat can never be untied,
And shadows shod in furs cannot be heard.
In life's dense forest fear can't be allayed.

So all that we have left to us are kisses,
Small furry ones, like tiny little bees,
That die the moment they have left their hive.

They rustle in the night's transparent thickets;
Dense forests of the Tayget are their home;
Their food is time and honey-plant and mint.

Accept for joy's sake this wild gift from me,
A dry, unlovely necklace of dead bees,
The bees that changed sweet honey into sun.

1920
Translated by Margaret Troupin

I was washing outside in the darkness,
the sky burning with rough stars,
and the starlight, salt on an axe-blade.
The cold overflows the barrel.

The gate's locked,
the land's grim as its conscience.
I don't think they'll find the new weaving,
finer than truth, anywhere.

Star-salt is melting in the barrel,
icy water is blackening,
death's growing purer, misfortune saltier,
the earth's moving nearer to truth and to dread.

1921
Translated by W. S. Merwin and Clarence Brown

Concert at the Railroad Station

I can't breathe; the hard earth crawls with worms,
And not a single star will speak.
But, heaven knows, above us there is music,
With the song of muses the station shakes.
And again, torn asunder by the engine's
Whistles, the violin-like air spills.

Enormous park. The station's glass dome.
The iron world enchanted once again.
Solemnly a freight car is being drawn
To a resonant feast in foggy Elysium.
Peacocks screech; the rumbling of grand pianos;
I'm late. I shudder. It's a dream.

And I enter the station's crystal forest;
The string choir is in tearful disarray.
Wild beginning of a nocturnal chorus,
And roses smell where greenhouses decay,
Where under a sky of glass a well-known shadow
Spends the night among the roaming crowds.

And, it seems, in all the music and the foam
The iron world trembles. Beggarly.
I press against the glass-walled waiting room...
Hot steam blinds the violinist's eye.
Where are *you* off to? To a dear shade's funeral.
It's the last time this music plays for us.

1921
Translated by Emery George

The Age

My age, my beast, to whom will it be given
To behold the pupils of your eyes,
To cement two centuries together,
Giving of his blood to glue their spines?
Out of earthly things the blood for building
Pours along the throat and gushes forth,
While the hanger-on can only tremble,
Standing at the new day's door.

To the end of life a creature
Has to bear his backbone's ridge,
While the playful wave keeps cresting,
Unseen vertebrae across its edge.
Like a baby's tender cartilage
Is the age of childish earth;
Now life's cranium's brought forth again
To be offered like a lamb and burnt.

So that a new world can take its place
And imprisoned life be broken loose,
Elbow-joints of knotted days
Must be bound together with a flute.
It's the age that rocks the wave
To the tune of man's lament,
And the golden measures of the age
There in the grass, on the viper's breath.

Still the buds will swell, and swollen
Shoots will burst, spreading their verdant spray,
But your backbone is already broken,
My beautiful, wretched age.
And behind your mindless smile,
Ruthless, of your strength bereft,
You look back now, like a beast once lithe,
On the tracks your paws have left.

1923
Translated by Struven Fehsenfeld

The Horseshoe Finder

We are looking at the forest and saying:
Here is a forest of ships, of masts,
Pink pines freed to their very peaks
Of shaggy burdens, they should screech in a storm,
Stone-pines isolated in unforested, raging air—
Under the wind's salty heel
The balance of the shipwright's plumb's kept fixed onto the dancing deck.

And the navigator,
In his uncontrollable craving for expanse,
Dragging a geometer's fragile instruments through drenched ruts,
Measures the sea's uneven surface against
The steady attraction of the mainland's lap.

But inhaling the odor
Of the resinous tears oozing out of a vessel's hull,
Admiring the planks arranged and riveted throughout the bulkhead,
Not by that peaceful carpenter from Bethlehem,
But by another one instead, father of travels and sailors' friend,
We are saying:
They too have stood on the land,
Awkward, like a donkey's spine,
Roots lost in a forgetfulness of peaks,
Atop some famous range of mountains,
And have moaned under the rainstorm's fresh water
Offering up their noble burden to the sky in vain
For a pinch of salt.

Where to start?
Everything gyrates and cracks.
The air is shaken with similes.
Each new word equals the next.
A metaphor drones in the earth.
Against the arena's snorting pets
Strain thickly-flocked birds
Harnessed to light
Two-wheeled carts that burst.

Thrice-blest the one who will name the song;
Bedecked with a name, a song lives longer in a crowd,
Distinguished in its companions' midst by that bandage on its brow,
Antidote for oblivion's too close, overpowering odor,
Whether of the nearness of a man,
The odor of a strong beast's wool,
Or simply the aroma of mint leaves rubbed between the palms.
Air is sometimes murk, all living things swimming in it like fish,
Their fins disturbing a realm,
Dense, warmed slightly, shapeless—crystal
In which wheels move, horses start,
Neaera's moist black loam tilled anew each night
With pitchforks, hoes, plows and tridents.
Air is kneaded as thick as earth—
Departure forbidden, difficult is entrance therein.
Like balls of green a rustling runs its game through the trees.
The children play pick-up-sticks with dead animals' backbones.
An era's delicate chronology is drawing to a close.
Thanks—for that which was.
I myself was wrong, got lost, mixed the count up.
The era was ringing, like a golden ball,
Hollow, molded, no one holding it up,
Answering every touch with ayes and nays.
The way a child answers:
"I'll give you an apple," or: "I won't give you the apple,"
His face an exact cast of the voice which just pronounced the words.

Still the sound rings, though its reason's vanished.
A stallion is lying in the dust and snorts in his lather,
But his neck's abrupt curve
Preserves the memory of a race, scattering legs,
Four hooves
Suddenly multiplied by the number of the cobblestones,
Or of a four-way relay, the pause,
Then the fire of new legs growing with each new lurch from the ground.

So—
The one who's found the horseshoe
Blows its dust off,
Rubs it to a gleam with wool,
Then hangs it up
Over a door
Where it can rest
And no longer must it strike sparks from flint.

Human lips,
        no longer having anything to say,
Preserve the last-spoken word's shape,
And a weighty feeling stays in a hand
Even though the jug
            spilt half its contents
                    on the way home.

In what I say now it's not I speaking.
It's ripped from the earth like grains of petrified wheat.
Some
    draw on coins a lion;
Others draw a head.
Miscellaneous gold, copper, and bronze wafers
Lie with like honors in the earth,
An age left them, trying to gnaw them in half, with the imprint on its teeth.
Time cuts me off, like a coin,
And already there's not enough of me left for myself!

Moscow, 1923
Translated by Struven Fehsenfeld

January 1, 1924

He who has kissed the wizened crown of time
Shall recall with filial tenderness
The moment time settled down to sleep
On a sheaf of wheat beneath his window.
He who has faced the age with lifted eyelids
(Those two enormous sleeping apples)
Shall know the voice of the river of time—
The eternal roar beguiling and certain!

The sovereign age has two sleeping apples
And an exquisite fragile clay mouth,
But the fingers of his aging son grow numb
As they grip him falling over, dying.
Life's breath grows weaker each passing day.
I know, little remains. My simple song
Of fragile clay wrongs shall never be sung,
And my lips shall be molded in tin.

O life, fragile as clay! O dying age!
How I fear you shall be apprehended
By a stranger flaunting the bloodless smile
Of a man forced to forfeit his soul.
What agony to search out a lost word,
What torture to lift my ailing eyelids
And, with quicklime congealing in my blood,
To gather herbs for an alien tribe.

The age. Quicklime congeals in the sick son's blood.
Moscow sleeps, like a wooden coffer;
There is nowhere to run from the sovereign age...
Snow smells of apples as in the olden days.
I want to run, to run far, far away.
But where? It is pitch black outside,
Though my conscience grows white before my eyes
As if someone were sprinkling the road with salt.

Past alleys, starling boxes, drooping eaves,
I finally set out, just a short way off;
A common man clad in a flimsy coat,
I need all my strength to fasten my laprobe.
One street flashes past, then another,
The hard sled resounds like a crunchy apple,
The narrow buttonhole just won't hold,
The button keeps slipping through my fingers.

Wintry night thunders through Moscow streets
Gliding along on frozen runners.
Now someone knocks offering fresh fish,
Now steam gushes from rose-colored taverns.
Moscow, Moscow. How warmly I greet her:
"Don't judge too harshly, the worst is over;
With time I've come to respect the brotherhood
Of severe cold and the pike's justice."

Raspberry drops ablaze in the snow,
And somewhere the clicking of an Underwood;
The driver's back, and snow half a yard deep:
What more can you ask? No one can touch you, kill you.
Winter's beauty, and the stars of Capricorn
Scattering goat's milk and sparkling;
Like a horse's mane rubbing frozen runners
My laprobe rustles and rings.

But the alleyways smoking from oil stoves
Gulped down the raspberries, ice and snow,
And devoured all that they came to know
Like a Soviet sonatina of the famine years.
Must I really condemn to shameful scandal
(Again the cold has the fragrance of apples)
That wonderful oath to the fourth estate
And those fierce vows confirmed only through tears?

Who else shall you kill? Who else shall you praise?
What other lies shall you invent?
There's gristle caught in the Underwood: quick,
Pull out the key—you'll find a pike's bones;
The quicklime congealed in the sick son's blood
Thaws and splashes his blissful smile...
But the typewriter's simple sonatina
Is but a shadow of the sonatas of old.

1924
Translated by Jane Gary Harris

Leningrad

I have returned to my city, known to me like tears,
Like veins, like childhood's swollen glands.

You've returned here—so then swallow, quickly,
The fish oil from Leningrad's river lamps.

Recognize quickly, then, December's tiny day,
Where egg-yolk is mixed in with sinister tar.

Petersburg! I don't want to die yet:
You still have my telephone numbers.

Petersburg! I still have the addresses
Where I can look up the voices of the dead.

I live by the back stairs, and the bell
Hits me in the temple and tears at my flesh.

And all night long I await the dear guests,
Shaking like handcuffs the chains on the doors.

December 1930, Leningrad
Translated by Emery George

Marina Tsvetaeva.

MARINA TSVETAEVA

Marina Tsvetaeva, the daughter of Ivan Tsvetaev, founder and director of the Alexander III Museum of Fine Arts (now the Pushkin Museum), and Maria Meyn, a talented pianist of Polish background, was born in Moscow in 1892. The eighteen-year-old Tsvetaeva, who had been writing poetry for a dozen years, published her first collection of verse, *Evening Album,* in 1910. Though published privately, the volume attracted the notice of some of the leading poets of the day, including Bryusov, Gumilyov and Voloshin. This collection was followed in 1912 by a second book, *The Magic Lantern* (1912), like its predecessor dedicated to memories of childhood and adolescence. In 1912 Tsvetaeva married the handsome Sergei Efron, whom she loved "boundlessly and forever," and for whom she would leave Russia in 1922 and return to Moscow in 1939.

Tsvetaeva, though a gifted and original versifier in her early books, attained her mature poetic voice in the 1920s and 1930s. Two of her best collections, *Craft* and *After Russia,* were published in emigration in 1923 and 1928 respectively. In addition Tsvetaeva began to concentrate on prose (literary essays, reminiscences and autobiography) during her last decade in France, prompted to a large extent by the greater monetary remuneration of prose. It is very definitely a "poet's prose": Tsvetaeva indelibly stamps the prose narratives with her poetic persona, be the subject early childhood, Pushkin, or her contemporaries Pasternak and Mayakovsky.

Tsvetaeva returned to Moscow in 1939 to be reunited with her husband, who because of his association with the Soviet secret police had been forced to flee France via Spain. Efron was ultimately arrested and shot. Tsvetaeva, who had never followed the path of political expediency (she praised Mayakovsky in emigration and glorified the White Army in the USSR), who was a former emigre with a decidedly dubious past, was unable to find suitable employment, much less publish her poetry in Stalinist Russia. Finally, on August 31, 1941, she hanged herself. She was buried without mourners in an unmarked grave in Elabuga.

Demesne of the Swans, a diary in verse, opens with the Tsar's abdication (1917) and ends on New Year's Eve 1920. Tsvetaeva during this time was separated from Efron who had gone to Crimea to join the White Army (the White Swans). The collection was first published as a whole only in 1957, although Tsvetaeva had read excerpts at public readings in Moscow and portions had appeared in emigre publications.

The Demesne of the Swans (Excerpts)

(2)

Clouds above the chapel—wisps of pale-blue air.
Screech of ravens...
And—drab cohort in their ashen, sand-gray wear—
Revolutionary troops pass there.
Ah, you loyal-dyed, you royal-dyed, my dark despair!

Faces they have none, no names have they,—
Songs they know not!
Kremlin bells, your peals have lost their way
In this hurst of banners where the wind doth play.
Pray then, Moscow, lay you, Moscow, down to sleep in aye!

Moscow, 2 March 1917
Translated by Robin Kemball

(35)

Better, my Lyre, to confess it freely!
It was the great ever stirred our feelings:
Masts, battle ensigns, churches, and kings,
Bards, epic heroes, eagles, and elders.
Those that are pledged to the realm, like soldiers,
Do not confide their Tent—to the winds.
You know the Tsar—do not toy with the hunter!
Loyalty has held us, firm as an anchor:
Loyalty to greatness—to guilt—to grief,
To the great crowned guilt—loyalty unswerving!
Those that are pledged to the Khan will serve him
—Their oath is not to the horde, but its chief.
We struck a fickle age, Lyre, that scatters
All to the winds! Uniforms ripped to tatters,
And the last shreds of the Tent worn thin...
New crowds collecting—other flags waving!
But we still stand by our word—unwavering,
For they are devious captains—the winds.

1 August 1918
Translated by Robin Kemball

(50)

This book I now confide unto the winds and
Unto the passing cranes.
So long, so long, my voice has drowned our parting
That now—no voice remains.

This book I fling, a bottle on the waters,
To wars' unbridled winds.
Long may it wander—like some feast-day candle—
No less: from hand to hand.

O wind, O wind, my well-founded faithful witness,
Make known to those I love

That in my dreams each night my steps still follow
The path—from North to South.

Moscow, February 1920
Translated by Robin Kemball

(51) To Blok

Like some faint ray through hells of dark foreboding—
Such is your voice amid the crash of shells exploding.

And, like some seraph, still, amid the noise,
He tells us in that strangely toneless voice

—Born of the morning mists of old—explains to us
How he has loved us—we, the blind, the nameless—

For dark-blue cape, for perfidy and sin...
And—most of all—for her caught deepest in

The toils of night—for her dire deeds' dark muster!
And how he has *not* ceased to love you, Russia!

Then runs his finger—distant, lost in thought—
Across his temple... Aye, and tells us what

Bleak days await us, and how God will fail us,
When we call on the sun—*no* sun shall hail us...

A lonely prisoner in his private keep,
(Or is it some child talking in his sleep?)

So spake to us—the whole assembled flock!—
The sacred heart of Alexander Blok.

April 1920
Translated by Robin Kemball

(61)

Hear Yaroslavna
Mourning her loved one
Ceaselessly—
Grief so impassioned,
Sighing, her sighs
Plaintive:

Who dashed the fair cup of health then
From my fingers?
Not mine to grow old but
Under cold stone, unto mould,
Igor!

Seal my red lips with clod and clay,
Now—and for ever.
It is over,
The White Crusade.

23 December 1920
Translated by Robin Kemball

* * *

My poems, which I wrote, not even knowing
I was a poet, for I was so young;
Which broke away like sparks, torn from a rocket,
Like spray, from fountains sprung,—

Which burst into the Sanctum's heavy incense
Like little devils, hampering its sleep,
My poems about death and adolescence,
Which no one ever reads,—

On dusty shelves, in gloomy bookshops scattered,
Ignored by all and taken out by none,
My poems stay like precious wine in cellars:
Their turn, their time will come.

1913
Translated by Lydia Pasternak Slater

I—a spotless page beneath your pen—
Will accept whatever you may offer.
As the guardian of your goods, I then
Will a hundredfold increase your coffer.

I'm the black earth of a village. You,
My lord and master, seem to pour your light on
Me, and you are like the rainy dew—
I'm black earth—and paper you may write on!

10 July 1918
Translated by Jamie Fuller

Just yesterday he gazed at me,
But now he turns away his glance!
Just yesterday he stayed till birds. . .
Now ravens take the place of larks!

I'm dumb—you're cleverer than I.
You are alive—I'm benumbed.
The howl of women of all times:
"My darling, tell me what I've done!"

Oh, water's tears and blood to her!
She's washed herself in blood and tears!
Not Mother, Step-Mother—is Love:
Expect no mercy and no trial.

Ships take our loved ones far away,
A white road takes them far from us. . .
And there's a groan across the earth:
"My darling, tell me what I've done!"

Just yesterday I seemed to him
Like China! He lay at my feet.
But he unclasped his hands and Life,
Just like a rusty coin, fell out!

Here, like the murderer of a child,
I stand on trial—not brave, not sweet.
In hell itself I'll say to you:
"My darling, tell me what I did!"

I'll ask the chair, I'll ask the bed,
"For what do I endure and want?"
"His kisses stopped—to torture you:
To kiss another," they'll respond.

You taught me first to live in fire,
Then threw me in the icebound steppe!
Yes, that's what *you* have done to *me!*
My darling, tell me what *I* did!

I know it all—don't contradict!
I see again!—I'm not your love!
Wherever Love has stepped away,
The Lady-Gardener, Death, steps up.

It's just like when you shake a tree!
Ripe fruit falls when the time has come. . .
Forgive me, love, for everything,
For all, my darling, that I've done!

14 June 1920
Translated by Margaret Troupin

Just like the hour of the Moon,
Of owls—of mist o'erall—
Is the Soul's hour... Like a tune
That David played for Saul.

In this the hour of chill, your rouge
Wash off, O Vanity!
This hour, like a storm's deluge,
Belongs, my child, to me.

The hour when secrets of the heart
Are freed from deep inside.
Things from their seams are torn apart,
All secrets from lips pried!

All curtains from the eyes are drawn!
All steps move to the rear!
The notes from off the staves are gone;
Misfortune's hour strikes clear.

Misfortune mine!—You summon me.
Thus by the doctor's knife
Alarmed, children reproachfully
Ask: "Why do we live life?"

And mother soothed the fever's burn:
"Because we must," she said.
Yes, in the Soul's hour I discern
The knife's unyielding blade.

14 August 1923
Translated by Jamie Fuller

Message

To Hippolytus from his Mother—Phaedra—the Queen—tidings.
To the capricious boy, whose beauty flees Phaedra
As wax does sovereign Phoebos... thus
To Hippolytus from Phaedra: the plaint of tender lips.

Quench my soul! (You can't but touch the lips
To quench our soul!) Stooping to the lips
You can't but stoop to Psyche, hovering guest of the lips...
Quench my soul: thus, quench my lips.

Hippolytus, I am tired... Shame on whores and priestesses!
No simple shamelessness cries out to you!
Simple are speeches and hands alone... Behind the trembling of lips and hands
Is a great secret, silence lies on it like a finger.

Oh forgive me, virgin youth! rider! despiser
Of delights! Not lust! Not the whims of a woman's breast!
Now she is the temptress! Now Psyche's illusions
To listen to Hippolytus' babblings at his very lips.

"Shame on you!" But it's too late! It's the last splash!
My steeds have charged off! From the sheer ridge—into the dust—
I am *also* a rider! So, from the heights of my breasts,
From the fateful double hill—into the chasm of your breast!

(Not my own?!) Be abler! Be bolder! Be gentler!
Rather than cut signs in a waxen tablet—not the wax of a swarthy heart?!—
With a pupil's stylus... Oh
May Hippolytus' secret be read by the lips of

Insatiable Phaedra...

11 March 1923
Translated by Robert Dessaix

Go, my son, not to the city and not
To the village—to your mother country,—
To the land which is opposite all lands!—
Where going *back* means
Going *forward,* especially for you,
Who have not seen Rus,

You, my child... Mine? *Her*
Child! That legendary life
In which "real" life is buried.
Bits of earth, ground down to dust—
Do you carry that earth in your trembling palms
To a child in his cradle:
"Rus—is ashes, honor—these ashes!"

January 1932
Translated by J. Marin King

Pasternak by Rodchenko.

BORIS PASTERNAK

Boris Pasternak (1890-1960) was born in Moscow to an artistic family: his father was a well-known painter, his mother a pianist. Pasternak always stood apart, even when he tried to be part of groups such as the Futurists. Beginning in 1922 he published work which led quickly to acknowledgement that he was the premier poet of the avant-garde. Never as popular as Mayakovsky or Esenin, he was chiefly valued by other writers, on whom he was a major influence. He combined early futurist colloquialism with musicality, the awareness of a classical tradition, and an utterly new way of looking at the world. Intensely subjective, he made few concessions to his readers. His metaphors are paradoxical at first glance, and then reveal themselves as carefully and logically thought out. He was criticized for individualism throughout his career, and in a sense his novel *Doctor Zhivago* (1957), which brought him attacks in the press and a Nobel Prize, is an explanation of his understanding of the poet's true mission.

From *My Sister—Life* (1922)
Translated by Mark Rudman with Bohdan Boychuk

About These Poems

I'll crush them against the pavement
grind them into sun and glass.
I'll shout them at the ceiling
into the cold, moldy corners,

until the winter attic bows,
declaiming to the window panes
as snowdrifts and ragged days
leap like omens in the cornices.

A month-long storm will sweep away
the beginning and the end
until, instantly, I'll remember: the sun!
Note, the world has changed.

Then Christmas glances like a jackdaw
opening the reckless day
that mystified
my love and me.

Bundled in a muffler, I'll screen
the sun's glare with my palm
and yell to the kids: "Hey,
what time is it in the playground?"

Who cleared this path to my door,
that hole all choked with snow,
while I was smoking with Byron,
drinking with Poe?

And then I came to Daryal,
that workshop, arsenal, hell,
and with Lermontov's death-quiver on my lips
dipped my life into Vermouth.

* * *

My sister—life today floods over
and bursts on everyone in spring rain,
while monocled folk in their grottoes of fine manners
snap and sting, like snakes in oats.

The grownups, of course, have their reasons.
Most likely, most likely your reason's naive,
that eyes and flowerpots turn violet in the storm
and the horizon smells of moist mignonette;

so that in May, on the Kamyshin branch-line
the schedule of trains you scan in transit
seems grander than the Holy Spirit,
even though you've read it before;

and only dusk draws swarms
of women crowding onto one platform.
Restless, I hear it's not my stop,
and the sun, setting, takes the seat beside me.

The last bell splashes and floats away
in a prolonged apology: "Sorry... not yet."
Night smolders under the shutters, and the steppe
stretches from the steps to the stars.

They flicker, blink: my love, a mirage,
and somewhere far away others sleep sweetly
while my heart pours onto every platform
scattering coach doors over the endless plain.

With Oars Crossed

The rowboat rocks in a drowsy creek.
Dangling willows kiss our wrists,
our elbows, collarbones, oarlocks—but wait,
this could happen to anyone!

This is the drift of song.
This is the lilac's ashes.
This is the beauty of dew crumbled on daisies.
This is to barter lips and lips for stars.

This is to embrace the horizon,
encircle Hercules with your arms.
This is to swirl through time,
squander sleep for nightingales' songs.

English Lessons

When it was Desdemona's time to sing,
and so little life was left to her,
she wept, not over love, her star,
but over willow, willow, willow.

When it was Desdemona's time to sing,
and her murmuring softened the stones
around the black day, her blacker demon
prepared a psalm of weeping streams.

When it was Ophelia's time to sing,
and so little life was left her,
the dryness of her soul was swept away
like straws from haystacks in a storm.

When it was Ophelia's time to sing,
and the bitterness of tears was more
than she could bear, what trophies
did she hold? Willow, and columbine.

Stepping out of all that grief,
they entered, with faint hearts
the pool of the universe and quenched
their bodies with other worlds.

The Definition of Poetry

It's a tightly filled whistle,
it's the squeaking of jostled ice,
it's night, frosting the leaves,
it's two nightingales dueling.

It's the soundlessness of sweetpeas,
the tears of the universe in a pod.
It's a Figaro from music-stands and flutes
like hail on garden plots.

And all that the night finds hard to find
on the sunken floors of bathhouses
is carried to the fish pond
like a star on damp, trembling palms.

It's a mugginess flatter than sunken boards,
alders banked over the horizon.
The laughter of the stars is welcome
in this universe—this soundless place.

The Thunderstorm

The storm, like a priest, burned the lilac,
and veiled eyes and clouds
with sacrificial smoke. Go,
mend the ant's sprained leg with your lips.

Pealing of toppled pails.
What greed: Isn't the sky enough?!
A hundred hearts beat in the ditch.
The storm burned the lilac, like a priest.

Enamel meadow—azure earth,
dimmed by frost and ice.
Even finches won't rush to shake
the crystal haze off the soul.

They still drink the storm from barrels,
from sweet tubs of plenty,
and clover turns deep burgundy
under the thunder's brush strokes.

Mosquitoes stick to raspberries.
That vicious malarial proboscis
thrusts itself—the pagan—
where summer's rosiest,

injects an abscess through a blouse,
pirouettes like a red ballerina

and jabs its stinger of mischief
where blood clots like wet leaves.

O, believe my game, and believe
that migraine raging at your heels!
The day's wrath burns
in the bark of wild cherry trees.

Do you believe? If so, lean your cheek
a little nearer, nearer still,
and in the dawn of your holy summer
my breath will fan it into flame.

I won't keep secrets from you,
who hide your lips in jasmine snow.
I feel that snow on my lips too:
it melts on mine in sleep.

What can I do with my joy?
Put it in poems? Ruled notebooks?
Its lips are already parched from poisons
on written sheets.

At war with the alphabet,
they burn as blushes on your cheeks.

The Substitute

I live with your photograph, the one with your sly laughter,
where wrist joints snap,
where knuckles crack but don't fall off,
and the guests feast and grieve.

It runs from the crackling logs, from the bravado of Liszt,
from the chandelier in the ballroom, from glasses and guests,
over the piano in flames and jumps—
from rosettes and dice, roses and knucklebones.

Your hair is ruffled, you're high on tea,
and with that fragrant bud pinned to your sash,
you waltz to fame, and jest like a dervish,
biting your scarf as if in pain.

Crumbling tangerine rinds in your fingers,
you gulp down the cool cool wedges,
then sweep into the mirrored hall
that smells of the perspiration of waltzes.

> This is how the gale subsides
> on a blind bet,
> enduring thorns like a Moslem monk
> without blinking.

And declares that not a horse,
not the wild murmuring of mountains,
but only roses on a slope
gallop over you.

Not it, not the murmuring mountains,
not it, not the clopping hooves,
but only that, but only that—
what's huddled in a shawl.

But only that, which runs like lace,
soul, or sash, to the rhythm
of whirlwinds and the tip of her runaway shoe
escapes upstream in dreams.

To them, to them—
laughing them off their feet,
to the envy of running sacks,
to tears—to tears!

Sparrow Hills

My kisses pour over your breast—as from a pitcher!
Not forever will the springs of summer turn.
Not, night after night, will we raise the dust,
stomp to the low bellow of accordions.

I've heard of old age—such blighted forecasts.
When no wave will raise its arms toward the stars.
They say—to deaf ears—there is no face in the meadows,
no heart in the rivers, no god in the groves.

Get your soul in motion, stretch it like a sail!
It's the world's midday—open your eyes!
Can you see, in the heights, thoughts simmer in the white foam
of woodpeckers, fir cones, clouds, pine needles, and heat.

This is where the rails for city trolleys end.
Beyond, pines hold sermons. Beyond, rails can't stretch.
Beyond that, it's Sunday. Snapping branches
the clearing scampers downhill, sliding on the grass.

Sifting the midday, Trinity's Day and the romping,
the grove begs, "Believe me—it's always like this."
It's divined by thickets, prophesied to clearings,
and sprinkled on our cotton by the clouds.

The End

Is it all real? Is it time now to drift away?
No—better to sleep, sleep, sleep, sleep,
and see no dreams.

Another street. Another night. Another canopy of tulle.
Once again—steppe, haystack, groan,
now and forever.

Wheezing in every atom the August leaves
dream of darkness and silence. The sound of the dog's
big paws awakens the orchard.

It waits—they'll settle down. A giant grows out
of the dark. . . then another. Footsteps. "Here's the bolt!"
Whistles: got it!

It literally drowned the road with our footsteps,
brought it all the way down and racked the fence
with images of you.

Autumn. The threading of gray-blue and yellow beads.
Decay, I long for oblivion. Like you I am sick
to death of living.

O and now is the worst time for trains to shuttle past,
switch tracks and wait, now, when in the rain each leaf
surges toward the steppe!

Windows frame senseless scenes. And to what end?!
To let the door spring from its hinges having kissed
the ice on her elbows?

Make known to me someone who's been reared, as they have been,
on the hard road at the end of southern harvests,
waste land and rye.

But with the bitter aftertaste, numbness, cold, and lumps
in the throat, but with the sorrow of so many words
you bring this friendship to an end.

Isadora Duncan and Sergei Esenin.

SERGEI ESENIN

Sergei Esenin (1895-1925) is in many respects still the national poet of the ordinary people of Russia. A peasant from Ryazan with a lyrical gift and a remarkable emotional appeal for Russian audiences, Esenin had a very colorful life. He was a handsome blond boy, who gained fame early from his poetry, then solidified it by several marriages to women who were also well-known,(Isadora Duncan, for one) and proceeded to make himself notorious for his drunken brawls and scenes. The despair that came up so often in his poetry was the key to his life, and at the age of 30 he hanged himself, the first of the famous suicides of this period.

Esenin sang the beauties of nature, the mysterious power of religion and foklore, and examined the sad truths which may be found among the sinners as opposed to the saints. He called himself "the last poet of the village," but what he really meant was the last poet of the pre-revolutionary village. When he went back home, he barely recognized it, so different had the atmosphere become. Despite an early infatuation with Bolshevism, he was not suited to either the revolutionary or NEP periods. He disliked industrialization and urbanization intensely, and indeed, was an anachronism in the brave new world of the five-year-plan. For twenty some years after his death he was not republished in book form, but once he was, the editions were immediately sold out, and he is popular to this day.

To Marienhof

I am the last poet of the villages.
I sing a modest plank bridge hymn,
And stand with the swinging birches
At a wake for the leaves of autumn.

The candle dies with a golden flame,
Consuming the human tallow.
Soon the wooden clock of the moon
Will sound my midnight hour.

The iron guest will shortly appear
On the track in the sky-blue plain,
And misted sadness will reap
The shining gold sown by the dawn.

In these lifeless alien hands
My simple songs will not last.
And only the nodding horse-oats
Will mourn for their old master.

The plaintive neighing will be swept away
By the wind as it leads the dancers.
And soon the wooden clock of the moon
Will sound my midnight hour.

1920
Translated by Nils Johnson, Jr.

Song of Grain

The time is stern and cruel and bled;
The people suffer in an empty rut.
A sickle slashing at a laden head
As under the neck a swan is cut.

Our fields are poor and dry and raw,
An autumn tremor in a morning lapse.
Our lands are bandaged like sheaves of straw,
Each yellow sheaf like a yellowing corpse.

Thrown onto buckboards for funeral cars
They travel men to the granary site,
The churchman screaming at the leading mare,
The driver barking out his funeral rites.

Carefully and without malice they brush
Those bright heads into the ground,
And separate the bones from the dead flesh.
Both piles glitter in a bright mound.

No one perceives, no one seems to mind
That the straw land is also flesh.
No one cares, no one sees that they grind
The land like bones till it's also dead.

And from the land they leaven bread.
They coax the bones and fry the meat.
They fill their jugs with the land that's dead
And poison stomachs so that men can eat.

The raw wheat poisons in their rotten craws,
As the reapers father the land by parts.
The meat that's poisoned and the flesh like straw
Burns like a fire on the human heart.

They whistle across the country like knells for the dead,
Murderers, charlatans, and our death, for what?
A sickle slashing at a laden head
As under the neck a swan is cut.

1921
Translated by Edward Hirsch with Dennis Whelan

Yes, it's done. There's no return.
I've left my native fields behind.
The winged poplar branches overhead
Have run out the last time.

Without me my stooped house sags lower.
My old dog died long ago.

I know that God has sentenced me to die
Upon the crooked streets of Moscow.

I love this old bridled city,
Though fat and decrepit it has grown.
Sleepy silent golden Asia
Dozes among the onion domes.

And at night when the moon shines,
As it shines... that devilish moon,
I walk through the alleys, head hanging,
To the same familiar saloon.

The noise in this lair is unearthly,
But, through the din, all night long,
To the whores I sing out my poems,
And I drink with the bandits till dawn.

My heart beats faster and faster,
And soon I awkwardly say:
"I'm just like you. I'm lost, I'm wasted.
I can't go back that way."

Without me my stooped house sags lower,
My old dog died long ago.
I know that God has sentenced me to die
Upon the crooked streets of Moscow.

1922-23
Translated by Nils Johnson, Jr.

Letter to My Mother

Hey, old lady, still alive?
Me too. Greetings to you, greetings.
May the ineffable light of evening
flow over your little old house.

They write me that though you don't show it
you're grieving sorely for your son,
that you're often walking out to the road
in your raggedy, old-fashioned coat,

that in the blue darkness of evening
you keep on imagining one thing,
that someone's stuck his Finnish knife
under my heart in a bar-room brawl.

Don't you worry, my dear, I'm alright.
You're just letting your mind run away.
I'm not yet such an out-and-out drunk
that I'd go die without seeing you first.

I'm still the same tender guy I was,
I just go on dreaming one thing—
that I escape this restless misery
and come back to our little old house.

I'll come back when our white garden
spreads out its branches all springlike.
Just don't you wake me at daybreak,
like that time eight years ago.

Don't you wake those dreamed-out dreams,
don't stir up what didn't seem true.
It was my fate to suffer weariness
and loss too early in this life.

And don't you teach me to pray, no don't.
To the old days there's no going back.
Only you are my help and my comfort,
only you are my ineffable light.

So forget all your worryings, please.
Don't you grieve so sore for me.
And don't you walk so much to the road
in your raggedy, old-fashioned coat.

1924
Translated by Richard Lourie

The Black Man

My friend, my friend,
I am very, very ill.
I don't know myself where this illness came from.
Whether it's a wind that whistles
over an uninhabited, empty field,
or whether, as through a September grove,
alcohol rains down upon my mind.

My head flaps its ears
the way a bird flaps wings.
It's more than it can bear any longer
to draw its feet to its neck.
The black man,
black, black,
the black man
sits down by my bed
and won't let me sleep all night.

The black man thumbs
through a loathsome book
and stooping over me,
as over a dead monk,

reads me the life
of a certain villain and rakehell,
piling melancholy and terror on my soul.
The black man,
black. Black.

"Listen, listen,"
he mumbles,
"there are many splendid concepts
and plans in this book.
This man lived in a country
of the most repugnant
crooks and charlatans.

"December in that country
has snow of a diabolic purity,
and blizzards make
the spinning wheels lively.
He was a man, that adventurer,
but of the very highest,
most uncommon distinction.

"He was refined
and a poet besides—
though with a not great
but nevertheless engaging talent.
he also called a certain
middle-aged woman a slut
and his own sweetheart.

"Happiness," he said,
"is sleight of hand and mind.
It is well known
that all clumsy souls are miserable.
It's no matter
if much torment
is brought about by false
and affected gestures.

"In the thunderstorm, the tempest,
the chill of the everyday grind,
when losses are heavy
and you are feeling down,
to seem simple then and smiling
is the highest art in the world."

"Black man!
Don't laugh at this!
It's not your business
to submerge yourself in mine.
What's a scandalous poet's life
to me?
Kindly go and read
your book to someone else."

The black man stares
at me point-blank.
His eyes are glazed over
with a vile blue discharge
as though he wishes to inform me
that I'm a rogue and a thief
who has just finished shamelessly
and savagely mugging somebody.

. . . .

My friend, my friend,
I am very, very ill. I don't know myself where this sickness came from.
Whether it's a wind that whistles
over an uninhabited, empty field,
or whether, as through a September grove,
alcohol rains down upon my mind.

It's a frosty night,
a peaceful hush at the crossroads.
I'm alone at the window
expecting neither friend nor guest.
The whole plain is dusted
with soft, dry lime,
and the trees congregate
like horsemen in our garden.

The evil night bird
is crying somewhere.
Wooden horsemen
sow their hoofbeats.
Once again the black man
sits down by my armchair,
tipping his tophat
and casually removing his frock-coat.

"Listen, listen,"
he wheezes, staring me in the face,
inclining himself
nearer and nearer,
"I haven't seen that anyone,
even among the cutthroats,
suffered from insomnia
so foolishly and without reason.

"Ah, suppose I am mistaken.
You know the moon is out tonight.
And what else does a small world need
in its drunken sleep?
Perhaps the mysterious
fat-thighed She will come
and you will read to her
your soppy, lifeless poetry.

"How I love poets!
Such a comic bunch!
They always remind me of a story—
I know it by heart—
of how a long-haired pervert
spoke down to a pimply little girl,
his student, about 'the worlds,' meanwhile
dying of horniness.

"I don't know, I don't remember,
but in a certain village,
perhaps in Kaluga,
or maybe it was Ryazan,
lived a blond, blue-eyed little boy
from a simple peasant family.

"And then he began to grow up
and became a poet besides,
though with a not great
but nevertheless engaging talent.
He also called a certain
middle-aged woman a slut
and his own sweetheart."

"Black man!
You interloper.
You've had a reputation
for quite a while now."
Rising to a fury
I let my cane fly
right into his snout,
right between the eyes.

. . . .

The new moon is dead,
the dawn shines blue at the window.
Ah, night!
Is there anything you haven't twisted?
I stand with my tophat on.
There's no one with me.
I'm completely alone,
and the mirror broken. . .

1925
Translated by David Rigsbee

Mayakovsky by Rodchenko.

VLADIMIR MAYAKOVSKY

·Vladimir Vladimirovich Mayakovsky (1893-1930) was born in Bagdadi, Georgia to a Russian family. Artistic from an early age, he had a strong public personality. Huge in size, energetic and dramatic, he early ran afoul of Tsarist authorities for engaging in various ineffective revolutionary activities. His first fame came as one of Russia's most visible Futurists, and he took a leading part in the battles which dominated Russian literary life in the 1920s. Mayakovsky had a firm and fatal belief in the necessary and desirable subjugation of art to politics. This literary self-destructiveness had its counterpart in his private life as well: he had attempted suicide a number of times in his life before he finally shot himself in 1930. Typically, Mayakovsky's death lent itself to contradictory interpretations: he either did it out of disappointment in love, or disappointment in his literary-political role.

Mayakovsky was a complex figure and would have been amazed at his tedious image with Soviet students today. He was both coarse and lyrical in his work, going from agit-prop jingles to serious poems about political subjects to his major theme—love. Mayakovsky is at his most original when he is most egocentric, proclaiming the miseries and joys of his overwhelming persona who emits ferocious energy in the form of realized metaphor, hyperbole, and neologism. For all its odd appearance (like most of the Futurists, Mayakovsky was also a painter) and striking colloquial phrasing and diction, Mayakovsky's poetry is often quite conventional metrically.

The poet was surprisingly sincere in his political attitudes, and surprisingly lacking in self-knowledge. Typical of him is his poem in protest against Esenin's suicide, an act which had obviously touched him in ways he did not wish to examine. In this poem he attempts to de-romanticize the poet's act, perhaps as a way of talking to himself.

As the political temperature of the late 1920s intensified, Mayakovsky tried to find some way to reconcile the social demands of groups such as RAPP with his often proclaimed beliefs about what the new literature should be. Perhaps partially as a reaction, Mayakovsky turned to the theater. Previously he had acted and written films, so it was not completely unexpected—although no one had ever known him to be an avid theater-goer. In a sense, of course, Mayakovsky had always been an actor, giving one-man shows, engaging the audiences in raucous debates and so on. Meyerhold, the most artistically radical director was the logical producer for *The Bedbug*, Mayakovsky's first play, produced in 1929. The critics were mixed in their reactions, but the general idea was that it was a flawed work, but worth seeing. Debates soon raged around the production, and Meyerhold was satisfied enough to plan another play with the poet, *The Bathhouse*, considered by many to be much inferior to *The Bedbug*.

There were many personal dramas in the year before Mayakovsky died. Where formerly he had been allowed to travel fairly freely, including to America, now he apparently could not get a visa to go to Paris to see a woman who mattered a great deal to him. His literary life was equally difficult. RAPP, which seemed to favor something suspiciously like what was later called Socialist Realism, was attacking Mayakovsky for his posterization of character, his directness, his lack of subtlety. Mayakovsky really had pledged obedience to the "demands" of his political leaders, but he had no use for second-rate imitations of Tolstoy, which is what was being asked of him. In the end he was reproached by his old comrades from the avant-garde LEF group for his decision to join RAPP—and a short time afterward, killed himself, leaving a note which, as always, joined the personal and the political.

In an edition of *A Cloud in Pants: A Tetraptych* published after the Revolution
Mayakovsky identified "the four screams of the four parts" as: "Down with your love,"
"Down with your art," "Down with your society," "Down with your religion." It made sense
for him to stress the anti-bourgeois social and political messages in the poem at this time.
Nevertheless, the poem is better seen as stressing the poet's screams rather than the targets of
the screams: it is a lyrical monologue that expresses the poet's anguished reaction in 1914-15 to
love, art, society and religion—his rage and anguish over unrequited love, criticism of his art,
the oppressive social structure and the absence of god and meaning in the universe. The poet
Mayakovsky is clearly the subject. More than any other poet of the day Mayakovsky
destroyed the poetic conventions of the nineteenth century. He restructured poetry
graphically, greatly varied rhyme schemes, created new rhymes, often using neologisms and
street language for this purpose. He made especially innovative use of metaphor. The lyrical
narrator of *A Cloud* may seem to ramble at first, but the poem's structure is extremely
complex and ordered and the work of a great poet.

"The Atlantic Ocean" was written on a ship while Mayakovsky was on his way to
America. Here the Revolution is seen as an elemental force, like the ocean, and offers the poet
temporary hope. The last poem, "It's almost two...," is a fragment from a poem Mayakovsky
was working on during his last weeks. He used four lines in his suicide note, changing the
"you" of "you and I are through" to "life."

A Cloud in Pants

A Tetraptych

I'll taunt your thought
with a bloody scrap of heart
as it sits musing on your besotted brain
like a paunchy lackey on a greasy couch;
arrogant and caustic, I will mock myself out until sated.

My soul does not contain a single gray hair,
nor any of an old man's tenderness!
Having shaken the world with the thunder of my voice,
I walk along—handsome
twenty-two years old.

Tender ones! You make your love on violins.
A brute does his on kettledrums.
But, unlike me, you can't turn yourselves inside out
to be just pure lips!

Come in cambric from your parlor
and learn—
prim little official of the angels' league.

You, who calmly turn your lips
as a cook leafs through a cookbook's pages.

If you like—
I'll be demented on meat
—or, changing shades like the sky—
if you like—
I'll be irreproachably sweet,
not a man, but—a cloud in pants!

I don't believe in a blossoming Nice!
Once again I sing the praises
of men as stale as a sickroom,
and women as worn out as proverbs.

1

You think I'm delirious from malaria?

It happened,
it was in Odessa.

"I'll come at four," said Maria.

Eight.
Nine.
Ten.

And then the evening
gloomy,
Decemberish,
turned from the windows
to nightly dread.

At my decrepit back
candelabras snort and cackle.

You wouldn't recognize me now:
a sinewy hulk,
moaning
and writhing.
What can such a clod be wanting?
Well, a clod can want a lot!

After all, it doesn't matter to the self
that it is bronze
or that its heart is of cold iron.
At night it wants to hide its clang,
to bury it in something soft,
in woman.

And so,
gigantic,
I hunch at the window,
forehead melting panes of glass.

Will there be love or not?
And what kind?—
Big or minute?
With a body like this, how can it be big:
it should be a small,
submissive pygmy-love.
A love that shies when car horns blow,
that loves the little bells on horses.

Burying my face
over and over
in the pitted face of the rain,
I wait,
splattered by the rumble of the city's surf.

Midnight, frantic, with a knife,
has caught me now,
has cut me down—
down with him!

The twelfth hour fell
like a head from the executioner's block.

Gray drops of rain howled
on the panes,
amassing into a grimace,
as though the gargoyles were wailing
on Notre Dame de Paris.

Damn you!
Isn't this enough!
Soon a shout will rip apart my mouth.

Then I heard—
quietly,
like a sick man from bed,
a nerve jumped.
I listened—
at first it barely moved
back and forth,
then it started to run,
agitated,
distinct.
Now it and two others
dance a tapdance of despair.

The plaster crashed on the floor below.

Nerves—
big ones,
small ones,
scads of nerves!—
mad nerves, galloping,
and before you know it
their very legs give way!

And night begins to ooze through the room—
my clogged-up eye can't get unstuck from the muck.

Suddenly doors began to clatter,
as if the hotel's teeth
chattered.

You came in,
as brusque as "take that!"
Crushing the suede of your glove,
you said:
"You know—
I'm getting married."

All right, go ahead.
Doesn't matter.
I'll manage.
See how calm I am!
Like the pulse
of a corpse.

Remember?
You used to say:
"Jack London,
money,
love,
passion"—
but I saw only one thing:
You were a Gioconda
that had to be stolen!

And you were.

In love again, I'll go play games,
the arches of my brow enflamed.
So what!
Even in a house that's been burned down
sometimes homeless hoboes live!

You're teasing me?
"You have fewer emeralds of lunacy
than a beggar has kopecks."
Just remember!
When they teased Vesuvius,
Pompei was destroyed!

Hey!
Ladies and gentlemen!
Lovers
of sacrilege,
crimes,
carnage—
have you seen
the worst horror of all—

my face,
when
I
am utterly calm?

And I feel
that for me
"I" is too small.
Someone stubbornly pushes his way out.

Hello!
Who is it?
Mama?
Mama!
Your son is marvelously ill!
Mama!
His heart has caught on fire.
Tell my sisters, Lyuda and Olya,—
that now he has nowhere to go.
Each word,
even a joke,
that he vomits from his blazing mouth,
hurls itself like a naked whore
from a burning brothel.

People sniff—
it smells like burnt flesh!
They've called out help.
Bright and shining!
In helmets!
Please, no big boots!
Tell the firemen:
A burning heart must be climbed caressingly.
I'll do it myself.
I'll pump out barrels of tears from my eyes.
Let me brace myself on my ribs.
I'll leap out! Out I'll leap! Out I'll leap! Out I'll leap!
They've collapsed.
You can't leap out of the heart!

On my smoldering face
From the crevices of lips,
a charred bit of kiss has risen to be thrown.

Mama!
I can't sing.
In my heart's chapel the choir has caught fire!

Scorched figures of words and numbers
rush from the skull
like children from a building ablaze.
Thus terror
thrust high
to grab for the sky
the burning arms of the Lusitania.

Into the apartment quiet
of quivering people
a hundred-eyed blaze bursts from the pier.
Howl a last scream
into the centuries ahead—
if but for this, that I am on fire!

2

Praise me!
I'm more than a match for the great.
I put "negate"
on all that's been done.

Never
do I want to read anything.
Books?
What good are books?

I used to think—
books are made like this:
a poet arrived,
parted his lips a bit,
and immediately the inspired dolt sang—
And that's it!
But it turns out
that before poets take to singing
they pace back and forth, getting corns from all their tramping,
and the foolish fish of the imagination
quietly flips and flops through the heart's slime.
And while they are boiling up some kind of brew
out of loves and nightingales, speaking with rhymes,
the tongueless street writhes—
it has no way to chat and shout.

Town towers of Babel
we raise again in our pride,
but god,
confusing words,
grinds towns
to ground.[1]

In silence the street vented torment.
A shout stood erect in its gullet.
Stuck in its neck,
pudgy taxis and bony horsecabs bristled.
Pedestrians trampled its chest
flatter than tuberculosis.

The city blocked up the road in darkness.

And when—
nevertheless—
the street coughed the jam up onto the square,
pushing aside the church porch that was stepping on its throat,
one thought:
In choirs of an archangel's chorale
a plundered god is coming to punish.

But the street just sat down and shouted:
"Let's go eat!"

The Krupps and little Krupps
grease-paint the city
with creases of menacing brows,
but in the mouth
tiny corpses of dead words rot;
only two live on, growing fat—
"bastards"
and also,
it seems, "soup."

Poets,
soaked in tears and sobs,
rushed from the street, mussing their locks:
"How to sing with two such words
a lady
and of love
and of sweet, dew-covered flowers?"

And behind the poets—
teeming streetfolk:
students,
prostitutes,
salesmen.

Gentlemen!
Stop!
You are not beggars;
how dare you beg alms!

Good-sized folk like us
with yard-long strides
shouldn't listen to them—
we should rip them apart,
stuck like no-cost supplements
to every double bed!

Are we to beg them humbly:
"Help me!"
Implore a hymn
or oratorio!
We ourselves are creators of an impassioned hymn—
the hum of factory and laboratory.[2]

What do I care about Faust,
gliding with Mephisto across the celestial parquet
in a fairy world of rockets!
I know
a nail in my boot
is more nightmarish than any fantasy of Goethe's!

I,
the most golden-tongued,[3]
whose every word
gives the soul a new birth
and celebrates the body's name,
I say to you:
the tiniest little speck of anything alive
is more valuable than all that I will do or have done!

Listen!
A present-day loud-lipped Zarathustra
is preaching,
rushing about and uttering moans!
We
who have faces like slept-on sheets
and lips that droop like chandeliers,
we,
prisoners of a leper-house city,
where gold and grime have festered sores,
we are purer than the azure of Venice,
washed at once by seas and suns!

I spit on the fact that there are no
people like us,
pockmarked with soot,
either in the Homers or the Ovids.
I know
the sun would dim, if it saw
the gold mines of our souls.

Sinews and muscles are truer than prayers.
It's not for us to plead for the charity of the day!
We—
each one—
grasps in our fist
the driving belts of the worlds!

This led me to Golgothas in the halls
of Petrograd, Moscow, Odessa, Kiev,[4]
and there wasn't anyone
who
did not shout:
"Crucify,
crucify him!"
But for me—
you people,
even those who have hurt me—
you are nearer and dearer to me than anything.

Have you seen
how a dog licks the hand that beats it?!

I,
who am laughed at by today's generation,
like a long
dirty joke,
I see something crossing the mountains of time
which no one sees.

There, where men's short sight breaks off,
at the head of hungry hordes,
marches the year Nineteen Sixteen
in Revolution's thorny crown.[5]

And for you I am its precursor,
I am wherever pain is—anywhere;
on every drop of flowing tears
I've nailed myself to a cross.
It's too late to forgive anything!
I've burnt out souls in which tenderness was bred.
That was harder than taking
a thousand thousand Bastilles!

And when
you step forth to meet the savior,
announcing his coming
with revolt—
I will take out
my soul for you,
stomp on it
to make it bigger!—
and, bloodied, give it to you for a banner.

3

Ah, why this!
Whence comes
this swing of dirty fists
in the face of bright joy?

It came
and draped my head in despair—
the thought of madhouses.

And
as in the wreck of a dreadnought
men in suffocating spasms fling themselves
through an opened hatch—
so out his own eye,
rent to the point of screams,
crawled Burlyuk, his senses spent.[6]

Having nearly stained his tearless lids with blood,
he crawled out,
stood,
walked,
and with a tenderness unexpected in a man so stout,
went and said:
"It's good!"

It's good when a yellow shirt
protects the soul from inspection!
It's good
to shout
on the executioner's block:
"Drink Van Houten's cocoa!"

And that second,
bright and bursting
like a Bengal light,
I wouldn't exchange for anything,
I wouldn't . . .

From the cigar smoke
Severyanin's soused face
extended like a liqueur glass.[7]

How can you call yourself a poet,
and, gray and dull, go chirping like a quail!
These days
the world in the skull
must be carved out
with brass knuckles.

You,
distressed by one thought—
"Do I dance gracefully?"—
see how I amuse myself—
I—
a common
pimp and cardshark!

From you
who wallow in romance,
from whom
a stream of tears for centuries has flowed,
I'll go,
placing the sun
like a monocle
in my wide open eye.

And decking myself in wild finery,
I'll walk the earth
to please and set aflame;
and out in front,
on a leash I'll lead Napoleon like a pug.

The whole earth will lie on her back like a woman,
her flesh trembling, ready to give;
things will live—
their lips
will lisp:
"Sweet, sweet, sweet!"

Suddenly
black clouds
and other cloud stuff
tossed about wildly in the heavens,
as if workers in white were raging
after having bitterly struck the sky.

Like a beast, thunder crawled from a cloud
and snorted briskly through enormous nostrils,
and for a moment the sky's face scowled
in the grim grimace of an iron Bismarck.

And someone
entangled in the paths of clouds
extended arms to a cafe—
somehow like a woman,
something somehow tender,
and somehow like a mounted gun.

Do you believe
it is the sun
that gently touches the cheeks of the cafe?
No, it's General Galliffet[8] once more advancing to shoot down insurgents.

Drifters, take your hands out of your pants—
grab a stone, a knife, or a bomb;
and you who have no arms—
come batter with your head!

Come, ye who are hungry,
sweaty,
humble,
spoiled in flea-infested filth!

Come!
We'll paint Mondays and Tuesdays
into holidays with our blood!
Let the earth remember at knife point
whom she wanted to debase!
The earth,
grown obese, like a mistress
Rothschild loved up!

Lamp posts, hoist higher
the blood-stained bodies of grain profiteers—
that flags may blow in the fever of fire
as on every proper holiday.

I swore and swore,
implored,
slit throats,
slid up behind someone
and bit into his flank.

In the sky, red as the Marseillaise,
the sunset shuddered, dying.

Madness again.

There won't be anything.

Night will come,
take a bite,
and devour you.

Look—
is the sky Judas again
with a handful of stars sprinkled by betrayal?
Night came.
It feasted like Mamai,[9]
seated with its backside on the city.
Our eyes cannot pierce the night
black as Azef![10]

I crouch, cast out into corners of bars;
I drench my soul and the tablecloth with wine,
and I see:
in the corner—round eyes—
with her eyes the madonna penetrates the heart.
Why bestow your radiant gaze, painted in a hackneyed art,
upon this tavern crowd!
Don't you see—that once again
they prefer Barabbas
to the spat-upon Golgothan?

Maybe it is intentional
that my face is not newer
than anyone's in this human brew.
I,
maybe,
am just the most handsome
of all your sons.

Give those
who have moulded in joys
a time of quick death,
so that children have leave to grow—
boys—into fathers,
girls—pregnant with child.

And let the new-born grow
the inquisitive gray hair of the wise men—

and they will come—
and they will baptize their children
with the names of my poems.

I, who have sung the machine and England,
maybe I am just
the thirteenth apostle
in the commonest gospel.

And when my voice
bawdily explodes—
from hour to hour,
for whole days,
maybe Jesus Christ sniffs
the forget-me-nots of my soul.

4

Maria! Maria! Maria!
Let me in, Maria!
I can't bear the streets!
You won't?
You'd wait
until my cheeks cave in,
until everyone's had a taste
and I come,
unsavory,
and toothlessly mumble
that today I am
"amazingly chaste."

Maria—
don't you see—
I've already begun to stoop.

In the streets
men will prick the fat of four-story maws,
poke out their little eyes,
worn from forty years of wear—
to hee-haw it up
at my chewing
—again!—
the stale roll of yesterday's caress.

Rain has covered the sidewalks with sobs—
a rogue, hemmed in by puddles,
wet, slobbering on the corpse of cobblestone-clobbered streets,
and on its gray eyelashes—
yes!—
on the hoary icicle eyelashes—
are tears from its eyes—
yes!—
from the downcast eyes of drainpipes.

The rain's mug licked every pedestrian,
but athlete after fleshy athlete flashed by in carriages:
people burst apart
having crammed themselves full,
and fat oozed through the cracks;
from the carriages in a roily stream
the gristle from old cutlets flowed
together with a chewed-on roll.

Maria!
How can I squeeze a quiet word into their fat-clogged ears?
A bird makes a living by song,
it sings,
hungry and resonant,
but I am a man, Maria,
a simple man,
spat out by consumptive night into the Presnya's dirty hand.[11]

Maria, do you want such a man?
Let me in, Maria!
Or I'll choke the doorbell's iron throat with fitful fingers!

Maria!

The common pastures of the streets turn beastly.
The fingers of the crowd have marked my neck.

Let me in!

It hurts!

Look—hat pins
are stuck in my eyes!

She let me in.

Baby!
Don't be afraid
that a wet heap of sweat-bellied women
is sitting on my ox neck—
through life I drag
millions of gigantic pure loves
and a million million little filthy loves.
Don't be alarmed
if again
in the foul weather of betrayal
I cling to thousands of pretty faces—
"Mayakovsky's fans!"—
after all, they are a dynasty
of queens ascended to a madman's heart.

Maria, closer!

In naked shamelessness,
or in shivers of fright,
give me the still fresh charm of your lips:
my heart and I have never reached May;
in my whole life
there is only the hundredth April.

Maria!
One poet sings sonnets to Tiana,[12]
but I—
all flesh,
every bit a man—
just ask for your body
as a Christian asks:
"Give us this day
our daily bread!"

Maria, give!

Maria!
I am afraid to forget your name
as a poet is afraid to forget
a word
as glorious as god
born in the torments of night.

I will love and cherish
your body
as a soldier
mutilated in war,
useless,
alone,
cherishes his one leg.

Maria—
you don't want to?
you don't want to?

Ha!

Then—once again
downcast and dark
I take my heart
watered with tears
and carry it,
as a dog
carries back
to its kennel
a paw run over by a train.

I brighten the road with my heart's blood,
its blossoms stick to my dusty smock.
Like Herod's daughter the sun
will dance a thousand times
around the earth—John the Baptist's head.

And when my measure of years
has finished its dance—
a million drops of blood will be spread
in a path to my father's house.

I'll climb out,
soiled (from spending nights in ditches),
stand at his side,
bend over,
and whisper in his ear:

Listen, mister god!
Aren't you bored
with dipping your fat eyes everyday
into cloud pudding?
Let's—okay?—
build a carousel
on the tree of knowledge of good and evil!
You'll be omnipresent in every cupboard,
and we'll have such wines on the table
that even grouchy Apostle Peter
will want to do the kickapoo![13]
We'll settle Eden with little Eves again:
just command it—
this very night
I'll fetch the prettiest girls on the streets
for you.

Do you want to?

No?

You shake your shaggy head?
Knit your gray brow?
Do you think
the one—
behind you with the wings
knows what is love?

I too am an angel, I was one once—
I had a sweet lamb's gaze;
but I no longer want to make gifts to mares
of vases cast painstakingly in Sèvres.
Almighty, you thought up a pair of hands,
arranged
for everyone to have a head—
but why didn't you fix it
so that without pain one could
kiss and kiss and kiss?

I thought you were a big all-powerful god,
but you're a dabbler, a little tiny god.
Look, I'm bending down,
from my boot
I take a cobbler's knife.

Huddle in heaven
you winged rascals!
Ruffle your feathers in fearful shivers.
You, reeking of incense, I'll rip you wide open
from here to Alaska!

Let me in!

You can't stop me.
Whether I'm telling a lie
or the truth,
I can't be any calmer.
Once more they've beheaded the stars
and slaughter has bloodied the sky!

Hey, you!
Heaven!
Take off your hat!
I'm coming!

Silence.

The universe sleeps,
its huge ear,
star-infested,
rests on a paw.

1914-15
Translated by Carl R. Proffer and Mary Ann Szporluk

Notes

1. In the Russian, God has to change only one letter to turn towers (*bashni*) into pastures (*pashni*).

2. The "we" refers to the Futurists.

3. An epithet used to describe preachers in Old Russian literature, in particular, St. John Chrysostom.

4. The Futurists toured Russia and provoked as much scandal as they could. Mayakovsky liked to wear black trousers, a yellow and black striped shirt, and a high silk hat.

5. Mayakovsky revised the date after the Revolution, thus making his prophecy more sound. See Edward J. Brown, *Mayakovsky: A Poet in the Revolution.*

6. David Burlyuk, painter, fellow Futurist and Mayakovsky's friend. Burlyuk was blind in one eye.

7. Igor Severyanin, a poet who considered himself a Futurist but whose poems Mayakovsky thought sentimental and superficial.

8. The French General Galliffet helped suppress the insurrection of the Paris Commune (1871).

9. Mamai, Khan of the Golden Horde. Mayakovsky alludes to the story that after a successful battle Mamai feasted on planks laid across the bodies of Russian prisoners.

10. Evno Azef (1869-1918) was an agent provocateur in the pay of the Tsarist secret police.

11. The Presnya was a working-class district of Moscow where Mayakovsky lived.

12. A reference to a poem by Severyanin.

13. A dance named after the Kickapoo Indians, an American Indian tribe that gave shows in Europe at the time.

The Atlantic Ocean

A blinding white is the Spanish rock,
like teeth of a saw its sides.
Now the steamer ate coal until twelve o'clock
and fresh water drank besides.
Then thrusting its iron prow forward, the steamer
at one,
weighed anchor, snorted and raced ahead, steaming.
Then Europe shrank, and was gone.
Alongside the ship the water chunks hurry,
and huge as the years, they pound.
Overhead the birds fly, underneath fish scurry,
water all around.
Sometimes hard-working and now a drunk blundering—
heaving and sighing for weeks and weeks—
from out its athletic chest the thundering
ocean speaks.
"I'd like to go to
the Sahara, creep up slowly...
Just let go and spit—
down below's a ship.
I might sink it,
or aid its trip.
Come out dry now, group—
you'll boil in soup.
We don't need people much—
too small for eating.
All right...don't touch them...
let them be then..."
Waves at agitation are expert:
splashing out one's childhood, or voice of a dear one.
Well, I'd like to have a banner to unfurl!
There—it's started, that is thunder we are hearing!
The translucent water again calms and levels
and there is no one whom we need to doubt.
And then from somewhere—who knows but the devil!—
a watery REVCOM rises from out
the depths. Water-partisans—a guard of droplets—
begin to climb up from the ocean's abyss;
they fling themselves up to the sky and then drop again
and tear the royal robe of foam into bits.

Commanding the wave to lead, strong and loud,
the waters in one stream have merged once again.
A huge wave crashes from under a cloud—
and orders and slogans it sends down like rain.
The waves vow their storm's force will not be abated,
to see that till victory it never stops.
And now they have conquered—around the equator
extends the power of Soviet drops.
The last waves grouped into little gatherings
are clamoring in a style that's exalted.
The ocean is smiling now after its lathering,
grows calm for a little while, its uproar halted.
I look past the railing. Strive onward, associates!
Below the ship's ladder, bridgelike, I discern
a wave committee that negotiates
and sweats over something, an ocean concern.
A coral palace in businesslike manner
beneath the waves is quietly growing,
that daily life may not be too demanding
for working whales and for the young whales not grown yet.
Already the moon like a path they've extended.
You almost could crawl on it, as on dry ground.
The watchful Atlantic eyes gaze, intending
to see that the enemy won't poke around.
You're chilled in moonlight's bright lacquered shining,
you're groaning, foam-drenched in wounds and in pains.
I look, I look at the sea, always find it
unchanged, dear to me it remains.
Your thunder always will fill my hearing.
Into my eyes I will empty you.
The brother of my revolution—in spirit,
in wideness, in blood, in the work you do.

1925
Translated by Jamie Fuller

It's almost two. You're probably in bed.
Tonight the Milky Way is like the silver Oka.
I'm in no rush, with lightning telegrams
I've no reason to wake and worry you.
And as they say, the incident is closed.
The daily grind has wrecked the love boat.
You and I are even. Useless the list
Of mutual wrongs and hurt and heartache.
And just behold the hush across the world.
The night has swathed the sky in starry tribute.
In hours like these one stands and speaks
To history, the ages, and the universe.

1927-30
Translated by Carl R. Proffer

NIKOLAI ZABOLOTSKY

Nikolai Zabolotsky (1903-58), a former member of the Leningrad literary fellowship known as Oberiu (The Association for Real Art) published his first and best-known book of poetry, *Scrolls,* in 1929. This was followed by the long poem *Triumph of Agriculture* (1933) and *Second Book of Verse* (1937), both of which, as had been the case with *Scrolls,* were viciously attacked in the press. The poet was arrested on false charges in 1938 and sentenced to five years hard labor. Zabolotsky published verse again after his release and began to receive favorable notice in the mid-1950s.

Etching

And it rang out through the whole deafening hall:
"The corpse has escaped from the royal house!"

The corpse goes proudly through the streets,
as the tenants lead him by the reins;
he chants a prayer in the voice of a trumpet
and wrings his hands upwards.
In copper spectacles, membrane frames,
he is up to his neck in subterranean water,
above him wooden birds with a knock
close the shutters like wings.
And round about is a thunderous battle,
the rattling of top hats, and a curly-headed sky,
but here is an urban box with an unfastened door
and behind the little window—rosemary.

January 1927
Translated by Christopher Fortune

Summer

The crimson sun hung full length,
and not only I enjoyed it—
peoples' bodies ripened like pears,
and their swelled heads swayed.
Trees turned soft. They grew fat
like greasy tallow candles. And it seemed—
that beneath them it was not a dusty stream running by,
but a thick stretch of saliva spreading.
Then night approached. In the meadows
prickly stars danced among the flowers,
furry sheep lay like balls,

curly candles of trees went out;
and a shepherd, sitting in a gully,
drew diagrams of the moon,
and dogs fought for posts
to keep watch...

August 1927
Translated by Christopher Fortune

The Bathers

What monk is this that forsakes the stove,
and climbs into a bath or a wash tub—
come, bathe in the river,
renounce all ugliness!

Who is plunging into the water
with a cuckoo hidden in his hand—
swimming at the head of a detachment,
with smoke coming from his groin.

Everyone, their clothes and bits of armor
removed for the first time,
is swimming out like ignoramuses,
but then success comes!

The water, like a tender goose,
nibbles parts of youthful bodies,
and leads you by a blue hand,
if you've come out in a sweat.

If someone doesn't wish
to stay wet very long—
he can rub himself dry with a kerchief
the colors of ochre and air.

If someone is tormented
by fear of temptation,—
he can quickly cool off,
while resting motionless.

If someone can't love,
and is devoured by anguish,—
he can now help himself,
as he quietly swims with a board.

O river, bride and wet-nurse,
holding everyone to your bosom,
you're neither maid nor spinster,
but a saint in an icon!

Neither are you maid or nurse,
but Saint Paraskovya,
O come and meet us bathers
where the sand and rushes grow!

1928
Translated by Christopher Fortune

Snowball Fight

A scuffle boils in the snow.
A dog flies by like an ethereal god.
An urchin hits his foe in the belly.
A black grouse lives in a fir tree.
Icy bombs whistle by.
It's evening. The snow gleams.
The urchin climbs onto his foe,
Digging catacombs in the snow drifts.
One, having pulled up his crooked legs,
Rolled down the hillock, and the other
Was stuck in the snow, and the two new,
Unkempt, contorted, crimson lads
Hit and grappled with each other,
But the wooden knife saved the day.

Sunset passed. And day ended.
And a shaggy horse approached like a giant.
The great hulk of an enormous peasant
Sat in the tresses of a painted sleigh,
And a spark smouldered in his copper pipe.

The battle ceased. The peasant sat immobile.

1928
Translated by Christopher Fortune

Beginning of Autumn

Old women, sitting by the gate,
Munch the fog of cabbage soup and cinders,
Here, hurrying to the factory,
A proletarian walked along the lane,—
Untouched by the center of O,
He walked, having fastened the periphery,
And the wind buffeted him.

Sable comes from Siberia,
And the Crimea gives us apples,
And a girl, taking four rubles,
Eats fruit as she admires the youth.

In his eyes—the rudiments of knowledge,
Then they sink into each others arms,
All the sciences gathered in his brain
In order to compete.
Like a dream of worldly geometry,
The axes of houses rattled above him,
In the unusually strong wind,
And in the center of O, autumn glimmered,
And touching it like a chord, perhaps,
A maple swayed, crying from pain,
The maple swayed, and like a flash of intellect,
The universe itself appeared to us!

1929
Translated by Christopher Fortune

Man in the Water

Who carved and forged
The contours of the body and the mind?
There, where the sea-kaurma is,
The wave rises like an idol.

His head a hairless skull,
Pale skin white as a maggot,
A man sat before the waves,
Straightening his tail.

Unfolding his palms,
Like white pancakes,
He swayed on a horse blanket
The whole length of his spine.

Every little joint
Was steamed and swollen.
And with the sea lashing his body
The man bathed.

The man dove to the bottom,
His body piercing the sea.
And the tide rose like an idol,
Obscuring the spot on the bottom.

The man, like a goose, like a crab,
His beak trumpeting joyously,
Left the bottom ravine,
And rose, tugging his little beard.

He swung his tail,
Stamped his foot,
And whirled like a wheel,
Hairless and naked.

And on his broiled back,
Laughing at the mad man,
The infusorias alone
Nibbled the skin of this bold fellow.

1930
Translated by Christopher Fortune

Cover of the Smithy journal *Kuznitsa*.

THE SMITHY POETS

The Smithy (*Kuznitsa*) was formed in 1920 by a group of proletarian writers, primarily poets, who had left Proletkult for ideological reasons. As their name indicates, the subject of the poetry is labor, the factory, the working class; that is, the elements necessary to forge a new society and art. Mikhail Gerasimov's "Iron," Vasily Kazin's "The Heavenly Foundry" and Vladimir Kirillov's "The Iron Messiah" are typical examples of the Smithy's cast-iron poetry. The Smithy issued a number of declarations and manifestoes on the definition and purpose of proletarian art, but this rhetoric had little bearing on their verse production, which drew heavily on Symbolist versification and revealed no new proletarian form of art.

Vladimir Kirillov
We

We are the countless, dread legions of Labor.
We are the conquerors of seas, oceans and land,
We have illumined cities with the light of artificial suns,
Our proud souls burn with the fire of rebellion.

We are in the hold of a terrible, passionate intoxication;
Let them shout: "You are the executioners of beauty";
In the name of Tomorrow—we will burn Raphael,
We will destroy museums and trample the flowers of art.

We have overthrown the weight of our oppressive inheritance,
We have repudiated the chimeras of bloodless wisdom;
Maidens in the radiant kingdom of the Future
Will be more beautiful than Venus...

Our tears have run dry, tenderness has been slain,
We have forgotten the scent of grass and spring flowers.
We love the power of steam and the force of dynamite,
The song of sirens and the motion of wheels and shafts...

O, poets-esthetes, curse the Great Boor,
Kiss the remnants of the past under our feet,
Wash the ruins of the felled temples with your tears,—
We are free, we are bold, we are alive with another beauty,

The muscles of our arms long for a gigantic task,
The collective breast burns with creative suffering,
We will fill the combs to overflowing with a wonderful honey,
We will find another, dazzling path for our planet.

We love life, its turbulent, intoxicating ecstasy,
Our spirit is tempered with stormy struggle and suffering.
We are all, we are in all, we are the flame and triumphant light,
We are God, Judge and Law.

Translated by Arthur Jacobsen

Mikhail Gerasimov

We will take all, we will know all,
We will pierce to the bottom of the depths.
Our vernal soul is intoxicated
Like the golden, flowering May.

There is no limit to our proud daring:
We are Wagner, da Vinci and Titian.
We will crown the new museum
With a cupola as tall as Mont Blanc.

In the crystals of the marble Angelo,
And all that was the grandeur of Parnassus,
Does not creative power sing
Like an electric current in us?

They cultivated orchids,
They rocked the roses' cradles,
Was it not we who were in Judea,
When Christ taught the lesson of love?

We raised the stone of the Parthenon
And the gigantic pyramids;
We cut the ringing granite
For all the sphinxes, temples, pantheons.

Was it not for us on Mount Sinai,
In the burning bush,
Like the sun, the Red Banner, shining,
Showed itself in storm and fire?

We will take all, we will know all,
We will pierce the turquoise of the heavens.
How sweet to drink, like flowering May,
The life-giving thunderstorm.

Translated by Arthur Jacobsen

Autograph of Pasternak's poem "My Sister—Life," from a handwritten copy given to Lily Brik by the poet.

Velimir Khlebnikov.

VELIMIR KHLEBNIKOV

In 1910 the young Velimir Khlebnikov (1885-1922) published his most famous poem "Incantation by Laughter," a work that was to become a touchstone for the fledgling Futurist movement. This poem (presented below in two translations), constructed entirely upon the root *smekh* (laughter) is the first of Khlebnikov's many experiments in which "a work of art is the art of the word" ("The Word as Such"). Khlebnikov soon entered into association with the Futurists, for whom he coined the term *budetlyane* (those who will be), and published in their first almanac *A Trap for Judges* (1910) and subsequent publications and manifestoes, including the scandalous "A Slap in the Face of Public Taste" (1912).

Judged an eccentric individual, even against the background of his bohemian confreres, Khlebnikov pursued several seemingly contradictory interests in his life and art. His mystical search for fundamental truth in the roots of words, which he believed had an extra-linguistic significance, led him to investigate the language and folklore of Old Russia and write futuristic utopias. The reduction (and expansion) of meaning as signified by linguistic roots also drew him to experiment with *zaum* (trans-sense; literally, beyond the mind), where entire compositions are constructed on the orchestration of sound qua sound (e.g., *Zangezi*). In addition Khlebnikov's interests included numerology, where he sought the "laws of history."

Khlebnikov was quite indifferent to the publication of his works, most of which were published posthumously by Yury Tynyanov and N. Stepanov (1928-33). Many works have been lost altogether. Vladimir Mayakovsky, in his warm remembrance of Khlebnikov, summarizes the poet's significance for his generation:

> Khlebnikov's poetical fame is immeasurably less than his significance.
>
> For every hundred readers, fifty considered him simply a graphomaniac, forty read him for pleasure and were astonished that they found none, and only ten (futurist poets and philologists of the "OPOYAZ") knew and loved this Columbus, this discoverer of new poetic continents that we now populate and cultivate.*

Incantation by Laughter

O laugh it out, you laughsters!
O laugh it up, you laughsters!
So they laugh with laughters, so they laugherize delaughly.
O laugh it up belaughably!
O the laughingstock of the laughed-upon—the laugh of belaughed laughsters!
O laugh it out roundlaughingly, the laugh of laughed-at laughians!
Laugherino, laugherino,
Laughify, laughicate, laugholets, laugholets,
Laughikins, laughikins,
O laugh it out, you laughsters!
O laugh it up, you laughsters!

Major Soviet Writers: Essays in Criticism, ed. Edward J. Brown (1973), p. 83.

Guffaw Incantation

O guff it out, you guffsters!
O guff it up, you guffsters!
So they guffaw with guffaws, so they gufferize disguffly.
O guff it up beguffably!
O the guffathon of the guffed-upon—the guff of guffed-off guffsters!
O guff it off outguffingly, the guff of guffed-at guffians!
Guffily, guffily,
Guffify, gufficate, guffolets, guffolets,
Guffikins, guffikins,
O guff it out, you guffsters!
O guff it up, you guffsters!

Zaklyatie smekhom (Transliteration)

O, rassmeites', smekhachi!
O, zasmeites', smekhachi!
Chto smeyutsya smekhami, chto smeyanstvuyut smeyal'no.
O, zasmeites' usmeyal'no!
O, rassmeshishch nadsmeyal'nykh—smekh usmeinykh smekhachei!
O, issmeisya rassmeyal'no, smekh nadsmeinykh smeyachei!
Smeievo, smeievo,
Usmei, osmei, smeshiki, smeshiki,
Smeyunchiki, smeyunchiki,
O, rassmeites', smekhachi!
O, zasmeites', smekhachi!

* * *

O the racing cloud's Dostoevskitude!
O the melting noon's Pushkinations!
The night is seen like Tyutchev
Pouring immensity into transmensity.

Liberty for Everyone

Whirlwind united, whirlwind immortal,
Everyone for freedom—swirl on!
Bearing the banner of labor,
Go men with the wind of a swan.
Burning with freedom their eyes shine,
The flame by comparison is cold,
Onto the ground go the icons!
Hunger paints new ones for old...
Toward fiery songs we are moving,
Everyone for freedom—ahead!
If we should perish—we'll be resurrected!

Each one will live life again.
We move down the pathway enchanted,
Harking to our stamping sounds.
If then the gods be encaptive,
Liberty we'll give to the gods...

The Lone Performer

And while above Tsarskoe Selo[1]
Akhmatova's[2] song and tears were pouring,
I, unwinding the skein of the sorceress,
Dragged through the desert like a sleepy corpse,[3]
There where impossibility lay dying:
An exhausted mummer
Determined to break through.
And meanwhile in dark caves
The curly brow of the underground bull
Bloodily champed and dined on people
Amid the smoke of threats immodest.
And wrapped in the will of the moon,
As in a sleepy cloak, the twilight wanderer
Jumped in his sleep above the chasms
And went from cliff to cliff.
Blinded, I went on while
The wind of freedom moved me
And beat with slanting rain
And the bull's head I took from mighty meats and bone
And stuck beside the wall.
Above the world I shook it, like a soldier of the truth:
Behold it, here it is!
Here is that curly brow which once inflamed the crowds![4]
And horrified
I understood that I was seen by none:
That one must sow the eyes,
That the eye-sower must go!

1. Tsarskoe Selo—a town outside of St. Petersburg, place of the lycée where Pushkin studied. Renamed Pushkin in 1937.

2. Anna Akhmatova's lyrics include a cycle titled "In Tsarskoe Selo."

3. *Kak sonnyi trup vlachilsya po pustyne*—an echo of Pushkin's "The Prophet" (1826): *V pustyne mrachnoi ya vlachilsya (*I dragged through the dismal desert).

4. Khlebnikov alludes to the myth of the Marathonian Bull and the Minotaur, both of which were killed by Theseus.

Zangezi (Excerpt)

Explanation: In the ninth section of this work Khlebnikov improvises on the Russian root "um" (mind), adding to it both conventional and unconventional prefixes. The translation below leaves the resulting neologisms as in the original and converts the standard Russian words into English ("razum" is the standard word for "reason"). The intended meanings of the "um" words are given in a list Khlebnikov attached to the work.

I

Goum.
Oum.
Uum.
Paum.
Soum of me
And of those I don't know
Moum.
Boum.
Laum.
Cheum.
Bom!
Bim
Bam!

II

Proum
Praum
Prium
Nium
Vèum
Roum
Zaum
Vyum
Voum
Boum
Byum
Bom!
Help, bell ringers, I'm tired.

III

Doum.
Daum.
Mium.
Raum.
Khoum.
Khaum.
Bang the glad tidings of the mind!
Here's the bell and the rope.

IV

Suum.
Izum.
Neum.
Naum.
Dvuum.
Treum.
Deum.
Bom!
Zoum.
Koum.
Soum.
Poum.
Glaum.
Raum.
Noum.
Nuum.
Vyum.
Bom! bom, bom!
It's the big booming bell of the mind.
Divine sounds flying down from above at the summons of man.
Beautiful is the tolling of the mind.
Beautiful are its pure sounds.

Khlebnikov's List (Translator's remarks in parentheses):

Vyum—an invention. Of course, the unlove of the old leads to *vyum*. *(Vy=*out, working out, outcome, etc.)

Noum—a hostile mind leading to other conclusions, a mind saying *no* to the first. (The Russian word *no=*but.)

Goum—high as those trinkets of the sky, the stars, which are invisible during the day. From fallen lords (*gosudari) goum* takes the dropped staff *Go*. (That is, the first two letters of *gosudari,* which Khlebnikov takes to mean "high.")

Laum—broad, flowing over the broadest area, knowing no confining shores, like a flooding river. (Khlebnikov has in mind the l-sound of *lit'*—to flow, pour; *lodka*—boat; *letat'*—to fly; etc.)

Koum—calm, binding, providing foundations, books, rules and laws. (These words have *k* as the first letter of their roots: *spo-koinyi=*calm, *s-kovyvayushchii=*binding, *knigi=*books, *za-kony=*laws.)

Laum—descends from the heights into crowds toward everyone. It tells the fields what is seen from the mountain.

*Cheum-*raising the cup (*chasa)* to the unknown future. Its *zori* (dawns) are *chezori.* Its *luch* (ray) is *cheluch.* Its *plamya* (flame) is *cheplamya.* Its *volya* (will) is *chevolya.* Its *gore* (woe) is *chegore.* Its *negi* (delights) are *chenegi.*

Moum—pernicious, destructive, devastating. It is forecast in the borders of faith.

Vèum—the mind of apprenticeship and faithful citizenship, of a pious spirit. (Perhaps the *v* from the word *vera*—faith, trust, belief.)

Oum—abstract, surveying everything around itself, from the height of one thought. (*Ozirat'=*to survey, look around.)

Izum—a leaping out of the borders of the everyday mind. (*Iz=*out of.)

Daum—affirmative. (*Da=*yes.)

Noum—argumentative. (See above.)

Suum—half-mind.

Soum—reason coworker. (*So*=with, co-.)

Nuum—commanding. (*Nu!*=Well!: Get on with it!)

Khoum—secret, hidden reason.

Byum—desiring reason, made not by what is, but by what it wants. (*By*=a particle indicating conditional mood.)

Nium—negative. (*Ni*=not, neither.)

Proum—foresight. (*Pro*=through.)

Praum—the reason of a distant land, a mind-ancestor. (*Pra* is a Russian prefix indicating origin, ancient times, equivalent to the German prefix *Ur-.*)

Boum—a nail of thought driven into the board of stupidity.

Vyum—a fallen hoop of stupidity, knowing no boundaries, no borders, a radiant, shining mind. (See above.)

Raum—its speeches (*rechi*) are *rarogi.*

Zoum—reflected mind. (Possibly from *zerkalo*—mirror.)

Some of the above meanings derive from Khlebnikov's theories on the meanings of individual sounds [see Khlebnikov's article "The Simple Names of the Language"]. Other meanings are based on common Russian prefixes and particles. Below are some Khlebnikov did not list:

Prium—the prefix *pri* indicates motion toward the speaker or thinker.

Zaum—transmind; the preposition *za* means "beyond"; the term *zaum* was used by the Futurists for "trans-sense" poetry.

Doum—the prefix *do* indicates action up to a given point, or to completion.

Neum—unmind; *ne*=not, non-, un-, etc.

Naum—the preposition *na*=on, upon; the interjection *na*=take this.

Dvuum—bimind; *dvu-* =two, bi-.

Treum—trimind; *tre-* =three, tri-.

Deum—the particle *de* indicates supposition, mention, rumor.

Glaum—*gla-* is probably taken from *glaz*—eye, glyadet'—to see, stare.)

Translations and Notes by Gary Kern

VLADIMIR MAYAKOVSKY

The Bedbug had its premiere February 13, 1929, at Meyerhold's theater. The sets were by Rodchenko and the Kukryniksy, the music by the young Shostakovich, and Meyerhold gave his best actors the major roles. There had been many plays about the reemergence of the bourgeois during NEP, most prominently *Zoya's Apartment* by Bulgakov, an artistic opponent of Mayakovsky. The material about the future world was also fairly shop-worn by this time, as were devices borrowed from Gogol's *Inspector General*. However, the use Mayakovsky made of this material was remarkable, through his exuberant imagination and his verbal energy. Mayakovsky's ability to divide himself into opposing characters was very suited to Meyerhold's technique of radical dissonance. It has been reported that both Mayakovsky and Meyerhold were a bit ironic about the "tasteful" world of the future, pallid as all such worlds tend to be, but it is not at all clear that the critics of the time noticed this irony.

Mayakovsky's personal dialectic—almost civil war in this work—was never more obvious than in the evolution during the course of the play of his anti-hero Prysipkin. From a thoroughly loathsome hustler in the first act, he gradually becomes the most human and touching figure in the work, especially when contrasted with the sterile world of the future. His vitality is his creator's vitality, and there is a sense in which one may conclude that the future will have no real use for either one of them.

THE BEDBUG
A COMIC FANTASY IN NINE SCENES

Dramatis Personae

Prisypkin (Pierre Skripkin), a former worker, a former member of the
    Party, now a fiancé
Zoya Beryozkina, a working girl
Elzevira Davidovna Renaissance, the fiancée, a manicurist, a cashier of a
    beauty parlor
Rosaliya Pavlovna Renaissance, the mother, a hairdresser
David Osipovich Renaissance, the father, a barber
Oleg Bayan (Bard or Accordian), a person of natural talents,
    from the houseowners
Policeman
Professor
Director of a Zoo
Chief of a Fire Brigade

Firemen
Groomsman
Reporter
Workers
Chairman of the City Street
Orator
College Students
Master of Ceremonies
Presidium of the City Soviet, Hunters, Children, Old Folks

I

(Center: huge revolving door of a department store, on the sides are display windows overstocked with goods. People are entering empty-handed and coming out with parcels. Private peddlers are walking about through the whole theater.)

BUTTON PEDDLER: On account of a button it's not worth getting married, on account of a button it's not worth getting divorced! Press the thumb and the index finger, and the pants will never fall down, citizens.
> Dutch,
> mechanized,
> self-sewing buttons,
> six for twenty kopecks...
> Here y'are, moosieu.

DOLL PEDDLER:
> Dancing people
> from the ballet studios.
> The best toy
> for in the garden or in the home,
> It dances to the order
> of the People's Commissar himself!

WOMAN PEDDLING APPLES:
> Pineapples!
>> ain't got any...
> Bananas
>> ain't got any...
> Antonov apples four for fifteen kopecks.
> What do you say, citizen lady!

MAN PEDDLING WHETSTONES:
> German
>> unbreakable
>>> whetstones,

Any
    one
        for thirty
            kopecks
Sharpens
    in any
        direction
            and style
razors
    knives
        and tongues for discussions!
Here you are citizens!
MAN PEDDLING LAMP SHADES:
Lamp shades
    of every
        color and size.
Blue for coziness,
        red for sweet passion.
Set yourselves up, comrades!
MAN SELLING BALLOONS:
Little sausage-balloons.
Fly without a care.
If General Nobile[1]
    had had
        such a balloon,—
They could have stayed
        longer at the North Pole.
Take one, citizens...
MAN PEDDLING HERRINGS:
Over here
    the best
        republican herrings,
indispensable
    with blini and vodka!
WOMAN PEDDLING LINGERIE:
Fur-lined bras,
Fur-lined bras!
MAN SELLING GLUE:
In our country
    and abroad,
        and everywhere else too,
citizens
    throw out
        broken crockery.
The celebrated

Excelsior
>powdered-glue
glues anything
>from a Venus de Milo
>>to a chamber pot.
Like to try some, madam?
WOMAN SELLING PERFUME:
>Coty perfume
>>by the quarter-ounce!
>Coty perfume
>>by the quarter-ounce!
MAN SELLING BOOKS: What the wife does, when the husband isn't around. A hundred and five hilarious stories by the former Count Leo Nikolaevich Tolstoi. Instead of a ruble twenty—fifteen kopecks.
WOMAN PEDDLING LINGERIE:
>Fur-lined bras,
>Fur-lined bras!

(Enter Prisypkin, Rosaliya Pavlovna, Oleg Bayan.)

WOMAN PEDDLER: Bras...
PRISYPKIN (*enthusiastically*): What aristocratic bonnets!
ROSALIYA PAVLOVNA: They're not bonnets, they're...
PRISYPKIN: Do you think I'm blind? Suppose we have twins? That one will be for Dorothy and that one for Lillian...I've already decided to give them aristocratic-cinematic names...so when they go out walking together. Right! My house must be a horn of plenty. Grab those bonnets, Rosaliya Pavlovna!
BAYAN *(tittering):* Grab'em, grab'em, Rosaliya Pavlovna! He doesn't mean to be crude. It's a young class, it understands everything in its own way. He brings into your home an ancient, unsullied, proletarian origin and a trade-union card, and you begrudge him a few rubles! Their house must be a horn of plenty.

(Rosaliya Pavlovna, sighing, makes the purchase.)

BAYAN: I'll carry them...they're really light...don't worry...it won't cost you anything...
MAN PEDDLING TOYS: Dancing people from the ballet studios...
PRISYPKIN: My future offspring must be brought up in a refined spirit. Go ahead! Grab one, Rosaliya Pavlovna!
ROSALIYA PAVLOVNA: Comrade Prisypkin...
PRISYPKIN: Don't call me comrade, citizeness, you haven't become related to the proletariat yet.
ROSALIYA PAVLOVNA: Future Comrade, Citizen Prisypkin, after all for

this money fifteen men could shave their beards, not counting the change—whiskers, and all. Wouldn't an extra dozen beers for the wedding be better?

PRISYPKIN (*sternly*): Rosaliya Pavlovna! I must...

BAYAN: He must live in plenty. Dancing and beer must gush forth like a fountain, like out of a cornucopia.

(Rosaliya Pavlovna buys.)

BAYAN (*seizing the parcels*): Don't worry, it won't cost you anything.

MAN PEDDLING BUTTONS:
On account of a button it's not worth getting married!
On account of a button it's not worth getting divorced!

PRISYPKIN: In our Red family there must be no petty bourgeois way of life and no trouser squabbles. Go on! Grab some, Rosaliya Pavlovna!

BAYAN: As long as you don't have a trade-union card, don't nag him, Rosaliya Pavlovna. He is the victorious class, and he sweeps away everything in his path, like lava, and the trousers of Comrade Skripkin must be a horn of plenty.

(Rosaliya Pavlovna buys with a sigh.)

BAYAN: Let me, I'll carry them and it won't cost...

MAN SELLING HERRINGS:
The best republican herrings!
Indispensable
with any kind of vodka!

ROSALIYA PAVLOVNA: *(loudly pushing everybody aside and cheering up):* A little herring—yes—of course! That's what you have to have for a wedding. I'll grab some of those, alright! Let me through, moosieus men! How much is this sprat?

PEDDLER: This salmon costs two-sixty a kilo.

ROSALIYA PAVLOVNA: Two-sixty for that overgrown sprat?

MAN SELLING HERRING: Really, madam, only two-sixty for this candidate to the sturgeon family!

ROSALIYA PAVLOVNA: Two-sixty for those marinated corset bones? Did you hear that, Comrade Skripkin? You were so right when you killed the tsar and drove out Mister Ryabushinsky![2] Oh! These bandits! I'll get my citizen's rights and my herrings at the State Soviet Socialized Co-op!

BAYAN: Let's wait here, Comrade Skprikin. Why should you get mixed up with this petty bourgeois element and buy herrings in such debatable fashion? For fifteen rubles and a bottle of vodka I'll organize a little wedding that'll suit you to a "t".

PRISYPKIN: Comrade Bayan, I'm against this petty bourgeois way of life— canaries and the rest...I'm a man with lofty needs...I'm interested in a dresser with a mirror.

(Zoya Beryozkina almost bumps into them while they are talking; surprised, she steps back and listens.)

BAYAN: When your wedding cortege...

PRISYPKIN: What are you chattering about? What card game?

BAYAN: Cortege, I said. That's what any procession is called in those lovely languages, Comrade Skripkin, and particularly such a solemn wedding procession as this.

PRISYPKIN: Ah! Well, well, of course!

BAYAN: So then, when the cortege approaches, I'll sing for you the epithalamium of Hymen.

PRISYPKIN: What are you chattering on about? What Himalayas?

BAYAN: Not Himalayas, but an epithalamium[3] about the god Hymen. That was a god of love the Greeks had; not these mad, brutish opportunists like Venizelos,[4] but the ancient republican Greeks.

PRISYPKIN: Comrade Bayan, for my money I demand a Red wedding and not any gods! Understand?

BAYAN: Yes of course, Comrade Skripkin, not only do I understand, but by the power of the imagination granted to Marxists, according to Plekhanov, I see as through a prism your class-conscious, lofty, elegant, and rapturous triumph!...The bride climbs out of the carriage—a red bride...all red...all steamed up, that is: a red escort, the bookkeeper, Yerykalov, is leading her; he's just a corpulent, red, apoplectic man...then red groomsmen lead you in, the whole table is covered with red hams and the bottles have red seals.

PRISYPKIN: *(agreeably)*: That's it! That's it!

BAYAN: Red guests cry "bitter, bitter," and then your red bride (already your wife) turns her red-red lips to you...

ZOYA *(confused, she seizes both of them by the arm. Both remove her hands, flicking the dust off their sleeves.)*: Vanya! What is he saying? What's this cuttlefish in a necktie chattering about? What wedding? Whose wedding?

BAYAN: The Red working-class nuptials of Elzevira Davidovna Renaissance and ...

PRISYPKIN:

> I, Zoya the Tub, I love another.
> She is more graceful and slender,
> and on her, an exquisite jacket
> holds her bosom tight.

ZOYA: Vanya! What about me? What does this mean: like a sailor you've loved me and left me?

PRISYPKIN *(pushing her off with an outstretched hand)*: We've parted like ships at sea ...

ROSALIYA PAVLOVNA (*She rushes out of a store, carrying a herring over her head*): Whales! Dolphins! (*To the merchant with the herrings.*) And now, show me! Let's compare it to your snail! (*She compares; the hawker's herring is larger; she throws up her hands.*) Longer by a tail?! What did we struggle for, Citizen Skripkin? Why did we kill the sovereign emperor and drive out Mister Ryabushinsky, eh? Your Soviet power will drive me into the grave... By a tail, longer by a whole tail!..

BAYAN: Dear Rosaliya Pavlovna, compare it from the other end—it's longer only by a head, and why do you need the head—it's not edible, you'll only cut it off and throw it away.

ROSALIYA PAVLOVNA: Did you hear what he said? Cut off the head. If I cut off your head, Citizen Bayan, nothing will be lost and it won't cost anything, but if I cut off the herring's head it costs ten kopecks to the kilo. Well! Let's go home! I really need a trade-union card in the family, but my daughter is in a profitable business—and that's nothing for you to shake a stick at.

ZOYA: We wanted to live together, we wanted to work together... So now it's all over...

PRISYPKIN: Citizeness! Our love has been liquidated. Don't interfere with my free civic feeling, otherwise I'll call the police.

(*Zoya, crying, grabs him by the arm. Prisypkin tears himself away. Rosaliya Pavlovna steps between them, dropping her packages.*)

ROSALIYA PAVLOVNA: What does this slut want? What are you clinging to my son-in-law for?

ZOYA: He's mine!

ROSALIYA PAVLOVNA: Aha!.. So she's pregnant! I'll pay her the alimony, but first I'll smash her mug!

POLICEMAN: Citizens, Stop this disgusting scene!

II

(*A dormitory for workers and students. An Inventor is wheezing and drawing. A Fellow is lolling about; a Girl is sitting on the edge of a bed. A Youth with glasses has his head buried in a book. When the doors are open, a corridor with doors and light bulbs can be seen.*)

BAREFOOTED FELLOW (*yells*): Where are my boots? Somebody's ripped off my boots again. What am I supposed to do, put them in the baggage room at the Kursk Station every night, is that it?

JANITOR: It was Prisypkin tramped off in them for a rendezvous with his she-camel. He swore when he put them on. The last time, he says. And in the evening, he says, I'll show up in a new look, more suitable to my new social position.

BAREFOOTED FELLOW: The bastard!

YOUNG WORKER (*tidying up*): And the rubbish after him has become kind of noble, delicate like. What did it used to be? Empty beer bottles and a fish tail, and now little Tezhe[5] jars and rainbowed ribbons.

GIRL: Stop twaddling; the fellow bought a necktie, so you curse him like he was MacDonald.[6]

BAREFOOTED FELLOW: He is a MacDonald! It's not the necktie that matters; the point is, the tie isn't tied to him, but he's tied to the tie. He doesn't even think—he's afraid to move his head.

JANITOR: He covers the holes with varnish; was in a hurry, saw a hole in his sock, so on the way smeared his leg with an ink pencil.

FELLOW: His is black even without a pencil.

INVENTOR: Maybe not black in that place. He ought to change his socks.

JANITOR: Found it right away—the inventor. Take out a patent. Look out less they swipe your idea. (*Swishes a duster over the table, knocks over a box—cards fall out fanwise. He bends over to collect them, holds them up to the light, bursts out laughing, scarcely able to call his comrades over.*)

ALL (*rereading, repeating*): Pierre Skripkin. Pierre Skripkin!

INVENTOR: That's the name he's invented for himself. Prisypkin. Well, what is Prisypkin? What good is Prisypkin? What's the point of Prisypkin? Who needs Prisypkin? But Pierre Skripkin—that's not a name, but a romance!

GIRL (*dreamily*): But after all it's true: Pierre Skripkin—it's very elegant and distinguished. You laugh now, but maybe he'll carry out a cultural revolution in the home.

FELLOW: With his mug he's even surpassed Pushkin. His whiskers hang like a dog's tail, doesn't even wash—he's afraid of mussing them up.

GIRL: Harry Piehl[7] has this culture all over his cheeks too.

INVENTOR: That's what his teacher in the hair department is developing.

FELLOW: And just what does this teacher's hair hold on to: no head at all but as much curliness as you want. Do they get hair like that from the dampness, or what?

FELLOW WITH A BOOK: No-o-o. He's a writer. I don't know what he wrote, I only know that he's famous! *Evening Moscow* wrote about him three times: they say he sold Apukhtin's[9] poems as his own, but when Apukhtin got angry, he wrote a denial. You're fools, he says, it's just not true—I copied it from Nadson.[10] Which one of them is right—I don't know. They don't publish him any more, but he's very famous now—he teaches young people. Some poetry, some singing, some dancing, some, well...to borrow money.

FELLOW WITH A BROOM: That's not a worker's way—to cover a corn with varnish.

(Locksmith, covered in grease, enters in the middle of the sentence, washes his hands, turns around.)

LOCKSMITH: He's got no connection with the worker, left his job today, he's marrying a girl, a hairdresser's daughter—she's a cashier, and a manicurist too. Mademoiselle Elzevira Renaissance will clip his claws for him now.

INVENTOR: Elzevira—there is a typeface called that.

LOCKSMITH: I don't know about typefaces, but she's got a body—that's for sure. He was showing her picture to the bookkeeper for speeding up the accounts.

> What a dearie, what a wonder,—
> Each breast weighs eighty pounds I'd guess.

BAREFOOTED FELLOW: He's fixed himself up!

GIRL: Aha! You're envious?

BAREFOOTED FELLOW: So what, when I too became foreman and get everyday boots, I'll also sniff out the best cozy little apartment for myself.

LOCKSMITH: Here's what I advise you: you get yourself little curtains. You could open the curtain when you wanted to look at the street. You could close the curtain when you wanted to grab a bribe. It's just boring to work alone, but it's more fun to eat your chicken by yourself. Right? Such people ran from the trenches to set themselves up too, only we slapped them back down. Well, what are you waiting for—take off!

BAREFOOTED FELLOW: I'm leaving, I'm leaving. But why are you posing as Karl Liebknecht?[11] Wave at you from a window with little flowers, and I'm sure you'd quicken your pace too... Hero!

LOCKSMITH: I'm not going nowhere. You think I like these rags and the stink? No. There is a lot of us, you see. You'll never have enough Nepmen's[12] daughters for all of us. We'll build houses and get on the move right away... Right away. But we won't crawl out of this trench hole with white flags.

BAREFOOTED FELLOW: At it again—the trenches. It isn't 1919 anymore. People want to live for themselves.

LOCKSMITH: What's this—these aren't trenches here?

BAREFOOTED FELLOW: Nonsense!

LOCKSMITH: Lice everywhere.

BAREFOOTED FELLOW: Bull!

LOCKSMITH: But they're shootin with noiseless powder.

BAREFOOTED FELLOW: Bull!

LOCKSMITH: And Prisypkin has already been hit by a double-barreled eyed woman.

(Prisypkin enters in patent leather shoes, in his outstretched hand he carries a pair of worn-out shoes by their laces, throws them to the Barefooted Fellow. Bayan enters with packages. He steps between

Skripkin and the Locksmith who is starting a little dance.)

BAYAN: Comrade Skriplin, don't pay attention to these vulgar dances, they will spoil the refined taste awakening in you.

(The youths in the dormitory turn away.)

LOCKSMITH: Stop bowing! You'll crack your noodle.

BAYAN: I understand you, Comrade Skripkin: it's difficult, it's impossible for you, with your tender heart, in their vulgar company. Try to keep your patience for one more lesson. The most crucial step in life is the first foxtrot after the marriage ceremony. You must leave an impression that will last a lifetime. And now, pretend you're with a lady. Why are you stomping like you're in a May Day parade?

PRISYPKIN: Comrade Bayan, I'll have to take off my shoes: in the first place, they're too tight, and in the second, the heels are wearing down.

BAYAN: That's it, that's it! Just like that, slowly, as if you were returning from a bar on a moonlit night in dreams and melancholy. Like that, like that! But don't wiggle your rear end, you're not pushing a lorry but a mademoiselle. That's it, that's it! Where is your hand? The hand is too low!

PRISYPKIN *(sliding his hand over an imaginary shoulder):* It won't stay in the air for me.

BAYAN: And now, Comrade Prisypkin, find the brassiere with a light reconnoitering and hook your thumb on it as if you were resting it; your sympathy is pleasant to the lady, and a relief to you—now you can think about your other hand. Why are you starting to shake your shoulders? That's no foxtrot, you're giving a demonstration of the shimmy "step" now.

PRISYPKIN: No. I was only... scratching myself on the way.

BAYAN: How could you, Comrade Prisypkin! If such an incident occurs with you in your dancing inspiration, show the whites of your eyes, as if you're jealous of the lady, step back like the Spanish to the wall, quickly rub yourself on some sculpture (in the fashionable society in which you'll be moving, there's always a hell of a lot of these different sculptures and vases piled up all over the place). Rub yourself, wince, flash your eyes and say: "I understand you, trrraitress, you are toying with me... but..." and start dancing again as if you are gradually cooling off and calming down.

PRISYPKIN: Like so?

BAYAN: Bravo! Well done! You have talent, Comrade Prisypkin! For someone like yourself in the conditions of bourgeois encirclement and the building of socialism in one country, you've got nowhere to turn. Is our Middlegoat Land really a worthy field for you? You need a world revolution, you need an outlet into Europe, you only have to crush the Chamberlains and Poincarés, and you will delight the Moulin Rouge and the Pantheon with the beauty of your bodily movements. So remember that, stand still like that! Excellent! But I must be going. I have to keep an eye on those groomsmen, they can have a glass before the wedding as an advance but not a drop more; once they finish their job, then they can guzzle from the bottle if they please. Au revoir. *(Leaves, yelling from the doors.)* Don't put on two neckties at once, particularly if they're different colored ones, and above all remember: you're not supposed to wear a starched shirt outside your trousers!

(Prisypkin tries on his new clothes.)

FELLOW: Vanka, stop this row; why turn yourself into such a scarecrow?
PRISYPKIN: It's none of your goddamn business, dear Comrade! What did I fight for? I fought for the good life. And now I have it within reach: both a wife, and a home, and real style. I'll always do my duty if the need arises. He who has fought, has the right to rest by a quiet stream. So there! Maybe I'll raise the standards of my entire class with my own comfortable arrangement. There!
LOCKSMITH:
>   A warrior! A Suvorov![13] Right!
>   I took the upper road,
>   I took the lower road,
>   I was building a bridge to socialism,
>   I didn't finish
>   and soon grew weary
>   and sat down by the bridge to socialism.
>   Along the bridge the grass grew high.
>   And the sheep passed by.
>   We wish
>   very simply
>   to rest by the stream...
>   under the bridge to socialism.
>   Isn't that so?
PRISYPKIN: Go to hell! Leave me alone with your crude propaganda ditties... There! *(He sits down on the bed, sings with a guitar.)*
>   On Lunacharsky Street
>   I remember an old house—
>   with a wonderful wide staircase,
>   with the most elegant window.

(A shot. They rush to the door.)

FELLOW *(from the door)*: Zoya Beryozkina has shot herself!

(All rush to the door.)

FELLOW: Oh. They'll come down hard on her now in the Party cell!
VOICES:

    Hurry...

    Hurry...

    First aid...

    First aid...

VOICE: First aid! Hurry! What! She shot herself! The breast. Right through. Middle Goat Street, No. 16.

(Prisypkin alone, hurriedly collects his things.)

LOCKSMITH: And such a woman killed herself on account of you, you hairy little bastard! There! *(Takes Prisypkin by the jacket, hurls him out the door and throws his things out right behind him.)*
JANITOR *(running in with the doctor, grabs hold of Prisypkin and lifts him to his feet, giving him his hat which flew off)*: You're certainly breaking away from your class with a bang, fellow!
PRISYPKIN *(turning away, yells)*: Cabman, Lunacharsky Street, No. 17! With my things!

III

(A large room in a beauty parlor. Mirrors on the sides. Paper flowers in front of the mirrors. Bottles on the shaving tables. To the left of the proscenium a piano with opened mouth, to the right a stove, its pipes winding through the whole room. In the middle of the room a round wedding table. Behind the table: Pierre Skripkin, Elzevira Renaissance, two Groomsmen and two Bridesmaids, Mama and Papa Renaissance. The Wedding Father—the Bookkeeper and the Wedding Mother, his wife. Oleg Bayan takes charge at the center of the table, his back to the audience.)

ELZEVIRA: Shall we start, Skripochka?
SKRIPKIN: Wait for a while.

(a pause)

ELZEVIRA: Skripochka, shall we start?
SKRIPKIN: Wait for a while. I wish to be married in organized fashion and in the presence of the personage of the Secretary of the Factory Committee, the esteemed Comrade Lassalchenko... There!
GUEST: *(running in)*: Dear bride and groom, generously forgive me for the delay, but I have been authorized to deliver to you the nuptial congratula-

tions of our respected leader, Comrade Lassalchenko. Tomorrow, he says, I could even go to church, but today, he says, I cannot come. Today, he says, is a Party day, and whether he wants to or not, he says, he must go to the Party cell. Now let us proceed, so to speak, to the immediate business.

PRISYPKIN: I declare the wedding open.

ROSALIYA PAVLOVNA: Comrades and moosieu, please, eat. Where will you find such pigs now? I bought this ham three years ago in case of a war with either Greece or Poland. But... there is still no war and the ham is already spoiling. Eat, moosieu.

ALL *(raising their glasses and wineglasses):* Bitter! Bitter!

> *(Elzevira clings to Pierre. Pierre kisses her gravely and with a feeling of class dignity.)*

WEDDING FATHER—THE BOOKKEEPER: Beethoven!.. Shakespeare!.. We beg you to play something. We don't celebrate your jubilees everyday for nothing!

> *(They drag out the piano.)*

VOICES: By the side, take her by the side! Ah, look at its teeth, what teeth! You'd like to smash 'em in!

PRISYPKIN: Don't trample on the legs of my piano.

BAYAN: *(gets up, staggers, and spills his wineglass):* I am happy, I am happy to see the elegant conclusion at this moment in time of Comrade Skripkin's path full of struggle. True, on this path he lost one particular Party card, but, on the other hand, he acquired a lot of State loan coupons. We succeeded in reconciling and linking their class contradictions—and the others, in which it's impossible for one armed with a Marxist view not to see, as in a drop of water, so to speak, humanity's future happiness, named by the common people socialism.

ALL: Bitter! Bitter!

> *(Elzevira and Skripkin kiss.)*

BAYAN: With what capital strides we are moving forward along our path of family construction! When we were all dying at the battle of Perekop,[14] and many even did die, could we have really supposed that these roses would bloom and be fragrant for us at this moment in time? When we were groaning under the yoke of autocracy, could really even our great teachers, Marx and Engels, have presumably dreamed or even dreamily presupposed that we would unite with Hymen's bonds unknown but great Labor with overthrown but enchanting Capital?

ALL: Bitter!.. Bitter!..

BAYAN: Dear citizens! Beauty is the motive force of progress! What would

I be as a simple worker? Botchkin—and nothing more! What could I do as a Botchkin? Moo! And nothing more! But as a Bayan[15]—I can do as much as I want! For example:

> Oleg Bayan is quite a sight
> once again he's drunk with delight.

And so I am now Oleg Bayan, and I enjoy, as an equal member of society, all the blessings of culture and I can swear, well no—I cannot swear, but I can converse just like the ancient Greeks: "Elzevira Skripkina, pass the fish would you dear." And the whole country can answer me, just like some troubadours:

> To whet your whistle,
> for elegance and delight
> we offer Oleg a glass of vodka
> and a herring's tail to enjoy tonight.

ALL: Bravo! Hurrah! Bitter!

BAYAN: Beauty is the mother...

GROOMSMAN (*jumping up, sullenly*): Mother! Who said "mother?" No swearing, please, in the presence of the newlyweds.

(They drag away the Groomsman.)

ALL: Beethoven! Kamarinsky!

(They drag Bayan to the piano.)

BAYAN:
> The streetcars drove up to the Registry Office—
> there was a Red wedding there...

ALL *(they join in)*:
> The groom was in his working clothes,
> a trade-union card was sticking out of his blouse!

BOOKKEEPER: I got it! I got it all! It means:
> Your health, Oleg Bayanchik,
> you curly-headed little ram-chik...

HAIRDRESSER (*pokes his fork toward the Wedding Mother*): No, madam, there are no real curly-haired people now after the Revolution. A chignon gaufre is done so... You take the curling-irons (he twists the fork), heat them on a low flame a la etoile (thrusts the fork into the stove's flame), and fluff up a hairy souffle on the crown of the head like this.

WEDDING MOTHER: You are insulting my dignity as a mother and as a girl... Stop it... Son of a bitch!!!

GROOMSMAN: Who said "son of a bitch?" No swearing, please, in the presence of the newlyweds!

(The Bookkeeper separates them, joining in the singing, trying to crank the handle of the cash register, spinning around with it as if it were a barrel organ.)

ELZEVIRA *(to Bayan):* Ah! Play something for us. Ah! The "Makarov's Longing for Vera Kholodnaya"[16] waltz. Ah, it's so charmant, ah, it's simply a petite histoire...

GROOMSMAN *(armed with a guitar):* Who said "pissoir?" Please, in the presence of the newlyweds...

(Bayan separates them and pounces on the piano keys.)

GROOMSMAN *(watching, threateningly):* Why are you playing only on the black keys? On half for the proletariat, but on all of 'em for the bourgeoisie, is that it?

BAYAN: What do you mean, what do you mean, citizen? I am trying especially on the white keys.

GROOMSMAN: So again it appears the white keys are better? Play on all!..

BAYAN: I am playing on all!

GROOMSMAN: So you're together with the Whites, opportunist?

BAYAN: Comrade... This is... D-flat.

GROOMSMAN: Who said "idiot?" In the presence of the newlyweds. Take that!!! *(He hits him on the back of the head with the guitar.)*

(The Hairdresser twists the Wedding Mother's hair on his fork. Prisypkin pushes the Bookkeeper away from his wife.)

PRISYPKIN: What're you doing sticking a herring into my wife's bosom? That's not a flower bed for you, but a bosom, and that's not a chrysanthemum you've got, it's a herring!

BOOKKEEPER: And did you treat us with salmon? Did you? Huh? And you're yelling yourself—huh?

(In the scuffle they push the gossamered bride onto the stove, the stove is turned over—flames, smoke.)

CRIES: We're on fire!!! Who said "we're on fire?" Fire! Salmon... The streetcars drove off from the Registry Office...

IV

(In the pitch black night, a fireman's helmet gleams from a nearby blaze. The Chief is alone. Reporting firemen come and go.)

FIRST FIREMAN: It's out of control, Comrade Chief! Nobody called us for two hours ... The drunken shits!! It's burning like a powder keg. *(Leaves.)*
CHIEF: Is it any wonder it's burning? Cobwebs and alcohol.
SECOND FIREMAN: It's dying down; the water's turning to icicles in the air. We flooded the cellar with water smoother than a skating rink. *(Leaves.)*
CHIEF: Found any bodies?
THIRD FIREMAN: Hauled off one, the whole skull smashed in. Must've been cracked by a beam. Straight to the morgue. *(Leaves.)*
FOURTH FIREMAN: Hauled off ... one charred body of undetermined sex with a fork in its head.
FIRST FIREMAN: An ex-woman with a wire crown on the back of the head was discovered under the stove.
THIRD FIREMAN: An unidentified person of prewar build was found with a cash register in his hands—apparently, in life he was a robber.
SECOND FIREMAN: No survivors ... One body is unaccounted for—since we didn't come across it I guess it burned to bits.
FIRST FIREMAN: Just look at the fireworks! Really a theater, only all the actors have burned up.
THIRD FIREMAN:

> A carriage drove them from the wedding,
> a carriage with a Red Cross.

(A bugler calls the firemen together. They fall in. They march through the theater, exclaiming.)

FIREMEN: Comrades and citizens,
    vodka is poison,
 Drunkards
  will burn up
   the Republic easily!
Living with fireplaces,
   living with primuses,
you'll burn down the house
   and cremate yourselves!
Fires start
 when
   you doze off,—
to take a snooze
  don't read
   Nadson and Zharov![17]

V

(A huge high-ceilinged meeting hall rising like an amphitheater. Instead of people's voices—radio loudspeakers, next to them several hanging arms like those sticking out of automobiles. Above each loudspeaker, colored electric lights; right under the ceiling, a screen. In the center, a rostrum with a microphone. On both sides of the rostrum, controls and switches for voices and light. Two mechanics—an Old Man and a Youth—are busy in the dark auditorium.)

OLD MAN *(flicking off the dust from the loudspeakers with a tattered feather duster):* Today is an important vote. Check the voting apparatus of the agricultural regions and oil it up. Last time there was a hitch. They were voting with a squeak.

YOUTH: The agricultural? Okay! I'll oil the central. I'll rub the throat of the Smolensk apparatus with a chamois. Last week they sounded hoarse again. Need to tighten up the arms to the auxiliary staff of the capitals, or else there is a little deviation: the right arm clings to the left one.

OLD MAN: The Ural factories are ready. We'll switch on the Kursk metallurgical works; they put in a new apparatus there of sixty-two thousand votes for the second group of the Zaporozhe power station. No trouble with them, the work is easy.

YOUTH: Do you still remember what it was like before? Must have been pretty ridiculous!

OLD MAN: Mama once carried me to a meeting in her arms. Not many people there—a thousand crowded together, sitting like parasites and listening. It was some big important question and it was passed by one vote. Mother was against, but she couldn't vote because she was holding me in her arms.

YOUTH: Well of course! Primitivism!

OLD MAN: Apparatus like this wouldn't have been any good before. Used to be, the first man had to raise his hand so they'd notice him, so he'd jab it under the chairman's nose. He'd stick both hands right up under his nostrils, just feeling sorry he wasn't the ancient goddess Isis so he could vote with twelve hands. But many people evaded voting. They tell a story about one guy who sat out a whole important discussion in the toilet—he was afraid to vote. He sat and pondered, trying to save his official hide.

YOUTH: Did he save it?

OLD MAN: He saved it!.. But they assigned him to another line of work. Seeing his love for toilets, they appointed him chief in charge there of the soap and towels. Ready?

YOUTH: Ready!

(They run down to the control boards and cables. A man with glasses and a beard, having thrown open the door, walks straight to the

platform; with his back to the auditorium, he raises his hands.)

ORATOR: Switch on all regions of the Federation simultaneously!
SENIOR AND JUNIOR: Okay!

(All the red, green, and blue bulbs of the auditorium light up simultaneously.)

ORATOR: Hello! Hello! This is the president of the Institute of Human Resurrections speaking. The question has been publicized via telegrams, has been discussed, and is simple and clear. At the intersection of Sixty-Second Street and Seventeenth Prospect, in the former Tambov, a brigade digging a foundation at a depth of seven meters discovered a buried, ice-filled cellar. Through the ice of this phenomenon a frozen human figure is visible. The Institute considers possible the resurrection of the individual, frozen to death fifty years ago.

Let's settle the difference of opinions.

The Institute considers that every worker's life must be utilized until the last second.

Radioscopy has shown calluses on the hands of the creature, formerly, half a century ago, the sign of a worker. Let us remind you that after the wars that spread over the world, after the civil wars, that created the Federation of Earth, by the edict of November 7, 1965, the life of a man became inviolable. I bring to your attention the objections of the Epidemiological Section, fearing threats of the spread of the bacteria which infested the former creatures of former Russia. Fully aware of my responsibility, I ask for a decision. Comrades, remember, remember and once again remember:
> We
> > are voting
> > for a human life!

(The lights are put out, a high-pitched bell rings, on the screen the resolution is flashed, repeated by the Orator.)

"In the name of research in the labor skills of working humanity, in the name of a graphic comparative study of the conditions of life, we demand resurrection."

(Voices of half the loudspeakers: "Right, passed!" Other voices: "Down with it!" The voices fall silent instantly. The screen darkens. A second bell, a new resolution is flashed. The Orator repeats it.)

"The resolution of the sanitation-control stations of the Donbas metallurgical and chemical factories. In order to avoid the danger of the spread of the bacteria of toadyism and braggadocio, characteristic of the year 1929, we demand the exhibit be left in a frozen state."

(Voices of the loudspeakers: "Down with it!" A few shouts: "Right!")

Are there any more resolutions or amendments?

(A third screen lights up, the Orator repeats.)

"The agricultural regions of Siberia request resurrection in the fall, upon conclusion of the work in the fields, to make possible the presence of the broad masses of interested people."

(Overwhelming majority of voices-speakers: "Down with it!" "Rejected!" The lights are turned on.)

I put it to a vote: Whoever is for the first resolution, I ask you to raise your hands!

(An overwhelming majority of iron hands are raised.)

Put them down! Who is for the amendment from Siberia?

(Two lone hands are raised.)

The Assembly of the Federation has adopted "Re-sur-rection!"

(Roar from all the loudspeakers: "Hurrah!" The voices fall silent.)

The meeting is closed!

(Reporters rush in through two flung open doors. The Orator cuts his way through, darting about joyfully in all directions.)

Resurrection! Resurrection! Resurrection!!!

(Reporters pull microphones from their pockets, shouting as they go:)

FIRST REPORTER: Hello!!! Wavelength 472.5 meters... *Chukotsky News*... Resurrection!
SECOND REPORTER: Hello! Hello!!! Hello! Wavelength 376 meters... *Vitebsk Evening Pravda*... Resurrection!
THIRD REPORTER: Hello! Hello! Hello! Wavelength 211 meters... *Warsaw Komsomolskaya Pravda*... Resurrection!

FOURTH REPORTER: *Armavir Literary Monday!* Hello! Hello!!!
FIFTH REPORTER: Hello! Hello! Hello! Wavelength 44 meters. *Chicago Soviet News* . . . Resurrection!
SIXTH REPORTER: Hello! Hello! Hello! Wavelength 115 meters . . . *Roman Red Gazette* . . . Resurrection!
SEVENTH REPORTER: Hello! Hello! Hello! Wavelength 78 meters. . . *Shanghai Poor* . . . Resurrection!
EIGHTH REPORTER: Hello! Hello! Hello! Wavelength 220 meters. . . *Madrid Farm Girl* . . . Resurrection!
NINTH REPORTER: Hello! Hello! Hello! Wavelength 11 meters . . . *Kabulsky Pioneer* . . . Resurrection!

(Newsboys rush in with newssheets fresh off the press.)

FIRST NEWSBOY:
            To defrost
                        or not to defrost?
            Editorials
                        in verse and prose!
SECOND NEWSBOY:
            Worldwide questionnaire
                        on the crucial theme—
            the possibility of a drift
                        towards epidemics of bootlicking!
THIRD NEWSBOY:
            Articles on ancient
                        guitars and romances
            and other
                        means
                        of gulling the masses!
FOURTH NEWSBOY: The latest news!!! Interview! Interview!
FIFTH NEWSBOY:
            Science Herald,
                        please don't be frightened!
            complete list
                        of so-called profanities!
SIXTH NEWSBOY: The latest radio broadcast!
SEVENTH NEWSBOY:
            The theoretical formulation
                        of an historical question:
            can
                        a cigarette
                        kill an elephant!
EIGHTH NEWSBOY:
            Sadness then tears,

laughter then colic:
explanation
of the word "alcoholic!"

VI

(A frosted-glass double door; the metallic parts of medical instruments shine through the wall. In front of the wall an old professor and an elderly assistant, still preserving the characteristic features of Zoya Beryozkina. Both in hospital white.)

ZOYA BERYOZKINA: Comrade! Comrade professor, I beg you, don't perform this experiment. Comrade professor, there'll be a brawl again ...
PROFESSOR: Comrade Beryozkina, you have begun to live in the past and you speak an unintelligible language. An entire dictionary of dead words. What is "brawl"? *(Looks for it in the dictionary.)* Brawl ... Brawl ... Brawl ... Bureaucracy, brotherhood,[18] bubliki,[19] Bohemia, Bulgakov ... Brawl—this is a kind of activity of people who disturb every kind of activity ...
ZOYA BERYOZKINA: Fifty years ago this "activity" of his almost cost me my life. I even went as far as ... attempted suicide.
PROFESSOR: Suicide? What is "suicide"? *(Looks for it in the dictionary.)* Self-advertisement, self-packing, self-taxation, sovereignty ... I found it— "suicide." *(Surprised.)* You shot yourself? Was there a sentence? A trial? A revolutionary tribunal?
ZOYA BERYOZKINA: No ... I did it by myself.
PROFESSOR: Yourself? Out of carelessness?
ZOYA BERYOZKINA: No ... Out of love.
PROFESSOR: Nonsense ... Out of love one wants to build bridges and bear children ... But you ... My, my, my!
ZOYA BERYOZKINA: Let me go; I really can't.
PROFESSOR: That certainly was ... How did you put it ... a brawl. My, my, my! A brawl! Society suggests you show all the feelings you have to make it as easy as possible for the defrosting subject to overcome fifty anabiotic years. Yes! Yes! Yes! Your presence is very, very important. I am glad that you were here and came. He—that's him! And you—that's her! Tell me, did he have soft eyelashes? In case of breakage during rapid thawing.
ZOYA BERYOZKINA: Comrade professor, how can I possibly remember eyelashes of fifty years ago....
PROFESSOR: What? Fifty years ago? That was yesterday!.. And how do I remember the color of the hair of a mastodon half a million years ago? My, my, my!.. Well, do you remember if he dilated his nostrils very much while

breathing in exciting company?

ZOYA BERYOZKINA: Comrade professor, how can I possibly remember?! Nobody has dilated his nostrils in such cases for thirty years.

PROFESSOR: All right! All right! All right! And you have no information about the size of the stomach and liver, in case of elimination of a possible content of spirits and vodka that might ignite from the necessary high voltage?

ZOYA BERYOZKINA: How can I remember, Comrade professor! I recall that there was a belly...

PROFESSOR: Ah, you don't remember anything, Comrade Beryozkina! At least, was he impulsive or not?

ZOYA BERYOZKINA: I don't know... Possibly, but... only not with me.

PROFESSOR: Yes! Yes! I see! I fear that while we're defrosting him, you in the meantime have been freezing up. My, my, my!.. Well, let's proceed.

(He pushes a button, the glass wall opens quietly. In the middle, on an operating table, a shiny galvanized box the size of a man. There are faucets around the box; under the faucets are pails. Electric wires are connected to the box. Cylinders of oxygen. Around the box are six Doctors, clad in white and calm. In the foreground in front of the box are six washstands. Six towels hang on an invisible wire, as if in mid-air.)

PROFESSOR *(going from doctor to doctor and speaking. To the First)*: On my signal switch on the current. *(To the Second.)* Bring the heat up to 36.4 degrees—fifteen seconds for every tenth. *(To the Third.)* Are the oxygen pillows ready? *(To the Fourth.)* Drain off the water gradually, replacing the ice with air pressure. *(To the Fifth.)* Open the lid immediately. *(To the Sixth.)* Observe in the mirror the stages of revival. *(The doctors nod their heads to show they have understood and disperse to their places.)* Let's begin!

(The current is switched on; they watch the temperature closely. Water drips. The Sixth Doctor stares at a mirror in the little right-hand wall.)

SIXTH DOCTOR: Natural coloration is returning! *(Pause.)* He's free from the ice! *(Pause.)* The chest is quivering! *(Pause. Frightened.)* Professor, just look at the unnatural violence...

PROFESSOR *(approaches, peers in, reassuringly)*: The movements are normal, he's scratching himself—evidently, the parasites peculiar to such individuals are reviving.

SIXTH DOCTOR: Professor, something incomprehensible: the movement of the left hand is separating something from the body...

PROFESSOR *(peering in)*: He and music joined together, they called that "a sensitive soul." In ancient times there lived Stradivarius and Utkin.[20] Stradivarius made violins, but Utkin made this, and it was called a guitar.

(The Professor examines the thermometer and the apparatus registering blood pressure.)

FIRST DOCTOR: 36.1
SECOND DOCTOR: Pulse 68.
SIXTH DOCTOR: Breathing even.
PROFESSOR: To your places!

(The Doctors walk away from the box. The lid is instantly thrown back, a dishevelled and surprised Prisypkin comes out of the box, looks around, clutching his guitar.)

PRISYPKIN: Well, I had a good sleep! Forgive me, Comrades, I was drunk, of course! What police division is this?
PROFESSOR: No, this is a different division entirely! This is the division from ice of the cutaneous integuments which you froze...
PRISYPKIN: What? It's you who've gotten frozen. We'll soon see which of us was drunk. As specialist-doctors, you're always hanging around the alcohol yourselves. And I can always prove my identity myself. Have my documents on me. *(Jumps out, turns his pockets inside out.)* Seventeen rubles, sixty kopecks on me. International Organization for Assistance to Revolutionary Fighters? Paid. Society for Assisting Defense and Aviational-Chemical Construction? Paid. "Down with illiteracy." Certainly. What's this? A certificate from the registry office! *(Whistles.)* Yes, that's right—I got married yesterday! Where are you now; who's kissing your fingers? Oh, I'll get a thrashing when I get home! Here's the receipt from the groomsmen. Here's my trade union card. *(His glance falls on the calendar; he rubs his eyes, looks around in horror.)* May 12, 1979! My unpaid union dues! I'm fifty years behind. Receipts, they'll demand receipts! The District Office! The Central Committee! My God! My wife!!! Let me out of here! *(Shakes hands with the Doctors, rushes for the door.)*

(Beryozkina, worried, follows him. The Doctors surround the Professor. The six Doctors and the Professor thoughtfully wash their hands.)

IN CHORUS: What was that he did with his hands? Grasping and shaking, shaking and grasping...
PROFESSOR: In ancient times it was an unsanitary custom.

(The six Doctors and the Professor thoughtfully wash their hands.)

PRISYPKIN (*running into Zoya*): And just what are you citizen? Who am I? Where am I? You wouldn't be Zoya Beryozkina's mother, would you?

(*The wailing of a siren turns Prisypkin's head.*)

Where have I come to? Where have they put me? What is this?.. Moscow... Paris?? New York?! Cabby!!

(*Blaring of automobile horns.*)

Neither people, nor horses! Just automobiles, automobiles, automobiles!!!

(*He presses against the wall, scratches his back, probes with his fingers, turns around, and sees a bedbug crawling from his collar onto the white wall.*)

A bedbug, a little bedbug, a darling little bedbug!!! (*Strums his guitar and sings.*) Don't go away, stay with me ... (*Tries to catch the bedbug with his fingers; the bedbug crawls away.*) We've parted, like ships at sea... He crawled away!.. Alone! But no one answers me, again I am alone... Alone!!! Cabby! Automobiles!.. Seventeen Lunacharsky Street! Without my things!!! (*Clutches his head, falls in a faint into the arms of Beryozkina, who has run from the door.*)

VII

(*The center of the stage is a triangular public garden. In the garden are three artificial trees. The first tree has huge plates on green square leaves; on the plates are tangerines. The second tree has paper plates; on the plates are apples. The third tree is green and has open perfume bottles resembling pine cones. The sides are the glass-fronted walls of houses. Along the edges of the triangle are long benches. A Reporter enters; behind him are four other people: Men and Women.*)

REPORTER: Comrades, this way, this way! In the shade! I'll tell you about all these dispiriting and astonishing events one after another. First ... Pass me the tangerines. The municipal government was right to make the trees tangerine today, because yesterday there were only pears—and they were neither juicy, nor tasty, nor nutritious.

(*A girl takes a plate of tangerines from the tree; the people sitting down peel and eat them, leaning towards the Reporter with curiosity.*)

FIRST MAN: Well, come on, comrade, tell us everything in detail and in order.

REPORTER: So now... What juicy little slices! Don't you want some?.. Well, okay, okay, I'll tell you. Just think, such impatience! Of course, as president of the press corps, I know everything... Over there, see, see?

(A man with a doctor's bag with thermometers walks by at a brisk pace.)

That's a veterinarian. The epidemic is spreading. Being left alone, this resurrected mammal came into contact with all the domestic animals of the skyscraper, and now all the dogs have gone mad. It taught them to stand on their hind legs. The dogs don't bark and don't play, but just sit up and beg. The animals pester everybody who's having dinner, nuzzling up to them and licking their boots. The doctors say that people bitten by such animals acquire all the primary symptoms of epidemic bootlicking.

PEOPLE SITTING: O—o—o!!!

REPORTER: Look, look!

(A man staggers by, loaded down with baskets of bottled beer.)

PASSERBY *(sings):*
> In the nineteenth century
> People lived wonderously—
> Guzzling vodka, beer, or rum
> Till noses hung like shrivelled plums!

REPORTER: Look at him! The man is sick—finished! He's one of the one hundred and seventy-five workers of the second medical laboratory. In an effort to ease its transitional existence, the doctors prescribed a mixture for the resurrected mammal to drink, poisonous in large doses and loathsome in small ones; it's called beer. Their heads began to spin from the poisonous fumes and by mistake they took a sip of this refreshing mixture. And since then they've already relieved the third batch of workers. Five hundred twenty workers are lying in the hospital, but the terrible epidemic, like some kind of beer plague, is still foaming, raging, and cutting people down.

PEOPLE SITTING: A—a—a—a!!!

MAN *(dreamily and languidly):* I would sacrifice myself for science—let them inoculate me too with this mysterious illness!

REPORTER: Ready! This one is ready too! Quiet.. Don't frighten that sleepwalker...

(A Girl goes by; she stumbles through the steps of a foxtrot and the Charleston and mutters verses from a book held by two fingers of her outstretched hand. She holds an imaginary rose in two fingers of the other hand; raises it to her nose and sniffs.)

Poor girl, she lives next door to it, right next to this crazed mammal, and now at night, when the city sleeps, she's begun hearing the thrumming of his guitar through the wall, followed by drawling heartrending sighs and sobs like singing—what do they call this? "Love songs," don't they. It got worse as time went on and the poor girl began going out of her mind. Her heartbroken parents meet with the doctors for consultation. The professors say it's acute attacks of "love"—a so-called ancient disease when human sexual energy, rationally distributed over one's entire lifetime, suddenly and explosively condenses in a week in one inflammatory process, leading to reckless and incredible acts.

GIRL (*covers her eyes with her hands*): I better not look; I can feel those terrible love microbes speading through the air.

REPORTER: Ready, this one's ready too ... The epidemic is swelling like an ocean.

(*Thirty dancing girls go by.*)

Look at that thirty-headed sixty-legged creature! Just think—they called this leg-lifting (*to the audience*) art!

(*A foxtrotting couple.*)

The epidemic has reached ... has reached ... has reached what? (*Looks in dictionary.*) Its a-po-gee, well ... It's already a bisexual quadruped.

(*The Director of the Zoo runs in with a small glass case in his hands. Behind the Director is a crowd equipped with telescopes, cameras and fire ladders.*)

DIRECTOR (*to all*): Did you see it? Did you see it? Where is it? Ah, you didn't see anything!! A party of hunters reported they saw it here a quarter of an hour ago; it was moving to the fourth floor. Considering its average speed of a meter and a half per hour, it can't have gone far. Comrades, check the walls immediately!

(*Observers extend their telescopes, jump up from the benches, look carefully, shading their eyes. The Director divides them into groups, leads the search.*)

VOICES: You think you'll find it!.. You need to put a naked man on a mattress in every window—it'll go for a man ...

Don't yell, you'll scare it!!!

If I find it, I won't give it up to anybody ...

You wouldn't dare: it's communal property ...

EXCITED VOICE: I found it!!! Here it is! It's crawling!...

(*Binoculars and telescopes are focused on one spot. Silence, broken by the clicking of photo and movie cameras.*)

PROFESSOR (*in a stifled whisper*):   Yes...That's it! Set up ambushes and a guard. Firemen, over here!!!

(*People with nets surround the spot. The Firemen extend their ladder, people climb up in single file.*)

DIRECTOR (*lowering his telescope, in a whining voice*): It escaped... Escaped to the next wall... SOS! If it falls down, it'll kill itself! Brave souls, volunteers, heroes!!! Over here!!!

(*They extend the ladder in front of the second wall, people scramble up. The onlookers stand stockstill.*)

EXCITED VOICE (*from above*): Caught it! Hurrah!!!
DIRECTOR: Quick!!! Be careful!!! Don't let it escape, don't crush the animal's legs...

(*The creature is passed down the ladder from hand to hand, finally ending up in the Director's hands. The Director puts the creature away in a box and raises the box over his head.*)

Thank you, humble servitors of science! Our Zoological Garden has been made very happy, has been enriched by a chef-d'oeuvre... We have captured a very rare specimen of an extinct insect, very popular in the beginning of the century. Our city can be proud of itself—scholars and tourists will flock to us... Here, in my hands is the only living bedbugus normalis. Step aside, citizens: the animal has fallen asleep; the animal has crossed its legs; the animal wants to rest! I invite you all to the solemn opening in the Zoological Park. A most important, most alarming capture has been accomplished!

VIII

(*The smooth, opalescent, translucent walls of a room. From above, from behind the cornice, falls an even band of bluish light. On the left, a large window. In front of the window, a worker's drafting table. A radio. A screen. Three or four books. On the right, a bed pulled out from the wall, on the bed, under the cleanest blanket, a most dirty Prisypkin. Fans. The corner round Prisypkin is a mess.*)

There are cigarette butts and overturned bottles on the table. There is a scrap of pink paper on the lamp. Prisypkin is groaning. A Doctor nervously paces the room.)

PROFESSOR *(entering):* How are things with the invalid?

DOCTOR: I don't know about the invalid, but with me they're rotten! If you don't arrange for a shift every half hour, he'll infect everybody. Whenever he breathes, my legs give way from under me! I've already installed seven fans: to dispel his breath.

PRISYPKIN: O-o-o!

(The professor rushes to Prisypkin.)

PRISYPKIN: Professor, oh Professor!!!

(The professor gets a whiff and staggers back in a faint, clawing the air with his hands.)

PRISYPKIN: A drink for the morning after...

(The professor pours a little beer into a glass and gives it to him.)

PRISYPKIN *(raises himself on his elbows. Reproachfully)*: Resurrected me...and now they mock me! What's that—it's like lemonade to an elephant!..

PROFESSOR: Society hopes to raise you up to a human level.

PRISYPKIN: To hell with you and your society! I didn't ask you to resurrect me. Freeze me up again! So there!!!

PROFESSOR: I don't understand what you're talking about! Our life belongs to the collective, and neither I nor anybody else can make this life...

PRISYPKIN: But what sort of a life is it when you can't even pin up a photo of your best girl on the wall? All the thumbtacks break on the damned glass...Comrade Professor, give me a shot for the morning after.

PROFESSOR *(fills a glass):* Just don't breathe in my direction.

(Zoya Beryozkina comes in with two piles of books. The doctors talk with her in a whisper, then leave.)

ZOYA BERYOZKINA *(sits down near Prisypkin, unpacks the books):* I don't know if this will do. They didn't have what you asked for and nobody knows about it. Only in the textbooks on horticulture is there anything about roses, and daydreams are mentioned only in medical books in the section on dreams. Here are two very interesting books from roughly the same time. A translation from the English: Hoover—*An Ex-President Speaks.*

PRISYPKIN (*takes the book and throws it away*): No, that's not for the heart; I want something that makes the heart stand still...

ZOYA BERYOZKINA: Here's the second one—by someone called Mussolini: *Letters from Exile.*

PRISYPKIN (*takes it, throws it down*): No, that's not for the soul. Leave me alone with your crude propaganda books. I want something that pricks the soul...

ZOYA BERYOZKINA: I don't know what that means. Makes the heart stand still, pricks the soul... pricks the soul, makes the heart stand still...

PRISYPKIN: What is this? What did we struggle for, shed blood for, when I, a leader supposedly, in my own society can't dance to my heart's content in a newly learned dance?

ZOYA BERYOZKINA: I demonstrated your bodily movement even to the director of the Central Institute of Calisthenics. He says he's seen such things in old collections of Parisian post cards, but now, he says, there isn't even anybody to ask about it. There's a couple of old women—they remember, but they can't demonstrate it because of their rheumatism.

PRISYPKIN: Then why did I bother to get myself a really elegant education? I was quite able to work even before the Revolution.

ZOYA BERYOZKINA: Tomorrow I will take you to see a dance by ten thousand male and female workers; they will be moving through the square. It will be a joyous rehearsal of a new system of field work.

PRISYPKIN: Comrades, I protest!!! I didn't get thawed out just so you could dry me up. (*Tears off the blanket, leaps up, grabs a pile of books and shakes them out of the paper in which they are wrapped. He wants to tear up the paper and suddenly stares at the letters, running from lamp to lamp.*) Where? Where did you get this?...

ZOYA BERYOZKINA: They were distributing it to everybody in the streets... They must have put it in the books in the library.

PRISYPKIN: Saved!!! Hurrah!!! (*Rushes to the door waving a piece of paper like a flag.*)

ZOYA BERYOZKINA (*alone*): I've lived fifty years ahead, but I could have died fifty years ago because of this miscreant.

IX

(*The Zoological Garden. In the center on a pedestal, a cage draped with cloths and flags. Behind the cage are two trees. Behind the trees are cages with elephants and giraffes. To the left of the cage a rostrum; to the right, a stand for guests of honor. There are Musicians all around. Spectators are approaching in groups. Ushers with arm bands assign them to their places—according to occupations and height.*)

MASTER OF CEREMONIES: Comrade foreign correspondents, over here! Closer to the stands! Step aside and give the Brazilians room! Their airship is just now landing at the Central Airport. *(Steps back, admires the arrangement of the guests.)*

Comrade Negroes, mix in with the Englishmen in handsome colored groups; their Anglo-Saxon whiteness will set off your olive coloring even better... University students—to the left; three old women and three old men from the Union of Centenarians have been assigned to you. They will supplement the professors' explanations with eyewitness accounts.

(The old men and old women ride in in wheelchairs.)

FIRST OLD WOMAN: I remember as if it was now...

FIRST OLD MAN: No—it's me who remembers as if it was now!

SECOND OLD WOMAN: You remember as if it was now, but I remember how it was before.

SECOND OLD MAN: But I remember, as if it was now, how it was before.

THIRD OLD WOMAN: And I remember how it was even before that, long, long before.

THIRD OLD MAN: And I remember both as if it was now and how it was before.

MASTER OF CEREMONIES: Quiet, eyewitnesses, don't lisp! Clear the way, Comrades, for the children! Over here, Comrades! Hurry! Hurry!!

CHILDREN *(marching in a column, singing):*

> We learn
> > our lessons
> to a "T"!
> But we know
> > better than all the rest
> how to go out
> > on a spree.
> Xs
> > and Ys
> were long
> > ago passed.
> We're on our way there
> > to the tigers
> and the elephants
> > at last.
> Here,
> > where there's lots of beasts,
> we can go
> > like other folks do
> to the zoological
> > garden.

> Come on!
>> Let's go!!
>>> Let's go!!!

MASTER OF CEREMONIES: Citizens wishing to afford the exhibits pleasure, as well as to utilize them for scientific purposes, will please obtain scientific instruments and exotic products in regulated doses only from the official zoo attendants. Dilettantism and hyperbole in large doses are fatal. We ask you to use only those products and instruments supplied by the Central Medical Institute and the Municipal Laboratories of Precision Mechanics.

(Attendants walk through the zoo and the theater.)

FIRST ATTENDANT:
>> It's stupid to examine
>>> bacteria
>>>> in your fist!
>> Comrades
>>> get
>>>> magnifying glasses and microscopes!

SECOND ATTENDANT:
>> Doctor Tobolkin[21]
>>> advises you have
>> a solution of carbolic acid
>>> in case you get spat on.

THIRD ATTENDANT:
>> Feeding the exhibits—
>>> an unforgettable scene!
>> Take'em
>>> doses
>>>> of alcohol and nicotine!

FOURTH ATTENDANT:
>> Give'em liquor,
>>> and the creatures are assured of
>> gout,
>>> idiocy
>>>> and cirrhosis of the liver.

FIFTH ATTENDANT:
>> A flaming carnation
>>> and a smoky rose
>> guarantee
>>> one hundred
>>>> percent sclerosis.

SIXTH ATTENDANT:
>> Give

your ears
            complete protection.
    Earphones
        muffle
            crude expressions.

MASTER OF CEREMONIES *(clears the way to the rostrum for the City Soviet):* Comrade Chairman and his closest colleagues have left their highly important work and, to the strains of an ancient national march, have come to our celebration. Let's welcome our dear comrades!

(All applaud; a group with briefcases goes by, gravely bowing and singing.)

ALL:

The burden
            of work
    hasn't aged us.
    There's a time—
                for work,
    and a time—
                for fun!
    Greetings to you
                from the city,
    brave trappers!
    We're proud
            of you,
    we—
            the city fathers!!!

CHAIRMAN *(comes to the rostrum, waves a flag, everything quiets down):* Comrades, I declare the celebration open. Our times are fraught with profound shocks and experiences of an internal nature. External events are rare. Mankind, wearied by preceding events, is even glad of this relative calm. However, we never deny ourselves a spectacle which, though it may be fantastic in appearance, conceals under its iridescent plumage profound scientific meaning. Regrettable accidents in our city, the result of the imprudent admittance of two parasites for a stay in it—these accidents have been overcome by my efforts and the efforts of world medicine. These accidents, however, glimmering with a faint reminder of the past, emphasize the horror of that rejected period and the power and the difficulty of the cultural struggle of working humanity.

May the hearts and souls of our young people be tempered by these ominous examples!

I cannot help expressing my gratitude and so yield the rostrum to our celebrated Director, who unraveled the meaning of these strange phenomena and made out of baleful phenomena a scientific and amusing pastime.

Hurrah!!!

(All cry "Hurrah," the band plays a flourish, the Director of the Zoo climbs to the rostrum, bowing to all.)

DIRECTOR: Comrades! I am delighted and embarrassed by your attention. Even taking into account my own participation, I still cannot help expressing my gratitude to the devoted workers of the Union of Hunters, who are the real heroes of the capture, and also to the respected professor of the Institute of Resurrections who conquered refrigerative death. Although, I cannot help pointing out that the esteemed professor's first mistake was the indirect cause of the well-known calamities. Owing to external mimetic characteristics—calluses, clothing and so forth—the respected professor mistakenly ascribed the defrosted mammal to the species homo sapiens and to its highest division—the working class. I do not attribute my success exclusively to my long experience with animals and my penetration of their psychology. Chance helped me. A vague, subconscious hope kept repeating: "Write up and publish an advertisement." And so I did:

"In accordance with the principles of the Zoological Garden, I am seeking a live human body to be constantly bitten for the maintenance and development of a newly acquired insect in the conditions habitual and normal for it."

VOICE FROM THE CROWD: Ah, how horrible!

DIRECTOR: I realize it's horrible; I myself did not believe my own absurdity, and then suddenly . . . a creature turns up! His appearance was almost human . . . Well, just like you and me . . .

CHAIRMAN OF THE CITY SOVIET *(rings a bell):* Comrade Director, I call you to order!

DIRECTOR: Forgive me, forgive me! I, of course, at once made certain by means of an interrogation and comparative bestiology that we were dealing with a frightful anthropoid simulator and that this was a most remarkable parasite. I will not go into details, especially since you will see them for yourselves presently in this, in the full meaning of the word, remarkable cage.

There are two of them—of different sizes but essentially identical: the famous bedbugus normalis and . . . and the Philistinius vulgaris. Both are to be found in the musty mattresses of time.

Bedbugus normalis, fattened and drunk on the body of one man, falls under the bed.

Philistinius vulgaris, fattened and drunk on the body of all mankind, falls on the bed. That's the whole difference!

When the toiling humanity of the Revolution was scratching and writhing, scraping the filth off itself, they built themselves nests and little homes in that same filth, beat their wives and swore by Bebel, [22] and rested and enjoyed themselves in the tents of their own riding breeches. [23] But Philistinius vulgaris is the more frightful. With his monstrous mimicry he lures victims he can bite, sometimes pretending to be a cricket-like versifier, sometimes a love-sick song bird. In those days even their clothes were mimetic—birdlike in appearance—wing ties and a tail coat with a white-white starched breast. Such birds built nests in theater boxes, perched on the oak trees of opera, scratched one leg against the other at the ballet of the "Internationale," hung down from the twigs of verses, clipped Tolstoi à la Marx, wailed and shrieked in shocking numbers and ...forgive the expression, but we are at a scientific lecture..., excreted in quantities which could not be regarded as mere bird droppings.

Comrades! However... look for yourselves!

(He gives a signal and the Attendants unveil the cage. The bedbug case is on a pedestal; behind it is a platform with a double bed. On the bed is Prisypkin with a guitar. From above, a lamp with a yellow shade hangs over the cage. Over Prisypkin's head is a shiny halo—a fan of postcards. Bottles are standing and lying about on the floor. The cage is surrounded by spittoons. On the walls of the cage— inscriptions, to the sides, filters and ozonizers. The inscriptions: 1."Caution—it spits!" 2. "No admittance without authorization!" 3. "Cover your ears—it swears!" The band plays a flourish; Bengal lighting; the crowd, rushing back at first, draws closer, struck dumb with delight.)

PRISYPKIN:

On Lunacharsky Street
There's an old house I know—
with a staircase broad and bleak,
with a curtained window!

DIRECTOR: Comrades, go up to it; don't be afraid; it's quite tame. Go up to it, go up to it! Don't worry: four filters on the sides keep the dirty words inside the cage and only a few get outside, but they're quite decent words. The filters are cleaned daily by special attendants in gas masks. Look, it's now going to have what's called "a smoke."

VOICE FROM THE CROWD: Ah, how horrible!

DIRECTOR: Don't be afraid—it's now going to have what's called "a swig." Skripkin—take a snort!

(Skripkin reaches out for a bottle of vodka.)

VOICE FROM THE CROWD: Ah, don't, don't! Don't torture the poor animal!
DIRECTOR: Comrades, it's not at all frightening: it's tame! Look, I'll bring it out now to the rostrum. *(Goes to the cage, puts on gloves, checks his pistols, opens the door, leads Skripkin out, brings him to the rostrum, turns him around to face the guests of honor.)* Now then, say a few words, imitating human expression, voice, and language.
SKRIPKIN *(stands submissively, coughs, raises his guitar and suddenly turns and glances at the audience. Skripkin's face changes, he becomes enthusiastic. Skripkin pushes the Director aside, throws his guitar down, and shouts to the audience):* Citizens! Dear brothers! My own! Dear ones! Where did you come from? So many of you?! When did they unfreeze all of you? Why am I in the cage alone? Darlings, brothers, come on in with me! Why am I suffering? Citizens!..
VOICES OF GUESTS:
> The children, take the children away...
> A muzzle... Get a muzzle on him...
> Ah, how horrible!
> Professor, stop it!
> Ah, only don't shoot!

(The Director, accompanied by two Attendants, runs onto the platform with a fan. The Attendants pull Skripkin off. The Director ventilates the rostrum. The band plays a flourish. The Attendants cover the cage.)

DIRECTOR: Forgive me, Comrades... Forgive me... The insect is tired. The noise and lighting caused him to start hallucinating. Be calm. Nothing's wrong. Tomorrow he'll calm down... Disperse quietly, citizens, until tomorrow.
> Music, a march!

(The End)

Translated by Joel Scannell 1928-29

Notes

Scene I

1. Nobile: Umberto Nobile was an Italian Arctic explorer. His dirigible crashed over the North Pole and the survivors were rescued by the Russian icebreaker "Krasin."
2. Ryabushinsky: P. P. Ryabushinsky was a Moscow millionaire.
3. Epithalamion: from the once popular opera "Nero" by Anton Rubinstein.
4. Venizelos: Elefterios Venizelos was the Greek Prime Minister for quite some time.

Scene II

5. Tezhe: a perfume shop.

6. MacDonald: British Prime Minister.

7. Pierre Skripkin: Prisypkin has changed his name to what he thinks is a more elegant one as an indication of his new social status. In Russian the word "skripka" means violin.

8. Harry Piehl: popular German movie actor.

9. Apukhtin: Alexis Apukhtin (1841-93) was a non-civic sentimental poet popular among the Russian gentry.

10. Nadson: Semyon Nadson (1862-87) was a sentimental poet of civic themes who for a period of time had many followers among the intelligentsia.

11. Liebknecht: Karl Liebknecht (1871-1919) was a German Socialist leader.

12. Nepmen: private businessmen during the period of the New Economic Policy (NEP).

13. Suvorov: Alexander Suvorov (1729-1800) was a famous Russian field marshal.

Scene III

14. Perekop: In 1920 the Red Army crossed the Straits of Perekop, defeated the Whites and drove them out of the Crimea.

15. Bayan: the name of an ancient Russian bard, also the Russian word for accordion.

16. Vera Kholodnaya: a Russian silent movie star.

Scene IV

17. Zharov: Alexander Zharov was a proletarian poet and the frequent target of Mayakovsky's satire.

Scene VI

18. Brotherhood: In the Russian text the word is "bogoiskatel'stvo," which means "God-seeking" or "seeking for the truth."

19. Bubliki: ring-shaped rolls.

20. Utkin: I. P. Utkin (1903-44) was a Russian poet whose once popular poem "The Guitar" was particularly detested by Mayakovsky.

Scene IX

21. Tobolkin: Y. A. Tobolkin was a Moscow veterinarian.

22. Bebel: August Bebel (1840-1913), one of the founders of the German Social Democratic Party.

23. Riding breeches: a status symbol in the post-Revolutionary and Civil War periods.

ISAAC BABEL
DIARY: 1920

(Excerpts)

Zhitomir. June 3, 1920.

At daybreak on the train, got my service blouse and boots. I sleep with Shukov, Topolnik, it's filthy, the burning morning sun, muck in the railroad car. The tall Shukov, the greedy Topolnik, the entire editorial staff—unbelievably disgusting people. Wretched tea in hidden kettles, letters to home, packages to Yugrosta, an interview with a Pole, operation assault on Novograd, the broken-down discipline in the Polish Army, Polish "White Guard" literature, booklets out of cigarette paper... Ukrainian Jews, commissars; they're all stupid, enraged, powerless, incompetent and remarkably unconvincing. Mikhailov's excerpts from Polish newspapers. The kitchen on the train, red-faced, fat soldiers, gutted pigs, stifling heat in the kitchen, mush-porridge, midday, sweat, laundresses with stout legs, apathetic women... To describe the soldiers, the fat, satiated, lethargic women. Love in the kitchen. In the afternoon off to Zhitomir. A clean city, not a sleepy, but a subdued, tamed city. I search for traces of Polish culture. Well-dressed women, white stockings. A church. Near Nushka I bathe in the Teterev, a detestable stream, there bathe old Jews with long skinny gray-haired legs. The young Jews. Women rinse clothes in the Teterev. One family, a beautiful wife, the husband carries the child. The open bazaar in Zhitomir, an old cobbler, bluing, chalk, twine. The synagogues, old architecture, how deeply all that touches me. An hourglass 1200 rubles. The market. A small Jew-philosopher. Incredible shops—Dickens, brooms and golden slippers. His philosophy—everyone says, they fight for the truth and yet everybody steals. If there were only a good government at least. Beautiful words, a little beard, we enjoy ourselves, tea and three pieces of apple cake—750 rubles. An interesting old woman, mean, enterprising, how avaricious they all are. To describe the bazaar, baskets full of cherries, the inside of an inn. Conversation with a Russian woman, who comes to borrow a washtub. Then weak tea. I eat, I'm alive, farewell, you dead ones. Brother-in-law Podolski, a degenerate intellect, something about trade unions, something about serving Budyonny. I am, of course, a Russian, his mother is a Jew, why? A pogrom in Zhitomir, plotted by the Poles, naturally afterwards also by the Cossacks. When our advance units appeared, the Poles occupied the city for three days, a pogrom, they cut beards off, that's only common. They apprehended 45 Jews at the market, drove them to the slaughterhouse, tongues were cut out, groaning throughout the entire place. Six houses were set afire, Konyukhovski's home on the cathedral square—I watched it, I wonder who saved it from being chopped up by the machine guns, it was entrusted to the caretaker, to whom the mother threw the infant child from the burning window. They were detained, the priest rested a ladder against the rear of the house, thus enabling them to escape.

The Sabbath is approaching, we are going from father-in-law to the Tsaddik's. The name I never did understand. A most unusual sight for me, although death and complete ruin are unmistakable. The Tsaddik's narrow-shouldered, haggard, petite figure. The son—a well-bred young boy in a small tallis, we look into the petit-bourgeois but spacious rooms. Everything's neat. The wife is an average Jew, has a tendency to be somewhat modern. The faces of the old Jews. Discussions about famine in the corner of the room. I'm lost in the prayer book. Podolski helps. A pine torch is used in place of candles. I'm happy—huge faces, aquiline noses, black beards shot with gray, I think about many things, farewell, you dead, Tsaddik's face, a real penny-pincher, where do you come from, young man? From Odessa. How are things there? One lives. Here things are dreadful. A short conversation. I leave stunned. Podolski, pale and sad, gives me his address, a wonderful evening. I walk, think about the quiet, unknown streets. Kondratev with a black-haired Jewess. The poor commander, with Papashka, he's got no luck. Then night, the train, the painted cries of communism (in contrast to what I saw at the old Jew's), machine gun fire, their own electric power station, their own newspaper, the movie's on, the train flashes, roars, big-lipped soldiers stand in line for the laundresses (2 days).

Zhitomir. June 4, 1920.

In the morning—letters to Yugrosta, information about the pogrom in Zhitomir, to home, to Oreshchnikov, to Narbut. I'm reading Hamsun. Sobelman tells me about the subject of his novel: Hiob's new manuscript, the old man who's been living for centuries, the students stole it in order to sham a resurrection, a gorged foreigner, the Russian revolution. Schulz, the most important thing, lust, communism is whenever we pilfer apples from our masters, Schulz tells me, his bald head, apples stuffed in his shirt, communism, a Dostoevsky-like character, there's something to it, you just have to think about it some more, this insatiable lust, Schulz on the streets of Berdichev. Khelemskaia, who had pleurisy, diarrhea, looks yellow, a dirty hood, applesauce, why are you here, Khelemskaia? You should have married, a man—accountant, engineer, abortion, or the first child, that was your life, your mother, you bathed twice a week, your novel, Khelemskaia—this is how you must live and adapt yourself to the revolution. The opening of the communist club in the editor's office. There it is—the proletariat—these unbelievably emaciated Jews, who crawled forth out of illegitimacy. Miserable, powerful race—onwards! Then to describe the concert, the women sing Little Russian songs. Bathing in the Teterev.

Belev. July 11, 1920.

Night, the staff works in Belev. What does Zolnarkevich mean? A Pole? His feelings? Touching friendship between two brothers. Konstantin and Mikhailo.

Z.—a war horse, exactly, works feverishly without growing tired, full of energy without being loud, a Polish moustache, thin Polish legs. The staff—there's Zolnarkevich, then three clerks who wear themselves out at night.

Lodging for the brigade's an immense problem, there are no provisions. Most importantly—the maneuver—goes unnoticed. The orderlies sleep at the headquarters on the ground. Thin candles burn, the commander of the divisional staff, with cap on, rubs his brow and dictates, dictates incessantly—operational reports, commands to the artillery division, we are going to march on Lutsk.

Night, I'm sleeping next to Lepin, the Latvian, in the hay, horses that have freed themselves roam about, eat away the hay from beneath our heads.

I spent the night in the hay with soldiers from the staff squadron. Slept badly, think of my manuscripts, depression, my energy weakens, I know that I'll make it, but when? Klevan, its ways, streets, peasants and communism—how far apart they are from one another.

Belev. July 12, 1920.

At dawn the journal of hostile actions was begun—I'm analyzing the official army communiques.

A mill—naturally not quite up to date. The Czech has heaps of receipts. A note to the district commissariat in Rovno that four horses have been seized, in place of a confiscated cabriolet—a broken-down machine gun wagon, three receipts for four and oats. A brigade arrives, red flags, a powerful, welded-together body, self-assured commanders, skilled, peaceful, Cossack eyes, dust, stillness, order, an orchestra, everything is to be sucked up by the barracks, the brigade commander calls to me, nothing is to be requisitioned, this is our territory.

Belev. July 13, 1920.

My birthday. I'm 26. I think of home, of my work, my life is just flying by. No manuscripts. Dismal melancholy, I'm going to make it. I keep up with my diary—that will be interesting.

I'm going to Yasienevishchi to exchange my touring car for a machine gun wagon and horses. Unbelievable dust, heat. We're driving through Peresopnitsa, what a joy to gaze at the fields, my 27th year, I believe the rye is ripe, the barley is growing quite well here and there, oats, the poppies are ready to bloom, no cherries, apples still green, much hemp, buckwheat, many trampled fields, hops. A rich land, rich with limitations.

The clerks—handsome, young. The young Russian field officers sing operatic melodies, everybody has been slightly spoiled by the field work. To characterize the orderlies—gossips, parasites, flatterers, gluttons, idlers, inheritors of the old system, they know their masters well.

Work of the staff in Belev. Well-coordinated machines, the wonderful staff commander, both a mechanical worker and a lively man. A disclosure—a Pole was set free, brought back under the order of the divisional commander, something that he can readily sense. He's not a Communist—a Pole, and serves loyally, like a watchdog, that one truly has to understand. The commander of the cavalry reserve Diakov—a fantastic sight. Red pants with silver stripes, belt with a golden embellishment, comes from Stavropol, built like Apollo, short, gray moustache, 45 years old, has a son and nephews, excessive cursing... Diakov, his soldiers love him, a devil of a fellow, our commander, was an athlete, almost illiterate... General, Diakov is a Communist, an experienced, brave Budyonny fighter. He once met a millionaire with a lady on his arm: Mr. Diakov, don't we know each other from the club? Was in eight states, wherever I appear all I have to do is snap my fingers—dancer, harmonica player, sly fox, boaster, extremely picturesque character. Barely decodes the commands, loses them constantly, this office junk, I'll just give up completely, what would they do without me, curses, conversations with peasants, they gape in awe. Machine gun wagons and a pair of emaciated horses.

Belev. July 14, 1920.

A shot-down American pilot, oh how that smelled of Europe, like a coffee-house, civilization, power, old culture, I ponder and observe, I see it all, barefoot, but elegant, his neck like a pillar, dazzling white teeth, suit covered with oil and dirt. Asks me fearfully whether it is a crime to fight against Soviet Russia. We have a strong cause... A letter from Major Font-le-Roy—things are bad in Poland, no existing system of government, the Bolsheviks are strong, the socialists in the center of interest, however not in power.

We study the new conduct of the war. What are the soldiers in Western Europe told? Russian imperialism, they want to destroy nations, to abolish customs, that's their main goal, they want to conquer all the Slavic lands—the same old nonsense. Endless conversation with Mosher, I'm engrossed in the old man, we'll bring you back to your senses, Mosher, ah, Conan Doyle, letters to New York. Whether Mosher pretends it or not, he's frantically trying to figure out what Bolshevism is. An impression—sad, but sweet. I'm familiarizing myself with the staff, I have a driver, Grishchuk, 39. Spent six years in a German prison, it's fifty versts to his home (he comes from the Krements District), he's not allowed to go there, he's silent. Divisional commander Timoshchenko on the staff. Colorful character. A colossal man, red leathery pants, red cap, slender, corporal, machine-gunner, was a cadet in the artillery. Legendary stories.

Budyonny's riders bring Communism, a woman cries.

Belev. July 15, 1920.

Life is dull here. Where is the Ukrainian gaiety? Harvest begins. Pilsudski's call intercepted: soldiers of the Rzeczpospolita, sentimental, sad, but without the iron-clad arguments of Bolshevism... A hearing about deserters. We present our flyers. Immense effect, the leaflet helps the Cossacks.

Novoselki. July 16, 1920.

I'm riding with the divisional commander and the staff squadron, we're chasing the horses, forests, horses, the red cap of the divisional commander, his strong stature, trumpeter, it's grand, the new army, the divisional commander and squadron—one body... To describe the ride with the divisional commander, the small staff squadron, the divisional commander's convoy. Bakhturov, the old Budyonny fighters, while decamping—a march.

Novoselki. Mal. Dorogostai. July 18, 1920.

Command from the southwestern front concerning movement into Galicia, for the first time Soviet troops cross the border. They treated the inhabitants well. We are not coming into a conquered land. The land belongs to the Galician workers and peasants and only to them, we are only coming to help them, to establish Soviet power. An important and shrewd command; are the boasters going to execute it? No.

We ride on dirt roads with two staff squadrons, the constant companions of the divisional commander. Special troops. To describe the cavalry equipment, swords in red velvet, scimitars, Cossack waistcoats, blankets on the saddles, poorly dressed, even though each one owns ten jackets, that most certainly is a part of the fashion.

Their grand comradeship, determination, love for horses, the horse alone takes up a fourth of the day, never-ending haggling, conversations. The role and life of the horse. The most unusual relation to authority—almost on a first-name basis.

At the priest's I ate my fill for the whole year. It's over for him, they say, he's trying to find a position, do you also have a regimental chaplain?

M. Dorogostai. Smordva-Beregi. July 19, 1920.

The wounded are arriving, units, bare bellies, patience, unbearable heat, constant bombardment from both sides, you can't recover your senses. Budyonny and Voroshilov on the small stairs.

Battle scene, the cavalrymen returning, covered with dust, soaked with perspiration, bloody, not a trace of excitement, war horses, professionals, everything proceeds in the greatest peace—that's the extraordinary thing, self-confidence, the difficult work, the nurses rush over to their horses, the glowing tank.

July 21, 1920.

Dubno's taken. Resistance was minimal, why? The prisoners say, and it's quite obvious—a small people's revolution. There would be a lot to say about that, the beauty of the pointed Polish gable-ends, touching the countess. Fate, honor, Jews, Count Ledóchowski? A proletarian revolution? How I inhale the fragrance of Europe, which emanates from there. And what about the Cossack? Traits: tale-bearing, boldness, professionalism, revolutionary spirit, bestial cruelty.

July 22, 1920.

In two hours I'll be riding to Khotin. Woodland path, restlessness. Grishchuk is apathetic and horrible. I'm riding Sikolov's difficult horse. I'm alone on the road. It's bright, clear, not hot, pleasantly warm. In front a small wagon, five men, look like Poles. A game, we ride, stop, where to? Fear and anxiety on both sides. At Khotin we discover our troops, we ride into it, haphazard fighting. A wild fight back, I pull the horse by the reins. The bullets zoom by, they whistle. Artillery fire, Grishchuk takes off at times, crazily, sullen, without saying a word, in dangerous moments he's sometimes incomprehensible, careless, morose, his hairy chin. Grishchuk grabs the torn reins and calls out in his unexpected clear and small tenor—we're lost, the Pole overtakes us.

July 23, 1920.

Then on to Dubno. I'm travelling with Prishchepa, a new acquaintance, coachman's coat, white hood, illiterate, Communist. The synagogues of Dubno. Everything demolished. Two small entrances have remained standing, centuries, two small rooms, full of remembrances, four synagogues, next to each other, and then pasture, fields, the sunset. Synagogues—obscure, old, little green and blue buildings. Hasidic, inside not a bit of architecture. I enter one of the Hasidic synagogues. It's Friday. What deformed small figures, what emaciated faces, everything that existed 300 years ago has risen from the dead for me, the aged run through the synagogue—no lamenting, for some reason they run from one corner to the other, a completely informal prayer. The ugliest Jews of Dubno have probably gathered here. I pray, I pray quickly and think of Hershele, in this way one should have to describe him. One quiet evening in the synagogue—that always has an unexplainable effect on me—four synagogues next to each other.

Here Grishchuk is fifty versts away from home. He doesn't escape.

July 24, 1920.

From Krivye I head toward Leszinów with Prishchepa, then further on to Demidovka. Prishchepa's mind—illiterate, just a lad, Communist, the cadets slew his parents, he tells me how he gathered up his things in the village. Decorative, hood, simple, like a blade of grass, one day he will become a boaster, despises Grishchuk, because he doesn't love horses and doesn't understand. We drive through Khorupan and Smordva towards Demidovka. To note the scene—baggage train, riders, half-destroyed villages, fields and forests, oaks, wounded here and there and my wagon. Towards evening we arrive in Demidovka. It's a Jewish place. I have to be on my guard. The Jews are exiled, everything's destroyed. We are in a house with many women. Liakhetsky, Shvekhvel, but no, that's not Odessa. The dentist Dora Antonovna reads Artsybashev, surrounded by Cossacks she is proud, bitter, tells of how the Poles wounded her honor, despises the Communists because they're too plebian for her, a number of daughters, the main worry—today is Sabbath. Prishchepa orders potatoes to be cooked, and I am silent, because I'm a Russian, and tomorrow is a time of fasting, the ninth of Av... The dentist, pallid from pride and dignity, announces potatoes will not be pulled out, it is a day of rest. Prishchepa, restrained long enough by me, breaks into a rage, Jews, lets out his complete arsenal of curses, they all hate us and me, how dare they not cook potatoes, do they fear in a strange garden, will they trip over crosses? Prishchepa has flown into a fit of rage. Everything's just distressing—Artsybashev and the secondary school girl, an orphan from Rovno, and Prishchepa in his hood. The mother wrings her hands—a quarrel on Sabbath, curses left and right. Budyonny was here and is gone again. An argument between a young Jewish boy and Prishchepa. The young boy with glasses, black hair, nervous, flushed with excitement, broken Russian. He believes in God, God is an ideal that we carry in our hearts, every man carries his own God in his heart—if you sin, God grieves for you, ecstatically and full of grief he tells us this nonsense. Prishchepa is embarrasingly dumb, he tells something about religion in antiquity, mixes up Christianity and paganism, the main point is—at that time there were the Bolshies, complete rubbish, naturally. They have absolutely no education at all—and the Jew with six classes in the secondary school in Rovno, speaks like Plato—sentimental and comical—birth, the ancients, Perun, paganism.

We devour the cooked potatoes like wolves, and each one has five glasses of coffee. . . the ninth of Av. The old woman howls, sitting on the floor, her son who idolizes his mother and says that he believes in God, in order to do something pleasant for her—sings in a pleasant small tenor and tells the story of the destruction of the temple: the frightful words of the prophet—they eat manure, the girls are raped, the men slain, Israel destroyed, angry, wailing words. The lamp smokes, the old woman howls, outside is Demidovka, Cossacks, everything like the time when the temple fell. . . .

July 25, 1920.

At morning departure from Demidovka. An agonizing two hours, the Jewish women were awakened at four o'clock in the morning and had to cook Russian meat, and that of all things on the ninth of Av. The girls run half-naked and sluggishly through the damp gardens. Prishchepa, lustful, assails the bride of the dishonest old man's son, in the meantime the wagon was ready, atrocious swearing, the soldiers eat meat out of the kettles, she—I shout, her face, he's squeezing her against the wall, sickening scene; she's frantically defending the wagon, he was hidden on the ground, she'll become a good Jewish woman someday. There's an argument with the commissioner, who maintains that the Jews didn't want to help the Red Army.

July 26, 1920.

The Galicians on the streets, Austrian uniforms, barefoot, tobacco-pipes in their mouths, the secret of lowliness, the triteness of obedience.

That remains to be thought through—Galicia, the world war, one's own fate.

Khotin. July 27, 1920.

They live poorly, primitively, a tiny room with a myriad of flied, abominable grub, and they don't need anything better—greed and the unaltered ghastly living conditions.

July 29, 1920.

The situation in Galicia is intolerably hopeless, destroyed churches and crucifixes, ominous sky. . . After a depressing and monotonous day—a rainy night, mud—I'm wearing half-shoes. Now it's really pouring, the majestic rain, the one and only victor. We wade through bog, penetrating, fine rain.

A new driver—the Pole, Gowinski, tall, skillful, talkative, restless and naturally, audacious.

Brody. July 30, 1920.

The city is destroyed, plundered. A very interesting city. Polish culture. An ancient, rich Jewish colony. These frightening bazaars, dwarfs in hooded coats, hoods and side-locks, the aged, a school street, 96 synagogues, all half-destroyed, and stories—American soldiers were here, oranges, cloth, thoroughfare, wire, deforestation and wasteland, endless barren land. Nothing to eat, no hope, war, everyone is equally bad, equally foreign, hostile, inhuman, before life was traditionally peaceful.

Brody, Lesniów, July 31, 1920.

At morning, before departing, my wagon stood on Zolotaya Street, one hour I was in the bookstore, a German store. All the beautiful books, film strips, the West, there it is, the West and Poland during the age of chivalry, anthologies, the story about all the Boleslaws, and I don't know why, it seems so nice to me, Poles, the old body clad with brilliant clothes. I act as if I were totally insane, run to and from, it's dark, the plunderings are in full speed, stationery is stolen, disgusting young boys of decidedly military manner from the requisitions commission. In desperation I tear myself away from the store.

August 2, 1920.

I'm getting the second squadron's first aid wagon, we drive to the forest, there I remain with my driver Ivan. Budyonny comes, Voroshilov, the deciding battle, not a single step back. Then the brigades break open, I speak with the staff commander. The atmosphere at the beginning of the battle—a giant field, airplanes, the cavalry attacks, our horsemen, explosions in the distance, the battle has begun, machine guns, sun, somewhere they are uniting themselves, a subdued hurrah, Ivan and I drive back, imminent danger, what I feel is not fear but passivity, he is obviously afraid to decide a course of direction, Koroshchaev's group retreats to the right, we to the left. The batle's raging, horses retrieve us—the wounded, one is deathly pale: brothers, take me along—his pants overflowing with blood, he threatens to shoot if we don't take him along, we lift him up, horrid sight, blood flows down Ivan's coat, Cossack, stop! I tie him up, he is only slightly wounded, stomach gunshot wound, right through the bones, we go for still another one, whose horse is dead. A long while we can't find our way (to describe the wounded) across the fields under fire, can't see anything. These indifferent roads and blades of grass, we dispatch messengers, who ride toward the thoroughfare—which way, to Radziwillów or Brody.

The administrative staff and the entire baggage train should be in Radziwillów, in my opinion it's more interesting to drive to Brody. Brody is being fought for. Ivan's opinion prevails. Some say the Poles are in Brody; the baggage train is fleeing, the staff is already gone. We drive back towards Radziwillów. We're there at night. The whole time ate carrots and peas—raw, biting hunger, covered with dirt, not having slept, I seize a cottage on the outskirts of Radziwillów.

An old man, a girl. The sour milk is great, we ate it up, then tea with milk. Ivan goes to get sugar. Shooting, uproar, we run out, the horse is lame, we flee in panic, hurry, they're shooting after us, everything's totally unexplainable, soon they'll catch up with us, we race towards a bridge. Collision, we stick in mud, wild panic, a corpse, deserted carts, grenades, machine gun wagons. Stoppage, night, fear, the endless line of baggage train cars, we make off to an open field, stop, sleep, stars. What I regret most from this whole episode is the tea we had to leave behind, in fact so much so that just the sound of the word is wonderful. I spend the whole night thinking about it and hate the war. What an unstable life.

August 3, 1920.

The battlefield. I meet the divisional commander, where is the staff, we lost Zolnarkievich. The battle begins, the artillery covers, grenade impacts close by, a frightful hour, the deciding battle—will we stop the Polish charge or not. Budyonny to Kolesnikov or Grishchin—I'm going to shoot you dead, they leave him looking pale.

Before that—a terrible field, dotted with maimed bodies, inhuman cruelty, monstrous injuries, caved in skulls, young, white naked bodies glistening in the sun, scattered notebooks, loose pages, paybooks, Bibles, bodies in the corn. I'm trying to rationalize my impressions. The battle begins, I'm given a horse. I see how the columns are forming, advancing in line, I feel sorry for these unlucky souls, not human beings but columns, the firing is at its peak, silence whenever the swords are at work. I ride forward, rumors about the recall of the divisional commander.

The beginning of my adventures. I ride with the baggage train to the highway, the battle is expanding, I found the supply center. Firing on the highway, the whistling of bullets, impacts twenty paces away, a feeling of hopelessness, the baggage train horses run away, I went over to the 20th regiment of the 4th division. To describe above all else on this day—the Red Army soldiers and the air.

Khotin. August 6, 1920.

From time to time Apanassenko emerges, he's different from the reticent Timoshchenko, he belongs to us—he's father, commander. In the morning Bakhturov rides, his entourage after him, I observe the work of the war commissioner, a dull, but proven Muscovite worker, therein lies his strength, he's a robot, but great goals, the three war commissioners.

Berestechko. August 7, 1920.

A memorable day. Morning from Sotin to Berestechko... Corpse of a slain Pole, horrible corpse, bloated and naked, ugly, Berestechko has seen several different occupants. The historical sites near Berestechko, Cossack graves. And above all, everything repeats itself—Cossacks against Poles, servant against master. I'll never forget this place, spread out, long, narrow, stinking yards. Everything's 100-200 years old, the population hardier here than in other places, most importantly—the architecture, white, waterblue houses, lanes, synagogues, peasant women. Life gradually returns to normal. It was good to live here—an honorable Jewry, rich Ukrainians, Sunday markets, a special class of Russian petite bourgeoisie—furriers, leather trade with Austria, smuggling. The Jews are less fanatic here, more elegant, more powerful, almost happier, aged old men, hoods, little old women, everything is redolent of the old times, of tradition, the place is enriched with the bloody history of European-Polish ghettos... The old church, graves of Polish officers at the church wall, fresh piles of dirt, ten days old, white birchwood crosses, everything's horrible, the priest's house destroyed, I find old books, valuable Latin manuscripts. Father Tuzinkiewicz—I find his apartment —plump and short, he has worked here forty-five years, lived at one place, scholastic, books, much Latin, editions from 1860, there also lived Tuzinkiewicz, an old spacious room, darkened pictures, photos from the conferences of the priests in Zhitomir, portraits of Pius X, an honest face, a beautiful picture of Sienkiewicz— there he is, the essence of the nation.

The plundering of the church was an awful event, the official robes torn to shreds, precious, brilliant material destroyed, on the floor a nurse drags away three bundles, lining torn out, the candles have disappeared, trunks forced open, papal bulls strewn about, money stolen, a wonderful church—200 years old—what hasn't it seen (Tuzinkiewicz's manuscripts), how many counts and peasants, beautiful, grand Italian painting, rosy-cheeked fathers, who rock the Christ child, a wonderfully mysterious Christ, Rembrandt, a Murillo-like Madonna, why not really Murillo, but most important are these well-fed, holy Jesuits, behind a veil of fearsome petite Chinese figure in a raspberry colored kontush, a bearded Jew, a reliquary broken into, a sculpture of St. Valentine.

Evening in this place. The church is closed. Towards evening I go to the castle of Count Raciborski. A seventy-year-old bachelor and his mother, ninety. They were alone, went mad, it was rumored. To describe the couple. The old Polish count's house, certainly over a hundred years, antlers, antique, brilliant painted ceilings, antler remains, the small servants' rooms upstairs, tiles, passages, excrement on the floor, young Jewish boys, a Steinway grand piano, sofas slit open to the feathers, not to be forgotten: the white, light, oaken doors, French letters from 1820... My God, who wrote them, when, the trampled down letters, I took the relics with me, a century, the mother countess. Steinway grand piano, park, pond.

I can't get away from it—think about the captain, Elga. Meeting in the castle park, the Jews of Berestechko, the gloomy Vinokurov, children running around, a revolutionary committee is chosen, the Jews curl their beards, the Jewish women eavesdrop on talks about the Russian paradise, about the international situation, about the rebellion in India.

Berestechko. August 8, 1920.

One has to look closely at Apanassenko. An ataman.

Laszków. August 9, 1920.

From Berestechko to Laszków, Galicia. The divisional commander's wagon, his orderly Lyovka—who loiters around and is crazy about horses. How he abused his neighbor Stepan, who was Denikin's watchman, insulted the people, and then returned to the village. They weren't allowed to cut his throat, therefore they threw him into prison, whipped him till his back bled, sprang all over him, danced, epic dialog: pleasant, Stepan? Bad. And those whom you've insulted—what became of them? Things went badly for them. And did you ever think that it could be bad for you? No. But you should have thought of that, Stepan, we believe, if we were arrested you would have cut our throats... but now, Stepan, we're going to kill you. They let him be only when he was almost cold dead.

We are hurrying, the first squadron is in my yard. Night, a lamp stands on my table, the horses are quietly snorting, everybody here is from the Kuban, we eat, sleep, cook together, it's a reserved community. Everyone is rustic, evenings they sing their songs in a full voice, they resemble church songs, devotion to the horses, small little heaps—saddles, bridles, adorned swords, coats. I sleep surrounded by them. Days I sleep outside. No operations, what a splendid and essential thing. Repose for the cavalry, horses rest from this inhuman work, men rest from the cruelty of war, they live together, sing softly, chat with each other.

Laszków. August 11, 1920.

About the Kuban Cossacks. A community, always together, outside the window horses snort day and night, the wonderful odor of manure, sun, sleeping Cossacks; twice a day they cook a giant cauldron of soup and meat. Nights they're guests somewhere. Continuous rain, they dry off and eat in my room.

Interview with Apanassenko. Very interesting. That I must bear in mind.

Apanassenko—thirsting for glory, that's it—the new class.

In spite of all operational duties, he frees himself and returns again and again, organized units, simply against the officers, four St. George's crosses, goes on duty, corporal, cadet under Kerensky, chairman of the regimental committee, tore off the soldiers' shoulder boards, long months in the steppe near Astrakhan, indisputable authority, professional soldier. About the atamans, there were many of them, they obtained machine guns, fought against Shukuro and Mamontov, merged with the Red Army, heroic epopee. That is not a Marxist revolution, but rather a Cossack rebellion, which would like to gain everything and lose nothing. Apanassenko's hate for the rich, the intellectuals, an undying hate.

August 12, 1920.

A free day, a good thing—correspondence, if one only didn't have to neglect it.
I also have to prepare Apanassenko's biography for the newspaper.
I'm still writing about tobacco-pipes, long since forgotten things.

August 13, 1920.

The whole day on horseback with the divisional commander. Khutor Porady. In the forest, four enemy airplanes, volleys. Three brigade commanders—Kolesnikov, Korochaev, Kniga.

[On the thirteenth of August Babel wrote a letter. It remained between the pages of the diary.]
Today my letterhead must read: at the edge of the forest, northwest of Starie Maidany. Since this morning both the staff squadron and the divisional staff are here. All day long we drive from brigade to brigade, pursuing battles, writing reports, we spend the night... in the forests, flee from the airplanes that bombard us. Above us an enchanting sky, a warm sun, the fragrance of firs all around us, hundreds of steppe horses snort—here one should live, however, our thoughts are occupied by the dead. This may sound silly, but war is, although in fact sometimes beautiful, in every respect destructive.
I have two weeks of total confusion behind me, it resulted from the raging cruelty which ceases not a single minute here, and from all of this I've clearly understood how unfit I am for the work of destruction, how difficult it will be for me to free myself from my old ways—from that which is perhaps bad, but which smells like poetry to me, as the beehive smells of honey, now I'm coming back to myself, what's there to worry about, some are going to cause revolution, and I am going to sing of that which is off to the side, which lies deeper, I have the feeling that I can do that and that there will be a time and a place for that... I recovered my senses, there's a storm raging in my breast, one hundred horsepower strong, again I continue with my thoughts, and the two demons, i.e., bombs, that exploded half an hour ago a hundred paces from us, even they are unable to keep me from them.

August 18, 1920.

In a night attack the second brigade took Toporov. Apanassenko's beaming. The second brigade rides by. Tufts of hair, uniforms out of carpets, red tobacco pouches, short carbines, the commanders on beautiful horses, Budyonny's brigade. Parade, orchestra, good day, sons of Revolution, Apanassenko's beaming.
The epopee with the nurse—and above all, much is spoken about her and everybody despises her, her own driver doesn't speak to her, her shoes, her aprons, she gives away Bebel's "The Woman and Socialism." One could write an entire book about women in the cavalry. The squadrons march into battle, dust, noise, drawn swords, atrocious swearing, with gathered up skirts they ride along from the very start, covered with dust, huge breasts, all whores, but comrades, and whores, because they're comrades, that's most important; they help with everything, in any way they can, heroes, even though despised, they water the

horses, fetch hay, clean the horses' bridles, steal in the churches and from the population. What's so special about the Galician cities? The mixture of the sordid and heavy flavor of the East with the German beer of the West.

Adamy. August 21, 1920.

Two from Odessa—Manuilov and Boguslavsky, district war commander of the air force, Paris, London, a handsome Jew, talks a lot, article in a Jewish newspaper, the Jews in the cavalry, I scout them. In waisted uniform—the extravagance of the Odessa bourgeoisie, bad news from Odessa. They were tormented. How are you father? Are they really going to take everything away from him. I must think of home.

August 26, 1920.

A synagogue—like it was 200 years ago, the same figures in loose robes, they pace up and down, gesticulate. That is the orthodox faction, they're for the rabbi from Belz, the famous one, who has fled to Vienna. The moderate ones are for the rabbi from Husiatin. It's their synagogue, a beautiful ark, carved by an artisan, brilliant green chandeliers, bruised tables. The synagogues of Belz—a vision of the past. The Jewish neighborhood, indescribable poverty, filth, isolation, ghetto... In Sokal—masters and workmen, Communism, they tell me, they'll barely get accustomed to. Such ragged, tortured people.

Komarov. August 28, 1920.

We ride on. Kulaczkowski's pillaged property near Labunie. White columns. Lordly furnishings, but very tasteful. Unbelievable destruction. The authentic Poland—administrators, old women, blonde children, rich, almost European-like villages with a village elder, all Catholics, beautiful women. They steal oats from the property, horses in the drawing room, black horses, what else can you expect—protection from the rain. The most valuable books in a suitcase, it would have been too late—a constitution from the beginning of the eighteenth century confirmed by the Seim, antique folio volumes from the time of Nicholas I, a Polish code of laws, valuable book bindings, Polish manuscripts from the sixteenth century, sketches by monks, old French novels.

Nothing has been destroyed upstairs, but everything has been searched thoroughly, all the chairs, walls, sofas are slit open, the floor torn up, nothing was destroyed here, it was searched. Exquisite crystal, bedrooms, oaken beds, a powder box, French novels on the tables, many French and Polish books about infant care, intimate women's apparel—everything shattered, bits of butter in a butter dish, were they young marrieds?

We're approaching Zamość. A terrible day. The rain is victor, it doesn't let up for a single minute. The horses barely make it. To describe this unbearable rain. We toil till late into the night. Thoroughly drenched, dead tired. Apanassenko's red bashchuk. We circle Zamość at a distance of three to four versts. We don't approach, armored trains beleaguer us with artillery fire. We stop in an open field, wait for messages—it's pouring in torrents. The brigade commander dictates a report in a tent. Commander! We aren't able to do anything against the armored trains. It turned out that we didn't know there was a railway line here, it wasn't on the map, that's how our reconnaisance works.

Chesniki. August 31, 1920.

A fruit garden, an apiary, the destruction of the beehives, it disgusts me, they buzz desperately, they're blowing up the hives with powder, they wrap themselves up in coats and go to attack the hives, a bacchanalia, the frame removed with the swords, honey flows out onto the earth, the bees sting, they're smoked out with tar rags. Circassian style. In the apiary—chaos and complete destruction, the ruins smoke. I write in the garden, a meadow, flowers, it pains me...

The story of a nurse—there are nurses who are strongly inclined to flirt, but we help the soldier, we endure everything together, I would shoot them if I could, but with what... we don't even have that much.

Budiatichi. September 7, 1920.

For two weeks now the report that the army has to catch its breath has become more and more emphatic.

V. Volynski. September 9, 1920.

The city is miserable, filthy, starved out, one doesn't get anything for his money anymore, one piece of candy is 20 rubles, cigarettes. Grief, army's staff, trade union council, young Jewish men. The way through the political economy councils and trade union commissions, sorrow, military tribunals; they kick over all traces. Impoverished young Jews.

A sumptuous repast—meat, groats.

One consolation—food.

The new war commissioner, of apelike appearance. The innkeeper and his wife want to make an exchange for my shawl. I don't give in.

My driver—barefoot and bleary-eyed.

Synagogue—I pray, bare walls, a soldier collects incandescent lamps. A bath. Damned life of a soldier, damned war. Conglomeration of young, plagued, primitive young people.

The life of my innkeepers, they make some kind of a profit, tomorrow is Friday, everything is being made ready, a good old woman, the husband's sly, they only act as if they're poor; but they say: better to starve under the Bolsheviks than to eat white bread under the Poles.

Translated by Nicholas Stroud   *1920*

OSIP MANDELSTAM
LITERARY MOSCOW: THE BIRTH OF PLOT

I

At one time monks would eat more or less lenten fare in their chilly Gothic refectories, while listening to excerpts from the *Book of Monthly Readings (Chet'i Minei),* [1] rather good prose for its day. The readings were provided not only for their edification, but because reading aloud was an adjunct to the refectory, like dinner music, and the seasonings offered by the reader helped maintain the harmony and order at the common table by refreshing the diners' minds.

But just imagine some enlightened and modern social group today that would like to resurrect the custom of reading at meals, and imagine that it invites a reader. In his desire to please everyone, the reader picks up Andrei Bely's *St. Petersburg.* [2] But as he begins to read, something incredible happens: someone gets a piece of food lodged in his throat; someone else starts eating his fish with a knife; a third person burns his tongue on the mustard.

It is impossible to imagine what kind of proceedings, what kind of work, what kind of group occasion could warrant the accompaniment of Andrei Bely's prose. His prose periods can only be intended for an age of Methuselahs, they are unsuitable for any human activity. Even the tales of Scheherazade are intended for three hundred and sixty-six days, one for each night of a Leap Year; and the *Decameron* is also amenable to the calendar, obedient to the succession of days and nights. But what of the *Decameron*! Dostoevsky is excellent for reading at meals; if not just now, then in the very near future when, instead of weeping over him and being moved by him, as chambermaids are affected by Balzac and by popular dime novels, he will be accepted for his literary merit; then he will be read and understood for the first time.

To extract a pyramid from the depths of your own soul is like having a cannula inserted into your stomach—an odious and antisocial activity. It is not work, but a surgical operation. Ever since the ulcer of psychological experimentation penetrated the modern literary consciousness the prose writer has become a surgeon and prose—a clinical catastrophe not at all to our taste. I would forego a thousand times over the psychological *belles-lettres* of Andreev, [3] Gorky, [4] Shmelev, [5] Sergeev-Tsensky, [6] and Zamyatin [7] for the sake of the magnificent Bret Harte in a translation by some unknown student of the nineties: "Without a word, with a single motion of hand and foot, he threw him down the stairs, then, completely calm, he turned to the unknown woman."

Where is this student now? I am afraid that he is unduly ashamed of his literary past and spends his leisure hours offering himself to the vivisectionists—the psychological authors— not the crude bumblers from the clinic of the *Anthologies of Knowledge (Sborniki znaniia),* [8] where the most minor operation, the removal of an intellectual's tooth, threatened blood poisoning; rather to the skilled surgeons from Andrei Bely's clinic, [9] equipped with the latest methods of Impressionistic antisepsis.

II

Mérimée's *Carmen* ends with a philological discourse on the place of the gypsy dialect in the family of languages. The highest tension of passion and plot is unexpectedly resolved in a philological tract which bears resemblance to the epode of a tragic chorus: "And everywhere are fateful passions, and there is no defense against the Fates." This preceded Pushkin.

Why should we be so surprised if Pilnyak[10] or the Serapions[11] introduce notebooks, construction estimates, Soviet circulars, newspaper announcements, manuscript fragments and God knows what else into their narratives? Prose belongs to nobody. It is essentially anonymous. It is the organized movement of the verbal mass cemented together by anything you please. The primary element of prose is accumulation. Prose is entirely fabric, morphology.

Today's prose writers are often called eclectic, that is, collectors. I think that no offense is meant by this, that this is a good thing. Every true prose writer is precisely an eclectic, a collector. Leave personality out of it. Make way for anonymous prose. This is why the names of the great prose writers, those contractors of grandiose literary plans, anonymous in essence and collective in their execution, like Rabelais' *Gargantua et Pantagruel* or *War and Peace*, are transformed into legend and myth.

The rage for anonymous, "eclectic" prose coincided with our Revolution. Poetry itself demanded prose. It had lost all perspective because there was no prose. It reached an unhealthy flowering and was unable to satisfy its readers' demands to align itself with the pure movement of verbal masses, bypassing the author's personality, bypassing everything incidental, personal, and catastrophic (the domain of the lyric).

Why precisely did the Revolution prove to be so favorable to the rebirth of Russian prose? Because it promoted the anonymous prose writer, the eclectic, the collector, who does not create verbal pyramids from the depths of his own soul, but is the Pharaoh's humble overseer assuring the slow but true construction of real pyramids.

III

Russian prose will advance when the first prose writer that is independent of Andrei Bely appears. Andrei Bely is the summit of Russian psychological prose—he soared upward with astonishing power, but merely perfected the groundwork of his predecessors, the so-called belletrists, with his varied and high-flown devices.

Are his disciples, the Serapion Brothers and Pilnyak, actually returning to the bosom of *belles-lettres,* thereby coming full circle? Are we really on the verge of new *Anthologies of Knowledge,* where psychology and "daily life" will resurrect the old novel, the novel of the convict and his wheelbarrow?

As soon as plot disappeared, "daily life" replaced it. Before Jourdain, no one guessed that people speak in prose, no one knew that there was such a thing as "daily life."

"Daily life" is a dead plot, a decaying plot, a convict's wheelbarrow that drags pyschology along behind it because it needs something to lean on; a dead plot will do if there is no living one. "Daily life" is always a foreignism, a false exoticism; it does not exist for its own native, domestic eye: a native notices only what is necessary and to the point. A foreign tourist (that is, a belletrist) tries to take in everything with his indiscriminate gaze and talk of everything with his pointless, inappropriate chatter.

Today's Russian prose writers, such as the Serapions and Pilnyak, are psychologists just as much as their pre-Revolutionary predecessors and Andrei Bely. They forego plot. They are unsuitable for reading at meals. However, their psychology is riveted to another convict's wheelbarrow—not to "daily life," but to folklore. I would like to discuss this distinction in more detail, for it is a very significant one. They are not at all the same. Folklore is superior, qualitatively better.

"Daily life" is a kind of night-blindness to things. Folklore is a conscious consolidation and accumulation of linguistic and ethnographic material. "Daily life" is the deadening of plot; folklore is the birth of plot. Listen closely to folklore and you will hear thematic life stirring in it, the plot breathing, and, in every folklore transcription, the rudiments of a plot are present—this is where interest begins, where everything is fraught with plot. It sets everything in motion, it intrigues, it threatens. The brood hen sits on a heap of straw, cackling and clucking; likewise a folklorist-prose writer cackles and clucks about something, and anyone who so desires may sit and listen to him. In actual fact, however, he is occupied with something more important—he is hatching a plot.

The Serapions and Pilnyak (their elder brother who does not need to be treated separately) are not suited for the serious reader. Their anecdotes are suggestive, that is, they threaten us with plot. Their work contains no trace of a plot, that is, of a larger narrative breath, but the anecdote twitches its whiskers from every nook and cranny, just as in Khlebnikov[12]:

> Winging his golden flourish of most delicate veins,
> The grasshopper laid his belly in a basket
> Of myriad herbs and faiths

Pilnyak, Nikitin, Fedin, Kozyrev and others, and Lidin (another Serapion, who for some reason did not join the brotherhood) and Zamyatin and Privshin are all "of myriad herbs and faiths." The beloved anecdote, the first free and joyous fluttering of plot, is the liberation of the spirit from the gloomy, funereal cowl of psychology.

IV

Meanwhile, we shall dig in. Folklore is descending upon us like a voracious caterpillar. A swarm of locusts is advancing toward us: a plague of observations, commentaries, notes, sayings, quotation marks, small talk. The crops are threatened by a great invasion of gypsy moths. Thus, the alternation of plot and folklore is canonized in literature,[13] and folklore gives birth to plot just as a voracious caterpillar gives birth to a delicate moth. If we did not notice this alternation previously, it was because folklore made no attempt to consolidate its strength and vanished without a trace. But as a period of accumulation, of voracious invasion, it preceded the flowering of any plot. And since it did not aspire to literature, not being acknowledged as such, it remained only within personal letters, in legends of native storytellers, in partly published diaries and memoirs, in petitions and office reports, in court protocols and on signboards. I do not know—perhaps some people like Pilnyak's discourses, so similar to those with which Leskov endowed his first railroad conversationalists, those who were breaking the monotony of the long haul. But to me the most endearing thing in all Pilnyak is the epic conversation in the bathhouse between the deacon and a certain Draube on the meaning of the universe: it does not contain a single "something," nor a single lyrical simile, so intolerable in prose, but it does consist of the elementary game of a plot being born, as in Gogol, where, if you recall, if you approach Plyushkin's, you cannot immediately discern "whether it is a man or a woman, no, a woman, no, a man."

To this day prose continues to vacillate between "daily life" and folklore. The Serapions, Pilnyak, Zamyatin, Prishvin, Kozyrev, and Nikitin should be forgiven all their differences because of the use of folklore which gives their work unity and serves as proof of their vitality. All of them, like the legitimate children of folklore, have a predilection for the anecdote. Vsevolod Ivanov does not have any predilection for the anecdote, and what was stated above regarding daily life applies to him.

If you listen carefully to prose during a period when folklore is flourishing, you will hear something like an intense ringing of grasshoppers coupling in the air—such is the universal sound of contemporary Russian prose. You do not want to dismantle this ringing sound, for it was not a watchmaker's invention, but was assembled from countless multitudes of winged herbs and faiths. During the period that inevitably follows, during the period when multitudes of plots flourish, the chirring of grasshoppers is transformed into the sonorous song of the skylark—of the plot, and then the skylark's high, ringing voice is heard, of which the poet said:

Lithe, frolicsome, sonorous, clear—
He has shaken me to the depths of my soul.[14]

Translated by Constance Antony   1922

Notes

1. *The Book of Monthly Readings (Chet'i Minei)* was the official church compilation of hagiography, patristic literature, homiletic and didactic works, even occasional apocryphal works, all arranged according to the days and months of the calendar.

2. Andrei Bely (1880-1934, pen name of Boris Nikolaevich Bugaev). Leading Symbolist prose writer, poet and literary scholar. He is best known for his prose fiction, including his novels, *Petersburg* (1913) and *Kotik Letaev* (1918), and for his highly original study of Gogol, *Gogol's Craftsmanship* (1934).

3. Leonid Nikolaevich Andreev (1871-1919). Russian novelist and dramatist interested in delving into pathological states of mind, including insanity, sexual obsession, suicide, and fear of death. Although very popular among middle-brow readers, he was despised by such intellectuals as Mandelstam.

4. Maxim Gorky (penname for Alexei Maximovich Peshkov, 1868-1936). Novelist and dramatist of the late nineteenth-early twentieth century, publisher, revolutionary, and literary activist, who wielded enormous influence over literary developments in the USSR.

5. Ivan Sergeevich Shmelev (1873-1950). Leading Russian emigre novelist. Shemelev's most important works are *The Man from a Restaurant* (1910) published in Russia and *The Sun of the Dead* (1925), published abroad.

6. Sergei Nikolaevich Sergeev-Tsensky (1875-1958), Russian novelist whose earlier thematic interests differed little from Andreev's, but whose style placed him close to the ornamentalist tradition of Bely and Remizov.

7. Evgeny Ivanovich Zamyatin (1884-1937). Novelist, dramatist and critic, best known in the West for his anti-utopian novel *We* (1920, published abroad in 1924).

8. An almanac published by Maxim Gorky under the auspices of the Knowledge Publishing House, which specialized primarily in realistic works of such writers as Gorky himself, Kuprin, Andreev, Veresaev, Chirikov, Shmelev, Bunin, Sugruchev, Skitalets and others.

9. Bely was considered the leader of the "ornamentalist" school of prose writing which dominated much of the fiction of the early 1920s.

10. Boris Pilnyak (penname of Boris Andreevich Vogau, 1894-1939). Novelist best known for his novel *The Naked Year* (1922), a modernist attempt to portray the dynamics and emotions of the Civil War years through narrative means, mainly via fragmentary episodes.

11. The group of young Soviet writers who called themselves The Serapion Brotherhood was formed with Evgeny Zamyatin's assistance in 1921 and included many of his students. The group included Lev Lunts, Mikhail Zoshchenko, Konstantin Fedin, Veniamin Kaverin, Nikolai Tikhonov, Nikolai Nikitin, Mikhail Slonimsky, Vsevolod Ivanov, Ilya Gruzdev, Elizaveta Polonskaya, Vladimir Pozner.

12. The preceding paragraphs owe much to Khlebnikov, in particular, to his interest in unearthing the linguistic and mythological foundations of Slavic culture, and to the Formalists, especially to Shklovsky's interest in "plot-construction." However, Mandelstam does *not* adhere to the rigid Formalist distinction between "plot" and "fable" ("siuzhet" and "fabula"), thus the English word "plot" is used here to denote Mandelstam's "fabula."

Mandelstam's own attempts at literary prose date from this period: See, for example, "Sukharevka" and "Cold Summer."

The citation is from Khlebnikov's popular poem, "The Grasshopper" ("Kuznechik," dated 1908-9 by N. Stepanov), which begins with the lines cited. This poem appeared in the Futurist manifesto "A Slap in the Face of Public Taste" (1912).

13. This type of generalization is very typical of the Formalist critics of this period.

14. This is a reference to Tyutchev's poem "A dark and rainy eve" (1836). In Russian folklore the skylark is the harbinger of spring.

HUMANISM AND THE PRESENT

There are epochs which maintain that man is insignificant, that man is to be used like bricks or mortar, that man should be used for building things, not vice-versa—that things be built for man. Social architecture is measured against the scale of man. Sometimes it may turn against man to enhance its own grandeur by feeding on his humiliation and insignificance.

Assyrian prisoners swarm like baby chicks under the feet of an enormous king; warriors personifying the power of the state inimical to man kill bound pigmies with long spears while Egyptians and Egyptian builders treat the human mass as building material in abundant supply, easily obtainable in any quantity.

Nevertheless, there is also another form of social architecture whose scale and measure is man. It does not use man to build, it builds for man. Its grandeur is constructed not on the insignificance of individuality but on the highest form of expediency, in accord with its needs.[1]

Everyone senses the monumentality of the forms of social architecture now approaching. The mountain is not yet visible, but it is already casting its shadow over us, and we who have grown accustomed to the monumental forms of social life, who have been trained in the governmental-juridical flatness of the nineteenth century, move in this shadow fearful and bewildered, uncertain whether this is the wing of approaching night or the shadow of our native city which we must enter.

Simple mechanical enormity and naked quantity are inimical to man, and it is not a new social pyramid which tempts us, but social Gothic: the free play of weights and forces, a human society conceived as a complex and dense architectural forest wherein everything is efficient and individual, and where every detail answers to the conception of the whole.

The instinct for social architecture, that is, for structuring life in grandiose monumental forms far exceeding man's immediate needs, as it were, has deep roots in human societies and is not dictated by idle whim.

Repudiate social structure and the simplest, the most necessary and universally accepted structure will collapse: man's home, the human dwelling place will fall.

In countries threatened by earthquakes people build flat houses and, beginning with the French Revolution, the tendency toward flatness, the repudiation of architecture, dominated the entire juridical life of the nineteenth century, which was spent entirely in the intense anticipation of some subterranean tremor, some social shock.

But the earthquake did not spare even the flat houses. The chaotic world burst in—into the English "home" as well as into the German *Gemüt*; chaos sings in our Russian stoves, banging our dampers and oven doors.[2]

How can we guard our human dwellings against such menacing shocks, how can we ensure their walls against history's subterranean tremors? Who dares to say that the human dwelling, the free house of man, should not stand upon the earth as its finest ornament, as the most stable element in existence?[3]

The juridical creations of recent generations have proven powerless to defend that for which they were created, over which they struggled and fruitlessly philosophized.

No laws concerning the rights of man, no principles of property and inviolability any longer protect the human dwelling, no laws preserve the house from catastrophe, provide it with any assurance or security.

The English, more than any people, are hypocritically concerned over the legal guarantees of individual freedom, but they forget that the concept of "home" arose many centuries ago in their own country as a revolutionary concept, as the natural justification of the first social revolution in Europe, a kind of revolution more deeply rooted and akin to our age than the French.

The monumentality of the approaching social architecture is conditioned by its calling to organize the world's economy to meet man's greater demands, broadening the scope of his domestic freedom to universal proportions, fanning the flame of his individual hearth to the dimensions of a universal flame.

The future appears cold and terrifying to those who do not understand this, but the internal warmth of the future—the warmth of efficiency, home economy and teleology—is just as tangible to the contemporary humanist as the heat of the incandescent stove of the present.[4]

If the social architecture of the future does not have as its foundation a genuinely humanistic justification, it will crush man as Assyria and Babylon did in the past.

The fact that the values of humanism have now become rare, as if taken out of circulation and hidden underground, is not a bad sign in itself. Humanistic values have merely withdrawn, concealed themselves like gold currency, but like the gold reserves, they secure contemporary Europe's entire circulation of ideas, and control them the more competently for being underground.

The transition to gold currency is the business of the future, and in the province of culture what lies before us is the replacement of temporary ideas—of paper banknotes—with the gold coinage of the European humanistic tradition; the magnificent florins of humanism will ring once again, not against the archaeologist's spade,[5] but when the moment comes, they will recognize their own day and resound like the jingling coins of common currency passing from hand to hand.

Translated by Jane Gary Harris   *1923*

Notes

1. This essay should be read in conjunction with Mandelstam's other essays treating the themes of social architecture, or what the author has also termed "Social Gothic"—"François Villon," "Morning of Acmeism," "Conversation about Dante"; the artist and society—"On the Addressee," "Government and Rhythm," "The Word and Culture," "A Revolutionary in the Theater"; and the nineteenth century—"The Nineteenth Century"—among others. It also demands comparison with Mandelstam's autobiographical prose, *The Noise of Time* and with his poetry of 1921-25.

2. Here, perhaps, the most pertinent chapters of *The Noise of Time* are "The Judaic Chaos" and "The Erfurt Program."

3. See Mandelstam's marvelous image of man's humble human dwelling place in the poem "To some winter is arrack and the blue-eyed punch" (1922).

4. The passage on the last page of *The Noise of Time* reads: "Looking back at the entire nineteenth century of Russian culture—shattered, finished, unrepeatable, which no one must repeat or dares to repeat—I wish to hail the century, as one would hail settled weather, and see in it the unity lent it by the measureless cold which welded decades together into one day, one night, one profound winter wherein the terrible State, like a stove, is blazing in the ice."

5. See the last section of Mandelstam's poem "The Horseshoe Finder," also dated 1923.

MIKHAIL BULGAKOV
MOSCOW IN THE TWENTIES

Introduction

It wasn't from the beautiful far away that I studied Moscow in the years 1921-24. Oh, no, I lived in her, I tramped through her from one end to the other. I went up to almost every sixth floor, floors on which only institutions were located, and since there was absolutely not a single sixth floor on which there mightn't have been an institution, those floors are definitely familiar to me. You ride, for example, by cab down Zlatouspensky Street to visit Yuri Nikolaevich and you recall:

"How do you like that building! Permit me, but surely I was in it." I was, honestly! And I even remember the particular occasion. January of 1922. If you please. It transpired when I went to work for a privately-owned trade-industry newspaper and asked the editor for an advance. The editor didn't give me the advance, but said: "Go to Zlatouspensky Street to the sixth floor, room no. . . ." or was it 242? or perhaps 180? . . . I forgot. It's not important. In short, "Go and get the notice in Head-Chem" . . . or Central-Chem? I forgot. Well, it's not important. "Pick up the notice, I'll give you 25 percent." If anyone said to me now: "Go pick up the notice," I would answer: "I will not." I don't want to go for notices. I don't like to go for notices. It is not my profession. But then . . . oh, then it was different. I submissively put on my hat, took that ridiculous pad of notices, and went, like a lunatic. The weather was absolutely, unbelievably freezing, the kind that rarely ever happens. I climbed to the sixth floor, found this room no. 200, and in it found a balding, red-haired man who, having heard me out, didn't give me any notices.

Incidentally, about sixth floors. Excuse me, is it true that there is an elevator in this building? There is. There is. But at that time, in 1922, only those with bad hearts could ride in the elevators. For one thing. And secondly, the elevators didn't operate. So that both those with proof of their defects and those with sound hearts (I am in this number) climbed to the sixth floor.

Now it is another matter. Oh, now it is quite another matter! I was at Patriarchs' Ponds, at my friends' place, not so long ago. Benignly ascending by foot to the sixth floor, about 100 feet above sea level, on the staircase between the fourth and fifth floors, in a shaft containing a network of wires, I saw a hanging, brightly illuminated, utterly motionless elevator. From it issued female weeping and a scowling male bass:

"They should be shot, the rascals!"

On the stairs stood a man who looked like a doorman, and near him stood another man wearing greasy pants who looked like a mechanic and some curious women from Apt. 16.

"How unexpected,"—said the mechanic, and he laughed, bewildered.

At nighttime, when I was returning from my visit, the elevator was still hanging right there, but it was dark, and no voices could be heard coming from it. Most likely the unfortunate pair, having hung there for two weeks, died from starvation.

God knows whether this Central- or Head-Chem exists now, or if it is no more! Maybe some sort of Chem-Trust is there, maybe there is still something. It's possible that for a long time there has been neither this Chem nor a balding, red-haired man, and that the rooms have been assigned by now, so that where there once stood a table with an inkwell now stands a piano or a soft divan, and in place of the chemist sits a fascinating young lady with bleached hair who is reading *Tarzan*. It is all possible. It's just as well that I no longer go there, not by foot and not by elevator, either.

Yes, a lot has changed right before my eyes. Just where haven't I been! To Myasnitskaya a hundred times, to Varvarka—to the Business Court, to the Old Square in Tsentrosoyuz, I dropped in on Sokolniki, and was thrown out of Devichye Pole. One desire propelled me through the strange, immense capital—the desire to make a living. And I made it, it's true, meager, dubious, unstable. I made it in the most fantastic and transient (like consumption) jobs, obtained it by strange, feeble means, many of which, now that things have improved, seem funny to me. I wrote a trade-industry events column in a small newspaper, and by night composed cheerful feuilletons (which to myself seemed no funnier than a toothache), submitted an application to L'no-trest, and one night, outraged at vegetable oil, potatoes, tattered boots, drafted a dazzling project of illuminated advertising. That this project was good is evidenced by the fact that, when I brought it to the attention of my engineer friend, he embraced me, kissed me, and said that I had wrongly missed the engineering profession: it turns out that my mind in one juncture had arrived at the very construction which already shines in Theater Square. What does this prove? This proves, simply, that a man, struggling for his survival, is capable of brilliant acts.

But enough of this. To the reader, of course, how I plunged into Moscow is not interesting, but I am relating all of this to a certain end: so that he believes me when I say that I know the Moscow of the twenties thoroughly. I turned her inside out. And I intend to describe her. But in describing her, I hope that they believe me. If I say something is so, it means that it is really so!

The next time that distinguished foreigners have freshly arrived in Moscow, I shall be ready as a guide.

I

The Question of Housing

... Hey, an apartment!
(Act II, The Barber of Seville)

Let us agree once and for all: a dwelling is the cornerstone of human life. We note the axiom: without a dwelling, a man cannot act. Now in addition to this, I report to all those living in Berlin, Paris, London, and other places,—there are no apartments in Moscow.

How then do they live there?

Here's how they live.

Without apartments.

* * *

But that's the least of it—the last three years in Moscow have convinced me that Muscovites have lost even the understanding of the word "apartment" by naively applying it to everything. So, for example: not long ago, one of my journalist friends received a paper in my presence: "Let to Comrade So-and-so the apartment in Building no. & (at the printer's)." A signature and a round, greasy stamp.

The room was let to Comrade So-and-so, and I visited Comrade So-and-so's place one evening. On a staircase without banisters were pools of cabbage soup, and across the stairway hung a ragged, thick (like a grass-snake) cable. On the upper floor, passing through a section of broken glass, past windows, half of which had been replaced with boards, I came upon a vacant, dark area and there let out a yell. A strip of light answered my cry, and going into somewhere, I found my friend. What had I entered? The devil knows. It was something dark, like a pit, divided by plywood partitions into five compartments, appearing to me like large oblong hatboxes. In the middle box sat my friend on a bed, next to my friend his wife, and next to the wife the brother of my friend; and the aforementioned brother, not rising from the bed, but merely extending his arm, was drawing a charcoal portrait of the wife on the opposite wall. The wife was reading *Tarzan*.

This threesome lived in a telephone receiver. Imagine to yourself, you, living in Berlin, how you would feel if they settled you in a receiver. A whisper, the sound of a match dropping to the floor, was audible in all the boxes, and theirs was in the middle.

"Manya!" (from the outermost box).

"What?" (from the opposite end).

"Do you have any sugar?" (from the end).

"In Lustgarten, in the center of Berlin, many thousand demonstrating workers with red flags assembled..." (from the neighboring box on the right).

"I have candy..." (from the opposite end).

"You swine" (from the neighboring left).

"Let's go together at 7:30!"

"Ignore him, please..."

In ten minutes' time commenced a nightmare: I ceased to understand what I was saying and what was not me, and my ear picked up strange things. The Chinese, specialists in the department of torture, are mere puppies. Never in their days did they contrive such a thing.

"How on earth did you get here?... Ho-ho-ho!... A Soviet delegation accompanied by a Soviet colony set off for the grave of Karl Marx... Well? Here's one to you! Thank you, I drank... With candy?!... Well, they can go to the devil!... Swine, swine, swine! Get him out! And where are you?... In Kyoto and Yokohama... Don't lie, don't lie, dolt, I've been watching you for a long time now!... What's that, there's no bathroom?!!"

My God! I left, not losing even a second, and they stayed there. I spent a quarter of an hour in that box, and they've been living there for seven months.

Yes, dear citizens, when I arrived back at my own place, I sensed for the first time that everything in the world was relative and conditional. I fancied that I was living in a palace where by every door stood a powder-faced lackey in red livery and that a deathlike silence reigned. Silence, this is a great thing, a gift of God and paradise, this silence. But in the meantime, there is only one door in my place (like in all the rooms), this door lets out directly onto a corridor, and catty-corner lives the illustrious Vasily Ivanovich with his illustrious wife.

* * *

I swear by all that I hold sacred, every time that I sit down to write about Moscow, the damned image of Vasily Ivanovich stands before me in the corner. The apparition in the jacket and striped drawers blocks my light! I lean my forehead against the stone wall, and Vasily Ivanovich is in front of me, like the lid on a coffin.

Imagine how impossible this man can make life in any given apartment, and he did it, made it impossible. All of V. I.'s actions are intended to harm his fellow creature, and in the code of the Republic there exists not a single paragraph which he would not violate. Isn't it wrong to swear loudly in harsh words? It's wrong. Yet he swears. Isn't it wrong to drink home brew? It's wrong. Yet he drinks it. Is getting violent allowed? No, it is allowed to no one. Yet he gets violent. And so on. It's a great shame that there is no clause in the code which prohibits the playing of harmonicas in apartments. Soviet lawyers take heed: I implore you to introduce it! There he played. I say—played, because he doesn't play anymore. Perhaps remorse stopped this man? Oh, no, cynics in Berlin: he sold it to get money for drink.

In short, he is not thinkable in human society, and I cannot excuse him, even taking his background into account. Just the reverse: particularly taking it into account, I cannot excuse him. I reason this way: he must show to me, myself a man of dubious background, an example of his good conduct, and by no means me to him. And let anyone prove that I am wrong.

* * *

And here it is the third year that I am living in an apartment with Vasily Ivanovich, and how many I will continue to live with him—is unknown. Possibly until the end of my life, but now, after the visit to the hatbox, it has become easier for me. You don't have to threaten me much, citizens!

Yes, it has become easier for me. I've become more patient and more sympathetic to others.

Doctor G., my friend, arrived at my place last week with the lament:

"Why didn't I ever get married?"

Coming from the lips of the foremost avowed nuptia-phobe in Moscow, such an utterance merited attention.

It seemed he'd been officially forced to double up. A partition had been installed in his room, and behind the partition had settled a married couple. In vain the doctor ranted and raved. Nothing happened. The housing chairman repeated one thing over and over:

"If you were married, now that would be a different story..."

But the third day, the doctor came by and said:

"Well, thank God I never got married...do you quarrel with your wife?"

"Hmm...sometimes...that is to say,.." I answered evasively and politely, looking at my wife, "generally speaking...it happens sometimes...if you see..."

"And who is at fault?" quickly asked my wife.

"I, I am at fault," I hastened to assert.

"A nightmare. A nightmare. A nightmare," the doctor started to say, swallowing some tea, "a nightmare. Every night, do you know that only one thing can be heard, and that is: 'Where were you?' 'At Nikolaevsky Station.' 'You're lying.' 'Honestly.' 'You're lying.' A minute later, again: 'Where were you?' 'At Anna's' 'You're lying'!!"

"The poor woman," said my wife.

"No, it is *I* who am poor," responded the doctor, "and I am leaving for Oryekhovo-Zuivo. The devil take them!"

"Who?" asked my wife suspiciously.

"Them...at the clinic."

* * *

He is at Oryekhovo-Zuivo, and his female friend L. E. is in Italy. Alas, for her there is no place even behind a partition. And a most beautiful woman, who could have adorned Moscow, rushes off to someplace like wretched Rome. Vasily Ivanovich will stay, but she will go away! And Natalya Egorovna flung a rag to the floor this winter, but wasn't able to unstick it because on the table it was nine degrees, while on the floor it was absolutely degreeless, and even one degree less than that. Minus one. And all winter she played the waltzes of Chopin in felt boots, whereas Pyotr Sergeich hired a servant and in a week's time dismissed her, but the servant didn't go anywhere! Because the chairman of the Board of Directors arrived and said that she (the servant) was a member of the housing development, that she was occupying her space, and that no one had the right to disturb her. Pyotr Sergeich, having completely lost his head, will now rush all about Moscow and ask everyone what he should do. But there is absolutely nothing for him to do. In the servant's trunk is a photograph of a brave-looking Red Army man, who took Perekop and a card from the housing development. The coffin-lid for Pyotr Sergeich!

And a certain young man, in whose "apartment" settled a meek little old lady, one Sunday, when the little old lady returned from mass, met her with the words:

"I'm fed up with you, meek little old lady."

And at this banged the little old lady on the head with a spring-balance. And of such events or events like it, I know recently—of four in all. Do I condemn the young man? No. Categorically—no. Because I feel certain that if a little old lady or even a second Vasily Ivanovich settled in my room, I too would seize a spring-balance, despite the fact that at home I was inundated from childhood with the idea that under no circumstances should one wield a spring-balance.

And Sasha offered 200 rubles simply to have Anfisa Markovna cleared from his room . . . However, enough.

* * *

Why does such a strange and disagreeable way of life come about? It comes about because of one thing only—overcrowding. Fact: in Moscow it is overcrowded.

What can be done?

Only one thing can be done: that is to activate my plan, and this plan I shall set forth now, having written another chapter called "On the Good Life" beforehand.

Moscow, 1924

II

On the Good Life

Yury Nikolaevich crossed his legs and, chewing his fruitcake well, asked:

"Well, I don't completely understand why you, a good-natured enough fellow, fly into a rage as soon as you begin to talk about apartments?"

I too slipped a piece of fruitcake into my mouth (an excellent thing with tea, but never at five o'clock in the afternoon, when a man arrives home from work and requires borshch, not tea with fruitcake. In general, Moscow citizens, we cast these "five o'clock's" to the devil!) and answered:

"I know this issue inside and out, and so I fly into a rage."

"Perhaps you would like some more tea?" cautiously suggested the hostess.

"No, thank you. I don't want any tea. I'm full," I answered with a sigh, feeling some strange sort of languor. The fruitcake debris floated around inside of me in a sea of tea and gave rise to a feeling of anxiety.

"It's easy for you to talk," I continued, lighting up a cigarette, "since you have a beautiful two-room apartment."

Yury Nikolaevich suddenly began to laugh convulsively, and, hurriedly swallowing some raisins, thrust his hands into his pockets. In one he didn't find anything. In another also. And in the third. Then he threw himself to the table, dove into the drawers, dove into some piles, and there didn't find it.

Instead of what he was looking for, he found the issue from two Mondays ago of *Nakanune,* admired it, and said:

"It's lost somewhere. Oh well."

With these words he knelt on the floor and clutched the feet of the armchair in the corner. A mangy cur rejoiced at all the fuss and began to race around and tug at his pants.

"Go away!" cried Yury Nikolaevich, reddening. The armchair came out to the side, and in a huge, ragged-edged hole, two-and-a-half feet in diameter, was discovered the dome of a neighboring church against a blue backdrop of sky.

"You don't say so."

"Before the repairs it wasn't there," explained the happy owner of two rooms with a hole, "but now they've made the repairs and the hole."

"It's possible to close that up."

"Well, no, I won't be able to close it up. Let the one who sent me the official notice close it up himself."

Again he slapped his pockets, but didn't find any offical notices. "They sent an official notice, telling me to move out of this apartment."

"To where?"

"It was written on the paper: it doesn't matter."

I confess: my soul became easier. I'm not alone after all.

* * *

Quite frankly: what is this "you move out.."?! Surely a place can't be empty? Yury Nikolaevich will move out, but won't Sidor Stepanich "move in" his place? And won't Yury Nikolaevich, turned out onto the street, naturally want to enter under a roof himself? But what if Fedosei Gavrilovich already sits under this roof? Does an evacuation paper to Fedosei Gavrilovich follow? Fedosei in the place of Ivan, Ivan in the place of Ferapont, Ferapont in the place of Pankratia...

No, citizens, this way you end up with complete nonsense!

* * *

From Christmas to summertime... (in the next room is heard a Komsomol voice: "He didn't exist!!") well, whether it was or it wasn't, in 1921, after coming to Moscow, and in the next years 1922 and 1923, I suffered, citizens, with acute envy. I, citizens, am a remarkable man, and I say this without false modesty. I obtained a work-book in three days, I stood all told only three times in six-hour lines, and not once in a line for six months, like all the other bunglers. I got work five times, in a word, I conquered everything, but an apartment, I have to say, I wasn't able to manage. Not three rooms, not two, not even one. And so I got into that celebrated neighborhood with Vasily Ivanovich, and there I was stuck.

(The voice of Yury Nikolaevich behind the scene: You really have an excellent room!!) The chorus of a Greek tragedy. The roomless:

"This is shocking!!!"

It's true, we won't argue. The fact remains that things could be better.

And so—I was stuck. Countless things occurred at that time in the sublunary world, and one of them, on the occasion of which I quite frankly celebrated, was the coming to trial of this, what did he call it now?.. Central-Living... yes, in short, that organization which distributed rooms in the years 1921-22 by warrant. I don't remember how many years they gave them, but I'm sorry that it wasn't twice as much. And then after this what happened to them?.. It seems that they cancelled this "Living." And notices soon emerged in *Izvestiia*: "I am seeking... I am seeking... I am seeking," and there I sat. I sat and tormented myself with envy. Because I saw the uneven distribution of blessed apartments.

* * *

Wouldn't you like an example? Sure Zina was wonderfully situated. Somehow in the center of Moscow there's not a little apartment, but a three-room bonbonnière. A bath, a little telephone, a husband. Manyushka prepares cutlets on the gas range and Manyushka has yet another little room. With knife to throat, I badgered Zina, demanding an explanation of how those rooms had survived whole.

Surely this was supernatural!

Four rooms—three people. And no outsiders.

And Zina related how one day someone arrived in a truck and delivered the official notice: "Move out!"

And she took it and...didn't move out.

Akh, Zina, Zina! If only you weren't already married, I would marry you. I would marry you, as God is holy, and I would marry the little telephone and the burners on the gas range, and they wouldn't be able to pull me by any force from those rooms.

Zina, you are an eagle, and not a woman!

The age of trucks has come to an end, like everything comes to an end in this world.

Sit, Zinyusha.

* * *

Nikolai Ivanovich recouped himself through his two nieces. He wrote to the province, and the two nieces arrived. One of them attached herself to some sort of institution of higher education, having proven by every seam her proletarian background, while the other entered a studio. Wasn't Nikolai Ivanovich smart weighing himself down with two nieces in so hard a time?

Not smart, but a genius.

Six rooms had been left to Nikolai Ivanovich. They arrived with briefcases as well as without briefcases, and wouldn't leave for anything. The apartment was crammed full of nieces. In every room stood a bed, and in the living room stood two.

* * *

In a few days' time, Yasha became noteworthy. Yasha didn't register any nieces. Yasha managed to sit alone in five rooms by sticking onto the door a warrant half-rotten with age (from 1918, it seems) which indicated that the studio was run by the aforementioned Yasha.

Yasha—you are a genius!

* * *

And Pasha...

Enough!

* * *

With the passage of time, I began to classify. And my classification is simple, as far as I can tell.

The two sorts of people living the good life:

(1) Those who had something and used all their faculties to keep it (Zina, Nikolai Ivanovich, Yasha, Pasha, and others...).

(2) Those who had nothing, arrived, and were given something.

An example: Nartsiss Johannovich arrives from Baku, immediately becomes the president of a trust, and receives two rooms (gas range and so forth) in a government building. Then the queen of clubs invariably brings troubles to the heart, then troubles in the government building, then a distant path and a final chord by the ace of diamonds (ten, according to the amnesty—two, in general—eight). In place of Nartsiss settles Sokiz. In the place of Sokiz—Abram, in Abram's place Fyodor....

Enough...

The Plan

Such things are, of course, inconceivable! There are many plans in the air: including official papers about the eviction of two by a certain date, insidious plans to crowd Fedul, and to move Valentin, and to evict Vasily.

This is not at all the thing.

My plan alone is effective.

Moscow needs to build up.

When white cards with the words

"For Let,"

crop up in the windows of Moscow, then everything will arrive at the norm.

Life will cease to seem like some sort of bewitched drudgery—for those on a trunk in the anteroom, for others in six rooms amidst a community of unexpected nieces.

Ecstasy

Moscow! I see you in skyscrapers!

Translated by Elyse Topalian   *1924*

ZAMYATIN ON SERAFIMOVICH

In every "literary-social" journal the belles lettres department is only a seasonal enterprise, it is merely a lobby in which those who have been announced stand before proceeding to the sanctuary of the next department. One would sooner expect to find literary documents in an almanac, where literature not only beckons the public to a concert-meeting (at one time such meetings were fashionable everywhere, but they now survive only in literature), but also persuades the public to come to the concert.

And so, here are the four latest almanacs: *Nedra,* No. 1; *Nashi dni,* No. 2; *Krug,* No. 3; and *Rol,* No. 3.

Nedra [*The Depths*] is clearly related to the former *Zemlya* [*The Earth*]. The name promises that the layer of black earth had now been dug deeply and that the treasures extracted from the depths of the earth have lain there for many years.

In one sense, at least, this promise is kept: the staleness of many years can really be felt in most of the treasures extracted from *The Depths.* This fully pertains to Veresaev's *Dead End,*[1] and this fully pertains to Serafimovich's *The Iron Flood*—a battle painting à la Vereshchagin,[2] 164 pages long, set in the year 1918.

The Iron Flood... Iron wrested from the earth—what, it would seem, could be better? But send just one small piece of this iron to the factory laboratory—and it will turn out that it has been rusting for quite a long time in *Znanie*'s basement.[3] In keeping with good old *Znanie* custom, for a good two pages they sing: "You have fallen victim in the fatal struggle", then they sing "How they yearned for and fought for, yet lost the Ukraine"; and "The mountain-high waves roared and crashed"; or: "So what if the mistress of the tavern doesn't have enough booze"; and finally one sings: "What does the Muscovite want"—for a whole page. Following *Znanie* tradition, going back to Andreev's *Red Laugh,*[4] are such things as: "mad sun," "the mother laughs with an inexpressibly-joyous, ringing laugh," "madly kisses her child," "enough of war, that's wildly understandable," "the light quivers madly," "over the blue abyss," "bottomless precipice," "the mirage flickers with fiery flickering."

However, it seems, there is something else here too, something not encountered in the Serafimovich of *Znanie.* When we read: "Elbowing his way out of the crowd toward the windmills, with an inexpressibly red face and with dark whiskers that had barely pushed their way through , wearing a sailor cap"—a sentence without a subject—we sense in Serafimovich someone obviously modern, almost a Przybyszewski.[5] And when we encounter phrases such as—"insuppressible amazement once again arose in those who were running amid tension toward salvation"—we detect here already the beginnings of instrumentation, almost in the manner of Bely.[6]

And what is more, in *Znanie* there was never any of that tinselling that we now find in Serafimovich's iron extracted from *The Depths.* The figure of the "infamous compromiser," Mikeladze, is built in accordance with all the codes of tinselling. But especially thickly tinselled is the end—the hero's apotheosis, pieced together in accordance with all the operatic rules, which, as is well known, require that "the heart be branded with a fiery stamp," and that tears "trickled down the weather-beaten faces of passersby and old-timers, and the eyes of young girls began to shine...."

The ore Serafimovich uses for his *The Iron Flood* is so rich that even his processing it by operatic methods could not depreciate it entirely: some scenes are memorable. There are a few effective images (Gorpino's husband has "hands like hooves"; the Cossacks have "frenzied, beefy eyes"); one lightning second in the mountains is done well. But these are as few as the righteous in Gomorrah.

Translated by Janis Eichelis   *1925*

Notes

1. V. Veresaev (pseud. of Vikenty Smidovich, 1867-1946) is best remembered today for his compilations of literary documents and memoirs of Pushkin and Gogol. His novel *Dead End (V tupike,* 1924) deals with the problem of the intelligentsia and the Revolution.

2. Vasily Vereshchagin (1842-1904) was famed for his paintings depicting battles in the War of 1812 and battles in Turkestan.

3. Serafimovich was an important contributor to Gorky's "Znanie" publishing house. whose authors also included Kuprin and Bunin.

4. "The Red Laugh" (1905) is Leonid Andreev's response to the Russo-Japanese war.

5. Stanislaw Przybyszewski (1868-1927) has been characterized as the "witch doctor" of the Polish Moderna by Czeslaw Milosz. Przybyszewski's ultra-decadent works enjoyed an enormous vogue in Russia.

6. Andrei Bely (1880-1934), one of the leaders of Russian Symbolism, is particularly noted for the instrumentation of his prose.

DMITRI FURMANOV ON SERAFIMOVICH

I. To Live is to Struggle

Serafimovich first embarked upon the broad path of literary creativity about forty years ago. The son of a Cossack, he did not find on the "free and quiet Don" that freedom he had been seeking since childhood. Pictures of harsh, everyday life, of barefaced, avaricious exploitation, of the complacency of some and the voiceless defenselessness of others, the savage customs of "cultured" society, drew him away from that life. But where? For a long time he did not know where he should turn. And helplessly, as in a severe illness, he tossed about in search of the true path.

Over the years he matured, his thoughts developed, he got the lay of the land, and right out of school he ended up in exile in Arkhangelsk: the path was found. This was that single path, along which in the course of decades with ever greater frequency and persistency, marched the best sons of the working people, scattered in exile, in prisons, in penal colonies— the long-suffering and thorny path of struggle.

All his long life, from the days of the tsarist underground to our days of triumph, Serafimovich remained faithful in unspoiled purity to the workers' cause. Never did this man of flint bend or surrender, neither in ordeals nor in wordly temptations. Never, not once did he stray from the path of struggle; never was he hypocritical in either life or in his literary work; he remained firm even at the time when the so-called "vanguard of society" lost heart and helplessly dropped its arms, after it had begun to deteriorate at the top.

From his first story, "On the Ice-Floe," to his last superb story, *The Iron Flood,* Serafimovich has remained the same singer of the struggle between labor and capital, between the free order and tsarist destitution, coercion and exploitation.

To shed light on the many years of Serafimovich's activity means to touch upon an entire epoch. We will not survey here his literary activity as a whole, but focus only on *The Iron Flood,* the first story of the broadly conceived cycle *The Struggle.*

Let us first of all consider the story's subject matter. It is founded on an historical event— the great, five-hundred-verst march of the Taman army, which was cut off by the Whites from Taman in 1918. With unbearable hardships, reckless heroism, and at the cost of great sacrifice the people of Taman made their way—through Novorossiisk, along the Black Sea coast, through Tuapse and Belorechenskaya—right up to their joining with the main forces of the Red Army, which had retreated there from the center of the Krasnodar district. "Kozhukh," the commander of the first column of the retreating mass, is the famed Civil War hero, Epifan Kovtyukh, presently commander of one of the red divisions. "Smolokurov" is the deceased sailor Matveev. "Prikhodka" is Kovtyukh's adjutant, Gladkikh, who had seen more than one ordeal of battle with him.

Everything—setting, characters, the events themselves—is a true copy of the epoch of the Civil War.

Serafimovich, knows beautifully the life, customs and language of the Ukrainian Cossacks, since he more than once had been to those places through which the Taman army had passed, and had spoken personally and several times with the actual participants of that heroic march, and particularly with Kovtyukh himself; Serafimovich, having thoroughly and conscientiously studied all the material about the march, succeeded in combining in his story the craftsmanship of an artist with the rich erudition of an ethnographer, the conscientiousness and broad competence of a historian with the wise, serious and sensible approach of a sociologist. This work, *The Iron Flood,* is both valuable and beautiful precisely because it offers rich food for the reader's thoughts and heart, it leads him into the events from all sides, reveals them in their entirety and manysidedness with an irresistible, natural simplicity and persuasiveness. The organic simplicity in Serafimovich's work stems from a deep understanding of the driving forces of life and human struggle.

Danger does not frighten him, "excesses" do not terrify him: he knows the ultimate goal toward which the tumultuous "iron flood" of life strives, no matter what it may encounter along the way. He looks upon everything as an *expert*, who sees the end results behind every event, as if he held firmly by its bridle a wild horse of the steppes that is bucking and racing about, but, and he knows this, the time will come one day when the violence will pass and the wild horse's arrogance will subside.

Serafimovich knows how to unravel the complicated and confusing tangle of life. Removing nearly imperceptibly one layer after the other, he uncovers the hidden core, and everything becomes distinct and clear. And often he shows the large and complex in the small, in the "secondary"; after all the sun is mirrored in the tiniest drop of water.

Here, for example, is Granny Gorpino, the old woman who marched with the army the entire way; at night, alone, by her wagon she muses:

> Who for, she'd like to know? For the Cossacks and their generals and officers. . . These had owned all the land, and the non-Cossacks were like dogs. . . Oh, what a life! They had worked with their eyes fixed on the ground, like oxen. Daily, in the morning and at night, she had mentioned the tsar in her prayers—her parents first, then the tsar, then her children, and then all Christians of the Orthodox faith. And he was no tsar after all, only a gray dog, so they kicked him out. Oh, what a life! She had trembled in every fibre, had been terrified when she heard the tsar had been kicked out, and then she had thought that it served him right—he was a dog, a mere dog. . . .*

Gorpino's feeling is directed on the true path: she is against the aggressors, against the "officers"; against exploitation. This "Granny Gorpino" stands before us as the personification of the "non-Cossack" Kuban, half-industrialized, half-peasant mass, which did not have a sharp and true class consciousness and merely through feeling intuited the directions of its historical path.

The same Granny Gorpino says:

> To hell with it if my samovar is lost! "Turn out for three days," they said, "and after three days everything will go back to normal again!" And here we are knocking about for a whole week, like lost souls. What kind of power is the Soviet power if it can't do anything for us? A dog's power! The Cossacks have risen, like the devils they are! My heart aches for my people, for Okhrim. . . and for that young fellow. . . Oh, dear Lord!

The artist-sociologist knows very well with what kind of material he is dealing. Once this problem is clear, then the forms fall into place by themselves, a lively language appears, and the broad canvas of a variegated, picturesque life unfolds.

But what is the nature of the "material" of the Taman army?

> This undisciplined, roaring torrent comprised demobilized men from the tsarist army who had been recruited into the Red Army, and others who had joined the Red troops, mostly small craftsmen, coopers, locksmiths, tinkers, carpenters, cobblers, barbers, and, more numerous than any, fishermen. All these were "outsiders" accustomed to living from hand to mouth, hard-working people for whom the coming of the Soviet

---

*All quotations from *The Iron Flood* are from the edition: Moscow: Progress Publishers, 1974, 4th revised edition.

power had pushed ajar the closed door of life, had made them think that life itself could be rendered less drab than it had always been. The overwhelming majority of these troops were peasants. With few exceptions they had all left their farms. Only the well-to do had remained in the villages; the officers and rich Cossacks did not molest them.

The scene is set, the foundation is revealed; it is now clear to the author how it should be constructed. And here he will never dissemble. He knows that he has before him no army of industrial workers, and he will give this army neither a heightened consciousness nor deep, organic discipline—no, for if he will accord them discipline, then exclusively the kind that is born in the face of danger, in the face of unavoidable, certain death. And if he will accord them "consciousness," then merely of an elementary sort, the only kind valid for the given "material."

The author knows that here too occur sudden changes, that here too ideological changes have a place, but he will show this carefully, without a shadow of false pathos and without any hypocrisy.

Here, for example, is a picture of the struggle between the old and the new worlds, of ideological stratification within one and the same social milieu. The situation occurs after a battle. They are preparing to bury the dead.

The baggage train and the refugees spread far over the steppe, in the groves and the undulations of the plain. Again there was blue smoke over the fires, again one saw the scarcely human sight of children's bony little heads on necks too thin to support them. Again, on white Georgian tents spread upon the ground, dead men lay with crossed arms, and beside them were prostrate women—other women this time—hysterically beating the earth and tearing their hair.

Soldiers crowded around some horsemen.

"Where are you going?"

"To get a priest."

"Kozhukh ordered that the band captured from the Cossacks should play."

"What's the good of a band? It's only a lot of brass trumpets, whereas the priest's got a live throat."

"What the devil do we want with his live throat? His voice gives you the belly-ache. Anyway, the band is a military unit."

"The band! The band!"

"A priest! A priest!"

They wrangled over the band or the priest with much cursing. The women got wind of the dispute and ran up, crying frantically:

"A priest! A priest!"

Young soldiers also ran up, clamoring:

"The band! The band!"

Eventually, the band got the upper hand.

The horsemen began to dismount.

Refugees and soldiers went in solemn procession behind the band which lifted its brazen voices to the brazen sky expressing sorrow and strength.

The hidden springs of action are clear to the author beforehand, the "material" itself never allows him to overreach himself: sociologist and ethnographer, historian and artist, live in harmonious agreement, in full harmony.

As Comrade Kogan has observed (*On Guard*, no. 5):

Serafimovich's objectivity is attuned to the scientific-materialistic thinking of our time. This is a deeply convinced consciousness of the natural progression of the historical process, of the inevitability of what is being accomplished. This consciousness allows him to transcend the particular, to look from above at the variegated arena of clashing interests, to preserve the calmness engendered by a vision of the path and goal. This is why he is serious and does not overextend himself with details: he does not sigh, comiserate, or show indignation. Everything will be resolved in the general, grandiose plan of history, in which everything is significant as a part of the whole, and everything is destroyed if approached with a barren, subjective frame of mind. He is attentive to everything, for him there are no primary and secondary phenomena. Everything—forces, moments of struggle—everything is taken into account. There is a burning fire in his objectivity, obtained through a knowledge of the facts and careful thinking, the inexhaustible source of firm, steady actions, and of persistent, progressive movement along the chosen path.

But "the path" was chosen forty years ago: it had been tried and tested in struggle. Along this path he traveled from the days of his youth to the time his hair turned gray.

This is the only path, there is no departing from it.

II. On Tendentiousness and "Agitation"

Serafimovich does not need to be tendentious—it is enough for him to be himself. He needs only to truthfully narrate what he has set out to do, the rest will come of itself. There is no need to "agitate" about the Taman army, it is unnecessary to glorify the march when a simple, truthful representation of the facts of historical reality represents the best document and makes for the best praise of the people of Taman. Perhaps the Taman people should have been presented as cultured people? Perhaps they ought to have been depicted as politically conscious, disciplined, and organized as a class? Perhaps as remarkably humane—as the "flower" of the revolutionary, struggling class.

Nothing of this kind is necessary. Just one thing is needed: to show them as they are. And if it was people like *that* who prevailed, it means the end of everything in the past, for this "incomplete" new phenomenon—the victorious toiling masses—will "complete itself"; for it everything is still ahead, the future is for it. And for this reason in Serafimovich one can sense, even behind the darkest facts of the masses' ignorance, its lack of culture and its cruelty, the reverse side of all this; one senses that which is coming to take the place of ignorance and darkness, and that it is coming precisely by this path of cruelty and suffering. He shows us this darkness like an artist—not like a judge—and for this reason "non-agitation" becomes agitational.

Serafimovich does not strive to and does not want to agitate—the material itself agitates for him.

And when this or that character in his work does stand out, you can always see the collective, the masses, behind him.

Both the living type and the whole social colossus that begot him are presented side by side. The actions of every person are concentrated, singular, and inimitable, but at the same time they interflow with the actions of the masses, because the individual and the masses are a single entity. All are responsible for the actions of one; the actions of one are characteristic of all.

And when the author focuses on an individual action, then it, too, inevitably "agitates," exerts an influence in the widest sense.

Artistic truth lies in the fact that everything essential is told without reserve and that it is told *correctly,* that is, from a definite point of view.

And Serafimovich proceeds in just this way: he tells it all, even that which at first glance appears to be most "disgraceful." But in the historical aspect that which appears to be "disgraceful" emerges as something *unavoidable,* and therefore as something that is natural as well.

And the haze lifts. The problem becomes clear without "tendentiousness," and "agitates" in a definite direction. Moreover, the author constantly senses the time, the conditions and the milieu in which the action is unfolding.

"What happens in war?—this is what happens," is his slogan.

In one place he writes:

> The huts, poplars, the dimly white church, all were emerging more and more distinctly from the twilight. Beyond the orchards the dawn was rose-tinted.
>
> From the priest's house people with ashen faces and golden shoulder-straps were being led—part of the Cossack headquarters' staff had been taken. Their heads were split open in the yard near the priest's stable, and blood soaked the dung.
>
> The din of the firing, the shouts, curses and groans drowned out the noise of the river.
>
> The house of the village ataman was searched from basement to attic—he was nowhere to be found. He had fled. Then the soldiers called out:
>
> "If you do not show yourself we'll kill your children."
>
> The ataman did not appear.
>
> They began to slaughter the children. The ataman's wife crawled on her knees, with streaming hair, clinging to the soldiers' legs. One of them said, his voice heavy with reproach:
>
> "Why're you yelling bloody murder? I also had a three-year-old daughter, just like yours. We buried her up there in the mountains, but I didn't yell."
>
> He slashed at the little girl and then split open the skull of the wildly laughing mother.

Or elsewhere:

> And behind, in the depths of the darkness, the firing and the shouts also grew fainter—the Cossacks, having no support, scattered, abandoned their horses, crawled under carts, scrambled into the black huts. Ten of them were taken alive. They were slashed with swords across their mouths which smelled of vodka.
>
> When dawn broke, a platoon of soldiers led the arrested commander to the cemetery. They came back without him.

These are the people of Taman, these are not the Whites. But is the same with the Whites: "What happens in war?—this is what happens!" In war the passionate wish in man to smash things awakes *inevitably*. It is impossible not to show this. But it must be shown with skill. And Serafimovich shows it *in a way* that for all the cruelty, despite the abyss of ignorance and want of culture of the masses, the reader's sympathies remain all the time, wholeheartedly, on the side of the Red Army—on the side of the people of Taman.

III. On Proportions

It can happen that the material is fine, that the treatment of the individual parts is also fine, but that as a whole the work is no good at all. And this frequently is a result of the fact that the individual parts are connected clumsily, that disproportionate attention is paid to them, that there is no artistic proportion linking the individual parts.

Precisely this proportionality of parts is so fascinating in *The Iron Flood*. It is as if the author somewhere from above takes in the entire field of action with a birds-eye view and knows precisely when to linger and when to press on. Essentially, in Serafimovich the masses remain active all the time. He more rarely dwells on the actions of individual characters—only out of necessity, and then in passing.

The masses of the Red Army, led by Kozhukh, is in the foreground; then Pokrovsky's army; then the troops of the Georgian division; the fighters of the main Red Army forces function when they join Kozhukh's troops. The masses are everywhere. And each acting force has its assigned place—no more and no less than is called for by artistic reckoning and sense.

There was a great temptation to show the march of the whole Taman army, that is, all three columns: the first, led by Kozhukh, and the second and third, under the command of Smolokurov, which followed Kozhukh. These last two groups had their special traits *all their own,* and the temptation to combine them with Kozhukh's column was not a small one. But the author did not proceed that way; and he presented the life of these two columns only to the extent necessary to render more vivid the background of the activity of the first column, the principle hero of all the operations. In this way an economy of means was achieved, and the reader's intense attention is always concentrated on what is important, on the primary.

Not that the "important" is being swept aside from the "unimportant"—here everything is equally important, and each action is merely a component part of the general flow of events. Here, only what is "necessary" to the artist is separated from the less necessary, and at the same time, the strength of the impression is increased ten-fold.

The author devised his story according to the system: "minimum of words, maximum of action."

He is sparing with arguments, he has no need of them: the dynamics of the unfolding events themselves show what is primary. Is it necessary to talk about the want of consciousness, which was so characteristic of the individual detachments to Taman? Is it necessary to speak of the horrors and the cruelty? The author supplies us with only one picture, and everything becomes clear: the Cossacks are already converging on the retreating people of Taman:

> A soldier whom the Cossacks had taken prisoner and then set free was brought to him. The soldier's ears, nose, tongue and fingers had been cut off, and on his chest was written in blood:
> "This is how we shall treat all you Bolshevik swine!"
> "That's fine, my boys... fine!" the voice within Kozhukh seemed to repeat.
> The Cossacks attacked furiously.
> Then a breathless messenger from the rear reported:
> "They're fighting at the bridge... the baggage train and the refugees...."
> Kozhukh's tanned face went as yellow as a lemon. He hurried to the spot. It was pandemonium. In a frenzied congestion at the approach to the bridge people were hacking with axes at the wheels of one another's carts, falling upon each other with poles and whips; roars, imprecations, shrieks, the dirge-like wailing of women, the screaming of infants; the bridge itself was blocked, carts locked together; snorting horses, which tore their traces, trapped people and children yelling in terror, unable to go either back or forward. And from behind the orchards came the menacing rat-tat-tat-tat.
> "S-t-o-p!... Stop!" roared Kozhukh in a voice that grted like iron. But he could not hear his own voice. He shot the nearest horse in the ear. The peasants turned upon him savagely with their poles.
> "You devil's bastard! Kill our horses, would you! Bash him, kill him!"
> Kozhukh with his adjutant and two soldiers retreated to the river, poles swishing through the air above their heads.
> "Bring a machine-gun," he ordered hoarsely.
> His aide slipped like an eel under carts and the bellies of horses. Presently a machine-gun and a platoon of soldiers came running up.
> The peasants roared like wounded bulls.
> "Go for them!" they cried, attacking viciously with their poles, trying to knock the rifles from the hands of the soldiers who, unable to shoot at their own people—their fathers, mothers, and wives—began to use their butt ends to good purpose.
> Kozhukh, agile as a cat, leapt to the machine-gun, adjusted it, and fired several bursts over the mob. The bullets whizzed low, and the wind of death made the

peasants' hair stand on end. They fell back. And from behind the orchards: rat-tat-tat-tat.

Kozhukh left the gun and began to curse the peasants at the top of his voice. They submitted to his authority. Some carts were inextricably locked together on the bridge; he ordered them to be thrown into the river. They obeyed. The bridge was cleared. He posted a platoon of soldiers at the approach to the bridge and the aide began sending the carts across in some semblance of order.

The reader sees right away what the masses before him are and what kind of man this iron commander, Kozhukh, is.

Frequently, Serafimovich will, with a single stroke, complete a whole picture, laying bare immediately what was still unclear.

Here, for example, is how the Taman people rest in camp:

"To each his own," says the author. And he shows how this *own* can be almost unusual in *such* a situation:

"Stepan, you must wake up. Your son is on a spree! Now... clumsy! Here, I'm putting your son at your side. Have a go at him, little son, pull his nose, and his lip. That's it... fine! Your father hasn't yet had time to grow a beard for you to play with, so tug at his lip, tug away."

And a man's voice, sleepy at first, then joyous and suggestive of smiles, began to speak in the dark:

"There, sonny, lie here beside me. We've no time to play with women, we two serious men. We'll go to war together; then we'll till the good earth. Hey, what d'you think you're doing?... Want to drown your daddy?"

The young mother burst into an inexpressibly merry laugh.

Or, when the troops are leaving on the road leading from Novorossiisk and they don't have the strength to take everybody with them:

A very tall soldier with a grim face and only one leg, his eyes fixed ahead, jerked himself forward on his crutches with big, determined strides, indefatigably advancing along the high-road and muttering:

"To hell with the lot of you, bastards... to hell!"

The baggage train gradually disappeared from view. One could see only the dust raised by the wheels of the last carts and hear faintly the creaking of the iron axles. The town and the bay lay far behind. There was only the high-road left and, at wide intervals, the corpse-like men slowly trailing after the vanished column. One by one they gave up helplessly, sitting down or stretching themselves out on the bank by the roadside, their dull eyes fixed on where the last cart had disappeared. The dust, reddened by the rays of the sinking sun, slowly settled.

Only the one-legged giant on crutches continued to jerk his body forward on the empty high-road, muttering as he went:

"To hell with the bloody lot of you. We shed our blood for you, bastards!..."

Cossacks entered the town from the opposite end.

The retreat would not be as vivid without this one-legged soldier. The cripple, doomed to certain death, has been unforgettably stamped in the reader's memory.

A third picture: a German battleship pounds at the departing column of the Taman people. People perish, cattle perish, good perishes. But this is not enough, it is necessary to fill in this picture of destruction with still one more stroke of the brush:

Another huge, blinding tongue flashed on the battleship, once more a crash shook the town, rolled among the mountains, and echoed back from behind the smooth sea;

again a snowy white puff appeared in the sparkling blue sky and several people fell moaning. In a cart an infant, greedily sucking the breast of a young woman with black eyebrows and earrings in her ears, suddenly became limp, his little hands fell away from the breast, his lips opened and let go of the nipple. The mother gave a wild animal cry. People rushed to her but she repelled them fiercely and obstinately pushed her nipple, from which the milk was dripping in warm white drops, into the baby's tiny mouth. The little face, with upturned eyes which had lost the sparkle of life, was already turning yellow.

This is the economical, skillful, proportional way in which the author directs his attention to different aspects of his epic. In this lies the art of the genuine artist.

IV. Mass Action

To construct a majestic epic such as the march of the people of Taman on the actions of individual characters would be unnatural: tens of thousands of people cannot be mechanically acting figures. Kozhukh is the hero because his will coincides with the wills of tens of thousands of fighters, whom he delivers from destruction. In Serafimovich it is precisely the whole Red Army that acts, having found in Kozhukh the most complete incarnation of its will.

Even Kozhukh's biography is very characteristic in this regard:

When Kozhukh was six he had been sent to work as shepherd to the village herd. The steppe, ravines, forests, sheep, the sailing clouds in the sky and their long shadows on the ground were his tutors.

Later, a bright and quick-witted lad, he was hired by a village kulak as assistant salesman in a shop; little by little he had taught himself to read and write. Then came military service, the war, the Turkish front. He became an ace machine-gunner. Once he climbed a mountain with his platoon of machine-gunners and got into a valley in the rear of the enemy. When the Turkish division began to descend from the range in retreat, he worked his machine-gun like a fury, mowing them down. They fell in neat rows like grass, and warm blood had poured down upon him. He had never before imagined that one could literally stand knee-deep in human blood—but that had been Turkish blood, and he had soon forgotten it.

And whether Kozhukh lets the commanders sign on paper that a firing squad awaits those who do not carry out an order; whether he is commanding in battle, whether he angrily refuses to carry out his "superior's," Smolokurov's, order—in all this there is not one thing uniquely Kozhukhovian or individual, but only that which is characteristically typical of the whole weather-beaten, iron mass of fighters. Each of them would act in the same way: the characteristic purpose is the same for all. Whenever one of them acts—the masses act.

The pictures of the masses in action are particularly well done in Serafimovich's novel. Take, for example, the above-mentioned picture of the chaos on the bridge. Or: when the people of Taman retreat with several thousand sailors from the Red Fleet that was sunk in the Black Sea.

In one place they are described in the following manner:

Even in the darkness one could feel that the confused, pale blur yonder was a rowdy crowd advancing. Their excited voices, raucous both from exposure to every kind of weather and drinking, preceded them, burdened with oaths. The men stopped dipping their spoons and turned their heads.

"The sailors!"

"Restless fellows, can't keep quiet a minute."

The sailors came up with a chorus of abuse.

"Loafers! Here you are, wolfing grub, not caring a straw about the Revolution. You spit on the Revolution, you bourgeois scum!"

"Why do you bark at us? Windbags!"

The soldiers glared at the sailors but were wary; the rowdies were hung with revolvers, bombs, and belts of cartridges.

"Where's your Kozhukh taking you? Have you thought of that? We started the Revolution. We sank the fleet, regardless of Moscow's instructions. The Bolsheviks are messing about with the German Kaiser, making secret plans, but we shan't allow the people to be betrayed. If a man betrays the people, he'll be shot on the spot. Who's your Kozhukh? An officer! And you are sheep straggling along, all huddled together. Bloody idiots!"

From the fire which licked the sides of the big company cauldron a voice retorted: "You've come with a lot of whores, a whole bawdy-house of them."

"It's no concern of yours. Envy us, do you? Don't poke your noses where you're not wanted, it might be bad for you. What we have, we've earned. Who was it that started the Revolution? The sailors. Who did the tsar shoot? Who did he drown. Who did he chain? The sailors. Who brought literature from abroad? The sailors. Who beat the bourgeois and the priests? The sailors. You're only beginning to see daylight, whereas we sailors have shed our blood in the struggle. And while we were shedding our blood for the Revolution, who but you fell upon us with your tsarist bayonets? You're no bloody good to anybody!"

Some soldiers put down their wooden spoons, took their rifles and stood up. The darkness around deepened and the fires seemed to have been swallowed up by the earth.

"Boys, let's go for them!"

They held their rifles ready.

The sailors whipped out their revolvers and began quickly to unfasten bombs.

A gray-moustached Ukrainian, who had fought throughout the imperialist war on the Western front and had been made sergeant for his fearlessness and who, when the Revolution broke out, had killed the officers of his company, took a mouthful of hot porridge, tapped his dripping spoon over the rim of the kettle, and wiped his moustache.

"Cockerels!" he cried at the sailors. "Cock-a-doodle-doo! Why don't you crow?"

His sally produced shouts of laughter.

"Why do they treat us like dirt?" said the soldiers angrily, turning to the gray-moustached man.

Again the long string of fires flashed to the eye. The sailors began to put their revolvers into their holsters and reattach their bombs.

"Bah, you bastards are not worth troubling about!"

They moved away, a riotous horde, dimly white in the dusk, and vanished. The string of fires stretched after them.

Kozhukh's troops joined the troops of the Red Army's main forces. The pictures of this meeting are indeed unforgettable. The unusually powerful force of the experience is clearly brought out:

And those who stood clothed and well-nourished, confronting the iron ranks of the emaciated naked people, were like orphans before this triumph which they had not experienced, and, without shame, tears welled up in their eyes and they broke their ranks, pressing forward, moving like an avalanche towards the cart on which stood the ragged, barefoot, and emaciated Kozhukh. And to the verge of the steppe their cry sounded:

"*Batko* ... lead us where you will! We will give our lives...."

Thousands of hands stretched out to him. They pulled him down, lifted him over their heads, and carried him. And the steppe was shaken for dozens of miles, shaken by innumerable voices.

"Hurrah—a-ah! Hurra-a—a—ah for *batko* Kozhukh!"

Kozhukh was carried past where the orderly ranks stood, and where the artillery was lined, he was carried past the horses of the squadrons, and the horsemen turned in their saddles and with shining faces and wide-open mouths yelled continuously.

He was carried past the refugees among the carts, and the mothers held out their children to him.

They carried him back again and set him upon the cart. Kozhukh opened his mouth to speak, and all gasped as if they were seeing him for the first time.

"Look, his eyes are blue!"

They did not cry this aloud because they were too simple to put their emotions into words, but indeed his eyes had turned out to be blue and gentle and with the smile in them of a child—they did not cry this aloud, but roared instead:

"Hurrah for our *batko!* Long life to him! We'll follow him to the ends of the earth. We'll fight for the Soviet power. We'll fight the landowners, generals, officers...."

Mass scenes are Serafimovich's native element.

As Prikhodko stepped outside, the sound of the water *grew* louder, permeating the darkness entirely. By the door on the *black* earth was a *dark* and *low* machine-gun. Two *dark* figures with *dark* bayonets stoody nearby.

It is impossible to say this any better and still make the reader feel it. Not a single word can be exchanged for another: through the repetition of epithets—black, low, dark—emerges a picture of the eerie situation.

The cottages loomed mysteriously, dimly white. The streets were black with cumbrous shapes. If you looked intently at them they turned out to be carts, from which came sounds of snoring and heavy breathing. Prostrate forms lay everywhere. A dark poplar seemed to tower in the middle of the street, or a church steeple—but it was only the raised shaft of some cart. Horses munched in a measured, lazy fashion; the cows sighed heavily.

Just try to put some other word in place of "the cottages loomed mysteriously, dimly white," and you will sense right away how the intense power of perception is weakened. Or again, an expression like "the streets were black with cumbrous shapes," which summons up a sense of chaotic disorder, of massiveness and of the nocturnal delusiveness of forms.

The sea, like a huge beast with gentle and wide wrinkles on its broad face, placidly approved of the splashing, shouting, and hooting and blandly licked the animated coast and the yellow human bodies performing their vigorous antics.

Whoever has been at the seashore will clearly sense how this huge beast "blandly licked the animated coast."

Or the description of the Georgian officer, who kept jabbering a lot about "freedom" and "culture," sincerely convinced that "Bolsheviks are enemies of mankind, enemies of world culture." He and his troops have gotten ready to "properly" confront the people of Taman and to finish them off at the mountain pass:

A Georgian officer with a short moustache and black almond-shaped eyes that made havoc, as he well knew, in the hearts of womenfolk, was strolling along the flat top of the massif. He wore a red Circassian coat that set off his narrow waist. On his shoulders were gold straps. Now and then he threw a glance around him. What he saw were trenches, ramparts, and well-hidden machine-guns.

Nothing more need be said of him.

The image, captured with just a few strokes, paints the Georgian, Menshevik-oriented officer more vividly than a detailed characterization.

The Caucasian sun was hot although it was autumn. But the steppe was translucent, the steppe was blue. Gossamer glittered delicately. Poplars with thinning leaves stood in meditation. The orchards were slightly tinted with yellow. The steppe gleamed white.

What a magnificent description in its precision of definition, in its harmony of style, in the severity and beauty of the epithets!

The picture of night is permeated with the same coloring, with the same spirituality:

Low red flames leapt in the velvet darkness, lighting up faces and bodies that looked as flat as if they had been cut from cardboard, the wheel of a cart, the head of a horse. The night was alive with voices, exclamations and laughter. Snatches of song rang out; someone played the balalaika; now and then an accordion struck up. Glowing fires here, there, and as far as the eye could see.

These examples can be multiplied ten-fold, but there is no need for this— *The Iron Flood* should not be quoted, but read in its entirety; from beginning to end—the whole story is written magnificently.

Serafimovich knows well the material that forms the base of his work. He senses beautifully the milieu in which the events unfold, he knows its customs and way of life, he knows the language, he knows the entire mysterious range of the workings of human thought and feeling; and for this reason he handles the material of his remarkable story with the ease and confidence of a genuine, great artist, setting standards of unsurpassed mastery.

To immerse oneself for a few hours in reading *The Iron Flood* is to refresh oneself with the experiences of heroic, revolutionary actions, to introduce oneself to the work of a great artistic talent.

Translated by Janis Eichelis   *1925*

A SLAP IN THE FACE OF PUBLIC TASTE

To those who read—our New First Unexpected.

We alone are the *face of our Time*. The horn of time blows through us in the art of words.

The past constricts. The Academy and Pushkin are less intelligible than hieroglyphics.

Pushkin, Dostoevsky, Tolstoy, etc., etc., must be thrown overboard from the Ship of Modernity.

He who does not forget his *first* love will not recognize his last.

But who will be so gullible as to turn his last Love to the perfumed lechery of a Balmont? Will he find a reflection of today's virile soul there?

Who will be so cowardly as not to dare to tear the paper armor from warrior Bryusov's black tuxedo? Will he find the dawn of an unknown beauty there?

Wash your hands which have touched the filthy slime of the books by countless Leonid Andreevs.

All those Maxim Gorkys, Kuprins, Bloks, Sologubs, Remizovs, Averchenkos, Chornys, Kuzmins, Bunins, etc., etc.,—need only villas on a river. That's the way fate rewards tailors.

From the height of skyscrapers we look at their insignificance!...

We decree that the following *rights* of poets be respected:

1. To enlarge the *scope* of the poet's vocabulary with arbitrary and derivative words.

2. To feel insuperable hatred for the language that existed before them.

3. To tear with horror from our proud foreheads the wreath of cheap fame which you have made from bathhouse switches.

4. To stand on the rock of the word "we" amid the sea of catcalls and outrage.

And if *for the time being* the filthy marks of your "common sense" and "good taste" remain in our lives, nevertheless, *for the first time* the lightning flashes of the New Future Beauty of the Self-Sufficient Word are already on them.

Moscow, December 1912

D. Burlyuk, Alexander Kruchenykh
V. Mayakovsky, Viktor Khlebnikov

OSIP MANDELSTAM
THE MORNING OF ACMEISM

I

Given the immense emotional excitement associated with works of art, it is desirable that discussion of art display the greatest restraint. A work of art attracts the great majority only insofar as it illuminates the artist's world view. The artist, however, considers his world view a tool and an instrument, like a hammer in the hands of a stonemason, and his only reality is the work of art itself.

To exist is the artist's greatest pride. He desires no other paradise than existence, and when people speak to him of reality he only smiles bitterly, for he knows the infinitely more convincing reality of art. The spectacle of a mathematician who, without seeming to think about it, produces the square of some ten-digit number, fills us with a certain astonishment. But too often we fail to see that the poet raises a phenomenon to its tenth power, and the modest exterior of a work of art often deceives us with regard to the monstrously condensed reality contained within. In poetry this reality is the word as such. Right now, for instance, in expressing my thoughts as precisely as possible, but certainly not in a poetic manner, I am essentially speaking with my consciousness, not with the word. Deaf mutes can understand each other perfectly, and railroad signals perform a very complex function without recourse to the word. Thus, if one takes the sense as the content, everything else in the word impedes the swift transmission of the thought. "The word as such" was born very slowly. Gradually, one after another, all the elements of the word were drawn into the concept of form. To this day the conscious sense, the Logos, is still taken erroneously and arbitrarily for the content. The Logos gains nothing from such an unnecessary honor. The Logos demands nothing more than to be considered on an equal footing with the other elements of the word. The Futurists, unable to cope with the conscious sense as creative material, frivolously threw it overboard and essentially repeated the crude mistake of their predecessors.

For the Acmeists the conscious sense of the word, the Logos, is just as magnificent a form as music is for the Symbolists.

And if, for the Futurists, the word as such is still down on its knees creeping, in Acmeism it has for the first time assumed a dignified upright position and entered the Stone Age of its existence.

II

The sharp edge of Acmeism is neither the stiletto nor the sting of Decadence. Acmeism is for those who, inspired by the spirit of building, do not like cowards renounce their own gravity, but joyously accept it in order to arouse and exploit the powers architecturally sleeping within. The architect says: I build, that indicates I am right. The consciousness of our rightness is dearer to us than anything else in poetry, and, rejecting the games [1] of the Futurists, for whom there is no greater pleasure than catching a difficult word on the end of a crochet hook, we introduce the Gothic[2] element into the relationship of words, just as Sebastian Bach established it in music.

What madman would agree to build if he did not believe in the reality of his material, the resistance of which he knew he must overcome? A cobblestone in the hands of an architect is transformed into substance, but a man is not born to build if he does not hear metaphysical proof in the sound of a chisel splitting rock. Vladimir Solovyov[3] experienced a peculiar prophetic horror before gray Finnish boulders. The mute eloquence of the granite mass startled him like sorcery. But Tyutchev's stone, which "having rolled down the mountain, lay in the valley, torn loose itself, or loosened by a sentient hand," is the word. The voice of matter in this unexpected fall sounds like articulate speech. Only architecture can answer this challenge. Reverently the Acmeists raise this mysterious Tyutchevian stone and make it the foundation stone of their own building.[4]

It was as if the stone thirsted after another existence. It revealed its own dynamic potential hidden within itself, as if it were begging admittance into the "groined arch" in order to participate in the joyous cooperative action of its fellows.

III

The Symbolists were poor stay-at-homes; they loved to travel, yet they felt unwell, uncomfortable in the cage of their own organisms or in that universal cage which Kant constructed with the aid of his categories.

Genuine piety before the three dimensions of space is the first condition of successful building: to regard the world neither as a burden nor as an unfortunate accident, but as a God-given palace. Indeed, what can you say about an ungrateful guest who lives off his host, takes advantage of his hospitality, all the while despising him to the depths of his soul, thinking only of how to deceive him? Building is possible only in the name of the "three dimensions," for they are the conditions of all architecture. That is why the architect must be a good stay-at-home, and the Symbolists were poor architects. To build means to conquer emptiness, to hypnotize space. The handsome arrow of the Gothic belltower rages because its function is to stab the sky, to reproach it for its emptiness.

IV

We perceive what is particular in man, that which makes him an individual, and we incorporate it into the far more significant concept of the organism. Acmeists share their love for the organism and for organization with the physiologically brilliant Middle Ages. In chasing after refinement the nineteenth century lost the secret of genuine complexity. What in the thirteenth century appeared to be the logical development of the concept of the organism—the Gothic cathedral—now has the esthetic effect of something monstrous: Notre Dame is the triumph of physiology, its Dionysian orgy. We do not want to distract ourselves with a stroll through the "forest of symbols,"[5] because we have a denser, more virgin forest— divine physiology, the infinite complexity of our own dark organism.

The Middle Ages, defining the specific gravity of man in its own way, sensed and acknowledged it for each individual regardless of his merits. The title of *maître* was given readily and without hesitation. The humblest artisan, the lowest ranking cleric possessed the secret knowledge of his own true worth, of the devout dignity so characteristic of that epoch. Yes, Europe has passed through the labyrinth of fine open-work culture, when abstract being, completely unadorned personal existence, was valued as a heroic feat. From this stems the aristocratic intimacy uniting all people, which is so alien in spirit to the "equality and fraternity" of the French Revolution. There is no equality, there is no competition, there is only the complicity of all who conspire against emptiness and non-existence.

Love the existence of the thing more than the thing itself and your own existence more than yourself: that is Acmeism's highest commandment.

V

A=A: what a magnificent theme for poetry! Symbolism languished and yearned for the law of identity. Acmeism made it its slogan and proposed its adoption instead of the ambiguous *a realibus ad realiora*.[6]

The capacity for astonishment is the poet's greatest virtue. Yet how can we not be astonished by the law of identity, the most fruitful of all poetic laws? Whoever has experienced reverence and astonishment before this law is a true poet. Hence, having recognized the sovereignty of the law of identity, poetry receives, absolutely and unconditionally, lifelong feudal claims over all existence. Logis is the kingdom of the unexpected. To think logically is to be perpetually astonished. We have come to love the music of proof. Logical connection for us is not some popular song about a finch, but a choral symphony, so difficult and so inspired that the conductor must exert all his energy to keep the performers under his control.

How convincing the music of Bach! What power of proof! The artist must prove and prove endlessly. The artist worth of his calling cannot accept anything on faith alone, that is too easy, too dull   We cannot fly, we can ascend only those towers which we build ourselves.

VI

The Middle Ages are very close to us because they possessed to an extraordinary degree the sense of boundary and partition. They never confused different levels, and treated the beyond with utmost restraint. A noble mixture of rationality and mysticism as well as a feeling for the world as a living equilibrium makes us kin to this epoch and encourages us to derive strength from works which arose on Romance soil around the year 1200. And we will prove our rightness in such a way that in answer to us the entire chain of cause and effect, from alpha to omega, will shudder. And we will learn to bear "more easily and freely the mobile fetters of existence."

Translated by Jane Gary Harris   *1913*

Notes

Although written in 1913, this essay was not published until 1919 in the Voronezh bi-monthly, *Sirena,* edited by Vladimir Narbut, a fellow Acmeist.

1. The Russian word is *biriul'ki,* the name of a game played with rules much like our "pick-up-sticks." Instead of sticks, the players use tiny hooks to pick up tiny replicas of household objects, such as pots and pans. This image emerges again in Mandelstam's magnificent poetic cycle *The Octets* of 1933-35, which contains his last poetic effort to define his esthetic vision.

2. The Gothic element is discussed in Mandelstam's essays on Villon and Dante, as well as in "Humanism and the Present." In the latter, the esthetic element is elevated to an essential aspect of Mandelstam's ideal vision of social architecture.

3. Vladimir Solovyov (1853-1900), outstanding Russian philosopher and mystic. He also wrote poetry explicitly intended to convey his mystical and religious experiences.

4. Fyodor Tyutchev (1803-73). The reference is to Tyutchev's poem "Having rolled down the mountain" ("S gory skativshis'").

5. A reference to Baudelaire's poem "Correspondances," a major "doctrinal" source for the Symbolists.

6. *Author's note:* Vyacheslav Ivanov's formula. See his "Thoughts on Symbolism" in the volume *Furrows and Boundaries (Borozdy i mezhi).*

Translator's note: An English translation of Ivanov's essay may be found in *Russian Literature Triquarterly,* No. 4 (1972), pp. 151-58. Mandelstam's essay is, at least in part, a rejoinder to this essay of Ivanov's.

Left to right: A. Surkov, A. Fadeev, Mayakovsky, V. Stavsky.

WHAT IS LEF FIGHTING FOR?

1905. A reaction followed. The reaction subsided in autocracy and the doubling of oppression by the merchant and the factory owner.

The reaction created an art, a world—in its own image and according to its taste. The art of the Symbolists (Bely, Balmont), the mystics (Chulkov, Gippius) and the sexual psychopaths (Rozanov) is the world of the petite bourgeoisie and philistines.

The revolutinoary parties waged war against the order of things, art has risen up *to wage war on taste.*

1909—the first impressionistic spark (the collection *A Trap for Judges*).

The spark was fanned for three years.

It ignited as Futurism.

The first book of the association of the Futurists—*A Slap in the Face of Public Taste* (1914—D. Burlyuk, Kamensky, Kruchenykh, Mayakovsky, Khlebnikov).

The old order correctly assessed the laboratory work of tomorrow's dynamiters.

The Futurists were answered with censorship, beheadings, *prohibition* of public appearances, *the barking and howling* of the entire press.

The capitalist, of course, never patronized our verse-whips, our paintbrush-splinters.

Being surrounded by a diocesan milieu forced the Futurists to mock with yellow coats, painted faces.

These hardly "academic" methods of fighting, the presentiment of the further sweep, immediately drove off the esthetes who had attached themselves (Kandinsky, the Jacks of Diamonds and so on).

But to make up for it those who had nothing to lose attached themselves to Futurism, or at least cloaked themselves in its name (Shershenevich, Igor Severyanin, The Ass's Tail and others).

The Futurist movement, led by people of art who have little investigated politics, has sometimes decked itself out in the flowers of anarchy.

People trying to make themselves look younger, who are screening esthetic mould with the left flag, have also marched alongside those of the future.

The war in 1914 was the first testing of public-mindedness.

The Russian Futurists had completely broken with the poetic *imperialism* of Marinetti, having already whistled him down during his visit to Moscow (1913).

The *Futurists* are the first and only ones in Russian art who, while drowning the clanking of the singers of war (Gorodetsky, Gumilyov and others), have *cursed war,* have fought against it with all the weapons of art (Mayakovsky's "War and Peace").

The war commenced a Futurist purge (the "Mezzanines" broke off, Severyanin left for Berlin).

The war ordered us to see the future *revolution* ("Cloud in Pants").

The February revolution extended the purge, broke Futurism into the "right" and the "left."

The right wing became an echo of democratic charms (their names can be found in *The Whole of Moscow*).

The left wing, waiting for October, wase christened the "Bolsheviks of art" (Mayakovsky, Kamensky, Burlyuk, Kruchenykh).

This Futurist group was joined by the first production-Futurists (Brik, Arvatov) and Constructivists (Rodchenko, Lavinsky).

The *Futurists* from the outset, as far back as Kshesinsky's palace, attempted to come to an agreement with the groups of proletarian writers (the future Proletkult), but these writers thought (while admiring the objects) that the revolutionary theme is exhausted by agitational content alone, and they have remained complete reactionaries in a state of formation and are in no way able to weld themselves together.

October cleansed, arranged, reorganized. *Futurism* became the left front of art. "We" began.

October taught us with work.

We had already started the work on October 25th.

It is clear that at the sight of the bolting intelligentsia's heels we were not asked much about our esthetic beliefs.

We created the then revolutionary "Iso," "Theo," "Muzo"; we led the participants on an assault on the academy.

Alongside organizational work, *we gave* the first *works of art of the October era* (Tatlin—the monument to the Third International, *Mystery-Bouffe* in Meyerhold's production, Kamensky's "Stenka Razin").

We did not esthetisize by making things for our own admiration. The skills we acquired were applied to the agitational-artistic works demanded by the Revolution (Rosta posters, newspaper feuilletons, etc.).

With the aim of propagandizing our ideas we organized the newspaper *Art of the Commune* and going round to plants and factories with debates and the reading of our works.

Our ideas have won the worker audience. The Vyborgsky District has organized a Committee of Futurism.

The advancement of our art has displayed our organizational strength to the bastions of left art throughout all of the USSR.

Parallel to this has proceeded the work of our Far East comrades (the journal *Creative Work),* who have affirmed the theoretical social inevitability of our course, our social oneness with October (Chuzhak, Aseev, Palmov, Tretyakov). *Creative Work,* having endured all manner of persecution, shouldered the entire struggle for a new culture in the Far East and Siberia.

Gradually losing heart with the two-week existence of the Soviet regime, the academics, alone and in small groups, began to knock at the door of the People's Commissariats.

Not risking to use them in responsible positions, the Soviet regime granted them—rather their European reputations—cultural and enlightenment outposts.

A persecution of left art has begun from these outposts, brought to a brilliant conclusion with the shutdown of *The Art of the Commune* and so on.

The regime, occupied by the war fronts and economic collapse, did not investigate esthetic feuds, but only tried to see that there was not too much noise on the home front and make us see reason out of respect for the "venerable" ones.

Now there is a respite in war and hunger. *LEF is obligated to demonstrate* the panorama of *art in the USSR,* to establish perspective and to assume our rightful place.

Art in the USSR—February 1, 1923.

I. Proletarian art. One sector has degenerated into official writers who are oppressive in their bureaucratic language and the repetition of political ABCs. Another has fallen completely under the influence of academicism, reminiscent of October only in the names of the organizations. The third is the best sector—leaving behind the rosy Belys, it is re-educating itself on our models and, we believe, will march with us in the future.

II. Official literature. Everyone has his personal opinion in the theory of art: Osinsky praises Akhmatova, Bukharin—Pinkerton. In practice the journals simply abound with all sorts of best-selling names.

III. "New" literature. (The Serapions, Pilnyak, etc.)—having assimilated and diluted our methods, they spice them up with Symbolism and respectfully and distressingly tailor them to light NEP reading.

IV. Changing Landmarks. An invasion of enlightened venerable people is approaching from the West. Alexei Tolstoi is already grooming the white horse of his complete collected works for a triumphant entry into Moscow.

V. And, finally, those who violate the successful perspective in various quarters—the *maverick leftists*. People and organizations (INUKH, VKHUTEMAS, Meyerhold's GITIS, OPOYAZ and others). Some heroically try to till virgin lands alone, others with nothing but files made of verse are severing the fetters of the old.

LEF must bring together left forces. LEF must inspect its ranks, after having thrown over the clinging past. LEF must unite a *front* for the destruction of the old, for the battle to dominate the new culture.

We will solve the questions of art not by the voice of majority of the left front, to this day only existing as an ideal, but by action, by the energy of our organizing body, year by year guiding the work of the left and always guiding it ideologically.

The Revolution has taught us much.

LEF knows:

LEF will be:

In our work of consolidating the achievements of the October Revolution, of fortifying left art, *LEF will propagandize for an art with the ideals of the commune,* thereby discovering for art the road to tomorrow.

LEF will propagandize the masses with its art, acquiring from them our organizational power.

LEF will confirm our theories with an effective art, having advanced it to its highest working qualification.

LEF will fight for the artistic structure of life.

We do not pretend to have a monopoly on revolutionism in art. We will prove ourselves through competition.

We believe that the correctness of our propaganda, the strength of our works *will prove: we are on the true path to the future.*

> N. Aseev
> B. Arvatov
> O. Brik
> B. Kushner
> V. Mayakovsky
> S. Tretyakov
> N. Chuzhak

LEF. The Journal of Left Art. No. 1, March 1923.

ALL-UNION ASSOCIATION OF PROLETARIAN WRITERS (VAPP)

Platform. January 1925.

(1) The era of socialist revolutions, which is a transitional period from a class to a classless, Communist society, began with the October Revolution that established the dictatorship of the proletariat with its system of soviets, thereby giving the proletariat the opportunity to become the organizer and rebuilder of society in all respects.

(2) Having adopted in the process of the class struggle the revolutionary-Marxist worldview in economics and politics, the proletariat in other areas has still not completely freed itself from the centuries-old, ideological influence of the ruling classes. Now, with the end of civil war and the process of intensifying the struggle on the economic front, the literary front has been brought forward, one that is particularly important in the context of NEP and the continuing ideological offensive against the bourgeoisie, in which connection the first priority for the proletariat is the building of its own class literature and, therefore, its own artistic literature, as a powerful means to profoundly influence the perception of the masses.

(3) Proletarian literature, as a movement, achieved the essential conditions for its appearance and development only as a result of the October Revolution. However, the cultural backwardness of the Russian proletariat, the centuries-old oppression of bourgeois ideology, the decadent phase of Russian literature of recent years and the decades before the Revolution—all of this taken together has influenced and continues to influence and makes possible the further influence of bourgeois literature on proletarian creativity. Moreover, it was impossible that no trace would be left of the influence of idealistic, petit-bourgeois revolutionism, brought about by the parallel task before the Russian proletariat—the conclusion of the bourgeois-democratic revolution.

Because of these conditions proletarian literature has inevitably presented and presents an eclectic nature, in both the spheres of ideology and, consequently, in form.

(4) However, with the beginning of the systematic, socialist construction in all spheres with the methods of NEP and the transition of the Russian Communist Party from agitation to a systematic and profound propaganda in the broad cross-section of the masses, the necessity has arisen to introduce a definite system into proletarian literature.

(5) Based on what has been put forward above, VAPP, as a part of the proletarian vanguard, imbued with its dialectical-materialistic worldview, is striving to create such a system and considers the achievement of this to be possible only with the creation of a single, artistic program, ideological and formal, which must serve as the basis for the further development of proletarian literature.

While understanding that such a program will take its final shape in the process of practical creative work and the struggle on the ideological front, VAPP proposes the following points of departure as the basis of its activity:

(6) In a class society artistic literature, as with everything else, serves the mission of a certain class, and only through that class does it serve all mankind. Hence, the only proletarian literature is that which inclines the psychology and consciousness of the working class and the broad cross-section of the laboring masses in the direction of the ultimate goals of the proletariat, as the rebuilder of the world and the creator of a Communist society.

(7) In the process of broadening and strengthening the dictatorship of the proletariat and approaching a Communist society, proletarian literature, while remaining fundamentally class-conscious, not only is determining the psychology and consciousness of the working class, but is also exerting an influence on the other strata of society, in this way removing the last piece of ground out from under the feet of bourgeois literature.

(8) Proletarian literature is the antipode of bourgeois literature. Bourgeois literature,

doomed together with its class, strives to conceal its essence by its isolation from life, its withdrawal into mysticism, to the realm of "pure art," to form as a goal in itself and so forth.

Proletarian literature, on the contrary, places as the basis of its creative work a revolutionary-Marxist worldview and takes its creative material from contemporary reality, of which the creator is the proletariat, as well as the revolutionary romanticism of the life and struggle of the proletariat in the past and its conquest in the future perspective. Naturally, to be a proletarian writer the artist must take an active part in public life, in the common struggle and construction of the proletarian vanguard.

(9) In connection with the rise in the social significance of proletarian literature, the main objective is the creation of broad canvasses, monumental works with a developed plot, taken primarily from the life of the proletariat. VAPP considers the fulfillment of these requirements possible only when a dramatic and epic approach to the creative material is placed alongside the lyric, which has dominated the last five years in proletarian literature. In accordance with this the work's form will also strive for the greatest possible breadth, simplicity and economy of artistic means.

(10) VAPP asserts the primacy of content. The content itself of a proletarian work provides the literary-artistic material and suggests the form. Content and form are dialectical antitheses: content determines form and artistically is shaped by it.

(11) The variety of forms of the class struggle and the transitional period demands that proletarian writers elaborate the most varied themes, thus making essential a thorough utilization of the artistic forms and devices in prose and poetry that were created by the preceding history of literature.

Therefore, VAPP will not take the course of embracing some single artistic form and setting boundaries according to a formal sign, by which to this time literary schools have been grouped, and which in essence is a transference of idealism and metaphysics to the literary creative process.

(12) Taking into consideration that the literary schools of decadence reduced to their component elements artistic forms that are in their essence united, that were created in the era of the historical rise of the ruling classes, and that they continue this reduction to the smallest particles, singling out some one of these elements as a self-sufficing principle, and also taking into account the fact of the influence of these schools on proletarian creative work and the danger of their further influence—VAPP in principle rejects:

(a) the degeneration of the understanding of the creative image to a self-sufficing, fragmented, pictorial ornament (Imaginism) and stands for a single, united dynamic image that develops throughout the entire work and is dependent on its socially-imperative content;

(b) rejects the isolation of the rhythm of the word as such, as a goal in itself, as a result of which the artist often withdraws into the realm of purely literary exercises that have no social significance, and passes them off for a true artistic work (Futurism), and stands for a united rhythm, systematically developed in relation to the development of the content of the artistic work in its unified, creative image;

(c) and also rejects the fetishism with sound that came into being during the period of the decline of the bourgeoisie and took root on the soil of an unhealthy mysticism (Symbolism), and stands for the organic confluence of the sound structure of an artistic work with the creative image and rhythm.

Only by taking the subject of an artistic work as a whole, in its full, concrete significance and in the process of a natural development can one achieve the historically supreme artistic synthesis.

(13) Thus, the task before VAPP is not the cultivation of forms that existed in bourgeois literature and have been eclectically introduced into proletarian literature, but the cultivation and revelation of new principles and types of form obtained by means of a practical mastery of the old literary forms and the transformation of them by means of a proletarian class content, and also by way of a critical interpretation of the rich experience of the past and works of proletarian literature, as a result of which must be created a new synthetic form of proletarian art.

Translated by Arthur Jacobsen   *1925*

ON PARTY POLICY IN THE FIELD OF BELLES-LETTRES

(Resolution of the Central Committee of the Communist Party)

(1) Improvement in the material well-being of the masses in recent times, together with the radical change of minds brought about by the Revolution, the intensified activity of the masses, and the gigantic expansion of the mental outlook, and so forth, is creating enormous growth in cultural interests and needs. We have, thus, entered the sphere of cultural revolution, which represents the precondition for continued movement toward a Communist society.

(2) A part of this cultural growth of the masses is the emergence of a new literature, for the first time a proletarian and peasant one, beginning with its rudimentary, but at the same time, unusually wide range of forms (worker correspondents, village correspondents, wall newspapers) and ending with an ideologically-realized literary production.

(3) On the other hand, the complicated nature of the economic process, the simultaneous growth of contradictory and even mutually inimical economic forms called forth by this development, the emergence and consolidation of a new bourgeoisie, the inevitable, though initially not always realized, attraction to it by a part of the old and new intelligentsia, the chemical isolation from the new social depths of new ideological agents of this bourgeoisie— all this must inevitably figure in the *literary* texture of the social life.

(4) Thus, just as our class struggle in general is not coming to an end, so it is also not coming to an end on the literary front. In a class society there is not and there cannot be a neutral art, although the class nature of art in general and literature in particular manifests itself in forms infinitely more diverse than, for example, in politics.

(5) However, it would be completely mistaken not to take into account a fundamental fact of our social life, namely the fact of the seizure of power, the presence of a proletarian dictatorship in our country.

If prior to the seizure of power the proletarian party kindled the class struggle and pursued a policy of exploding the whole social fabric, then in the period of the proletarian dictatorship the proletarian party is faced with the problem of how to accommodate and slowly remake the peasantry; of how both to tolerate a certain amount of cooperation with the bourgeoisie and slowly supplant it; of how to put in the service of the Revolution the technical and all other kinds of intelligentsia and ideologically seize it from the bourgeoisie.

Thus, although the class struggle is not coming to an end, it is changing its form; for prior to the seizure of power the proletariat was striving to destroy the given society, whereas in the period of its own dictatorship it is placing in the forefront "peaceful, organizational work."

(6) While preserving, strengthening, and ever further broadening its leadership, the proletariat must take up a corresponding position in a whole series of new areas on the ideological front. The process of the penetration of dialectical materialsim into completely new fields (biology, psychology, the natural sciences in general) has already begun. *In exactly the same way the conquest of positions in the field of belles-lettres must sooner or later become a fact.*

(7) It should be borne in mind, however, that this task is infinitely more complicated than other tasks the proletariat is trying to resolve; for already within the framework of capitalist society the working class had been able to prepare itself for a victorious revolution, set up cadres of fighters and leaders, and work out superb ideological weapons for the political struggle. But it could not solve problems in either the natural sciences or in technology; and in a similar manner the culturally-suppressed class has been unable to devise its own artistic literature, its own special artistic form, its own style. If the proletariat already possesses infallible criteria for judging the socio-political content of any given literary work, it still lacks

the same definite answers to all questions regarding artistic form.

(8) The policy of the leading party of the proletariat in the field of belles-lettres must be determined from the above. Primarily, the following questions are germane to the problem: the relationship between proletarian writers, peasant writers, and the so-called "fellow travellers," and others; the policy of the Party with respect to proletarian writers; the question of criticism; the questions of style and forms of works of art and the methods of devising new artistic forms; finally, questions of an organizational nature.

(9) The relationship between different groupings of writers according to their social class or social group is defined by our general policy. However, it must be borne in mind here that leadership in the field of literature belongs in general to the working class as a whole, with all its material and ideological resources. A hegemony of proletarian writers does still not exist, but the Party must help these writers *earn* the historical right to this hegemony.

Peasant writers should receive a friendly reception and enjoy our unconditional support. The task consists of transferring their growing numbers onto the rails of proletarian ideology, *while in no way, however, extirpating from their work the peasant literary forms, which are also the necessary precondition for influence on the peasantry.*

(10) With respect to the "fellow travellers" it is necessary to bear in mind: (1) their differentiation, (2) the significance of many of them as qualified "specialists" in literary technique, (3) the presence of a certain degree of vacillation in this group of writers. The general directive here should be one of a tactful and cautious attitude toward them, i.e., an approach that would ensure all the conditions for a swift transition on their part to the side of Communist ideology. While weeding out anti-proletarian and anti-revolutionary elements (which are now quite insignificant), and while combatting the germinating ideology of the new bourgeoisie in those "fellow travellers" who adhere to the views of the Changing Landmarks movement, the Party should treat these temporary ideological forms tolerantly, patiently assisting these inevitable, numerous forms to be eliminated in the process of more comradely cooperation with the cultural forces of Communism.

(11) With respect to proletarian writers the Party should take the following position: While doing all it can to encourage their growth, supporting them and their organizations in every way, the Party must forestall by all possible means the emergence of Communist snobbery among them, for it is the most ruinous of phenomena. The Party, precisely because it sees in the proletarian writers the future ideological leaders of Soviet literature, must fight with all its means against a frivolous and contemptful attitude toward the old cultural heritage, and thus toward the specialists of the artistic word. Equally deserving of censure is the position that undervalues the very importance of the proletarian writers' struggle for ideological hegemony. Against capitulation, on the one hand, but against Communist snobbery, on the other hand—this must be the Party's slogan. The Party must also fight attempts of a purely hothouse "proletarian" literature; the framework of proletarian literature should provide for: a broad scope of phenomena in all their complexity; it should not be confined within the bounds of one factory; it should be a literature not of the guild, but of the struggling great class that is leading millions of peasants.

(12) The above-mentioned by and large determine the tasks of *criticism,* one of the chief educative weapons in the hands of the Party. Never for a moment abandoning Communist positions, not retreating one iota from proletarian ideology, but revealing the objective class thought of different literary works, Communist criticism must struggle relentlessly against counter-revolutionary manifestations in literature, expose the liberalism of the Changing Landmarks group, and so forth, but at the same time, display the greatest tact, caution and tolerance in its relations with all those literary stratifications that can march with the proletariat and will march with it. Communist criticism must banish from practice the tone of literary command.

Criticism will have a deep educative meaning, only when it is able to rely upon its ideological superiority. Marxist criticism must root out from its midst all pretentious, semi-literate and complacent snobbery. Marxist criticism must take up the slogan—"Learn"; and it must reject all literary pulp and self-important formulations from its midst.

(13) Unerringly discerning the class content of literary currents, the Party on the whole cannot in any way commit itself to endorsing any given trend in the sphere of literary form. While guiding literature as a whole, the Party can no more support any *one* literary faction (classifying these factions according to different views on form and style) than it can decide through resolutions problems about the form of the family, even though in general the Party guides and must guide the building of a new way of life. Everything compels one to expect that a style that corresponds to the epoch will be created, but it will be created through other methods, and a solution to this problem has as yet not begun to emerge. Any attempts to bind the Party in this direction during the present phase of the country's cultural development must be rejected.

(14) Therefore, the Party must declare itself in favor of free competition among the different groups and currents in this area. Any other solution of the question would be a bureaucratic pseudo-solution. Equally inadmissable would be a *legalized monopoly* of the business of literary publishing by any group or organization through Party decree or Party resolution. While supporting materially and morally a proletarian and proletarian-peasant literature, while helping the "fellow travellers," and so forth, the Party cannot grant a monopoly to any one of these groups, not even to the most proletarian of the groups as far as its ideological content is concerned: that would spell the ruin of proletarian literature.

(15) The Party must in every way possible root out attempts at makeshift and incompetent administrative interference in literary matters; the Party must take pains to carefully select the personnel of those institutions that manage the press so as to ensure a truly correct, useful and tactical guidance of our literature.

(16) The Party must point out to all workers in the field of belles-lettres the necessity for the correct delimitation of functions between critics and writers of literature. For the latter it is necessary to shift the center of gravity of their work to literary production in the true sense of the word, and in doing so they should make use of the vast material of the present. It is essential to pay increased attention as well to the development of a national literature in the numerous republics and provinces of our Union.

(17) The Party must stress the necessity of creating an artistic literature designed for the truly mass reader, for the worker and peasant; it is necessary to break more boldly and decisively with the prejudices of the gentry in literature, and, utilizing all the technical achievements of the old mastery, devise a corresponding form that is understandable to millions.

Soviet literature and its future proletarian vanguard will be able to fulfill their cultural-historical mission only when they find a solution to this great task.

Translated by Janis Eichelis   *June 18, 1925*

BULGAKOV AND ZAMYATIN: LETTERS TO THE GOVERNMENT

BULGAKOV'S LETTER TO GORKY

From 1927 on, Bulgakov was viciously attacked in the press, along with many other writers. By 1929 he had become a non-person, deprived of his livelihood: his plays were banned, and there was no possibility of getting other work since he was effectively black-listed. In March of 1930, he wrote his famous letter to Stalin, which, however, has not survived. What is known are fragments of various drafts strung together. His wife, L. E. Belozerskaya, as well as some of his friends, has repeatedly stated that the real letter to Stalin was short and to the point. But a letter which has survived is one in which Bulgakov asks Gorky's help in letting him go abroad. In form and content, this letter is apparently very close to the one sent later to Stalin.

September 28, 1929

Much Esteemed Alexei Maximovich!

Evgeny Ivanovich Zamyatin has told me that you received my letter, but that you wish to have a copy of it. I have no copy, but the contents were basically this:

"I have submitted a Petition through Svidersky[1] to the Government of the USSR in which I ask them to give attention to my unbearable situation, and to allow me and my wife, Lyubov Evgenievna Bulgakova to go abroad for however long the Government wishes to prescribe. I had wanted to write in detail about what is happening to me, but my bottomless exhaustion does not permit me to work. I can only say one thing: why keep a writer in the USSR when his works cannot exist in the USSR? In order to condemn him to extinction?

I earnestly ask for a humane resolution—let me go. I ask you to intercede for me. I ask you to be so kind as to let me know if you receive this letter."

I would like to add the following to the letter: all my plays are banned, not one line by me is printed anywhere, I have no work ready, I receive not one kopeck of royalties from anything. Not one institution, not one person has answered my petitions. In a word—everything I've written during ten years of work in the USSR is destroyed. All that remains is to destroy the last thing left—me myself.

I ask that a humane decision be taken—let me go!

Yours respectfully,

M. Bulgakov[2]

1. A. I. Svidersky was briefly head of Glaviskusstvo, a censorship board for the arts under Narkompros.

2. This letter is taken from the text printed by Lesley Milne in *Novyi zhurnal*, No. 111, 1973.

Evgeny Zamyatin's Letter to Stalin

Dear Iosif Vissarionovich,

Condemned to the maximum penalty, the author of this letter appeals to you with a request for a commutation of this sentence.

My name, most likely, is known to you. For me, a writer, to be deprived of the opportunity to write is precisely a death sentence, but circumstances have arisen that make it impossible for me to continue my work, because no creative work is conceivable, if one must work in an atmosphere of a systematic persecution that becomes more intense with each year.

I in no way want to depict myself as an injured innocent. I know that in the first 3-4 years after the Revolution there were things among the works written by me that might have given occasion for attacks. I know that I have the very unfortunate habit of not saying what is advantageous at a given moment, but what seems to me to be the truth. In particular, I have never masked my attitude towards literary servility, obsequiousness and opportunism: I have considered—and continue to consider—that this equally degrades both the writer and the Revolution. Precisely this question, once put forth by me—in a form that was harsh and offensive to many—in one of my articles (in the journal *House of Art,* No. 1, 1920) was a signal for the beginning of a newspaper and journal campaign against me.

This campaign, on various grounds, continues to this day and has finally resulted in something that I would call fetishism: just as the Christians once created the devil as a more convenient personification of all evil, so the critics have made me the devil of Soviet literature. To spit on the devil is considered a good work, and everyone has spat as best he can. Some diabolical design turns up in each of my published works. The critics in this search have even conferred upon me prophetic gifts: thus, in one of my stories ("God"), published in the journal *Chronicle*—in 1916—a certain critic has contrived to find. . . "a mockery of the Revolution in regard to the transition to NEP"; in a story ("The Monk Erasmus"), written in 1920, another critic (Mashbits-Verov) has seen "a parable of leaders who have grown wiser after NEP." My signature alone has become sufficient to declare the work criminal—regardless of the content of this or that work of mine. Recently, in March of this year, the Leningrad *Oblit* [Regional Literary Organization] undertook measures so that no doubt would be left: I had edited Sheridan's comedy *The School for Scandal* for the Academia publishing house and had written an essay about his life and work: it goes without saying that there was nothing, nor could there be anything, scandalous in this essay—and nevertheless *Oblit* not only forbade the essay, but also forbade the publisher to even mention my name as the editor of the translation. And only after my appeals to Moscow, after *Glavlit* [Main Literary Censor], apparently suggested that, after all, one cannot act with such naive obviousness, was permission granted to publish the article, and even my criminal name.

I cite this fact here because it shows the attitude towards me in a completely bared, so to speak, chemically pure form. From my extensive collection I will cite here one more fact, connected not with an incidental essay, but with a large-scale play on which I had been working for almost three years. I was certain that this play of mine—the tragedy *Atilla*— would finally force those who like to make me out to be some sort of obscurantist to be silent. I had, it seemed, every reason for such certainty. The play had been read at a meeting of the Artistic Council of the Leningrad Bolshoi Theater; representatives of 18 Leningrad factories were present at the meeting—here are excerpts from their comments (quotations are from the minutes of the meeting on May 15, 1928).

The representative of the Volodarsky Factory: "This is a play by a contemporary author, who is treating the theme of class struggle in ancient times, which resembled that of our contemporary era... The play, ideologically, is entirely acceptable... The play makes a strong impression and does away with the reproach aimed at contemporary dramatists that they do not write any good plays..." The representative of the Lenin Factory, noting the play's revolutionary character, finds that the "play by virtue of its artistic importance, recalls Shakespeare's works... The play is tragic, extraordinarily full of action and will fascinate the viewer." The representative of the Hydro-Mechanical Factory considers that "all elements in the play are strong and exciting" and recommends that the production be made to coincide with the theater's anniversary.

Even if the comrade workers praised it excessively as far as Shakespeare is concerned, in any event M. Gorky wrote about the same play that he considers it "highly valuable in both its literary and social aspects" and that the "play's heroic tone and its heroic subject could not be more useful for our time." The play was accepted by the theater for production, it was approved by the Main Repertory Committee, and then.... Was it shown to the worker audience who had given it such a high appraisal? No: afterwards the play, already half through rehearsals, already announced on the posters, was banned at the insistence of *Oblit.*

The death of my tragedy, *Atilla,* was truly a tragedy for me: after that the futility of all attempts to change my situation became entirely clear to me, particularly since shortly afterwards followed the well-known incident with my novel *We* and Pilnyak's *Mahogany.* It goes without saying that any crooked dealing is allowable for the exorcism of the devil—and my novel, written nine years earlier, in 1920—was presented alongside *Mahogany* as my latest, new work. The persecution that was organized, then without precedent in Soviet literature, was even noted in the foreign press: everything possible was done to close for me any possibility of further work. My former friends, publishing houses and theaters began to fear me. My play (*The Flea*), which had already run for four seasons in the Moscow Art Theater's Second Studio with invariable success, was withdrawn from the repertory. The publication of my collected works by the Federation publishing house was brought to a halt. Every publishing house that attempted to publish my works was subjected to immediate fire, which was the case with Federation, Land and Factory, and particularly the Publishing House of Leningrad Writers. The latter publishing house risked having me on its board of directors for another year, it made so bold as to utilize my literary experience by entrusting to me the stylistic correction of young writers' works—including the works of Communists. This spring the Leningrad branch of RAPP secured my removal from the board and the discontinuance of this work. *The Literary Gazette* triumphantly gave notice of this with the completely unambiguous addition: "the publishing house must be preserved, but not for those like Zamyatin." The final door to the reader was closed for Zamyatin: the writer's death sentence had been published.

In the Soviet codex of law the step below the death sentence is deportation of the criminal from the country. If I am really a criminal and deserve punishment, I nevertheless do not think that I deserve such a severe one as literary death, and, therefore, I ask that this sentence be commuted to deportation from the USSR—with the right for my wife to accompany me. If I am not a criminal, I ask that my wife and I be allowed, temporarily, for at least one year, to go abroad—with the right that we may return as soon as it becomes possible for us to serve great ideas in literature without waiting on little men, as soon as there is at least a partial change in the view of the role of the artist of the word. And this time, I am certain, is already near, because following the successful creation of a material base, the question will inevitably arise of creating a superstructure—of an art and literature that would truly be worthy of the Revolution.

I know: it will not be easy for me abroad either, because I cannot belong to the reactionary camp—my past says enough about this (membership in the Russian Social Democratic Party in the tsarist era, prison, two exiles, trial in time of war for an antimilitaristic novella). I know that due to my habit of writing according to my conscience, and not on command, I have been proclaimed to belong to the right here, and that for the same reason sooner or later there they will probably proclaim me to be a Bolshevik. But even under the most difficult conditions there I will not be sentenced to silence, there I will be in a position to write and be published—even if it is not in Russian. If circumstances make it impossible (I hope, temporarily) for me to be a Russian writer—perhaps, I will succeed, like the Pole Joseph Conrad, in becoming, for a time, an English writer, especially as I have already written in Russian about England (the satirical novella *Islanders* and others), and for me writing in English is only slightly more difficult than in Russian. Ilya Ehrenburg, while remaining a Soviet writer, has for a long time now worked principally for European literature—for translation into foreign languages: why, then, can I not be permitted what Ehrenburg has been permitted? At the same time I recall yet another name: Boris Pilnyak. He has fully shared with me the role of the devil, he was the critics' chief target, and for respite from persecution he was permitted to go abroad; why can I not be permitted what Pilnyak has been permitted?

I could have based my request to go abroad on other reasons more ordinary, but no less serious: I need to be treated abroad in order to rid myself of a long-standing, chronic illness (colitis); again, I myself need to be abroad to see through to production two of my plays, translated into English and Italian (the plays *The Flea* and *The Society of Honorary Bell Ringers),* already mounted in Soviet theaters; the proposed production of these plays, in addition, makes it possible for me not to burden the People's Commissariat of Finances with a request to be given hard currency. All these motives are in effect: but I do not want to conceal that the principal reason for my request for permission for me and my wife to go abroad is my desperate position as a writer here—the death sentence has been delivered to me as a writer here.

The exceptional consideration you have shown to other writers who have appealed to you allows me to hope that my request will also be granted.

Translated by Ronald Meyer   *June 1931*

BIBLIOGRAPHY

This bibliography is not intended to be comprehensive for either the period or the writers included, but is rather a compilation of suggested further readings. In the case of the bibliographies for individual authors, translations are listed first, followed by critical studies and biographies.

HISTORIES AND CRITICISM

Avins, Carol. *Border Crossings. The West and Russian Identity in Soviet Literature 1917-1934.* Berkeley: Univeristy of California Press, 1983.

Barooshian, Vahan D. *Russian Cubo-Futurism 1910-1930.* The Hague: Mouton, 1974.

Bowlt, John E., ed. *Russian Art of the Avant-Garde. Theory and Criticism, 1902-1934.* NY: Viking, 1976.

Brown, Edward J., ed. *Major Soviet Writers: Essays in Criticism.* NY: Oxford University Press, 1973.

———. *The Proletarian Episode in Russian Literature, 1928-1932.* NY: Columbia University Press, 1971.

———. *Russian Literature Since the Revolution.* Revised and enlarged edition. Cambridge: Harvard University Press, 1982.

Edwards, T. R. N. *Three Russian Writers and the Irrational: Zamyatin, Pil'nyak and Bulgakov.* Cambridge: Cambridge University Press, 1982.

Erlich, Victor. *Russian Formalism. History—Doctrine.* New Haven: Yale University Press, 1981.

———. *Twentieth-Century Russian Literary Criticism.* New Haven: Yale University Press, 1975.

Ermolaev, Herman. *Soviet Literary Theories 1917-1934. The Genesis of Socialist Realism.* NY: Octagon, 1977.

Folejewski, Zbigniew. *Futurism and Its Place in the Development of Modern Poetry. A Comparative Study and Anthology.* University of Ottawa Press, 1980.

Hingley, Ronald. *Nightingale Fever: Russian Poets in Revolution.* NY: Knopf, 1981.

Kaun, Alexander. *Soviet Poets and Poetry.* Berkeley: University of California Press, 1943.

Kern, Gary and Christopher Collins, eds. *The Serapion Brothers: A Critical Anthology of Stories and Essays.* Ann Arbor: Ardis, 1975.

Maguire, Robert A. *Red Virgin Soil. Soviet Literature in the 1920s.* Princeton: Princeton University Press, 1968; 2d ed. Ithaca: Cornell University Press, 1987.

Markov, Vladimir. *Russian Futurism. A History.* Berkeley: University of California Press, 1968.

Mirsky, D. S. *Contemporary Russian Literature, 1881-1925.* NY: Alfred A. Knopf, 1926.

Oulanoff, Hongor. *The Serapion Brothers.* The Hague: Mouton, 1966.

Patrick, George Z. *Popular Poetry in Soviet Russia.* Berkeley: University of California Press, 1929.

Poggioli, Renato. *The Poets of Russia, 1890-1930.* Cambridge: Harvard University Press, 1960.

Slonim, Marc. *Soviet Russian Literature: Writers and Problems, 1917-1977*. NY: Oxford University Press, 1977.
Struve, Gleb. *Russian Literature under Lenin and Stalin. 1917-1953*. Norman: University of Oklahoma Press, 1971.
Williams, Robert C. *Artists in Revolution: Portraits of the Russian Avant-Garde, 1905-1925*. Bloomington: Indiana University Press, 1977.
Zavalishin, Viacheslav. *Early Soviet Writers*. NY: Praeger, 1958.
Zhirmunsky, Viktor. "Symbolism's Successors," in *The Noise of Change,* ed. & trans. Stanley Rabinowitz. Ann Arbor: Ardis, 1985.

ANTHOLOGIES

Bannikov, Nikolai, comp. *Three Centuries of Russian Poetry*. Bilingual edition. Moscow: Progress, 1980.
Friedberg, Maurice and Robert A. Maguire. *A Bilingual Collection of Russian Short Stories*. Volume 2. NY: Random House, 1965.
Glad, John and Daniel Weissbort, eds. *Russian Poetry: The Modern Period*. Iowa City: University of Iowa Press, 1978.
Glenny, Michael, ed. *"Novy Mir." A Selection 1925-1967*. London: Jonathan Cape Ltd, 1972.
Guerney, Bernard Guilbert, ed. & trans. *An Anthology of Russian Literature in the Soviet Period from Gorki to Pasternak*. NY: Random House, 1960.
———— and Merrill Sparks. *Modern Russian Poetry: An Anthology with Verse Translations*. Indianapolis: Bobbs-Merrill, 1967.
Pomorska, Krystyna, ed. *Fifty Years of Russian Prose*. 2 vols. Cambridge: MIT Press, 1971.
Proffer, Carl R. and Ellendea. *The Ardis Anthology of Russian Futurism*. Ann Arbor: Ardis, 1980.
Russian Literature Triquarterly. Translations, criticism, documents. See in particular: No. 1 (1971)—Acmeism; No. 2 (1972)—Prose of the Twenties; No. 4 (1972)—Symbolism; No. 8 (1974)—Unread Classics; No. 12-13 (1975)—Futurism and Constructivism; No. 14 (1976)—Satire and Parody; No. 15 (1976)—Bulgakov.

ANNA AKHMATOVA

Poems. Selected & trans. Lynn Coffin. Intro. Joseph Brodsky. NY: W. W. Norton, 1983.
Poems of Akhmatova. Selected, trans. & intro. Stanley Kunitz with Max Hayward. Boston: Little Brown, 1973.
Selected Poems. Ed. & trans. Walter Arndt. Ann Arbor: Ardis, 1976.

Driver, Sam N. *Anna Akhmatova*. NY: Twayne Pubishers, 1972.
————. "Akhmatova: A Selected Bibliography." *Russian Literature Triquarterly*, No. 1, pp. 432-55.
Haight, Amanda. *Anna Akhmatova: A Poetic Pilgrimage*. NY: Oxford University Press, 1976.
Leiter, Sharon. *Akhmatova's Petersburg*. Philadelphia: University of Pennsylvania Press, 1983.
Verheul, Kees. *The Theme of Time in the Poetry of Anna Akhmatova*. The Hague: Mouton, 1971.

ISAAC BABEL

The Collected Stories. Ed. & trans. W. Morrison. Intro. Lionel Trilling. NY: Criterion Books, 1955.

Forgotten Prose. Trans. & ed. Nicholas Stroud. Ann Arbor: Ardis, 1978.
The Lonely Years, 1925-1939. Trans. Andrew R. MacAndrew & Max Hayward. NY: Farrar
    Straus, 1964.
You Must Know Everything. Stories 1915-1937. Ed. Nathalie Babel. Trans. Max Hayward.
    NY: Farrar, Straus, Giroux, 1969.

Carden, Patricia. *The Art of Isaac Babel.* Ithaca: Cornell University Press, 1972.
Falen, James E. *Isaac Babel. Russian Master of the Short Story.* Knoxville: University of
    Tennessee Press, 1974.
Grongard, R. *An Investigation of Composition and Themes in Isaak Babel's Literary Cycle
    "Konarmija."* Tr. D. R. Fickelton. Aarhus: Arkona, 1979.
Luplow, Carol. *Isaac Babel's "Red Cavalry."* Ann Arbor: Ardis, 1982.
Mendelson, Danuta. *Metaphor in Babel's Short Stories.* Ann Arbor: Ardis, 1982.

Terras, Victor. "Line and Color: The Structure of I. Babel's Short Stories in *Red Cavalry.*"
    Studies in Short Fiction 2 (1966), pp. 141-56.

ALEXANDER BLOK

Selected Poems. Trans. Alex Miller. Moscow: Progress, 1981.
Selected Poems of Aleksandr Blok. Ed. James B. Woodward. Oxford: Clarendon Press,
    1968.

Chukovsky, Kornei. *Alexander Blok as Man and Poet.* Trans. Diana Burgin and Katherine
    O'Connor. Ann Arbor: Ardis, 1982.
Mochulsky, Konstantin. *Aleksandr Blok.* Trans. Doris V. Johnson. Detroit: Wayne State
    University Press, 1983.
Orlov, Vladimir. *Hamayun. The Life of Aleksander Blok.* Trans. Olga Shartse. Abridged
    edition. Moscow: Progress, 1980.
Pyman, Avril. *The Life of Alexander Blok.* 2 vols. NY: Oxford University Press, 1979-80.
Reeve, Franklin D. *Aleksandr Blok: Between Image and Idea.* NY: Columbia University
    Press, 1962.
Sendich, Munir. "Blok's *The Twelve:* A Bibliography of Criticism (1918-70)." *Russian
    Literature Triquarterly,* No. 4, pp. 462-72.
————. "Blok's *The Twelve:* A Critical Interpretation of the Christ-Figure." *Russian
    Literature Triquarterly,* No. 4, 445-61.
Vickery, Walter N., ed. *Aleksandr Blok Centennial Conference.* Columbus, OH: Slavica
    Publishers, 1982.
Vogel, Lucy. *Aleksandr Blok: The Journey to Italy.* Ithaca: Cornell University Press, 1973.
————., ed. *Blok: An Anthology of Essays and Memoirs.* Ann Arbor: Ardis, 1982.

MIKHAIL BULGAKOV

A Country Doctor's Notebook. Trans. Michael Glenny. NY: Bantam, 1975.
Diaboliad and Other Stories. Trans. Carl R. Proffer. Bloomington: Indiana University Press,
    1972.
The Early Plays of Mikhail Bulgakov. Trans. Carl R. & Ellendea Proffer. Bloomington:
    Indiana University Press, 1972.
Flight and *Bliss. Two Plays.* Trans. Mirra Ginsburg. NY: New Directions, 1985.
The Heart of a Dog. Trans. & intro. Michael Glenny. NY: Harcourt Brace & Wolff, 1968.
The Master and Margarita. Trans. Mirra Ginsburg. NY: Grove Press, 1967.
Notes on the Cuff. Trans. Alison M. Rice. Ann Arbor: Ardis, forthcoming.
White Guard. Trans. by Michael Glenny with an epilogue by Victor Nekrasov. NY: McGraw-
    Hill, 1971.

Natov, Nadine, comp. "A Bibliography of Works by and about Mikhail A. Bulgakov."
     Canadian American Slavic Studies, 15 (1981), pp. 456-65.
_____. *Mikhail Bulgakov.* Boston: Twayne Publishers, 1985.
Proffer, Ellendea. *Bulgakov. Life and Work.* Ann Arbor: Ardis, 1984.
_____. *An International Bibliography of Works by and about Mikhail Bulgakov.* Ann
     Arbor: Ardis, 1976.
Russian Literature Triquarterly, No. 15 (1976). Special Bulgakov issue: translations, criti-
     cism, documents.
Wright, A. Colin. *Mikhail Bulgakov: Life and Interpretation.* Toronto: University of
     Toronto Press, 1978.

SERGEI ESENIN

Confessions of a Hooligan. Trans. & intro. Geoffrey Thurley. Cheadle, England: Carcanet,
     1973.
Selected Poems. Trans. J. Davies. Derbyshire, England: Hub Publications, 1979.
Selected Poetry. Trans. Peter Tempest. Moscow: Progress, 1982.

Davies, Jessie. *Esenin: A Biography in Memoirs, Letters and Documents.* Ann Arbor: Ardis,
     1982.
McVay, Gordon. *Esenin: A Life.* Ann Arbor: Ardis, 1976.
_____. *Isadora and Esenin.* Ann Arbor: Ardis, 1980.
Visson, Lynn. *Sergei Esenin: Poet of the Crossroads.* Würzburg: Jal-Verlag, 1980.

NIKOLAI GUMILYOV

On Russian Poetry. Trans. David Lapeza. Ann Arbor: Ardis, 1977.
Selected Works of Nikolai S. Gumilev. Selected & trans. Burton Raffel & Alla Burago, with
     intro. Sidney Monas. Albany: SUNY University Press, 1972.

Sampson, Earl. "Gumilev: A Selected, Annotated Bibliography." *Russian Literature Tri-
     quarterly,* No. 1, pp. 433-34.
_____. *Nikolay Gumilev.* Boston: Twayne Publishers, 1979.

ILF AND PETROV

*The Complete Adventures of Ostap Bender; Consisting of the Two Novels: The Twelve
     Chairs* and *The Golden Calf.* Trans. John H. C. Richardson. NY: Random House,
     1963.
Little Golden America. Trans. Charles Malamuth. NY: Farrar & Rinehart, 1937.

VSEVOLOD IVANOV

The Adventures of a Fakir. NY: The Vanguard Press, 1935.
Selected Stories. Comp. Elena Krasnoshchekova. Intro. V. Shklovsky. Moscow: Raduga,
     1983.

Maguire, Robert A. "The Pioneers: Pil'nyak and Ivanov," *Red Virgin Soil.* Princeton:
     Princeton University Press, 1968.

VENIAMIN KAVERIN

Two Captains. Trans. E. Leda Swan. NY: Modern Age Books, 1942.
The Unknown Artist. Trans. P. Ross. Intro. Gleb Struve. London: Westhouse, 1947.

Oulanoff, Hongor. *The Prose Fiction of Veniamin Kaverin*. Cambridge: Slavica Publishers, 1976.

VELIMIR KHLEBNIKOV

The King of Time: Selected Writing of the Russian Futurian. Trans. Paul Schmidt.
    Ed. Charlotte Douglas. Cambridge: Harvard University Press, 1985.
Snake Train: Poetry and Prose. Ed. Gary Kern. Intro. Edward J. Brown. Ann Arbor: Ardis, 1976.

Markov, Vladimir. *The Longer Poems of Velimir Khlebnikov*. Berkeley: University of California Press, 1962.
Russian Literature. Vol. IX, No. 1 (1981). Special Khlebnikov issue.
Vroon, Ronald. *Velimir Xlebnikov's Shorter Poems: A Key to the Coinages*. Ann Arbor: Michigan Slavic Materials, 1983.

OSIP MANDELSTAM

The Complete Critical Prose and Letters. Ed. Jane Gary Harris. Ann Arbor: Ardis, 1979.
Complete Poetry of Osip Emilevich Mandelstam. Trans. Burton Raffel & Alla Burago. Intro. Sidney Monas. Albany: SUNY Press, 1973.
The Prose of Osip Mandelstam. The Noise of Change, Theodosia, The Egyptian Stamp. Trans. with a critical essay by Clarence Brown. Princeton: Princeton University Press, 1965.
Selected Poems. Trans. Clarence Brown and W. S. Merwin. NY: Atheneum, 1974.
Stone. Trans. & intro. R. Tracey. Parallel Russian and English texts. Princeton: Princeton University Press, 1981.

Baines, Jennifer. *Mandelstam: The Later Poetry*. Cambridge: Cambridge University Press, 1977.
Brown, Clarence. *Mandelstam*. Cambridge: Cambridge University Press, 1973.
Broyde, Stephen Joseph. *Osip Mandel'stam and His Age. A Commentary on the Themes of War and Revolution in the Poetry, 1913-1923*. Cambridge: Harvard University Press, 1975.
Cohen, Arthur A. *Osip Emilievich Mandelstam: An Essay in Antiphon*. Ann Arbor: Ardis, 1974.
Mandelstam, Nadezhda. *Hope Against Hope*. Trans. Max Hayward. Intro. Clarence Brown. NY: Atheneum, 1972.
———. *Hope Abandoned*. Trans. Max Hayward. NY: Atheneum, 1974.
Przybylski, Ryszard. *An Essay on the Poetry of Osip Mandelstam: God's Grateful Guest*. Trans. Madeline G. Levine. Ann Arbor: Ardis, forthcoming.
Ronen, Omry. *An Approach to Mandelstam*. Jerusalem: Magnes Press, 1983.
Taranovsky, Kirill. *Essays on Mandelštam*. Cambridge: Harvard University Press, 1976.

VLADIMIR MAYAKOVSKY

The Bedbug and Selected Poetry. Ed. & intro. P. Blake. Trans. Max Hayward and George
     Reavey. Bloomington: Indiana University Press, 1975.
The Complete Plays of Mayakovsky. Trans. Guy Daniels. NY: Simon & Schuster, 1968.
Poems. Trans. Dorian Rottenberg. Moscow: Progress, 1972.

Barooshian, Vahan D. *Brik and Mayakovsky.* The Hague: Mouton, 1978.
Brown, Edward J. *Mayakovsky: A Poet in the Revolution.* Princeton: Princeton University
     Press, 1973.
Jangfeldt, Bengt and Nils Ake Nilsson. *Vladimir Majakovskij: Memoirs and Essays.*
     Stockholm: Almqvist and Wiksell, 1975.
Shklovsky, Viktor. *Mayakovsky and His Circle.* Ed. & trans. Lily Feiler. NY: Dodd, Mead,
     1972.
Stahlberger, Lawrence L. *The Symbolic System of Mayakovsky.* The Hague: Mouton, 1964.
Woroszylski, Wiktor. *The Life of Mayakovsky.* Trans. Boleslaw Taborski. NY: Orion Press,
     1970.

YURY OLESHA

Complete Plays. Trans. Michael Green and Jerome Katsell. Ann Arbor: Ardis, 1983.
Complete Stories and Three Fat Men. Trans. Aimee Anderson. Ann Arbor: Ardis, 1979.
Envy. Trans. T. S. Berczynski. Ann Arbor: Ardis, 1975.
No Day without a Line. Trans. Judson Rosengrant. Ann Arbor: Ardis, 1979.

Beaujour, Elizabeth Klosty. *The Invisible Land. A Study of the Artistic Imagination of Iurii
     Olesha.* NY: Columbia University Press, 1970.

BORIS PASTERNAK

The Correspondence of Boris Pasternak and Olga Freidenberg, 1910-1954. Comp. & ed.
     Elliott Mossman. NY: Harcourt Brace Jovanovich, 1981.
Doctor Zhivago. Trans. Max Hayward and Manya Harari. NY: Pantheon, 1958.
Fifty Poems. Trans. Lydia Pasternak Slater. NY: Barnes & Noble, 1963.
Letters. Summer 1926. Boris Pasternak, Marina Tsvetaeva, Rainer Maria Rilke. Ed.
     Yevgeny Pasternak, et al. Trans. Margaret Wettlin & Walter Arndt. NY: Harcourt
     Brace Jovanovich, 1985.
My Sister—Life and *A Sublime Malady.* Trans. Mark Rudman with Bohdan Boychuk. Ann
     Arbor: Ardis, 1983.
Pasternak on Art and Creativity. Ed. Angela Livingstone. Cambridge: Cambridge University
     Press, 1985.
Selected Poems. Trans. Jon Stallworth & Peter France. NY: W. W. Norton, 1983.
The Voice of Prose. Early Prose and Autobiography. Ed. Christopher Barnes. NY: Grove
     Press, 1986.

Davie, Donald and Angela Livingstone, eds. *Pasternak: Modern Judgements.* Nashville:
     Aurora, 1969.
Erlich, Victor. *Pasternak: A Collection of Critical Essays.* Englewood Cliffs, NJ: Prentice-
     Hall, 1978.
Gifford, Henry. *Pasternak: A Critical Study.* Cambridge: Cambridge University Press, 1977.
Hingley, Ronald. *Pasternak. A Biography.* NY: Alfred A. Knopf, 1983.
Mallac, Guy de. *Boris Pasternak. His Life and Art.* Norman: University of Oklahoma Press,
     1981.

BORIS PILNYAK

Mother Earth and Other Stories. Trans. Vera T. Reck and Michael Green. NY: Doubleday, 1968.
The Naked Year. Trans. A. R. Tulloch. Ann Arbor: Ardis, 1975.
Tale of the Unextinguished Moon and Other Stories. Trans. Beatrice Scott. Intro. Robert Payne. NY: Washington Square Press, 1967.

Browning, Gary. *Boris Pilniak: Scythian at a Typewriter.* Ann Arbor: Ardis, 1985.
Jensen, Peter Alberg. *Nature as Code: The Achievement of Boris Pilnjak, 1915-1924.* Copenhagen: Rosenkilde & Bagger, 1979.
Reck, Vera T. *Boris Pil'niak. A Soviet Writer in Conflict with the State.* Montreal: McGill—Queen's University Press, 1975.

ANDREI PLATONOV

Chevengur. Trans. Anthony Olcott. Ann Arbor: Ardis, 1978.
Collected Works. Trans. Thomas P. Whitney, et al. Preface Joseph Brodsky. Ann Arbor: Ardis, 1978.
Fierce, Fine World. Comp. Maria Platonova. Intro. E. Evtushenko. Moscow: Raduga, 1983.
The Foundation Pit. Trans. Mirra Ginsburg. NY: Dutton, 1975.
The Foundation Pit/Kotlovan. Bilingual edition. Trans. Thomas P.Whitney. Preface Joseph Brodsky. Ann Arbor: Ardis, 1973.

Jordan, Marion. "Andrei Platonov." *Russian Literature Triquarterly,* No. 8, pp. 363-72.
———. *Andrei Platonov.* Letchworth. Bradda Books, 1973.

MARINA TSVETAEVA

A Captive Spirit: Selected Prose. Ed. & trans. J. Marin King. Ann Arbor: Ardis, 1980.
The Demesne of the Swans/Lebedinyi stan. Bilingual edition. Ed. & trans. Robin Kemball. Ann Arbor: Ardis, 1980.
"Epic and Lyric in Contemporary Russia: Mayakovsky and Pasternak."Trans. Anya Kroth. *Russian Literature Triquarterly,* No. 13, 519-42.
Letters. Summer 1926. Boris Pasternak, Marina Tsvetaeva, Rainer Maria Rilke. Ed. Yevgeny Pasternak, et al. Trans. Margaret Wettlin & Walter Arndt. NY: Harcourt, Brace Jovanovich, 1985.
Selected Poems. Trans. E. Feinstein. Rev. & enlarged edition. Oxford: Oxford University Press, 1981.
Tsvetaeva: A Pictorial Biography/Tsvetaeva: Fotobiografiia. Ed. Ellendea Proffer. Ann Arbor: Ardis, 1980.

Brodsky, Joseph. "Footnote to a Poem," in his *Less than One. Selected Essays.* NY: Farrar Straus Giroux, 1986.
Karlinsky, Simon. *Marina Cvetaeva. Her Life and Art.* Berkeley: University of California Press, 1966.
———. *Marina Tsvetaeva. The Woman, Her World, and Her Poetry.* Cambridge: Cambridge University Press, 1985.
Marina Cvetaeva: Studien und Materialen. Wiener Slawistischer Almanach, Sonderband 3. Vienna, 1981.

NIKOLAI ZABOLOTSKY

Translation of 8 poems by Robin Milner-Gulland and Peter Levi. *Russian Literature Triquarterly*, No. 8, pp. 1-13.

Milner-Gulland, Robin. "Grandsons of Kozma Prutkov: Reflections on Zabolotsky, Oleynikov and Their Circle" in *Russian and Slavic Literature*, ed. Richard Freeborn et al. Cambridge: Slavica Publishers, 1976.
_____. "Zabolotsky and the Reader: Problems of Approach." *Russian Literature Triquarterly*, No. 8, p. 385-92.

EVGENY ZAMYATIN

The Dragon. Fifteen Stories. Trans. & ed. Mirra Ginsburg. Chicago: University of Chicago Press, 1976.
A God-Forsaken Hole. Trans. W. Foard. Ann Arbor: Ardis, forthcoming.
Islanders. Trans. T. S. Berczynski. Ann Arbor: Trilogy, 1978.
A Soviet Heretic. Essays by Yevgeny Zamiatin. Ed. & trans. Mirra Ginsburg. Chicago: University of Chicago Press, 1970.

Brown, Edward J. *Brave New World, 1984 and We: An Essay on Anti-Utopia*. Ann Arbor: Ardis, 1976.
Collins, Christopher. *Evgenij Zamjatin. An Interpretive Study*. The Hague: Mouton, 1973.
Kern, Gary, ed. *Zamyatin's "We": A Collection of Critical Essays*. Ann Arbor: Ardis, forthcoming.
Shane, Alex M. *The Life and Works of Evgenij Zamjatin*. Berkeley: University of California Press, 1968.

MIKHAIL ZOSHCHENKO

"About Myself, My Critics, and My Work." Trans. J. D. Cukierman. *Russian Literature Triquarterly*, No. 14, 403-6.
Before Sunrise. Trans. & afterword Gary Kern. Ann Arbor: Ardis, 1974.
A Man Is Not a Flea. A Collection of Stories. Trans. Serge Shishkoff. Ann Arbor: Ardis, forthcoming.
Nervous People and Other Stories. Ed. & intro. Hugh McLean. Bloomington: Indiana University Press, 1975.
Youth Restored. Trans. Joel Stern, intro. Gary Kern. Ann Arbor: Ardis, 1985.

Murphy, A. B. *Mikhail Zoshchenko: A Literary Profile*. Oxford: Meeuws, 1981.
Shklovsky, Viktor. "On Zoshchenko and Major Literature." Trans. J. D. Cukierman. *Russian Literature Triquarterly*, No. 14, pp. 407-15.
Titunik, Irwin R. "Mixail Zoščenko and the Problem of *Skaz.*" *California Slavic Studies*, 6 (1971), pp. 83-96.
Wiren, V. von. "Zoshchenko in Retrospect." *Russian Review* 21 (1962), pp. 348-61.

FIRST ANTHOLOGY IN ENGLISH
OF THE MOST EXCITING PERIOD
IN SOVIET LITERATURE

This is the first anthology devoted to the prose and poetry of the richest and most diverse period of Soviet literature. The anthology covers the period from just before the Revolution to the end of NEP and the start of the First Five-year Plan.

From Zamyatin's dazzling science-fiction satire *We* to Mayakovsky's comedy *The Bedbug* (both provided in new, accurate translations), most of the works included here became classics of twentieth-century Soviet Russian literature. Styles range from the modern dislocations of the Futurist poet Khlebnikov to Ivanov's Socialist-realist classic, *Armored-Train 14-69*.

While the material is extremely diverse, certain concerns resurface again and again, chief among them the question of what was lost in the Revolution as compared to what was gained. In the works of Pilnyak, Mandelstam, Babel and Platonov, we see a very real concern that culture itself was thrown out along with the old world. At the same time, these writers feel the vitality, energy and justice of the Revolution—and this ambivalence fuels their work. In these years especially all writers could afford to argue both side of the issue with a fair degree of sincerity. As the documents included show, despite all the manifestoes, the Party had decided to let the various literary groups fight it out among themselves, and the history of the literary press in this period shows that they did just that.

Themes which would go underground during the 1930s are very striking here: the idea that violence is sometimes both necessary and attractive (Blok, Babel, Ivanov, Serafimovich, Zamyatin), anger at the ways in which craftsmanship is destroyed and inefficiency rewarded in the name of political correctness (Pilnyak, Platonov), and lyrical despair (Mayakovsky, Esenin, Akhmatova).

"All major genres were being cultivated. And much of this literature still comes across as fresh and invigorating. One reason is that it deals with issues we have come to think of as quintessentially "modern," issues like the quality of life in industrialized societies, the bankruptcy of old values, or savagery masquerading as civilization. Such issues are the very stuff of twentieth-century literature, of course; but in the context of the Soviet 1920s, they became intensified and sufficiently defamiliarized to make an even greater impact on the foreign reader. For instance, the novel *We* compellingly demonstrates that the theme of *1984* was not invented by Orwell, but had been cast in its now chillingly familiar terms by Zamyatin in 1920."

From the introduction by Robert A. Maguire